Australian Genesis

Australian Genesis

Jewish Convicts
and Settlers
1788–1860

John S. Levi
G. F. J. Bergman

New edition

MELBOURNE UNIVERSITY PRESS

MELBOURNE UNIVERSITY PRESS
PO Box 278, Carlton South, Victoria 3053, Australia
info@mup.unimelb.edu.au
www.mup.com.au

First published by Rigby Limited 1974
This edition, Melbourne University Press, 2002
Text © John S. Levi 2002
Design and typography © Melbourne University Press 2002

Designed by Lauren Statham, Alice Graphics
Printed in Australia by Openbook Publishers

National Library of Australia Cataloguing-in-Publication entry

Levi, John S., 1934– .

   Australian genesis: Jewish convicts and settlers, 1788–1860.

   2nd ed.
   Bibliography.
   Includes index.
   ISBN 0 522 84777 3.

   1. Jews—Australia—History. 2. Jewish criminals—Australia.
   3. Australia—Exiles. I. Bergman, G. F. J. (George F. J.), 1900– . II. Title.

994.004924

Contents

Illustrations

Colour Plates

Text Illustrations

Maps

Preface

Australian Genesis was first published by Rigby in Adelaide in 1974. Dr George Bergman and I spent more than seven years working together on the project. In those days we found ourselves delving into material that had been ignored for more than 150 years. Documents were still covered with the chalk-dust used to dry the ink on the pages. I found the first records of a magisterial court in New South Wales in a brown paper parcel tied up with string. We were warned not to publish information about convicts or settlers that could embarrass their great grandchildren. Australia was just beginning to understand that its history was broader than lists of the kings and queens of England, and even more colourful and complex than the heroic stories of intrepid explorers who traversed our distant deserts.

To our pleasure the first edition quickly became a collector's item and there has been a persistent and constant demand for a new edition. Week after week I would receive queries about the Jewish origins of Australian families. With this growing interest in genealogy came new clues, new information and new resources. The book and the research took on a life of their own.

In 1979, to my great sorrow, Dr George Bergman died. As the new edition developed and grew, his influence has continued to be profound. He is still the co-author of this book, which now appears so many years after his death. In this project I have been greatly encouraged and assisted by Dr Eva Raik and her husband Ivor Bitel of Sydney. Eva is the daughter of the late Mrs Millie Bergman and stepdaughter of George Bergman.

When I became Rabbi Emeritus of my congregation in Melbourne in 1997, it was possible to devote more time to the project, which promptly grew into two books. This is the first of them. The second will be a biographical dictionary of the Jews of colonial Australia, 1788–1850. I am very grateful to Melbourne University Press and to its Commissioning Editor, Teresa Pitt, for their enthusiastic support. Jean Dunn, a senior editor of Melbourne University Press who had already worked with me on my biography, *Rabbi Jacob Danglow: 'the uncrowned monarch of Australian Jews'* (MUP 1995), has been my 'right and left hand'.

In the first edition of this book Dr Bergman and I acknowledged the help we had received from all the major Australian libraries, and I gladly do so again. The collections of the Mitchell Library, the Dixson Galleries and Library and the Archives Office of New South Wales, at the State Library of New South Wales are the essential core of any study of colonial Australia. The staff of experts were unstintingly helpful and kind. My particular thanks go to Fabian Lo Schiavo of the Archives Office and to Jennifer Broomhead and Kevin Leamon of the Mitchell Library. In Victoria, the La Trobe Librarian Dianne Reilly immediately offered to help in the publication of material gathered from the great collection of the State Library of Victoria, including the newspaper collection and the print collection. I have spent many happy, and often exciting, hours in Hobart's Archives Office of Tasmania, and I am most grateful to the staff in the Hobart Library and to Mrs Marian Jameson, the Senior Librarian of the magnificent Allport Collection and Museum of Fine Arts at the Tasmanian State Library. In the United Kingdom I was able to study at the Oxford Centre for Hebrew and Jewish Studies at Yarnton Manor, while the Bodleian Library readily granted me access to their collection. My thanks are due to the Australian National Library in Canberra, the J. S. Battye Library, State Library of Western Australia, and the Art Gallery and Library of South Australia.

The kindness and generosity of many friends must be acknowledged. Sam Stiglec of Melbourne greatly assisted me with the digital imaging of many of the pictures. David Same has been my computer 'guru'. Anne McCormick of Horden House Rare Books in Sydney has been of great assistance. I would like to thank people who have shared treasures with us: Ruth Simon and Peter Simon of Sydney; Mr and Mrs Stuart Cohen of Melbourne; Rabbi Raymond Apple of the Great Synagogue in Sydney and Marcelle Jacobs, curator of the synagogue's archives; Michael Walford of Basingstoke in the United Kingdom; Heidi Fixel of Hobart and all the members of the Hobart Synagogue; Susan Hood, archivist at Port Arthur; Rabbi Jeffrey Cohen, former Chief Executive Officer of the Jewish Museum in Sydney, and Dr Helen Light, Director of the Jewish Museum of Australia in Melbourne; Justice Howard Nathan of Melbourne; the late Rabbi Ron Lubofsky of Melbourne; John G. B. Perry of Melbourne; Alisa Jaffa, former curator of the Alfred Rubens Print Collection at the Jewish Museum in London, Diana and Richard King of London, Jane Walters and David Kingston.

The two major Australian Jewish communities in Melbourne and Sydney sustain twin Jewish historical societies and, as will be obvious, their journal and proceedings provides an extraordinarily rich source of primary and secondary material. Dr Howard Freeman and Mrs Lorraine Freeman together with Mr Trevor Cohen and Mrs Heather Cohen have generously and enthusiastically supported the publication of this book. Howard is the President of the Victorian Branch of the Australian Jewish Historical Society and Trevor the Immediate Past President. From Sydney came a most generous grant from Rabbi Jeffrey Cohen, in honour of Moshe-Lieb and Miriam Cohen.

There is a Hebrew expression that the last to be mentioned is especially beloved. In this case, the truth is almost self-evident as I express my gratitude to my wife Robyn for her unfailing support and critical assistance. Together we dedicate this book to our 3-year-old grandson Joshua, whose great, great, great grandparents were in Melbourne when European settlement began.

John Levi
Melbourne

The Outcasts

AN OMINOUS SPECTRE of hatred bedevilled the synagogue and its shadow fell across the tiny Jewish community of London. For English Jewry the most critical years of the Industrial Revolution were haunted by the Old Bailey, the hangman and the convict hulks.

A secret debate in the highest circles of Whitehall about a plan to settle a colony of convicts on the eastern coast of Australia coincided with a time of rapid expansion and severe distress for the Jewish community of London. In 1753, during the ministry of Henry Pelham and his brother, the Duke of Newcastle, legislation was introduced into Parliament to exempt Jews from taking the sacrament before they could be naturalised. This 'Jew Bill' created a storm of protest even though its very limited goal was to enable a few members of the small Spanish and Portuguese elite in London, who had supported the government, to compete as equals in the commercial life of the capital.[1]

Jews ventured beyond their homes in the streets east of the City of London at their peril. In November 1753 a pedlar, Jonas Levi, was brutally mutilated and murdered in Monmouthshire. In 1757 Israel Hart, a Jewish pencil-maker, gave evidence at the Old Bailey that 'it was a common thing . . . when Jews came to offer pencils to sell, to take them away and throw the pencils out the window'. In 1776 the landlady of a public house was convicted at Westminster Quarter Sessions for assaulting a Jewish customer and forcing him to eat pork. In 1763 a mob pursued a clumsy Jewish pickpocket from Tower Hill to Duke's Place, where London's two synagogues were to be found. The crowd was at first beaten back by Jews and then returned to plunder three Jewish homes and throw the women and children into the street. These may have been isolated events; however, on a Saturday evening in the latter part of 1771 a new and more sinister era began. The author of the *New Newgate Calendar* recalled that it was 'just as the Jewish Sabbath was ended' when a band of 'eight foreign born Jews' raided and ransacked the farmhouse of a Mrs Hutchings at Chelsea Fields. 'The most sanguinary villain' stunned and then shot one of the farm labourers, while the rest of the gang shouted, 'Shoot him! Shoot him!' For years after, Jews on the streets of London were followed by the raucous cry of 'Go to Chelsea!'.[2] A visitor to London wrote to his family: 'Dogs could not then be used in the streets in the manner in which the Jews were treated'.[3]

A reward was posted at the Public Office, Bow Street, the home of the famous Bow Street Runners who were the precursors of Scotland Yard. The London *Public*

Advertiser of 8 November 1771 led a report of the investigation with the words 'House-breakers and Murderers' and mentioned that 'It appears from the Examinations already taken that this same gang was increasing to a dreadful degree, and that even fresh Miscreants have been sent for from abroad and are arrived and that they had formed some very daring and Mischievous Plan'. The offenders were described as 'all Jews', and listed and detailed:

> Asher Wyld, 5 feet 9 inches high, middling in person, red face, wears a wig, some-times clubbed, dressed sometimes in Blue and Gold, and sometimes Green and Black Velvet breeches. Abraham Linevil; a little thin man about 28 years of age, thin visaged and commonly wears grey clothes and a blue Great Coat. Hyam Lazarus, about 28 years of age, low in Stature, rather thin, round faced, his own brown hair short and generally wears brown-grey clothes. One Coshey, a little man, born in England, of German parents. Mark Ashebury, a tall lusty man about 50 years of age. Solomon Lazarus, commonly called blind Zelick, about 60 years of age, rather tall and thin, marked with smallpox.

The reward caused one of the villains to betray his companions, and they were soon taken. Hyam Lazarus and Ashebury were acquitted for want of evidence, while the leader of the gang was found to be Doctor Levi Weil, a graduate of the University of Leyden and a physician who had practised in London. It was said that he had brought his companions from Amsterdam to form his sinister gang of robbers.

Levi Weil and three of his fellows were carted to the gallows at Tyburn on 9 December 1771. No rabbi would stand with them, as on the previous Sabbath they had been formally cut off from their people by the solemn curse of excommuni-cation: 'A rabbi went to them in the press-yard of Newgate and delivered to each one of them a Hebrew book; but declined attending them to the place of death, nor even prayed with them at the time of his visit'. Mournfully, and defiantly, they sang a Hebrew hymn before an 'immense crowd'. Then the hangman set about his work and they tumbled to their deaths.[4] Their bodies were delivered to the anatomists for dis-section. A letter from James Northcote to Sir Joshua Reynolds concludes the episode on a bizarre note by mentioning that one of those executed Jews served as the demon-stration subject for a crowded anatomy lecture in the newly founded Royal Academy.[5]

Levi Weil was one of the first of scores of Jews to perish on Tyburn Tree and on the scaffold erected outside the Debtors' Gate at Newgate Prison. Those who died on that December day were part of a new and unwelcome Anglo-Jewish community, which was swelling rapidly through natural increase and the constant influx of des-perate newcomers escaping the nightmare of European ghettos. The rate of increase can be estimated through various authorities.

In 1660 there were about 35 Jewish families in London and by 1684 about 90. The guilds of the City of London required that a tradesman take a Christian oath prior to receiving the freedom of the City, thus ensuring that no Jewish merchant could carry on a business there. In order to make sure that Jews could not evade the prohibition by converting to Christianity, the Court of Aldermen ordered, in 1785,

'The Robbery at Chelsea, committed by Levi Weil & his Associates', 1771. The Judge 'prefaced the sentence with a just and judicious compliment to the principal Jews, for their very laudable conduct in the course of this prosecution, and trusted no person would ignorantly stigmatise a whole nation for the villains of a few ... on the Sabbath prior to their execution, an anathema was pronounced at the Synagogue in Duke's Place against the criminals'. (James Picciotto, Sketches of Anglo-Jewish History.)

that even baptised Jews could not be admitted. The City Corporation's prohibition against Jews enjoying the freedom of London lasted until 1831 and the first synagogues were carefully placed just east of the City's boundary. Between 1790 and 1850 the Jewish population of England grew from 12 000 to 35 000, and this steady increase placed intolerable burdens on the small Anglo-Jewish community of London.[6] It was small because, in the centuries between Edward I and Oliver Cromwell, England had seen few Jews. After Richard I's return from the Crusades the Jews of England faced a continual deterioration in their way of life, which culminated in their brutal expulsion in 1290. More than three hundred years were to pass before the edict was allowed to lapse. The first Jewish families to live in London in the seventeenth century called themselves by the proud and nostalgic name of 'Sephardim', derived from the Hebrew word for Spain. Some were merchant princes of Spanish and Portuguese stock, a portion of those whom the fires of the Inquisition had driven to seek refuge in northern Europe and North Africa. For centuries to come, in memory of their ancient link with the cultural and spiritual renaissance of the Iberian Jewish civilisation, the Sephardim kept their communal records in Spanish rather than English.

A growing respect for financial facts and property rights persuaded the English to allow their small Jewish community to become part of the nation's economic life.

The right of English Jews to live within the United Kingdom gained official recognition during the eighteenth century, when they were permitted to use the normal law courts for recovery of debts. It was the era when London was developing into the financial capital of the world, and the city began to attract Jews of substance from Hamburg and Amsterdam: the 'Ashkenazim', a communal name (from the Hebrew word for Germany) given to Jews whose ancestry was central or eastern European. Both Sephardi and Ashkenazi Jews became directors of Lloyd's of London and the Honourable East India Company, and news of English economic tolerance and the opportunities that were opening spread rapidly among European Jews.

The picture changed even more rapidly during the second half of the eighteenth century. The inexorable process of persecution which reached its nightmarish climax in the extermination camps of the Third Reich was heralded by the massacre of Poles and Jews by the Ukranian warrior Bogdan Chmielnicki in the seventeenth century, and continued in numberless ways. Wave after wave of Jews moved across Europe from east to west. It was a spiritual and physical migration. They moved 'from the self-sufficient world of rabbinic tradition and corporate autonomy to the desacrilized world of the modern European state'.[7] They dreamed of a world that bore them no contempt and where they would be safe. These were not the merchants and financiers whom the English had accepted easily, but penniless migrants who brought no money and few skills. They had survived the ghettos of Europe, but were ill-equipped to face the rigours of Georgian London. In the towns they had left, they were forbidden to enter any respectable trade or profession, so they knew only how to deal in money-lending, trinkets or old clothes. In many parts of Germany they did not dare frequent places of public amusement, and in several towns had to pay a special tax if they stayed outside the walls of the ghetto overnight. Until 1824 only fifteen marriages a year were permitted among the thousand Jewish families living in the Protestant city of Frankfurt. They had to pay a poll tax to enter some cities, and were given a receipt marked 'Jews and swine'. While revolutionary France prated of Liberty, Equality and Fraternity, its leaders vigorously debated whether such liberty should be extended to Jews.

By 1771, one and a half million Jews lived in Europe, two-thirds of them in eastern Europe.[8] Those of western Europe were crippled by the pressures of prejudice and rapacity, and on the eve of their political emancipation they were deeply divided by religious and class enmity.[9] The crowded ghettos bred a feeling of kinship and communal awareness, but only freedom could release the full Jewish contribution to the spiritual and intellectual life of the world.

When the Netherlands granted citizenship to Jews, and it was seen that Britain treated all her subjects as equal in sight of the law without regard to their political emancipation,[10] the temptation to emigrate across the English Channel became overwhelming. Those who entered this promised land encountered some rude shocks. Unable to speak the English language and without money or skills, the Jews were obliged to scratch a living by 'picking up unconsidered trifles'. The Jewish pedlar, dealer and old-clothes man became a familiar sight. Plodding into country areas, he was the only foreigner the yokels ever saw. His strange accent, clothes, customs and mannerisms brought a glimpse of a baffling world, and the rural folk often reacted with the scorn, suspicion and hostility which are human reactions towards the unfamiliar. On Easter Sunday the boys of one venerable London school would rush out of chapel after prayers singing, 'He is risen. He is risen. All the Jews must go to prison!' And so they did!

A letter written from London in 1807 describes the streets and crowds which produced Australia's first Jews:

> Some of their lower orders let their beards grow and wear a sort of black tunic with a girdle; the chief ostensible trade is as old clothes but they deal also in stolen goods, and not infrequently in coining. A race of Hebrew lads, who infest you in the streets with oranges and red slippers or tempt schoolboys to dip in a bag for ginger bread nuts, are the great agents in uttering base silver ... You meet Jew pedlars everywhere travelling with boxes of haberdashery at their back, cuckoo-clocks, sealing wax, quills, weather glasses, green spectacles, clumsy figures in plaster of Paris ... even the Nativity and Cruxificion ... Some few of the wealthiest merchants are of this persuasion.[11]

'Old Clothes!', engraving by Thomas Rowlandson, London, 1794. 'We see him (the Jewish pedlar) in innumerable contemporary sketches, cartoons, engravings, silhouettes, even terra-cotta groups and porcelain ... He is unmistakable, with his straggling reddish beard and the shapeless hat at the back of his head. He is wearing a long blue coat, and carries a heavy stick in his hand; and one of his worsted stockings has slipped inelegantly down to his ankle. Suspended from his back is his pack, ready to be swung around in front should a potential client appear.' (Cecil Roth, Essays and Portraits in Anglo-Jewish History, Jewish Publication Society of America, Philadelphia, 1962, p. 132.)

Benjamin Disraeli asked the readers of his novel Tancred to imagine what it was like to live as a Jew in London's slums:

> Conceive of being born and bred in the Judenstrasse of Hamburg or Frankfort, or rather in the purlieus of our Hounsditch or Minories, born to hereditary insult, without any education, apparently without a circumstance that can develop the slightest taste, or cherish the least sentiment for the beautiful, living amid fogs and filth, never treated with kindness, seldom with justice, occupied with the meanest, if not the vilest, toil, bargaining for frippery, speculating in usury, existing for ever under the concurrent influence of degrading causes which would have worn out, long ago, any race that ... did not adhere to the laws of Moses.[12]

The novelist Charles Dickens was less sympathetic, and one of his earliest childish recollections was an encounter with the unfamiliar figure of a Jewish pedlar, 'a dreadful old man, with a long tangled, reddish grey beard'. Later he mused, 'Carrying the bag, crying "old Clo'"' seems to be a sort of novitiate or apprenticeship which all Hebrews are subject to ... Every Jew, millionaire as he may become afterwards, seems to begin with the bag'.[13]

But worst of all was the reaction of the established leaders of English Jewry towards the newcomers. It was determinedly hostile. The respect and status won by the 'old' Anglo-Jewish community was in danger of being swamped by the strange, unpopular invaders.[14] Destitute Jewish refugees were greeted by a resolution from the wardens of the London Synagogue that no financial relief could be extended to foreign Jews 'who had left their country without good cause', as though prejudice and poverty were groundless reasons for despair.

As Levi Weil and his gang were brought to trial, the General Vestry of the London Synagogue inserted in the *Public Advertiser* of 15 November 1771 a notice disclaiming responsibility for the actions 'of foreign miscreants who stain our Religion by calling themselves Jews'. The Vestry implored:

> Every Honest member of our Community to aid and assist us in this pious Cause, in which the Lives and Property of his Majesty's subjects are deeply concerned; and in order if possible, to strike Terror into the wicked Hearts of these abandoned Offenders, we hereby declare our determined Resolution to grant them no Burials, or any other Religious Indulgence whatsoever after Conviction, that they may be forever excommunicated from our Community, as well as to deter every Jew from receiving stolen Goods, or concealing such, or harbouring any Persons guilty of any Theft, and to the utmost of our Power to extirpate such vile Miscreants forever from our Congregation, for the Glory of God and the Peace and Safety of Society in General.

But such threats had little effect. Many of the invaders could not read them and others were obliged by sheer force of circumstance to seek a living outside the law. The lazy tolerance developed by the English towards a small and therefore harmless community was sharply reversed. Towards the end of the eighteenth century, while the first convicts were arriving in Australia, some English voices were raised to question the right of Jews to live in England at all.

Even among the enormous displaced criminal population of Georgian London, a Jewish element had become noticeable. Patrick Colquhoun, the distinguished London magistrate, wrote in *A Treatise on the Police of the Metropolis* in 1796 that there were over 100 000 criminals in London, a substantial proportion of a population which at that time numbered 640 000. Colquhoun estimated that 50 000 were prostitutes, 8000 were thieves and 2000 were 'itinerant Jews, wandering from street to street, holding out temptations to pilfer and steal, and Jew boys crying Bad Shillings, who purchase articles stolen by Servants, Stable Boys etc. etc. generally paying in base money'.

Colquhoun believed that Jewish religious observances were partly to blame for their criminal proclivities. Because the Jewish Sabbath falls on the Christian Saturday,

'Get Money, Money Still, And then let Virtue, if she will', cartoon by Thomas Rowlandson. The three dishevelled and bearded Jews stand in the street where London's Great Synagogue was located.

young Jews could not be apprenticed to trades or become servants. Their religion forbade them to work on the Sabbath, whereas Christian employers, in that era of the six-day week, would certainly expect them to work on Saturdays. And in those days it was customary for apprentices, servants and many other types of employee to live on their master's premises and be fed by him, a practice which would have caused many problems if the employee expected kosher food. Colquhoun made this assessment:

> There are about twenty thousand Jews in the City of London besides perhaps about five or six thousand more in the great provincial and seaport towns . . . These exist chiefly by their wits, by living upon the industry of others. Educated in idleness from their earliest infancy, they acquire every debauched and vicious principle which can fix them for the most complicated acts of fraud and deception. From the orange boy, and the retailer of seals, razors, glass and other wares in the public streets, to the shopkeeper dealing in wearing apparel or in silver and gold, the same principles of conduct too generally prevail.

He was of course right, though his estimate of the Jewish population was high.[15] Young European Jews had too often been 'educated in idleness' because in Poland and the German kingdoms and principalities they were barred from most professions and trades. In the ghettos, Jews had been forced to hone their native intelligence to razor sharpness merely to survive, and in their new country they were obliged to use similar tactics.

Patrick Colquhoun noted that 'Jews of the higher class', i.e. those of the old Anglo-Jewish community, viewed 'with horror and distress the deplorable condition and growing depravity of their own society'. It was a horror which prevented the wealthier, established Jews from helping their poorer and newly arrived brethren. They turned on them with the vigour of men whose status was threatened by undesirable intruders. They were reserved, prudent, as inconspicuous as possible and infinitely respectable. They protested to the Home Office about this invasion of unfortunates, and not only excommunicated the convicted but aided their conviction by giving information to the police. On 25 May 1766 the Bow Street magistrate Sir John Fielding (brother of the novelist Henry Fielding) wrote to Napthaly Franks and Napthaly Hart Meyers, Presidents of the Great Synagogue, to thank them for their help in the detection of receivers of stolen goods. He assured the Presidents that he knew the practice was carried on 'by a few persons only'.[16]

The *Newgate Calendar* gives a succinct description of how London Jews were regarded in those days:

> Those unacquainted with the ways and customs of the metropolis will be surprised when we say that on a moderate calculation it contains about twenty thousand Jews. They are generally a set of cheats, and the lower order are to be found lurking in every street, lane and alley, pretending to buy old clothes, old metal, glass, hares' and rabbits' skins, old hats and shoes, but their real object is to corrupt servants to pilfer from their masters. These itinerant Jews are ever ready to purchase anything they are offered for sale; and where the article has been stolen of which they are excellent judges, they seldom give the thief more than a third of its value. They also carry

'St James, Duke's Place', c. 1770. An iron gateway leads to the hidden courtyard in front of the synagogue. Only the presence of bearded figures in the street give tangible evidence of a Jewish place of worship.

about base money, which they pay for stolen goods, and circulate it by every poss-ible deception. Denying the divinity of Christ, they seldom scruple at committing perjury, and hence the expression of 'cheap as Jew's Bail'.[17]

In 1804 a particularly bitter letter to the 13–15 May edition of the London St James Chronicle, signed 'Catharticus', actually seems to have provoked a meeting between the two main synagogues. Minute Book No. 1 of the Board of Deputies of British Jews (November 1760 to April 1828) records that the aristocratic Sephardi congregation and the more plebeian Ashkenazi Great Synagogue met to discuss the possibility of a libel action. The letter had made this suggestion:

> Whoever will give themselves the trouble to examine the Districts in the Metropolis inhabited by the low Jews, will observe enough to convince them that the followers of Moses are the most nasty and filthy people under the canopy of Heaven. It would be kind to endeavour to give them some idea of cleanliness and decency as well as honesty; and if they be found incorrigible, they should have a town to themselves and we should oblige them as the old Romans did, to wear a mark whenever they came into the city.

But not even such dangerous insults, yet another link in the long chain leading towards the 'Final Solution', could bridge the social gap between the Sephardim and Ashkenazim. No legal action was taken, and the well-established British Jews did not consider any method of upgrading their foreign brethren. A note written in the back of the Minute Book lists 'The principal causes of the separation which exists between the Spanish and Portuguese Jews, and the German Jews' and states that the communal funds of the Sephardim were not 'for the purpose of encouraging German, Dutch, or Jewish adventurers . . . within the last fifty years the German Jews have increased prodigiously in number, coming from all parts of Germany, and mostly of the poorer class . . . they have nothing and want for everything'. The comment betrays the well-founded fear of the Sephardim that they would be swamped by the northern invaders, and it is understandable that they did not wish to pay for the process.

As each European outbreak of persecution sent Jews to England, the leaders of London Jewry tried to stem the apparently inexorable invasion. Whilst the wealthier, established and more tightly knit Sephardim had their own charitable institutions, the Ashkenazim desperately ex-communicated law-breakers and applied to the government for aid to help prevent the migration of impoverished Jews to England. By 1779 poverty had become such an acute problem within the Ashkenazi community of London that riots broke out and a society was set up to supply food and coal to the Jewish poor. In 1807 a Jewish hospital was established to receive and support the aged poor and for 'the education and industrial employment of the youth of both sexes'.[18]

An anonymous *Essay on the Commercial Habits of the Jews*, published in London in 1809, describes a community in the depths of a social crisis:

> The number of intricate lanes and alleys near Whitechapel, and other parts of the town entirely occupied by these [Jewish] miscreants and their associates, render them formidable to the officers of justice, and at the same time impervious to the public eye. From these depositors of filth and iniquity, the approach of morning sends them in herds over the whole face of the capital . . . the baneful and immoral effects upon society with such a race of men need not be insisted upon.

In a letter of 10 July 1863 to Mrs Eliza Davis, Charles Dickens answered her question as to why, in 1838, he had made Fagin a Jew: 'Fagin in *Oliver Twist* is a Jew, because it unfortunately was true of the time to which the story refers, that that class of criminal almost invariably *was* a Jew'. In her reply, Mrs Davis wrote, 'Perhaps we are over sensitive, but are we not ever flayed?'[19]

Dickens may have exaggerated, because Britain in those years had a formidable number of law-breakers—though most of them broke it in the light-fingered way in which Fagin trained his gang of youngsters rather than with the brutality of Bill Sikes. Throughout the entire transportation era, the most frequently heard story in the law courts of England was that of the pickpocket or petty thief. Gangs of young criminals roamed the city streets, jostling pedestrians and 'dipping' their watches, purses, money or handkerchiefs. Agile fingers played on shop counters and pavement displays, messenger carts and the luggage racks of coaches, and thieves who could not run fast enough produced a rich crop of convicts. During the first eighty years of settlement in Australia, more than 160 000 men, women and children were sent there from the British Isles and from many of her colonies.[20] In some ways they were the lucky ones, because transportation was in many cases used by the judges as an alternative to public execution. Death by hanging was the punishment for a wide variety of crimes, so those who were transported were only a proportion of the criminal population.

It may have been disingenuous of the British to blame so much of their crime on the Jews. It is truer perhaps to say that, for countless people in that era of vast social inequalities, crime was a way of life because they had no other way of making a living, and that a number of Jews took to it for that reason.

So, on most convict ships which carried Britons to Australia, there were Jews who shared their fate. In this bizarre, haphazard way, Australia became the only community of European·people in which Jews were present from the moment of its establishment. It was the prelude to history's mildest struggle for Jewish emancipation, and the beginning of a unique Jewish experience.

Interior of the Great Synagogue, Duke's Place, drawn and engraved by A.W. N. Pugin and Thomas Rowlandson; acquatint by Sutherland for Microcosm of London, 1809. The interior of the Ashkenazi synagogue in Aldgate was refurbished in 1767. The synagogue was carefully located just beyond the boundary of the City of London. It was only in 1831 that Jews were admitted to the freedom of the city and allowed to carry on retail trade within it.

THE EARLIEST RECORDS of Australian settlement describe the destiny of Jews dubbed as 'vile miscreants' by their own congregational leaders in London. The Jews formed a tiny yet very noticeable part of Australia's convict community. The convict dossiers, the little colonial newspapers and the voluminous records of colonial administrators paint a finely detailed portrait of an early nineteenth-century European Jewish community as it emerged from the ghetto and blossomed into new life in Australia. Through the documents of Australian history, we can trace the stories of people torn from the narrow confines of London's Jewish quarter and forced to create a new life in what was to them a completely alien world. We see that the transportation of Jewish men often caused the migration of whole families, drawn by ties of kinship or friendship to make the arduous voyage.

Of the 145 000 Britons transported to Australia from 1788 to 1853, at least 700 were Jews. Most were men and boys born within a small London community that numbered, at most, 3000 families.[21] This steady winnowing must have been one of the Jewish community's most shameful problems, yet no reference to it can be found in the records of the English Jews of that period. They erected a wall of total silence—the defence fostered by centuries of persecution.

Only in 1788 did the Jews constitute more than 1 per cent of the total colonial community, and this came about because most of the convicts sent out in the First Fleet were selected from the prisons of London. The largest number of Jewish convicts to arrive in a single year was in 1818, when 28 out of 2550 sent to Australia from Great Britain can be identified as Jews.

The rolls of the convict ships show that English Jews had begun to overcome the lack of skills typical of refugees from northern Europe—though apparently this had not saved them from temptation. The trades or skills of most of the earliest Jewish convicts are recorded in the colonial records. No less than 400 Jewish convicts arrived in the first forty years of European settlement in Australia, and 50 free settlers. Nine out of ten of the convicts had been sentenced in London. Their average age at the time of deportation or transportation was twenty-five. Nearly all were pickpockets or thieves. There were only 30 Jewish women among that first generation of convicts. Very few of that Jewish group could be classified as 'middle class'. The list includes 16 tailors, 11 watchmakers, 12 cobblers, 11 glass-cutters, 8 jewellers, 8 furriers, 9 grooms and 9 butchers. There were no less than 50 street fruit-sellers, pedlars and old-clothes men. There were bakers, an actor, a chimney sweep, two dentists, a musician, a sailor, a silversmith, a spectacle-maker, hatters, pencil-makers, unskilled labourers and prostitutes.[22]

The Jews of Europe were accustomed to making a living within a hostile environment. They possessed a deep respect for education, so that it was common for the poorest Jews to be able to read and write when illiteracy was the rule rather than the exception, and a sense of kinship was heightened by familiarity with poverty, exile and sudden expulsion. Their names and faces were distinctive and their social background and economic status very similar. All these qualities, which merge into a flexible ability to make the best of circumstances, they brought with them to Australia. For decades there was no organised Jewish community, and yet Australian Jews maintained helpful social contact and a feeling of shared responsibility.

It would be romantic to say that transportation to Australia redeemed the miserable offenders against the laws of England, for many convicts died in poverty, either before or after the completion of their sentences. Many died in chains. The gallows claimed its share of victims, and harsh and often bloody discipline was imposed through the cat o' nine tails, the chain gang, the treadmill and solitary confinement. Of those who completed their sentences, very few could scrape together the price of a passage home—for the law made no provision for repatriation. In the Jewish group, perhaps one in ten managed to find his way home again. But some of the Jews who remained in Australia did extraordinarily well, and the colonial freedom from snobbery and prejudice enabled their children to take their places on the Bench and in the legislative chambers of their country, and to found some of the notable families of the new land.

The Jews in colonial Australia were not the only outsiders in the early community. There were a number of significant minorities, not all of whom were convicts. The chasm between Protestant and Catholic was widened by the constant 'Irish problem'. A good many of the early Irish and Scottish settlers spoke Gaelic, and some lacked even a rudimentary knowledge of English. The early records have numerous references to 'men of colour' who came as convicts, often from other British colonies. As time went on, two new and different breeds evolved. The emancipists were convicts who had served their time and whose uncertain status bred the bitterness and self-consciousness typical of minority groups. The 'currency folk' were those born in the colony to parents who were either free settlers or emancipists; they were the first true Australians of European stock, and in many cases showed a wild independence and intolerance of restraint.

Nevertheless, apart from the indigenous peoples, the Jews would form the only substantial non-Christian community on the continent until thousands of Chinese arrived during the gold rushes. Until that time the Jews were also a minority within a minority. For they were part of an embryonic mercantile class in a military dictatorship that evolved into a pastoral community.

Australia's seminal period, from 1788 to 1860, has a lustily flamboyant character. In the small colonist population, the deeds of simple men and women assumed heroic proportions. Their lives formed patterns for the future social development of the nation, just as their actions and achievements shaped its folklore and culture. For this reason, the story of Jewish settlement in early colonial Australia can be read most clearly in the lives of individuals, whose adventures illuminate an era that ended when gold attracted a multitude of migrants from many parts of the world. By 1861, following the gold rush, official colonial census figures showed 5486 Jews in Australia: just less than half of 1 per cent of the total population.[23] Yet, as will be seen, this tiny community provided Australia with one of the most colourful and unusual strands in its heritage.

The First Fleet

IT WAS A GRIM BEGINNING to a new world. The coastline of the great southern continent was barely known. Its interior was an uncharted mystery. When the first convicts landed in Australia, the British government had long been accustomed to the transportation of prisoners to distant penal colonies. During the first three-quarters of the eighteenth century, over 60 000 men and women had been transported to the plantations of Virginia and Maryland. They were Britain's unwanted population and the sad by-products of the Industrial and Agricultural revolutions, who were to be removed from the scene of their distress and disgrace.

In 1775 the American colonists closed their ports to British ships, British cargoes and British convicts. As a 'temporary' measure, which was to last for several decades, the convicts were consigned to the hulks of old ships anchored in the Thames Estuary and other English ports. The crumbling gaols overflowed with prisoners, as is described by a medical visitor in the *London Gazetteer* of 11 January 1776:

> Vagrants and disorderly women of the very lowest and most wretched class of human beings, almost naked, with only a few filthy rags almost alive with vermin, their bodies rotting with the bad distemper, and covered with itch, scorbutic and venereal ulcers; and being unable to treat the constable even with a pot of beer to let them escape, are drove in shoals to gaols . . . In the morning . . . the different wards . . . are more like the Black Hole in Calcutta than places of confinement in a Christian country.

In a search for suitably remote destinations to replace the lost American colonies, the authorities considered Gibraltar, Gambia, Senegal, South America and the Cape of Good Hope. Each presented its own set of problems. The major one arose from the British experience that convicts rarely were reformed by imprisonment and that, when they had served their sentences and were released in a new country, they returned to a life of crime.

Joseph Banks, the wealthy scientist and naturalist who sailed with Captain James Cook on his 1768 expedition to the South Seas, solved the problem for the British government. He optimistically told a parliamentary committee that Botany Bay, near the great harbour around which the city of Sydney was to arise, would be 'best adapted . . . in case it should be thought expedient to establish a Colony of convicted Felons in any distant part of the Globe, from whence their Escape might be difficult, and where, from the fertility of the Soil, they might be enabled to maintain themselves, after the First Year, with little or no Aid from the Mother Country . . .' Banks,

The Discovery, etching, 1829. This vessel carried Captain Cook on his last voyage to the Pacific. Deemed to be unseaworthy, it was then beached at Deptford near Greenwich and used as a prison or convict hulk. Most convicts transported to Australia spent time on the hulks before their deportation.

who believed that the soil could support 'a very large number of people' and that the natives were 'extremely cowardly' mentioned, as an additional inducement, the fact that there were 'no beasts of prey'.[1]

The use of New South Wales as a convict colony already had been suggested by James Matra, an American loyalist who had been displaced by the War of Independence. The idea was officially adopted in 1785, abandoned, and then, in 1786, taken up again. In London, indignant and courageous opposition to the plan to transport convicts to New South Wales came from Lord George Gordon, the well-known aristocratic convert to Judaism.[2]

Gordon had been imprisoned in the Tower of London on a charge of high treason for his leadership of the notorious 'No Popery' riots of 1780. Following his acquittal, Gordon became aware of the plight of those in prison awaiting death or transportation. At the same time, the noble and highly eccentric gentleman began a process that would lead him to become a Jew. The importance of his story is reflected in a cartoon, 'Non Commissioned Officers Embarking for Botany Bay', published in November 1786. It lampoons Gordon's protests against transportation.

'Non Commission Officers Embarking for Botany Bay', cartoon by H. Humphreys, 1 November 1786. This is the first public reference to the British government's secret plan to settle an outpost on the east coast of Australia. On board the small rowing boat sit members of the British Establishment: the forlorn Prince Regent (George IV) with the Archbishop of Canterbury and sundry aristocrats. Two Jews, one of whom may well be Lord George Gordon, lament the group's fate while Lady FitzHerbert, the Prince's mistress, bewails his departure.

In 1787 the noble dissenter published a twenty-two page pamphlet entitled *The Prisoner's Petition to the right honourable Lord George Gordon, to Preserve their lives and Liberties, and Prevent their Banishment to Botany Bay*, in which he accused the judiciary, and therefore the King, for 'having condemned prisoners to death contrary to law' through the subterfuge of transportation'. Gordon quaintly chose the gist of his protest with words from the Jewish prayer book and the Hebrew Bible:

> We the prisoners whose names are underwritten, galled with fetters of iron, and appointed to death in England or condemned to perpetual exile and arbitrary government in a barbarous country abroad, where the remainder of our lives is determined to be made with hard bondage, most earnestly intreat your Lordship to hear our sighs and groans . . . For verily we have sinned, we have been guilty, we have deceived, we have spoken falsely; we have way-laid the unwary in his footpath, we have arrested the traveller on the high way, we have committed iniquity and wickedness . . . We have departed from the Commandments of God and refused to keep His laws.

A sensational trial for 'a libel on the Judges and the administration of the law' followed, in which Gordon's counsel maintained that his client was insane and could not be properly sentenced. While the jury agreed that his offence did not amount to high treason, they believed he was guilty of being a 'malicious, seditious and ill disposed person'. Rather than wait for the sentence of the law, the noble lord fled across the Channel to find refuge among the Jews of Amsterdam. The Dutch authorities promptly returned the bearded, grotesquely behatted, black-robed English nobleman to face the verdict of the court, which found him guilty and sent him to Newgate Gaol. Curiously, Gordon scored one small triumph and actually delayed the birth of a nation in his 'barbarous country'. It seems that the authorities waited to see what would be the outcome of the trial and whether Gordon was correct when he alleged that 'divers laws of this realm, punishable by death, were made contrary to the laws of God, and the rightful power of the king and the parliament of this realm to make such laws'. The *Public Advertiser* of 29 March 1787 reported that 'Governor Phillip is still in town, and it is supposed his sailing with the fleet to Botany Bay will be postponed til after Lord George Gordon's trial on the second libel he is charged with by the Attorney General'. In prison, Gordon defiantly held court, but five long years later, in 1793 at the age of forty-two, he died of gaol fever. Spurned both by the official Jewish community of London and his mortified family, a contemporary newspaper commented that 'his last moments were embittered by the knowledge that he could not be buried among the Jews, to whose religion he was warmly attached'.[3]

The need to dispose of the increasing number of convicts packed into the hulks was not the only reason for colonising New South Wales. Profound social changes brought about by the Industrial Revolution led to a search for new ways to dispose of the dispossessed and disobedient criminal class. The procession of the condemned prisoners from Newgate to the gallows at Tyburn was discontinued in 1783 because the crowds in the streets of London had become too difficult to control, and many executions brought public cries of protest. The first executions in front of Newgate Gaol, adjacent to the Old Bailey, took place on 3 December 1783. The burning to death of women was finally abolished in 1790, but between 1783 and 1790 the victims were hanged and then burnt. A few weeks after the first settlement in New South Wales, the *Gentleman's Magazine* of Wednesday 23 April 1788 proudly told its readers of a wonderful new invention involving a portable platform with a trap door':

> This day the malefactors ordered for execution on the 18th were brought out of Newgate, about eight in the morning, and suspended on a gallows of a new construction. After hanging the usual time, they were taken down, and the machine cleared away in half an hour. By practice the art is much improved, and there is no part of the world where villains are hanged in so neat a manner, and with so little ceremony.

The growth of British commercial and national interests demanded the continuation of an expansionist policy, despite the deeply felt loss of the American colonies. The centuries-old confrontation of Britain with France, Holland and Spain was spreading to Asia and the Pacific, creating the need for new trading ports. British merchants hankered for the riches of the Orient, which for so long had been the

'*A Fleet of Transports under Convoy*', *watercolour by Andrew Dighton, c. 1771. Transportation of England's unwanted criminals was sanctioned by Act of Parliament in 1717, only to be briefly interrupted by the American War of Independence. This procession of tied convicts is being led into exile past London's Newgate Prison by a villainous guard. The first two figures in the line are clearly identifiable as Jews.*

exclusive preserves of the Dutch in the East Indies and the Spaniards in the Philippines and other Pacific islands. The Royal Navy, which protected England's trade, would need a ready source of flax, hemp and timber in the South Seas, and it was believed that New South Wales and tiny Norfolk Island, a thousand miles to the east of Botany Bay, would supply these. There was undoubtedly a sense of empire in the creation of the Australian colony. This was felt by Captain Arthur Phillip—the son of Jacob Phillip, a Frankfurt language teacher, and an English mother—who, when he was appointed to be its Governor, wrote to the Colonial Office:

> As I would not wish convicts to lay the foundation of our Empire I think they should ever remain separated from the Garrison and other settlers that may come from Europe and not be allowed to mix with them even after 7–14 years for which they are transported may be expired.[4]

Like so many of Phillip's recommendations, it was ignored.

The sense of destiny faded as the eleven ill-equipped and overcrowded ships of the First Fleet sailed from Portsmouth on Sunday 13 May 1787, and must have been replaced by a sense of relief. Britain was ridding herself of some of her unwanted citizens, who would be dumped 12 000 miles away and safely forgotten. The process of deportation was carefully explained to the Parliamentary Select Committee on Transportation in July 1812:

> When the hulks are full up to their establishment and the convicted offenders in the different counties are beginning to accumulate a vessel is taken up for the purpose of conveying a part of them to New South Wales.
>
> A selection is, in the first instance, made of all the male convicts under the age of 50 who are sentenced to transportation for life and for 14 years and the number is filled up with such from amongst those sentenced to transportation as are the most unruly in the hulks or are convicted of the most atrocious crimes. With respect to female convicts, it has been customary to send, without any exception all whose state of health will admit, and whose age does not exceed 45 years.
>
> The owner of a vessel provides a surgeon. The sick are visited twice a day. He is paid a gratuity of ten shillings and 6 pence for every convict landed at New South Wales. From 1795 to 1791 the death toll was one in ten. Since 1801 the death toll is one in forty.

And so, for the first thirty years of Australia's existence most of her settlers arrived either in chains or in uniform. Among the 759 convicts transported in the First Fleet at least 13, and possibly 14, can be identified as Jews. Esther Abrahams, Henry Abrahams, Aaron Davis, Daniel Daniels, John Harris, Frances Hart, John Hart, David Jacobs, Flora Larah, Amelia Levy, Joseph Levy, Peter Opley and Thomas Josephs were certainly Jews. John Jacobs may have been Jewish.[5]

The Jewish convicts shared the hardships of the colony of which Major Robert Ross, the senior military officer in New South Wales, wrote on 10 July 1788 in a 'Private and Secret' letter to Lord Evan Nepean, Secretary of the Admiralty, from 'Camp Sydney Cove':

> I am convinced that if it even is able to maintain the people sent here, it cannot be in less than probably a hundred years hence. I therefore think it will be cheaper to feed the convicts on Turtle and Venison at the London Tavern than be at the expense of sending them hence . . . all the seeds put in the ground had rotted and I have no doubt but [we] will like the wood of this vile country when burned or rotten, turn to sand.[6]

Despite the plans laid down in London the First Fleet did not land its convicts in Botany Bay, for no fresh water could be found there; but just to the north a great harbour was discovered with space for the entire British navy. A deep bay tucked well within the densely wooded cliffs and watered by a rivulet was duly named Sydney Cove and became the site for the first settlement. The harbour named Port Jackson held no promise of ease or comfort. The seasons were strange, the soil poor, and water scarce. The white man could find little sustenance in the bushland that supported the shy Aborigines, to whom they brought disease and death in many novel forms. Rations dwindled, expected replenishments failed to arrive, European seed would not grow in the dry, rocky soil, and within two years the colony faced starvation. The convicts and their guards shared hunger alike. Facing starvation and despair, Surgeon John White bitterly described Australia as a land 'so forbidding and so hateful as only to merit execration and curses ... the wood is bad, the soil light and sandy, nor has it anything to recommend it'.[7]

Of those Jews who landed in Sydney Cove, Joseph Levy had the doubtful honour of being brought before the second sitting of any court in Australia. He seems to have been a clumsy thief though a man of some self-confidence. He was transported because at 1 a.m. on 1 May 1784 he stole a copper kettle worth eight shillings from its hob in a London street. He was caught as he ran away with kettle in hand and sentenced to seven years transportation,[8] but he did not sail until three years later, aboard the *Scarborough*.

Events leading to Levy's trial in Australia began on the evening of 20 February 1788. The convict Daniel Gordon complained to the overseer William Parr, also a convict, that he had lost some possessions and had seen them in one of the tents. He led Parr to the tent and pointed them out, just as Levy arrived and abused them 'in insolent and infamous language' and threatened to kill Parr.[9] At his trial Levy denied the charge and said that he had been in trouble before but had escaped punishment —'no thanks to Parr'. He had cause to be grateful to Parr on this occasion for Governor Phillip remitted the sentence of one hundred lashes on the request of 'Mr Parr, the prosecutor', who must have seen that Levy was frail. Two months later, on 15 April 1788, Levy was dead. He was the first Jew to be buried in Australia.[10]

The lives of the First Fleet Jews can be traced through the records, which show that all of them—like many of the convicts—were transported for crimes which nowadays would be regarded as paltry. David Jacobs, a lemon-seller, was exiled for stealing two livery greatcoats from the side of a coach in Thomas Street. From Sydney, as Convict No. 73, he was transferred to Norfolk Island aboard the *Sirius*, and landed there on 13 March 1790. Three years later he was returned to Port Jackson in the *Kitty*, and on 5 July 1802 he was buried at Parramatta. Such bald details are all that remain of a man who must have known experiences and emotions which we can imagine only vaguely.[11]

Henry Abrahams had been convicted in London of three acts of highway robbery committed at or near Chelmsford, Essex in 1785. He had been caught in London and, on being brought back to the scene of the crimes earned himself a reprieve from the gallows by warning the authorities of an escape plot hatched by several fellow prisoners. Abrahams was brought before the fourth sitting of the Criminal Court of New South Wales on 26 May 1788 to give evidence against a fellow convict accused of stealing a pound and a half of flour. He was back before the Bench in September in the guise of 'James Abram' to give evidence in a case of two women who, he said, were continually quarrelling.

Abrahams will not be forgotten for his part in an investigation into a quarrel that was the subject of a hearing on 23 October 1788. He was an overseer of a work gang when he came across a line of wooden stakes put across a road on the orders of another convict overseer named James White. Abrahams ordered them removed. White challenged him and said that he would kick Abrahams' arse. He also said that Captain Tench would not be pleased if the stakes were pulled up. Abrahams knew better and declared, 'Damn and Bougre Captain Tench and Mr Long. I would knock their blocks off'. As it happened, White was in the wrong and was sentenced to be publicly reprimanded the following Saturday, but Abrahams was charged with making use of disrespectful words when speaking of the two officers, Captain Tench and Lieutenant Long. When the case was heard Abrahams mustered a formidable defence. The Captain of his convict transport ship, the *Scarborough*, agreed to give evidence and testified that Abrahams had kept himself distant from the other convicts and was always very clean. He had come out with only a single iron on his ankles. Lieutenant Kellow grudgingly testified that Abrahams had behaved 'reasonably well'. Lieutenant Davey said he was the 'best and quietest'. On 1 November 1788 the Bench ruled that Abrahams was not guilty, 'suffering that good character to weigh against so contradictory a testimony', and declared that 'Had there been any clear proof he would have met with the severest punishment'. Abrahams was sent to Norfolk Island in February 1789 and by July 1791 he was able to maintain himself and not rely on the government stores. He remained on the island until 1796 and then appears to have returned to England.

Daniel Daniels stole a copper pot, a pewter porringer and a pair of shoes from Joseph Solomons in 1784 and was sentenced to seven years transportation. Having spent some time on board a hulk in the Thames Estuary, he arrived on the *Scarborough* with only three years of his original sentence still to serve.[12] In December 1789 the *Gloucester Journal* published what was probably the first favourable news of the convict colony at Port Jackson by means of a letter from Daniels sent through the good offices of a Mr Levy in Amsterdam. Daniels wrote that in the convict colony 'no person was without habitation . . . If the smiths had a plentiful supply of coals and iron hardly any utensils would be wanting'. The letter had been sent on to a Mr Ephraim Daniel, a Jew, of Mile End from his nephew in Port Jackson, 'who left you with the transport for Botany Bay':

> he has settled at Port Jackson, and has leave to teach the children of some of your nation to read and write Hebrew.—The place is very much improved since you had any letters from it. Except wearing apparel very little is wanting but business . . . The Christian Church is quite finished and he thinks if there were enough of your

people, they might have a place for themselves in that he had received permission to teach the children of some of his nation to read and write Hebrew. There had also been a report that several Jewish families in Batavia intended to settle in the new colony and if there were enough . . . they might have a place to themselves . . . He expects several of your people will go from Batavia to settle there very soon and wonders a way for sending old clothes is not found out. Norfolk Isle is so thinly inhabited that it is not worth a stranger's while to settle there . . .

Alas, there were no Jewish children to teach and no Jewish migrants from Java, and Daniels' last recorded appearance was on Norfolk Island in October 1796.[13]

Frances Hart, a mantua-maker of thirty-six, was sentenced at the Old Bailey to fourteen years transportation for receiving two pairs of stolen boots and a pair of shoes. She seems to have been in prison before. A woman of that name had been sentenced to two years imprisonment in Newgate in January 1782. A David Hart, who was probably her husband, was hanged a week later after escaping from a prison ship. Undeterred by David's death Frances was also involved in an escape from a prison hulk when the convicts on board the *Mercury* mutinied in April 1784. She was recaptured at Torbay and, following a special investigation into the mutiny, was sent on to the hulk *Dunkirk*. She had learned her lesson. She was now behaving 'better than formerly' and during her journey to Australia was described as one of 'the Six Very best Women we have in the Ship [*Friendship*]'.

'*Newgate Prison, Old Bailey*', c. 1800. *Newgate, built in 1770, replaced a squalid predecessor. It stood beside the Old Bailey, or the Central Criminal Court, and only a few yards away from the Fleet Prison and the Bridewell. As London grew, carrying a prisoner through the city to Tyburn Tree beside Hyde Park became increasingly risky. In 1783 a platform was built outside the gate to the debtors' prison, and crowds would gather outside Newgate to witness each execution.*

It seems that either the long voyage or the sudden arrival in a strange land sparked off a number of romances, because ten marriages were celebrated during the convict women's first week ashore at Sydney Cove. The marriage of Frances Hart to her fellow convict William Robins was the tenth: on 13 February 1788. On 7 November 1788 she gave evidence at a trial, and in recognition of her religion was sworn in on the Old Testament. As Frances Robins, she and her husband embarked for Norfolk Island in March 1789 in the *Supply*, and on 21 October 1792 were returned to Sydney in the *Atlantic*.[14] Robins was a sailor and would have had no difficulty in finding a place on a ship travelling home to England, and Frances Robinson [Robins?] vanishes from the colonial records.

Amelia Levy, an illiterate furrier of nineteen, was tried with Ann Martin at the Quarter Sessions at St Margaret's Hill, Surrey, on 9 January 1787 for having stolen some silk handkerchiefs from a shop at Southwark. Obviously her sentence of seven years transportation did not cause her to mend her ways, because on Tuesday 11 November 1788 she was described in the colonial records as 'a loose girl', though she was sinned against as well as sinning. Her hut companion saw a man enter their room and assumed he had come with Amelia, but he was a thief who quickly departed with an apron, trousers and some sheets. In the trial on Monday 2 March 1789 it was noted that Amelia took the oath on the Old Testament.

During the convicts' first Christmas in Australia, Amelia was accused of stealing a shirt belonging to a corporal who had spent the night with her. Brought before the court on 17 January 1789, Amelia said that the shirt was in payment for favours received, a statement which was accepted. But two weeks later she was found to be wearing a shift worth one shilling belonging to Ann Ward, another convict. Amelia could hardly use the same excuse in this case, and confessed her guilt. She was punished by '50 lashes at the cart's tail' on three successive Saturdays, while the provisions were being issued. This means that she was tied to the back of a tumbril and whipped in sight of the other convicts, but she had Sundays to get over it before returning to work on Mondays. It is hard to imagine how anyone was able to stand upright after fifty or one hundred lashes by the cat o' nine tails.

As so often happens, such savage punishment did not seem to have the desired effect. In November, Levy received a further fifty lashes because she 'uttered scandalous and abusive language to a sergeant of a working party', despite her defence that her workmates had 'pelted her with stones'. From 1790 to 1794 she was stationed on Norfolk Island, but she was not receiving public stores for this period so it may be assumed that she was living with one of the soldiers. By November 1795 she was back on the mainland again, still attracting enough official attention for her name to be recorded in the proceedings of the Criminal Court as living with a free settler near Parramatta.

John Pascoe Fawkner, pioneer of the settlement of Melbourne, whose father's back was forever scarred by the terrible punishment he had suffered in his youth, recalled the destructive physical and spiritual impact of the cat o' nine tails. 'You lose the last hold of an unrelenting and immoral character when you break his remaining sense of personal honor by a lashing which degrades him to the level of a hound'.[15]

Peter Opley, 'of the Jewish persuasion', was an 18-year-old butcher who, together with a friend, stole a woman's printed cotton gown. He was sentenced at Maidstone, Kent to seven years transportation on 13 March 1786. At the end of April 1788 he was given one hundred lashes for having stolen a tin pot which he said he found on the beach. The authorities were determined to break his spirit. In January 1789 he was found to be absent from the work camp at Rose Hill for three days and was given another hundred lashes, and twenty-five more in March for the theft of half a loaf of bread—and passage to Norfolk Island. Surprisingly, his dispatch to that isolated place of secondary transportation brought blessing. Within a year he was able to take himself off government rations and in 1793 took out a three-year lease for land, finding sufficient money to buy some livestock and furniture. In March 1794 he found work with Aaron Davis and surrendered his own leaseholding. Opley worked briefly as a sawyer and in 1796, having more than served his sentence, was able to return to England.[16]

Flora Larah of Whitechapel was sentenced at Westminster Sessions to transportation for seven years for having stolen a mahogany tea-chest and a half-guinea gold coin. She arrived at Newgate with the name of Flora Sara and unenviable description as 'an evil disposed person ... not minding to gain her livelyhood by truth and honest labour'. Evidently she had persuaded a Mrs Sarah Blackwell to hand her large sums of money on the pretext that she could multiply it mightily by magical means in an imaginary island called Salvadee. On 13 February 1788 Flora married John Hart at Port Jackson. Hart was able to sign his name; Flora made a mark in place of a signature. It was a strange ceremony arranged by the authorities to give some sort of legitimacy to the scenes of debauchery that followed the landing of the soldiers and convicts of the First Fleet. Nevertheless there is no doubt that this marriage, celebrated by the chaplain two-and-a-half weeks after the arrival of the First Fleet, was the first contracted between two Jews on the Australian continent.

Sadly, the ceremony brought only fleeting joy. Nobody could have taken it very seriously because four days after the wedding the bridegroom was sent to work at Norfolk Island and Flora did not succeed in getting permission to join him until November 1789. John Hart had been born in 1740 and claimed to have served in the British army. He was working in London as a porter when he stole a package from the Stratford coach as it stood in a Whitechapel street. He was sent from Newgate to the *Ceres* hulk on 5 April 1785, and two years later gathered up from the hulk to be sent to Australia. By 3 January 1795 John Hart was dead. Flora is recorded in a colonial muster as being single and living in Parramatta in 1814. Could she have been related to James Larra of Parramatta whose successful story will soon be told? Flora seems to have remarried, and by 1821 the inaccurate muster records of New South Wales tell us of the death of a 'Laura Ford'.[17]

The next generation of Jewish arrivals in Australia fell into the pattern set by the convicts of the First Fleet. Old Jewish religious and family loyalties were erased by the pressures of penal life, the struggle for existence precluded the development of a Jewish community, and the rigid colonial hierarchy had no place for religious dissent. At the foot of English gallows the bizarre had mingled with the tragic, but some of those who escaped the noose were to find, in their incredibly harsh place of exile, the will to fashion a recognisably different way of life.

The whip, the cat o' nine tails, the treadmill, the punishment of solitary confinement on bread and water, produced a fellowship of suffering. A new society was shaped in the chain gangs who were forced to build the colony's first roads, bridges and gaols. The military measured out a brutal discipline and the victims inevitably created their own slang. Twenty-five lashes were disparagingly called 'a tester'. Fifty lashes were 'a bob'. Seventy-five lashes and the victim roared like 'a bull' and with a hundred lashes you sang like 'a canary'.

Prisoners transported for seven years were free to go home when their time was up, and many did so after advertising their departure in the colony's semi-official gazettes to ensure that their debts had been paid. Most of the convicts who left Australia paid their way home to England by working as deck-hands or sailors on the convict transport ships or whalers that sailed the Pacific. Others stowed away and were dumped at sea or at the first port of call by nervous sea captains who could be severely punished for unwittingly allowing a prisoner to escape. A system of pardons and recognition of good behaviour gave the convicts a glimmer of hope. A Ticket of Leave served as an internal passport within the boundaries of a town or district. A Certificate of Freedom was the next step up the ladder towards a normal life. A Conditional Pardon could follow and, for the very few, an Absolute Pardon entitled its owner to leave Australia and even to return as a free settler.

The birth pangs of Australia's Jewish community are recorded in the dossiers of those lonely men and women who, like so many non-Jews, laid the foundations of life in an alien land. Two of those convicts who arrived with the First Fleet have detailed histories because they had extraordinary careers in their new homeland. They were Esther Abrahams and John Harris, Jewish convicts whose children and grandchildren would rank among the highest in Australia. Harris founded the Australian police and was the enemy of a colonial governor. Esther Abrahams' tragic life reads like dramatic fiction.

The First Lady

THE OMINOUS PAGEANTRY of the Old Bailey was months away in memory and 12 000 miles away by sea when the convict James Ruse splashed out of the boat sent to the shore of Sydney Harbour, bracing himself as Lieutenant George Johnston climbed on his back and was carried dry-shod to the sheltered beach. A nation was being born when, on that southern summer's day of 26 January 1788, Johnston became the first British officer to set foot on Sydney Cove.[1]

For the young lieutenant it was the beginning of an extraordinary career, in which he rose to be Lieutenant Governor of the colony and to be tried for rebellion against the Crown. His life was shared by Esther Abrahams, the Jewish convict girl who sailed to Australia in the same ship, became his mistress, bore his children and, after twenty-five years, became his wife.[2]

Two lengths of lace sent Esther Abrahams to the penal colony. On 27 July 1786 she walked into a London drapery shop in which Hannah Crockett was an assistant. Esther had taken two cards of black silk lace from an open box that lay on the counter and asked their price. Hannah said that the measured material would cost twenty-five shillings; Esther haughtily replied that she would pay no more than a guinea, and quickly left the shop. Within a few seconds a suspicious Hannah discovered the lace was gone, and rushed after Esther, whom she caught only two doors away. The angry and anxious shop assistant accused her of the theft, saying to onlookers, 'I insist on having this woman searched'. Esther quickly put her hands under her cloak and denied her guilt, but her fright betrayed her. 'I heard them drop', Hannah said in her evidence at the Old Bailey, 'And I said, "There, you wicked devil, you have dropped two cards of lace"'.[3]

Despair had driven Esther to the theft. She was fifteen years of age and she may have just discovered that she was pregnant. Despite the very strong character references given her by three witnesses at her trial, she was sentenced to seven years transportation, and her baby girl was born inside the walls of Newgate Gaol on 18 March 1787. It may merely have been a coincidence, but it should be noted that the trial following her own in the Newgate Calendar was of Joseph Abrahams. A petition to the Home Secretary for Royal mercy was of no avail. The official negative response did not come until sixteen months later and was forwarded by the Recorder of London to Lord Sydney when Esther was already on her way to Australia. The birth of her baby had delayed her departure because, although 'Esther Abrahams and child' were 'discharged' from Newgate 'to be sent to New South Wales' on 30 April 1787, her assigned ship had already sailed from Woolwich. It was some weeks before she joined the 102 women waiting aboard the *Lady Penrhyn* for the voyage to Australia. All that can be traced of Esther at this time is a note in the log of the ship's surgeon, Arthur Bowes, stating that she was on board, that she was a milliner, and that she was '20'. With a child in her arms she must have thought it wiser to add some years to her age.[4]

Many of the convicts had come from the prison hulks and were so badly clothed and so dirty that sickness raged among them. Their condition, in the words of the forthright Captain Arthur Phillip, 'stamped the magistrates with infamy', and 'nothing but clothing could have prevented them from perishing'. Most of the women were thieves, transported for offences ranging from pocket-picking to shoplifting, from fraud to robbery. A number were prostitutes. According to the surgeon, Arthur Bowes, the women were punished on board, for thieving, fighting and abusive language, by being placed in fetters or thumb screws. On 26 April 1787 five women were put in irons for prostitution and the Second Mate was demoted, but it was obviously impossible to keep the women and the ship's company apart.[5]

For Esther Abrahams, with a newly born baby in her arms, the voyage must have been a terrifying experience. It is little wonder that she was glad to accept whatever

'Cattle Not Insurable', cartoon by Thomas Rowlandson. The anchors are hauled up and the sailors' visitors are leaving the man o' war, which is bound for distant ports.

help and protection were implied in becoming the mistress of Lieutenant Johnston. A portrait painted in Sydney in 1820 shows her as a woman of dignity, with dark hair framing a long, finely featured face with almond eyes, small lips and a long straight nose. Lieutenant George Johnston was a handsome and ambitious blond 23-year-old who, despite his youth, was a veteran of years of colonial warfare. His fateful choice of a shipboard mistress would found a colonial dynasty.

George Johnston was born at Annandale, Dumfriesshire, Scotland, on 19 March 1764, the son of a Scottish officer who had been aide-de-camp to Lord Percy. This connection would have been useful in an era when commissions in the armed forces were secured through purchase and influence, and he was made Second Lieutenant in the Royal Marines in 1776, at the age of twelve. George saw his father fall wounded at the Battle of Bunker Hill in June 1775. The teenager served in New York, Halifax and Nova Scotia. In 1781 he fought against the French in the East Indies, and was severely wounded in action. After six months leave in England he was appointed to command the Royal Marines detachment ordered to garrison the new settlement on the other side of the world.[6] Ironically, among his instructions was a strict order to keep the women convicts and the sailors separate.

No mention of his affair with Esther Abrahams can be found in the diaries and log books of the First Fleet—perhaps because their relationship was too common-place to warrant even a gossipy footnote. The only clue that remains is a note that he bought a she-goat from stock purchased by the *Lady Penrhyn*. Esther was already expecting a second child, so milk would have been important. In May 1789, in Sydney, the goat would be stolen and eaten by convicts.[7]

The child was a son, and Johnston had no hesitation in acknowledging him as his own. Pointedly they gave the baby his father's first name, and he was baptised as 'Abrahams or Johnston, George, son of George Johnston, Captain Lieutenant of Marines and Esther Abrahams, convict' on 4 March 1790.[8] Two days later Johnston left Sydney for the convict settlement on Norfolk Island, accompanied by Esther and his son. As the mother of an officer's child, Esther was not to be included among the convict establishment. Her name was only pencilled in the lists between numerals 88 and 89, and 'George Abrams' was recorded in the same way, without any number, at the top of the list of 'convict children'. But Esther had to pay the price of leaving her daughter Rosanna, for whom there is no record of baptism, with a Sydney foster-parent whose identity is still unknown.[9]

Johnston stayed on the island for almost a year. He returned to Sydney in February 1791, and the Norfolk Island Victualling Book shows that Esther and young George followed him in May. On 9 March 1792 she gave birth to her second son. This time there was no ambivalence in the naming, and the baby, who would become the first Australian officer in the Royal Navy, and live to be eighty-nine, was baptised Robert Johnston. His godfather was Governor Arthur Phillip, the only child thus honoured.[10]

In February 1793 George Johnston received one of the 100-acre grants of land bestowed upon the officers of the first garrison. The land he chose, four miles along the road from Sydney to Parramatta, was eventually increased to 390 acres. He named it Annandale, after his birthplace. No doubt he and Esther made many plans for its development, but for the time being he was still engaged in his duties as a King's officer. In 1796 he was sent to Norfolk Island again, taking his son George, now six, to accompany him. By this time it seems that George was fully recognised as his son, because page 72b in the Norfolk Island Victualling Book records the 'military child, Geo. Johnston', instead of the 'convict child, Geo. Abram'.

It seems that Esther remained behind to supervise Annandale, because by 1799 the small family was able to move into a fine home built on the estate. One of the first large brick buildings to be constructed in Australia, it was a colonial mansion built in the style that was to become characteristic of the country: single-storeyed and surrounded by wide verandahs. Within a few years Annandale resembled a little township. Its buildings included a slaughterhouse, butchery, bakery, blacksmith's shop and stores, and an orange grove and vineyard were flourishing. A magnificent avenue of Norfolk Island pines, the first to be grown in New South Wales, led up to the house. In 1832 the estate was considered 'one of the most complete farms in the neighbourhood of Sydney'. This achievement had been helped by the assignment of sixteen convicts to Johnston in 1800, one of the largest groups of convict servants in the colony—a fact which signifies Johnston's status.[11]

The third son of George Johnston and Esther Abrahams was born in 1800. They named him David, and he later became a well-known grazier living at George's Hall, near Bankstown, on the family's Georges River estates. During the next ten years they

Annandale. The grand house and garden established by George Johnston and Esther Abrahams was named after Johnstone's place of birth in Scotland. Sadly, the estate was replaced by an inner Sydney suburban development which still bears its name.

had four daughters: Maria in 1801, who was to marry Captain Brotheridge of the 44th Regiment; Julia in 1803, who did not marry but lived to be seventy-six and died at Horsley in 1879; Isabella in 1804, who died in 1806; and Blanche in 1809. She married Captain G. E. N. Weston of the East India Company, who became a judge in India after retiring from the Company's militia. Eventually they returned to New South Wales, where Blanche, like most of Esther's family notable for longevity, was the last of them to die, at the age of ninety-five on 29 August 1904.

George Johnston snr had transferred out of the Royal Marines into the New South Wales Corps, the regiment raised for the protection of the colony and notorious for the commercial preoccupations of its officers. Its commander, Captain William Paterson, did little to control them[12] and there were frequent quarrels over matters of protocol and profit. In one of these, Johnston crossed swords with Paterson, who ordered his arrest and sent him to England for trial in 1800. The London authorities saw that it was no mere disciplinary matter, and found that he could not be tried in England. He was returned to Sydney, where he was reconciled with Paterson and the case was politely ignored. During his absence Esther lived quietly, receiving her stores from the government and being listed by the colonial authorities as Hester Julian.[13]

The proportion of Irish convicts in the colony had been rising steadily and in March 1804 a number attempted an uprising which became known as the Castle Hill rebellion. Governor King proclaimed martial law and George Johnston took a leading part in suppressing the 'rebellion', which added considerably to his charisma. In London on 13 April 1812, Johnston told the story of his part in the Battle of Castle Hill in the course of evidence he gave the Select Committee convened to investigate Johnston's behaviour towards Governor Bligh:

> When the rebellion broke out in March 1804 I was sent against them with my 25 soldiers. They had 136 stand of arms, beside bayonets, pistols and reap hooks tied to poles. I received the two ring leaders, firing took place leaving 16 dead, 10 or a dozen wounded, took about 30 prisoners and ten of them were hanged.

It was not one of Australia's most glorious military triumphs. Fame held its dangers as well as its rewards and, in Johnston's case, danger was heralded by the appointment of Captain William Bligh to replace King as Governor of New South Wales.[14]

Bligh, whose violent and arrogant behaviour had already brought him to disaster when the crew of his ship *Bounty* mutinied and set him adrift, soon came to grips with the self-made aristocracy of the colony. Measures he took to make it easier for the smaller settlers to dispose of their produce for cash, instead of having to barter it for tea, sugar, rum and other commodities imported by officers of the New South Wales Corps, soon brought about the 'rum rebellion'—a bitter power struggle. At first Bligh attempted to have the Corps disbanded or withdrawn and threatened to cancel the five thousand acre grant of land to his principal enemy, John Macarthur— who was as arrogant and intemperate as Bligh himself, and probably the wealthiest and most powerful man in the colony. Macarthur clashed so constantly and violently with the Governor that Bligh at last ordered his arrest on a number of charges.

There were serious matters of policy at stake. On the one side were the small farmers who struggled to exist. Most were emancipists who were granted thirty acres of land when they were released from servitude. This reward for time spent in chains or assigned service achieved three goals. If the emancipists became farmers, their produce would reduce the dependency of the colony on supplies sent from England. The British government hoped the convicts would stay in Australia and not return home to contribute to the growing ranks of the unemployed. It was also hoped that the redemptive power of work on the land would rehabilitate the offenders.

This vision of a new land filled with sturdy yeomen was flawed. Thirty acres of Australian bushland did not equal the promise of thirty acres in England, nor were English and Irish convicts likely to become successful farmers. Yet the British government had decided to encourage the migration of small farmers to Australia with the promise of a land grant and assigned convict labour. When John Macarthur signed an address of welcome to Bligh upon his arrival in the colony on behalf of the free inhabitants of the colony, the small farmers protested:

> John Macarthur was not chosen by us, we consider him an unfit person to step forward upon such an occasion, as we may chiefly attribute the rise in the price of mutton to his withholding the large flock of wethers he now has to make such price as he may choose to command.

Bligh opened the government stores and broke the prices levied by the private traders. He encouraged the use of the plough, permitting government oxen to be bought for this purpose. He sold government livestock at reduced prices and threatened to break the monopoly of those who sold rum, tobacco, sugar and tea at outrageous prices. The colony's economy was fueled by alcohol, and in February 1807 Bligh forbade the exchange of rum or any other liquor for food, grain, clothes or labour. It was a declaration of war against the officers of the New South Wales Corps, led by John Macarthur, who held a monopoly on trade, imports and liquor.

William Paterson was now in command of the settlement at Port Dalrymple in Van Diemen's Land, and Johnston, now second-in-command of the New South Wales Corps, had entitled himself Lieutenant Governor during Paterson's absence. In Sydney the legal confrontations between the Governor and Macarthur and the officer corps multiplied. One such confrontation involved a chartered ship that had forfeited its bond when its captain had allowed stowaway convicts to disembark in Tahiti. The compulsory bond of eight hundred pounds had been put up by Macarthur, who refused to pay. Handing the warrant back to the constable Macarthur thundered:

> You will inform the persons who sent you here with the warrant . . . that I will never submit to the horrid tyranny that is attempted until I am forced: that I consider it with scorn and contempt, as I do the persons who have directed it to be executed.

On the night before the trial, Macarthur held a mess dinner complete with wine and music. Colonel Johnston fell out of his carriage on the way back to Annandale. The court assembled the next morning and Macarthur refused to recognise the authority of Judge-Advocate Richard Atkins, accusing him of being party to a conspiracy.

Johnston, the commanding officer of the Corps, refused to answer Bligh's summons on the grounds that he had met with an accident the preceding night. Macarthur was arrested once again by a loyal Provost Marshal. An attempt to reconvene the court with six officers of the Corps was thwarted by Bligh, and Macarthur remained in custody throughout the day. That evening the news caused Johnston to fall into 'a state of temporary forgetfulness because of my bruises' and he ordered Macarthur's release. At Johnston's trial in England in 1811 he managed to recall:

> an immense number of people, comprising all the respectable inhabitants, except those who were immediately connected with Captain Bligh, rushed into the barracks and surrounded me, repeating with importunate clamour a solicitation that I would immediately place the Governor under arrest.

According to Macarthur's evidence Johnston exclaimed 'God's curse! What am I to do? Macarthur, here are these fellows advising me to arrest the Governor'. Johnston ordered the Corps to assemble under arms and with colours flying and the band playing 'The British Grenadiers'. Accompanied by Macarthur and his allies, they marched on Government House. Bligh was at dinner. When warned that the enemy was literally outside the gates he hurriedly drank a toast to the King and rushed upstairs to change into his full dress uniform. He then hid in a servant's room in the hope of eluding his captors and rallying his allies. Colonial gossip spoke of Bligh hiding beneath his bed when the soldiers arrived.

Bligh was kept prisoner in Government House for more than a year, with self-appointed Lieutenant-Governor George Johnston nominally in charge. In fact, Macarthur acted as Johnston's colonial secretary and ran the colony. As a colonial ditty observed:

> That Turnip head fool
> Jack Bodice's tool
> Stepped into Bligh's station—*he dared not oppose.*[15]

Eventually replaced by William Paterson, Johnston was given full military honours on 23 March 1808 when he embarked for England, there to face a court martial for his part in the revolt against Bligh. The trial, held in May 1811, found him guilty of mutiny. Such a military offence could have been punished by death, but the court seems to have been sympathetic towards Johnston and to have recognised, tacitly at least, that he had not engineered any plot nor challenged the rule of law and order, apart from his arrest of Bligh. He was cashiered from the army but permitted to return to New South Wales as a 'free settler' in continued enjoyment of the seven thousand acres which by this time had been granted to him by the Crown.

No one knows how Esther Abrahams felt about the caprices of a fate which had carried her from the convict hold of the *Lady Penrhyn* to her position as unofficial First Lady of the colony in which, for six months, she would have been acutely aware of protocol and precedent and of the rigid demarcation between bond and free. But perhaps some hint of her feelings may be found in her use of the name Mrs Julian

'The Red Coats Arrest Governor Bligh', a contemporary cartoon, 1808. There is no real evidence that on the evening of his arrest at Government House, on 26 January 1808, Bligh hid under a feather mattress. Apparently he had changed into full dress uniform, complete with decorations, to confront the posse and declare that George Johnston, and all those involved in the 'rum rebellion', were committing treason.

from 1800 onwards. The origin of the name is unknown. It may have been her mother's maiden name, or that of the father of her first child. She may simply have adopted it because she was in a society which would have carried all its religious prejudices as part of the First Fleet's cargo. It was, of course, less obviously a Jewish name than Abrahams, even though there were some English Jews with that surname. Curiously, the convict dossier of Ann Solomon, wife of the notorious criminal Ikey Solomon, showed that her father was 'Moses Julian, a coach master of White-chapel'.[16] And Esther may have called herself 'Mrs' Julian as a way of explaining to the world why she was not married to George Johnston.

She used the name when, immediately after Johnston's departure for his court mar-tial, she made a hasty application for a grant of land. Faced with the very real possibility of her protector's conviction and disgrace, accompanied by the withdrawal of his land grants, 'Mrs Julian' was moving to safeguard her family. On 30 June 1809 Lieutenant Governor William Paterson granted Mrs Esther Julian 570 acres of land on the Georges River near Bankstown, adjoining a farm owned already by George Johnston.[17] While Johnston awaited trial in England, numerous advertisements in the colony's press of 'caution to trespass Annandale' show that unscrupulous persons were encroaching upon her family's land and property and that Esther's fears were not unfounded.[18]

Nor were such trespasses the only harassment she experienced. On 13 October 1809 an otherwise unknown Mr Browne complained in a letter to the Secretary of State, Viscount Castlereagh, about corruption that had followed the deposing of Governor Bligh. Among other points, he claimed that 'Johnston's woman, a Jewess, offered to sell since he went, two hundredweight of kidney fat, taken out of Government bullocks, at two shillings and sixpence per pound. This she saved during his Government'.[19]

Whether this charge was justified or not, it seems certain that Esther had by this time developed into a capable woman of affairs. As will be seen later, one of her friends was prepared to testify that she bore the brunt of the administration of Annandale, and that 'the red jacket' (her husband, in scarlet military tunic) left the hard work to her.

It is indeed possible that Johnston, like most Britons of that era, associated wealth with land, without giving much thought as to how wealth was to be extracted from the land. It may well be that Esther, with an instinct for making the best of whatever came to hand, acted as his unpaid agent and land steward as well as his mistress. As also will be seen, it seems that her family life suffered in the process and, with too much on her mind, she sought relaxation in the bottle.

Sadly, Paterson's grant of land was short-lived. Late in 1809 Colonel Lachlan Macquarie with seven hundred men of the 73rd Regiment arrived in Sydney as the new Governor and began, as he meant to continue, by reorganising the New South Wales Corps. It was the beginning of a soberly progressive era in which political power was moved firmly from military to administrative hands, and a by-product of the process was cancellation of all grants and leases made between Bligh's arrest and Macquarie's arrival.[20] On 30 October 1810 Esther sought 'confirmation of her land grant' from the new Governor, stating that she had 'a large family, and it is her intention to settle in the country'. As an additional persuasion she mentioned that she had 'received a considerable stock of cattle which will be at a serious loss for grazing land, if deprived of the said land'.[21]

The appeal failed to stir Macquarie's stern Scottish soul. In his Proclamation No. 4, published in the *Sydney Gazette* on 24 February 1810, he wrote:

> the Governor has seen with great Regret, the Immorality and Vice so prevalent, among the lower Classes of the Colony: the scandalous and pernicious custom . . . of persons of different sexes cohabiting and living together.

Undoubtedly he knew that Esther was the mistress of a leader in the revolt against Bligh, and he had strong views about marriages 'unsanctioned by the ties of matrimony'. Esther could not conceal herself behind her alias of Esther Julian, and her petition bears only a short note in Macquarie's handwriting: 'Inadmissible'.

Defiantly Esther decided to ignore the vice-regal decree, and remained in illegal occupation of the land until 1813. By that time, George Johnston had returned to Australia and, as so often happens after one man has made a snap judgement on another, the Governor had found, to his surprise, that Bligh's usurper was a fine fellow after all. He reversed his ruling against Esther, the grant was unconditionally confirmed, and to this day the Bankstown parish map that registers the original grants shows Esther Julian as grantee of the 570 acres.[22]

The friendship between Johnston and Macquarie had another unexpected result. The Governor's friend and comrade could hardly remain the father of a large family of illegitimate offspring, and so, twenty-five years after the First Fleet arrived in Australia, 'George Johnston of Annandale married Mrs Esther Julian of the same place' at Concord, their marriage being registered at the Church of St John's, Parramatta on 12 November 1814. The witnesses were Mr Isaac Nichols and his wife Rosanna, and their reason for being there sheds light on Esther's oldest secret. Mrs Rosanna Nichols was the child whom Esther bore in Newgate Gaol.

Rosanna's husband had arrived as a convict in 1791 and for some years was assigned to Johnston's household, where he met Rosanna when she was still a little girl. By the time they married he was a well-to-do merchant who had been appointed the first Postmaster of New South Wales, even though in 1799 he had crossed swords with the law in a case in which George Johnston attested that 'for near two years and a half that he [Nichols] was under my direction he always behaved with the Outmost Honesty, Attention, and Sobriety'.[23] The Marriage Register of Sydney's Church of St Philip shows that on 18 February 1805 he married Miss Rosanna Abrahams, though the *Sydney Gazette* reported the marriage of Mr Nichols to Miss Rosanna Julian. The fact that Rosanna was, occasionally at least, known under this name, gives some support to the theory that it was her father's surname. She must have given this name to the parish clerk, who entered it in the register; but the wily chaplain who performed the ceremony, Reverend Samuel Marsden, was aware of the truth and crossed it out, substituting 'Abrahams'. Rosanna, then eighteen, signed the register as Abrahams.

Samuel Marsden's change in the Marriage Register makes it fairly obvious that people in the little Sydney community were well aware of the true name and origin of the 'Julians', but the incumbent did not dare to correct Esther when she signed the register under that name. The risk of offending Johnston, by that time an even more powerful man in the colony, would have been too great.

As Mrs Johnston, Esther and her family continued a close association with Isaac and Rosanna Nichols. When Isaac died in 1819 it was found that he had named George Johnston as one of his executors,[24] and when Rosanna married again the ceremony was witnessed by Blanche Johnston, one of her half-sisters. This wedding also was at St Philip's, on 13 August 1820, to the farmer James Stewart.[25] Rosanna's children subsequently lived for varying periods with the Johnstons at Annandale. Unlike most of Esther and George's children, Rosanna died comparatively young. After all, she had been born in Newgate Gaol, travelled to Australia on the First Fleet and survived those first years of famine, after which she had been fostered while her mother was at Norfolk Island. Rosanna died on 11 April 1837, aged forty-nine, and is buried in the Nichols family vault in Rookwood Cemetery, Sydney.

Much of what we know of Esther as a person must be gleaned from a sensational trial after the death of George Johnston in 1823. By that time the children were all well grown, apart from a daughter who died as an infant and the eldest son, George. In the manner of those days, George snr had applied to the Governor for his son to be given a commission as an Ensign (presumably in the New South Wales Corps) when he was only six years old, describing him rather vaguely as 'well grown', and the application was recommended to England.[26] Probably because of Esther's status, it was never approved. George had to wait for a government appointment until he was of age. He was made a clerk in the Commissariat General Department, and five years later Macquarie appointed him Superintendent of Government Flocks and Herds.[27] The position was rather appropriate because his family had been supplying a large part of the government's beef requirements for some years, but it was also to be the death of him.

On 19 February 1820, while mustering government cattle at Brownlow Hill near Camden, young George was killed by a fall from his horse. His death moved Macquarie to write that he had been 'by far the most rising and promising young man to which this country has ever given birth'. The regard in which Macquarie held the Johnston family is shown once more by the fact that he appointed the third son, David, to fill George's position.[28]

George Johnston died on 5 January 1823 'after a short but severe illness', and left to 'the mother of his children ... for the term of her natural life the estate of Annandale'. Robert was to succeed her in this inheritance, while David received the family land on the Georges River, where he was to become a leading grazier.[29]

Apparently Robert resented the fact that Annandale was left in his mother's care and to her benefit, and perhaps Esther did not run it as well as she might have done. Possibly the woman who had been a convict girl was weary of the bucolic life, because on 10 February 1829 she placed an advertisement in the *Australian* to say that she wanted to 'mortgage her property for her lifetime'. A subsequent advertisement, no doubt on legal advice, changed the period to 'five or seven years', as she intended to return to England.[30]

This spurred Robert and his sisters to action. An undelivered mortgage could mean that he would receive Annandale under a heavy encumbrance, if at all. He asked the court to declare his mother insane, and less than a week later the inquiry opened at what the *Australian* of 11 March 1829 described as 'the residence of this unfortunate lady'. Esther certainly had enough wits about her to engage David Poole, a Jewish lawyer who had arrived as a settler in 1828, as solicitor in her defence. Poole was well regarded, and in 1830 was offered the position of Solicitor-General, which he refused. In the Johnston case he had to face W. C. Wentworth, of the family which, for two hundred years, remained prominent in Australian law and politics.

The spectacle of two members of one of the colony's leading families hanging out their dirty washing in public aroused avid interest and, in the uninhibited manner of the period, was fully reported in the *Sydney Gazette* of 19 March 1829. If both parties were to be believed, there were considerable faults on both sides.

The principal witness for the children's application was the physician Dr William Bland, who said that Esther was 'of rather eccentric habits, hasty in temper, and with an abrupt mode of expressing herself'. He had seen her 'driving most furiously through the streets' and, although he distinguished 'excitement caused by drinking and that which is the effect of insanity' he considered her to be 'in such a state that she ought to be under personal restraint'.

Even David Poole admitted that Esther had eccentric habits, heightened by the occasional practice of drinking too freely. But 'If all persons in the habit of drinking or committing extravagances in consequence were to be supposed mad, he believed it would be difficult to find Jury men enough to decide upon their cause'.

Esther's only witness was an unfortunate choice. He was Jacob Isaacs, an elderly convict who had received his ticket of leave from the government in the previous year. His wife, Esther, had followed him to Australia in the year after his conviction, and her arrival in Sydney in 1816 made her the second free Jewish settler in Australia.

Jacob and Esther Isaacs owned a public house and fifty acres of cleared land at Petersham, on the Parramatta Road. As he gave his evidence he 'kept the court in long continued laughter by his very precise but comical manner of delivering himself'. He told the court that Esther had frequently sought refuge in his home, 'craving protection' from her son Robert, complaining about his behaviour, and showing Isaacs 'Various bruises and kicks and describing other acts of violence'. Isaacs testified that she had 'accumulated her property by hard struggling, that it was not the red jacket who got the money'. He had seen her 'personally superintending the concerns of the farm, and considered her a woman fully capable to minding her own affairs . . . she takes a glass, so do we all, the higher classes as well as the lower'.

Robert's counsel, Wentworth, called two of Robert's assigned servants to the witness box, and even her grandson Charles Nichols, to give evidence against Esther. According to the report, the young man testified that his grandmother 'was always a strong industrious woman, but of late she had become altered . . . she had frequently complained to him of things occurring at Annandale, and raving against her son Robert'.

Sensing that his case was not going well, Poole spoke for some length in asking for an adjournment so that more witnesses might be called, but Wentworth pressed for a decision. The jury retired and, 'after a lapse of one hour, during which much anxiety pervaded the auditors', returned with the finding that Mrs Esther Johnston, although she had lucid intervals, was 'not of sound mind, nor capable of managing her affairs'. Whatever hopes Robert might have had were frustrated by the appointment of trustees for the estate, and the declaration that he was not the heir at law. At least he had prevented his mother from mortgaging Annandale and returning to England.[31]

Esther lived for another fifteen years, most of them at her son David's estate, named appropriately George's Hall. When she died, on 26 August 1846, Robert obeyed the instructions in his father's will that she was to be buried at Annandale, and her body was interred there on 31 August 1846. She lay undisturbed for many years until Annandale was subdivided and a new family vault built at Waverley Cemetery, where she lies by her husband's side, described as 'Esther, his relict'.

There is a fitting sequel to her story. Rosanna, born in Newgate Gaol, gave birth on 27 October 1809 to her second son, George Robert Nichols. Before Isaac Nichols died in 1819 he sent two of his sons, Isaac David and George, to England.[32] George returned in 1822 and was articled to the Crown Solicitor to prepare him for what was to be a successful and prosperous legal career. In the 1830s he was closely associated with W. C. Wentworth and Dr William Bland (who had been transported for killing a man in a duel) in Australia's first organised political party: the Australian Patriotic Association. In 1839 he became editor and part-owner of the *Australian* as well as being a prosperous lawyer, and his newspaper did not fail to report on 27 May 1841 that he had appointed George Moss, the Honorary Secretary of the Sydney Synagogue, as his secretary.

In 1848 George Nichols was elected to the New South Wales Legislative Council to represent East and West Maitland and Morpeth, and in September 1853 this son of an illegitimate Jewish girl and a convict used his powerful oratory to plead for Jews to be placed on the same footing as

George Robert Nichols, charcoal drawing by Charles Rodius, 1850. The grandson of Esther Johnston and son of Rosanna Abrahams of the First Fleet became the first native-born Australian to be admitted as a solicitor in New South Wales. An eloquent and forceful speaker, Nichols defended in the Legislative Council the cause of Australian Jewish emancipation and legal equality.

Christians in the distribution of State aid for public worship, since Jews and Christians contributed equally to the revenue of the colony. George Moss wrote to the *Jewish Chronicle* in London describing the debate on the motion for a stipend for a Jewish minister of religion:

> Mr Wentworth who introduced the motion is well entitled to the thanks of our co-religionists, wherever located, for his exertions in our cause; as is also Mr Nichols, another member. This gentleman is of Jewish descent and had recently given £100 to the proposed [Sydney] Hebrew Grammar School.

The motion, which was the final step to full Jewish political emancipation in Australia, was successful and the sum of £200 was placed on the government estimates to pay the stipend of a minister to Sydney's Jewish congregation. The Letter Book of the Sydney Synagogue recorded that the grandson of Esther Abrahams, whom the minister certainly would have known, was presented with a silver cup and a written testimonial of the synagogue's gratitude.[33]

George Nichols died on 12 September 1857, after serving as Auditor-General in the New South Wales ministry formed when responsible government was granted to the colony in 1856.[34] Seventy years had passed since his grandmother was arrested for stealing two cards of lace from a London shop.

A more recent echo of the past concerns Admiral Sir David Martin, chief of naval personnel, who was the first naval man to become a governor of New South Wales since its first decades and the last governor to be knighted. Before he died he established, in 1990, a foundation in his own name to fund centres for needy and homeless youth. It was a fitting memorial to the pride he felt in being the great-great-great grandson of George Johnston and a starving pregnant waif named Esther Abrahams.[35]

A Policeman's Lot

I F THE BRITISH GOVERNMENT gave any thought to the policing of their new colony, no doubt they believed that the two hundred Royal Marines landed from the First Fleet would do the job. But the Marines, members of one of Britain's oldest and proudest military formations, had no taste for such inglorious work. As Winston Churchill observed when First Lord of the Admiralty, British discipline was traditionally controlled by a judicious combination of rum, sodomy and the lash. Major Ross, their commander, certainly displayed a furious contempt for the colony and everything in it. Within a few months of landing in Sydney Cove, Governor Phillip wrote to ask the government to form a special force to cope with the problems of controlling a penal settlement.

This force was mustered in England by the customary manner of offering a bonus to recruits, and was named the New South Wales Corps. Most of its officers had transferred from other regiments, and included such men as Francis Grose, Nicholas Nepean, Edward Abbott, John Macarthur, George Johnston and William Paterson, whose names are inseparable from the early history of New South Wales.

The first hundred men of the Corps arrived with the Second Fleet in June 1790, and another detachment, under Corps commander Major Francis Grose, in February 1792. By one of those tricks of circumstance which have far-reaching results, Phillip was under the impression that his much-desired permission to leave the colony had been granted, and sailed for England in December of that year. As the senior officer remaining in New South Wales, Grose became Lieutenant Governor and the colony automatically became a military dictatorship.

Before the Corps arrived, one other attempt was made at solving the problem of keeping public order, as Judge Advocate David Collins recorded:

> after frequent commissions of offences in the settlement and these depredations continuing, a convict of the name of Harris presented to the Judge Advocate a proposal for establishing a night watch, to be selected from among the convicts with authority to secure all persons of that description who should be found straggling from the huts at improper hours . . . This proposal being submitted to the Governor, the plan thoroughly digested and matured and the first attempt to form a police force in the settlement commenced on Saturday, 8 August 1789.[1]

John Harris, the man who made the suggestion and who may be described as Australia's first policeman, had the unenviable record of being twice sentenced to death. A labourer of St Marylebone, he was tried at the Old Bailey on 15 January 1783 for 'feloniously stealing on December 30th, 1782, eight silver spoons, value three shillings and a penny, the goods of Peter Livies Esq. in his dwelling house'.[2] His death sentence was commuted to fourteen years transportation to America, but on 22 February 1785 Harris was again condemned to hang—this time for 'feloniously returning from transportation'. Whether he had in fact been sent to the American plantations and had found his way back again, or whether he had merely escaped from the hulks cannot now be known.

His luck held good, because on 19 March 1785 he appeared in court again and was sentenced to deportation to Africa for life. This was the period when the British were attempting to establish penal colonies in West Africa. For some reason Harris was spared certain death by malaria, the fate of many convicts and their guards sent to Africa, and in 1788 he was among the convicts herded aboard the *Scarborough*, to fulfil the sentence passed on him for stealing spoons worth three shillings and a penny.[3]

The night watch that Harris had suggested to Governor Phillip soon proved successful. Seven days after its institution, Harris appeared as a witness before the Bench of Magistrates to give evidence in the 'Complaint of Mrs Sarah Bellamy'. Her home had been broken into by two drunken gentlemen, Captain Meredith and Mr Kettie, and 'The offenders were apprehended by Harris as he was going on his duty of the watch' between one and two on a Thursday morning. The minutes record that John Harris was sworn on the Old Testament.[4] David Collins wrote:

> The night watch was found of infinite utility . . . the fear and detestation in which they were held by their fellow prisoners was one proof of their assiduity in searching for offences and in bringing them to light; and it possibly might have been asserted with truth, that many streets in the metropolis of London were not so well guarded and watched as the small but rising town of Sydney, New South Wales.[5]

Apparently it was a case of 'set a thief to catch a thief', because all the members of the night watch were convicts, no doubt wise in the ways of the felonious community.

Governor Phillip listed the names of the night watch on 1 February 1790, but John Harris' name was not included because he had been sent to Norfolk Island.[6] In those early years of settlement, the little Pacific island was a tranquil and beautiful haven, despite the associated hard work and isolation. The comparatively few men on the island distributed the land among themselves and managed to work it productively enough to support both soldiers and convicts when the supply ships failed to arrive, as they often did. Harris married a convict woman, later identified as Mathilda, and they were to have two daughters and a son.

The island was commanded by Captain Philip Gidley King, later to be Governor of New South Wales, and on 23 August 1793 he selected some of the 'Officers, Settlers, and Inhabitants' of Norfolk Island to be constables, and swore them in. They included John Harris, who became leader of the night watch.[7]

Harris was a man of initiative and independent spirit. By 1794 he was listed as an 'overseer', but in the same year was 'deprived' of two acres of land which he appears to have taken over without benefit of formal grant or purchase. Harris

The first settlement on Norfolk Island, 1790. The remote island became Australia's place of secondary punishment. High hopes held for its native pine trees and flax would never be fulfilled, but its isolation secured it as a place of exile from which there was no escape.

appealed to Captain King, with such self-confidence that he requested a free pardon as a reward for his services on the island. King passed the application to Sydney, but it was more than a year before Harris and his family were allowed to leave the island. They arrived back in Sydney on 19 February 1796, and seven months later, to quote his own words, he received 'from His Excellency Governor Hunter an absolute and unconditional emancipation bearing the date of 13 September, 1796'. This had been granted 'in consideration of good services as principal of the Night Watch at Norfolk Island and at the recommendation of Lieutenant Governor King'.[8] Five years later, when King was Governor of New South Wales, he was to write querulously to London complaining that his former convict night-watchman, John Harris, had 'gone to England with the intention of persecuting me'.[9]

When Harris received his freedom, the New South Wales Corps was well established in the colony. As a military force, it performed its duties efficiently enough. By protecting the settlers against attacks by Aborigines it enabled the settled areas to be extended and, when the Corps had to put down the Castle Hill Rebellion it manoeuvred swiftly and effectively against a considerable threat to the safety of the community.

But the officers of the Corps exerted an altogether unexpected influence upon the colony. In part, this stemmed from Governor Phillip's system of encouraging agriculture by granting land to servicemen whose period of duty had expired. When

Grose, commander of the Corps, became Lieutenant Governor after Phillip's departure for England, this policy was extended to grant land to serving officers. At about the same time, Grose made John Macarthur the Inspector of Public Works, thus giving him control of the convict labour force. The result was fairly predictable. Macarthur and his fellow officers were ensured of an endless source of what was virtually slave labour to clear and develop their land grants. For an opportunist like Macarthur this was a passport to fortune. It did have some advantages for the colony, as the amount of land brought into production increased rapidly, so that Sydney became less and less dependent upon imported provisions.

In the hands of the New South Wales Corps, this new power carried inbuilt temptation. It stemmed from the fact that the colony's economy was based on barter rather than currency, and that the most popular item of barter was rum. For the convicts, who for the most part were illiterate and ignorant men and women existing under conditions of gruelling hardship, rum was a comfort, a relaxation, an occasional anodyne. In those hard-drinking days, it was almost a necessity of life for people who before their conviction had been able to buy spirits more cheaply than food. The convicts would barter their meagre rations for rum, which was brought into the colony partly as official supplies and partly by shipmasters, some of them American, who exchanged it for whatever cash or produce the settlers could provide. The officers of the Corps lost no time in seizing the rum monopoly, and soon became the sole purchasing agents and importers of rum and other goods into the colony. They rationalised their actions by explaining that they were protecting the settlers from the demands of unscrupulous shipmasters, who could earn higher prices by playing off one purchaser against another.

This was only one step in the New South Wales Corps' takeover of the colony. Macarthur was paymaster of the Corps, so the officers could tap a reserve of credit which they put to good use. Grose's administration of the land grants was so easy-going that land was granted to serving soldiers who then sold it to their officers. When Grose returned to England he was succeeded as commanding officer and Lieutenant Governor by William Paterson, who was equally lax about the commercial activities of his officers. When Captain John Hunter, a naval officer who already had served in the colony, arrived from London in September 1795 as Governor, the Corps had completed its economic domination and blandly ignored his attempts to control the trade in spirits and the abuse of land grants. Hunter reported the situation to England, mentioning that small settlers were being obliged to sell their farms because of the monopolistic prices being charged for every necessity, and recommended that the New South Wales Corps be withdrawn and replaced by a force of marines.

When John Harris returned to Sydney from Norfolk Island he must have been fairly quick to assess the situation. It would not have been difficult for him to take up his old position in the Night Watch, which was still in existence, especially since the authorities seem to have found it hard to discover constables of suitable calibre. In the official Encouragement to People acting as Constables at Sydney, Parramatta, Toongabbie and the Hawkesbury, 1796, recruits were offered an additional suit of clothing 'in order to have a respectable appearance' and a pint of spirits every Saturday. Any convict serving a seven-year sentence who acted satisfactorily as a constable for three years was to be at liberty to leave the colony, while those transported for life were to have conditional emancipation after ten years satisfactory service in the constabulary.[10]

But Harris had secured his freedom and no doubt could see where the colony's power and profit lay. He became an agent of Captain John Macarthur, together with James Larra, a Jew who came to New South Wales as a convict with the Second Fleet, and whose story is told in Chapter 5. In 1797 Harris settled at the little town of Windsor in the Hawkesbury District, thirty-five miles from Sydney. It was the first rural hinterland of the colony, irrigated and often flooded by the Hawkesbury River, and evidently it was there that Harris became involved in early Australia's only flourishing trade, the traffic in liquor.

On 1 January 1798 Harris received official confirmation of his right to the $6\frac{1}{2}$ acres of land that he occupied, for the annual rent of five shillings.[11] As soon as he received the grant he moved from Windsor to a district closer to Parramatta and his friend Larra. Plans were being made to license persons dealing in liquor, and in June 1798 Harris and Larra were among the first ten licensed victuallers in New South Wales. Harris and a man named John Livingstone made the requisite sureties of twenty pounds each for Larra, and Larra and Livingstone performed the same office for Harris. The licence granted to Harris was for the 'Sub Division of Parramatta', but the name of his tavern is not given, although it appears to have been located near Toongabbie.

For the time being, Harris and Larra were comfortably established in the New South Wales Corps network of liquor distribution. They sold the spirits while Macarthur and his cronies carried on their power struggle with Governor Hunter, a struggle which they won in September 1800. While Hunter had been reporting on the activities of the Corps, the Corps had been complaining to London about the maladministration of Hunter. Since they themselves were largely responsible for Hunter's inability to control the colony's economy, this cynical act succeeded only because the Corps and the civilian officers of the government, who shared in the profits of the rum trade, could wield more influence in London than was at Hunter's command.

The twelve-year-old settlement was in a sorry state. There were 4930 Europeans in New South Wales, of whom almost half were convicts and their children and the remainder were emancipists, free settlers, the New South Wales Corps and government officials. The convicts included about fifty Jews. Nine thousand acres of land were under cultivation, but prices were so high that government stores were imported from England rather than bought from local farms and businessmen. Money was scarce, spirits were being made from locally grown grain, and alcohol was such a common currency that it was used to induce assigned servants to work overtime. Troubles in Ireland had resulted in an increasing number of Irish political prisoners being shipped to the colony, and there was so much fear that these men would plot an uprising that one of Hunter's last acts as Governor was to sentence some of them to brutal floggings, totalling thousands of lashes.

Hunter was replaced by Philip Gidley King, who already had clashed with the New South Wales Corps when in command of Norfolk Island. His first significant administrative action was an attempt to stem the flood of liquor by enforcing an old General Order of 1796 which forbade convicts to trade their rations for rum. He also instructed that settlers were to be provided for from government stores. The results of these reforms were overwhelmingly positive. As one of the settlers wrote:

> The inconveniences and embarrassments which fettered the growth of this infant colony are now daily disappearing. Population rapidly increases, agriculture begins to flourish, and industry is actively embraced . . . We enjoy the most complete tranquillity. The conduct of a number of convicts is truly exemplary. They feel the value of regaining some footing in society here distant from their native land; and endeavour, by a course of honest and diligent exertion, to earn the esteem of the other settlers, and to atone for the errors of the former part of their lives.[12]

The emergence of a new and more settled civilian economy was a direct challenge to the monopoly and hegemony held by the 'Rum Corps'. Led by John Macarthur, the officers set to work to have King removed in the same way as Hunter, and John Harris was to be the first victim of this renewed struggle for power.

The police reported to King on 13 November 1800 that they had received a letter accusing Harris of having 'sent a Cask of Spirits to a convict' and denouncing him for having 'offended against the regulation forbidding the removal of spirits'; Harris 'had defended himself in saying that no such Order be in existence'. Another report soon followed, probably from the senior chaplain, the Reverend Samuel Marsden, who was one of the colony's magistrates. It stated that 'John Harris, being sent for, admits that he purchased from 2 men 2 lbs of Porke from each. The Charge being admitted, it does not seem necessary to send for the prisoners from Toongabbie. We have therefore sent Harris up to your Excellency'.[13]

Thus far, Harris may have felt himself safely under the protection of John Macarthur, and even when taken to Sydney his self-confidence may have been reinforced by his previous happy association with King. If so, he was in for a rude shock. After King had interviewed Harris, the Governor went to the ex-convict's tavern at Toongabbie with several soldiers. He ordered all the wine and spirits to be dragged into the street, where every cask was staved in and every bottle emptied. When some casks could not be easily moved through the door, the Governor peremptorily directed one end of the house to be torn down. The total destruction represented a prime cost of four hundred pounds, a very substantial sum for those days and, in the words of Harris, 'the whole of the hard earned reward of many years of frugality and industry'.

After the event, King and Harris gave totally different reasons why the Governor had acted so harshly. In December 1803, by which time he was in London, Harris wrote a memorial to the Colonial Secretary, Lord Hobart, in which he petitioned for help and justice.[14] He gave an account of how he had settled in Sydney and become a licensed victualler, 'in which exercise and trade he continued for five years until Governor King began to officiate as Governor of the Colony'. Harris claims that after a few months the Governor sent for him and instructed him to return immediately to the police force and take charge of it. But Harris, having a large family, was unwilling to abandon a trade which afforded a comfortable and decent subsistence, and humbly requested that he might be excused from accepting the office. Eight or nine days later, Harris was suddenly arrested, brought before the Governor, and told that he would be tried before a Court of Criminal Judicature for trading spirituous liquors for convict rations. Harris, 'entirely innocent of any such offence', denied the charge and asked to be tried in any manner the Governor might think proper, but King disregarded this and demanded the key of his cellar. Knowing that resistance was in vain, Harris handed it over and was kept under detention while King and his soldiers wrecked the tavern. King then broke open Harris' bureau and confiscated his licence to sell wine and spirits and, on returning to Sydney, had Harris brought before him to be told that he was discharged and could take possession of the empty casks. When Harris returned to Toongabbie he found that his home was partly in ruins and his property, 'the source of his own and his children's support', destroyed.

Though the truth can never be known, it is possible to believe Harris' side of the story. It is quite likely that King wanted a proven man to take charge of his police, and that when Harris refused he decided to teach him a lesson. On 31 December 1800 King issued a public justification for his action in the form of a General Order:

> John Harris, a licensed victualler and retailer of spirituous liquors, having given spirits to two convicts for their week's ration of salt meat from the public stores, is deprived of his license and the Governor has directed all his liquors be staved. There is every reason to be assured that this transaction has long been carried on . . . If the convicts who have no means of maintenance but by the rations they receive from the stores, are invited to part with it for a taste of spirits, they must consequently rob those who are nearest to them for support during the remainder of the week, which consequently leads to a train of other evils that must be put a stop to . . .[15]

King's persecution of Harris did not end with the destruction of his business. He also deprived him of his land grant. It was an ill thing for an ex-convict to be in the Governor's disfavour, so Harris made hasty preparations to quit the colony. Before doing so he complained bitterly to John Macarthur about his maltreatment, and Macarthur seems to have advised Harris to take legal action against King as soon as he reached England. Macarthur himself was embroiled with King by this time, and no doubt took savage satisfaction in telling the Governor about the advice he had given to Harris. It prompted King to take evasive action by writing to London:

> A dealer, or rather the agent of a dealer, is gone to London with the intention of persecuting me for ordering about two hundred gallons of liquor to be staved, he having in disobedience to orders, purchased some convict salt provisions, just as it was received from the stores, for spirits.[16]

Evidently the matter was much on King's mind, which lends some weight to the suspicion that he acted unjustly. He wrote to London again in November 1801 when Macarthur had been ordered home to stand trial for wounding his commanding officer, William Paterson, in a duel fought over Paterson's refusal to back up Macarthur's quarrel with King. King must have known the lengths to which Macarthur was capable of carrying a vendetta, and feared that he would back up Harris' charges, because he wrote to confess that he had acted 'without a single written instruction':

> [existing orders] were very unequal to meet a hundredth part of the excesses I wanted to remove, one instance of which is a prosecution I am threatened with in the Court of the King's Bench for staving a quantity of spirits belonging to a licensed agent who was detected buying up the convicts' provisions as they were issued from the stores, for which purpose the huckster is gone to England and is to be supported by Captain John Macarthur'.[17]

But Harris was nowhere near England. He had left his two daughters, Elizabeth and Hannah, in the care of James Larra, with whom the family was so friendly that he had come to call the girls his nieces. With his son John, Harris had taken passage on the first available ship leaving the colony, the little *Plumier* of only 250 tons, which had been taken from the Spaniards as a prize of war and towed by a British warship to Sydney. There it was sold to Thomas Fishe Palmer, a clergyman who was one of the five famous 'Scottish Martyrs' exiled to New South Wales in 1794 for sedition against George III. With his sentence nearly expired, Palmer was anxious to leave Sydney and snapped up the *Plumier* with the idea of making the voyage pay for itself by buying timber in New Zealand and selling it at Cape Town en route for England. The only flaw in this canny plan was the little ship herself. She was so rotten that they had to spend six months in New Zealand carrying out repairs, while they ate up most of the ship's stores. So Palmer sailed northwards in the hope of some profitable business in the South Seas, but battling unfavourable winds they were wrecked at Guam, then a Spanish possession and thus an enemy port, where Palmer fell ill and died. Harris' adventures did not end until nearly three years after his flight from Sydney, when he and his son reached London in October 1803.[18]

Macarthur had reached London before him, and Harris hurried to consult his patron. They decided not to 'persecute' Governor King in court, possibly because Macarthur had some uneasy feelings about matters which might appear to his own discredit, but in November 1803 Harris submitted a petition to the Secretary of State, Lord Hobart. This 'Memorial of John Harris, a settler of New South Wales . . . most humbly and respectfully sheweth' the story of his life and misadventures, and concludes:

> That your Lordship's memorialist has been since shipwrecked and made a prisoner at the Spanish island of Guam from whence he reached this island only a few days ago in great penury and distress. That your memorialist can appeal with confidence to Cap'n Hunter, the predecessor of Governor King, and to Captain Macarthur and Mr Balmain, the late principal surgeon of the settlement, for their testimony of his honesty, industry and propriety of conduct . . . In consideration of the distress and misery in which he and his family are most innocently involved, and of the great cruelty and oppression he has suffered, your Lordship will be pleased to bestow upon him such relief as your Lordship's humanity and regard to justice shall dictate . . .'[19]

This appeal is the last recorded utterance of John Harris, and he is not mentioned again except for the brief note published by Governor King in the *Sydney Gazette* of 27 January 1805, which described Harris' offence and punishment. No doubt King believed the battle to be over and that this was the official seal on his victory. And so it was, for Australia's first policeman never returned from England.

But his daughters remained, and James Larra adopted them into his own family. In April 1804 Governor King granted him a hundred acres in the District of Bankstown, and Larra called the property Harris Farm. He may have had his friend's interests in mind, because he could not know that Harris would never return. Five years later no doubt remained, and in 1808 he consolidated and increased the land he held for his 'nieces', Elizabeth and Hannah Harris.[20]

The *Sydney Gazette* recorded Elizabeth's marriage by special licence to Mr Walter Lang at St John's, Parramatta, on 17 June 1812. It must have been love at first sight, because Lang had arrived in Sydney only six weeks earlier. A Scotsman, he carried such impressive letters of recommendation that he was immediately granted seven hundred acres and some cattle from the government herd.[21]

Lang's recommendations were well founded, because when he died only four years later he left Elizabeth a considerable fortune. She returned to Parramatta to live with James Larra and there, on 19 December 1816, eight months after her husband's death, she was delivered of her son John George Lang. He was to become Australia's first native-born novelist, and his book *Botany Bay, or True Stories of the Early Days of Australia* is a remarkably detailed work of early Australian literature.

The wealthy widow must have been a good catch, but when she married again it was to even greater wealth. On 12 August 1820 the *Sydney Gazette* reported the wedding of Elizabeth Lang and Joseph Underwood, one of the colony's leading merchants, and Elizabeth became his partner in managing his vast land holdings and his mercantile and shipping ventures. The huge estate upon which the Underwood mansion stood is now occupied by three or four Sydney suburbs.

This rise by the daughter of an ex-convict into the highest strata of Sydney society brought with it an all-too-human taint of snobbery. When Elizabeth died on 31 August 1858, at the age of sixty-seven, she was buried in the churchyard of St John's in Ashfield, a church she had endowed despite her part-Jewish parentage. When the incumbent, her son-in-law the Reverend T. A. Wilkinson, filled in the particulars on the certificate he wrote that Elizabeth had been born at sea, 'the daughter of John Harris, Paymaster in the 73rd Regiment'.

One hesitates to believe that the cleric would have written deliberate untruths, so the answer is probably that Elizabeth had long since disseminated such a story in a society which was becoming ashamed of its convict ancestry. History reveals her deception, because there was no paymaster named John Harris in the 73rd Regiment, which did not even land in New South Wales until Elizabeth was eight.

A less easily soluble mystery is that of the modest tombstone standing in the enclosure behind Elizabeth's elaborate stele, and incised 'Elizabeth Harris, aged 78, died 24.10.50'. The *Sydney Morning Herald* of 26 October 1850 reported that the deceased had 'resided as housekeeper in the family of Mrs Underwood for upwards of 20 years', but it is difficult not to wonder whether the name Harris was merely a coincidence. So far no trace has been found of what happened to Mathilda Harris, the mother of Elizabeth, though her name is given on Elizabeth's death certificate. The woman buried behind Elizabeth would have been nineteen when the latter was born, in 1791. Yet Elizabeth Harris arrived in Sydney in the *Providence* on 8 January 1822, having been sentenced at Portsmouth on 5 March 1821 to fourteen years transportation. Is it possible that she was really the convict girl who had become Mathilda Harris, and that she had returned to England after her husband and run foul of the law once more? Stranger things happened in those days, and it is amusing to speculate on the embarrassment of the wealthy merchant and his wife when mother turned up as a convict. To take her on as a 'housekeeper' would have been a feasible solution, and the 1828 census lists Elizabeth Harris, at fifty-four years old, as living with Mrs Underwood at George Street, Sydney.

In the same enclosure, a large memorial and a small tomstone mark the graves of Elizabeth Underwood and Elizabeth Harris. We may never know whether Elizabeth was really a niece of James Larra or the daughter of John Harris. But there is no doubt that Elizabeth was a devoted and loyal member of the Larra household. Elizabeth was the mother of Australia's first native-born novelist.

An odd sidelight is cast on this part of the Harris family story by the fact that Mrs Elizabeth Harris was one of the witnesses who signed the Register when John Harris, grandson of the original John, was married to Catherine Underwood, a niece of Underwood. It is hard to imagine why, in those class-conscious days, a wealthy colonial family would have given this honour to a woman who was ostensibly a convict servant.

The John Harris whose marriage she witnessed was brought to Australia with his brother George in 1833 by their father John, who was perhaps attracted back to the country by the successful marriages of his sister Elizabeth. A place was found for young John in the commercial empire of the Underwoods, and obviously he was personable and promising enough to be linked with it by marriage.

George Harris went to the newly formed colony of Queensland, where he became a prominent citizen and a member of its Legislative Council. His daughter Evelyn Jane married Richard Gardiner Casey, and their son, who was also named

Richard, is one of the best-known Australians of the twentieth century. He was a member of Winston Churchill's War Cabinet and, as Lord Casey, was a Governor-General of Australia.[22]

This speculation on the provenance of Elizabeth Harris may sound far-fetched, but the true story of Hannah Harris, the second 'niece' of James Larra, reads like a romantic novel. Only one year old when her father left her at Parramatta, she moved to Sydney when her sister married and, at the age of seventeen, fell passionately in love with Captain Thomas Ritchie, master of the *Greyhound*. She smuggled herself on board the ship and, according to one witness, 'for a month or more she remained in the Captain's Cabin without coming on deck ... when she did she wanted to return and offered a sailor a hundred pounds if he would get her back'. But apparently the captain was sated with love, because he somewhat ungallantly had her dumped ashore at Timor and sailed away, though she desperately waded 'up to her middle in water' in pursuit of him.

Like many another sailor, Captain Ritchie was to find that the ocean was not wide enough to save him from a determined woman. Hannah found her way back to Australia by way of India,

This portrait carved on whale tooth is said to be of Hannah Harris (Ritchie). Scrimshaw portraits and sentimental designs scratched by sailors on tooth and tusk became an art form on the high seas. The story of Hannah's teenage romance with a sea captain became the talk of two colonies and her ten children founded a pioneer Tasmanian dynasty.

and Ritchie was held to account for his actions. He was fined and, with honors even, he took her into his bunk again. He sailed with her to Launceston, then called at Port Dalrymple in Tasmania, where his brother Captain John Ritchie had been Commandant of the Port. They settled at Scone, near Launceston, where their son Thomas was born on 1 February 1820. Four sons followed, with monotonous regularity. But Captain Ritchie, almost as though he did not believe that it was entirely his business, still refused to marry his passionate pursuer. By 1830 he had been granted a total of 2000 acres of land and had purchased a further 1630 acres, but despite this prosperity he was so annoyed by a refusal of further grants that he impulsively sailed all the way to London in January 1831 to complain to the Colonial Secretary. He returned to his estate in June 1831 and, perhaps with a sigh of resignation, married Hannah on 11 August 1831 at St John's, Launceston. Four more children appeared before he died on 19 February 1851, to be out-lived by Hannah by more than thirty years. She died on 25 August 1882 at the age of eighty-five, ninety-nine years after John Harris' conviction for stealing three silver spoons—as the mother of a wealthy and respectable pioneer family of Tasmania.[23]

As for the New South Wales Corps, it was reorganised by Governor Lachlan Macquarie with the 73rd Regiment behind him. He gave the men of the Corps the option of joining the Regiment, or another unit he organised called the Veteran Corps, or of return-ing to England. All the officers and about half the other ranks returned to England, where eventually the Corps was renumbered as the 100th Regi-ment, then disbanded in 1818.

Elizabeth Ritchie, by Thomas Bock. Elizabeth was the daughter of Hannah and the granddaughter of John Harris.

The Honest Jew of Parramatta

JAMES LARRA'S LIFE depended upon the value of a silver tankard which he had stolen from a coffee house at Charing Cross. Were it to be valued at more than forty shillings, he could be hanged. As he stood in the dock at the Old Bailey on 12 December 1787, he conducted himself towards the Bench in a composed and almost courtly manner. Perhaps this gives some clue as to why, among the hundreds of Jewish convicts who served their time and became part of the life of New South Wales, he was one of the few to gain a measure of social recognition and material success. In answer to the charge he declared:

> To deny the fact would be very horrid; at the same time I leave myself entirely to your mercy; the time the act was committed, which my witnesses will prove, I was very much intoxicated, or else no man in the world could attempt to do a thing of the kind, to put a tankard in his pocket, where there was forty or fifty people in the room; as such I leave myself entirely at your mercy; I never was guilty of such a crime before. I never was in the house before in my life.

The Bench was not impressed, particularly as the witnesses disagreed as to the extent of Larra's intoxication. Mr Justice Heath observed, 'I do not think that will be of any use to you, if you was to prove that you was ever so much intoxicated; because an honest man, if he was ever so drunk, would not steal'. To which Larra answered graciously, 'Very just, my lord'.

The trial was brief and the verdict was inevitable. Three witnesses gave Larra a good character, and it is interesting that one of them mentioned Larra as being a 'shipbroker'—that is, an agent who puts those with cargoes to carry in touch with ships to carry them, and vice versa. This placed him in a social and professional capacity above almost all the Jews transported to Australia in the following thirty years. In the transcript of the trial his surname is given as Lara, and his birthplace as France. It should be remembered that one of the Jewish convicts on the First Fleet was Flora Larah, and in London, Hamburg and Bayonne there are records of an important Sephardic family of this name. The family was exiled from Spain by the Inquisition and derived its name from the illustrious Spanish noble family of Manrique de Lara, who played an important protective role during the conversion of the Jews of Spain and Portugal. Many Marranos (secret Jews) adopted the name Lara, and kept it after their escape from the Inquisition and their return to Judaism. It is probable that our James (Jacob) Lara migrated to London some time during the latter half of the eighteenth century from France. Larra's work as a shipbroker may have occasioned

'Adieu Adieu my native land', an unsigned and undated lithograph of convicts in chains about to be deported.

his move to England, but it is not known how long he had lived there before his trial at the age of thirty-seven.

Larra was found guilty, with a 'humble recommendation to mercy' by the jury. This recommendation probably saved his life.[1] He went to prison, and in September 1789 his name appeared among those convicts who had accepted 'Royal Mercy upon condition of their being severally transported to the Eastern Coast of New South Wales or some one or other of the islands adjacent for and during the term of their respective natural lives'.

According to the 1828 census of New South Wales, Larra arrived in Sydney in the *Scarborough* on 28 June 1790. The ship was one of that second fleet of convict transports which was so anxiously awaited by the hapless survivors of the First Fleet. They had expected food and other supplies to be brought to them, because the stores and provisions landed by the First Fleet were almost exhausted. But the Second Fleet brought a horrifying cargo and, when the *Scarborough* anchored in Sydney Cove, 'afforded a scene truly distressing and miserable'. Judge Advocate David Collins wrote:

> Upwards of thirty tents were pitched in front of the hospital . . . all of which, as well
> as the adjacent huts, were filled with people, many of whom were labouring under
> the complicated diseases of scurvy and dysentery, and others in the last stages of

either of those terrible disorders or yielding to the attacks of an infectious fever . . .
Several of these miserable people died in the boats as they were rowing on shore or
on the wharf as they were lifted out of the boats; both the living and the dead exhi-
bited more horrid spectacles than had ever been witnessed in this country . . . sixty-
eight men had died on the *Scarborough* during the voyage.[2]

Larra, at forty, was a good deal older than most of the male and female convicts
who sailed with him. He must have had a sturdy constitution to withstand the
rigours inflicted by dishonest contractors and corrupt magistrates who allowed the
Second Fleet to sail so woefully short of necessities—and hard work, education,
maturity and a forceful personality all had their effect. Judge Advocate Collins records
that in September 1794, four years after Larra's arrival, he received a conditional
pardon together with James Ruffler and Richard Partridge, two other 'convicts for
life'.[3] So Larra was one of the first convicts in Australia to regain his freedom, and in
June 1800 he received his full and final pardon. This mentions his 'unremitted good
conduct which induced Lieutenant Governor Grose to grant him a conditional emancipation in 1794, and the faithful discharge of his duty as a Principal of the Night
Watch'.[4] It seems therefore that he succeeded John Harris when Harris left for
Norfolk Island, so Australia's first two chief constables were both Jews. No doubt
their friendship began when they served in the night watch together.

Larra's conditional emancipation brought him first happiness, and then prosperity. On 19 November 1794, within two months of his first pardon, he married
Susannah Langford, widow of the convict John Langford who had died at Parramatta
only four months earlier. As Susannah Wilkinson, she was sentenced on 29 October
1790 at Middlesex Assizes to seven years transportation for stealing three pairs of
shoes worth four shillings,[5] and she married Langford on 20 December 1792.

The wedding of James Larra and Susannah Langford was solemnised by the
Reverend James Bain, in the presence of Zaddock and Sarah Pettit. Despite their first
names, the witnesses were not Jewish; it was the common custom to use biblical
names. They, like Susannah, were illiterate, and signed the wedding certificate with
simple marks. Larra's well-written surname is the only signature on the document.[6]
It is possible that Susannah was a relative of John Harris or his wife, and it may have
been through her that the Harris girls became part of the Larra family.

As a free and married man, Larra applied for a grant of land, but although there
was a desperate need for land to be worked the government must have felt wary of
granting it to such a rare bird as an emancipated convict who had the right to ask for
a portion. It took two-and-a-half years for his application to be approved, but on
1 May 1797 he received '50 acres in the District of the Field of Mars at a quit rent of
one shilling, with the implication that he should reside upon and cultivate the land,
and any sale before 5 years would be void'.[7]

Perhaps if the government had not been so tardy in making the grant the destinies of both James Larra and John Harris would have been different, because by the
time Larra received his fifty acres the liquor trade was well established and it was
obvious that there was a better living to be made in selling spirits than in working

the hard soil. John Harris had returned from Norfolk Island and, with the help of John Macarthur, the two friends were granted liquor licences at the general meeting held in the Judge Advocate's office on 19 September 1798, at which the colony's first licences were issued.[8]

Larra's tavern was in a place which he had cause to know very well. Collins gave this account regarding convicts of the second fleet:

> [those] in a tolerable state of health were sent to Rose Hill to be employed in agricultural and other labour. There the Governor in the course of the month [July 1790] laid down the lines for a regular town. Huts were to be built on each side of the principal street, this was to be the foundation of Parramatta.

So Larra the road-making convict now became Larra the first publican of Parramatta, which was then the seat of government and the colony's second-largest township, just fifteen miles west of Sydney. He built his tavern on land which John Macarthur had leased from the Crown, and named it The Mason's Arms. Macarthur's lease was cancelled, and on 20 March 1800 Larra received a new lease allowing him to use the land for fifteen years at a quit rent of five shillings.[9]

The tavern stood on what is now the corner of George and Marsden streets, the later site of Parramatta Courthouse. After Larra had secured the lease, he changed the tavern's name to the more dignified Freemason's Arms. He may have belonged to a Freemason's lodge in England, because Jews had held high offices in English lodges from as early as 1723. Freemasons' meetings may have been held at Larra's tavern, though it is doubtful whether he would have participated because the only early Australian lodge (no. 227) consistently refused to accept emancipists.[10]

The inn is mentioned three times in the memoirs of Joseph Holt, the 'General' of the Irish rebels who, during the disastrous rising of 1798, had hoped for support by a landing of Napoleon's troops.[11] Holt was deported to New South Wales, where he became an overseer of workers on a farm near Parramatta. Obviously he was a man of strong stomach, because after witnessing the savage flogging of an Irish convict named Galvin, he walked with Provost General Smyth to 'a tavern, kept by James Larra, an honest Jew, where we dined upon a nice lamprey and some hung beef'. Holt became one of Larra's regular customers. In July 1803 he took his convict labourers to the tavern of the 'honest Jew' and treated them each to 'a glass of rum at parting'. When he returned from Norfolk Island, where he had been sent after the abortive rising of the Irish convicts in 1804, his first call was for 'a bottle of wine at James Larra's Hotel at Parramatta'.

Governor Hunter granted Larra a Final Pardon on 4 June 1800, and once again it mentions his service to the police and details his relationship to the colony's power-brokers:

> John Hunter taking into Consideration the unremitted good conduct of James Larra which induced Lt. Governor Grose to grant him a conditional emancipation in 1794 and the faithful discharge of his duty as a Principal of the Night Watch, together with a recommendation from Lt. Colonel Paterson, Major Foveaux, W. Balmain Esq.,

the Magistrates in general and several others, the Principal Officers of the Colony, do hereby ABSOLUTELY remit the remainder of the term or time which is yet un-expired of the original sentence or order of transportation passed on the said James Larra in the year 1789.[12]

Even though Britain was fighting for its life against Napoleon, in 1800 the British government issued passports for a French scientific expedition to Australia. One of the naturalists who accompanied the expedition was Monsieur F. Péron, who in 1809 published *A Voyage of Discovery to the Southern Hemisphere*. The work was published in London, which was another example of the remarkable way in which citizens of both countries seemed able to co-operate on unwarlike business even though their governments were pledged to destroy one another. It must be hoped that the scientific researches of the expedition were more accurate than Péron's recollections of James Larra, about whom he wrote:

> Before leaving Parramatta, it may perhaps be amusing if I say something of the singular host with whom we lodged during our stay in this town. This was a French Jew, named Larra, who as he told me himself, had been a thief and forger of bank-notes, and as such had been transported to Port Jackson, in the fleet under Commodore Phillip. After having fulfilled his time of condemnation and slavery, Larra became free and a good citizen. Having obtained a grant of land, he began to cultivate it with much success, and soon joined his fate to that of a woman of his own nation and religion who, like him, had been transported for her infamous conduct . . . this couple tilled a fertile portion of soil, and an abundant harvest was the fruit of their labours. Larra then directed his industry to other objects, and engaged in commercial speculations, which succeeded beyond his hopes. In short, by the most honorable means, he gradually acquired a fortune, and he is now generally considered as one of the richest landholders in New South Wales . . . It is necessary to add that Mr Larra does not keep a 'public' Tavern or Inn, though all persons who have business at Parramatta, and wish to be well treated, put up at his house; we were recommended to him by Colonel Paterson who had written to him without our knowledge . . . we were served with an elegance, and even a luxury, which we could not suppose obtainable on these shores.
>
> The best wines such as Madeira, Port Xerxes, Cape and Bordeaux, always covered our tables; we were served on plate, and decanters and glasses were of purest flint; nor were the eatables inferior to the liquors. Always anxious to anticipate the tastier wishes of his guests, Mr Larra caused us to be served in the French style; and this act of politeness was the more easy for him, because amongst the convicts who acted as his domestics, was an excellent French cook, a native of Paris, as well as two other of our countrymen.[13]

Larra may have taken a sly pleasure in spinning a yarn to the Frenchman, or perhaps the latter was overwhelmed by the hospitality he received. Susannah Larra was neither French nor Jewish, nor had Larra been a forger of bank-notes. His fifty acres hardly made him one of the richest landowners in the colony, though there is no doubt that he enjoyed a modest prosperity. Governor King did, on 9 September 1803, allot Larra a piece of ground adjoining his lease for the purpose of enlarging his inn, but good staff was hard to find and in the *Sydney Gazette* Larra desperately advertised, 'Wanted a single man as Cook and to wait at Table occasionally, Liberal Wages will be given and, if his conduct merits approbation after serving a certain time, a passage to England will be procured for him'. The Muster records that in 1806 he had $80\frac{1}{2}$ acres, of which 6 were sown to wheat, 40 to maize, 6 to barley, and 3 to oats. He had $2\frac{1}{2}$ acres of garden and $22\frac{1}{2}$ acres of fallow land, owned 4 horses, 3 cattle, 194 sheep, 5 goats, and 24 pigs, and had four free men and three convicts in his employment.[14]

Long before the Irish convicts actually attempted their rebellion, the fear of such a rising grew steadily in proportion to the number of prisoners shipped out of Ireland. Volunteer corps were formed in Sydney and Parramatta, and equipped with arms and uniforms. By 1802 Larra was listed as a sergeant in the Loyal Parramatta Association, and in 1804 he appears as the 'Senior Non-commissioned Officer' with the rank of Sergeant-Major.[15] He was becoming a substantial citizen. The Freemason's Arms was the centre of many Parramatta activities, which would always have to be lubricated with a glass of grog, and auctions were held at 'the house of Larra'. Farms, stock, furniture and even a ship were sold on the premises. He was probably Australia's first newsagent when he began to distribute the *Sydney Gazette*, and he was a trusted commission agent when he opened a store and began to supply the government with grain and stock-feed.[16]

When the officers of the New South Wales Corps rebelled against Bligh, Larra, as an agent and partisan of Macarthur, promptly signed the petition to George Johnston asking him to depose the Governor. When Johnston had done so, Larra was one of the

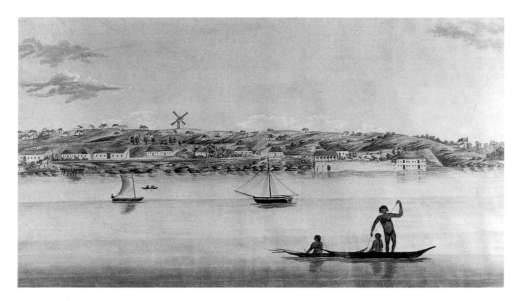

View of Sydney, watercolour, c. 1804.

signatories of an address of thanks to him. The rebel regime was generous to its supporters, and on 11 November 1808 Lieutenant Governor Foveaux granted Larra 13½ perches at Parramatta for 'having erected at considerable expense an excellent dwelling house and office, and in making improvements thereon'. An additional 33 acres of valuable Parramatta land was leased to Larra 'in trust for the use and benefit of his nieces Elizabeth and Hannah Harris', and during 1809 a further 300 acres was issued to be held in this trust. To gain this grant, he surrendered the land he had called Harris Farm when he received it from Governor King. In January 1809 he was appointed the 'Vendue Master for the District of Parramatta', which meant that he was the first official assignee and auctioneer in the district, and in June he was granted ten cattle and in December 300 acres of rich farmland in the Upper Nepean district.[17]

For the time being, nothing could go wrong for James Larra. Even when Macquarie cancelled all land grants received during the 'rum rebellion', thus forcing all who had profited from it to apply to him for confirmation of their status and benefits, Larra continued to prosper. As an ex-convict he bore out Macquarie's strong belief in the rehabilitation of offenders, and the Governor not only reaffirmed Larra's right to his Parramatta property and the grant of six hundred acres but also confirmed the land held in trust for his 'nieces', who had been born at Norfolk Island. Apparently Larra had transferred the name 'Harris Farm' to this new grant, because he wrote in his application, 'Harris Farm, I have proceeded to cultivate for the benefit of my orphaned nieces Elizabeth and Hannah Harris and have expended a considerable sum in erecting buildings on and cultivating the same'.[18] His use of the word 'orphaned' seems to show that he had received word of the death of the girls' father —unless he was assuming it to play on Macquarie's sympathies. At the time, the colony was a tight-knit community where everybody knew everybody else. The story of John Harris and his quarrel with Governor King was well known, and it is extremely unlikely that Larra would have written to Governor Macquarie claiming to be the girl's uncle if they were not, in fact, related. That relationship is still a mystery. Larra's first wife was Susannah or Hannah Langford, who may have been a sister or sister-in-law of John Harris.

Not long after this halcyon time, James Larra's life began to take on the classic proportions of tragedy, in which one event after another leads inevitably towards disaster. It began with the death of his wife Susannah on 12 June 1811, after what the *Sydney Gazette* of 15 June called a 'long and painful illness which she endured with exemplary fortitude and resignation'. The eulogy which appeared in the newspaper read:

> This worthy woman had been many years an inhabitant of the place in which she breathed her last; and was universally esteemed through all classes of society. Notwithstanding the very heavy rains, great numbers had gone from Sydney and other settlements to her funeral.

Susannah Larra was buried in the Common Cemetery at Parramatta, but no trace of her grave can be found, despite the fact that Larra had generously contributed to a fund to build a fence around the cemetery.

Larra had no children of his own, and was now over sixty. When Elizabeth Harris married Walter Lang and left for Sydney, taking Hannah with her, the 'honest Jew' must have felt deserted and lonely. On 26 June 1813 he advertised in the *Sydney Gazette* for a 'sedate middle aged Woman, capable to undertake the management of servants in a Tavern of Respectability'. The result of his search for companionship was his marriage on 25 September to Mrs Phoebe Waldron, the well-to-do widow of a Sydney innkeeper who had died twelve months before. They were married by special licence at the Church of St Philip, Sydney. But she died eleven months later, and Larra's life and reputation were ruined by a rumour that he had murdered her.

The story going the rounds of the little community was that Larra's wife had died as the result of his bizarre sexual assaults, and was given so much credence that he was arrested and charged with 'feloniously and wilfully and of his malice aforethought killed and murdered his wife'. Larra was tried on 15 September 1814 before the Court of Criminal Judicature, but his prosecutors had nothing to go on but the rumoured sexual aberrations which he had inflicted upon the second Mrs Larra—'not having the fear of God before his eyes, but having been moved and seduced by the instigation of the Devil'.[19] It would have been difficult for even the most malevolent gossip to confess to having witnessed the sexual activities of a married couple and, after a very brief trial, Larra was found to be not guilty and discharged.

But the ultimate effect of the trial was to be devastating. Two days after his release, Larra set into motion a series of plans to sell up and leave Australia. In the *Sydney Gazette* of 17 September he advertised his 'valuable and commodious' premises at Parramatta for sale or lease. His property included two houses, a bakehouse, stables for nine horses, a stockyard, vineyard and orchard. He also owned a house and garden in Sydney. But, perhaps because popular prejudice against him was so strong, no one offered to buy or rent his property, and on 1 October 1814 the *Sydney Gazette* reported that he had been 'removed' from the office of auctioneer at Parramatta. A boycott may be suspected by the fact that, only three months later, he mortgaged the Freemason's Arms, which had been the most popular and thriving hostelry in Parramatta, to his friend Samuel Terry. He could not have made a more unfortunate choice. Terry, like Larra an emancipated convict, had set himself up as a sly-grog seller and pawnbroker when he obtained his freedom. In 1828 he owned 21 580 acres of land, obtained by acting 'as a usurer who lent money to friends and then sold their properties when they did not promptly pay back'.[20] Terry soon added the Freemason's Arms to his holdings when Larra failed to pay off the mortgage, but despite Larra's troubles the heart of the old Frenchman remained young.

Faithfully following the dictum that 'there's no fool like an old fool', at the age of sixty-eight he married young Mary Ann Clarke on 18 March 1817. Apparently Mary Ann was a girl of spirit: she had been transported to Australia for helping a French officer to escape during the Napoleonic Wars.[21] Even though he had mortgaged the Freemason's Arms, Larra must still have been a man of property and a good catch for a young woman. In his statement to the Governor concerning Hannah Harris and her escapade with Captain Thomas Ritchie, which took place soon after Larra's third marriage, he described himself as having 'one of the best homes and largest farms at Parramatta'.[22]

Larra's third marriage showed fairly early signs of disintegration, and it seems that Mary Ann behaved in a manner which allowed scandal to accumulate around her name. A note written in 1836 describes her as fulfilling the description of the Samaritan woman in the Gospel of St John (4:18): 'For thou hast had five husbands, and he whom thou cast, is not thy husband: in that saidst thou truly'. The note continues, 'Ultimately she married a Jew named Larra; they lived at Parramatta, but in connexion with a freed convict she robbed the Jew and bolted to London; here the fellow robbed her and left her'.[23]

Like most scandalous stories these statements seem to be based only tenuously on the truth. While a woman who lives an upright life does not attract scandal, it must be presumed that Mary Ann's behaviour flouted the conventions of the time. But, for a few years, James Larra seems to have recovered from the prejudice directed against him and to have regained his place in the community. On 1 March 1819 he was one of the signers of a 'Memorial of the Mercantile and other inhabitants of this Colony', asking Governor Macquarie to act against the importation of trade goods by convict ships. In January 1821 he was selected to give evidence before a British government inquiry, headed by Commissioner John Thomas Bigge, into the affairs of the colony. As the publican established longest in the colony, he was called on to give evidence as to the sale of spirits by unlicensed dealers.[24]

But this was only one side of the picture. The amount of provisions which the government purchased from him dwindled year by year. In 1815 he supplied 3000 pounds of meat to the stores, but he did not even submit a tender after 1819. In February 1821 his name appeared for the last time on the list of those licensed to sell liquor. And in June 1821 Samuel Terry foreclosed on the Freemason's Arms.[25]

While on the other side of the world Napoleon was marching from Paris towards Waterloo, the Provost Marshal's Office published an advertisement in the *Sydney Gazette* on 2 June 1815. 'Terry versus Larra' described Larra's brick house, weatherboard house, one brick kitchen, one stable and several small outhouses. Larra lost everything, and a month later the tavern was taken over by Andrew Nash of Parramatta, who renamed it The Woolpack.

Larra's loss of his property to a fellow-emancipist may have inspired the gossip that his wife had robbed him 'in connexion with a freed convict', because it coincided with Mary Ann's departure for England. But it was hardly fair to describe her as 'bolting', because her forthcoming departure was advertised in the *Sydney Gazette* on 19 May 1821. This was standard practice, so that people could not 'skip the colony' and leave debts unpaid.

She stayed in England only six months, and on 11 February 1823 returned to Sydney aboard the *Skelton*. Once home again, she devoted herself during the next two years to ruining her elderly husband. The law still contained the peculiar provision that a man could be imprisoned for his own or his wife's debts, and on 18 August 1825 the *Gazette* reported that Larra had been sent to prison for debts incurred by his wife. From prison he issued a bitter public notice disclaiming responsibility for any further debts:

> since Mrs Larra's return from England he has supplied her with every Necessary she required, besides Money and Cattle, sufficient to have maintained herself comfortably, had she been provident therewith, which Supplies have left him wholly dependent upon the Bounty of Mr Joseph Underwood. He therefore trusts that his long residence in the colony together with the general knowledge the public have of the arrangements between Mrs Larra and him to live separate and apart from each other, will operate against their giving Credit to her in future. And he further wishes the Public to be apprized that he has been for some weeks past, and is now confined in His Majesty's Gaol at Sydney, for a debt contracted by her, which he is wholly unable to pay, and which at his advanced age he feels very hard.

Very hard indeed! Obviously Larra was now dependent upon the bounty of his 'niece', Elizabeth Underwood. Apparently Underwood settled the debt for which Larra was imprisoned, because he lived with the Underwoods for at least three years after his imprisonment and the 1828 census shows him as a 79-year-old member of the Underwood household. His experiences do not seem to have robbed him of his business acumen, because on 29 August 1828 a *Gazette* advertisement announced that if the debts owed by a Mr O'Meara to James Larra were not settled, a 'town allotment with good house' would be sold to satisfy the account. Perhaps Larra was following in Terry's footsteps and, with the help of Elizabeth, had become a moneylender.

The remainder of Larra's long life, for he lived to be ninety, seems to have been uneventful. He is not recorded again until 1837, the year in which he was listed as a resident of Parramatta. He must have returned to the place of which he had become the 'commercial nabob',[26] and in which he had spent most of his life. When he died on 11 February 1839, Elizabeth Underwood arranged for him to be buried by the synagogue in the Devonshire Street Cemetery. Not a single newspaper recorded the passing of one of the most successful and best-known men of the early decades of New South Wales. However, Mary Ann remained in the public eye for many years as one of the colony's most popular actresses.

James Larra, 'an honest Jew', had seen his erstwhile prison change into a thriving community. He was, without doubt, the most prominent Jew of Australia's early years and among the first convicts to turn exile into prosperity. His downfall had been as dramatic as his success.

The Man They Couldn't Hang

THE GALLOWS STOOD by Brickfield Hill in Lower George Street on the road from Sydney to Parramatta. At nine-thirty in the morning of Monday 26 September 1803, a crowd of men, women and children followed the armed units of the New South Wales Corps which escorted the convicts James Hardwicke and Joseph Samuel to the place of public execution. None of them would forget the events which followed, and which caused Joseph Samuel to be remembered in Australian history as 'the man they couldn't hang'.[1]

Samuel's escape from public strangulation can hardly be ascribed to any merit in the man himself. His life had been a miserable one of violence and poverty. He was only fourteen when arrested in Petticoat Lane as an accomplice of two housebreakers who stole bed and table linen, some cloth and two silver tablespoons, worth a total of seventy-five shillings. On 20 May 1795 he was found guilty at the Old Bailey, and sentenced to seven years transportation. Perhaps because of his age he was not transported immediately but sent to prison instead, and he did not arrive in Australia until December 1801 with only a few months of his full sentence left to serve. Obviously he had behaved badly in his English prison to have been deported at such a late stage of his servitude.[2]

In Sydney, Samuel soon became friendly with Isaac or Ikey Simmons, otherwise known in Cockney dialect as Hikey Bull—an illiterate Jewish convict who had become a constable. Simmons, when thirty-two, had helped a friend attack and rob a pedestrian in Gracechurch Street after they saw him exchange a bank-note in a shop. They stole a purse containing notes worth thirty pounds, though it was not in Simmons' possession when he was caught and identified. This did not help him, because his guilt was established by several eye-witnesses and his declaration to the court that he was 'as innocent as the child unborn' made no impression. He was sentenced to death, but this was subsequently commuted to transportation and he arrived in Sydney in March 1801, on the *Glatton*.[3]

Constable Isaac Simmons of Sydney soon earned a reputation for cruelty, and in 1803 it brought him before the Bench of Magistrates. In May of that year he met a drunken man weaving his way through the dark, and challenged him with, 'Who comes there?' 'A friend', the drunk replied, to which Simmons said, 'Damn your eyes —why don't you go home?' and whacked him over the head with his staff of office. Witnesses testified that Simmons had acted with brutality, and he was 'advised for the future not to beat prisoners'.[4]

Brickfield Hill in Lower George Street on the road to Parramatta. Public executions were held on this hill beside the busy road to the second settlement in New South Wales. Child convicts were sent to 'Carters' barracks' which was built by Brickfield Hill.

Simmons lodged at the home of Sarah Laurence, near his friend Joseph Samuel. With two or three of their cronies they became intrigued by the career and profits of Mrs Mary Breeze, one of Sydney's most successful prostitutes, and before long her home was ransacked. A desk in which she had stowed 24 guineas against the proverbial rainy day was stolen.

The Chief Constable stationed constables at Mrs Breeze's home to trap the thieves if they tried again. One of these policemen was Constable Joseph Luker, and when he went to the house on the night of 28 August 1803, he told Mrs Breeze that Hikey Bull and his mates were the prime suspects in the case. He set out on his midnight patrol of the land behind her house, and early next morning was found as 'a breathless corpse, shockingly mangled, and with the guard of his cutlass buried in his brain'. Near to his body was the missing desk, now empty of money, and the bloodstained wheel of a barrow. Evidently he had disturbed the thieves as they attempted to dispose of the desk.

The little lonely community was in an uproar. The militia was called to arms, road blocks were set up, and a search for the assassins begun. When a barrow without a wheel was discovered at Constable Simmons' lodgings, the ominous words of Constable Luker were soon recalled. Further inquiries soon discovered witnesses who had seen Joseph Samuel at the end of Mrs Breeze's garden on the evening before the murder. Samuel claimed that he and his friends had been with Simmons until eight o'clock, after which they went to bed in a nearby house. An interview with Isaac Simmons soon resulted in his detention, and the two Jews, Samuel and Simmons, were locked in the same cell. Next day Simmons told the magistrate that Samuel had confessed to the robbery, and then Samuel showed the constables where the money had been hidden. But at the same time he declared adamantly, 'I didn't even know Luker was dead. I didn't even see him. I only took her money'.

Samuel, Simmons and two of their cronies were brought to trial. The discovery of bloodstained clothing seemed to implicate Simmons and one of the others in the murder, but Simmons blandly claimed that the blood-spots on a shirt and three handkerchiefs were the result of a nosebleed. His friend had a similar excuse, and explained away the blood on his clothes as the result of slaughtering a pig.

In those days there was no way of identifying blood, and circumstantial evidence was not enough to satisfy a British court, even when dealing with rogues. There were no witnesses to the crime or its aftermath, and the fact that Simmons was off duty at the crucial time was not evidence. The court released Simmons and the other two men, but Samuel's confession of the robbery brought him the death sentence.

Even in the convict colony, it appears that the administration was sometimes reluctant to kill men for the vast range of petty crimes which under English law could be punished by death. The court sitting at which Samuel was sentenced was a sensational one because eight death sentences were pronounced, even though six of them were later mercifully commuted. Joseph Samuel had to face the gallows with James Hardwicke, a thief who had been convicted for the most unlikely sounding of robberies: that of cash from a debtor's room in the prison. The Australian-born colonial novelist John George Lang recalled the events of an execution:

> On the Monday morning, so early as half past six, the rocks which overlooked the gaol-yard in Sydney, and commanded a good view of the gallows, were crowded with persons of the lower orders; and when at a little before seven, the hangman came out to suspend the rope to the beam, and make other preparations, he was hailed with loud hisses and execrations: so emphatic was the demonstration of the multitude in favour of the condemned man. By seven 'clock the mob was doubled; and when the under-sheriff or any other functionary was seen in the court yard the yells with which he was greeted were something terrific.
>
> At five minutes to eight, the culprit was led forth, and at the foot of the gallows, and near his coffin (according to the custom prevailing in the colony), was pinioned preparatory to ascending the ladder. Whilst this ceremony was being performed the shouts of the populace were deafening.[5]

Sometimes condemned men faced their last journey with bravado, cheering and shouting to the crowd, joking with their friends, and mocking the solemnity of the law, but Samuel and Hardwicke 'conducted themselves with becoming decency'. Although they were accompanied by the Reverend Samuel Marsden, one of the colony's most eminent Protestant chaplains, Samuel, it was reported, was also 'prepared by a person of his own profession' on his arrival at the dreadful hill. That person was undoubtedly Samuel's fellow-convict Joseph Marcus, a former student of rabbinical seminaries in Germany and in Jerusalem who would act as Australia's first rabbi and conduct Australia's first Jewish funerals. Ironically, it was Monday 26 September, the Day of Atonement, 1803.

Once Samuel had been 'prepared', Marsden took over and attempted to obtain a confession from the two condemned men. This was the usual practice, and perhaps it eased the conscience of the executive when a victim of the harsh colonial system of justice confessed to the crime which up until then he had denied. Such confessions were frequent from men faced with the immediate prospect of divine judgment, and many of them exhorted the crowd to live in a way which would avoid the same fate. Possibly some of them hoped that their repentance would bring a last-minute reprieve; certainly, the confessions often gave the police interesting information about the colony's underworld.

Samuel's confession gave the awe-stricken crowd its fill of drama. Isaac Simmons, who had been brought there specially to witness the awful fate of his friend, stood close to the gallows, and Samuel made an impassioned declaration to Marsden. It was an imaginative story in which he said that when he was in prison with Hikey Bull they had exchanged 'an oath of secrecy in the Hebrew tongue', after which Simmons told Samuel where the money was hidden and that he had killed Luker. Samuel added bitterly that he would not be facing the gallows if Simmons had not told him about the money, and 'as it was, he would hang 500 Christians to save himself'.

Simmons must have been a man of great self-possession. Suspicion against him had been strong since the day of the murder, and at Luker's funeral there was nearly a riot when Simmons had unwisely stepped forward to help to 'lower the mangled body into the grave'. But now, when a man about to die was accusing him in front of the crowd, Simmons repeatedly tried to interrupt 'with mildness and composure . . . untinctured with acrimony'. So strange is the way of crowds that his composure seemed to bring him sympathy rather than the effect that Samuel may have desired.

'Convicts of New Holland', sketched in Sydney by the Spanish artist Juan Ravenet in 1793.

At last, Samuel had no more to say:

> [he] devoted the last awful minute allowed to him to the most earnest and fervent prayer; at length the signal was given, and the cart drove from under him, but by the concussion, the suspending cord was separated at the centre, and the corpse fell to the ground on which he remained motionless with face downwards.

The executioner, who was himself hanged in 1807, called back the cart, and Samuel was hoisted into it and supported by two men until another rope could be fastened to the gallows and the noose dropped around his neck. The cart drove off again but, as Samuel fell, the rope unravelled and slipped until his legs touched the ground and his unconscious body was only half-suspended.

The crowd was in an uproar, with some calling out that Samuel's last declaration had been true and that providence was saving him from death. But the cursing executioner hurried to fit another rope while Samuel was lifted once again. This time, as though in hope of avoiding a further embarrassing incident, the body was 'gently lowered'—but as soon as the rope took the strain it snapped, close to Samuel's neck, and he fell prostrate.

This third failure caused pandemonium. The Provost Marshal galloped off to tell the Governor what had happened, while Samuel lay on the ground and the crowd milled around him. The Provost Marshal returned with news of a reprieve:

> Samuel . . . was incapable of participating in the general satisfaction. By what he had endured, his reasonable faculties were totally impaired, and when his nerves recovered from their feebleness, he uttered many incoherencies and was alone ignorant of what had passed. Surgical assistance has since restored him. And may the grateful remembrance of these events direct his future course.[6]

The ropes which had broken were later tested, and each supported seven weights of 56 pounds each without breaking. 'It would seem there has been Divine intervention', said Governor King when he commuted Samuel's sentence to life imprisonment.

Samuel's future course was not 'directed by grateful remembrance' of his escape. He was transferred to the dreaded penal settlement of Kings Town, later named Newcastle, on the Hunter River north of Sydney. The convicts worked under fearful conditions in the recently discovered coal mines, and in August 1805 Samuel was charged with taking part in the theft of a chest belonging to Mr John Green of Kings Town. His admission of guilt came 'After much evasion'. After incriminating an accomplice he revealed that the chest had been hidden on the beach, but it could not be found. Samuel was whipped, and in December of that year he escaped in a boat with seven other convicts. Fate caught up with him at last: in May 1806 it was announced in Sydney that the eight men had been drowned in a storm.[7]

Isaac Simmons, or Hikey Bull, was more fortunate. He had escaped the gallows, but as a constable he had 'harboured in his home persons of infamous character, and had concealed and encouraged their ill doings'. So he was sent to George's Head for hard labour in the Battery Gang, until in 1817 he applied to Governor Macquarie for remission of his sentence. He stated that he was 'never convicted in this Colony' and that he had rendered 'long service' to the government.[8] His appeal succeeded, and in the Muster of the colony in 1818 he is listed as holding a free pardon. Yet he is not mentioned in the first comprehensive Australian census, held in 1828, though he must have become a person of some consequence by that time. (In fact, the 1828 census was anything but accurate and many convicts who were in the country are not listed.) In 1831 Simmons applied to Governor Sir Richard Bourke for two male convicts to be assigned to him as servants for the following year, a request that was granted together with a further application for one servant.[9] The map of the Jewish portion of the Old Devonshire Street Cemetery shows that 'Isaac Simmons or Bull' was buried there on 13 October 1833, at the age of sixty-eight.

Long after the gallows had gone from Sydney's Brickfield Hill, the inscription on the tombstone of Constable Joseph Luker reminds us of the drama of his death. The name of the Judge of all the earth must have been included to point an accusing finger at his attackers:

> My midnight vigils are no more
> Cold sleep and Peace succeed;
> The pangs of death are past and o'er.
> My wounds no longer bleed.
> But when my murderers appear
> Before Jehovah's Throne
> Mine will it be to vanquish there—
> And theirs t'endure alone.

Joseph Samuel was not the only Jew to be brought to the Sydney gallows. The next to be executed was Elias Davis in 1806. Decades later, in 1841, the Jewish bushranger Edward Davis, whose story will soon be told, was hanged in Sydney.

Elias Davis broke into a blacksmith's house in Whitechapel and stole some clothes. He was seen leaving the house, chased, caught, and sentenced to seven years transportation.[10] Like so many convicts he was not reformed by the experience. On 1 August 1806 he was arrested for breaking and entering, and the Proceedings of the Criminal Court of New South Wales for 29 August 1806 record that he was seen breaking the lock on government stores and was caught in the act of stealing meat, wheat and sugar. The *Sydney Gazette* reports thus of the trial and its outcome:

> The Judge Advocate acquainted the prisoner that the offence for which he stood convicted was capital and that the pains of death were a retribution which the law required, the present situation of the colony was such as to render example necessary to the security of Society . . .

The Judge Advocate reminded Elias Davis of 'a very recent similar act of atrocious outrage which he had been permitted to escape under a hope . . . of his contrition and amendment . . . he was now on the very brink of eternity and the work of his own salvation became his only duty'.

On Thursday 4 September 1806, at eight in the morning, Elias Davis 'was taken to the place of atonement and being of Mosaic persuasion was attended at his own desire by a friend of the same religion'. This, and prayers uttered at the gallows for Joseph Samuel in 1803, are the first recorded instances of public Jewish worship in Australia.

On a dark winter's night in London in 1823 the 17-year-old Abraham Aaron hid himself under the seats of the Duke's Place Synagogue in Aldgate and waited until the prayers had all been chanted and the way was clear to steal a silver Torah pointer that lay on the reading desk. The pointer was made of gilt and set about with fragments of rubies and diamonds, and valued at about seventy pounds. It was a stupid act. The moment the boy tried to sell the pointer to a jeweller he was denounced to the police and immediately brought to trial at the Old Bailey. Aaron was illiterate and a pauper and therefore had no legal representation in court. Weeping, he vainly asked for the rabbi of the synagogue to be brought to the court so that he would have someone to plead on his behalf for mercy. Confronted with the strange, glittering Jewish ritual object, officials at the Old Bailey erroneously estimated its worth at between four and five thousand pounds: a fatal mistake. The error was carefully recorded in Aaron's colonial prison dossier and clearly demonstrated that he was a villain. Aaron sailed for Van Diemen's Land with a sentence of transportation for seven years. His behaviour on board the *Phoenix* caused the ship's surgeon to report that Aaron had lost his mind and had received more than 200 lashes in the course of the voyage.

Worse was to come. On 18 January 1825 in Van Diemen's Land he was found out of prison after hours and, when caught, attempted to escape from the constable's grasp. Aaron was sentenced to 50 lashes. On the next day a small piece of stolen silk, possibly a handkerchief, was found in his possession and he was sentenced to a further 35 lashes. On 30 March 1826 Aaron refused to go out to work and 'for his impudence' was sentenced to a further 50 lashes. On 24 July 1826 he was found guilty of 'improper conduct and neglect of duty' and received another 25 lashes. In October 1827 he stole a quantity of yarn from the convict clothing factory and was sentenced to receive a further 50 lashes. On 18 July 1828 a charge of theft earned him a sentence of colonial transportation and he was sent to the penal settlement on Maria Island. There, on 18 July 1828, he stole some clothes from a gaoler while in the island's grim Colonial Hospital. Taking into account the enormity of his previous crime in England, he was sentenced to death. The condemned man was brought back to Hobart Town in chains and, in the process of being prepared for the gallows, was persuaded by the Protestant prison chaplains to convert to Christianity and to be baptised. Aaron was publicly executed in Hobart Town on 1 August 1828. A journalist was appropriately impressed:

> This morning at 8 o'clock the awful sentence of the law was carried into execution on Abraham Aaron who was lately convicted of robbery at Maria Island. He was attended by the Reverends Bedford and Carvosso and appeared to meet his fate with resignation. He shortly addressed the spectators, particularly the Jews, and assured them there is no salvation but through the redeeming blood of our Lord Jesus Christ. He appeared to be about 27 years of age, but extremely frail and emaciated.

In truth, Aaron was only twenty-one when he died on the gallows; in the brutal course of hundreds of stripes from the cat o'nine tails, the blood that had been shed was his own.[11]

Izzi, the 'Noted Trap Man'

Fact and fiction linked John Harris with Israel Chapman, Australia's first detective. Several stories by John George Lang, the grandson of John Harris, contain a character named George Flower, the Thief Taker, who clearly is modelled on Israel Chapman. Lang was a Sydney schoolboy when Chapman, Inspector of Police, was known as 'the flower of the colonial constables'. The name of Lang's character may have been fortuitous, but his adventures and characteristics frequently are reminiscent of those of Israel Chapman.[1] Lang wrote:

> George Flower was a great character in the colony of New South Wales. He had been transported for discharging, in cold blood, the contents of a double barrelled gun into the body of a young squire who had seduced his sister . . . a handsomer lad had rarely breathed. Flower had received a conditional pardon . . . for capturing single handed, three desperate bushrangers, for whose apprehension a reward of £100 had been offered in the *Government Gazette*. Flower was now a 'sworn constable', and as a thief-taker was without a rival in the colony. So many attempts had been made upon his life, that, like Macbeth, Flower used to boast of having a charmed existence. His sagacity was on a par with his courage and personal prowess; and in many points he strikingly resembled the blood-hound. He walked about the police-office in Sydney with a swagger which spoke of a consciousness of a superiority in his profession. He was a hard drinker, but liquor . . . never interfered with the exercise of his faculties. Although he made a great deal by capturing the runaways and claiming rewards Flower was always, to use his own phrase, 'without enough to pay turnpike for a walking stick'. . . . He had no fixed residence; but was generally 'to be found' about sunset, at a public house kept by a Jew, called Pollack,[2] immediately opposite the police-office. No great man was ever more easy of access than George Flower, and no one more popular with informers, for he invariably 'acted on the square'. His word was his bond; and he never made a promise, either to do a favour for a friend, or bring about an enemy's ruin, without completing it to the very letter . . . It was a prominent feature of Flower's character, that he had no petty pride—none of that vulgar prejudice which most emancipated constables entertained against men in an *actual* state of bondage . . . no informer dared to name his price for putting Flower upon a scent. His terms were well known: half a crown out of every pound.

Whether Lang's portrait of the clever, knowledgeable George Flower betrays a sense of kinship between author and subject cannot be proved, but when Lang was a youngster he must have heard a good deal about the Sydney underworld. He would have known that his grandfather was a Jewish convict who founded the Sydney police, and he spent some of his childhood in the same house as James Larra before his mother, Elizabeth Lang, who was one of Larra's two 'nieces', became Elizabeth Underwood. He must have heard many stories of the early police and the bushrangers, and his interest in 'thief taking' may have developed out of these.

Like so many others, Israel Chapman's adventures in Australia began at the Old Bailey. On 14 January 1818, when twenty-four, he was arraigned with George Scott for having 'feloniously assaulted James Palmer, a Captain, on the King's Highway at the Parish of St Botolph Without, Aldgate, putting him in fear and taking from his person, against his will, one bag value one penny and 14 shillings and a penny and halfpenny in monies numbered, his property'. The two men were said to have followed the sea captain out of a tavern into the courtyard, where Chapman tried to steal his watch and Scott took his money. They must have been cool customers, because Chapman was arrested after going back into the tavern and 'taking a bason [sic] of soup for my supper, when the night constable came in and the prosecutor swore to me'.[3]

Chapman, who described himself as a coachman and groom, was a small man of 5 feet $3\frac{3}{4}$ inches, with a 'dark ruddy complexion, black hair, dark eyes'.[4] Both Scott and Chapman were sentenced to death, later commuted to transportation for life, and Chapman landed in Sydney in September 1818 on the *Glory*.

Even at twenty-four, Chapman must have been able to make his presence felt. Within a year he was Chief Wardsman at the Prisoners' Barracks in Sydney's Hyde Park with a salary of fifteen pounds per annum and an assistant at his side. A few months later he was appointed Principal Overseer of the Government Lumber Yard. He was delighted with his new vocation, which meant that even though he was still a convict he was paid a wage and could marry the convict girl Catherine Martin in St Philip's Church. The ceremony was witnessed by his Jewish friends Aron and Ann Barnett, neither of whom could write and so signed the marriage register with their 'marks'.[5]

Chapman's future seemed assured. By the end of 1821 he had received a conditional pardon for 'good conduct and work',[6] and the *Sydney Gazette* of 18 January 1822 reported that he had been awarded one pound for helping in the capture and arrest of a bushranger—the first of many such rewards. But early in 1822 something went wrong. Apparently he quarrelled with some superior and was dismissed by the Colonial Secretary, Major Frederick Goulburn. His search for suitable work must have been fruitless, because on 7 June 1822 he advertised in the *Sydney Gazette* offering himself for 'a situation in the avocation of General Overseer, or in any other capacity, so as to make himself beneficial to his employer'.

It seems that only the government needed overseers, and Chapman approached Dr D'Arcy Wentworth, a physician who was one of the earliest emancipists and who acted as Principal Superintendent of convicts in the colony. Wentworth must have promised to help him because Chapman promptly and obsequiously wrote to Major Goulburn:

> With your kind submission being Dismissed By you Sir from His Majesty's Lumber Yard I hope you will take It in consideration Being Out of a Place Ever Since and a Wife to Maintain Which I Cant got no Employ Whatever and Doctor Wentworth will

give me a Situation in the Police Force With Your Sanction as I have got particion [sic] Sign by Many Gentlemen which have known My Activity I will make It my Constant Study to wards the public at Large to Detect all Robbery. Sir, I am your most Obedient and Humble Servant, Israel Chapman.[7]

Major Goulburn relented, and Chapman commenced his career as Sydney's first detective.[8] He began with gusto, and soon fulfilled his promise to make it his 'Constant Study' to 'Detect all Robbery'. The *Sydney Gazette* and the more recent *Australian* carried frequent stories of his adventures, and the underworld soon came to know and fear him—and to disseminate threats to do away with him.

The newspapers told how he found a stolen shirt in a convict's hat and how, in pursuit of a party of escaping convicts, he had his hand mangled by an exploding gun. Years before Sherlock Holmes was even dreamed of, the eager little detective stalked his quarry in disguise. This caused some curious complications in the unsophisticated streets of Sydney, and on one such occasion a prisoner was charged with using impertinent and indecent language to a constable of the law.[9] The *Gazette* reported:

> It appeared in evidence that Israel was masquerading and was so disguised that his mother would not have known him, much less the prisoner, who stated, in his defence, that he mistook the 'Knight of the Staff' for an old cripple, belonging to the barracks with himself. He was sentenced by way of improving his powers of vision, to two days exercise on the tread mill. A little later pedestrians outside Joseph Raphael's general store in George Street were startled to see an elegantly dressed loiterer suddenly cast aside his cane and gloves and throw himself upon a departing customer who had tried to dispose of some stolen jewellery.

Chapman also became known as Izzy the Hebrew Dreamer, and on 26 October 1827 the *Sydney Gazette* began to publish stories about the Antipodean Joseph:

> Israel Chapman, the fidelity of whose dreams has become almost proverbial, was for three successive nights, tormented with a vision, in which he beheld a man who had been appointed guardian in the shop of Mr Dillon carrying off sundry goods and chattels. This renowned dreamer, certain that the three warnings were not to be disregarded, watched about the premises three nights, and on the third night made a prisoner of the alleged thief and detected the stolen property . . .

The penalty for being a good policeman is usually unpopularity and, in a community such as Sydney in the 1820s, when many citizens still bore 'the marks of the irons', Israel Chapman became the butt of malicious gossip and rumours. One was started by *The Blackwood Magazine*, published in London, which on page 157 of its eighth volume published a story about a man described as Izzi C. The magazine said that he was a 'bodysnatcher, drinker and burglar' who had died on his way out to New South Wales. This began the rumour that Chapman was a former 'resurrectionist' who unearthed the newly buried dead and sold them to medical schools for dissection. People yelled after him as he walked the Sydney streets and, when he arrested a lout who had knocked down an old man and stolen his money, the crowd turned on Chapman and tried to release his prisoner.[10]

Treadmill at Brixton Prison. The treadmill was introduced into Australia in 1823. Convicts were condemned to perform an endless macabre march uphill which inflicted agonising suffering upon them. Officialdom was delighted, and use of the treadmill spread rapidly through the convict settlements and prisons of Australia.

In 1826 he became involved in the infamous Sudds–Thompson affair.[11] This began when soldiers Joseph Sudds and Patrick Thompson deliberately stole cloth from the shop of Michael Napthali in the hope that they would be discharged from the army and allowed to stay in Australia after they had served their colonial sentence. Australia had become more attractive than service in another colony or even demobilisation in England. The plan was not original, and its success would have effectively destroyed the morale of the military establishment that supervised and controlled the entire colony.

It was Chapman's duty to arrest the miscreants. First he assembled the evidence against them by taking a sergeant of the 57th Regiment with him to the Watchhouse at the Military Barracks and searching the soldiers. Chapman took some stolen material from Sudds while the Sergeant took a similar piece of shirt cloth from Thompson. Governor Darling felt bound to make an example of both men in order to prevent other soldiers from following the same course. They were solemnly and spectacularly drummed out of the regiment and sentenced to seven years hard labour in the chain gang. The Governor ordered them to be placed in irons of a type which would not allow them to sit, stand or lie down except in cramped and painful positions. It was summer and they were locked in an airless cell, where Joseph Sudds died of exhaustion. This provided a fine opportunity for attacks on Governor Darling, who was in some circles an unpopular administrator, and the political storm caught up Israel Chapman in its flurries. A band of drunken soldiers clamorously attacked his house in Kent Street, but he fought them off with a brace of pistols. It seems that nothing would daunt the Jewish detective.[12] As an expression of sympathy Governor Darling wrote personally to Lord Bathurst, the Colonial Secretary, asking for an absolute pardon to be granted to Chapman 'for his indefatigable exertion as a constable of the Sydney Police'.[13] Lord Bathurst approved, and Chapman was a free man a little less than ten years after having been sentenced to death at the Old Bailey.

During that year, the convict ship *Speke* arrived in Sydney. Among the convicts was Chapman's 17-year-old brother Noel, who was sentenced at Surrey Special Sessions on 10 December 1825 to seven years transportation, for having stolen a watch. He promptly applied to be assigned to his brother and his request was emphatically refused. He too had been a groom and was below average height, but had a fresh complexion, brown hair and brown eyes, unlike his brother's darker colouring. Small wiry men usually were favoured as grooms because they could move easily among horses and ride without tiring them, so it is possible to picture Israel and his brother as a brisk, alert pair. It seems that Noel Chapman had a taste for the sporting life, because he had two pugilists tattooed on his arms, a blue ring on his left hand and the sun and seven stars on his chest. Even though he was not allowed to work for his brother he must have shared Israel's predilections, because Governor Darling's despatches record that on 16 May 1828 he was given his ticket of leave 'in consideration of having apprehended six runaways'. Israel was fearless:

> About 1 a.m. on Sunday 3 February 1826 in consequence of some information he had received, Chapman went together with some other constables to Mr Haslam's house in Parramatta Road to search for some bushrangers. On approaching the house, the party divided, one half taking the back, the other coming from the front of the house, armed with cutlass and pistol and cried out 'here is Chapman—who is going to kill him now?' The bushranger Roberts seized the cutlass and a struggle ensued in the course of which Chapman wounded Roberts severely in the groin. He also wounded Morison and Mackay and secured them in the outside room.[14]

The captured bushrangers were later tried and sentenced to death.

Chapman's luck ran out in the following month, as the *Sydney Gazette* reported:

> active constable Chapman met with a serious accident last week on the Parramatta Road. A party of constables of whom Chapman was one, had been in pursuit of some runaways overnight, and on the following morning, returning into town, Chapman was in the act of drawing the charge from a fowling piece belonging to one of his companions, when it accidentally went off and shattered his hand almost to pieces.[15]

But there was more to life than the grace and favour of a governor. In May 1827, after a particularly dangerous skirmish with some bushrangers, Chapman went on strike. The *Australian* reported that 'Chapman, the flower of the Colonial Constables, has resigned the Staff of Office. Hard work and little pay do not suit an active policeman; and he properly resolves to shew his employers the void that is created by his

Joseph Sudds and Patrick Thompson and their punishment, 1832. Governor Darling's savage punishment of the two soldiers, arrested by Israel Chapman, caused a scandal in London.

resignation. He is perfectly right'. Obviously it did not take the administration long to perceive the 'void', because on 18 June the *Gazette* could report that Chapman was back on duty in the newly created position of Police Runner with a salary of one hundred pounds per annum, which for those days was quite a comfortable wage.

Early in the new year, on 26 January 1829, Israel Chapman's wife Catherine died at the age of twenty-eight. She had been in Australia just under nine years, having arrived in the *Morley* in July 1820 under sentence of fourteen years transportation. Her death must have loosened whatever ties he had with the colony, because he resigned from the police and on 29 March sailed for England in the *Henry Wolseley* with his precious absolute pardon safely in his pocket. Ever-malicious rumour said that his voyage was connected with the impending recall of Governor Darling to face an inquiry into the Sudds–Thompson affair, and there may have been some truth in this. Two years later, with a newly acquired wife, Chapman was en route for Sydney again, having been granted a free passage through the patronage of the ex-governor of New South Wales. However, it is possible that like many a returned migrant he had found London too gloomy and restricting after the blue skies of the south, because there is another story that after a few months in the metropolis he had asked Solomon Levey for a berth in one of his Australia-bound ships.[16]

The *Currency Lad*, a short-lived Sydney newspaper, reported on 30 March 1833 that, 'Izzi Chapman, the celebrated thief catcher formerly designated "the Hebrew dreamer" has been sworn again into office'. This followed an earlier comment in the *Gazette* that 'The villains who infest the town practising their delinquencies had better mind their P's and Q's. They will not be able to elude this vigiland, this very active officer, for a very long period. They had better take the hint and betake themselves to honest industry'.

But Chapman did not fulfil this gleeful forecast. A vital spark had gone out of him. Perhaps his second wife, Mary Ann Chapman, had something to do with it, because she seems to have been hard to handle. She was twice sued by neighbours for quarrelling violently with them, and on at least one occasion Chapman gave her the beating which was the traditional fate of a brawling wife. The press reported that she charged him with having 'thrashed her most unmercifully', and he was bound over to keep the peace.[17] His lack of enthusiasm caused him to be demoted to Conductor, but then he became an Inspector for three years before moving to the country in the hope of an easier life. The government was not grateful to their formerly ardent servant, because when he retired in 1840 it was without a pension.

He went to live in Berrima, where his brother was Chief Constable. Noel Chapman had been rising as Izzi fell. With his ticket of leave in his pocket he went to Windsor on the Hawkesbury, and in 1831 married Rebecca Armfield—the daughter of James Armfield and Isabella Ruse and granddaughter of James Ruse, the first convict to set foot on Australia and recipient of the first land grant in the Hawkesbury District. They had two sons, Benjamin and Henry.

Israel applied to the government for assistance, writing, 'In many engagements I found myself with bushrangers and I became several times severely wounded. I was

TICKET OF LEAVE.

No. *28/89*   *16th May 1828.*

Prisoner's No. ——
Name, ——————   *Noel Chapman*
Ship, ——————   *Speke (3)*
Master, ——————   *McPherson*
Year, ——————   *1826*
Native Place, ——   *Chelsea*
Trade or Calling,   *Groom*
Offence, ——————
Place of Trial, ——   *Surry Sessions of G.D.*
Date of Trial, ——   *10th December 1825*
Sentence, ——————   *Seven years*
Year of Birth, ——   *1809*
Height, ——————   *five feet 2½ Inches*
Complexion, ——   *fair Ruddy*
Hair, ——————   *Brown*
Eyes, ——————   *Brown*
General Remarks,   *Granted in pursuance of the Govr order dated 1 Janry 1827 & also in consideration of his having apprehended 6 Bushrangers —*

Allowed to remain in the District of *Sydney*
On recommendation of *Sydney* Bench,
dated *31st December 1827*

Noel Chapman's Ticket of Leave. Chapman received his ticket-of-leave within two years of arrival as a reward for having helped capture six 'runaways'. By 1839 he was Chief Constable of Berrima, and ten years later held the same position at Yass.

shot in the head and my right hand is crippled besides other wounds of a more trivial nature'.[18] There was no answer, and in 1847 he wrote again. 'I am now getting very old and in proportion to the increase of age so are my pecuniary resources decreasing', he said, but the administration closed its ears to the plea of the man who had served so ardently. He was now fifty-seven, and his hard life was to become harder.

At the end of 1849 his brother died at Yass and Izzi returned to Sydney where he found the strength to become a bailiff.[19] This was a sad descent for the 'flower of the constabulary'. In those days, bailiffs were the lowest-ranking officers of the law, hated and despised because so much of their work involved the forcible collection of debts and the dispossession of those who could not pay. Yet it was an office which Jews occupied quite frequently in London, perhaps because it was a first step up from the degraded trades in which many had had to find a living. The early issues of *Punch*, of the 1840s and 1850s, always depict a bailiff with caricatured Jewish features.

The unsavoury nature of this new work led Israel into evil ways. He may have felt some inspiration for revenge on the system which had rejected him. In June 1852, with two of his fellow bailiffs, he found himself on the wrong side of the dock in the Sydney Police Court, accused of robbing 'an aged shoemaker of very sanctimonious appearance named Amen Willock' of seven £1 notes and two pairs of boots. The press which had once lauded him now turned on him, and wrote of Izzi Chapman and his confederates that they were 'as ugly looking rips as ever composed a trio'. The magistrate agreed, and sentenced him to six months hard labour in Darlinghurst Gaol. Prison must have been a terrible fate for Sydney's first detective, and the rest of his life was endured in broken-spirited poverty. He died at the Liverpool Asylum in 1868, and the Sydney Synagogue granted him the boon of a free burial.[20]

In the stories by John George Lang, Izzi Chapman is disguised as George Flower. The convict poet Frank MacNamara had no such compunction. 'Frank the Poet' had been a guest of His Majesty in most of the prisons of New South Wales and Van Diemen's Land, and gained intimate knowledge of the names and histories of the enemies of those condemned to suffer the agonies of the Australian penal system. In bitter reprisal he wrote 'The Convict's Tour of Hell', and there we meet Israel Chapman:

> *He next beheld that noted trap man*
> *And police runner, Israel Chapman*
> *Steeped was he standing to his head*
> *In cauldron hot of boiling lead.*
> *'Alas!' he cried. 'Behold me, stranger,*
> *I've captured many a bold bushranger*
> *For which I now am suffering here.'*
> *But Lo! now yonder snakes appear*
> *Then Frank beheld some loathly wax worms*
> *And snakes of various shapes and forms*
> *All entering at the mouth and ears*
> *To gnaw his guts for endless years.*[21]

The Redemption of Sydney Sam

OR SAMUEL LYONS, the foul torment of the long voyage from London to Sydney in the *Marquis of Wellington* was only endurable because it gave him time to plan an escape. Unaware that each mile carried him closer to immense riches, the 23-year-old tailor plotted and schemed with others in the convict hold.

A thin, intense man, 5 feet 5 inches tall, with dark brown hair, hazel eyes and a pale pockmarked complexion,[1] Lyons had been sentenced to transportation for life for the theft of a handkerchief worth five shillings. But evidence given at the Old Bailey revealed that Lyons, the son of Levy and Hannah Lyons of London, was the youngest of a gang of three men 'well known to the police'. They had been under observation when they picked the pocket of Mr Robert Goodsall on London Bridge.[2]

When Lyons arrived in Sydney he was assigned as a servant to a Mrs Armitage. Three months later, on 22 April 1815, the *Sydney Gazette* reported that he had absconded. Another convict, a boy of ten, disappeared at the same time. He was John Morris, who had been the youngest of a group of eight or nine Jewish prisoners in the *Marquis of Wellington*. At eight, he had been old enough to earn some kind of a living as a 'quill winder' in London—and to be sentenced to death at the Old Bailey. He was 3 feet 10 inches tall when he was sent aboard the convict ship instead of to the gallows.[3]

The British government may have thought that the establishment of a penal colony 12 000 miles away would keep its inmates out of mischief, but it is hard to destroy the human hope for freedom. A good many convicts attempted to escape, though very few were successful. Some went inland, in a forlorn effort to find freedom beyond the Blue Mountains. They either perished or were recaptured. Others tried to escape by sea, and some of these were no doubt helped to stow away by sailors who were either bribed or sympathetic. Four men and a woman got as far as Calcutta in this manner, but were handed over to the authorities there and sent back to Sydney in the brig *Kangaroo*, commanded by Lieutenant Charles Jeffreys, RN. As the *Kangaroo* was passing the desolate Prince of Wales Island, off Cape York in the waters between Australia and New Guinea, she was hailed by a naval vessel and ordered to add two more escaped convicts to her party. The escapees were Lyons and Morris, but it is not known how they came to be aboard the naval ship. Presumably they had stowed away aboard a north-bound vessel, and had been transferred when discovered.[4] On 17 February 1816 the *Gazette* reported that 'the men were corporally punished for their delinquency and the woman sent to the Factory'.

It was Lyons' first taste of the lash, but it did not reform him. A year later he was aboard the *Kangaroo* again, together with another shipmate from the *Marquis of Wellington*: the convict Moses Moses.[5] They were part of a cargo of convicts being taken to Van Diemen's Land, which had become a place of secondary punishment for unruly prisoners.

By that time, Lieutenant Jeffreys had learnt enough about colonial conditions to discover that there were considerable fringe benefits on offer to enterprising sea captains. The *Kangaroo* carried two thousand gallons of rum to be smuggled into Hobart Town, and Jeffreys negotiated with his convict passengers over the cost of a clandestine passage to England.

Some kind of a bargain was struck and arrangements made. The prisoners were landed. When the *Kangaroo* returned to the Derwent River in May 1817, preparing for the long voyage home, Samuel Lyons asked for permission to visit. His request was refused as 'contrary to standing regulations',[6] but when Jeffreys heard of this he sent one of the ship's boats to bring Lyons, Moses and three other convicts out to the brig. They were hidden below decks.

The sudden disappearance of five convicts from the tiny settlement could not be overlooked for long. The Port Master went out to search the *Kangaroo*, and after a brief scuffle recaptured the missing men. When Jeffreys was confronted with Lyons, the two men played out a straightfaced farce for the benefit of the officials. 'How long have you been on board?' asked the 'astonished' shipmaster. 'Three days', replied Lyons, and Jeffreys commented, 'I thought you were a long time making me a pair of pantaloons'.

It was an embarrassing affair, because Jeffreys was an officer of the Royal Navy and a sense of *esprit de corps* inhibited the administration from taking drastic action. The convicts were charged with secretly planning to leave the colony, and were lucky to escape with a month in prison.[7]

This narrow escape from another flogging, or worse, jolted Lyons back to the path of virtue. He worked out his period of assigned service in Hobart Town and then, as a ticket-of-leave man, attempted to earn an honest living by his old trade of tailoring. In October 1817 he and his friend Moses Moses attempted to win some easy money by entering one of the colony's earliest recorded public exhibitions of boxing. The *Hobart Town Gazette* of 4 October told of a grand field-day: Moses won his match. The battle between 'Stewart, a Hibernian and Lyons, a tailor of the Jewish persuasion' was a long and evenly matched contest which ended when the tailor's 'seams were completely flattened, and Pat was declared victor'. Perhaps there was no great demand for tailoring in a community whose members were mainly clothed by His Majesty in grey or yellow hessian decorated with broad arrows. Lyons seems to have become a general dealer and his name appears on a list of traders, published in the *Hobart Town Gazette* of 9 January 1819, who provided the colonial Police Department with supplies. Lyons sold the police a quantity of pencils.

He then made plans to build a tavern in the heart of Hobart Town, and set up house with a woman known as Ann Lyons who advertised that she was his 'agent' when the time came to collect his debts. Unfortunately he had not yet rid himself of an itch for other people's property. Even while the building materials for the tavern were being assembled, he became involved in a robbery of the government stores in Hobart Town and, as his trial approached, he realised that he had no hope of acquittal. He advertised the sale of 'a most valuable Piece of Ground situate in the most centrical street in Hobart Town [Liverpool Street]'. On the land were 53 loads of excellent foundation stone, about 40 000 bricks, 40 bushels of lime, and a quantity of seasoned timber. His address was given as 'the Plough, Argyle St'.

The crime and the trial are reported in the *Hobart Town Gazette* of 12 June and 24 and 31 July 1819. Lyons' partners in crime were John Fawkner, who had been transported with Lyons, and Fawkner's remarkable son, John Pascoe Fawkner, later to become one of the founders of Melbourne and a consistent friend of the Jews. They were found guilty by the full Bench of Magistrates, and Lyons and Fawkner snr, received the savage sentence of two hundred lashes each and four and three years respectively in the dreaded Hunter River coal mines near Newcastle, New South Wales.[8]

Surprisingly, it seems that the punishment had its desired reformatory effect, Lyons behaved well enough to receive permission to live in Sydney, where he was assigned to Joel Joseph of Pitt Street. In 1822 he petitioned for mitigation of sentence describing himself as being 'by trade a taylor', and that, having saved some little property sufficient to carry on his trade, was about to be married to a young woman born in the colony.[9]

The young woman was Mary Murphy, probably the daughter of an Irish convict of an earlier era of transportation and apparently only about fifteen or sixteen when she married Lyons, who was at least thirteen years older. The records of the family of Samuel Lyons are preserved in a family bible,[10] which shows that Mary Murphy was a Catholic and that the marriage was celebrated 'according to the rites and ceremonies of the Holy Catholic Church'. Presumably Samuel the Jew and Mary the Catholic reached some kind of compromise, because their children were all baptised in the Church of England. They had three children in three years: George Joseph Lyons on 4 April 1823; Hannah Lyons on 10 October 1824 and baptised 2 November 1824; and Samuel Lyons on 9 June 1826 and baptised 2 July 1826. George was not baptised until 16 April 1832, shortly after the death of his mother in March of that year, so it is quite possible that the religious compromise was not complete when he was born.

As a married man, Lyons began to tread the paths of respectability, and on 5 June 1823 the *Sydney Gazette* records that he was among the subscribers towards the erection of a Catholic chapel in Hyde Park. He gave one pound. On the principle that there is no one more virtuous than a reformed rake, he took some part in preventing crime and in his petition for a pardon claimed credit for the 'discovery of various offenders', including the Jews Benjamin Lee and Henry Phillips who had tried to escape from the colony and eight other convicts for various offences.[11] Perhaps this was why a ticket-of-leave man, Martin Bryant, was reported in the *Sydney Gazette* of 14 March 1825 to have committed a violent and unprovoked assault upon him.

Ten days later Lyons appeared in the *Gazette* again, this time to announce that he had received his conditional pardon. And on 16 June came the announcement that he had opened a shop at 92 Pitt Street. Like many of the Jews of Sydney he sold millinery and drapery, and he did so well that on 1 September he took space in the *Gazette* to advise 'his numerous friends and the public in general' that he had moved to 75 George Street and opened a general store to sell cotton goods, cloth, groceries and 'a variety of articles too numerous to mention'.

The year 1825 was an auspicious one for Samuel Lyons, and the new year was only two days old when the *Gazette* reported that he had been granted a licence as Auctioneer and Vendue Master. It was his key to fortune, because the Sydney retailers obtained most of their stock at the auction rooms. Officers of the British Army were not above turning an honest penny by participating in the auctions, and in Lyons' first year as an auctioneer the officers of the 40th Regiment tried to commandeer a part of his auction room. Civilians and soldiers came to grips, and the Jewish dealer Lewis Solomon was thrown downstairs by the regimental paymaster. Solomon summoned his assailant to court and called Lyons as a witness, but inevitably the court found in favour of the military.[12]

Lyons was becoming a substantial member of the community, and the *Gazette* of 1 March 1826 listed him as one of a meeting of 'respectable . . . landholders, traders, etc.' at which free settlers like the haughty Gregory Blaxland rubbed shoulders with Jewish settlers like Barnett Levey and such wealthy emancipists as Simeon Lord, Samuel Terry and Dr William Redfern. In a book written a quarter of a century later, a grudging tribute was paid to Lyons by Lieutenant Colonel Godfrey Charles Mundy, who rarely had a good word to say for anyone whom he considered to be beneath him socially. In *Our Antipodes, or Residences and Rambles in the Australian Colonies*, he wrote of Lyons:

> He was not deported for a heinous offence, but, while under probation, had the character of the most incorrigible of the chain gang he belonged to. He was whipped at the cart's tail through the streets of Sydney. He was drafted as irreclaimable to the pandemonium of Norfolk Island. Yet he reformed, who shall say through what agency? Perhaps the devil was whipped out of him. Perhaps reflection cast the foul fiend out . . . At any rate, in process of time, and by a mixture of good conduct, good luck and address, the branded and scourged felon became a wealthy capitalist. He takes a public house, dealing meanwhile in various other money making pursuits. He buys up cattle . . . lends money. He builds, buys, and sells houses . . . in the height of his prosperity his house rentals alone bring him £120 a week. He purchases shares in a great banking company. He possesses high store houses in the City, a beautiful villa in a fashionable suburb. The above is no fanciful portrait. It is from nature.[13]

Some of what Mundy wrote must have been hearsay, because he served in New South Wales from 1846 to 1851 as Deputy Adjutant-General of the army and did not know Lyons in the early days. This could be why he makes the erroneous statement about Norfolk Island, which had been abandoned as a penal settlement during Lyons' period as a convict. But the rest of his account encapsulates the commercial success of Samuel Lyons. During 1827 Lyons became an important part of Sydney's business life, and the story of his transactions can be picked up from the *Gazette* and the

Australian of that year.[14] In January he auctioned household furniture, thoroughbred horses, and properties in Cumberland and Prince's Street; in February the stock-in-trade of Mr Cobb and the furniture and stock of the Woolpack Inn, George Street; in March the stock-in-trade of Lewis Solomon of the Manchester Arms; in May, shares in the Bank of New South Wales; in June the whole of the remaining stock of Barnett Levey and four cottages in Pitt Street owned by David Kelly; in July the three boats *Ann*, *Betsey* and *Catherine*; in August, houses and premises at 68 Pitt Street, hats and other goods at J. B. Montefiore & Co., iron at Barnett Levey's and clothing at Vaiben and Emanuel Solomon's. In September he auctioned the sloop *Sally* at King's Wharf, damaged goods at Simeon Lord's and fresh butter at T. Ferris of George Street, and in October calico at Aspinall, Brown & Co. and cigars at A. B. Spark's store.

'Sydney Sam, Who has Knocked Down Thousands', from Heads of the People (Sydney), 1847. Samuel Lyons was convicted for transportation for life for stealing a handkerchief worth less than five shillings. He arrived in Sydney in 1815, and by 1835 was the city's leading auctioneer averaging a cash turnover of twelve thousand pounds a month.

The list shows that his talents as an auctioneer were recognised by a wide range of businessmen. Simeon Lord, for example, was actually in direct competition with Lyons, yet called him in to help dispose of stock. Aspinall, Brown & Co. was an old established firm and their confidence was no small tribute to his ability. The *Gazette* of 14 August 1827 mentioned that Lyons was 'getting a tolerably fair share of the public patronage', and that he was 'deserving what he is acquiring by his extraordinary application to trade'. The auctions were an integral part of Sydney's economy, and professional buyers formed cartels which were hard for an outsider to break. In the 1840s Mundy wrote, 'The chief attendants at these public sales are brokers and keepers of miscellaneous stores, many of them Jews either by persuasion or descent . . . the Sydney Gentlemen had no chance at these auctions'.

His growing prosperity induced him to invite two of his brothers and his widowed sister to join him in Australia. First to arrive was Saul Lyons, twenty-eight when he stepped ashore in 1827 as one of the earliest free Jewish settlers in New South Wales—despite the fact that in the 1828 census he described himself as a Protestant. Although Samuel brought him to Australia, Saul went into business by himself. He obtained a publican's licence, opened a tavern in Pitt Street, and in October 1828 married Esther Nettleton at St Philip's Church, in which nineteen years

The yard at Bristol's Newgate Prison, attributed to Francis Howard Greenway. Greenway was a talented artist who had become a forger. He was arrested in 1812 and transported to New South Wales. This unsigned painting shows male and female prisoners, visitors to the gaol, and manacled children.

ABOVE LEFT: Esther Johnston, attributed to Richard Read snr, c. 1820. This is Australia's only portrait of a prisoner who came out on the First Fleet. If the date is correct, Esther Johnston was almost fifty years of age when paintings of the Johnston family were commissioned. The artist had been transported to New South Wales in 1813 and was highly regarded by Governor Macquarie and by the gentry of the colony. Read claimed to have been a pupil of Sir Joshua Reynolds. He received an Absolute Pardon in 1825.

ABOVE RIGHT: George Johnston, attributed to Richard Read snr, c. 1820. Handsome and popular, Johnston was a professional soldier whose world turned upside-down when, in 1808, he overthrew Governor Bligh and assumed the post of Lieutenant Governor. Johnston was cashiered by a court martial in London and allowed to return to New South Wales. He became a close friend of Governor Macquarie, who suggested that this prominent landowner, and otherwise respectable member of society, marry his mistress, the mother of his seven children.

earlier she had been the first child christened. Despite Saul's claim to be a Protestant he contributed to the building fund of Sydney's York Street Synagogue, and became a seat-holder in 1845.

The early 1830s were eventful years for Samuel Lyons. In 1831 Governor Sir Ralph Darling considered that he deserved an absolute pardon as 'a man in good circumstances, industrious and respectable in business transactions'. Lord Goderich accepted the recommendation, and from 5 May 1832 Samuel Lyons became a free and equal citizen of New South Wales.[15] His freedom was granted only two months after his first legal wife, Mary Lyons, died in March 1832 and was buried in the Protestant section of the Devonshire Street Cemetery. In a manner worthy of a popular romance Samuel Lyons sent to Van Diemen's Land for Ann, the woman with whom he had lived in Hobart Town; but, as though he wished to make amends to his deceased wife, the daughter born to 'Samuel Lyons, auctioneer, and Ann Lyons' was christened Mary in St Philip's on 27 February 1834.[16]

Samuel Lyons was now the talk of the town. The *Australian* of 21 October 1831 reported his purchase, for £1700, of the block on the corner of George Street and Charlotte Place (now Grosvenor Street) where in earlier days the Lieutenant Governor had lived. Fashionable architect John Verge had been commissioned to plan a residence and auction rooms to be built on the site, and the newspapers kept enthusiastic track of progress. On 22 May 1832 the *Gazette* wrote:

> We have seen a drawing of the plan and elevations of the shop . . . it promises to be by far the most spacious and superb building in the town. For elegance of design and essential convenience as a family dwelling it will be unrivalled by any edifice we know in the Colony, and from the very conspicuous part of the town it is to occupy, it will form a striking ornament to the Capital of Australia.

On 3 November, when the building was taking shape, the journal declared that, 'The splendid building . . . will constitute a noble example of what industry, combined with integrity, is able to achieve', while the *Monitor* of 23 June judged it was second only to Levey's Waterloo warehouse, though fashioned with far more elegance and style. It was a proud year for the man whose back still bore the scars of two lashings.

When the building was opened as Lyons Auction Mart it drew further plaudits. The residential portion contained a rare device which brought colonial fame: a large marble bath sunk in the floor of one of the ground-floor rooms and entered by elegant steps. In the cellar beneath the building a deep spring-fed well provided the family with the luxury of constant fresh water.

Lyons Auction Mart, from Joseph Fowles, Sydney in 1848.

But the Auction Room attracted most comment. It was the largest in Sydney, and with its cedar panelling, carved shutters and 'marvellous' chandeliers was described as 'the finest room south of the Line'. It became the venue for innumerable important meetings, including those concerned with the establishment of responsible government, the founding of the colony's railways, the development of education for the masses, the cessation of transportation of convicts and of importing cheap Asian labour and, in 1851, the meeting of merchants who planned Sydney's Stock Exchange and the Sydney Chamber of Commerce. The spaciousness of the Auction Room was characteristic of the whole building, which was so lavishly designed that two generations later Lyons' grandson was able to convert a butler's pantry into a 'convenient office'.[17]

As Samuel Lyons progressed, so did his family. His brother Saul was already in Australia, his nephew Lewis Samuel had arrived in 1829 and, when *The Brothers* anchored in Sydney Harbour on 25 August 1832, she carried Lyons' eldest brother Abraham, born in 1782, his widowed sister Mrs Lydia Samuel, and Lewis Samuel's younger brother Saul, who would become Sir Saul Samuel, Bt. A good many business discussions would have preceded Saul Lyons' announcement that he was turning over the retail side of his tavern, The Governor Macquarie, to Lewis Samuel, and that he was joining Abraham Samuel in a wholesale business at 9 Pitt Street. The firm of Abraham and Saul Lyons advertised itself as Wine and Spirit Merchants, but also exported wool and built houses and hotels and developed into one of the six largest Jewish firms in Sydney.

A bitter family quarrel broke out in June 1833 between Samuel Lyons and his brother Saul when Samuel claimed that Saul had promised to contribute to the cost of bringing out their sister Lydia and their hapless brother Abraham. Sadly, the matter ended up in the Supreme Court when Samuel sued Saul for the passage money and sustenance amounting to £369. The court found that no proof of an agreement existed, and the quarrel remained unresolved. In 1835 Saul Lyons became one of the six lessees of the Theatre Royal in Sydney. He took an interest in the early development of Maitland, took out a licence for the Rose Inn there in 1833, owned a farm in 1834, and received land grants in West Maitland. Saul's marriage was childless and Abraham did not marry; when Saul died in 1887, predeceased by Abraham by thirty years, he left to the children of Sir Saul Samuel the tidy little fortune of £30 000.

In those seminal days of the Australian wool industry, Samuel Lyons astutely recognised its importance. On 20 October 1833 he advertised in the *Australian* that he would 'obtain the highest prices the market can give', and declared that he would charge no store rent, sell small consignments, advance money when he received wool for sale, guarantee a sale, and charge only a 5 per cent commission on actual sales. It was a typical play for the widest possible market, and by 1834 he was kept busy both with real estate auctions and with wool sales.

Auctions were not always carried on in the comfort of the new Sydney Market. Often a country sale demanded a long journey into the bush, which meant that stamina and some courage had to back up the skill of an auctioneer. When Lyons was returning home from such a sale in late December 1834 he was held up on the

Parramatta Road. His assailants were two soldiers of the 17th Regiment, who seized his horse's bridle and demanded his cash. He gave them some silver but concealed a packet of bank-notes, and when they asked for his watch he refused them. His firmness surprised and unnerved them so much that they took to their heels with Lyons after them. They escaped, but later were arrested and punished.[18]

Lyons was now doing so well that he commanded colonial power and influence, and aroused the concomitant jealousies. The *Australian Almanac and Directory* of 1835 reported that of private land sales worth £115 537 during 1834, Lyons had handled sales worth £61 872. However, Lyons revealed that his business was even more valuable. Including sales of livestock, furniture, general goods, and private unadvertised property, his turnover amounted to £110 000 in 1834, £156 000 in 1835 and £165 000 in 1836.[19]

The first move against him was an indirect one. In December 1833 the *Sydney Herald*, reporting on completion of the North Shed of the new Sydney Market complained, 'On Friday last slips of wood, reaching from one pillar to the other, bore in chalk the names of the intended occupants and here, at the antipodes, that trading "Commoonity", the Israelites taking a striking lead, almost to the exclusion of the Gentiles'. In March 1834 the *Sydney Herald* harrumphed, 'the present market is too crowded and there is evidently an unjust monopoly on the part of the tribe of Israel'. Lyons hit back. Writing to the *Australian* under the pseudonym Shibolet, he asked, 'Why have the Gentiles a deed of settlement more than the infidels? Or do they pay more taxes, are they more patriotic? But those days of religious persecution belong to the last century, the banner of religious toleration floats triumphantly, and the Hebrew ranks with his fellow citizen in spite of bigoted clergy'. On 14 March, Mr Hall, the editor of the *Monitor*, told Lyons to watch his language lest he ruin the status of the entire Emancipist population: 'You may build a palace and your store may be breaking down with the goods of your customers, but you will not dictate the press!'

Quill pens spluttered and the nimble fingers of compositors flew over the type-cases as Lyons and the newspapers came to grips. In the *Australian* and the *Sydney Gazette* of 17 March, Lyons said that the *Monitor* attacked him only because he refused to assist the newspaper by buying its advertising space. He denied that he was 'ever a member of any faction of political nature'. In the same issue of the *Australian*, an editorial comment supported him by declaring that although Lyons might be an auctioneer and an emancipist, there was no reason for him to be led by the nose in his political opinions.

The antagonism simmered quietly for a couple of years, and evidently there was growing resentment against the system of auction sales wherein the retailers of the colony had to buy their goods: on one hand it ensured the highest possible price for the importers, because retailers had to bid one against another, and on the other hand enabled the existence of 'rings' which could manipulate prices by prior agreement and gain a monopoly over certain goods. The system still exists today, especially among art and antique dealers in various countries.

But the system was a direct inheritance from the New South Wales Corps, and many years of ill-feeling burst into print when the *Sydney Herald* of 20 June 1836 published several articles entitled 'Auctioneers and Agents'. It wrote feelingly of 'low, disreputable persons who were enriched at the expense of British exporters', and declared that 'with few exceptions Auction Rooms may well be designated "Dens of Thieves" [where] the property of the British capitalist and of resident colonists is parcelled out among a band of transported felons'.

In the course of the attack the *Sydney Herald* was indiscreet enough to refer to a Mr L, and followed this up on 26 October by stating that Lyons was the 'foster father' and financier of a pamphlet entitled 'Extracts from Humanitas, or Party Politics Exposed, by an Immigrant of 1821'. This pamphlet, later identified as having been written by a Mr William Williams, accused Commissariat Officers of sending putrid salt beef to the convicts of distant Moreton Bay and claimed that Norfolk Island had seen 'new butcheries' and that a 'Cabal' of the powerful Macarthur family and its friends manipulated the administration through bribery and corruption.[20]

In fury Lyons announced that he was about to retire and return to England, and required that all accounts be paid by 12 August 1836. He also took the *Sydney Herald* to court, and with the help of four barristers obtained a verdict of libel and damages of two hundred pounds. He was, by this time, not at all likely to attack such a symbol of wealth and status as the Macarthur family. The ex-tailor who had been transported for stealing a handkerchief had become very reactionary in his politics. He was much impressed by the power of money and property and was contemptuous of those who failed to accumulate them, and in 1842 he circulated a petition advocating that the franchise for the City of Sydney be restricted to those who could claim property worth one hundred pounds. This campaign, described by a contemporary as 'an act of the blackest ingratitude ever put on record'[21] had no success, so he then waged war against the whole idea of a democratically elected city council. But at eleven o'clock on the night of 3 March 1842, after the votes had been counted for the council that he opposed, a mob of two hundred angry citizens shouted threats and threw stones at his George Street house.[22]

This episode was part of the second stage of Samuel Lyons' Sydney career. Obviously his vitriolic treatment by the press had bitten deep, and he must have abandoned hope of seeing his convict origins ignored or forgotten. But it seems that his preparations for departure kept him out of the public eye for eighteen months, and in this peaceful period his determination to shake the dust of Australia from his feet may have weakened. He decided to lease his auction rooms instead of selling them, and he purchased a choice piece of land in the centre of Sydney.[23]

Lyons sailed from Sydney aboard the *James Pattison*. But the cold and busy anonymity of London repelled him, and after only a few months he set sail for Australia on 20 March 1839, with his brother Abraham Lyons, in the *Indemnity*. Samuel would have been briefly reunited with his children while in England, for in January 1834 the *Australian* reported that he had sent George, Hannah and Samuel junior 'home' to be educated. This must have been a heartbreaking voyage for the three motherless, Australian-born children, then only eleven, ten and eight years old; perhaps Ann

Lyons, Samuel's second wife or mistress, insisted that they be sent away before her own daughter Mary was born. The three children were not brought up as Jews.

Home again in Sydney, he plunged into even more ambitious building plans. The *Australian* of 11 July 1839 announced that he had begun a row of magnificent terrace houses in Liverpool Street, opposite Hyde Park, perhaps inspired by the noble terraces of London's West End. Twenty-one years later a book called *My Experiences in Australia*, by 'A Lady', described Lyons Terrace as 'the Park Lane of Sydney', and for seventy years it was favoured by the city's most prominent professional men.

Apart from this venture, Lyons encountered some problems in re-establishing his business during the year of his return. His vicissitudes and successes were faithfully recorded by the *Australian*, which on 5 and 8 October told how he was unable to evict the tenants from his auction rooms. By 25 January 1840 he had tried to take over the premises of Isaac Simmons, another Jewish auctioneer, who hauled him into the Police Court, but soon after that he regained his own premises and his business soared again. On 20 March his day's sales totalled £5464 2s 10d.

The colony was beginning to totter towards the economic collapse of the early 1840s, but Samuel Lyons continued to auction wool, land, ships, shares, hotels, wheat, and even a shipload of Glasgow beer. The *Monitor* thanked him for starting the

Lyons Terrace facing Hyde Park, Sydney.

practice of hanging out a flag on sale days instead of ringing a noisy bell, but on 3 January 1841 an over-enthusiastic description of some real estate brought him a fine of two hundred pounds for misleading the public. As the depression grew worse he concentrated on the sale of land, until in 1844 the nadir came with the failure of the Bank of Australia. Lyons was the only Jewish shareholder on its register.[24]

The Jewish community in general had little love for the 'exclusivist' Bank of Australia, but Lyons had maintained widespread banking interests since early in his career, when his extensive dealings necessitated banking and credit facilities. In 1826 he attended a meeting called to establish a 'Sydney Banking Company' to counter the restricted policies of the new Bank of Australia. By 1828 he was a proprietor of the Bank of New South Wales, holding thirty-five shares valued at seven hundred pounds, and in April 1829 he bought five shares from Jacob Josephson. He took an active part in the meetings of this bank during the next twenty years and became an important shareholder in the rival Bank of Australia.[25]

The depression hit Lyons hard. He escaped, or scorned, the bankruptcy of many other businessmen, but at the inquiry into the failure of the Bank of Australia he testified that his credit was not acceptable in Sydney.[26] In Lieutenant Colonel Mundy's reminiscences of the era he wrote that 'at the time of the general money quake' Lyons failed for an immense sum, which he estimated at not less than £50 000 and probably twice as much. This may be mere guesswork, but he pays tribute to the fact that after 'reduction to beggary' Lyons rose again and by hard work succeeded in paying his creditors twenty shillings in the pound, unlike other men who escaped their debts by going into bankruptcy.

This, if it is true, must mean that a large part of Lyons' remaining years was spent in paying off his debts, but he was still able to find enough to donate a silver pointer to the York Street Synagogue for the Torah Scrolls.[27] For Samuel Lyons, despite his self-description as a Protestant in the 1828 census and the baptism of his children in the Church of England (probably to please his wife), had returned to his ancestral faith. The death of his wife, the absence of his children in England, the presence of his brothers and sisters in Australia, and the organisation of a Jewish congregation all must have helped to bring him back to admission of an allegiance which for some time had been apparent only in his readiness to denounce anti-Semitism. He donated a hundred pounds to the building fund of the York Street Synagogue, joined its committee at the time of its dedication, and helped to start Sydney's first Jewish library. In 1844, when the congregation met to consider a request for State aid to Jewish education, Lyons seconded the main resolution, was a member of the deputation to the government, and displayed a copy of the petition at his Auction Rooms so that anyone might sign it.[28]

Lyons had never been afraid to involve himself in colonial politics, and his name crops up again and again in newspaper reports of the period. In an 1830 petition asking for the ancient British rights of trial by jury and no taxation without representation, Samuel Lyons was listed in the *Australian* of 3 February and the *Gazette* of 4 February. The *Sydney Times* of 19 August 1834 and the *Australian* of 22 August named him as one of a large number of influential emancipists protesting against the mis-appropriation of waste lands by the Crown, and the *Gazette* of 2 June 1835 reported that he had subscribed fifty pounds to the Australian Patriotic Association, which intended to represent Australian interests at Westminster and in England generally. The report of the Association's Directory Committee in 1836 shows that he was one of its directors and that in the previous year he had collected donations exceeding five hundred pounds. Lyons was believed to have engineered the election of W. C. Wentworth and Dr W. Bland to the legislature. By this time, his house, his grooms, his butlers, his cooks, his wealth had caused most people to forget his convict origins.

On 27 July 1851 Samuel Lyons advertised his last auction sale, in the *Sydney Morning Herald*. A week later the same newspaper reported that 'at his residence, George Street, after a short but severe illness, Mr Samuel Lyons, for many years auctioneer in this city' had died on 3 August, aged sixty. On 6 August the *Herald* reporter wrote:

> We were not prepared for the marked respect which was paid to his memory by a large portion of the mercantile and trading as well as professional community. The cortege consisted of a hearse, nine mourning coaches, sixty private and hired carriages and ten gigs, altogether 80 vehicles. The body was deposited in the Jewish burial ground, accompanied by the usual ceremonies of that community.

Lyons' special interest was education. He was a founder of Sydney College and the first large contributor to its library, and in his will made generous provision for a scholarship at the new University of Sydney. He would have been dismayed to know that his descendants withheld the legacy.[29]

Of his progeny, no trace can be found of his second daughter Mary nor of her mother Ann. Hannah and George stayed in England, where George studied law at Cambridge and later became a barrister. It may have been easier to stay in England, free from the stigma of convict parenthood, and practise the same law which once had condemned his father.[30]

Only Samuel Lyons jnr, who had studied at Liège and Cambridge, returned to Australia. It was expected that he would carry on his father's business, but apparently he lacked his father's business acumen. The quiet backwaters of Cambridge would not have been the best training ground for the quick-witted crossfire of a colonial auction mart, and as soon as possible he sold the business and settled down to live on the rents he received from the great Auction Rooms and his father's many other properties in Sydney. He dabbled in politics, was twice elected to the legislature of New South Wales, and became associated with Sir Henry Parkes. When his fortune dwindled he used Parkes' influence in his search for a steady job. Ironically, he was appointed Official Assignee in Bankruptcy.[31]

Though it would have pleased Samuel Lyons to know that his son would sit in parliament, Samuel Lyons jnr remained a backbencher and never attained the pol-itical eminence of his cousin Saul Samuel, who became one of the colony's most dis-tinguished parliamentarians, was knighted for his services, and eventually was made a baronet. Yet it is extremely unlikely that Saul would have been brought to New

South Wales by his mother, Samuel Lyons' sister, if Samuel had not been transported for his 'crimes'.

Samuel Lyons felt that his wealth and success expunged his convict origins and made him a member of the élite. In fact, he was one of the emancipists who seized the opportunities offered by the new country and in doing so revolutionised the whole social system of colonial Australia. The military officers and civil administrators who established themselves as the first ruling class attempted to transplant the traditional English system in Australia: a system based on the ownership of land and buttressed by hereditary privilege and status. The emancipists relied instead upon energy and ability, and in doing so founded a new tradition—the Australian belief that any man is entitled to a 'fair go' regardless of his origins.

Samuel Lyons and Solomon Levey were among Sydney's most important emancipists. It is an odd coincidence that they arrived on the same convict transport, though Levey's Australian career was ending just as Lyons was tasting success. Lieutenant Colonel Mundy summed up Samuel Lyons when he wrote:

> The calling he has adopted brings him in contact with persons of every grade. He is extensively employed by the Government as well as by Companies and individuals, and has always been cited as a punctual respectable and upright man of business as well as a singularly clever one. He is the landlord of many of the aristocrats of Sydney who find him both liberal and correct in dealings. In the only transaction of this kind I had in the Colony, involving several hundred pounds of property, I deliberately selected this meritorious person from among 26 of the same profession, possessing the highest qualities of character and capacity.

'Mr Levey is a Jew'

A STOUT AND PROUD Mr Solomon Levey was bound for home. At the age of thirty-two he stood on the deck of his own ship and watched as the familiar buildings that clustered around the southern shores of the great harbour faded astern. Less than a dozen years before, he had been sent to New South Wales with shackles on his feet and seven years of servitude ahead. Now it was May 1826, and in Sydney the titles to buildings and land in his name were worth more than £30 000. During the previous year, his income had exceeded £60 000. In his stables stood the vice-regal carriage of the previous governor of the colony. He had been co-partner in the creation of one of the great mercantile houses of New South Wales. Solomon Levey's prison had become his promised land, and he was now bound for London, where he would become the architect of the first fumbling attempt to establish a British colony on the western coast of the continent. Australia had been incredibly generous in rewarding his endeavours, and in future years he was to pour out most of his fortune in an effort to keep a colony in Western Australia alive.[1]

Solomon Levey was born in the squalid, turbulent heart of the little London ghetto, as one of the eight children of Deborah and Lion Levy of Wentworth Street, Whitechapel. In that narrow street which still winds through the crowded East End, Solomon and his brothers and sisters acquired their smattering of education and the ambition to escape from the noisy poverty that surrounded them. Solomon was the first to try. On 18 August 1813 'Solomon Levy alias Levy Levy' and a James Skinner were arrested at Solomon's house on a charge of having taken a tea-chest from a delivery cart, emptied the tea into a bag, and then sold it to Solomon's mother for four pounds. In October the 19-year-old culprit stood before Judge Baron Thompson at the Old Bailey and told the court that he had merely 'held the bag for two young men that I had never seen before' and then gone to the yard behind his house to play ball. The tea was worth over thirty-five pounds, so there was no doubt that its theft was a capital offence. But Solomon and his family were lucky. The witnesses for the prosecution were not entirely convincing, and it is difficult to identify a quantity of tea once it has been removed from its container. So Mrs Levy escaped a charge of receiving stolen property, and Solomon escaped with his neck and a sentence of seven years transportation.[2]

It may be pointless to speculate on what might have happened if Solomon Levey had not been transported, but the chain of events begun by his arrest is a classic example of how the Old Bailey judges unwittingly caused whole chapters of British and Australian history to be written. In the years ahead, Solomon's brothers Barnett, Isaac and Philip, his sister Rebecca and his nephews and nieces by his sister Susannah, would all follow their convict kinsman to Australia as free settlers. The boisterous and unfortunate Barnett Levey is generally regarded as the father of the Australian theatre. Isaac Levey became a respected leader of the Sydney Jewish community, and the founder of a prominent Australian family.

After sentencing, Solomon was taken to the prison hulk *Retribution*, where the slender young man, dark and pale with hazel eyes, spent six anxious months while human cargo was collected for the convict transport *Marquis of Wellington*.[3] It was to include eight Jewish males, the largest single group of Jewish prisoners sent to the Antipodes since the sailing of the First Fleet, and they formed an extraordinary party.

All eight were Cockneys. Solomon Levey had the only sentence which gave much room for hope, because the rest were being transported for life. The savagery of the age is illustrated in the fact that two of them, Moses Solomon and John Morris, aged respectively ten and nine years, had, with another child been sentenced to death for stealing a pair of shoes from a shop in Holborn. Moses Solomon subsequently escaped from the colony, was recaptured at the Cape of Good Hope, and brought back to receive one hundred lashes.[4] Abraham Levey was a 19-year-old 'fruitman'. Solomon Solomons, aged twenty, was a pedlar who married in Sydney in 1821 and whom, five years later, John Macarthur was to describe was to write in a letter to the Colonial Office as 'a Jew publican—lately deprived of his licence for keeping a disorderly house'.[5]

The remainder of the sad little band were to make their marks in the new country, and perhaps prove the theory that transportation brought reformation. James Simmons, at sixteen, helped to rob the Hanover Square home of the Countess of Hillsborough, and was sentenced to death. His father Nathan was found guilty at the same trial and sentenced to fourteen years transportation, though there is no record of his arrival in Australia. James Simmons began the life sentence to which he was reprieved by working as a servant to the architect Francis Greenway. He married Agnes Thorley at St Peter's, Richmond, in 1821, and eventually became a successful businessman, a pillar of the Sydney Jewish community and Sydney's first Jewish alderman, having been elected to the Municipal Council in 1848.[6] He died in 1849.

Samuel Lyons, whose extraordinary career was told in Chapter 8, was a semi-literate tailor transported for stealing a handkerchief. Moses Moses, a 22-year-old glass-cutter, was sent from Sydney to Hobart Town to serve his sentence. He was pardoned in 1832 and returned to the mainland to become a pioneer of the town of Yass and one of its most respected early citizens.[7] But the brief Australian career of Solomon Levey would eclipse those of his shipmates.

Levey was fortunate to arrive in January 1815, as Governor Macquarie looked benevolently upon convicts who seemed capable of building a new life in exile. According to later colonial gossip, he began his business career as a street hawker of confectionery after his initial period of servitude. Obviously he was successful, because by 24 November 1817 'Solomon Levey of Pitt Street' had found the requisite four hundred pounds wherewith to buy his first allotment of land at 72 George Street.[8] The George Street property was to become his home, and later the site of his brother Barnett's disastrous attempts to build in one place a mill, a hotel, a warehouse and a theatre.

Levey built a cottage and entered into partnership with Edward Franks, a convict shipmate from the *Marquis of Wellington*, as 'general dealers'. The partnership was brief but profitable. A little more than a year later it was dissolved. Franks bought himself a hotel and Solomon purchased his second property: the house of Joseph Marcus at 52 Kent Street. Marcus was one of the oldest Jewish inhabitants of Sydney and, as he had studied to become a rabbi, actually served as a rabbi to the Jews of Sydney. The *Sydney Gazette*, with the remarkable freedom of the press of that era, described him in 1820 as a 'palsied and infirm old man' whose wife Jane, a 'most profligate character', was sentenced to six months hard labour for cruel treatment of her husband.[9] Possibly Levey did not have to pay much for his house and land.

Now a two-fold man of property 'by servitude' at the age of twenty-five, Levey had only another month to wait for the free pardon granted by Governor Macquarie, in which he was described as a 'trade broker'. Three days later he married Ann Roberts, the 14-year-old daughter of wealthy emancipist William Roberts. Roberts had been in Sydney from the earliest days, having arrived in the *Scarborough* with the First Fleet, and after serving his seven years was granted land at Mulgrave Place in 1796. He settled in the Hawkesbury District and in 1813 became a contractor for building the road to Liverpool and also was granted that sure passport to fortune, a liquor licence.[10]

Roberts endowed his daughter with farmland and stock, which proved to be a valuable addition to Levey's capital, and in October 1820 the official List of Convicts Who have Become Landowners contained Solomon Levey as the owner of 1000 acres. Samuel Terry, the moneylender, is listed as holding 19 000 acres.[11]

Levey's relations in England were thrilled by news of the transformation of his life from convict to man of property, dignity and marriage. His brother Barnett signed on as a clerk aboard the convict transport *John Bull*, arriving in Sydney in December 1821, and thus became the first free Jewish male to land in Australia. Only the wife of the convict Jacob Isaacs had preceded him as a free Jewish settler.[12]

Unfortunately it was not a propitious time for Barnett Levey to arrive. Solomon's son John had been born on 13 November 1819, Ann was pregnant with her second child, and the marriage was on the rocks.[13] His wife had taken up with another man, whom Solomon later described as her 'seducer'. On 25 August 1821, after the birth of his daughter Jane Ann Levey, Solomon advertised in the *Gazette* to warn the community against 'giving trust or credit to my wife, Mrs Ann Levey'. Ann had left him and, although he remained the guardian of John, the baby became a stranger to him. He saw no need to mourn when Jane Ann died at the age of two.

Even though Barnett could help him in the George Street shop and was living with him, Solomon's commercial life was as much in the doldrums as his family life.

A letter written in 1820, after the dissolution of his partnership with Franks, illustrates the struggle he was having in finding a footing in the mercantile community. In the young colony, the most important source of money was the administration, which had to provide the military, police and prison establishments and a variety of government servants with the necessities of life. Solomon complained to the Governor that the commissariat purchased tea and sugar at prices higher than those he had tendered, but the Commissioner-General denied this. He told the Governor, 'I frequently receive tenders of different articles in this place, from [persons] whom I am assured at the time, do not possess a single ounce of the article they offer for sale'.[14] Apparently some merchants did not purchase goods until tenders had been accepted, and then bought them on credit. As the government paid on delivery of the goods, the credit could be used for other purposes. The Commissioner concluded triumphantly, 'and from this class of Dealers it may be supposed complaints are not to be unexpected'.

It is impossible to say whether Levey was one of 'this class of dealers', but in any case it seems that he soon grew impatient with the limitations of the somewhat incestuous trade within the colony. In January 1821 he took the obvious step and sank whatever he had by way of 'risk capital' in the purchase of the schooner *Mary* and a share in the brig *Campbell Macquarie*, in order to import goods from overseas.[15]

His companions in the new venture were two emancipist brothers, Robert and Daniel Cooper, and it was the beginning of an association that would mature into the partnership of Daniel Cooper and Solomon Levey. The two men brought together a

A bank-note issued and signed by Solomon Levey and Daniel Cooper in the name of their Lachlan and Waterloo Mills Company, Sydney, December 1825. Cooper and Levey boldly challenged the citizens of New South Wales by issuing bank-notes whose security was greater than the subscriptions raised by the shareholders of any colonial bank.

formidable combination of capital, energy and speculative ability, and their business grew into one of the most successful joint stock ventures in the colony. Both men had considerable colonial business experience. Daniel Cooper, who had been a store-keeper while his brother was a brewer, was an original member of the partnership that began in flour milling and then developed into a large general business called the Waterloo Company that issued its own bank-notes in order to cope with the volume of its trade and the calls on its credit. It was upon this company that Daniel and Solomon would base their Sydney business.

Levey's shipping interests soon transformed the bustling young general dealer into a merchant with his sights raised far beyond the comparatively limited horizons of the little New South Wales community. In 1822 he established a trading post at Tahiti, and soon had two small vessels busy in the Pacific Island trade. In the same year he became the owner of Sydney's only rope works, and planned to supply it with fibres imported from the Pacific Islands. He owned a watermill in the rural town of Liverpool, and even though Ann Levey had left his bed and board she had perforce to leave him in possession of her dowry, which now had grown to more than 1000 sheep and 200 cattle.[16] His brief marriage had helped him to found a commercial empire which was beginning to arouse the jealousy of his rivals. They were delighted to take up the story spread by South Sea Island missionaries that he was selling watered-down gin. His indignant answer, published in the *Gazette* of 30 October 1823, was replete with religious symbolism.

> I trust that eight or nine years conduct in the colony is sufficient testimony to show whether a reformation has taken place or not . . . I challenge the impartial to prove me guilty of a dishonest act . . . I am quite at a loss to know where you take your text from, in reporting that Cooper and Levey were the christeners of your gin. I disavow the knowledge of such an unrighteous deed; and I do not wish to benefit by your baptized spirits . . . I live by honesty.

The accusation struck deeply, because Levey took his social obligations and status very seriously. Time and again the lists of subscribers to charitable appeals, published in the *Sydney Gazette*, showed his name near the top. In 1824 he was recorded on 5 February as subscribing to the Scots Church building appeal, on 19 February to the Wesleyan Missionary Society and the Roman Catholic Chapel, on 26 February to the Sydney Benevolent Society and on 22 April to the Sydney Public Free Grammar School. The *Australian* of 3 March and 30 June 1825 reported that he had subscribed to the commit-tee for building a monument to his emancipator, the former Governor Macquarie, and that he had 'very humanely sent a quantity of bread and beer to the prisoners confined in gaol'. On 1 April 1826 the same journal showed his name among the list of sub-scribers to the proposed school for the education of female servants.

The year 1824 was both tragic and rewarding for Solomon Levey. In the shadow of the death of his infant daughter, and with his estranged wife fatally ill, he helped to preside over the annual dinner given by the colony's leading emancipists in which they defiantly celebrated the First Fleet's arrival in 1788. Each year, on 26 January, these former convicts recalled the foundation of the nation which had begun as their prison. There is no doubt that this annual event marked the germination of an Australian consciousness. A tradition had developed that a song should be composed for each dinner and should mention the names of the organisers. As reported in the *Gazette*, Solomon Levey's was:

> *Defaulters may tremble, if ever they shrink*
> *From the feat that swells every glass to the brink.*
> *We admit no excuse for transgressing so heavy*
> *For the wine we impose, we determined to LEVI.*

Four days later, Solomon's young wife was dead. She died ten days after her daughter, and in a *Gazette* announcement of 5 February 1824 Solomon wrote bitterly, 'Her complaint originated in the brutal treatment of her seducer, joined with his inhumanity in not allowing her medical advice . . . she sincerely repented of her conduct to an injured husband and fervently prayed for forgiveness'. It is hard to imagine a deserted husband placing such an announcement in a modern newspaper, or even to envisage the newspaper accepting it, but in those days people had less reluctance about displaying their emotions in public and, in any case, the small Sydney community would be well acquainted with all the circumstances of Ann Levey's 'seduction'.

Despite Ann's deathbed contrition, the *Gazette* noted that her funeral cortège was to begin at the home of her mother, not of her husband. Nobly, Solomon concluded his announcement by asking 'such persons as may have claims against the late Mrs Levey to present the same' to him. No corresponding offer was made by Ann's lover, who must remain forever unknown.

Levey, who had found himself executor of his father-in-law's estate soon after his marriage, maintained close contact with his wife's family and never forgot the foundation of his wealth. In his own will he made large bequests to his brothers-in-law, and ordered that all the property which Ann had brought as her dowry should be returned to the Roberts family.

Among Levey's ventures was a partnership with John Grono, a well-known shipbuilder, in a seal-hunting enterprise for which they supplied the ship *Elizabeth*.[17] The sealing ship was one of eight sailing out of the colony, which caused an anonymous correspondent to the *Gazette* to voice his opinion that there would be a glut of sealskins. Levey wrote a rebuttal, to which the anonymous author replied on 15 July 1824: 'I am sorry that Mr Levey, whom, as a trader, I consider liberal and respectable, is not better advised than to dabble with authorship . . . He may be a Pharisee, a very "Nathaniel" in guileless integrity, but "he is no Scribe"'.

The liberal Mr Levey's maritime interests had increased considerably in March 1824, when the payment of a thousand pounds completed the purchase from the government of HM Sloop *Snapper*.[18] He expanded his intercolonial and Pacific Island trade by sending his ships into 'any part of the Hawkesbury River' to buy 20 000 bushels of wheat from the farmers of the colony's hinterland. He paid them city prices with no charge for freight,[19] but trade with farmers and rural clients often brought complications. On 16 September 1824 he took space in the *Sydney Gazette* once more, for an advertisement which begged leave 'to solicit his country customers to come forward and say when they will pay the balance of their Accounts. He trusts they will recollect his forbearance for the last 18 months, there being 120-odd Country accounts in the book, not twenty of them yet been settled'. By way of an exasperated postscript he wrote, 'It having been reported by a Great Man that the undersigned has made large bargains, by purchasing the Settlers wheat in prospect of the coming harvest, I declare it is not so'.

During that year Levey began an even closer association with the Cooper brothers, and as a part of this the three businessmen chartered a brig to bring sugar from Mauritius to New South Wales. The cargo arrived safely, but a small private venture of the ship's master compromised his employers. Levey found himself being accused of smuggling tobacco, and as usual took to the *Gazette* to air his side of the matter. 'In my opinion it is a bad case in this Colony, when a man of business has to hold up his honesty in the newspapers ... I am not inclined to have the name of smuggler', he wrote on 9 December 1824.

Levey and his partners shared far more than commerce. On 15 December 1824, together with six other emancipists, they began a long and ultimately successful legal battle to gain the privilege of serving as jury men alongside fellow-citizens who had landed as free settlers.[20]

The steady rise of emancipists who had sufficient energy and acumen to take advantage of their opportunities did not always gain the applause of the other settlers —or even of officials, who might be expected to approve of these examples of reformation. G. T. W. Boyes, the sharp-tongued Deputy Commissioner in Sydney, wrote to his wife on 16 January 1824:

> I see a great many faces among the prisoners and emancipated convicts that are familiar. There are several Jews here, rich, keeping a handsome Tilbury [a type of carriage] etc. There is among them a fellow by the name of Raphael, rather stout and not tall, two or three Levis, a Josephson and some others.[21]

Josephson was Barnett Levey's father-in-law, so the association of the two surnames was natural. One may imagine the comments made a few months later when Solomon Levey was the successful bidder at the auction of the stately carriage imported by the late Governor, Sir Thomas Brisbane. He paid what was then the huge sum of £370, roughly equivalent to buying a Rolls Royce at today's prices.

Daniel Cooper and Solomon Levey signed a deed of co-partnership on 28 June 1825, which was to expand their operations enormously. It was based upon a capital of £4700 in Spanish dollars valued at five shillings each, presumably because these coins had been a common medium of exchange during the long years in which the colony was always short of British currency. Their business was based on the 'spacious' Waterloo warehouse that Daniel Cooper had built three years before for an earlier partnership.[22]

The new partnership imported shiploads of goods from India, Mauritius, New Zealand, Van Diemen's Land and the Pacific Islands. Because of the favourable north-east monsoon winds from September to March, the Indian Ocean island of Mauritius was a convenient entrepôt at which European goods could be trans-shipped for Australia, besides being a ready source of sugar, of which very little was then grown in the colony. 'Twenty thousand silver dollars worth' of cargo came from Mauritius in 1828; 700 sealskins were collected from hunters on the islands between Van Diemen's Land and the mainland in February 1829, and 16 000 bushels of wheat were imported from India in the same year. Long before New Zealand was a British possession, Cooper and Levey were among the first to trade with the Maori chiefs. In fact they received official encouragement to do so, in the hope of obtaining the flax which was so important for making many types of cloth, from shirt linen to sail canvas. Their trading posts caused the partners' names to be written on the earliest maps of the New Zealand islands, and Port Cooper and Port Levey are now long-forgotten names for bays near Christchurch on the South Island.[23]

The two men moved with Napoleonic daring and rapidity to extend the scope of their business. On 5 May 1826, less than a year after forming the partnership, the lawyer W. C. Wentworth prepared for them another deed of co-partnership, providing that each partner should advance £30 000 for joint stock operations. They became pivotal to the colony's import trade, and when in 1826 they sent wool to England they were among the first woolbrokers in Australian history. They bought and sold ships, and served as agents for other ships trading to Australia. They built their own vessels, including the *Australia* built 'of colonial produce' in 1827 by John Grono, who repaired their ship *Minerva* in the same year. The *Australia*, which was among the earliest vessels of any size to be built in the colony, was to become an important trader between Sydney and England. Later she was used for yet another of the partnership's ventures: the hunting of whales.[24]

Even in those days, businessmen were the mainstay of the governments. When in 1825 Solomon Levey submitted a petition for a land grant to the Governor, he mentioned that he had paid almost £30 000 in taxes to the colonial exchequer during the previous four years.[25] So there was another side to the story of 'rich Jews with their Tilburys'.

In a community increasing naturally, and added to by the growing number of free settlers and the steady influx of convicts, there were innumerable opportunities for men with ideas and the capital to back them up. Solomon Levey already owned a flour mill operated by water power, but the partners leapt into the age of technology when they began to build the colony's first mill operated by a steam engine, costing in all more than £15 000. It was one of Australia's first examples of any propulsive power outside human, animal, wind or water.

Prosperity brought power to both partners. In 1826 a colonial scandal brought them the richest reward so far. Captain John Piper, RN, known as the Prince of New South Wales because of his vast landholdings and the pomp and circumstance of his official and commercial positions, was the Naval Officer in Sydney and had the task of collecting the harbour dues and customs and excise duties for the continent's principal port. Also he had been the Chairman of Directors of the Bank of New South

Wales. An inquiry revealed that he had mismanaged his affairs so badly that the government had not received more than £12 000 in revenue, and an official claim was lodged against him.

The colony was going through a temporary depression. Property was hard to dispose of, and Piper was unable to raise the money. He turned to Cooper and Levey for help, and they were able to raise the £10 000 in cash which he needed to free himself from debt. In return they gained an estate worth between £60 000 and £70 000, so beginning their accumulation of enormous property holdings around Sydney Harbour and in the developing rural districts, including what are now known as the inner suburbs of Sydney: Alexandria and Redfern.[26] Daniel Cooper bequeathed the Point Piper property to his nephew, Sir Daniel Cooper, first Speaker of the Parliament of New South Wales. Part of the estate is now occupied by the Cranbrook School.

The most spectacular proof of the power possessed by the Cooper–Levey partnership came only a month after their acquisition of the Piper estate. The Bank of New South Wales had been far too conservative to issue more stock to increase its capital, and in consequence the whole colony suffered from a shortage of money. Cooper and Levey attempted to solve this by issuing their own bank-notes.[27] The Bank of New South Wales and the recently founded Bank of Australia reacted violently against this transgression on their privilege, and no doubt the partnership's capture of the Piper estate, the property of the first bank's former chairman, added piquancy to the encounter.

The partnership was vehement in defence of its action. In what would nowadays be known as 'public relations', the two men followed Solomon Levey's old tactic of telling his side of an argument to the public by taking newspaper space. In an advertisement in the Monitor of 13 October 1826 they set out their side of the story:

> And the said Firm feeling indignant that a private Banking Company though bearing the high sounding title of the Bank of Australia should, with only an Eighth of the real capital of themselves presume to interfere with the mode in which the said Cooper and Levey choose to carry on the concerns request the above mentioned parties—to settle—forthwith. Cooper and Levey having claims on the Trading Community of Thirty Thousand Pounds . . . the bank only three months experience.

They announced, justifiably, that they could command more capital than the two banks put together and, as part of the battle, abruptly and brutally recalled the £30 000 due to them. They maintained an insistent pressure, which included Daniel Cooper's successful election as a director of the Bank of New South Wales in August 1828, but the struggle was really won in April 1827 when the banks agreed to accept Cooper and Levey bank-notes at face value as colonial currency.[28]

The affair went deeper than normal commercial competition and the banks' feeling that the issue of currency was their own private preserve. The contest for control of the means of exchange was partly a contest between the privileged classes, as represented by the free settlers and landowners, and the 'upstart' emancipists who were former convicts. As usual in human affairs there was an undercurrent of emotion which had nothing to do with the facts of the case, and this was defined by the Sydney *Monitor* on 28 July 1826: 'The emigrants of the colony are ridiculously afraid of the emancipist interest. Hence in forming a new Bank a directory, or a committee—pass laws of perpetuity of office . . . the emancipists are honoured by being allowed to put down their dumps to pay the piper'. ('Dumps,' or small coins made by punching out the centre of a dollar, were one of the colony's solutions to the recurrent shortages which were so persistent that Cooper and Levey continued to issue their own bank-notes until 1834; 'Piper' was a veiled allusion to the ill-fated Captain Piper.)

Despite this quarrel with the Bank of New South Wales, Solomon Levey had been a shareholder in it since 1820. Almost immediately after the granting of his free pardon he had applied to the Board of Directors for a financial share in what was then the colony's only bank.[29] This was quickly granted, and his name began to appear regularly in the minutes book of the bank. Repeatedly he expressed faith in the future of the colony, and argued vigorously in favour of lower interest rates and the introduction of British capital. As the *Gazette* wrote on 22 March 1826, 'Mr Solomon Levey took, as usual, a very advanced view of the country'. In that year, as he prepared to leave for England, he became interested and involved in the foundation of the Sydney Commercial Bank, and at a meeting called to discuss the subject he suggested that they should 'open a correspondence with an English Bank' to gain additional capital, and with characteristic bluntness added that it was only 'narrowness of idea' which prevented them from doing so. He offered to engage in the sale of three hundred shares in the new bank while in England, but the chairman was not persuaded. With what Levey must have found to be frustrating conservatism, he said politely, 'It was a pleasure to hear the sentiments of Mr Levey taking so wide a stretch, but it was in vain to talk of subscribing such a large sum, without showing gentlemen that a great advantage was to be derived from it'.[30] The meeting must have been shortsighted indeed if it could not see what 'great advantages' Levey and Cooper had gained from risking huge capital investments.

The departure of Solomon Levey for England was an event worth noticing throughout the scattered colonial communities. In Van Diemen's Land, the Hobart Town *Colonial Times* recorded on 30 March 1826 that 'Messrs Cooper and Levey have chartered the large ship *Mangles* for England for the sum of 4,000 guineas. The enterprising colonists will load her entirely with their own property, with the exception of a few tons of timber. She is said to sail in May. Mr Levey proceeds in her to England to form mercantile arrangements with an eminent London house, upon a grand scale, from which the most important benefits may be expected'.

The departure was on an equally grand scale. The Sydney newspapers reported the large parties of friends who waved farewell from the headlands of Sydney Harbour, the firing of a salute from guns on Point Piper, and its acknowledgment by Solomon and his son John aboard the *Mangles* as she sailed on 27 May 1826. In one of his *Gazette* announcements, on 8 April 1826, Solomon had stated that he hoped to 'return in 18 months and never more to leave Australia'. This was to be a forlorn hope. Levey's dazzling vision of Australia's future was to blind him to practical problems and to dissipate his fortune as he strove to transform vision into reality. He would never see Sydney again.

At first everything went splendidly. His first year back in London was busy and successful, and in metropolitan society his former criminal record seemed far less important than in Sydney. Britain was in the midst of the lengthy trade recession which followed the Napoleonic wars, and Levey's huge purchases of goods for Australia were most welcome. In 1827 he had to charter four ships to carry his cargoes to the colony.

The colonists were able to read about his activities in reports which, it may be assumed, were extracts from his letters given to the newspapers by Daniel Cooper. On 13 April 1827 the *Monitor* wrote, 'Mr S. Levey, of this colony, is a constant caller at Mr [Solomon] Polack's at the Strand where he was entertained on his first arrival with a splendid entertainment to meet Mr Rothschild jun., Mr Samuels jun. and other gentlemen of the first mercantile respectability'. The *Gazette* reported on 6 August that he was about to arrange a loan of £100 000 for the firm of Cooper and Levey, and on 28 December that he was sending 2000 'mechanics', i.e. skilled tradesmen, out to Sydney under government contract. 'People thinking of migrating, pay frequent visits to Mr Levey, and he has induced several to try their fortune in the new colony. All this will tend to the good of the Colony, and entitles Mr Levey to the good wishes of his fellow colonists', the *Australian* wrote on 26 June 1827.

To the London Jews who went to see him, Solomon Levey's reappearance as a wealthy and respected merchant must have been convincing proof that a Promised Land lay beyond the sea. His brimming faith in the new country, and the advice which he gave to so many, precipitated the birth of the free Jewish community of Australia. Within a decade of his return to London, the free Jewish settlers outnumbered those Jews who had reached Australia as convicts, even though the transportation system continued in full swing.

But Levey did not only meet Jews who were eager for a more spacious and rewarding life than was offered by the narrow, wretched lanes of Whitechapel. The ex-convict began to move in far more illustrious circles of society, and in 1828 he was introduced to Thomas Peel, a first cousin once removed of Sir Robert Peel, Home Secretary in the ministry of the Duke of Wellington.[31] For Levey, this meeting with a man whose ambition was as great as his own, but whose splendid visions arose from more selfish impulses, was eventually to be fatal.

Peel had been planning to go to Australia since early in 1828, when he left his home in Scotland and travelled to London to prepare for a voyage to New South Wales. He proposed to settle there and develop an estate worthy of his name and status, but in London he heard talk of a new settlement to be founded on the unpopulated western coast of Australia. By helping in its creation, he saw the possibility of being in on the ground floor, and with three members of his London club he formed a syndicate to exploit the possibilities. They were Colonel Thomas Potter Macqueen, Sir Francis Vincent, and E. W. H. Schenley.[32]

The four men planned on an imperial scale, and in due course submitted a memorandum to the Colonial Office. This proposed that they be permitted to ship

10 000 people to Western Australia and to give each male 200 acres of land. The community thus established would foster trade with the East Indies. All that Peel's syndicate asked from the Crown was a grant of land based on the calculation that each colonist would cost them thirty pounds, and that each acre of land should be given to them 'at a valuation of one shilling and sixpence per acre to the full quantity as a payment in the value for their trouble'. In plain English, which the memorandum did not use, this proposal meant that Peel and his friends would be granted four million acres of land. And, as negotiations developed, it became obvious that the syndicate wanted the right to choose the land before any settlement was made, which was a wise precaution on their part to avoid gaining possession of four million acres of desert.

The Colonial Office hesitated.[33] Whitehall was under pressure from Captain James Stirling, the original explorer of the Swan River district, who had made the first suggestion to establish a settlement on the river. He too claimed first choice of land.

Peel's approaches showed the British government that sooner or later Britons would press for a settlement in Western Australia and that all the trouble and expense of founding a colony was inevitable. The outcome was a characteristic government compromise. Peel was told that a colony would be established, that Captain Stirling would be its administrator and governor with the right to choose the first 100 000 acres for himself and his own needs, but that Peel's syndicate could select 500 000 acres as soon as they landed not less than four hundred men and women in the colony.[34] Stirling's success and imminent departure for Western Australia exploded Peel's hopes, and his three partners withdrew from his syndicate.

With his hopes of an Australian empire momentarily frustrated, and his finances at a low ebb after a fruitless year in London, Peel's hopes must have flared anew when he met the wealthy Jew from Sydney. Solomon Levey would have been proof positive that there was a fortune to be made on the other side of the world, and it is easy to imagine the eagerness with which he described his scheme to Levey—although the latter was to claim that the whole plan had been his own and that Peel's original syndicate had submitted it to the Colonial Office 'with little alteration'.[35] This is hard to follow because Levey does not seem to have met Peel before the collapse of the syndicate, but in any case it is certain that the two men lost no time in forming a strange and unequal working partnership.

Peel's first move in the new partnership held a bad omen for the future. On 28 January 1829 he wrote to the Colonial Office to reopen the matter, but did not mention Levey and said that he was 'desirous of carrying on and completing the whole project by himself'. Though no one would question the word of a gentleman, it was obvious that Under-Secretary Twiss of the Colonial Office was irritated by the persistent Peel and his plans, because he replied immediately to say that he was ready to deal with Peel 'on the same terms' as before, but the 'identical grant' on the Swan River was reduced to 250 000 acres. Next day he wrote again, setting a deadline for the project. Peel was warned that if he did not arrive at Swan River with his first four hundred settlers by 1 November 1829, then he would receive only 'as many acres of the tract so reserved for him, as his actual number of settlers and amount of investment would cover at the rate of 40 acres for every three pounds invested'.[36]

By this time the public was well aware of what was going on, and criticism began to mount. Caricatures of Thomas Peel 'plucking the Swan' were sold in the streets, and Sir Robert Peel was forced to defend himself in Parliament against charges of favouritism towards members of his family. This encouraged Twiss to set forth the conditions of his grant even more precisely to Peel, and the force of his antagonism is unmistakable:

> I am told that your impression only to take out 400 souls and that under this denom-ination you might include children of tender age ... 'If you will turn to the Correspondence you will find that my expression has always been not souls but persons, secure persons capable of all the work necessary for a new settlement. The 400 therefore whom you are to land, must be persons of more than 10 years of age'.[37]

It was, to say the least, a curious definition of the well-known English word 'soul'.

As negotiator for the partnership, Peel continued to play a double game. He failed to tell Levey about his deadline and the new conditions of settlement, which are not mentioned in the subsequent contract between him and Levey or in Levey's later correspondence with the Colonial Office. Nor did he tell Under-Secretary Twiss that he was working in partnership with a rich Jewish ex-convict, though this omis-sion may be explained by the snobbery and prejudice of the era. Peel's fraudulent and deceitful behaviour now knew no limit. He had found an ambitious alternative to his former financial backers who was clearly dazzled by his relationship to someone of the ruling class.

Thomas Peel and Solomon Levey signed a deed of partnership on 27 April 1829. It included the story of the failure of Peel's first syndicate and quoted from relevant corre-spondence with the Colonial Office—with the notable exception of the letter of 29 January 1829. Despite Peel's knowledge of the restricted grant, the contract refers to a land grant of a million acres, out of which Peel was to choose 20 000 acres and Levey 5000 acres. The remaining—and non-existent—975 000 acres was to form the capital stock of the co-partnership. Peel was to be 'the sole manager with power to employ or dismiss staff', with a salary of £1500 a year and an advance of £2000. He was entitled to draw £2000 from the profits of the venture wherewith to build himself a house and office on his own land, and to draw £3000 for salaries and wages. He was to give a proper account of his dealings at the end of each year. Levey was to finance the project with £20 000 to begin with, and promised 'upon requisition and demand of Mr Peel' to 'furnish funds and supply at or from Sydney or the nearest and best market ... to the extent an amount of £50,000 in addition to the £20,000 ... Provided that if the provi-sions and other necessary articles of life cannot be obtained in Australia then the same shall be supplied from such market as Levey shall think expedient'. Peel was entitled to send competent persons to the establishment indicated by Levey to select cattle and stores.[38] Levey formally agreed 'not at any time during the continuance of the partner-ship to do any act ... whereby ... the co-partnership can or may be in any manner prej-udiced except so far as carrying on his present trading and other transactions at Sydney'.

Peel was now in the classic position of a businessman who has negotiated a shady deal and has to make it work, and he set about the task with enormous energy.

'Plucking or Peeling', 1829. Cartoonists in London had no illusions about the plan to settle Western Australia, and pictured Thomas Peel preparing to feather his nest at Swan River.

An office was opened in Piccadilly, ships were bought or chartered, families with two children were promised 400 acres for the cost of their passage money. Artisans, fishermen and labourers were promised wages of three to five shillings a day with tools and other necessities provided. Shops in London advertised clothing suitable for settlers on the Swan River. Solomon Levey arranged for the engraving and printing of bank-notes for the settlement, payable 'on demand here or at Messrs. Cooper and Levey, Sydney, N.S.W.'

News, as usual much belated, reached Australia of the great project, and it became the talk of Sydney and Hobart Town. The *Hobart Town Courier* of 16 January 1830 reported that 'Mr Levey of Sydney has united with Mr Peel in his speculation to Swan River, having advanced £10,000 in London, with an undertaking to forward livestock etc. from Sydney to the new settlement to the amount of £50,000'.

By the time that report appeared, Peel was at the Swan River, still trying desperately to make the project work. Before he left London he took care to write to the Colonial Office with details of the departure of the first ship, which carried two hundred emigrants, and gave an impressive list of supplies for the settlement. They included 500 bullocks, 1000 heifers, 200 sheep, 100 horses, 20 tons of salt beef, 4 tons of sugar and 4 bags of pepper. These goods, he said, would have cost £180 000 'if sent from England', but he did not mention where the supplies were to come from. Obviously he was more than tripling their cost, which Levey had agreed to meet from Sydney. Peel concluded by asking for an extension of the time limit imposed for the disembarkation of his first four hundred settlers but this was promptly refused, and as usual he hid the bad news from Levey.[39]

But it may be that Levey already was beginning to have misgivings. The second ship had to put into Falmouth for repairs to her foreyard, and Levey wrote to the Colonial Office as Peel's 'agent' and 'attorney' to tell them of the mishap and also to ask whether there was any truth in the rumours of 'great distress' in Western Australia and the proposed abandonment of the colony. If so, he offered to travel to Falmouth and tell the ship not to proceed.[40] Under-Secretary Twiss replied that 'no other information has been received by His Majesty's Government from or respecting the New Settlement at Swan River than what had already appeared in the public Newspapers',[41] To a letter received eight days later from a Mr Gardener, who had no connection with Peel's expedition, he wrote far more explicitly, stating that the government had no intention of abandoning the Swan River settlement.

Obviously Twiss's dislike of Peel extended to Levey and anyone else connected with the expedition, which had been doomed by the Colonial Office's refusal to extend the deadline, and its instructions to Governor Stirling that the tract of land reserved for Peel should not be kept for a single day beyond the stipulated time.[42]

Peel's first ship arrived on 15 December 1829, exactly six weeks too late for him to have free choice of land. But when he asked Governor Stirling for land, Stirling promptly made him a grant of 250 000 acres. This was to be known as Cockburn Sound, Grant Location 16, but to Peel's eye it appeared to be useless wasteland. Ironically, the land was later to prove much better than originally estimated.[43] Peel protested, but the whole concept of his settlement collapsed during the weeks in which he attempted to argue Stirling into granting him a more promising piece of land. The hapless migrants, landed on an arid coast in summer heat, received neither farms nor wages. In the miserable months that followed, Peel saw thirty-seven of his workmen and tenants die from malnutrition, and the second of his three ships wrecked. The news of his failure reached Sydney, and on 2 June 1830 the *Monitor* wrote that Peel's 'head or heart or both must be made of very singular material thus to consent to delude and be deluded or something worse'.

Times were hard in Sydney, and Daniel Cooper was not anxious to see any of his partnership profits dissipated in the new colony. On 22 April 1830 the *Gazette* had printed a facsimile of one of the bank-notes which Levey had had printed for the Swan River settlement, and on 18 May Daniel Cooper inserted a notice addressed to 'the inhabitants of Swan River and the Public in general' to say that he had no connection with the firm of Peel & Co. other than being their Sydney agent, and that goods would be supplied only on Levey's written order and against his personal account, not against funds 'invested in or belonging to the Firm of Cooper and Levey'.

In July the Barrack Master and Storekeeper at Perth wrote a letter home in which he described Peel as 'a ruined man, in the very sense of the word, unless some person arrives here speedily to manage his affairs, one who has general knowledge of trade, agriculture, and the management of men. He is totally incapable of conducting such an enterprise'.[44] On 20 September 1830 Adam Emslie, Peel's disillusioned confidential clerk, wrote from Swan River to Daniel Cooper and warned him that 'the whole

'Florishing [sic] State of the Swan River Colony', cartoon, c. 1835, London. A family in tatters sits forlornly beside the Swan River with 'water unfit to drink', while the sun blazes down on them and the settlement on Australia's west coast appears doomed.

concern then, from the beginning to the present time has been merely a dead outlay of money without any profitable return whatever hitherto or in expectancy'. With this warning the promised supplies from Sydney remained in New South Wales.

Despite Peel's duplicity it is possible to feel sorry for him, because he had deluded himself as well as others. He was among the first of a long line of men who, without the slightest practical knowledge of Australia, believed that the country would somehow make their most grandiose dreams come true.

In London, the true fate of the Swan River venture remained tantalisingly obscure, particularly to its principal supporter. No news reached Solomon Levey from either Perth or Sydney and, if Cooper felt a justifiable annoyance at Levey's neglect of their common interests in London in favour of the Swan River speculation, he could hardly have guessed that Peel had not written a line to Levey since leaving London. In the meantime, the wildest rumours circulated. On 11 December 1830 the *Sydney Gazette* reported that 'A London journal claims that Messrs Peel and Levey have cleared nearly ninety thousand pounds net profit by their Swan River Scheme'. With heavy sarcasm, and considerable inaccuracy, the *Tasmanian and Austral-Asiatic Review* of 5 March wrote:

> Mr Peel, the great Mr Peel, next to the greatest of all possible great men, Mr Peel the Home Secretary of State, has actually entered into partnership with Mr Levey, the gentleman of whom mention was made at the Philosophers' dinner as having risen by his honest industry from a retailer of Lollypops about the streets of Sydney while a crown prisoner some years ago, to a state of most independent affluence. Mr Peel and his partner Mr Levey are now about to colonise at Swan River upon a grand scale. Levey's Botany Bayism is no impediment of his forming so high a connexion . . .

But slowly the truth became apparent to everyone but Solomon Levey, who retained his faith until the last. In October 1831, Daniel Cooper sailed for London from Sydney on board the *Dukenfield*. On his arrival Cooper gave Levey the most definite and trustworthy news that he could expect from anyone. Yet it took him a further full year to acknowledge that something was seriously wrong with the Swan River settlement. Perhaps he had written to Peel with a final appeal for information, and when no answer came he turned to the authorities.[45]

Levey wrote to Viscount Goderich, the Secretary for the Colonies, on 14 January 1833. His letter explicitly claimed responsibility for the initial plan for the settlement at Swan River. Patriotically, he explained that when Peel's first syndicate collapsed, 'feeling as a merchant and a British subject [I] never for a moment supposed that these Gentlemen had any just cause for retiring from a proposal solemnly made to H.M. Government'. Levey explained obsequiously:

> My Lord, The Undersigned begs most humbly and respectfully to state that, in the year 1828, he was applied by certain Gentlemen who stated to him they were authorised by the Secretary of State Sir George Murray to say that the British Government was most anxious to give great encouragement to them, if they could cause Emigration to a sufficient extent to take place as would lead to the formation of a Colony on the West Coast of Australia, and it was also stated that the importance of

such a step was the greater in consequence of information having reached H.M. Government that the French Government was about to take possession of that part of New Holland . . . The Undersigned has faithfully acted up to the words and assurance then made, namely to assist with his fortune in furthering His Majesty's benign intention of making the settlements of Western Australia a refuge for honest and willing industry.

He now sought to know the contents of 'such correspondence' that might have passed between Thomas Peel and Governor Stirling, or between the settlement and England.

A note written by Under-Secretary Twiss for the information of his minister, in the Colonial Office papers relating to the affair, shows that the fate of the Swan River settlement was well known in London by this time—together with Peel's cavalier treatment of his partner. Twiss observed:

This is the first official information made to this Department of the connection of the writer (Mr Levey) with Mr Thomas Peel—altho' it has often been mentioned to me by persons in conversation that Mr Thos. Peel derived all his funds from Mr Levey who had nearly ruined himself by the large sums which he had advanced and who had never received one single line from Mr Peel since his departure from this country. In the agreement between the Department and Mr Thomas Peel on the secession of Mr Potter Macqueen, Sir Francis Vincent and Edward Schenley from the Speculation, Mr Levey's name does not appear nor have we by accepting in the manner alluded to in the beginning of his Memorandum any information as to Mr Levey's connection with Mr Peel. Mr Levey is a Jew. He called on me a few days before I left Town. I had directed him to tell in writing what he has to say.[46]

The words 'Mr Levey is a Jew' may be seen as the clue to all that had passed and was still to come. Thomas Peel had not hesitated to disclose to the Colonial Office the names of his first three partners, but when he accepted the aid of a Jew he took pains to conceal the fact. His failure to inform Levey of the changes in Colonial Office conditions for the settlement, followed by his constant neglect to tell Levey what was happening at Swan River, may be ascribed to the same feeling: a contempt for Levey because he was a Jew, and therefore not entitled to the consideration one would offer to other humans.

The behaviour of Twiss was not to be much better. Twiss had all the facts at his fingertips, but 'Mr Levey was a Jew' and therefore, by implication, a tricky person who was not to be trusted. At no stage in this acrimonious exchange of information was it ever mentioned that Solomon Levey had been a convict, although that may well have been an additional reason for Levey's absence from public view. It is astonishing that no official ever seems to have asked Peel where he had found the money or the stores to finance his enterprise. Twiss acknowledged, in his note to the Colonial Secretary, that he knew of Levey's financial backing of Peel, but the Colonial Office's next move was to request Levey to 'submit the fullest information' so that his right to see the relevant correspondence could be assessed.

Levey submitted what must have seemed to be convincing proof of his involvement with Peel: the co-partnership indenture into which they had entered. The British government countered this with the kind of tactic in which governments are expert. The Colonial Office politely replied that 'however binding upon Mr Peel' the partnership might have been, the Secretary of State would deal with Peel alone. Solomon Levey, however, was 'at liberty' to apply to Governor Stirling at Swan River 'for information'.[47] Levey then asked to see the deed of grant for the 500 000 acres he understood from Peel to have been granted to the partnership. Even though Twiss knew full well that the original grant had been slashed and subjected to a deadline which Peel had not met, Levey was told to apply to Sir James Stirling for the 'Deed of Grant to Mr Thomas Peel, of the land to which he may be entitled . . .'[48]

It is impossible to say whether the pettifogging callousness of Twiss' behaviour can be ascribed to religious or social prejudice. It is certain, however, that like countless public servants before and since, he preferred to abide by the strict letter of administrative procedure rather than show common humanity towards a man whom he was supposed to serve. He knew all the facts of the case, yet would not assist Levey beyond referring him to a man 12 000 miles away in distance and at least five months in time, for an answer could not be expected in less than that.

In contrast to Solomon Levey, the colonial authorities in London harboured few illusions about Thomas Peel. In an undated private note to the colony's Governor, Under-Secretary Hay warned Stirling not to trust Peel: 'I cannot but think that the impetuosity, indiscretion, to use no harder words, which he has betrayed in his communications with the Department, will render him an unsafe member of a body whose deliberations are likely to involve both General and individual interests of great and yearly increasing importance'.[49]

Levey continued to act with humanity and dignity. Although it seems that he was still unaware of the full extent of the disaster which Peel's colony had suffered, he heard of Governor Stirling's advances of money to the survivors. Immediately, he offered and arranged help. He wrote to Sydney to order the sale of two of his farms, with the proceeds to be paid to Cooper & Levey.[50] When this had been done, tenders were called on 9 December 1833 by Cooper & Levey 'for the conveyance of certain goods and livestock from this port to the Swan River'.

The Colonial Office was told of this action in a letter from Levey which remarked that, although he was Peel's partner, no demands had been made on him to help the settlers in their need. Nevertheless, he said, he was informing the Colonial Office 'for fear of death or any other misfortune', so that the government might feel free to take possession of the consignment of supplies when it arrived at Swan River.[51]

This letter establishes that Levey did not even know whether Peel was dead or alive, or whether he was still at Swan River. Through the Colonial Office, Levey sent a packet to Peel, and on 13 November 1833 the Colonial Secretary in Perth wrote to Levey to tell him that 'Mr Peel is still in the Colony, at the Murray District . . . the packet addressed to him will be delivered into his hands at his first arrival in Perth'.[52] Whether or not the packet reminded Peel of his obligations will never be known, because Levey had died in London on 10 October 1833 at the age of thirty-nine.

It was left to Solomon Levey's son, John Levey, to settle accounts with the heartless betrayer of his father, but the reckoning would take another eighteen years. John

Levey had been brought up as a Christian, and after his twenty-first birthday he added his mother's surname to his own and became John Levey-Roberts. However, his heritage ran deep. On 25 November 1842 the *Sydney Morning Herald* reported that John Levey-Roberts had married Miss Minna Cecilia Goodman at St George's Church in Spitalfields. The bride, who was Jewish, was the sister of George Barron Goodman, the first photographer in Australia and son-in-law of the emancipist Abraham Polack. Ties with Australia also lingered. In 1851 an agreement was concluded in Perth between Thomas Peel and John Levey-Roberts 'to avoid litigation'; it is obvious that John was unflinchingly committed to pursuing Peel. Peel had no money, but John's right to share the Cockburn Sound land grant was at last confirmed.[53]

Peel was at least consistent and constant in his chicanery. He had not kept any of the agreements in the co-partnership deed and, after it was signed, had behaved as though Levey did not exist. On 31 July 1832 he asked for the grant of 250 000 acres, about which he had been arguing with Governor Stirling, to be 'prepared and executed in his favour to enable him to forward the same for final approbation to the Government at home'.[54] Levey was not mentioned, and the land was granted to Peel.

Levey's faith in Peel may have survived his endless silence, but the officials of the embryonic colony of Western Australia were under no illusions. On 12 August 1833 the Colonial Secretary, Lord Stanley, wrote to Governor Stirling:

> If Peel should claim further land to the extent of one million acres this would not be considered, as he is without financial means and so, as far as his undertaking has proceeded, he has not fulfilled any of the conditions in the manner H.M. Government has the right to expect. His 400 settlers became nearly immediately a charge to the Government.[55]

Daniel Cooper remained a loyal friend of the Levey family. The partnership had of course to be dissolved, though the firm continued to exist until 1848. It had been one of the most important businesses in Australia and the last mercantile venture that included banking as one of its departments. Cooper steadfastly tried to help Levey's erratic younger brother, Barnett, by purchasing Barnett's building ventures in Sydney, and after Solomon's death he generously supported his brothers and son in London. In 1841 he was named sole executor of Solomon Levey's mother's estate.[56] In 1844 the firm of Cooper and Holt gave five pounds to the building fund of the York Street Synagogue. Daniel Cooper died on 13 November 1853 and his estate went to his nephew, Sir Daniel Cooper, Speaker in the first New South Wales Parliament.

Sydney retains very little by way of memorial to the remarkable Solomon Levey, and there is nothing whatsoever in Western Australia that recalls his name. Levey Street, in the Sydney suburb of Redfern, which stands on property once owned by Cooper & Levey, may recall his name. It took nearly twenty years to sell Solomon Levey's extensive real estate. A bequest of £500 which Levey left to 'Sydney College', the Free Grammar School of which he was a trustee, was transferred in 1853 to the new University of Sydney. It was the university's first endowment, and the interest is still distributed each year as a scholarship for a second-year student in natural science.

'Enter Barney!'

SUCH A FLAMBOYANT CHARACTER deserves a chapter on his own. Unlike his brother Solomon, Barnett Levey had no memory of lollipops at the beginning of his career, nor would he ever return to England in triumph. His empire was the Australian stage. His painful battle to establish a theatre in Sydney sheds light upon the astonishingly large number of Jews involved in the first years of Australian cultural and theatrical history, yet his life was far more than a mere prologue for the performance of others. His plans, quarrels, schemes and adventures all had a grandiose quality. Everything he did seems larger than life, and it is appropriate that he should be regarded as the father of Australian theatre.[1]

Barnett Levey was tempted to Australia by the success of his brother Solomon. He arrived on 18 December 1821 aboard the *John Bull*, a ship carrying female convicts and some free passengers, and was the one of the first Jewish males to make the voyage of his own free will. He had paid for his passage by signing on as the captain's clerk, and upon his arrival in Sydney gained official permission to settle in New South Wales.

His brother Solomon, who was generous with gifts but cautious in his selection of a business partner, enabled him to taste success during his first four years in Sydney, by having him work at the George Street shop. At the end of that apprenticeship Barnett was able to back up his petition for a land grant with the claim that he owned property worth £2000 and that his brother assured 'further support'. He stated in the petition that he was anxious to 'purchase cattle and to cultivate land'.[2] On 22 June 1825 Barnett Levey announced that he 'intended commencing business on his own account at 72 George St, the former residence of his brother Mr S[olomon] Levey'.[3] The following week he advertised that he would be selling grain, pork and bullocks that he would take in exchange for merchandise at market price.

The colonial administration granted him 640 acres at Lapstone Hill in the lower Blue Mountains. He had begun to build a house, clear the land and fence the property when he applied for permission to buy 350 acres adjoining his grant so that there would be 'no interruptions from an unpleasant neighbour'. The government agreed, and the 27-year-old migrant from the East End became the second member of his family to be a substantial landholder. Though he was anything but religious he called his property Mount Sion, its brook Kidron, and its valley Jehosapath.[4] Such a property required a mistress, and the *Sydney Gazette* duly reported the marriage of Barnett

Levey, merchant, of Macquarie Street, to Sarah Emma Wilson, daughter of Mrs Josephson and stepdaughter of Jacob Josephson, at the Church of St John's, Parramatta, in a ceremony solemnised by the Venerable Archdeacon Scott on Saturday 25 June 1825.

Solomon Levey would have been well aware of his brother's strengths and weaknesses. While Barnett was building his house, Solomon was concluding his partnership arrangements with Daniel Cooper. With his usual mixture of canniness and generosity, Solomon did not take Barnett into partnership but provided him with a considerable amount of stock and capital to enable him to set up business on his own account. It must have been a wedding present, for in the week before his marriage Barnett took over his brother's store and made his debut as an independent merchant.[5]

The colony was flourishing and Levey's business developed rapidly. As a general dealer he was able to sell spirits and a wide range of necessities, and he also built up Sydney's first lending library.[6] He was present at the founding of the Sydney Banking Company, and he and Solomon were shareholders in the Bank of New South Wales. This interest in banking had become apparent quite early, as indicated by the *Sydney Gazette* on 11 March 1825.

> A meeting of proprietors of the contemplated Bank of Australia met at the Sydney Hotel . . . Mr Barnett Levey of George Street unquestionably deserves the thanks of that portion of the public with whom he sympathises for making such liberal proposals to them, which his extending business, we are glad to see, enables him to accomplish without any great sacrifice to his concerns.

The same newspaper had frequent occasion to mention Barnett Levey's effervescence of ventures and ideas. On 27 July 1825 he took out an auctioneer's licence, which would ease his way through many periods of stress in the future. On 16 July 1827 he became interested in a plan to grow cheap vegetables for the Sydney market on a 60-acre property on the South Head Road, and submitted it to the government in the form of a memorandum. The *Gazette* on 12 December and the *Australian* on 22 December 1825 reported his scheme to issue bank-notes based on rupees imported from Mauritius by Colonel Dumaresq of the Colonial Land Board. The rupees were overvalued by Levey at two shillings and sixpence apiece, and the note issue, which was Australia's one and only issue of bank-notes based upon rupees, was a complete failure. The issue was abandoned, but curiously enough counterfeit copies of the notes were still appearing in 1830.

But while one side of his mind was devoted to commerce, Levey was discovering a more glamorous aspect of life. During 1825 and 1826 he gave a series of concerts which transformed him into 'the general favourite'. He sang, gave recitations and, according to the *Gazette* of 25 June and 6 December 1826, performed 'with infinite drollery' and was 'greeted with universal plaudits'. He was 'applauded to the very echo that did applaud again'. He dreamed of building a theatre that would be a fitting showcase for his talents, and that dream became an obsession.

Whether by coincidence or not, it seems that Barnett's tact, financial security and business sense left him when Solomon sailed for England. Even while Solomon prepared for departure, Barnett embarked upon a huge and fantastic building project, possibly with the aid of a parting gift from his brother.

Sydney was first appraised of what was to come by an advertisement in the *Gazette* of 8 March 1826 calling for tenders for the supply of 100 000 bricks. With the assistance of a mortgage held by Daniel Cooper, work began in June 1826 on what was to be a combined warehouse, public house and flour mill. The Colchester Warehouse was a five-storey construction behind Levey's home and store on George Street. As soon as it was completed, Levey rebuilt his George Street premises as the Royal Hotel. One floor of the warehouse was designed as a theatre, for which Barnett asked Solomon to send him a chandelier from England. The theatre, known as Levey's Theatre Royal, was connected to the Royal Hotel by a saloon 60 feet long. A hall for Masonic meetings, a large supper room, and kitchens were surmounted by a loft, 200 feet long, which covered both buildings and was the base for a windmill. The windmill formed the sixth storey of the building and has been called Sydney's first skyscraper. It has been estimated that the entire building, including the mill, towered 90 feet above the street.[7]

As a new home to replace the redesigned George Street premises, Barnett built himself a two-storey Georgian mansion on land he owned near the heart of today's Bondi Junction. In tribute to his favourite author, Sir Walter Scott, he named it Waverley House. On 1 June 1826 a daughter was born and 'a ball and supper' was held 'to a very

Waverley House. Built and named by Barnett Levey in 1827, this was the first building in what is now the Sydney suburb of Waverley. By the time it was completed Levey's financial troubles had overtaken him, and he would never live in the house of his dreams.

large concourse of friends on the gratifying occasion of their heiress being admitted to the rite of baptism, within the pale of the Church'. In the 1828 census Levey registered that he was a Jew, but his four children were brought up in the Anglican faith.

Sydney citizens, and their newspapers, applauded the construction of the huge George Street building. The *Gazette* of 27 June 1827 recorded the laying of the foundation-stone for the Royal Hotel by Samuel Terry, Master of the Masonic Lodge No. 26 attended by his brethren in full regalia, amid 'loud cheers for the owner of the Colchester Warehouse'. On 8 May 1830 the journal described the whole building as 'a stupendous structure with its proud windmill turret'. Some 1200 people were to be seated in Levey's Theatre Royal and another 500 in the Royal Hotel saloon. By the time Levey's building spree was over, he had erected Sydney's tallest building at a cost of nearly £20 000.[8]

The government took a less optimistic view of Levey's venture. He had not asked for building permission nor submitted plans. Not only were the authorities dismayed by the sight of such an enormous building rising upon such a small block of land, but they even doubted whether he had title to that land. Levey's relationship with the colony's autocratic Governor Darling was already somewhat tense because of Levey's own foolhardiness. Even while planning his building, he had crossed swords with Darling on the issue of ticket-of-leave men being licensed as publicans.[9] As the loyal brother and beneficiary of a former convict, Levey publicly, and foolishly, announced in the *Australian* of 16 March 1826 that he would use his licence to supply such men with liquor.

The government's first move came when the windmill was being installed, and one of its sails fell off. The Attorney-General filed a complaint of nuisance against Levey, who was ordered to stop constructing immediately.[10] Levey reacted with scornful fury, and threw fuel on the fire by seeking legal representation by William Charles Wentworth. Wentworth, the colony's first Australian-born lawyer and a champion of representative government, was already at loggerheads with Governor Darling over the Sudds–Thompson affair, which he had exploited as proof of vice-regal despotism. The result of Levey's approach to him was, in Darling's words, one of the most impertinent letters ever written to the colonial authorities.

Levey declared that even though the mill had taken nine months to build, no notice had ever been received from the government disapproving of its construction.[11] He enclosed a certificate from his neighbours, stating that they did not consider the mill to be a nuisance. The letter continued:

> if it be a nuisance the Government Windmill is an equal nuisance; and I will take care [it] shall meet the same fate as mine. I decline furnishing you with the particulars of my Title to the Yard, upon which this Building is being erected. I believe it to be as good a title as any in the Town, and I will take care to defend it, if it be sought to be impugned. If this notice had been given me in due time, I might have desisted. To desist now would be next to ruin; and, if the Government is really so anxious about the Lives of His Majesty's Subjects, as is pretended, let them pay for their default in not giving me notice sooner, and I will then leave off.

ABOVE LEFT: *Robert Johnston, attributed to Richard Read snr, c. 1820. The second son of Esther Abrahams and George Johnston, born on 9 March 1792, Robert Johnston was the only godson of Governor Phillip and the first Australian-born officer in the Royal Navy. He died at Annandale on 8 September 1882.*

ABOVE RIGHT: *Julia Johnston, attributed to Richard Read snr, c. 1823. Julia Johnston stands in the garden at Annandale in front of the mausoleum and family vault, designed by Francis Greenway, where her father, George Johnston, was buried in 1823.*

ABOVE: A convict distributes used military clothing to the Aborigines, unfinished sketch by an unknown artist. The grey convict uniform indicates that the sketch was made in New South Wales. It resembles sketches by Augustus Earle, who visited Australia in the 1820s.

BELOW: The Convict Barracks, Hyde Park, Sydney, possibly by J. Lycett

It was an impudent and foolish letter which precipitated Levey into the feud between Wentworth and Darling and destroyed any possibility of government good-will for the future. Levey was destined to regret it bitterly. Darling saw at once that the letter had been inspired by Wentworth, and promptly sent a copy to London as an awful illustration of the opposition he faced. In an accompanying note to the Under-Secretary of the Colonial Office, Darling described Barnett Levey as 'a man of the Lowest Class, having commenced erecting a Wind Mill in the Centre of the Town of Sydney on Ground to which he has no claim . . . the style and tone of the letter speak for themselves'.[12]

The Governor never forgave Levey for his insolence, and quite soon found an opportunity for revenge. After six months procrastination, Levey submitted the plans of his windmill to the authorities on 12 June 1827, but avoided any embarrassing confrontation at an official level by writing that he was 'too sick to bring them personally'.[13] On 23 July he applied for permission to obtain a licence to distil spirits, and said that 'having the interests of the settlers at heart' he would produce it for a third of the usual price of twenty to thirty shillings a gallon.[14] Darling promptly rejected the application, and noted upon it:

> I have fully considered the whole of this man's proceedings and think it would be an act of weakness on the part of government to grant him any indulgence. He has erected his Mill in defiance of the warnings of government, and now looks for indulgence . . . I remember . . . how he allowed Mr Wentworth to make a tool of him to abuse the government. Inform him that I have declined complying with his application.

Public opinion about the 'stupendous structure' began to change, and a mocking note crept into newspaper reports. On 31 December 1827 the *Gazette* wrote that 'Mr Barnett Levey's whirl about thing-um-bob was put in motion' on Christmas Day. It was a vain gesture on Levey's part, because government opposition was becoming a formidable obstacle. But he continued to complete the building, to fight for its operation, and to carry on normal business life. On 6 March 1828 the *Gazette* reported that 'Mr Levey, not of steam engine, but of windmill notoriety—the brother of the Australian Rothschild—has contracted with the settlers already, for 15,000 bushels of wheat of the growth of the ensuing season at seven shillings the bushel'. This gamble, involving Levey in an enormous capital outlay, was a failure. The mill could not be made to work and very little of the wheat was ground into flour.

Governor Darling was still on the offensive. A special statute was promulgated to prohibit 'theatrical representations of any kind unless the houses are licensed' and stating that 'persons frequenting unlicensed houses' were 'to be deemed rogues and vagabonds'. This, of course, was aimed at preventing the opening of Levey's Theatre Royal.[15] Ill and bitterly frustrated, Levey organised a petition, signed by Sydney folk, urging that he be allowed to hold performances in his theatre.[16] In December 1829 Barnett received a licence permitting him to present plays so long as he was able to keep public order—and provided that the plays had already been seen, and therefore

'Sydney from the West', a sketch by John Thompson, 1832. The view shows St James' Church, the Rum Hospital, and Levey's 'frightfully lofty' windmill sitting on top of his warehouse and theatre.

passed, by the Lord Chamberlain's office in London, which acted as censor. This provision meant that Levey would not be able to perform on his own stage.

It was crushing evidence that the enemy in Government House remained implacable. Levey wrote to him in terms very different from the letter inspired by Wentworth, and his words reveal that he was looking into a bleak and desperate future:

> I have received yours of yesterday, enclosing a license for one year to have Balls and Concerts at my House, the Royal Hotel—for which I return you my sincere thanks. But at the same time I must respectfully beg leave to say that it will be of no benefit to me—unless allowed to give entertainments SOLO . . . I was the only person who amused the public on that Evening and who gave moral recitations and Loyal as well as Humerous Songs . . . What with severe losses in trade by frauds practised on me— a protracted illness—Disappointments in my Mill, Will Truely (if not already) be the ruin of me unless you grant me permission to amuse the public, not in a Theatrical way, but separate from any other person . . . I have a Wife and three children to support and were it not for their Sakes I should rest satisfied . . .[17]

The Governor refused to relent, and on 21 January 1830 the *Sydney Gazette* reported that 'Mr Levey, proprietor of the Royal Hotel, wishes to retire on account of ill health'. It was a vain hope, because as the months passed he failed to find a buyer for his bizarre construction. The *Monitor* of 3 February borrowed from the playbills of the era when it mockingly described the first unsuccessful auction as 'Positively the last time Mr Levey's performance'. The same newspaper shows that on 17 February

'New Theatre Royal Sydney', from Maclehose, The Picture of Sydney . . . *Levey's theatre in George Street waits for its licence from a hostile governor.*

he was obliged to sell his plate, wine and furniture and that on 10 March even his library, a rich collection of novels and historical works, went under the hammer. The journalists recorded the shipwreck of his ambitions as faithfully as they had reported his first bold ventures, but he was still not short of imagination. The *Sydney Gazette* of 8 May outlined a scheme to sell the Royal Hotel by issuing shares to subscribers. As each subscriber died, his shares and any further interest payable upon them were transferred to the surviving shareholders, until the one who lived the longest owned all the shares and the property. This method, known as a Tontine because it was devised by the Neapolitan financier Lorenzo Tonti in 1650, was popular in the early nineteenth century, but in Levey's case it was unsuccessful through lack of public confidence in its proprietor.

Levey now swallowed his pride completely, and with heavy heart wrote to Governor Darling on 30 September 1830 that 'from circumstances which would be painful for me to relate' he had been compelled to quit his premises, and begged leave to stage a few evening entertainments called At Homes, at which he would be the only performer.[18] He stated pathetically that 'it would be the means of affording me some Assistance', but one may imagine the vengeful pleasure with which Darling wrote on the petition, 'It cannot be allowed'.

It seems that one of Darling's objections to the theatre in Sydney was his fear that convicts or former convicts could appear on the stage and receive the applause of free men.[19] In the case of Barnett Levey, who had arrived a free man, that objection could hardly be sustained, and in any case convicts had given theatrical performances from the earliest years of settlement. In 1789 the convicts of the First Fleet presented

The Recruiting Officer for the edification of their superiors and, in 1824, a mud and bark theatre was built at Emu Plains, where the convicts gave regular performances of comedy, drama and melodrama.[20] This point was noted by the *Monitor* on 10 July 1830:

> Mr Levey built a theatre in Sydney, the non-licensing of which had ruined him. His was a theatre at which free and freed persons only were to perform and be present. Yet he, and the Colony through him, was refused the pleasures of the Drama on the score of their being irreligious and immoral. Not so with the convicts. They, worthy men, are allowed to have a Theatre, and at Emu Plains too, a demi-penal settlement, where discipline in flogging etc has always existed to a comfortable degree.

The trustees of the under-subscribed Tontine requested in December 1830 that the Royal Hotel and its subsidiary buildings be sold by public auction. They were bought by the mortgagor, the loyal and ever helpful Daniel Cooper, who would thus have released Levey from part of his burden of debt. As the *Sydney Gazette* observed on 18 December, 'Mr Levey has a large, young family to support, we trust public sympathy will help repair his broken fortunes'.

The sale of the burdensome building seemed to give Levey a new lease of life. Perhaps he had realised secretly what was not to be said publicly until after his death: that a combined flour mill, warehouse, theatre and hotel simply was not a workable proposition. The *Sydney Times* wrote on 31 October 1837:

> The Theatre and the windmill were in one respect alike; they were both useless. The mill at the top of an immense house was found inconvenient and ill-adapted; and moreover endangered the whole building, and would not have contributed much more to the safety and satisfaction of persons in the Theatre immediately underneath; than would the noise of the Mill, and dust from the flour, to the comfort and edification of an audience.

Windmills, of which there were a number in Sydney at that time, were among the very few pieces of large machinery so far invented by humanity. The huge sails, sometimes spun round by the wind so fast that they could not be seen, were harnessed by a system of belts and gearing to huge grindstones which rumbled thunderously as they ground the wheat. It is little wonder that the authorities were unhappy about such a mechanism being poised on top of a building planned to hold nearly two thousand pleasure-seekers.

But Levey was not yet free from the desire to build. With his 'whirl about thing-um-bob' behind him, he began to promote yet another project. The *Australian* of 10 December 1830 told the Sydney public of his proposal to build a range of terrace houses on the land he owned at today's Bondi Junction.[21] The terrace was to adjoin Waverley House—which he built in 1827 but never lived in and which, like most of his possessions, had been sold early in 1830—and was to be called Waverley Crescent. But Sydney folk were sceptical about his projects by this time, and had already named his house and other buildings Levey's Folly. His Waverley Crescent scheme resulted in no more than two or three cottages, and their sale in 1834 ended his interest in real estate.

He was busy with other dreams. 'The exertions of Mr Levey in everything he undertakes are indefatigable', the *Gazette* noted on 9 October 1830, by which time he had resorted to his skill as an auctioneer. In February 1831 he plucked yet another of the many strings to his bow. He opened a watchmaking and jewellery shop and, with a flair for public relations which was decades ahead of his time, spent the full first month of business in organising raffles. These called for twenty customers to pay four shillings each to enter, which gave them the right to throw dice for sets of jewellery. Unfortunately it seems that there were not enough gamblers in Sydney, though the *Gazette* said that his 'skill and assiduity' merited public support. On 7 May the journal reported that he had sold his stock of watches and jewellery and opened a Reform Auction Mart. Explanation of this reform was withheld, by the *Gazette* at least, until 31 December, when the public was told that those who bought goods from Barnett Levey could also borrow money from him—at interest, naturally.

Levey's struggles to recoup his fortune were lightened by one bright spot: the departure of Governor Darling for England on 22 October 1831. He had been one of the most unpopular rulers the colony had suffered, and when in 1830 his recall was announced a petition was circulated summoning colonists to a public meeting at which to express their delight. Not surprisingly, Barnett Levey's name appeared on it, and gave Darling the opportunity for another stab at one of his many enemies. Darling took a copy of the petition home to the Colonial Office, together with a pungent analysis of numerous people who had signed it. He called Barnett Levey 'An insolvent Jew—came out to the colony to join his brother who was a convict'.[22] Since Darling was at least partly responsible for Barnett's insolvency, the remark is a fair illustration of why the Governor was so disliked.

Darling was replaced by Sir Richard Bourke, a man with far more liberal opinions and benevolence of nature. Levey continued to live by auctioneering while he studied the lie of the land. When Bourke had been in office for six months, Levey petitioned him for permission to open a theatre 'for entertainment of an amusing nature governed by virtue and morality'.[23] Permission was promptly granted, and on 26 August 1832 Levey triumphantly took space in the *Sydney Herald* to announce the arrival of his long-awaited Theatre Licence, 'for which I shall ever feel thankful . . . I am satisfied that the Public are aware of my losses for attempting to introduce into Australia a species of Entertainment, Amusements both moral and entertaining, and that, too, at my individual expense'. Levey solemnly promised the Governor that his stage would be a 'mirror of virtue', to which the administration returned a warning that the two problems of ready identification and possible public acclaim prohibited convicts from appearing in any dramatic presentation or masquerade.[24]

Characteristically, Levey now began to plan grandiose theatre ventures. Though he was no longer the owner of the Royal Hotel or the untried theatre attached to it, he began to publish newspaper notices to inform the public of his vision of how the theatre should be rebuilt and enlarged. The owners of the building were understandably reluctant to spend any money on the theatre, but allowed Levey to perform in the large saloon of the hotel. To his mingled chagrin and delight, his first three At

Homes played to packed houses, with crowds of would-be patrons turned away at the door. The loss of such potential revenue, after so many years of financial struggle, emboldened him to tell his reluctant landlord that he would open a new theatre within six months. Solomon Levey was now in London and deeply involved with his ill-fated scheme to settle Western Australia with the help of Thomas Peel, but Solomon had harboured a soft spot for his younger brother. The firm of Cooper & Levey, faced with the prospect of losing the only theatrical client in the colony, hastily agreed to allow him to enlarge and rebuild the Theatre Royal.[25]

The history of Australian professional theatre began on the day after Christmas 1832, in the saloon theatre of the Royal Hotel. Barnett Levey presented the drama *Black Eyed Susan, or All in the Downs*, by D. W. Jerrold, followed by the farce *Monsieur Tonson*, by W. T. Moncrieff, to a packed audience of more than five hundred people who had paid 5 shillings each for box seats or 3 shillings for pit seats. The *Currency Lad* of 22 December advised that 'Those who expect to see a "Drury Lane" or even an "Adelphi" [the two best-known London theatres] will find themselves egregiously deceived, but those who may go with no higher expectation than to witness the first playhouse in a new colony will be agreeably surprised'. It has been estimated that the auditorium could not have been more than 40 feet long and 33 feet wide.[26]

Levey was understandably anxious to move to the real theatre in his former warehouse, and his ambition was consummated on 5 October 1833 when he opened to an audience of twelve hundred. Perhaps his anxiety to see the curtain go up had prevented proper rehearsal, because the *Gazette*'s issue of 7 October reported:

> '*The Miller and his Men*' by I. Pocock, and '*The Irishman in London*' by W. Macready, were chosen for the opening night. It may be generally said of the first piece that it was rather run through than acted. The burning of the mill failed, pistols were fired off, and one squib in miniature as the curtain fell hid the confusion of those behind it. '*The Irishman in London*' made some amends for the deficiencies of the first piece.

It is not certain whether the 'squib in miniature' was a firework or a sketch performed on the stage, which in those days sometimes were called 'squibs'.

Starting with *Othello* on 26 July 1834, followed by *Hamlet* on 18 August of the same year, many Shakespearean dramas were performed on his stage, which excelled in its variety. An astounding 342 comedies, operas, operettas, ballets and dramas were performed on the stage of the Theatre Royal between 1833 and 1837. The list included first performances of no less than seven Shakespearian plays. Levey's theatre performed *The School for Scandal*, *The Rivals* and *She Stoops to Conquer*, and plays by contemporary French and German authors. Defending Levey's extraordinary role in Australian theatrical history, Eric Irvine concludes that 'Far from being negligible as a theatre, or a theatrical company, Levey's had a repertoire unequalled by any single Australian theatre company since it was established'.[27]

Sydney's metropolitan population was then less than 17 000, so keeping the theatre going was an endless and heartbreaking battle. On 3 January 1834 Levey advertised in the *Australian* for a partner to help him because he was ill, and found that

The first Play Bill
as Theatre Royal
printed in this Colony
D. Oley.

THEATRE ROYAL,
SYDNEY.

ON WEDNESDAY, DECEMBER the 26th, 1832,
THIS THEATRE
Will open for the first time, with New Scenery, Machinery,
Dresses, and Decorations, under the management of
MR. MEREDITH.

The Pieces selected for the opening are first:
THAT MUCH ADMIRED
Nautical Melo - Drama,
IN THREE ACTS,
CALLED,
BLACK-EYED SUSAN;
OR,
ALL IN THE DOWNS.

ADMIRAL, by Mr. Vale.
CAPTAIN CROSSTREE, by Mr. Cooper,
LIEUTENANT PIKE, by Mr. Raymond.
BLUE PETER, by Mr. Richardson.
SEAWEED, by Mr. Taylor.
QUID, by Mr. Kirby.

DOGGRASS, by Mr. Buckingham.
JACOB TWIG, by Mr. L. C. Cook.
GNATBRAIN, by Mr. Vale.
PLOUGHSHARE, by Mr. Varley.
RAKER, by Mr. Hollingsworth.
HATCHET, by Mr. Hill.
YARN, by Mr. Sykes.

WILLIAM, BY MR. MEREDITH.
BLACK-EYED SUSAN, by Mrs. Love.   DOLLY MAY-FLOWER, by Mrs. Weston.

Captains, Midshipman, Sailors, Villagers, &c. &c.
To conclude with that Far-famed Highly Comic Farce,
IN TWO ACTS,
FROM TAYLOR'S CELEBRATED POEM, ENTITLED,
MONSIEUR TONSON.

MORBLEU, by Mr. Meridith.
TOM KING, by Mr. Cooper.
JACK ARDOURLY, by Mr. Buckingham.
USEFUL, by Mr. Raymond.
WANTOM, by Mr. Taylor.
TRAP, by Mr. Kirby.

MR. THOMPSON, by Mr. Vale.
RUSTY, by Mr. Hill.
NAP, by Mr. Ryder.
FIP, by Mr. Hollingsworth.
WAITER, by Mr. Barnard.
SNAP, by Mr. Barns.

ADELPHINE DE COURCY, Mrs. Weston.   MADAME BELLEGARDE, Mrs. Love.
MRS. THOMPSON, by Mrs Ward.

The Performance to be supported by the Band of His Majesty's 17th Regiment, kindly
allowed by COLONEL DESPARD, and conducted by Mr. Lewis.

BOX SEATS, 5s.   PIT SEATS, 3s.

The first playbill of the Theatre Royal, 1832.

partner in Joseph Simmons. On 31 October the same journal reported that he had paid a brief visit to Hobart Town in search of help and money. His vicissitudes over the next twenty months may be traced through the columns of the *Australian*. On 21 July 1835 he lost control of the theatre to six trustees and returned to conducting land sales and auctions; on 19 April 1836 he was appointed a director of the new Sydney Gas Company; in May he resumed control of the Theatre Royal, and on 3 June proudly advertised the names of those in his new extensive Corps Dramatique. A week later his children, 'Master and Miss Levey,' appeared on stage in *The May Queen* by J. B. Buckstone.

Levey perceived a sad decline in the standards of his theatre, and worried about the effect on his previous licence. He warned the public:

> Parties frequenting the Gallery, making use of obscene expression, will be not only sent to the Watch House, but excluded from the House from that time. It is a pity to see Persons, who, by education, and general deportment, should know better, smoking in the upper boxes. I hope this hint will have the desired effect.

In the *Gazette* of 26 November 1836 he confessed that he was seriously considering 'setting a part of the upper tier of boxes exclusively for accommodation of women of disreputable character, after the fashion practised in Berlin, so that no mistake can take place as to the real circumstances of the partner'.

But the 'patriarch of the drama of New South Wales', who worried about bad manners and immoral liaisons in his theatre, was himself increasingly open to public criticism. Like so many others in colonial Australia he turned to the bottle for relaxation and encouragement, and was frequently seen to be drunk. 'Enter Barney—Sober!!!' was a malicious note in a court report in the *Sydney Gazette* of 31 August 1837. Less than a month later, on 23 September, the newspaper carried an advertisement by the stage manager, who said that it had been found 'absolutely necessary' to exclude the proprietor from behind the scenes, and that he must cease all 'intermeddling'.

The sands, or was it the gin, were fast running out and, in the words of one Sydney newspaper, Barnett Levey 'played his last part and quitted the stage for ever' on 2 October 1837. He was only thirty-nine, the same age at which his brother Solomon had died. Both men had packed a lot into their brief lives.

His only detailed obituary appeared in the *Sydney Times* on 21 October 1837, which in the forthright manner of the period wrote, 'His constitution was completely shattered . . . He was, and everybody knows it, a hard drinker. He has rendered the colony, by the introduction of the Drama, a service, let us in justice to his memory support liberally his widow and four orphan children'. The reporter mentioned that the Governor had sent a 'handsome present of a ten pound note' to Barnett's widow, as he was unable to attend a public benefit for her family. When probate was granted on his estate, the total value failed to exceed £500.[28]

Barnett Levey was buried as a Jew, but his relationship with the emerging Jewish community in New South Wales had been tenuous. He had not hesitated to emigrate to a land in which there were no eligible Jewish women for him to marry, and he married Emma Wilson, the stepdaughter of the apostate Jew and a former convict, Jacob Josephson.

Notwithstanding baptisms, and the addition by both Barnett and Solomon Levey of the extra 'e' to their name while in Australia, no one seems to have doubted Barnett Levey's Jewishness, and in his theatrical performances he capitalised upon his knowledge of the mannerisms and accents of his people and the prejudice of the crowd. In June 1838 he was called 'a little Jew thief' in a public brawl, in which he threw a pair of candlesticks and a decanter at his persecutor and subsequently was bound over to keep the peace.[29] In the *Gazette* of 21 October 1829 and the *Sydney Herald* of 10 September 1832 it is possible to see the development of his stage character, Mishter Isaacs, a 'shew [Jew] pedlar' who spoke such monologue as 'Oh vat a mash, oh ma properte, here's all my shleeve buttons run up to my very packpone; oh dat I vas a little poy again'.

Barnett Levey's tombstone still lies among the graves moved to the shore of Botany Bay when the old colonial cemetery made way for Sydney's Central Railway Station. There is nothing to tell the visitor that it is the grave of Australia's first free Jewish male migrant and the founder of Australian theatre—though he gave Sydney more glamour, drama and pathos in his daily life than ever on the stage. But his tombstone, together with those of Joseph Marcus and Samuel and Abraham Lyons, were saved from destruction by their re-erection in the Pioneer Park at Botany Cemetery.

Judah's Voice

HE JEWS who crowded the galleries at London's Drury Lane Theatre and Covent Garden provided Australia with an impressive proportion of its first actors, singers, musicians and playwrights. Barnett Levey's painful battle brought other Jews to his side. They included John Lazar, the future Mayor of Adelaide and one of Australia's earliest professional actors. The exiled Isaac Nathan became the first composer. Jacob Levi Montefiore, merchant and parliamentarian, translated the libretto for Australia's first opera. Joseph Simmons, an auctioneer, managed Sydney's second theatre, acted in many of Australia's first serious theatrical productions, and wrote some of Sydney's earliest plays.[1]

JOSEPH SIMMONS first appeared on the London stage at the age of twelve, in the ready succession of minor roles available to bright and versatile young actors. Nevertheless in 1830, at the age of twenty, he set sail for Sydney to work with his successful older brother, the emancipist James Simmons. Within a year Joseph was ready to strike out on his own as an auctioneer, announcing to the commercial world that he had 'devoted a considerable time to a series of studies in respect to mercantile affairs in one of the first wholesale and retail houses in the colony'.

Experience was a harsh tutor. The older Jewish auctioneers were formidable competitors and, for a young Londoner, Sydney was a dull and provincial outpost with no theatre and no eligible Jewish girls. So Simmons set sail for home, after placing an advertisement in the *Sydney Gazette* of 10 April 1832 for the sale of his 'household furniture, glass and china ware, elegantly framed pictures, English chairs, a handsome pianoforte, an excellent horse, silver watch, gold chain, and seals'. On the voyage he stopped briefly in Van Diemen's Land to delight Hobart Town and Launceston with a series of popular, pioneer theatrical evenings.

In London, Simmons married the daughter of Henry Cohen, a wealthy broker. His Australian experience proved valuable to his father-in-law, who within the year was arrested and sentenced to transportation for possession of stolen promissory notes. Simmons set sail with his new wife and all her relatives, arriving in Sydney on 21 December 1833 in the *Brothers* in time to see Henry Cohen sent off in chains to the prison settlement at Port Macquarie. A hurried petition to have Cohen assigned to his son-in-law was refused, and Simmons settled in Sydney to set up in business again.

Either his marriage or his wealthy brother James endowed him with sufficient capital to open Paddington House and Fancy Bazaar in George Street, which offered 'fancy and other goods, unequalled in Sydney for variety, quality and cheapness'.[2] Barnett Levey's Theatre Royal was one year old, and within weeks of his arrival Simmons succumbed to the lure of the stage and began work as stage manager and one of Levey's principal actors. In the space of a few months he appeared, with varying degrees of critical acclaim, as Iago, Macbeth, Lorenzo, Mercutio, Hotspur and Petruchio.[3] But when it came to raising money on his own behalf, on a Simmons Night at the Theatre Royal in October 1834, he shrewdly spurned a Shakespearean role and announced in the *Gazette* of 11 October that he would appear as Long Tom Coffin with Horn Pipe.

Theatrical gossip alleged that Levey was not firm enough to control the 'ambitious and turbulently disposed Thespian', and the *Gazette* of 21 March 1835 forecast the establishment of a second theatre in Sydney with Simmons in command. Levey temporised and made Simmons the manager of the Theatre Royal for 1836. It was a hopeless partnership. Fierce battles flared and the volatile Simmons sued Levey for malicious libel, for which he was awarded one farthing damages. The *Gazette* of 11 October 1836 again wrote of the 'warmth' of his temper and the 'impetuosity of his disposition'.

A business journey to Van Diemen's Land in the same month enabled him to perform several At Homes in Hobart Town and Launceston, but when he returned he entered into an ill-fated partnership as a dealer and ironmonger with Solomon Marks of King Street. The *Gazette* reported hopefully that 'Mr Simmons has abandoned all thoughts of theatrical glory and taken to himself the more lucrative employment of auctioneer. We will have a little peace and quietness in theatrical matters'. However, the partnership ended in bankruptcy after little more than a year.[4]

Perhaps this was because Simmons had been unable to abandon his theatrical ambitions. He had become a tavern-keeper and, according to the *Gazette* of 30 October 1836, the 'Simmons saloon' offered Sydney folk 'a choice collection of glees, duets, and solo, serious and comic . . . such as George Street Courtship or The Strictest Propriety presented in person by Mr Simmons'. In May 1834 he bravely opened the City Theatre with Joseph Belmore, former stage mechanic of the Theatre Royal but, unable to compete with the well-established Victoria Theatre, closed it down after a few weeks. On 21 July the *Sydney Morning Herald* reported that the two partners had to file for bankruptcy.

Back at the Royal Victoria Theatre in August 1844, Simmons presented his own melodrama *The Duellist*, which he described as 'The first truly original drama ever produced in the colony'. It was performed only twice and was in fact a badly written and laboured melodrama.[5] The standard of its dialogue is shown in the following excerpt:

> FARMER: Don't you know my mother? Lawks I thought every fool in the Parish knowed my mother.
> VISITOR: Very pleasant—what's her name simpleton?
> FARMER: No, it beant, nothing of the sort. It be Henley—Dame Henley and a right good mother she be.

When the visitor gets his face slapped he declares: 'Confound the slut. She has left the marks of her right hand fingers perfectly visible on my left hand cheek'.

A month later Simmons became the owner of the Tavistock Hotel on the corner of King and York streets, while occasionally appearing in comedy parts at the theatre until a final battle with the owner in April 1845 induced him to announce that his theatrical career in New South Wales was finished. Instead, he became a country shopkeeper, with three Wholesale and Retail Cheap General Stores at Bathurst, Carcoar and Canowindra. Sometimes his large advertisement in the *Bathurst Advocate* covered half a page filled with details of the bargains available At Simmons. He was very active in Bathurst's business and civic affairs, and his name appeared frequently in the *Advocate*. On 4 March 1848 it reported that he had founded a 'boiling down establishment', which he sold within a year; on 24 June his part in forming a copper-mining company; on 30 June 1849 that together with Chief Constable John Davies he was on a committee to form a night watch in the town; and on 31 March 1849 that he was one of the six commissioners for regulating and managing the Bathurst markets.

He started to liquidate his interests in the district in 1849. His store in Carcoar was disposed of to Solomon Meyer, who would later become a member of the Legislative Assembly. He entrusted the management of his Bathurst store to Raphael Tolano and, as the *Advocate* reported on 23 February 1850, 'having determined upon taking his residence again in Sydney at the end of February' left Bathurst at a most ill-chosen moment: three months before the gold rush. Simmons hastened to return, and the *Bathurst Free Press* of 4 January 1851 noted that he had become a gold buyer. He remained there until the first alluvial gold in the district was exhausted and companies, instead of individuals, had taken over the mining and purchase of gold. On 4 March 1854 he used the *Bathurst Free Press* to inform 'his old friends in the gold-mining settlements' that he had returned to George Street, Sydney, where his new premises as 'importer and wholesale storekeeper could be found opposite the old burial grounds'.

Simmons became deeply involved in the affairs of the Sydney Synagogue and was its President in 1859, when the Jewish community was split by dissension that led to the foundation of a separatist synagogue in Macquarie Street. Despite his communal duties, Simmons did not lose his love for the theatre. In June 1879 he appeared on stage at a Grand Complimentary Benefit given in his honour at Sydney's new Theatre Royal—built and managed by Samuel Lazar, the son of John Lazar—where he was hailed as 'the old favourite actor and manager'.

Simmons died on 9 August 1893, at the age of eighty-three, having lived for over sixty-three years in the colony. In his old age he worked as an 'elocutionist', and was seventy-three when he opened a Dramatic Academy in Elizabeth Street.[6] The newspapers published no obituary notice. Joseph Simmons had long been forgotten.

JOHN LAZAR, or Lazarus, another stage-struck pioneer, emigrated to Australia in the migrant ship *Lady McNaughton* in 1836.[7] It was a tragic voyage, with appalling conditions resulting in the death of three of his six children among the 123 migrants who perished on board the crowded ship.[8]

Lazar was a silversmith and jeweller by trade but claimed to have worked on well-known London theatre stages, and in Sydney soon worked as a professional actor with Barnett Levey's Theatre Royal. His first appearances in Shakespearean roles were not applauded; the *Sydney Gazette* of 27 May 1837 wrote:

> When we saw him in the Jew, we gave him much credit for adapting his voice to the Jewish style, not supposing he was playing in his usual tone. We however find that Mr Lazar not only personates the Jew on the stage, but that he is a Jew off it so that when playing the Moor he was unable to disguise his being a true son of Israel, which is a considerable drawback to his personification of such characters as Othello . . . he invariably pronounces hearse, erse, house, ouse, but this it is very evident he can break himself of because he does pronounce the H in many words, and in some where it should not be; for instance he calls arm, harm; of this habit Mr Lazar should break himself, for he never can play Shakespeare's characters well, till he does. But he also has another drawback—he lisps. We could not find fault with him in Shylock for this, but it is very remarkable in his Othello.

But the *Gazette* made up for this criticism by noting that his 10-year-old daughter Rachel, who appeared at the Theatre Royal as a dancer, was 'most vociferously encored'. A handbill dated 25 June 1839 proclaims: 'At Nash's Rooms, Parramatta—Miss Lazar dances the celebrated cachousa Dance and sustains six different characters in one sketch'. She was to remain the darling of Sydney's audiences.

By the time Barnett Levey died, Lazar was manager of Sydney's Theatre Royal—while under his full name of Lazarus he conducted a small general business in Kent Street. Lazar's productions did not equal those of Barnett Levey and Joseph Simmons, and the Gazette commented sourly on 13 March 1838, 'We shall not stay to discuss the accuracy of Mr Lazar's grammar but he persists in bringing out still more of the trashy absurdities dignified with the name of melodramas which have lately disgraced the Sydney Stage'. He was then engaged as stage manager of the Royal Victoria Theatre.

The construction of Adelaide's first theatre was completed in 1840 by Emanuel Solomon, who brought Lazar from Sydney, to be its manager and principal actor. Before leaving Sydney, Lazar staged a 'benefit' for himself and chose to put on a play about the Rothschilds called *The Rich Man of Frankfurt*, in which he took the title role

John Lazar. Lazar's abiding passion was the stage. Shortly after his arrival in Sydney he became manager and actor in Barnett Levey's Theatre Royal, then moved to South Australia and leased Emanuel Solomon's theatre.

of Isaac Ben Samuel. No one could take offence at his lisp or his accent when he appeared on the stage as a Jew.

South Australian theatrical history began at Emanuel Solomon's Queen's Theatre in January 1841 with John Lazar's production of *Othello*. Lazar played the Moor and his young daughter danced.[9] The *South Australian Register* of 30 January 1841 described Lazar as the 'indefatigable manager' of Adelaide's 'very elegant and commodious place of amusement', though it would have been difficult for him to have arrived at a worse time. The economic depression that crippled New South Wales hit South Australia even harder, and on 12 February 1842 the *Register* reported that Emanuel Solomon and John Lazar had opened the theatre for a public meeting to 'take into consideration the calamitous state of the colony'. Lazar took over the management of the theatre's bar and on 1 October the *Register* announced the performance of a benefit for himself and his family. In a desperate attempt to fill the theatre, his program included the trial scene in the *Merchant of Venice*, the third act of *Othello*, the third act of *King Lear* and the fifth act of *Macbeth*, with Lazar taking the principal role in each. His 18-year-old son Abraham made 'his first appearance on the stage in an entirely new comic dance' and the performance concluded with 'a laughable farce' with Lazar and his daughter.

Lazar returned to Sydney in 1843 with ambitious theatrical plans. He applied to the Colonial Secretary for permission to stage some new plays and wrote, 'There is a great scarcity at the present moment of printed plays and I am anxious that all asperants [*sic*] for dramatic literature in New South Wales should have every encouragement'.[10] He enclosed with his letter a farce he had written called *Contradiction or a Wife upon Sufferance* and two more serious plays translated from the French by Jacob Levi

The Queen's Theatre of Adelaide, opened by Emanuel Solomon in 1841.

Montefiore. Lazar was in his theatrical heyday, and while manager of the Royal Victoria Theatre he presented Sydney with some of the best operas and musical comedies of the day. They ranged from Shakespeare to Schiller, from contemporary French comedies to dramas from the English stage. Probably his greatest theatrical moment was his Sydney production of *The Last Days of Pompeii* in October 1844. His only original productions were pantomimes written and staged by himself. The Easter Pantomime of 1846 was ecumenically entitled *St. George and the Dragon or Harlequin and the Seven Champions of Christendom* and the Christmas program for the same year was called *Za, Ze, Zi, Zo, Zu*.[11]

Returning to Adelaide in 1847 to lease Solomon's Theatre, Lazar began a tour of the Australian colonies, and the *Register* reported that he had entered into partnership with George Coppin, the theatrical giant of the nineteenth-century Australian stage. But perhaps the strain of keeping up with Coppin was too great, because Lazar soon decided to leave the stage and settle down. He opened a jewellery business in Adelaide's Hindley Street, took an active role in the Jewish life of the city, helped to conduct the High Holyday services of 1848, and became a member of the City Council in 1851. From 1855 to 1857 he served as Mayor of Adelaide. It was his greatest role, and a prelude to the failure of his business investments. He was forced to migrate to New Zealand to become town clerk in Dunedin and later in Hokitika, where eventually he died in 1879.

SYDNEY'S MOST PROFESSIONAL theatrical personality was Barnett Aaron Phillips, who arrived in Sydney in 1835. On 12 November 1836 he announced in the *Gazette* that he had been foreman of the Drury Lane Theatre in London for eight years and was ready to work as 'a carpenter, joiner, venetian blind maker, furniture repairer, locksmith and ball hanger'. He soon became Levey's stage carpenter and built Australia's first stage scenery, while his children appeared as actors in a series of juvenile performances staged by Levey. With true theatrical versatility he was ready to turn his hand to anything, and on 15 September 1838 advertised in the *Gazette* that he had 'imported a well built hearse and mourning coach' from London and was ready for business.

Another theatrical personality of the same name but apparently no relation was Morris Phillips, a Jewish colonial playwright who staggered from one disaster to the next. A printer by trade, he arrived in 1838 and announced himself as the man 'from whose pen many of the new acting spectacles in our London theatres are taking great runs'. He announced the presentation of a Grand Historical Drama written by himself called *The Massacre of Jerusalem*, which the *Gazette* scornfully described as 'dull, absurd and stupid mass of nonsense . . . without a plot or design . . . the repeated allusions to the distinguished abilities of the Jewish people are absolutely disgusting . . . the sooner Mr Phillips returns to his printing the better it will be'.[12]

After this gruesome drama, in which Phillips appeared as Mattathias the high priest, came the anti-climax. It was usual in those times for a drama to be followed by some kind of farce or dance. And so Phillips danced after his drama, and the *Sydney Gazette* wrote on 15 September 1838 that 'Phillips' dance with the hard name

Cat-Choca was vulgar in the extreme'. The following year *Fidelio* from the pen of Mr Morris Phillips was presented at the Royal Victoria Theatre and, though the play itself was ignored, the *Commercial Journal* commented that 'the scenery and dresses are admirably conceived and well executed'.

Melbourne's theatrical history includes the names of John Davies, Michael Cashmore and John Lewis Jacobs. The draper Cashmore was said to have 'felt himself equal to anything, from Hamlet or Shylock down to executing a hornpipe' and joined in Melbourne's first theatrical production in 1842. Although Davies also appeared in this pioneer effort, he was most famous for his Grand Guignol performance as a body-snatcher at the Pavilion, Melbourne's first theatre. In August 1845 Davies had applied to open a new theatre in Melbourne but, as the township was about to welcome 'a new and respectable theatre', this request was seen as an unnecessary threat to public morals, and was refused. He was consoled by being allowed to open Melbourne's new Queen's Theatre Royal on 21 April 1845 with a special benefit performance for himself, 'on a scale of splendour not to be surpassed in the colonies', on the eve of his departure for Hobart Town. Davies left a curious reputation in Melbourne:

> In running a benefit for himself, it would not be easy to find his equal. Very little could be said in praise of his performance, but the patronising public were, or affected to be, well pleased with what they got for their money, and as the bene-ficiary was sure to pocket the lion's share of it, there could be little doubt of his being pleased too.[13]

The story of John Lewis Jacobs, a professional actor, magician and dancing teacher from London and Liverpool who called himself 'professor', is linked with both Davies and Lazar. Jacobs staged Launceston's earliest theatrical evenings and, in 1839, was engaged by John Lazar to appear at Sydney's Royal Victoria Theatre, where he apparently took delight in masquerading on stage as a member of the military. 'Professor' or 'Wizard' Jacobs was soon on tour, combining prodigious feats of memory with character sketches, conjuring tricks, dancing and singing, and often appearing in the ubiquitous comic Jewish role. From Sydney he went to Melbourne, where he appeared first at the Pavilion and later at the Queen's Theatre Royal. In 1848 he became manager of Adelaide's Royal Victoria Theatre and two years later, in a fit of professional jealousy, disgraced himself by charging John Lazar with having per-formed a lewd act on stage. As it was quickly shown that Jacobs had not even been in the theatre on the night of the alleged offence, the 'Wizard' found himself on a serious charge of perjury.[14]

JACOB LEVI MONTEFIORE, born in 1819 at Bridgetown on the island of Barbados in the West Indies, joined his uncle J. B. Montefiore in 1837 and was promptly sent by him to his Wellington Valley properties. This was little to his liking and he soon started trading on his own account until, untouched by the depression of the 1840s, he went into partnership with Robert Graham in the firm Montefiore Graham & Co.

Jacob Levi Montefiore combined a talent for the theatre with business acumen and a remarkable grasp of political theories and economic principles.[15] Together with his excursions into the theatrical world, he entered politics and served as a member of the Legislative Council of New South Wales from 1856 to 1860 and from 1874 to 1877. In this capacity he became a close friend of the powerful politician Henry Parkes, and many of their letters are preserved. In Parkes' *Fifty Years in the Making of Australian History* he wrote, 'in 1852 I began to take an active part in the constitutional discussion outside the Legislature. The gentlemen who took part with me in these agitations were certainly not demagogues or men wanting in social influence. Among them . . . Mr J. L. Montefiore'. Montefiore was certainly one of the most important Australian Jews of the second half of the nineteenth century. He wrote one of the earliest Australian books on economic theory, *A Catechism of the Rudiments of Political Economy*. He enthusiastically preached the doctrine of Free Trade with the aid of his pamphlet *A Few Words upon the Finance of New South Wales, Addressed to the Members of its First Parliament by one of Themselves*, printed in Sydney in 1856. In it he suggested the establishment of a central or national bank and the construction of a railway from Sydney to Melbourne. But he was no mere theorist, becoming one of the directors of the Bank of Australasia and a president of the Sydney Chamber of Commerce.

Montefiore's name appears on the title-pages of many of the first plays written in Australia. Most of his work was based upon French light operas and comedies of the type he must have seen and enjoyed in Paris, and include *The Duel*, a drama in two acts, *The Duchesse de Chevreuse*; and *Marguerite, or He Might do Worse*, a comedy in three acts. In collaboration with the musician Isaac Nathan he produced the libretto of the opera *Don John of Austria*, the first opera to be written in Australia. Its theme, which comes from Jewish history, is the story of a Sephardi girl whose family is still secretly Jewish and who falls deeply in love with a prince. Miraculously the young man reveals that he has been adopted and shares the same background. The rather feeble plot includes a romantic elegy written by Montefiore that might be the first Jewish poem composed in Australia:[16]

> *The days are gone when Judah's voice*
> *From crowded Temples rose on high*
> *When heartfelt prayer on incense borne*
> *Soared upward to the deep blue sky*
> *Those days are gone and Israel's song*
> *Uprises from the stranger's sod*
> *Outcast alike from land and home*
> *Their only Temple is no more*
> *That like their strength has passed away*
> *And strangers now rule o'er the land*
> *Where Israel's mighty ones held sway*
> *But though despised, condemned and reviled*
> *Dispersed where'er in life or death*
> *Judah still clings with trusting hope*
> *Made clear by sorrow to his faith.*

J. L. Montefiore returned to London in 1875, and he died there on 24 January 1885.

Jacob's brother Eliezer Levi Montefiore settled in Adelaide in 1843 and set himself up as a commission and shipping agent. Later he was to manage the Pacific Fire and Insurance Company. Eliezer, a talented artist himself, took an active part in the creation of the art galleries of Melbourne and Sydney and in 1892, towards the end of his life, was appointed the first salaried Director of the Art Gallery of New South Wales. He died in Sydney on 22 October 1894, the only important member of the Montefiore family to settle permanently in Australia.

Eliezer Levi Montefiore. A talented amateur artist and astute businessman.

AT THE CONSECRATION of the Sydney York Street Synagogue in 1844 the congregation was stirred by the sound of the choir directed by Isaac Nathan, son of the cantor of the little Anglo-Jewish community of Canterbury.[17] But Nathan's fame reached far beyond the synagogue, because he had been a friend of Lord Byron and a former teacher of music at the Court of St James. The first man to bring serious music to Australia, he was a composer, a conductor, a teacher and a performer of music in colonies that had heard very little music apart from the sound of regimental fifes, bugles and drums.

Nathan was born in 1790 and sent to London by his father to receive a traditional Jewish education at the school of Rabbi Solomon Lyon. There his musical talents were discovered, and his father arranged for him to become a pupil of the Italian composer Domenico Corri, a now-forgotten celebrity. Soon he began to write music himself.

The young composer summoned up the courage in June 1814 to ask the famous Lord Byron to send him one or two songs which he could set to 'a considerable number of very beautiful Hebrew melodies of undoubted antiquity', so giving his work 'great celebrity'. Byron agreed, and the two men collaborated on a group of poems which eventually numbered twenty-six. The music consisted of rather clumsy adaptations of familiar and far-from-antique synagogue hymns and non-Jewish folk tunes from Europe, probably used by Nathan's father in the chanting of the synagogue service. Yet the connection with Lord Byron, and interest in Judaism and the service of the synagogue, brought fame to Nathan and the 'Hebrew Melodies'.

He began to publish operas and melo-dramas, some of which were staged at Covent Garden and Drury Lane. His *Sweethearts and Wives* and *The Illustrious Stranger* were performed in Barnett Levey's Theatre Royal long before Nathan arrived in Sydney. The Musical Catalogue of the British Museum contains no less than twelve pages listing his compositions and literary works.

Nathan became a teacher of singing and then blotted his copybook by elop-ing with a well-born 17-year-old pupil, Elizabeth Rosetta Worthington. They were twice married: first in a church and then, three months later when Elizabeth had converted to Judaism, in a synagogue. Isaac was appointed librarian of music at the Court of the Prince Regent, and singing teacher to Princess Charlotte, daughter of the Prince Regent and heiress to the throne.

'Hebrew Melodies'. An English parody of Isaac Nathan's setting of Lord Byron's poetry.

As he moved in these exalted circles, Nathan became romantically involved with a Lady Langford, who was very much his senior, and in 1829 he was slightly wounded in a duel he fought on her behalf. In 1835, fifteen years after his liaison had first become public knowledge with the publication of cartoons lampooning a young David and an older Bathsheba, Nathan came to blows with Lord Langford. Legal proceedings against him were withdrawn only after appropriate apologies had been offered and accepted.

Meanwhile the young musician found time to produce a great deal of work. In 1823 he published a *History and Theory of Music*, and in 1829 his reminiscences of Lord Byron were published, including 'critical, historical, theatrical, political and theo-logical remarks, notes, anecdotes, interesting conversation and observations, made by that illustrious poet'.

Nathan's position at court survived the Regency and the reigns of George IV and William IV, but after the death of the latter he became involved in a mysterious affair with the British government. He later claimed £2326 from the Prime Minister, Lord Melbourne, for work which he said was on the King's behalf. He may have been employed as a spy, or connected with bogus bonds issued by the King while still Duke of Clarence and in need of ready cash. Whatever the truth, Nathan was rewarded with the paltry sum of £326, dismissal from his position at Court, and a hopeless financial tangle which induced him to 'bolt'.

He suddenly left England for Australia in 1840, together with his wife and eight children of whom, strangely enough, none was Jewish, all having been baptised at birth. When his first wife died in 1824 Nathan had an understandable problem in convincing the Jewish authorities that she should be buried in the Jewish cemetery. When he married Henrietta Buckley in 1826 there was no synagogue ceremony. Henrietta and her son Charles were both devout Christians, and after Nathan's death it is alleged that she destroyed all unpublished writings and music that might reflect his Jewish background.

Nathan and his new wife brought to Australia a story of aristocratic descent, claiming that his father had been the illegitimate child of Stanislaus Augustus Poniatowski, the last King of Poland. There is a family tradition that Menahem Muna had to flee from Poland, when Poniatowski lost his throne. This happened in 1795. Apart from the fact that the story was not known before Nathan migrated to Australia, the tombstone of Menahem Muna records that he was the son of Rabbi Judah Muna, 'the Pollack'. And Isaac Nathan's birth at Canterbury in 1790 makes the story unworthy of belief.

His claim to royal blood may have been inspired by his years at the British Court, by memories of the Polish monarch's reputation as a ladies' man, and by a remarkable resemblance of the young Nathan to the young Poniatowski. It is also not impossible that the story may originally have been circulated by Nathan in the hope of becoming more acceptable to colonial society. The name of Nathan had allegedly been adopted by the family in honour of people who had been kind to Muna on his arrival in England.

When Nathan reached Australia he was greeted with extravagant praise. The *Port Phillip Gazette* wrote of the 'exquisite' Hebrew melodies and their 'eminent composer', and his piano was especially brought into Melbourne from his ship for a series of concerts. In Sydney the *Australian*, one of whose owners was the secretary of the Sydney Synagogue, understandably glowed with pride at his migration.[18] The *Sydney Gazette* on the other hand was disposed to criticise Nathan for his readiness to perform in St Mary's, the Roman Catholic cathedral of Sydney. On 9 September 1841 the *Gazette* dismissed his advance publicity as 'quackery':

> His musical performances have not sustained his high reputation. What care we about his royal descent and his having been the friend of princes—we only know him as an organist and music master, in which character he will no doubt prosper in Sydney. If he does not swamp himself in this evil quackmire of self adulation.

Despite such criticism, there is no doubt that Nathan brought to the Australian colonies an entirely new standard of musical knowledge and professionalism. No sooner had he arrived in Sydney than he was invited by the clergy of St Mary's to conduct an oratorio on the occasion of the inauguration of the new organ in the principal Roman Catholic church in the colony. Undaunted by a rowdy audience accustomed to simpler fare, Nathan presented an ambitious program of classical music, including a Mozart symphony, a Kyrie Eleison by Beethoven, some songs by

Handel and several of his own compositions. The *Australian* wrote on 3 July 1841 that 'this concert was superior to anything of the kind yet produced in the Colony' and cast a jaundiced Protestant eye on the liturgical language of the church by remarking 'one was glad that Mr Nathan had selected English singing for an English audience'.

Nathan founded the St James and St Mary's choral societies and in the *Australian* of 1 May and 28 October 1841 announced first the establishment of his Classical Music Academy and then its extension to Windsor and Parramatta. He delivered a series of lectures at the Sydney College on the theory and practice of music, and continued composing. When in 1845 the explorer Ludwig Leichhardt was lost on his way to the Gulf of Carpentaria, Nathan composed an elegiac ode on a poem by Lieutenant R. Lynd entitled '*Leichhardt's Grave*'. When the explorer triumphantly returned, he quickly set to music the poem '*The Greeting Home Again*', by E. K. Sylvester. The *Sydney Free Press* reviewed the first composition on 6 September 1845.

In 1849 he simultaneously published in London and Sydney his best-known work, partly literary and partly musical, grandly entitled *The Southern Euphrosyne and Australian Miscellany, containing oriental Moral Tales, original anecdotes, poetry and music. An Historical Sketch with examples of the Native Aboriginal Melodies put into modern rhythm and harmonised as solos, quartettes, etc.* In this curious work Nathan not only repeats tales from the Talmud but combines stories of Jewish history and quotations from rabbinical commentators with a large collection of Aboriginal songs. It was the first sustained attempt by a musician to capture and convey the music of the first Australians, although the published account of Péron's explorations included a musical setting of the cries of the Aborigines. In his *Southern Euphrosyne* Nathan transcribed the notes of the well-known cry 'Coo-ee', and songs of the Moneroo and Wollongong tribes. In his madrigal concert in the hall of the present Sydney Grammar School on 27 May 1842, the Aboriginal song of joy, 'Koorinda Braia' was first performed, and pessimistically acclaimed by the *Australasian Chronicle* on 2 July as 'a memorial of ancient Australian melody after the race of ill fated aborigines shall have ceased forever to sing and hold their corroborees on their invaded territories'.

Nathan arranged the musical part of the service at the consecration of the Sydney York Street Synagogue on 2 April 1844. The opening prayer, 'Baruch Haba . . . Blessed be he who comes in the name of the Lord' and the concluding Hallelujah psalm were both especially written for the occasion and were greatly admired by the press. Unfortunately both hymns have vanished.

Australia has never been an easy land for a musician and Nathan was not unscathed by the great economic depression of the 1840s. His musical academy and the sale of his books failed to bring him enough money to support a large family, and in May 1844 he was declared insolvent. Evidently his friends rallied to his side for within a few months he was able to apply for a discharge. Patriotically he composed an Australian national anthem, 'Star of the South, An Australian National Melody', and compassionately set to music a series of poems that told of the fate of the Aboriginal people.

Nathan was a disappointed and embittered man; his colonial exile had come upon him when he was over fifty and not easily able to adapt. After eight years in

KOORINDA BRAIA,

A GENUINE ABORIGINAL NATIVE SONG,

SUNG BY THE

MANEROO TRIBE, OF AUSTRALIA:

PUT INTO MODERN RHYTHM,

ARRANGED AS A SOLO AND GLEE,

WITH CHARACTERISTIC HARMONY,

AND RESPECTFULLY INSCRIBED TO MRS. E. DEAS THOMSON,

BY

I. NATHAN.

Maneroo, pronounced by the aborigines *Mineroo*, signifies an open space or plain; hence the Maneroo Tribe literally means, "The Tribe of the Plains." What *Koorinda Braia* imports I could never ascertain; many persons whom I have consulted are of opinion that it is the name of one of their ancient chiefs, whom they venerate, and always eulogise in song.

This genuine aboriginal melody, which I have faithfully put into modern rhythm, is sung by the Maneroo Tribe. Before they commence the air, which is in common time, they first, by striking two pieces of wood against each other, beat two or three bars of perfect measure in treble time, as if trying to excite inspiration, and they continue marking the rhythm with great accuracy while singing the Koorinda Braia; which, without the slightest variation of time, measure, or rhythm, they repeat several times, with increased energy and gestures, until they become completely exhausted by their enthusiasm.

"*Cooey*," which I have introduced into the 4th page, to small notes, may be either sung or omitted. Neither the word nor the notes have any connexion whatever with the original melody; and the only apology I can offer for its introduction is the singular use of the word, so peculiar throughout the whole colony of Australia, a word unknown in any other part of the world. The "Cooey," in Australia, is a term used to call a person far off, and is equivalent to our *holla* in England, with this difference, and, I may add, advantage, the cooey, from the acuteness of sound its pronunciation affords, can be heard at a greater distance than the holla. It is surprising to hear an Australian sailor at sea draw attention for several miles off by the peculiar shrill sound of his *Coo——ey*, and it is equally astonishing to witness at what distance the cooey is carried on land. The manner of producing the cooey is merely sounding the highest note in the compass of voice, and after pausing a considerable

time, at pleasure, on that note, let the voice fall to the octave, thus :—

Coo - - - ey.

The natives of Port Phillip differ, they reverse the sound, thus :—

Coo - - - ey.

No. 4.

Price 3s.

SYDNEY:

PUBLISHED FOR THE COMPOSER, ADA COTTAGE, PRINCE STREET.

'Koorinda Braia', title-page, 1848. Of Nathan's many musical compositions with Indigenous themes, this was the best known. Derived from an Aboriginal song of rejoicing, it was first sung at a concert at the Sydney College in 1842, accompanied by a detailed eye-witness description of the associated corroboree. The familiar bush call 'Coo-ee' makes its first appearance on a title-page.

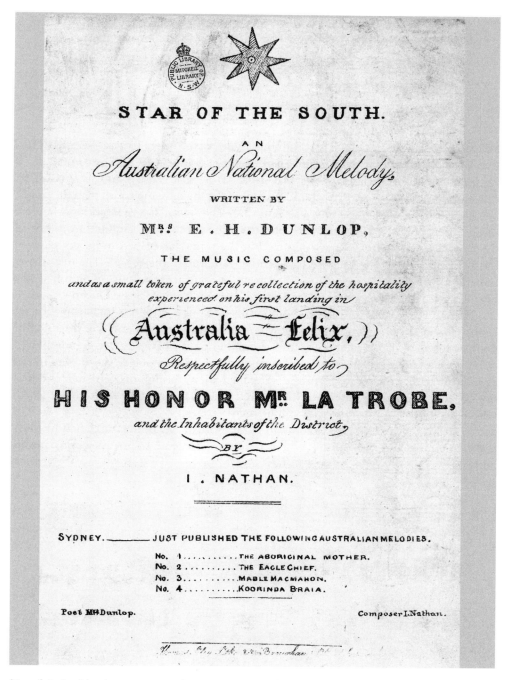

'Star of the South', title-page. Isaac Nathan wrote the music for Australia's first national song. The words were by Mrs Eliza K. Dunlop and the work was published in Sydney in 1845. Nathan's enthusiastic reception in the infant colony of Melbourne induced him to dedicate the anthem to the Administrator of the Port Phillip District.

Australia his frustration is vividly expressed in a poem entitled 'New South Wales' which he published in his *Southern Euphrosyne*:

> *A sordid spirit rules this barren land!*
> *No love of art, nor worship of the wise,*
> *No moral virtues, nor domestic ties*
> *Nor any sense of greatness doth expand*
> *The sterile minds that seek this distant strand!*

Perhaps he was reacting to the ignominious failure of the opera *Don John of Austria*. It had not been greeted with the enthusiasm history assumes on the presentation of Australia's first opera. The *Atlas* of 8 May 1847 wrote that Nathan's music was 'heavy, dull and uninteresting' and 'much more adapted for the drawing room than the stage'.

Isaac Nathan died at the age of seventy-four. The *Sydney Morning Herald* reported that on the afternoon of 15 January 1864 the 'celebrated composer' alighted from one of the first of Sydney's horse-drawn trams, but the tram started before he got clear of the rails and Nathan was crushed to death beneath one of the wheels. The newspaper remarked that his last composition had been 'A Song to Freedom', which had just been forwarded to the Governor Sir Richard Young for Her Majesty Queen Victoria.

Nathan left a large and flourishing family of twelve children including Charles Nathan, who became a prominent New South Wales physician and had fifteen children of his own. Eight of them founded families, and Charles' great-grandchildren remember being told that Isaac would pray wrapped in his prayer shawl even in old age. So the 'father of Australian music' remained a Jew, though his Christian children buried him at a private funeral in the Church of England cemetery at Camperdown, where his modest tombstone may still be seen.

With his fellow Jews, from Levey to Lazar, Nathan began the Australian involvement in music and the theatre which continues to send so many world-famous performers into the international scene.

Judah's Face

IN A TRIBUTE to folk memory of the religious savagery of the Tudor and Stuart periods, the people of Georgian England, including those who went willingly or otherwise to New South Wales, preserved most of their antagonism for the Catholics. But there was plenty to spare for the Jews and it included basic attitudes not unique to the English. The legends of Europe had been passed by word of mouth through London to Sydney, and Jews were generally seen as aliens belonging, until eternity, to a different nation concerned with usury or old clothes, rarely honest, and usually rich.

The convict dossiers constantly and superfluously characterised Jewish prisoners by their religion. In a note from the police at Port Macquarie, the convict Lyon Abrahams is described as 'an able Jew but so lazy as to preclude the possibility of his obtaining a call for his services from any person requiring a labouring hand'. The prisoner David Solomon's trade was described as a 'Jew hawker', and Joseph Abrahams was a 'Jew thief'.[1]

Such names as Jacky Jacobs, Izzi the Hebrew Dreamer, Groggy Hyams, Money Moses, Long Levy, Blackguard Levi, Little Mo', Old Yankiff, Hikey Bull and Old Sam, some of whom already have been described, were familiar in the Australian colonial community. Occasionally the nicknames denoted an affectionate respect, but more often they perpetuated a sinister stereotype and were brands which their owners wore for ever.

Jacky Jacobs was John Jacobs, who lived in Elizabeth Street, Sydney, in the 1840s and was said to be a dealer in stolen goods. We can only guess why John Hyams bore the nickname Groggy, but it went with him to the grave and was dutifully recorded in the cemetery records of the Sydney Synagogue. Money Moses was Emanuel Moses, of whom the *New Newgate Calendar* wrote in 1841, 'There were very few people well acquainted with the vicinity of Covent Garden to whom the person of this man was not familiar, although his peculiar character and practices may not have been so well known'.[2]

Long Levy was Samuel Levy, who was buried in the Sydney Jewish Cemetery in April 1849. The synagogue burial register notes that he was so known even to his wife, and that he was almost eighty. Blackguard Levi, or Lazarus Levi, earned his nickname because of his 'inability to utter a sentence uncluttered by profanity'. He was delivered to Hobart Town by the *Lord Lyndoch* in August 1836, and the indent describes

'An Old Clothes Auction in the Country'.

him as 'A labourer and pencil maker, 5 feet 3 and three quarter inches tall, age 24, dark complexion, large head, black hair and whiskers, large nose, freckled face—a Jew'. His brothers Samuel and Philip followed him to Van Diemen's Land, where Philip opened a pawnbroker's shop and, in contrast to his brother Samuel, became known as Gentleman Levi. Samuel, with a clothing shop on the same street, almost inevitably was nicknamed Intermediate Levi. According to the Hobart Synagogue minutes of 17 November 1845, poor Blackguard made such a 'disgraceful disturbance in the Synagogue on *Simchat Torah* [the Festival of the Rejoicing of the Law]' that he was barred from enjoying any future congregational honours until Passover.[3]

Little Mo' was so called because of his diminutive stature, which must indeed have been slight in an age when the average Jewish convict was less than 5 feet 4 inches tall. His real name was George Lewis, and the *Commercial Journal and Advertiser* of 7 November 1840 reports that, 'George Lewis, a diminutive Jew appeared before their worships to answer the complaint of his master (another of the tribe of Israel) for absenting himself from his hire service. Poor little Mo' in a most emphatic manner denied the charge', but he was sentenced to four years imprisonment.

Old Yankiff was Jacob Jonas (Yankiff being the Yiddish version of Jacob), who arrived in Sydney in the *Cornwallis* in June 1801, became a dealer in Parramatta, and was buried in the Sydney Jewish Cemetery on 25 May 1833.[4]

James Larra was not the only 'honest Jew' in colonial Australia. Abraham Polack claimed this distinction for himself in what must be one of Australia's earliest advertising jingles, which he published in the *Australian* on 28 June 1825:

> *To keep A.P. upon his ground*
> *From apes, lions, jackals, and monkeys too*
> *By paying twenty shillings in the pound*
> *And be called still the honest Jew*

And when in 1828 Joseph Aarons extended his business by opening a branch store one hundred miles from Sydney, the *Gazette* of 18 August wrote enthusiastically of 'An honest Israelite yclept Joseph Aarons . . . we know of no one more industrious in his attention "Advance Australia"'. It is interesting to speculate as to whether the same correspondent would have written of 'an honest Christian', as though that too was something slightly remarkable.

Anti-Jewish stereotypes withstood the tests of time and truth. The press rarely failed to label as Jews those whose misdeeds brought them to the public eye. The pattern appears in the first newspapers and can be traced through the years to the anti-Semitic cartoons and jokes printed in Australian journals during the first flowering of national consciousness at the end of the nineteenth century. So deeply did prejudice wound its victims that for a century the synagogues in Australia all called themselves by the more polite alternative of 'Hebrew congregation', and throughout the twentieth century the census returns of the modern Commonwealth of Australia still delicately referred to Hebrews instead of Jews.

In one of the earliest issues of the *Sydney Gazette*, of 25 November 1804, a rare humorous poem was published. It tells of an atheist and a Jew who both arrive at the gates of hell at the same time and argue about who should take the first step:

> . . .
> *Moses begs that his Friend*
> *Might have the first leap,*
> *As he'd fain see his end:*
> *Then his motive demanded . . .*
> *He answers 'Go' Knows*
> *My motives is just—*
> *For to py his old Cloaths'.*

No one could dispute the fact that the status of colonial Jewry was low. On 6 November 1846 Jacob Levi Montefiore wrote in a private letter to T. Cohen in England, 'in respectability our community . . . [is] still very far from what they might be'. Although the free population had increased considerably and the character of Australian society was beginning to change, still most of the adult males in the Jewish community were of convict origin.

Of course in matters of status a great deal depends upon the point of view. In 1842 the devoted secretary of the Sydney Synagogue, George Moss, attempted to publish an Australian Jewish newspaper, the *Voice of Jacob*, but with less than a thousand Jewish men, women and children in all the Australian colonies his effort was doomed from the start. Moss lamented editorially on 27 May 1842 that 'our number is too small, and with one or two exceptions, our wealth is too inconsiderable'. Whereas J. O. Balfour, a Christian settler of exactly the same era, noted without malice in his book *A Sketch of New South Wales* that there were 'a great number of Israelites in Sydney, most of whom are wealthy' and that the small 'but handsome' Sydney Synagogue would 'before long' be followed by 'other and larger Synagogues'. The myth of Jewish wealth was believed throughout the community. At the time of the consecration of Sydney's first synagogue, the Catholic *Morning Chronicle* wistfully wrote on 6 April 1844:

> We wish that some of our religious firebrands would imitate that respectable, wealthy and orderly community . . . in not disturbing their neighbours with perpetual attacks and insults . . . The Jews very properly trouble nobody's religion, but only mind their own.

The few score Jewish families in Sydney, Hobart Town and Melbourne in the 1830s and 1840s formed a very noticeable part of the Australian merchant community. In the census of 1841, only 1774 shopkeepers and other retail dealers were listed for the whole of New South Wales.[5] At least one-fifth of this emerging middle class was Jewish.

Jews had simply to exist to be noticed—and blamed. In 1841 the little town of Port Macquarie mustered less than 30 Jews of all ages in a population of 1053, yet when a shopkeeper advertised she proclaimed, 'Who has broken up the iron monopoly so long held by the Jews and forestallers in the trade of every necessary of life—Georgina Kinnear'.[6] The *Sydney Gazette* of 15 November 1832 wrote:

> What thorough bred cockney is there, who is unacquainted with Duke's Place that abode of Ephraimites and Ishmaelites, of Benjaminites and Gaddites? It is proposed to apply the same designation to that portion of George Street between the St John's Tavern and the Baker's Arm public house in which limited space will be found, the residence of no less than twelve industrious, enterprising children of Israel.

Maclehose's *The Picture of Sydney and Stranger's Guide in New South Wales* for 1838 even attempted to explain the reasons for a 'Jewish quarter' in town:

> George Street . . . is decidedly the first street in Sydney . . . there are numerous ranges of buildings on each side, of considerable extent and uniformity of design which are not to be met with in any other part of town . . . A little above are the premises where the *Sydney Gazette* and *Herald* newspapers are printed; the opposite side of the street is still occupied by a row of indifferent wooden cottages, for which however a good rental is obtained, being well situated for the sale of seaman's slops etc., they are mostly occupied by Jews.

George Street became synonymous with Sydney's Jewish community. An indignant 'new chum' wrote bitterly to the *Sydney Gazette* of 18 February 1841:

> certain ill looking hook nosed fellows . . . make a regular system of entreating, stopping and pulling even the passers-by into their cribs . . . Strangers of all classes, but chiefly those with sailors toggery, are the persons pounced upon . . . I am, in all

sincerity, afraid to budge out of my lodgings; if I was to walk the whole length of George Street, I would not think my life worth ten minutes purchase.

Exaggeration, envy and ignorance are the progenitors of prejudice. The new colony in Western Australia yielded one of the most startling examples when Eliza Shaw wrote querulously to England on 10 March 1830:

> disappointments . . . no land to be given away . . . what land is given, is given to Jews, Stockbrokers, and man-of-war's men . . . We have lots of Jews settling here and gents who some time since in England rode in their carriages are now weighing out a $\frac{1}{4}$ pound of tea and $\frac{1}{2}$ pound of rice.[7]

Yet the two young Samson brothers were the only Jews in the whole colony, so the other migrants must have been overwhelmingly conscious of their presence.

An even more blatant example of anti-Jewish prejudice occurred in December 1832, in the early years of migration of free Jewish settlers to Australia, when the arrival of a small group of Jewish migrants in Van Diemen's Land was greeted by a violent outburst. The *Palambam* brought to Australia eleven or twelve Jewish adults and ten children, of whom only three adults and four children disembarked in Hobart.[8] The *Tasmanian and Austral-Asiatic Review* of 14 December wrote wildly that the ship had brought 'an entire colony . . . 75 in number . . . to replace their brethren of the money lending tribe about to return to England', and on 22 December the *Colonial Times* seized the chance to denounce 'the beardless shylocks with whom the Colony swarms' and 'might have been content with fobbing their pelf and sneaking out of the colony without burthening us with more of the same race, who like an incubus have fastened, or who rather as vultures, have preyed on its vitals'.

But the *Launceston Independent* of the same date showed a more liberal spirit, even though the writer did not know how few Jews had in fact arrived:

> We cannot help expressing a regret that the feeling of the newcomers should be hurt immediately upon their arrival, by being twitted about their nation and peculiar tact of trading in money . . . Surely it is only as just and as reasonable a wish in a Jew to live easy in his after-years, without the drudgery of commercial life, as in a Christian . . . whether Christian, Jew, or Gentile, an honest man's the noblest work of God.

The Jews of eighteenth-century England had discovered with their fists that there was one immediate path to fame and fortune that bypassed all the laborious efforts of the socially respectable. For almost twenty years the great Jewish pugilist Daniel Mendoza dominated English boxing and won fame and fortune—though his daughter Sophia was to find a tragic way to Australia as a convict. She was sentenced at the Old Bailey on 29 May 1828 to seven years transportation for larceny, and was described as a 'servant of all work, 5 feet 1 inch in height, age 36, dark complexion, dark brown hair, oval face, high cheekbones, aquiline nose, Jewish countenance'. She was unmarried with three children and was one of seven children of 'Daniel Mendoza the noted bruiser'. Sophia arrived in Van Diemen's Land in the *Harmony* in 1829 and, perhaps because she was repeatedly in colonial courts on various offences, she did not receive her Certificate of Freedom until 1855.[9]

As previously described, the ambitious Samuel Lyons and his shipmate Moses Moses both fought with their bare fists in an attempt to wrest fortune for themselves in Van Diemen's Land. Both were ignominiously defeated. On 7 September 1832 *Bell's Life in New South Wales* described how 'the Children of Israel mustered very strong' near the Parramatta Road to watch the twice transported convict Abraham Davis fight against a baker named Jackson. The contest provided the Jewish community with one of its first public appearances.

> The Israelite walked steadily into the ring and although not so fair in his proportions as the man of dough, exhibited an iron bark trunk which seemed to put all the baker's elements at defiance. The match had been circulated as one of great interest, the tribe of Israel looking forward to their country man as the national prep . . . There were 25 rounds and at the 26th Davis sent doughey to doss, with as fine a beating as a man would wish to receive. The Jews hoisted their clansman on their shoulders and with clamorous hurras, bore him away from the ring . . . If the Jews won heavy sums at the battle, they were less fortunate on their return from the scene of action. The more lucky Israelites challenged all whom they chanced to meet at the various public houses on the Parramatta Road . . . Mr. McC——he placed a hundred in the Bank of N.S.W., the fruit of his industrious earnings on this occasion.

The most spectacular exhibition of fisticuffs, and by no means a one-sided display, occurred in October 1834 at Barnett Levey's Theatre Royal. The Jewish community had been incensed by the refusal of one of Levey's regular actors to participate in a special theatrical benefit evening for Morris Phillips. When the same actor readily appeared in a subsequent benefit for a locally born boy called Jones, the Jewish community turned up in force to disrupt the show and hiss their enemy. With cries of 'Throw the bloody Jews overboard!' and 'Murder!' the theatre divided into two partisan battling groups and the evening ended in turmoil. As most of the audience were local lads who had come to see their friend perform on the stage, the newspapers and the court saw the incident as a battle between 'the natives' and 'the Jews'. By way of apology, Vaiben Solomon collected five pounds and seven shillings from his friends and presented it to Master Jones, while Lewis Cohen narrowly escaped conviction for bloodying the head of a Mr Hayes.

Paradoxically no more patriotic section of the community could be imagined than the often beleaguered, and as yet unemancipated, Jewish citizen of the vast British Empire. When word of the appointment of a new Chief Rabbi in London reached the Jewish community in Melbourne in 1846, every Jewish male, all twenty-one of them, rallied to sign an illuminated vellum Address expressing hearty congratulations, beginning with the ringing phrase 'We, the undersigned British Jews residing in Port Phillip Australasia'. Dr Adler's appointment was deemed to be opportune as religious reform had begun to shake the Jewish world. The British Jews of Melbourne looked forward to his guidance to end discord.

When the irrepressible Jacob Josephson was scornfully accused of being 'a foreign Jew' by a nonconformist preacher in Sydney, Josephson did not deny the charge and publicly replied to his persecutor:

Surely he ought to know that all Jews are foreigners, and as a good Christian, it behoves him to believe, as a foundation stone of his religion . . . that Jews are to be foreigners and wanderers over the whole world and the greatest mystery is that though Jews are everywhere foreigners yet are they everywhere at home. For, let the poor Jew arrive in a foreign town or place he instantly begins to do something for the support of himself and his family.[10]

The assumption that the Jews were aliens was always present. The *Monitor* of 20 March 1830 published a letter by A Briton of the True Breed writing from Gentile Town who alleged that a Sydney Jewish businessman had refused to sign a petition requesting trial by jury and an elected house of representatives. 'In this country', wrote the Briton about the Jews, 'they are not at present debarred from holding lands, nor from any privileges which are enjoyed by genuine Englishmen who believe in that religion which is the law of the land . . . Let him therefore ponder the effects of his present policy ere it be too late'. On 3 April the newspaper reported that all the Jewish merchants had expressed 'their warmest wishes' in favour of the petition.

The reluctant Jewish notables may well have been J. B. Montefiore and David Poole, both of whom had been harshly criticised in the previous year for having meddled in colonial affairs when they supported Governor Darling in his battle with W. C. Wentworth. 'We will be glad to know', the *Monitor* had said on 18 July 1829, 'what Mr Montefiore and Mr Poole signed the address for, seeing they are hardly fixed in the Colony? What can these gentlemen know of Sudds and Thompson, or indeed of any other of the subjects of the address?' The press was by no means consistent in its liberalism.

The only recorded instance of malicious destruction of Jewish communal property in colonial Australia occurred in 1832 when vandals destroyed the gravestones erected above the graves of children of Michael Phillips and Vaiben Solomon in the Sydney Jewish Cemetery. The newspapers of Sydney were horrified. The *Herald* of 23 July wrote that 'it was one of the greatest violations of all that is held sacred in all climes and countries' and the *Sydney Gazette* of 24 July claimed that it was 'one of the most infamous and inhuman outrages that has ever disgraced the colony'.

Yet the *Herald* was disturbed by the presence of Jews at the old Sydney market, and complained of 'an unjust monopoly on the part of the tribe of Israel'. When a new market was completed the newspaper was alarmed to see evidence that even 'at the antipodes that trading "commoonity" the Israelites, taking a striking lead almost to the exclusion of the Gentiles'. The paper felt that the market's fine new buildings were to be 'perverted' and turned into 'a fair'.[11] To the newspaper's credit it published the courageous reply of Samuel Lyons:

it is no disgrace to be a member of a trading community, and if the Jews do monopolise the retail trade of vending sundry goods in the Market, it is a more creditable and legal manner of obtaining a livelihood than the forestallers who have the honour and the distinction of being members of other sects . . . calculating on the census the solitary Israelite stands at the ratio of 1 to 273?

145

Forcefully, and perhaps foolishly, Lyons seized upon the popular resentment towards a government scheme to entrench the Church of England in Australia by granting it one-twelfth of the colony's land. Hopefully, he declared:

> the banner of religious toleration floats triumphantly, and the Hebrew ranks with his fellow citizen in spite of a bigoted clergy burdened with Bishops and Archdeacons who drain the last penny from the poor in order to revel in luxury.

On the whole the Australian newspapers could see little sense in delaying Jewish emancipation. The German anti-Jewish riots of 1819 were described in the *Sydney Gazette* of 12 February 1820 with 'a sense of outrage', even though the paper also published the observations of a Scottish gentleman who saw in the appearance, circumstances, and character of the Jews of Europe 'the greatest proof that now exists upon the authenticity of Sacred Writ'. By which was meant that God's rejection of Israel was quite obvious. Commenting upon the political situation of the Jews in England in 1829 the *Gazette* wrote on 10 January, 'To ask a man what religion he is before you allow him to open a shop for the retailing of wares (as in the City of London) would be only ludicrous if it were not tyrannical and oppressive. But these things cannot last'.

John Pascoe Fawkner was at that time the owner and editor of the *Launceston Advertiser*, and on 8 November 1830 he used his paper to declare that bigotry was the only bar to Jewish political emancipation in England. He concluded, we wish the Jews much success, they never injured England but England has been, and is obliged to them'.

The *Gazette* had shown that bigotry in Australia was likely to be answered by force, legal action, or both. On 17 October 1827 it published the case in which Constable Lewis Solomon was abused while he stood at his post in the Sydney Market. It was alleged that David Hayes had driven past him and shouted out 'Look here, you Jew looking scoundrel. I've a load of pigs'. Solomon promptly knocked Hayes off the cart and arrested him on a charge of driving dangerously and took him to the watch house, but his charge was not sustained.

At Oatlands in Van Diemen's Land the respectable tavern-keeper Henry Samuel Benjamin was called 'a bloody Jew Bastard' and 'that little Jew Benjamin [who] robbed me' by a fellow publican. This time the court awarded Benjamin £65 damages.[12] On 21 January 1846 the *Hobart Town Courier* described how a Mr Mooney had been fined ten shillings for having kicked Morris Benjamin, an 8-year-old Jewish boy, and sung at the same time 'that well known ditty':

> *If I had a piece of pork*
> *I'd stick it on a fork*
> *And give it to a Jew boy, Jew*

This was not the only appearance of the poem in an Australian court of law. In Adelaide in 1848 it caused the merchant Lewis Joseph to blacken the eye of a Captain Carew in the course of a fracas at the theatre. Mr Joseph was fined forty shillings.

The courts were not immune from outbursts of prejudice. In 1818 Judge Barron Field characterised a fraudulent sale of tea by Solomon Davis to Joseph Raphael as 'a mere juggle among Jews' and a little later the learned judge assailed an antagonist of a gentile by publicly dubbing him 'a grasping Jew'. In another court case, concerning Jacob Josephson, an unfriendly solicitor cast doubt on Josephson's evidence by speaking scathingly of 'the testimony of a foreign Jew' which was 'not worth a straw'. *The Sydney Gazette* commented dryly, 'It is much more to the honour of a man to be designated "a foreign Jew" than "a colonial swindler"'.[13]

The same newspaper objected on 16 July 1839 when the Attorney-General laid stress on a debatable point with the words, 'even any Jew must acknowledge the fact', and then turned to stare at Samuel Lyons who happened to be in the court and, not unnaturally, was seen to blush. The Chairman of the Court of Quarter Sessions, in his advice to the jury, dismissed a principal witness as being 'only a Jew boy'. These were not isolated comments. *Bent's News* of 20 July 1839 wrote:

> Certain members of the legal profession, for reasons best known to themselves, are much given to abuse the members of the Jewish persuasion, which is most unfair, for they are as a body, as respectable and reputable a class as any other of the community . . . Such remarks . . . belong to an age long since gone by.

When in 1846 the news reached Australia that Sir Moses Montefiore had been raised to the baronetcy by his friend and admirer Queen Victoria, the *Hobart Town Advertiser* wrote:

> [It was] a tribute not to his wealth, but to his merit—to his open charity—his persevering efforts for the freedom, the rejuvenation of his race. This is as it ought to be. The Hebrew is now what he should be. He is one of the people. His character, not his creed, is the distinction in society. Pity it should be so long coming; that the industry, the energy, the intellect of the Hebrews should so long have been forced by national injustice into channels unworthy of them, calculated to injure the community in which they were placed, to deteriorate their own character.[14]

The Birth of the Synagogue

A USTRALIA'S RELIGIOUS HISTORY began badly. Sydney's first church was no sooner built than it was burned to the ground. Governor John Hunter wrote to the Duke of Portland in November 1799:

> About a month past, some wicked and disaffected person, or persons, in conse-quence of a Strict Order which I saw it absolutely necessary to issue, for Compelling a decent attention upon Divine Service, and a more soberly and orderly manner of Spending the Sabbath Day, took an opportunity of a Windy and dark Evening and Set fire to the Church . . . and it was completely consumed.

Sadly the Governor observed, 'a more wicked, abandoned and irreligious set of People have never been brought together in any part of the world'.[1]

The burning of the church may be understood better against the background of church-going in the colonial prison system. For convicts, church parade was a grim and repulsive affair without promise of comfort and succour. Every Sunday morning, before Divine Service, the convicts were mustered and checked. Each prisoner was inspected to make sure that he had not bartered or sold parts of his uniform. Punish-ments were meted out to those who appeared on parade too dirty to be marched into church. During the muster the overseers of the chain gangs and road parties made their reports upon the behaviour of those in their charge,[2] and these reports held a further threat of punishment.

But for countless people, high and low, religion was far more than lip-service. Belief in the Supreme Being who watched over every human activity was deeply in-grained. Unfortunately for Roman Catholics, Jews and nonconformists, the Supreme Being of the penal settlements was a Church of England God, and most of the officials had inherited an abiding fear and hatred of popery. Many of the prisoners were Irish Roman Catholics, and a large proportion of these were political prisoners sentenced during Ireland's seemingly interminable struggles to rid herself of the 'Saxon yoke'. So the established church in early Australia was regarded as one of the bulwarks of law and order as well as the portal to salvation, and the early ecclesiastical establish-ment pontificated as impressively upon the magisterial bench as it did in the pulpit.

Week after week, Roman Catholics, Jews and nonconformists sat as prisoners through the Sunday church parades in which only Anglican beliefs and practices were followed. For the colonial authorities it was as though the words of Henry Fielding's Parson Thwackum were held to be self evident: 'When I mention religion I mean the Christian religion; and not only the Protestant religion; but the Church of England'. For decades this church ministered haphazardly to the spiritual needs of the whole population. For more than thirty years Catholics were baptised and married by parsons ordained by Canterbury. Presbyterians waited twenty years for their first kirk to be built. The government could see no purpose in fostering ancient religious division, and in 1810 the colony's chaplain, Samuel Marsden, complacently described to the London Society for the Propagation of the Gospel how 'Roman Catholics, Jews and persons of all persuasions send their children to the public schools where they are all instructed in the principles of our established religion'.[3]

In *The 1845 York Street Synagogue Report*—issued after the consecration of that synagogue (the first in Sydney)—a summary was given of the earliest years of the Jewish community. The report recalled that 'in 1817 there were about 20 Hebrews in the Colony, but little versed in the faith of their ancestors; however they formed themselves into a Society, and raised a subscription for the interment of their dead'. Certainly no one remembered, or wanted to remember, that by 1820 there were more than 200 Jews in New South Wales, of whom only one or two had landed voluntarily.

Obviously the creation of Australia's first Jewish congregation had to wait for the arrival of free men who felt that it was their right to worship as they pleased. The convicts, even after serving their sentences, were hardly the material from which Jewish communities were to be formed. Many of the older convicts had left families in England, and returned to them as soon as they were free to scrape up the money for the passage. Most of those remaining were very young, often illiterate, and they had been brought up under such conditions in the London ghetto that preservation of the body rather than the soul was of prime importance. Their average age when they were transported was just over twenty-five. There were nine men to every woman. In only two of the early colonial households were both husband and wife Jewish. Of the first 250 Jewish convicts who arrived before 1820, only 45 married in Australia. The records, incomplete as they are, show that just over 60 children born in Australia carried the names, but not the faith, of the first Jewish settlers. Only one convict went back to England, and then returned to Australia with his family.

The establishment of a synagogue arose slowly out of the inevitable need to bury the dead. Joseph Levy, a convict of the First Fleet, was the first Jew to be buried in Australian soil, on 15 April 1788. The convict Uziel Baruch, known as 'Husser Brewe', died two weeks after arrival and was buried on 13 July 1790 in the now forgotten piece of land designated as a cemetery by Governor Phillip near Sydney Cove. The Reverend Richard Johnson, who kept the births, deaths and matrimonial registers of the colony, noted in June 1791 that on 16 June he had buried 'Solomon Bockron (or Bockroh), convict, a Jew'. This was the first time a Jew was specifically described as such by the registers of the colony. The actual name of the convict was Solomon Bockerah. He left behind him an infant daughter, Sarah, who was one of the first children of a Jewish parent born in the colony. Her mother, Ann, was buried at St John's, Parramatta, on 21 February 1793.[4]

A new tract of ground was set aside by the government in the sandhills beyond Brickfield Hill in 1818, and two years later this cemetery was consecrated by the Church of England. It was not until 1820 that 'on application to the Rev. Dr Cowper, the right corner of the Christian burial ground was allocated to the Hebrews' and there was buried Joel Joseph, erstwhile companion of Ikey Solomon and landlord of the St Paul's Hotel in Pitt Street. In the decade that followed, even though there was no congregation in existence, at least five Jewish burials took place in the little Sydney cemetery.[5] An early visitor to Australia recalled that melancholy place which would be abandoned and callously replaced with the city's main railway station:

> Just outside Sydney, south, there is a large uneven tract of sand, the Sand Hills. Everybody in New South Wales knows the import of the name *the Sand Hills*. It is one of the still trophy yards of death—one of the stillest—one of the saddest. Here in a cold winter day, a chiller and more wail like breeze goes stealing along each knoll that breasts up along the barren hollow; and here too in the summer prime the sand, gathering the solar heat, glows upward again into the descending beams, till it is faintness and blindness and something near suffocation to stand still anywhere within the dread precinct. If the world were searched from end to end, nowhere could you find such another volume of unutterable woe is bound up in this little spot. In yonder corner lie the Jews, in this the Protestants; here the Presbyterian, there the Catholic: but *all* wanderers far from home and kin.[6]

In Australia the shared experience of distance was far more important than denominational difference.

The colony's assistant chaplain, the Rev. William Cowper, wrote to the London Society for Promoting Christianity Amongst the Jews in 1821, giving us the first glimpse of the first Jewish religious services in Australia and an introduction to Sydney's first 'rabbi':

> Sydney, 26 February 1820
>
> A number of Jews now reside in this town; about thirty of whom have lately agreed to meet together once or twice each week to have their own prayers and the Scriptures read to them. Their only acknowledged Levite, Joseph Marcus, who I have known for some years is an intelligent, peaceable and well disposed man. He had devoted much of his time to the study of the Scriptures in Hebrew, and in English, and is favourable to the Christian Doctrines. I think half a dozen copies of the New Testament in Hebrew, and two or three Old Testaments (i.e. the Hebrew Bible) might be of service to some of them ... Who can tell if God will be gracious to them in this land of their captivity and bondage for sin (Deut. 4:31).
>
> I have had much candid, pious, edifying conversation with Marcus. He now voluntarily, as his bodily infirmities permit him, attends our Church and expresses his appreciation of our mode of worship ... All the Jews are most respectful in their conduct towards me and I felt it is my duty to serve them.[7]

No organised Jewish community was formed until 1832. The *Sydney Gazette* of 23 June 1828 reported that a public meeting was called by Walter Jacob Levi to discuss the tsarist oppression of the Jews in Eastern Europe. In the audience sat 26-year-

The tombstone of Jacob Marcus, Australia's first 'rabbi', now stands in the Pioneers' Cemetery beside Botany Bay. Four lines of expertly carved Hebrew are from the final stanza of the medieval synagogue hymn 'Adon Olam' (The Lord of All):

> The Lord of all who reigned supreme
> Before all was shaped and formed
> Into His hand I place my spirit, both when I sleep and when I wake;
> And with my spirit, my body also. The Lord is with me, I will not fear.

It is the earliest Australian Hebrew inscription and it poses a puzzle. Who chose the words and who carved them on the stone?

old Philip Joseph Cohen, who had arrived in the brig *Alexander Henry* only a month before, and who would soon help create the congregation. Sadly Levi could not know that he had only six weeks to live, though he might have anticipated the outcome of the demand that his audience bestir themselves on behalf of the persecuted Jews of Russia.

Levi felt that 'the more frequently they met together, the better would they cultivate that feeling of kindness and good will which should distinguish the house of

Israel'. Piously he declared that the causes of their misfortune were 'their sins and the sins of their forefathers. Not the persecutors, but the God of Israel should be feared'. There was 'only one cure' and that was to be found in the latter chapters of the Book of Deuteronomy. Despite the protests of the young Philip Cohen that 'sympathy was but poor help in the face of Czarist oppression', a further meeting was arranged at the emancipist Abraham Polack's London Tavern.

With the sudden death of Walter Jacob Levi, those at the next meeting turned for leadership to their obliging host. Despite his convict origin, Abraham Polack had built up a prosperous business, and was well known throughout Sydney. Cohen had arrived far too recently to be considered the leader of the group, so it was Polack who wrote on 29 August 1828, 'on behalf of myself and other members of the Jewish persuasion', to the Colonial Secretary in the hope of finding accommodation for a Jewish congregation before the High Holydays of 1828:

> It is a well known fact that although every other sect in this Colony have a place of Worship wherein Divine Service can be celebrated the Jews are the only denomination who at present are without it, and are therefore in great measure prevented from paying that adoration to their Maker which is so requisite and essential in a Colony like this . . .[8]

Polack asked for permission to hold Jewish religious services in a little building that had recently been used by a government department.

His letter was studiously ignored. A note scrawled on its back by Governor Ralph Darling reads, 'It is hard if they cannot procure some other representative' and then, in place of a reply, the brutal words 'Put away' tell of its fate and bear silent witness to Darling's prejudice. The *Monitor* of 9 August had anticipated Polack's letter in its report, 'We are informed that those members of our community who are of the Jewish persuasion are joining in contributions to erect a place of public worship and that a building for this purpose will shortly be commenced on'. A year passed before anything more was done. On 28 June 1829 the *Gazette* noted, 'The respectable Jews of the Colony are anxious to form a congregation that they may observe the solemnities of their own Sabbath, but many difficulties are in their way'. A major difficulty must have been the manifest bigotry of Governor Darling, who was never slow to stigmatise an opponent as 'a Jew'.

Though Polack was eventually to be elected the President of the Sydney Synagogue in 1836, the obstacles placed in the way of forming a Jewish congregation must have appeared insuperable. On 27 July 1829 Polack and his wife took their infant daughter Sarah, born on 24 July, to be baptised at St James' Church in Sydney. In spite of her baptism she grew up within the Jewish community and married George Barron Goodman, Australia's first professional photographer and daguerreotype-maker.[9] Yet though the Polacks had turned to the Church of England to receive their baby into its spiritual fold, only a month earlier another Jewish family had brought its son into the covenant of Abraham.

The continent's first Jewish circumcision ceremony was performed in June 1829 by the recently arrived free settler, Michael Hyam, and the *Australian* of 19 June described the event in a quaint paragraph which managed to be incorrect in almost every particular:

> Yesterday, we hear, there was a Jewish Sabbath—the first instance, we believe, of the kind on record in the annals of the Colony. Hitherto the children of Jewish parents could not receive the benefit of baptism here; owing to there being no competent priest; but we understand that Mr Hyam, of George St., has been duly authorised by the High Priest at London to perform the ancient rite of circumcision.

On 16 October the *Australian* again reported that Michael Hyam had been called upon to 'perform the office of the High Priest', this time at the circumcision of the 8-day-old son of Joseph and Rachel Aarons. These early naming ceremonies were certainly a more hopeful omen than the establishment of a burial society and the previous abortive attempt to create a congregation.

When Polack lost faith in the whole project, its leadership was taken by the free settler, P. J. Cohen. He had begun to trade as a general dealer at what is now the corner of George Street and Martin Place, and the heart of the modern metropolis of Sydney. There, during 1829, the first regular Jewish religious services in Australia were held. In April 1830 the first public notice was taken of the gatherings. It was Passover, and the *Gazette* of 8 April wrote:

> All the Jews in Sydney, and many from the country, will meet at Messrs Cohen and Spyers, in George Street, who have kindly accommodated their brethren with the use of their large rooms as a temporary synagogue; and Mr Cohen will officiate as reader on the great occasion.

This report precipitated a letter to the *Monitor* on 10 April, signed by 'a Hebrew'. The writer heaped praise upon the emancipist merchant James Simmons, and stated that there had been three Sydney 'banquets' at the time of Passover. As the editor of the *Monitor* was beholden to Simmons for his freedom following a libel case, the tone and publication of the letter is hardly surprising. It said that the 'whole of the congregation' had met at Mr Simmons's, at Messrs Vaiben and Emanuel Solomons's, and at Messrs Cohen and Spyers's, though the 'unbounded hospitality' of Mr Simmons outdid that of the others. The writer said that Simmons had taken the trouble to send 'letters of invitation' to the whole of the 'Jews up the Country', thus indicating that someone had bothered to keep in touch with the isolated Jewish emancipists scattered through the remote interior. Whimsically the letter about these first Australian communal Passover meals ends, 'We had plenty of *matza clice* but alas! no *coogle*'. These popular Jewish foods had had another public mention, as a pseudonym for a person who paid a shilling and threepence costs in a libel suit between the *Monitor* and Hannibal Macarthur, as reported in the *Monitor* on 29 December 1829.

The 1845 *Report*, which celebrated the opening of Sydney's new synagogue, records that though religious services had begun at the home of P. J. Cohen, 'divine services were occasionally performed in a room hired by Messrs A. Elias and James Simmons' and that 'some difference in the opinion then existing amongst members of the faith' produced two infant Jewish congregations.

Once again, however, the memory of the compiler of the 1845 *Report* was at fault. Only Simmons lived in Sydney in those early years. Abraham Elias did not leave his general store in the country town of Windsor and move to Sydney until the middle of 1831. 'Mr Abraham Elias of Windsor thanks all classes at the Hawkesbury and intends to move to Sydney', he advertised in the *Gazette* on 15 March. In Sydney, despite his marriage to a non-Jewish woman, Elias became one of the honoured members of the Sydney Synagogue Committee. Both Simmons and Elias were former convicts who came to Australia at almost the same time. The two men married out of their faith, prospered, and later were both concerned with the management of the Sydney Synagogue. So it is easy to understand how, when the Sydney Jewish community divided, Elias became associated with Simmons. There was one important difference between the two men. Elias was childless, while Simmons eventually had eight children and felt so deeply about their Jewish status that he specified in his will that they would be disinherited if they married out of their faith.[10]

There can be no doubt that Simmons was deeply conscious of his Jewish identity. In July 1828, together with his old shipmate Samuel Lyons, the aristocratic Michael Phillips, the wealthy Walter Jacob Levi and the mighty firm of Cooper & Levey, he supported the tottering fortunes of the Bank of New South Wales. Proudly, Simmons called his large store in George Street Jerusalem House. He was the only Jew in Sydney to call attention to his faith by the name of his business.

Understandably, the old emancipists did not want to be taught religion by a 25-year-old newcomer. But probably the vital issue upon which the nascent community split was that of the children. Traditional Jewish law recognises the Jewish status only of the child of a Jewish mother, and some years later, when P. J. Cohen collated a birth register for the York Street Synagogue, he carefully omitted all mention of the children of James Simmons. Cohen may have been very strict on such points. He officiated at the first and third Jewish marriages in Australia, but did not preside over the second, in which one of the partners was a convert to Judaism. We know that the early congregation had great difficulty defining who was entitled to join it and who could be married in a Jewish ceremony.

A number of meetings were held in 1839 to discuss Jewish identity. In July the committee discussed the case of Eliza Hyam, whose mother had not been Jewish but whose father, Michael Hyam, was a stalwart member and the community's Mohel. It was decided on 6 November that 'in consequence of her father being Jewish' she could be admitted 'without any restriction'. Samuel Barnett made an application in April 1840 that his wife and children 'be received within the pale of our holy religion' and mentioned that his son had been duly circumcised by Michael Hyam and his daughter named within the congregation. He wrote, 'mine is no novel case, for several parties who are now the leading members of the congregation have been placed in the same situation as I am in'. On 10 June the committee of the synagogue came to the decision, seconded by John Lazar, that 'no converts shall be made among the congregation unless the father or mother shall be born a Jew or Jewess'. Moses Joseph added an amendment, which was passed, that this rule should apply only to 'unmarried persons having been respectably married any length of times and requiring to have their wife made a *Geyurise* [convert] should not be excluded, but subject to the approval of the committee'.

Even if there had been no marriages contracted with Christian women, the little community would still have been deeply divided. The question of convicts in the life of the synagogue must have caused deep heart-searching. The Jews of Christian Europe, from which many of the Australian Jews were only two or three generations removed, had for centuries to eschew any actions which might give Christians an excuse to punish their communities. The Jews feared and hated criminals of their own faith as possible triggers of annihilation, and when in 1663 the first Jews returned to Restoration England they decreed that a Jewish criminal should be 'punished by the law according to his crimes, as an example to others, and that thereby the stumbling-block in our midst be removed and God's people be free'.

In this same fearful spirit, the Jews of eighteenth-century London had excommunicated those found guilty by due process of the civil law, and abandoned them to their physical and spiritual fate. But there were too few Jews in Sydney to maintain such barriers for very long, especially since the convict and emancipist communities contained plenty of potentially respectable and useful folk who had been transported for very minor transgressions. Many of the free newcomers were related to convicts, and had come to Australia either to help them or to share their new prosperity. It was hardly realistic to expect such migrants to discriminate against their own brothers, sisters and cousins.

Division in the infant community concluded with the arrival in Sydney of Rabbi Aaron Levy, the youngest member of the London Beth Din, the Jewish Rabbinical Court, sent by the Chief Rabbi to arrange a religious divorce.[11] During the first half of 1831 Levy brought a measure of unity to the affairs of Sydney's Jewish community, and the 1845 *Report*, written by Philip Joseph Cohen, summed up his visit in glowing terms:

Rabbi Aaron Levy in old age.

> [He] corrected many of the errors and abuses which then existed, and endeavoured by his judicious management to instil into the minds of the Hebrew community a taste for Religion. His efforts were successful, a Scroll of the Law was purchased from him by subscription, Hebrew books of prayers were also sold by him to different persons who had no previous opportunity of possessing them and thus Divine Service was more regularly conducted.

A properly constituted congregation came into being following meetings in 1831 and 1832, and was defined in *Laws and Rules for the Management of the Sydney Synagogue*, drawn up and printed in Sydney in 1833. Its first recorded officers were Joseph Barrow Montefiore as President, Abraham Elias as Treasurer and George Moss as Secretary. The general committee consisted of Moses Brown, P. J. Cohen, Abraham Lyons, Michael Phillips and Vaiben Solomon. Emanuel Phillips was the collector of membership dues. Montefiore, Cohen and Michael Phillips were representatives of the upper strata of Anglo-Jewry; Lyons was the brother of a convict; Elias and Solomon were emacipists. Both Emanuel Phillips and Brown were dealers with shops in George Street. This balance between the various sections of the community could hardly have been coincidental.

Apart from the fact that the congregation had no home, many problems were reflected in the congregation's first book of laws. There was the need to decide upon the way in which the services were to be conducted. In a letter sent by the President and the committee to the authorities of the Sephardi Spanish and Portuguese congregation and the Ashkenazi Great Synagogue in London, dated 28 November 1832, the form of service was stated to be 'the same as read by the German Jews in England, subject to such curtailments modifications and abridgements as may be found necessary by the committee'. In other words, the committee was going to run its own synagogue. It was the establishment of a pattern that was to exclude rabbis from the inner councils of every synagogue in Australia for the next century and a half.

The regulations grappled with one of the most complex of all questions in the early years of each Australian Jewish community. Who was to be admitted? Membership, for which there was to be an entrance fee, was barred after Passover 1833 to 'all persons marrying contrary to Judaical Marriage Rites, violating the laws of Brith Milah [circumcision] or neglecting to have their daughters named agreeably to the prescribed Hebrew ritual'. There were other laws permanently excluding illegitimates and people who had been baptised. Nevertheless the children of Jews who had been married in the years prior to the congregation's formal existence could, with the President's permission, be accepted as proselytes even if their parents could not be accepted as members.

Any member who refused a congregational honour, or any committee member 'not attired in a decent and respectable manner', was to forfeit a guinea for each offence. No person could officiate as a reader of a service without permission of the President, who would nominate 'a worthy and competent person', nor could anyone be married without his written permission. The rules concluded with an exhortation to 'those Gentlemen who being the junior branches of their families will take especial care they behave themselves in a manner becoming a place of Divine Worship'.

The creation of a congregation made it possible for the Jewish community to gain official recognition. The Jewish corner of the Devonshire Street general cemetery, granted in 1832 on application by J. B. Montefiore and Michael Phillips, became the responsibility of the synagogue, and the Crown appointed trustees nominated by the congregation. In addition the authorities saw no reason to withhold their permission to convicts and settlers who wished to marry within the Jewish tradition.

The Ketuvah (marriage document) of Mary Connelly and John Moses, 10 July 1831. The document was written by Aaron Levy during his Australian visit. Mary was given the Hebrew name of Rebecca and signed the certificate with a **X**. John Moses, an emancipist, had arrived as a convict in Van Diemen's Land in 1820. The couple married in an Anglican Church in 1826 and the date on the document has been changed in an attempt to protect the Jewish status of their first two children.

The altar of the Church of England at Parramatta had been the incongruous setting for the second marriage in Australia between a Jewish bride and a Jewish groom in July 1826, but when Samuel Marsden performed the ceremony there was no other legal way in which they could be joined together. [12] They were a diminutive couple, with the groom, Solomon Lyons, only three inches taller though six years younger than the 4 feet 9 inches, 35-year-old Phoebe Benjamin. Solomon, who was club-footed, had been a weaver until at the age of sixteen he was transported for life after being caught in the act of stealing a woman's purse in Newgate Market. He arrived in the *Tottenham* in 1818. Phoebe, a silk-glove maker and also serving a life sentence, had arrived in the *Mary Ann* in 1822. Both bride and groom had hazel eyes, but Phoebe's complexion was 'florid' while that of Solomon was 'dark'. [13]

The first Jewish wedding to be conducted beneath the traditional marriage canopy was on 31 January 1832, between the bonded convict Moses Joseph and his first cousin, the free woman Rosetta Nathan, twenty-two, who had come to Sydney to join him. The 'clergyman' is recorded as P. J. Cohen 'by authority of the Rev. Solomon Hershell [Herschell] Chief Rabbi of the Jews in London'.

Apart from being Australia's first Jewish marriage, it was an occasion fraught with awesome practical consequences for Jewish life in both Australia and New Zealand. Moses Joseph, a jeweller by trade, had hawked his wares through provincial England until he increased his stock by stealing jewellery from another pedlar and was sentenced at Warwick Assizes on 25 March 1826 to transportation for life. Like so many of the Jews listed in the early records, he had a 'ruddy dark complexion, black hair, brown eyes', and was five feet three inches tall. Twenty-three years old when he arrived in the *Albion* on 4 February 1827, he was able to read and write. [14]

When he landed in Sydney, Moses Joseph was assigned to the firm of Cooper & Levey, and he completed his term of servitude working for the firm. Rosetta Nathan arrived in Sydney in 1831, and on 24 January 1832 Moses applied for permission to marry. [15] In his own words Rosetta, 'a respectable and virtuous woman', had by her journey shown 'the continuance of her attachment to share the fate and misfortune of petitioner Moses Joseph'. Proudly and carefully Moses pointed out to the Governor that 'your petitioners are of the Jewish persuasion and with your Excellency's sanction are to be married according to the laws, rights and ceremonies of that religion'.

Rosetta Nathan's story is remarkable. She was the daughter of Nathan Lyon Nathan, alias Nathaniel Newton. He was 16 years old when sentenced at the Old Bailey in 1799 to seven years transportation for snatching a bag from an old lady in the Cornhill. He returned to London in 1810 and married his first cousin Sarah Nathan. It was therefore not an astonishing decision to allow their daughter to set out to New South Wales. After all, her father had spent ten years of his life in Sydney. In time, Sarah's brother Henry Nathan gave each of his many nephews and nieces one hundred pounds as working capital when they migrated to the Antipodes. [16] Rosetta's eight siblings all migrated to Australia and New Zealand between 1835 and 1845.

Shortly after his first official step towards freedom, as the holder of a ticket of leave, Moses Joseph opened a tobacconist's shop. Prosperity came so easily to him that many of the members of his family were quickly tempted to try their luck. Of his five brothers, only one remained in England. One settled in America and three in Australia and New Zealand. All his four sisters married migrants to Australia. Louis Nathan, his brother-in-law and first cousin, became one of the most eminent businessmen in colonial Hobart. Another brother-in-law, David Nathan, founded New Zealand's mightiest merchant dynasty. Moses' brother Jacob Joseph, blind but courageous, built the first brick store in Wellington, and virtually founded the Jewish community in New Zealand. Yet another brother, Israel, helped to officiate at New Zealand's first Jewish wedding.

Moses Joseph himself received a rare absolute pardon from the Governor in 1848. By that time he had completed almost a decade of service as the respectable President of the Sydney Synagogue. In 1849, 108 000 acres of grazing land in the New England district was listed in the name of Moses Joseph. In 1853 he was the largest gold buyer in New South Wales, sending more than a thousand ounces of gold in that year alone. After the gold rush, Joseph returned to England from his land of exile with a fortune at his command and, when he died in London in 1862, his Australian estate alone was worth almost £200 000. He would have been worth more than twice that amount had he not picked the wrong side in the American Civil War and invested £250 000 in the Bonds of the American Confederate States.[17]

Once the congregation had been organised and the various factions brought together, the next step was to establish a place of worship. P. J. Cohen's shop was too small, and reminded the emancipists of their former quarrel. With his usual aristocratic aplomb, the President of the congregation summoned a meeting and 'implored his brethren to build a special house of prayer'. Montefiore's plea was out of place in the small new world of Sydney's Jewish community. J. J. Maclehose wrote in 1837 that his plan was defeated by a 'cabal'. Probably because of this 'cabal' and because the bulk of his congregation belonged to a different class from his own, J. B. Montefiore was soon to lose interest in Sydney's Jewish community. By 1836 Abraham Polack had assumed the presidency, followed in 1837 by Isaac Simmons, brother of James Simmons. The High Holydays of 1832 were therefore celebrated in a synagogue 'elegantly fitted up' in rented premises 'over Mr Rowell's shop in George Street'.[18]

The solemn prayers had practical and appropriate consequences. Following the Day of Atonement, a Jewish Philanthropic Institution was established 'for allowing permanent relief to aged, decayed and meritorious objects of the Jewish persuasion'. A circular was printed and, though no copy exists, it was the earliest known Jewish publication in Australia. The society was given the Hebrew name of Ezroth Avyounim (Aid to the Poor), and it was announced that six aged or blind Jews in New South Wales were being provided with sustenance.

The little synagogue served the community for five years, until the Jewish population in Sydney increased and the congregation was forced to rent a modest two-storey house in Bridge Street. From 1833 to 1837 their part-time minister and reader of the synagogue services was the dealer and auctioneer Solomon Phillips, brother of

Emanuel and grandfather of the Australian impressionist painter Emanuel Phillips Fox.[19] The congregation was able to remodel the premises and constructed a synagogue capable of holding a hundred male worshippers and a ladies gallery that seated almost thirty, but even at its first service in 1837 the Bridge Street building must have been too small to serve as the only synagogue in a town with an adult Jewish population of between three and four hundred. To make matters even more difficult the building did not belong to the congregation, and probably it was no surprise when it was sold within the year and the congregation given notice to quit. Obviously this nomadic existence was unsatisfactory, so a building committee was formed and in 1839 an appeal launched to raise enough money to construct an 'elegant and stately' synagogue which would 'accommodate with comfort and ease, a congregation at least, of Five hundred persons, at their daily service'.

On 23 February 1840, members of the congregation asked their solicitor and co-religionist David Poole to apply to the government for a grant of land for the building of a synagogue. Generously the Governor responded with the grant of an allotment in Kent Street, next to a quarry behind the Military Hospital. But although it was a fine commercial site, it was felt that the shape, plan and slope of the land made it unsuitable for the building of a house of worship. A second equally unsuitable site, at Church Hill, was granted for a school, and thirty years later the congregation received permission to sell it and use the proceeds for the building of Sydney's Great Synagogue.[20]

Bridge Street in Sydney, looking east, c. 1835. The gabled two-storey building at the extreme left is the first synagogue in Austraila. Alongside, with a verandah supported by columns, is the mansion of the wealthy emancipist Simeon Lord.

Moses Joseph, who in 1840 had become the President of the congregation, paid a thousand pounds in November 1841 for a more suitable block of land in York Street, and in April 1842 the foundation-stone was laid for what was later inaccurately but proudly called 'the first place of public worship for the Hebrew nation in the Southern Hemisphere'.[21] Two years later, on 2 April 1844, two days before the festival of Passover, the new Sydney Synagogue was consecrated. The service had been arranged by George Moss, the Honorary Secretary, 'whose exertions in all Jewish concerns really appear indefatigable.'[22] A choir trained by Isaac Nathan sang music he had written 'expressly for the occasion'. Sadly no trace of this music remains. The cantor Mr Leon, a pupil of Isaac Nathan, 'chanted psalms'. Commenting on synagogue's appearance, Sydney's Roman Catholic newspaper the Morning Chronicle displayed a deeper sense of history than both the architect and the congregation's elected committee when it reported on 6 April 1844:

> The building is somewhat in the Egyptian style. It does seem rather complimentary to the memory of the tyrant Pharaoh. However the Jews are people well known to have taste in the fine arts, and it hardly becomes us to give this hasty opinion.

Aside from the synagogue's appearance, which was more the product of a Masonic symbolism than Jewish tradition, York Street itself was an odd choice for a place of worship. The synagogue stood opposite the old Central Police Court, and very close to the George Street Market. No less than five taverns clustered around this busy corner of Sydney, and the noise on Saturday must have been deafening. Nevertheless, popular guides to the town described the synagogue as 'chaste and classic', 'beautiful' and 'a handsome building'. A similarly styled synagogue had been built in Philadelphia in 1825.[23] The synagogue, apart from the price of the land, cost almost four thousand pounds. Most of the money came from over 120 Jewish individuals and families in New South Wales, but more than 100 Christians generously joined in the synagogue's appeal for funds, and donations came from the small Jewish communities throughout Australia and even 'per Messrs L. & S. Spyer from London'.

The Jews of New South Wales built their synagogue during the colony's bleakest years. The great J. B. Montefiore had already left Sydney and his name is missing from the 'list of donations' for the building fund. The formidable Samuel Lyons and the hard-pressed George Street shopkeeper all faced the commercial indignity of empty pockets and angry creditors. The longer a settler had been in the colony the more vulnerable he seemed. The more complex his business the less chance there was to escape. It was therefore not surprising that even after the surprisingly successful building appeal the synagogue found itself faced with an apparently insurmountable shortfall of one thousand pounds.

With great trepidation the Jews of Sydney turned to the Legislative Council of the colony for the liquidation of their debt.[24] The Sydney Examiner of 4 October 1845 was puzzled by the community's 'senseless bickering' about approaching the government and reminded its Jewish readers, 'Ask and it shall be given says the Holy Writ'. It was good advice, though the editor might have remembered that the Gospels were not exactly

The York Street Synagogue, looking south, watercolour by John Rae, 1842. The brand new synagogue can be seen over the old Sydney Burial Ground. Close by was the domed Police Office designed by Francis Greenway, and next to that stood the bustling Sydney Market. York Street ran parallel with George Street, Sydney's commercial heart. Sadly, the synagogue was built in a noisy, dusty and undesirable locality.

Jewish 'Holy Writ', nor was the matter as simple as it seemed. The Jews knew full well that such a request would have been pointless if made in Britain, and the role of the church in these new British colonies was far from clear. The congregation submitted its petition in the knowledge that a new kind of society was taking shape in Australia.

Citing the precedent of Jamaica, where the House of Assembly had supported the island's synagogue on more than one occasion, the Hebrew Congregation of the City of Sydney pointed out that though they had been in existence for fourteen years, they had neither solicited nor received official assistance. They had been granted some land, but they had not used it and the deeds were not in their possession. They had contributed to the revenue of the colony, had paid their rates and taxes and so felt they were entitled to receive some support for their religious establishments.

Money was allocated annually within the colonial budget for the purposes of 'public worship', so the Jews appeared to have a strong case. In the Legislative Council it was moved that £1000 be allotted to liquidate the building debt, and that £150 be voted for a minister's stipend. The motion was carried by eight votes to five, and may have been influenced by an impassioned speech from Robert Lowe (later Viscount Sherbrooke and Chancellor of the Exchequer in Westminster). Lowe proclaimed that the Jewish claim to such monies took precedence over that of their Christian fellow citizens. The *Sydney Morning Herald* of 25 October 1845 quoted him as saying, 'Their warriors had ceased to fight, their poets had ceased to sing, their own greatness as a nation had passed away, at least for a season, before the most prized record of ancient history had obtained an existence'.

The vote presented Governor Sir George Gipps with constitutional problems. He felt that funds could be allocated only to Christian worship, and a dispatch from W. E. Gladstone at the Colonial Office agreed with this opinion. From Government House in Sydney on 4 November 1845 the Governor firmly declared:

> Gentlemen—I regret I do not feel that I have the authority to pay any money towards the erection of a Jewish synagogue or towards the maintenance of a Minister of the Jewish religion out of the sum which by schedule C of the 5th and 6th Vict. C.76 is secured to Her Majesty for the purpose of public worship.

A solution was found by providing the grant out of the general supplementary estimates, and the successor of Governor Gipps, Sir Charles FitzRoy, wrote to England explaining that 'I considered it advisable to accede ... the members of the Jewish religion being a numerous, respectable and influential class in the community, contributing largely to the public revenue'. But this explanation met with disapproval from Whitehall, and in an icily polite note Lord Grey told his colonial representative, 'I should have been glad if you had not consented to make provision for the liquidation of the debt incurred in building the synagogue'.[25]

The battle for State aid for the synagogue continued for more than a decade and came to a climax when George Robert Nichols, the grandson of Esther Abrahams and member of the New South Wales Legislative Council, persuaded the House to place the Jews on the same footing as other faiths in the allocation of money to support religion.[26] Once again the motion ran counter to precedent, and the place of the Church within the English constitutional framework. But the legislature of New South Wales felt that colonial conditions were different and for three brief years, 1855–58, the State subsidised the salary of Sydney's Jewish minister. The question was not resolved until 1862, when State aid to religion came to an end in New South Wales.

The Sydney Synagogue literally set the pattern for Jewish worship throughout the colonies. Within five years of its dedication the same distinctive 'Egyptian synagogue' style appeared in Hobart Town, Launceston and Adelaide. Some of the earliest Jewish settlers in Melbourne and Adelaide travelled to Sydney to find their brides. Sydney's efforts to obtain financial assistance from the government were watched with close interest by the Jews of the neighbouring colonies.

Beyond all the financial, legal and architectural preoccupations of the Sydney Synagogue, there remained its spiritual welfare. There was no rabbi, no teacher and no standards. There was a place to pray and there were Jewish families, there was a committee and there was a cemetery, but a synagogue is more than the sum total of all these essential ingredients. Religious leadership and guidance became the special concern of the congregation's secretary, George Moss.

Moss was the son of a London cantor, and his fine sense of history was eclipsed in everyday life by his poor head for business. He migrated to New South Wales in 1831, became a publican in early Maitland and a tavern owner in George Street. He had been a ticket collector at Levey's Theatre Royal and a bill collector for the Sydney City Council and for the *Australian* newspaper. For a short time during 1842 and 1843 he had even been an owner of the paper, and finally became shipping and customs-house agent.[27]

But Moss' main preoccupation was clearly the Sydney Synagogue. He battled valiantly to create congregational institutions that would enable Judaism to survive in Australia. On 27 May 1842, while working in the newspaper business, he published an Australian edition of a London Jewish weekly newspaper called the *Voice of Jacob*. Apart from being Australia's first Jewish newspaper, and therefore almost fifty years ahead of its time, it was an intelligent attempt to educate the young Australian Jewish community. Moss wrote anxiously of the need to 'secure a competent person to deliver religious discourses in their synagogue, in the English language' and hoped that his newspaper would make up for the lack of a spiritual teacher and leader. It took a wise man to be disturbed enough to print an article decrying the sight of the first Australian-born generation of Jewish boys coming to the synagogue on the day of their Bar Mitzvah 'not being at all acquainted with the ordinances of the Mosaic religion, or the object of confirmation'. On 5 September 1842 he reminded his readers that he had been the secretary of the Sydney Synagogue from its first properly organised meeting in 1833 and, with only a brief interruption, remained in that post. As the editor of the *Voice of Jacob*, he was 'desirous of knowing if all the young men of our community pay attention towards our religious establishments? We fret to say no! The subscriptions are indeed very limited and are all derived from Sydney residents'. Nobody seemed to care and hardly anybody bought his newspaper.

Apathy and the deepening economic crisis silenced the Australian *Voice of Jacob* after three slim issues, although Moss continued to correspond with the English edition of the paper and presented to its London readers a vivid picture of Jewish life in New South Wales.[28]

In March 1854 he wrote an article for the *Sydney Morning Herald* which he entitled 'Jewish Intelligence'. He was angered by the Hobart Synagogue's obtaining a rabbi dubbed Presiding Rabbi of the Australian Colonies by the Chief Rabbi in London. Moss declaimed for all the world to know:

> Alas! The Sydney Synagogue has no Minister to expound the sacred Scriptures on the sabbath and festival; the community attend the Synagogue, they retire from it not better or wiser men. Is there no balm in Gilead? Is there no physician in Tyre? Tell it not in the streets of Gath; relate it not in the highways of Ashkelon.

And Moss sarcastically signed the column 'A Reformed Israelite.'

The committee of the Sydney Synagogue was far from amused. They felt that they had been disgraced in public. The secretary was suspended. Moss apologised. The committee was adamant. A general meeting of the congregation voted to pay Moss a hundred pounds a year for life. This was subsequently changed to fifty pounds, to be approved each subsequent year. They had no need to worry. The battle had broken Moss' health and snapped his mind and he died in the Tarban Creek Lunatic Asylum on 5 November 1854. The congregation authorised that his tombstone should read that he was 'secretary of the Synagogue until infirmity overtook him' and, a little later, reluctantly granted his young children a temporary stipend. Moss had been Australian Jewry's first public servant.

Moss must have known that the community was far from viable. In 1841 he wrote that there were 90 subscribing members of Australia's first and, at the time, only Jewish congregation. The official government census showed that in all of eastern Australia there were 856 Jews, of whom 462 lived in Sydney and 414 outside the metropolis. Moss estimated that there were 60 Jewish couples living in Sydney, 200 children, 200 single Jewish males, a small number of single women and 100 Jewish convicts. Undaunted by his own statistics, Moss believed that Sydney's Jewish community was worth preserving if only because of its destiny in the burgeoning glory of Britain. In the first issue of his ill-fated paper he wrote, 'It is evident that Providence has reserved the British Jews for the execution of some great purpose in His vast designs and that they hold a proud position among their brethren'.

In the 1845 *Report* of the York Street Synagogue, a sub-committee (which included Moss) surveyed the state of Jewish affairs in the colony and deplored the condition of Jewish education. There was no religious school, no library of Jewish books, no public lectures or sermons 'either within or without the walls of our synagogue'. The congregation was told that 'as British Jews, it is necessary we should not throw off the connection which binds us to our Mother country, and that having no spiritual guide of our own, we should place ourselves under the protection of the Chief Rabbi of England'.

At the same time Moss wrote, in a letter published in the London *Voice of Jacob* of 22 May 1846, that the Sydney congregation faced a dilemma. He had hoped 'That two or three members will undertake to deliver a series of discourses during our winter . . . I am aware that those who are competent are not so rigid and orthodox as to have weight; while the majority of those who would attend are not conscious of the necessity of preaching'. Sadly he observed, 'For too many years we have been wholly absorbed in ceremonials'.

The only professional Jewish religious leadership came from men such as Michael Rose, who were unable to preach or to teach. Rose was Sydney's, and therefore Australia's, first Jewish 'minister', though in the manifest of the barque *Mary* in which he and his wife had travelled to Sydney, arriving on 22 September 1835, he was more accurately described as a 'dealer'. Nevertheless, Rose brought with him credentials from the Chief Rabbi in London declaring that he was a 'reader' and that he could conduct a traditional Jewish religious service and slaughter livestock for kosher meat. He remained in Sydney for three years, supplementing his income as a shopkeeper by serving the young Sydney congregation as its first salaried officiant. When Rose left Sydney for India, the congregation battled on alone.[29]

Two years later help arrived once more in the person of Jacob Myer Isaacs, another licensed 'reader', who wrote that he had been 'led to suppose' in London that the congregation was in need of assistance.[30] For fifteen years Isaacs helped conduct the synagogue services, chant the prayers, perform the wedding ceremonies and slaughter the animals required for kosher food. At the same time he, like Rose, conducted a business and therefore, in spite of a building debt of seven hundred pounds, the congregation was forced to bring the young but knowledgeable Moses Rintel out from England to be the Hebrew teacher for their children.

Several early settlers attempted to copy Anglo-Jewish practice and employ private tutors for the religious education of their children. On 1 April 1830 the *Gazette* reported that Isaac Simmons had 'a Jewish priest of the name of Sebbett' staying with him. Nothing at all is known about this 'priest'. Barnett Phillips applied for the assignment of the Cracow-born convict Thomas Harris, alias Herscht, to be the Hebrew tutor of his nine children. His request was refused by the Principal Superintendent of Convicts who 'disapproved of convicts teaching children'. Though Jacob Myer Isaacs had offered to 'fill my vacant time by opening a school for teaching Hebrew or English or giving lessons private', no Jewish school was established until the arrival of Moses Rintel in 1845. He began to give private Hebrew and religious instruction three times a week to five children, and conduct group instruction to twenty-four boys aged between five and twelve and sixteen girls aged between seven and thirteen. This was the first Jewish school in Australia.[31]

The Sydney Synagogue began in 1845 to plan the establishment of a full-time denominational school supported by the same government aid that was already extended to other church schools. The Jewish community was far from united in its attitude toward denominational education and the place of a Jewish day-school. P. J. Cohen believed it would be 'far better to have a system where all might be taught where all religious creeds might meet' while George Moss was 'bound to state, though it was generally disapproved by his co-religionists, that he himself was far more disposed towards the educational system that would give them an opportunity of teaching their children agreeably to their own views'. Nevertheless, dissatisfaction with the Christian orientation of the colony's existing schools led to a long struggle to establish a Jewish communal school.[32]

A Jewish request for a grant of land 'to erect and found a school at their own expense in a central part of Sydney' was speedily approved and an architect was commissioned to design 'a Public School for both sexes, with a master's residence . . . to consist of a ground floor for the Boys School, to contain 100 pupils, an upper floor to contain 80 girls . . . besides dormitories for 6 Boarders'. Ten quarrel-laden years later, the Sydney Jewish day-school finally opened its doors.[33]

Isolated from the mainstream of Jewish life, the Australian Jewish community prior to the gold rush remained myopically unaware of changes being wrought in Europe as Judaism, both orthodox and liberal, faced the challenge of emancipation. When an English-born and German-trained rabbi was appointed to be London's new Chief Rabbi, George Moss wryly commented in a letter to the London *Voice of Jacob* of 22 May 1846, 'Dr Adler's portrait has been received. Some of my old fashioned friends were surprised at seeing the worthy Rabbi minus a beard, a fur cap and a Polish peltz'.

Emigration

IN A WORLD reserved for felons a flourishing colony of free men arose. To the adventurous traveller to the Antipodes the streets and fields of New South Wales seemed hard to reconcile with the persistent notion that Australia meant little more than exile, convicts and kangaroos. As one Briton wrote, 'The extraordinary rapid growth which has followed upon the settlement of the scum of the Earth on the shores of Australia would almost make it appear that in colonising it is as in gardening, the more your foundations consist of dung the more rapid and striking is the production'.[1] A contributor to the *Gentleman's Magazine* in 1804 was deeply impressed by the transformation of the country and the reformation of its population:

> It is now eighteen years since the first establishment was made in New South Wales and the colony is already England in miniature ... This useful colony increases in wealth and convenience much more rapidly than that country did, which is now termed the United States of America. Bad and unprincipled as are the convicts annually transported, a very flattering reformation appears to have been wrought among them on their arrival at New South Wales and favourable hopes may be cherished of the progress of that settlement.[2]

It was certainly true that in little less than forty years a lonely open-air prison had been transformed into a complex and dynamic colony. The end of the Napoleonic Wars in 1815 caused a trade depression in Britain, with a consequent rise in emigration by those seeking a better life overseas—to say nothing of a rise in crime which increased transportation. The expanding population gave the Australian economy its first real chance to develop. It had taken a long, precarious twenty years for the settlement to reach a total of 10 000 inhabitants. It took only another ten years for the population to pass a total of 40 000. Between 1788 and the end of 1814 a total of 12 476 male and female convicts were transported to Australia, while in the six years from early 1815 to the end of 1820, 14 277 male and female convicts were embarked. Government works expanded rapidly, local need for food quickly surpassed the ability of farmers to keep pace, and the export of wool to England began to bring substantial financial rewards to the colony.[3]

The first free adult Jewish arrival to New South Wales was sent back home on the ship that brought her. Mordecai Pass was sentenced at the Old Bailey in 1790 to seven years transportation for stealing a box from a cart, and was consigned to be deported on the convict transport *Active*. Esther, his wife, then contacted the Master of the ship, John Mitchinson, and paid him to find space for her. The records show that it was a terrible journey. The ship encountered appalling weather after it left the Cape of Good Hope, and the sparse rations almost ran out. Twenty-three of her passengers died of malnutrition and the surviving prisoners were carried ashore at Sydney in an emaciated condition.

Esther Pass' arrival at Sydney Cove on 26 September 1791 caused some official anger and not a little consternation. After all, transportation was supposed to be a punishment and, even though children were transported with their mothers, accommodation was not provided for other family members. The colony itself was starving, and food and shelter were in very short supply. The colony was too young to cope with someone who was neither a convict nor part of the military establishment. Esther was therefore 'allowed' to leave New South Wales after Lieutenant Governor King had been convinced that she was not a convict in disguise. Governor Phillip wrote to Under Secretary Nepean on 24 November 1792 telling him that 'The Master of the *Active* Transport having made Oath that a woman of the name of Esther Pass, whom came out in that Ship, is not a convict and never was intended to remain in the Settlement, she is permitted to proceed with him'. Esther left Australia shortly after. Mordecai became known as James Pass in Sydney. He was still in Australia in 1813 when, on 30 January, he was charged and found guilty of receiving stolen goods. He then vanished from sight as did Esther, our first free Jewish immigrant.[4]

There were isolated free Jewish immigrants in the mid-1820s. Barnett Levey hastened to share his brother's success and Esther Isaacs chose to share her husband's fate. Several children had come with their convict fathers. The 4-year-old Joshua Frey Josephson arrived with his father in 1818. His brother-in-law Barnett Levey allowed the boy to perform at some of his concerts and soon Joshua was well known as a local child prodigy. He was to become a teacher of music, a publican and a lawyer; Mayor of Sydney in 1848, member of the Legislative Assembly in 1864, and Solicitor General in 1868. He retired from politics to become a District Judge, and died in 1892.

The four small children of Joseph and Rachel Aarons arrived with their mother on 18 October 1823, on the convict transport ship *Mary*. They were Rachel aged seven, Rosina aged five, Hannah aged four and Aaron Joseph two. Their parents were penniless foreigners transported for stealing cloth from a London warehouse.[5] By 1827 these children and the two adults, who had come to join their convict relatives, were the only free Jewish settlers in the colony of New South Wales. *Bell's Weekly Messenger* in London described the colony to its readers:

> The temperature of the climate is very agreeable, except occasionally during the summer months, when the heat is very oppressive. But extremes of this kind seldom continue long. Most of the inhabitants appear to enjoy uninterrupted good health . . . the farmer gives his Government servants £10 wages and a weekly ration consisting of four to seven pounds of meat, from ten to fourteen pounds of wheat or a certain portion of maize . . . Most farmers set them task work, as they will do little

otherwise . . . Highway robbery and burglary are very common . . . I am inclined to think that the drunkenness of the market people encourages many of the robberies we hear committed from time to time. Scores of carts regularly attend the Sydney market, from 20 to near 50 miles distant. A journey to the market of 40 miles is as little thought of in this country, as the distance of half a dozen miles in most parts of England. There is little doubt but in the course of time this Colony will rise to considerable magnitude and the people of this land become great and mighty.[6]

As some former convicts began to consolidate their fortunes in Australia, free men in England began to wonder whether honesty did, in fact, bring its own reward. And so, between the years 1820 and 1830, 7654 free immigrants arrived to settle in New South Wales and Van Diemen's Land. During this decade the first 56 free Jewish adults and their 25 children landed in New South Wales. With their arrival, a Jewish community was born.

The trickle of free Jewish immigration to New South Wales began in London on 7 November 1826 when Walter Jacob Levi of 4 Finsbury Square wrote to Earl Henry Bathurst, Secretary for the Colonies, asking for assistance in his plans to develop two new crops in New South Wales.[7] Levi was not a young man but he cited his extensive colonial experience. He had worked for 'many years' in the West Indies as a dealer in military clothing and real estate and as a plantation owner. For the previous ten years he had lived in Barbados, and claimed to be well known to the vice-regal authorities on the island. It was, he wrote, his hope to grow cotton and sugar in Australia, as he had seen a sample of cotton grown in New South Wales. He knew of the cost involved in importing sugar to the colony, and he had heard about the ideal place to begin his work. Levi's financial capital consisted of five thousand pounds, 'with the command of as much more as may be required'. In return he hopefully asked for a grant of five thousand acres of land at Port Macquarie, with the option of purchasing an additional ten thousand acres, and the assistance of seventy to one hundred Crown servants or convicts. Levi failed to mention, because it would have been widely known, that his wife Rebecca was the daughter of the extremely wealthy Mr Lemon Hart who held the contract to supply the Royal Navy with its daily ration of rum.

Downing Street was appropriately impressed, and Governor Darling was asked to extend towards Levi the help 'you may deem proper upon consultation of the probable success of his undertaking, with reference to the amount of Capital, which he may have at his disposal'. And so the pioneer, his wife Rebecca and his three young children set sail for New South Wales in the *Medway* in 1827, happily unaware that despite money, social status and high hopes, only tragedy and disappointment awaited them. They were the first Jews to reach Australia who had no connection with any convict or emancipist family.[8]

The *Medway* was held up in Hobart Town, so Levi went on ahead in the *Emma Kemp*, and arrived on 22 September 1827. Rebecca arrived on 2 October. Within a month of his arrival Levi wrote to Governor Darling applying for the grant of land, and immediately struck trouble. Perhaps the Governor doubted that Levi would really settle on the land and had never heard of a Jewish farmer. In any case the land that Levi wanted at Port Macquarie was not to be released yet, because it was too close to a colonial convict establishment. Levi had been misled by his English informant. On 2 November 1827 Levi began his battle for acknowledgment that he had come in good faith to the colony to be a farmer. He wrote to Darling:

> having a large and extensive family, I feel the need to do something until Port Macquarie be open [for settlement] . . . How then His Excellency the Governor can doubt my intentions I cannot conjecture . . . if my views are not in future purely agricultural it will be from a total failure of those facilities I expected to receive from His Excellency . . . had I entertained any doubt of the possibility of a disappointment I should not have emigrated to this colony.[9]

It must be admitted that there were grounds for the Governor's scepticism. On 10 December an advertisement appeared in the *Sydney Gazette* to notify the public that paint, oil, calico, wine and other goods had been brought to the colony by Levi and set up for sale in his store room in Macquarie Place. When Levi found that his land ventures were not progressing, he at once ordered goods from England and registered himself as a shipping agent and merchant.[10]

As his plan to grow sugar and cotton seemed doomed, Levi began negotiations with the appropriate colonial committee for a grant of choice grazing land that he had seen on the banks of the Manning River. As his capital was ample, and as he proposed to 'reside upon the land and manage it in person', the Land Board wrote that it had no objection to such a grant of land 'as His Excellency may be pleased to order'. Governor Darling was not so pleased. Levi's application was passed over in favour of two undistinguished rivals, a retired civil servant from India and a far less affluent immigrant from the West Indies. He continued to search for land, while the cattle he had bought in anticipation of a grant were scattered on the pastures of many different properties. In June 1828 he applied to the government for some land in Sydney itself on which to build a residence for his family. His cotton seed was about to arrive and suitable land of his own was not available, so he generously offered the seed at cost to anyone who would buy and use it.[11] The proceeds from the sale of the seed would be put aside and prizes were to be awarded for the best cotton produced.[12]

Levi's social status and activities indicate that he encountered little religious prejudice in his life in the colony. When the *Sydney Gazette* of 25 April 1828 announced the formation of the Australian Racing Club, with the Governor as patron, Levi was listed as one of its foundation members. At the second annual meeting of the Female School of Industry, attended by the Governor and Mrs Darling, the *Gazette* of 16 April reported that the two principal chaplains of the colony and Mr Walter Levi were the only three speakers. His last public duty was recorded in the *Gazette* of 16 July, when he took an active role in resolving a financial crisis caused by the creation of the colony's second bank. Less than a month later he was dead, and the newspapers of 4 August dolefully declared that an illness lasting four days had robbed the colony of one whose 'wealth, intelligence and public spirit constituted a superior and valuable colonist'. A 'long and respectable funeral train' accompanied the body to the new Jewish Cemetery. Levi's fourth child had only recently been born, in time to be recorded in the colony's first census. It was three years before the Monitor of 2 February 1831 recorded that his widow had settled his estate and left for home. Rebecca would remarry in England. For Sydney's first free Jewish family, Australia had been a harsh and sad experience.

The glittering return of Solomon Levey to England had, as we have seen, far-reaching repercussions upon the business community of London and upon the future course of Australian development. In distant Sydney the newspapers reported in detail Levey's enthusiastic reception, and on 26 June 1827 the Australian wrote:

> He has met with very handsome treatment from some of the first mercantile houses in the City of London . . . Messrs Samuel and Phillips, relatives of the Rothschilds, have acted very liberally towards Mr Levey, and in the full confidence of the stability of the firm Cooper & Levey, are likely to have extensive trade with him.

The list of the earliest free Jewish settlers shows that Levey made his greatest impression upon those who lent him money. No sooner had the triumphant emancipist set foot in London than Michael Phillips, a young scion of the banking family whose wife had been born a Samuel, applied to the Colonial Office for an initial grant of four thousand acres of Australian land.[13] References attesting to his 'character, respectability and means' were supplied by the family firm of Samuel and Phillips, and the young man set sail to spy out the land. Australia's impact upon him was immediate, and no doubt he wrote glowing reports to the Anglo-Jewish community. Little more than six months passed before the Colonial Office in London received an application for a grant of land in Australia from the London merchant Joseph Barrow Montefiore, a young member of the small circle of London Jewish grandees to which Michael Phillips belonged.[14]

In the opinion of a Secretary of the Treasury, the 25-year-old Montefiore was 'a most respectable gentleman . . . a most valuable acquisition to the colony'. Joseph's older brother Jacob had become interested in colonial trade and Joseph himself had become impatient with life in the City of London, even though only two years before at the cost of fifteen hundred pounds he had become one of the twelve 'Jew brokers' permitted to belong to the Stock Exchange.[15] The chance to extend business to a new land, backed by the security of dealing with his own family, was irresistible. Fully aware that the British Colonial Office had begun to regard the Australian colonies as sources of primary produce rather than mercantile wealth, the astute young businessman wrote to the colonial officials as an 'agriculturalist'. He asked for five thousand acres of land, and said that he would take with him a capital of ten thousand pounds, being 'persuaded of the vast importance of the fast rising colony' and intending to grow 'drugs, marino [sic] sheep, breeding of horses and horned cattle'.

An imposing group of wealthy and well-connected young Jews had arrived in Australia by the end of 1830. It consisted of Joseph Barrow Montefiore with his wife Rebecca and their two children; his 14-year-old brother-in-law George Mocatta; his young cousin John Israel Montefiore with wife and child; and his partner David Ribiero Furtado with his wife Sarah, who had gone to Hobart Town to found a branch in the southernmost colony. Mrs Michael Phillips with her six children and her brother-in-law Moses Phillips and 19-year-old brother Samuel, as well as Horatio Samuel, also arrived during that first decade of free Jewish settlement. Suddenly Australian Jewry had an 'aristocracy', and the humbler free Jewish settlers were able to see men and women of their own religion associating as equals with the colony's class-conscious élite.

These few families represented a third of all Jewish migrants in the first decade of free Australian expansion, and their arrival made the creation of a Jewish congregation inevitable. The respectability of their community depended upon their recognition as a group of citizens united by religious affiliation and not, as so often has been the case with Jews, by historical misfortune.

Each family was to make a name in its own way. George Mocatta, who arrived in the *Jupiter* on 22 February 1829, became a manager of J. B. Montefiore's rural properties in New South Wales between 1837 and 1839, and then a grazier in his own right in what is now Queensland. In the late 1850s he returned to Sydney, became a produce merchant, and in 1857 married a widow, Mrs Lydia Harriet Voss. After a lengthy stay in Europe he went to New Zealand and bought Tauranga Station, and died in Sydney aged seventy-nine on 21 March 1893. Although never baptised he was buried in the Congregational Cemetery, Gore Hill. His second son, W. Hugh Mocatta KC, became a District Judge in 1922.

David Ribiero Furtado was an important member of the commercial community of Hobart Town between 1831 and 1845. He was elected a director of the Bank of Van Diemen's Land, was one of the directors of the Bank of Australia, and manager of the Van Diemen's Land Company. As a partner in the bankrupt firm of Montefiore, Breillat & Co., his estate was sequestrated in 1844. He was present at the laying of the foundation-stone of the Hobart Synagogue and gave the synagogue £6 3s 6d, but by 1845 had moved to the new colony at Port Phillip and worked as a private banker buying and selling foreign currency at his home in Flinders Lane. Furtado was appointed auditor of the City of Melbourne without his knowledge or consent in 1853, and was fined twenty-five pounds when he refused the honour. Busy with other tasks, the press announced on 17 January 1853 that he was to be the manager of the newly formed Commercial Bank of Australia. In his *Sketches of Anglo-Jewish History*, James Picciotto names the Furtado family in London as one of those which became Christians for the sake of 'exaggerated notions of self importance, unbounded pride and expectations of worldly advancement'—but in Melbourne, David Ribiero Furtado would remain a Jew.[16]

Though Joseph Barrow Montefiore was witty, imaginative and possessed of the flair for business and leadership typical of his family, his Australian career was curiously unsuccessful. Inevitably, Montefiore had the capacity to raise high hopes whenever he made the vaguest financial move or speculation. Perhaps this was the key to his own failure, for there was more than a hint of euphoric greed in the *Sydney Gazette's* note on 22 July 1834 that 'We understand that Mr Montefiore is the brother of Mr Jacob Montefiore who married the daughter of a Rothschild, and son-in-law of Mr Mocatta, an opulent bullion broker'.

No sooner had Montefiore arrived in New South Wales in 1829, and taken possession of a large grant of land, than he began to prepare for new conquests.[17] He began to learn the Maori language and then sailed across the Tasman to establish one of the earliest trading stations on the west coast of the North Island of New Zealand. Deeply impressed by the country's beauty and natural resources, he persuaded his cousin John Israel Montefiore to proceed to the Bay of Islands in 1831 and establish an important trading post. Joseph Montefiore returned to London in March 1836 and gave evidence to the Select Committee of the House of Lords appointed to inquire into the state of New Zealand. Montefiore patriotically believed that the North Island should become part of the British Empire and dubbed New Zealand the Britain of the South. He observed that the island's missionaries had enriched themselves and acquired vast tracts of land with no visible spiritual results, and he believed that political controls were necessary.

Montefiore's estates in Australia were based upon the maximum grants of land that the government could give and augmented by a series of purchases, so that within ten years he owned over eleven thousand acres in the Wellington Valley in New South Wales.[18] He quickly became one of the leading merchants and shipping agents of Sydney. During the 1830s he was one of the few Jewish businessmen whose name regularly appeared beside the lists of cargoes imported and exported from the colony. Montefiore was associated with the founding of the Bank of Australia and, through his English family and its connections, was one of the sources through which English capital flowed into the colony. When Montefiore returned to Sydney in 1840 after an extended stay in England, the newspapers wrote that 'an old and esteemed colonist had returned'.

To the great consternation of the London business world, Montefiore Brothers in London 'temporarily' stopped payment in February 1841. In Sydney the *Australian* of 24 and 29 June reported the circumstances and regarded them as 'the most startling event to the mercantile community'. The London newspapers hoped that funds would come from the sale of Montefiore land in New South Wales, but Joseph returned to London to tell his family that their hopes were vain. It was the eve of the colony's great depression and he had hopelessly over-extended the firm's capital investment in land. In the Wellington Valley a village called Montefiores testified to the sale of some parts of the great estate to private, and smaller, settlers. At the new township of Melbourne, Montefiore was forced to sell speculative land purchases made when he returned from England in 1840. Finally, in December 1844 the estates of D. R. Furtado and Thomas Breillat, 'two of the partners in the firm of Jacob Montefiore and Joseph Barrow Montefiore, trading under the firm of Montefiore Breillat & Co. of Sydney', were sequestrated.[19] Joseph Barrow Montefiore made a second and less spectacular attempt to build up an Australian fortune in 1846 when he returned as a merchant to South Australia, and his life there forms an important part of the story of the Jewish community in Adelaide.

The promising Australian career of Michael Phillips ended even more miserably. Unlike the insolvent Montefiore, Phillips was not spared a term in debtor's prison, though like Montefiore he had at first met with a great deal of respect and financial success. The purchase of a cargo from an American ship in 1832, which he paid for in colonial produce, raised high hopes for an 'extensive trade with American ports'. He had sufficient capital to warrant receiving a grant of 2560 acres of land adjoining Joseph Montefiore's land at Wellington. In Sydney he built a home and store 'replete with every comfort and convenience', and he travelled to England several times and returned with shiploads of merchandise.[20]

With his five children and his pregnant wife, Phillips went to Hobart Town on business in 1837.[21] His credit in Sydney was low and a rumour spread through the town that he was about to leave the colonies. Samuel Lyons acted quickly, followed him, and served him with a summons for the recovery of £658 in four promissory notes. It was the first time that Phillips had been in Van Diemen's Land, where he was unknown. He may well have been in some slight financial difficulty, and certainly was not carrying a large sum of money with him. So, being unable to satisfy the court that he could pay his bills, he was placed in the Debtors' Prison, where he languished for nine months whilst Lyons callously returned to Sydney. The court refused to release Phillips, on the grounds that he had contracted debts without knowing how he was to repay them: a law which applied in Van Diemen's Land but not New South Wales. So Phillips lay in gaol in Hobart Town, unable to care for his wife or to be with her when the time came to bear a new child, and it is not surprising that when he was released he quickly left the colony for England. Presumably his family in London had ransomed their despairing son. Meanwhile Samuel Lyons returned to Sydney to mete out similar treatment to Lawrence and Stephen Spyer in the Supreme Court, where he succeeded in preventing their release from prison after they had served three months for being unable to meet their debts.[22] There were old scores to be settled between the emancipated and the free.

Closely associated with both Phillips and Montefiore in those early years of free settlement was Philip Joseph Cohen, who probably was the son of a Cambridge pedlar. It is reasonable to assume that he and his shipmate Lawrence Spyer may have been attracted to Australia by Solomon Levey. He most certainly knew Phillips and Montefiore, and upon his arrival in Sydney he found himself obliged to deny that he had come 'under the auspices' of the Rothschilds. Nevertheless, on the basis of the capital he brought with him, Cohen applied for a grant of land adjoining the properties secured by Montefiore and Phillips.[23]

Cohen's first colonial experiences were not auspicious. His ship had battled with bad weather in the Irish Channel for a month and it had taken the 'tremendously long time' of six months to complete the journey to Sydney. Some of the passengers claimed that the captain had starved the passengers, a report that Cohen and Spyer denied. The two friends became partners in July 1828, rented a shop next to the Customs House in George Street and announced that they 'daily expected . . . the most exclusive collection of European goods which . . . they will be enabled to sell at very reduced prices', but it was five months before the goods arrived.[24]

The two young men were not accustomed to the trading conditions of a remote colony that suffered from a chronic lack of cash and a haphazard dependence upon credit. The *Australian* of 31 July 1829 reported that they had sold six hundred acres of land to satisfy the first of a stream of anxious colonial creditors. On 11 March 1831 a notice in the same paper showed that their business was in ruins. The partnership was over and their stock-in-trade was sold by order of the trustees in their insolvency.

The Jews were not lacking in pioneer spirit, and on 8 July 1831 the *Australian* mentioned that Cohen had put Sydney behind him and opened a general store in the two-year-old township of Maitland, then an agricultural settlement in the Hunter River Valley and located twenty miles north of the former prison settlement of Newcastle. His departure was a great loss to the Jews of Sydney for, as recorded in the 1845 *Report* of the York Street Synagogue, 'Divine worship according to the Hebrew form' had been regularly held in his house.

Cohen was rarely successful in business but he was certainly a knowledgeable and pious Jew. During his twelve years in Maitland he never lost his interest in the affairs of the Sydney Synagogue, and his later financial failure may well have been caused by his continual absences from his business to participate in the life of its Jewish community. Armed with the authority of London's Chief Rabbi he officiated at Australia's first Jewish wedding, in Sydney on 1 February 1832, and on 31 December 1835 he travelled from Maitland to Sydney to officiate at the marriage of his former partner Lawrence Spyer to Angelina de Metz.

In Maitland, Cohen's first years were happy and prosperous. His success was noted by the Jews of Sydney, and Maitland soon had a second Jewish family when Solomon Levien, his wife Harriet and their five children, arrived to become the postmaster and the licensee of the Rose Inn.[25] Cohen must have welcomed the move, for on 18 October 1833 the *Australian* reported a ceremony in Sydney conducted by Michael Phillips in which Cohen was married to Annette Abigail Levien, the 16-year-old daughter of his new neighbour.

Married life began well. Cohen opened a soap factory, then took over his father in-law's hotel and kept control of the general store. In 1835 he became the town's postmaster and in 1840 was appointed secretary of the Maitland and Newcastle Steam Navigation Co. that planned to develop shipping along the Hunter River and from Newcastle to Sydney.[26] The Jewish community in Maitland continued to grow, and among those tempted to the township by Cohen's prosperity were his step-brother Simeon Joseph Cohen and his brother-in-law Alfred Levien. The two new arrivals formed a partnership, and soon shared in the economic catastrophe of the 1840s. They were declared insolvent in January 1843, with debts totalling £2458, and Cohen met the same fate in July, with debts estimated at £4178.

The courts permitted Cohen to retain his clothes, his household furniture and his wife's trinkets, and above all the happy memory of a farewell dinner at his Maitland Hotel where fifty local gentlemen drank his health and wished him success as he set out once more for Sydney.[27] There was an interesting Hibernian tinge to the Hebraic farewell, perhaps because of the background of many of Cohen's customers. His chair was adorned with the motto 'Auld Lang Syne', and the walls were ornamented by a large green flag with the Irish harp hanging above the words 'Erin go Bragh', the inscription 'Maitland's Friend', and the sign 'Success Attend Him!' It is thought to have been Simeon J. Cohen, an amateur actor, who immortalised his brother's adventures in a popular ballad entitled 'Billy Barlow, An Old Hand's Chaunt' first published in the *Maitland Mercury and Hunter River General Advertiser* on 18 May 1844 and clearly containing the sad story of his brother's colonial career:

> The interest was due, and as
> I couldn't pay, you see, sir,
> They sold the farm the other day,
> To pay the mortgage, sir.
> So after twenty years have past
> With all my pains and toiling,
> I'm left without a stick at last,
> 'to keep the pot a-boiling.'
> So thus you see we've floored at last
> By over speculation—
> With discounts, auction companies
> And Steamboat Navigation
> And once more hard work we'll go
> And forward we will creep yet,
> And when we get some cash again
> We'll know the way to keep it
> So, if the truth you'd understand
> If wisdom you'd discover
> Take warning by the oldest hand
> Upon the Hunter River.[28]

The *Sydney Morning Herald* of 23 July 1844 reported that Cohen had returned to Sydney to become the publican of the Saracen's Head, a hotel and coffee-house near the centre of the town. Later he became a Customs House agent. He continued to take an active role in the life of the synagogue. He argued forcibly for State aid, he belonged to the committee that compiled the congregation's first history and finally, in 1859, he was embroiled in the creation of a secessionist synagogue. It was a move accompanied by great bitterness and it ended in his dismissal as a 'perpetual member' from the York Street Synagogue which he had helped to build and create.[29]

P. J. Cohen died, a poor man, on 13 November 1864. His last years had been spent peacefully and happily as manager of the Hunter River New Steam Navigation Co., and when he died the *Sydney Morning Herald* of 15 November reported that flags on the Sydney waterfront flew at half-mast. He left ten surviving children, several of whom became leaders of Sydney's Jewish community in the latter part of the nineteenth century and the first part of the twentieth. The prayer book and Bible that he used in the first regular Jewish services of worship in Australia is preserved in the Mitchell Library in Sydney.

Curiously, Walter Levi's few years in Australia brought to New South Wales a young capitalist, Michael Hyam, who was of a very different class. Perhaps his dreams were not as grandiose as those of Phillips, Montefiore and Cohen, but he may have been made of sterner stuff. Certainly he was almost the only one of the early Jewish

settlers who benefited by free settlement in Australia. A 28-year-old shoemaker, he sailed from London with a
large consignment of general goods for
Levi and impressive personal recommendations from the Chancellor of the
Duchy of Lancaster and from Horace
Twiss, the senior civil servant at the
Colonial Secretary's Office.[30]

Hyam arrived in December 1828
to be told the shattering news that
Walter Levi had died only a few months
before. The young migrant was
stranded with merchandise worth fifteen hundred pounds that had been
ordered by the dead merchant for a
market about which Hyam knew nothing.[31] Fortunately the little Jewish community rallied to his side. Michael
Phillips, the executor of Levi's will,
quickly and helpfully declared that the
consignment belonged to Hyam, and
the auctioneers Vaiben and Emanuel
Solomon disposed of the goods on his
behalf at a most respectable price.

As Hyam overcame the unfamiliar
problems of trade in the colony he also

*Michael Hyam. A maker of boots and shoes, Hyam had
the temerity to come free to the colony with a
considerable sum of money, and dared to ask for a land
grant. Far from impressed, Governor Darling wrote that
he was 'a perfect Jew'.*

turned to the task of 'establishing a respectable Boots and Shoe warehouse' and asked
for government assistance.[32] At the same time he advertised in the *Sydney Gazette* of
27 January 1829 to declare that 'any gentleman wishing for a responsible manager
may meet with a person of the highest respectability and extensive knowledge of
both in [sic] agriculture and affairs and accounts'. It was a fanciful self-description,
as the next four years were to show.

Armed with capital provided by the sale of the consigned goods, Hyam applied
to Governor Darling for a First Class Land Grant. Darling was not pleased, and in a
scathing letter to Under Secretary Twiss characterised Hyam as a 'perfect Jew' because
he had 'the ingenuity', though a shoemaker, 'in qualifying himself to become a man
of landed estate'. The Governor believed that people of this class 'should confine
themselves to their proper calling and defer becoming landed proprietors until they
have done making shoes and selling stockings'.[33]

Nevertheless, Hyam's request was brought before the Land Board, which recommended his application. Reluctantly Darling relented, and an order was made out for
a grant of 1280 acres at Minnamurra near Kiama in the Division of Illawarra, about
sixty-five miles south of Sydney. The 'ingenious' shoemaker ingenuously refused the

offer. Hyam notified the Governor that he would prefer another section of land as he 'had been informed that the country in which he received that grant is not adapted for the growth of wool which I intended turning my whole attention to'. Fortunately for Hyam his complaint was rejected, because the grant proved to be a valuable source of Australian cedar timber. But, as Governor Darling wrote to England, his direst predictions had come true because 'in consequence of the grant to the shoe-maker Hyam, an Irish tailor named Flanagan had applied to become a landholder'. It is obvious that to this English gentleman of the old school the idea that Jews and Catholics could become landholders was anathema.[34]

Despite his new status as a landowner, Hyam remained in the more familiar urban environment of Sydney. But, like Cohen and the Spyers at the same time, he appeared to be quite out of his depth. On 7 April 1832 the Monitor reported that Michael Hyam was an inmate of the Debtors' Prison. He had been ruined by the speculative purchase of the cake and confectionery shop of John Moses in George Street, by a robbery, and by his total neglect of basic book-keeping procedures. The four convict servants assigned to Hyam to work on his property, which he had named Sarah's Valley in honour of his mother, were withdrawn as a token of the Governor's disapproval at both his bankruptcy and his failure to leave Sydney and to settle in the country.[35]

No doubt Governor Darling felt a certain satisfaction in reports of the chaotic state of affairs at Sarah's Valley. Hyam had established a store on his property and illegally stocked it with liquor. He had hired labourers and sawyers to cut the cedar and transport the logs by bullock teams to Kiama where it was shipped to Sydney, but most of these men were rough and unmanageable former convicts and Hyam's English-born overseer was unable to cope with them. Hyam panicked when the magistrate at Kiama failed to deal sternly enough with a group of men who broke into his store and stole a quantity of liquor, assaulted the overseer and his wife, and threatened the life of their employer. Hyam implored 'the Governor's protection as his life and property are both in danger', to which Darling replied that 'his establish-ment in Illawarra required to be looked after by him'.[36]

Hyam took the hint. His commercial reputation in Sydney was damaged by his bankruptcy and so, in 1833, he personally took charge of his grant. He felled the remaining cedar, cleared his land, and began to prosper. He built a proper store and public house, which he called The Harp, employed shoemakers and cobblers, estab-lished a tannery, and formed the nucleus of the township called Jamberoo.[37] Although Hyam could not be counted as a pastoralist he was nevertheless the first free Jew to own, live on and work a rural property in New South Wales.

He found companionship in his isolated bush settlement. In 1835 he travelled to Sydney to marry Catherine Mary Broughton, a convert to Judaism, at the temporary synagogue in George Street.[38] Together they managed the inn and, once most of the timber had been removed, leased their land. Alexander Brodie Spark, a Sydney merchant, left some impressions in his diary of Hyam and his inn:

> 28.10.1837: The Jews made us as comfortable as they could, but the place is small, not very clean and very expensive. 1.11.1837: Settled our expensive bill and received from Mrs Hyams a pair of beautiful Regent Birds stuffed.[39]

LEFT: *The Ark of the York Street Synagogue, Sydney. The Ark for the scrolls of the Torah was made from Australian cedar. It is a superb example of colonial craft and is a larger version of the ark designed for the Bridge Street Synagogue in 1830.*

BELOW: *Isaac Nathan, by an unknown artist. Considered (by himself) to be the composer laureate of the colonies, he was certainly the first musician of significance to settle in Australia. His opera* Don Juan of Austria, *the first to be written and performed in Australia, was performed at Sydney in May 1847. It is a romance about two lovers who are amazed to discover that they are both descended from Jewish families in hiding from the Inquisition.*

ABOVE LEFT: Rosetta Joseph, née Nathan. Rosetta Nathan was born in London in 1800, the daughter of Henry Lyon Nathan who had been transported to Australia in 1794. In 1830 she travelled to Australia in order to marry her first cousin, Moses Joseph. She could well be called the mother of Australasian Jewry. Her relatives founded and led congregations in Sydney, Melbourne, Hobart Town, Wellington and Auckland.

ABOVE RIGHT: Moses Joseph. Australia's first legally sanctioned Jewish marriage was of convict Moses Joseph and Rosetta Nathan on 30 January 1830. Joseph became a member of the Bridge Street Synagogue in 1837 and was president from 1840 to 1848, when the York Street Synagogue was built. He amassed a fortune during the gold rush as a licensed gold buyer.

LEFT: Phillip Joseph Cohen. Cohen officiated at Sydney's first public Passover Seder in 1829. He boasted that he had inaugurated Jewish worship in Australia—a claim that was not strictly true. Nevertheless, his Pentateuch is still cherished by the Great Synagogue and his portrait is kept in a place of honour.

BELOW: Plan of the Jewish Section of the Devonshire Street Cemetery in Sydney.

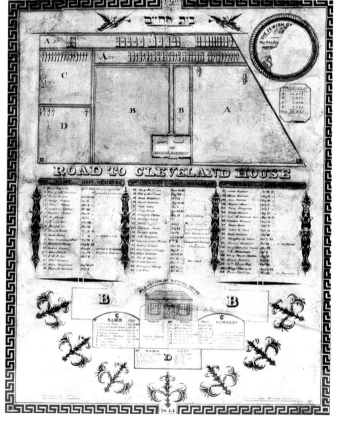

'Synagogue, York Street', watercolour by Joseph Fowles, 1845 (from his Sydney in 1848, p. 66). 'At length the Hebrews became so numerous and respectable a portion of the community, that it was thought necessary to erect a new synagogue, subscription lists were opened and to which many names, belonging to various denominations of Christians were added, displaying a liberality rarely to be met with even in England . . . and the present chaste and classic edifice . . . was erected.'

Hyam sold his land in 1841, a process marked by a fierce battle with a Dr Alley who had originally leased Hyam's farm at Illawarra and then gone bankrupt. Bitterly Alley alleged he had been 'a near neighbour to the daily scenes of drunkenness and vice at Hyam's House when one of my own free servants and day labourers have been artfully seduced from their propriety by Hyam'. Hyam booked his passage to England, hoping to have all his purchase money paid over before leaving, but the deal collapsed when the purchaser, Captain William Wilson, lost several of his ships in a storm, and was forced to forfeit Hyam's deposit.[40]

Captain Wilson's misfortune was Michael Hyam's good luck. He had to cancel his passage to England, and later learned that the ship upon which he was booked had been lost at sea with no survivors. Three years later Hyam's property was advertised for sale in the *Sydney Morning Herald* of 29 September 1844. It included one hundred fenced acres that were cleared and partly cultivated, a farmhouse of thirteen rooms, a large store, stockyard, piggeries, a good tanyard and many smaller buildings. By the time Hyam sold the farm, in 1846, prosperity had begun to return to the colony and he obtained a good price. He moved to Kiama, built a racecourse, and raced his own horses at Kiama, Wollongong and Dapto. In 1847 he moved to Shoalhaven and established a hotel. He built a store at Greenhills and a hall at Terara. When Michael Hyam died at Nowra on 3 September 1878 at seventy-nine, he was survived by five sons and three daughters. One branch of the family remained Jewish. The descendants of his daughter Rebecca constitute one of the oldest Jewish families in Australia. Other descendants, not Jewish any more, are still farmers in the Illawarra district.

Like Michael Hyam, many early free Jewish settlers were quite indistinguishable from their emancipist fellow-Jews. Some were closely related to the convicts, for the Old Bailey cast a long shadow and the ghetto was only one or two generations away. For example, Henry Cohen was a free settler of 1828 who prospered and whose jeweller's shop in George Street, next to Michael Hyam's boot shop, was conveniently located near the Sydney wharf. Cohen had established a branch store in Parramatta by March 1833, but on 18 June the *Sydney Gazette* reported that he had been accused of stealing a watch and had fled to Van Diemen's Land. Quite soon, Cohen was in trouble again. This time it concerned a quantity of stolen meat, and the *Colonial Times* of 7 October 1834 said he only escaped conviction because of 'defective evidence'. Evidently he learned his lesson, for he forsook the life of the town and became a farmer near Hobart Town. His grave may be seen in St John's churchyard, New Town, where he was buried in 1847.

In the mixed society of those days, which included wealthy ex-convicts and bankrupt free settlers, there were many partnerships between the fettered and the free. In 1842 a traveller in New South Wales noted:

> If an individual is known to have acquired wealth, as many hundreds have done, who originally belonged to the class of emancipists, his name upon a bill is received with as much confidence by the merchant or banker as that of any other colonist in good circumstances. The wisdom of forgetting or of abstaining from all unnecessary reference to the past circumstances of individuals has forced itself upon the minds of all.'[41]

Free family members came out to join a convict husband or father, and it sometimes happened that the relation of a free settler would arrive as a convict.

The emancipist Abraham Polack was the son of a Dutch-born painter and engraver, Solomon Polack, who became a fashionable artist in Georgian London. It was at his home in the Strand that, according to the *Monitor* of 13 April 1827, Solomon Levey was 'entertained on his first arrival with a splendid entertainment to meet Mr Rothschild and other gentlemen of the first mercantile respectability'. Abraham's brother Joel Samuel had come out to Sydney as a free settler in 1830; after running a merchant's and ship-chandler's business he travelled on to New Zealand, where he became one of the North Island's first European traders. Polack had quickly learned to speak the Maori language and, together with Joseph Barrow Montefiore, appeared as expert witnesses before the Select Committee of the House of Lords that was considering the colonisation of New Zealand. His book, *New Zealand: Being a Narrative of Travels and Adventures during a Residence in that Country between the Years 1831 and 1837*, was published in London in 1838. A second book, *Manners and Customs of the New Zealanders*, printed in 1840, helped to influence the British annexation of the country.[42]

The nephew of Abraham and Joel Polack, William Jones alias Lewis Myers, arrived in Sydney in 1831 as a convict, having been transported for picking pockets. He was an 18-year-old fishmonger, but in Australia became a carrier working between Parramatta and Sydney.[43]

And Abraham Polack's family further blurred the boundaries between bond and free when his brother-in-law David Poole, aged fifty-two, arrived in the *Sarah* in 1828 with his 27-year-old wife Elizabeth and three children. Like Montefiore, Phillips, Levi and Hyam, the Pooles belong to the earliest group of free Jewish settlers.[44] Poole was admitted as an attorney and solicitor of the King's Bench, Westminster, in 1795, and was to practise as a lawyer in the colony for seventeen years. From the beginning, he had close links with the Jewish community. Five days after his admission to the Bar of New South Wales he was nominated by Walter Levi's widow to be her proctor, and he represented Esther Johnston when she was arraigned by her sons. He became the Sydney Synagogue's solicitor, who made the formal request to the government for a grant of land and was presented with a 'handsome silver salver' for his work for the congregation. In Hobart, the *Tasmanian and Austral-Asiatic Review* of 5 March 1830 even reported that, 'Mr Poole (who, we are informed, is of the Israelite persuasion) has been offered the vacant position as Solicitor General in Sydney. Mr Poole has refused it, considering his practice as Attorney more profitable'. No Sydney paper reported this news.

Poole maintained a discreet distance from the synagogue and in the 1828 census described himself as a Protestant. He pledged fifty pounds to the synagogue building fund, but did not honour his promise and did not join as a member or seat-holder. Yet he found time and money to be an active member of many other organisations. He helped to found the Legislative Assembly, became vice-chairman of an Australian Steam Conveyance Company, and was a director of the Australian Wheat Company and the Sydney Gas Company. He was an active Freemason, and in January 1840 he became the agent in Sydney of the new settlement at Port Phillip.

His commercial interests extended to New Zealand and Tahiti—which included a fascinating family link. His wife's nephew Alexander Salmon, made trading visits to Tahiti and in 1843, at the age of twenty-three, married Princess Arii-taimai. Their daughter Marau became the wife of King Pomare V, and as such was the last Queen of Tahiti. Salmon may have travelled to Tahiti in the footsteps of Solomon Polack, a convict and probably a relative, who arrived in the Second Fleet, escaped from Sydney and was shipwrecked at Tahiti. His presence there was noted by Captain Bligh in 1792 and by a visiting missionary. David Poole's son David also spent some years in Tahiti and was given 'the public and private seal of the Queen of Tahiti'.[45]

David Poole's unsuccessful attempt at election to the Sydney Municipal

David Poole. Poole was the first Jewish member of the legal profession in Australia. In one of his earliest courtroom appearances he unsuccessfully defended Esther Johnston against her son's attempt to declare her incapable of acting reasonably.

Council was reported on 19 September 1842 by the *Australian*, which gave an account on 31 December of his invitation to be chairman at the Mayor's Dinner. In 1843 the *Colonial Observer* of 4 March reported his election as auditor for one of Sydney's municipal districts, but Poole was now an old man and anxious to go home. The economic prospects of the colony were clouded and in 1845 he sailed for England, stopping briefly in Van Diemen's Land where he and his family were induced by the very respectable Louis Nathan, President of the new Hobart Town Synagogue, to become seat-holders. It is easy to understand Poole's self-imposed separation from the Jewish community. Even after ten years of free migration to Australia, few Jews were known beyond the confines of George Street and the bustle of the Sydney market. His last mention in Australian papers was when the *Sydney Morning Herald* of 13 January 1860 reported his death in London on 31 October 1859.

Apart from Poole, the only Jew who was a member of a profession to arrive before 1850 was Mr Jacob (John) Emanuel, who arrived in 1842 as an Examined Surgeon-Dentist Brevette du Roi d'Hollande. He came from Paris, and the *Sydney Morning Herald* and the *Australian* of 21 June 1842 announced that he had obtained his diploma in Leyden and that he would work as a surgical and mechanical dentist in the manner 'as practised by the most eminent dentists in Europe'.

His sole competitor was the Jewish ex-convict Simon Lear, who had been born in Amsterdam and transported by the Devon Assizes on 5 August 1816 for fourteen years. He was described as a 'Dentist and corn operator', presumably corns on the feet, and extended his talents to officiating at some of Sydney's earliest circumcisions. He regularly hawked his services as a 'Corn operator, oculist, and dentist' in Macquarie Street, and the *Sydney Gazette* of 29 July 1820 reported that Australia's first officially constituted Medical Board had forbidden him to practise 'Surgery and Physic', which perhaps makes him the first Australian 'doctor' to be struck off the register.[46]

The Jewish community of New South Wales took an active part in the expansion of the Australian economy. Samuel Benjamin and Elias Moses, of Sydney House, George Street and of the London General Store of Windsor, announced that they could open a store at Goulburn, and so in 1837 established Australia's first retail chain-store. In the same year Montefiore & Co. notified the public that they were dispatching the First Wool Ship for London Direct. In London itself Jacob Montefiore, brother of J. B. Montefiore, became one of the directors of the Bank of Australasia. In Sydney J. B. Montefiore became an agent for the Alliance Life Assurance Company of London, of which N. M. Rothschild and Sir Moses Montefiore were directors.

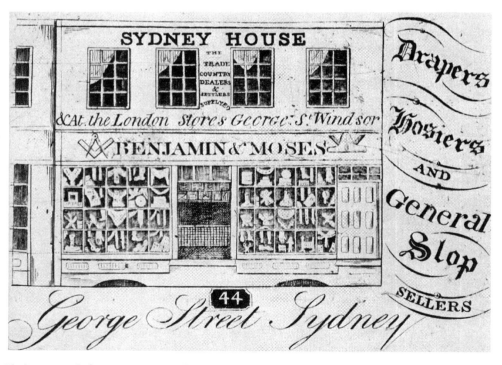

The business card of Benjamin & Moses, showing their premises in busy George Street.

By 1837 the main auctioneers in Sydney were Abraham Polack, Samuel Lyons, Isaac Simmons, Joseph Simmons and Solomon Marks. Solomon Levien, by then in Sydney, was proprietor of the popular Pulteney Hotel. His non-kosher turtle soup was a speciality of the house, and one may imagine how he impressed Sydney folk when he announced he had purchased a 'very large turtle' weighing five hundred pounds which he had patriotically reserved for His Excellency the Governor.

The Sydney *General Trade List* from 1835 to 1840 noted the larger Jewish firms and their imports from London and exports to England and the Australasian colonies. A. & S. Lyons imported lead pipe, cider, wine, clothing, saddles, groceries, pickles, billiard balls, sulphuric acid, and even furs. Montefiore, Breillat & Co. imported iron bars, blankets, liquor, sugar, glassware, pianos and carriages from London, potatoes and hay from Van Diemen's Land, and spices from Java and Sumatra. Other prominent Jewish importers were Moses Joseph, Benjamin & Co., Joseph Simmons, Abraham Polack, Abraham Cohen, Moses Lazarus and Isaac Simmons.

A number of well-known jewellers included Joel John Cohen of the Temple of Fashion, the brothers Lewis and Maurice Birstingl. There was Phillip Levy's Looking Glass and Furniture Warehouse, and Edward Daniel Cohen's City Hall of Arts, known by its two 'mechanical clocks' and the large mirror at the end of the shop. J. G. Raphael managed the Old Established Seaman's Shipping and Registry Office in Lower George Street. He was an alderman and known as a great philanthropist. In 1834, Andrew de Metz with the assistance of his six daughters founded Sydney's first boarding school for girls, where for sixty pounds per annum young ladies were taught, with the most arduous care, writing, arithmetic, geography, French, pianoforte, drawing, painting, mezzo and oriental tinting, dancing, plain and fancy needle work, and every other branch of polite female education.

As the colony flourished, speculative pressures gathered force. When drought affected the availability of grain the price of wool on the English market fell steadily. Oppressive interest rates, and the high cost of labour after Britain discontinued the transportation of convicts, brought unemployment and financial instability. A catastrophic depression loomed and one of the first firms to go under, due to the failure of the parent business in England, was that of Joseph Barrow Montefiore. In November 1841 the large non-Jewish firms of Duke & Co. and the Australian Auction Mart were declared insolvent and dragged many Jewish businesses down with them. Soon many Jews appeared as creditors in the Insolvency Court, and their inability to cover their debts led to a dismal chain reaction.

The list of insolvencies for the year 1842 demonstrates the extent of the damage done to the little Jewish community of New South Wales. The Jews on the list were: in February, Moss Marks and John Moses; in March, Lewis Cohen and Joseph Aarons; in April, Samuel Henry Cohen, John Moses, Solomon Marks, Coleman Zadok, Abraham Jacob, and Henry Barnett; in May, Samuel Cohen and Samuel Levy; in June, Baron Cohen; in July, P. J. Cohen and Solomon Levien; in September, John Barnett; in October, David Collins; in November, Phillip Meyers; and in December, Simeon J. Cohen and Alfred Levien. More than 4 per cent of the 1500 firms declared bankrupt during the 1840s were owned by Jews. As the total Jewish population of the colony was less than 0.5 per cent the impact of the depression upon the Jewish community is obvious.

By the end of 1844 it was all over and the country breathed again. Most of the merchants had obtained their discharge from the Insolvency Court and were able to start afresh. Many of the old and well-established emancipists, like Samuel Lyons, Moses Joseph and James Simmons, had proved tough enough to survive. Clever and cautious businessmen like Isaac Levey and Jacob Levi Montefiore rode the storm. By March 1845 Moses Joseph, was advertising that he wished to buy a farm capable of carrying twelve thousand sheep, while Isaac Simmons wanted to purchase tallow and hides at his City Mart. Sixteen Jews received publicans' licences for hotels in Sydney in 1845. Judah Moss Solomon was the agent for his uncle Emanuel Solomon's ship, the *Dorset*, at the South Australian Packet Office. In 1848 the Jews mustered strongly enough to put up their own candidate for the municipal elections, and in November the old emancipist James Simmons was duly elected to the Sydney Municipal Council.

The *Shipping Gazette* for 1849 reflects the upward trend. David Cohen & Co. exported 108 bales of wool, Isaac Levey together with Lewis and Saul Samuel sent 103 casks of tallow to London, and Moses Joseph sent a very large consignment of goods to his partner in Auckland, receiving in return 1000 bushels of maize and a cask of 'Curiousities'. The diversity of goods exported is illustrated by a shipment sent to Liverpool in September 1849 by Montefiore Graham & Co. It included 1 ton of pearl shell, 50 casks of coconut oil, 4 casks of sperm oil, 49 bundles of whalebone, and 216 bales of wool. On the same day the same firm sent to London 74 casks of tallow, 19 casks of coconut oil and 12 casks of sperm oil. Rum, brandy and tobacco were sent to Tahiti and Valparaiso. The 1849 list of colonial shipowners mentions four Jews of whom Moses Joseph was the most prominent. He was not only owner of the brig *Louis and Miriam* and of the barque *Rosetta Joseph* but part-owner of the barque *Australian*. J. Joseph owned the cutter *James and Amelia*, Henry Cohen owned the steamer *Thistle* and Solomon Faulk the cutter *Young Queen*.

But Jewish shipowners, exporters, auctioneers and merchants were a minority within Sydney's Jewish community, of whom most were small dealers and pedlars who worked hard to provide the basic necessities for their families and themselves. Mrs Rebecca Solomon, the daughter of Joseph Levy of Berrima, was interviewed in Sydney on her ninety-seventh birthday in March 1930. In recalling Sydney of the 1840s, the old lady said:

> In George Street there was a pillory for prisoners and we children had fun by tickling the feet of the chained prisoners with straw. The Jewish community was like one big family. The majority of the congregation was poor and all alike strove to assure fellowship in religion.

She was correct. The Jews of colonial Australia were one big family related by blood, by marriage and by memories of England.

Myer David Isaacs, a former graduate of the Liverpool Hebrew Academy, was one of the thousands of young men who tried their luck in the first decade of the Australian gold rush. In 1853, on the eve of the sixty-fifth anniversary of Australia's settlement, Isaacs wrote lyrically about his new home:

In justice I must own,
That from the cove there's not a prettier town
O tis a striking scene, when from the sea
You enter first, and view the scenery
Wrapt in a trance, you gaze with fond delight
For all at once then breaks upon the sight
The finest port in new and ancient world
When ev'ry fleet might float with sails unfurled
Thus nature form'd the scenery of the place
And in her happy step art walks apace
The Cath'lic Chapel and the Sydney school
(I should say College but my rhyme's the rule),
And Wool Mooloo and all the villas there,
And windmills, too, that court the morning air,
Smile on the cove; while in the southern sky,
The town of Sydney greets the strangers' eye.[47]

Isaacs added, 'It is indeed a beautiful place, and it appears more so to the care-worn voyager who feels that here he can have a home, like unto the homes of his native land. But for all that it is a most beautiful land, yes, even "a land flowing with milk and honey"'. He concluded with a warning: 'I would not advise any young man not having a capital—or, what is of more value, a trade, to come to Sydney. Any trade will prosper here'.

High hopes; that were hardly ever fulfilled, brought the first small band of free migrants to Australia. The success of former convicts, the tales told in London by those who had returned, and the ambitious dreams of well-born young men combined to create Australia's first Jewish community. Common experiences and hopes united them. With the exception of Poole they were all interested in agriculture and anxious to build up great landed estates. They took their place in colonial society and yet they voluntarily associated with former criminals and emancipist families in the founding of the Sydney Synagogue. The first free Jewish settlers in Australia were not fugitives escaping from persecution. They were pioneers.

The Lost Sheep

THE CHRISTIANS OF LONDON were so perturbed by the spiritual darkness of the increasing number of Jews in England that in 1807 they founded the London Society for Promoting Christianity among Jews. Men of good will would visit the synagogue in Duke's Place and emerge from the disorderly service determined to rescue the Jews from their obstinate obduracy. One such shocked Christian visitor wrote:

> Instead of the beauty of holiness, a magnificent service, and a Temple filled with immediate presence of Jehovah, they should see a rabble transacting business, making engagements, and walking to and fro in the midst of public prayers—children at their sports—every countenance, with a very few exceptions, indicating the utmost irreverence and unconcern—and their chief rabbi sitting by, and seeming to care for none of these things: though (to speak without any intentional exaggeration) the modern synagogue exhibits an appearance of very little more devotion than the Stock Exchange, or the public streets of the metropolis at noon-day.[1]

It was therefore with the very best of motives and with very little sensitivity to a totally different cultural tradition that the Church of England girded its evangelical loins to convert the stiff-necked unbelievers who lived in their midst. Collections were taken up on designated Sundays and all the corners of Europe were explored to find Jews who were prepared to lead their people to the Christian Saviour. They could hardly imagine that ten years after they began their society, one of its most notable converts would arrive in chains at Botany Bay.

Jacob Josephson was born in Breslau in 1778. After working as a silversmith in Hamburg he migrated to London, where he fell under the spell of Joseph Samuel Frey, formerly Levi, who had become a Christian non-conformist clergyman and the mainstay of the Society for Promoting Christianity among Jews. Within a few months Josephson had become a paid 'teacher of scripture' to members of the society, a part-time jeweller, and a salaried clerk at the Parish Church of Stanstead Park.[2] He knew very well that he would only hope to bring salvation to a limited number of the Jews of the East End and in 1808 he warned his well-meaning benefactors, 'It is chiefly amongst this class of Jews ie the poor and ignorant we must look for success at first and there is no doubt but afterwards, some of the rich, the wise and the mighty will listen to the joyous sound'.[3]

Even the 'poor and the ignorant' failed to be moved by Josephson's efforts, and evidently three professions were not enough to sustain his body and soul. In 1817 he and his wife Emma were detained near Oxford after paying for their hotel accommodation with a forged pound note. A search of their luggage revealed twenty more false bank-notes and a suspicious collection of glass, lace, ribbons and silver. The Oxford Quarter Sessions duly decreed that Josephson be transported to serve a sentence of fourteen years. His downfall, needless to add, was noted with glee by the Jewish opponents of his proselytising activities. A pamphlet written by a Hebrew teacher, M. Sailman of Southampton,[4] and published following his conviction alleged that Josephson was not only a dealer in forged currency, but that his light fingers had made away with the communion plate at the Parish Church of Stanstead Park. With an authoritative air, the pamphlet salaciously added that Emma Josephson had been the mistress of Joseph Frey, and that 'the circumcised and the uncircumcised were equally partakers of her favours'. Emma had certainly been previously married, and her oldest daughter, who bore the surname Wilson, very emphatically pointed out in the *Sydney Gazette* of 12 June 1823 that she was Jacob's stepchild and not his natural child.

The convict indent concerning Josephson's arrival in the *Neptune* noted that he was 'Sentenced at Oxford Quarter Session, 13 October, 1817. 14 years sentence of transportation. Born Breslau. Hebrew teacher, age 39, 5 feet 4 inches in height, dark ruddy complexion, black hair, dark eyes'.[5] His age alone would have set him aside from his convict shipmates, and obviously the officials had translated his profession of 'teaching the gospel to the Hebrews' into that of 'Hebrew teacher'.

It was his good fortune to arrive in Sydney during the latter part of Governor Macquarie's clement régime. He was freed within a year, and opened a jewellery shop at 3 Pitt Street where, the *Gazette* of 3 October 1818 noted, jewellery and silver were made and repaired, and gold and perfume bought and sold. Josephson was a shrewd and colourful businessman, whose German accent, eloquence and fondness for litigation constantly brought him before the public eye. He was granted his conditional pardon on 30 June 1820,[6] and in 1821 his wife Emma and their sons Lewis, three, and Joshua Frey, six, arrived in the *Morley*. Lewis died soon after landing, but Emma soon produced Emanuel in 1821, followed by Isaac (John) in 1824.[7]

It was both a lucrative and a risky business to maintain a jeweller's shop in the convict colony. The lawyer W. C. Wentworth was said to have recovered bad debts amounting to two thousand pounds for his client Jacob Josephson in 1823, but in 1824 the tables had turned and Josephson owed his creditors almost ten times that amount. His business affairs appeared to be in complete confusion. His readiness to strike a bargain brought him continual trouble, and in 1824 for 'the second or third time' he was brought before a Sydney court, accused of perjury. The magistrates dismissed the charge as 'cruel, malicious and infamous', though one witness later wrote of 'the difficulties of prosecuting such a man as Josephson who, by his wealth, has created many friends'.[8]

Friendly or not, his creditors did not take kindly to Josephson's declaration that he was unable to pay his debts. Arrangements were announced for sealing obligations amounting to what the *Australian* of 22 April 1824 called 'the enormous sum of between £11,000 and £12,000', and on 21 October the paper reported that his business was to be allowed to continue. At the very least this was welcome news to members of the Sydney underworld, as on 26 November 1824 Josephson's shop was robbed.[9] The victim quickly offered five hundred pounds reward. He alleged that goods worth almost twenty thousand pounds had been stolen, and that Abraham Polack, his former assigned convict clerk who had become a business rival with a shop close to his own, had pilfered stock and aided the thieves. Josephson appealed to his anxious creditors for 'patience and I will pay you all' and, casting himself into the role of a benevolent martyr, added that 'Their late requital of the kindness of a now calumniated Jew is no very honourable commentary on Christian gratitude'.[10]

As a ticket-of-leave man, Polack could not ignore Josephson's accusations, and he threw himself upon the protection of the court, declaring that he would 'a tale unfold'. The *Australian* described Josephson as 'loudly lamenting his misfortunes, weeping, wailing, wringing his hands, heaving piteous sighs and protesting his innocence', to which he responded, 'The description of me . . . may be very ludicrous and amusing but it wants one discriminatory feature, that of veracity!' But doubt also was cast upon Josephson's veracity, because Polack swore on oath that the robbery could not possibly have happened without some prior collusion as his former master always removed valuable property from his shop at night.

Unexpectedly the legal proceedings turned into a wrangle about the admissibility of evidence from a Jew. The Chief Constable affirmed that Polack had made his declaration 'as a Jew . . . with his hat on'. It was then questioned whether the volume of the Bible upon which he was sworn included the New Testament and, if so, whether this invalidated his oath. Josephson had by this time produced enough evidence to contradict Polack's accusation, and it was only by sheer luck that Polack was not found guilty of perjury and imprisoned.[11]

In his efforts to pay his debts, Josephson had expanded his retail business. The *Australian* of 4 November 1824 announced that he was selling linens, silks, gloves and guns, as well as gold and jewellery. The following year was a busy one. In June he saw his stepdaughter marry Barnett Levey at St John's in Parramatta, and in August he petitioned the Governor for mitigation of sentence in a fruitless attempt to return to Europe and recover two thousand pounds of rents allegedly owing to him on his property at 49 Ridings Mart, Hamborough. W. C. Wentworth supported his petition with a letter to testify that Josephson had repaid debts totalling fifteen thousand pounds.[12]

But by the end of the year the patience of his major creditors was exhausted. They obtained an order for the seizure of his goods, but it was discovered that most of his 'very large stock of plate and jewellery' had unaccountably vanished from his shop.[13] The fury of his creditors knew no bounds. His new step-relative-in-law, Solomon Levey, wrote provocatively of Josephson's 'unparalleled conduct' while the accused publicly lamented in the *Australian* of 24 November 1825, 'What is to become of me—a husband and father, destitute . . . who five years ago was master of thousands of pounds of my own. I have all along been governed by the perfect principle of doing unto others as I wish they should do unto me'.

A reward was offered to any person, other than Josephson, who could uncover the missing treasure, and it was unearthed almost immediately. The *Sydney Gazette* of 24 November and 26 November 1825 reported that some of the jewellery had been hidden at a tavern at Parramatta, where the innkeeper self-righteously declared, 'it is evident that Josephson was making a hiding hole of my House in a most unjustifiable manner'. The balance was found at the home of the Rev. Dr L. H. Halloran, who claimed to have been innocently misled by his friend Jacob Josephson. Although Halloran was no saint, having been sent to New South Wales for forgery, Josephson turned upon him in scorn. Likening himself to David, he appealed to 'the Almighty Disposer of Events ... to discomfort my enemies'. He accused Halloran of having made indecent proposals to his wife, and declared:

> In the memoirs of private treachery he will stand first and unrivalled ... what then became of his once well quoted decalogue! and the meekness of Christianity ... How could Jacob Josephson, an ignorant man and a foreigner, mislead a Reverend Doctor of Divinity—impossible!

It was the end of Josephson's career as a Sydney businessman, but he was able to avoid his inevitable destination for almost a year because the Debtors' Prison was so dilapidated that it was deemed unfit for use. When at last he had been lodged in prison he was visited by an apprehensive businessman who was financially embarrassed, and who asked Josephson what he had done when he had been robbed. The *Gazette* of 19 November 1827 reported the scene:

> Josephson, it is said, then asked Mr. Campbell of how much he had been robbed? He was told. Mr. Josephson, remembering what Mr. Campbell once on a time observed to him, answered 'Upon my void I don't pelieve you have been robbed of one farthing', and away Old Croesus walked. This alleged visit and reported retort, are in every mouth in town.

In his heyday Josephson had given generously to the memorial to Governor Macquarie, to the building of Scots Church and the first Roman Catholic chapel, to the Bible Society of New South Wales, to the Benevolent Society and to the Public Free Grammar School. As one of the trustees of the new Wesleyan chapel in 1821, he earnestly asked for financial aid from the government 'that the common cause of our Lord Jesus Christ may increasingly prosper'.[14]

When Josephson's son-in-law Barnett Levey died, the old man moved to Sydney to protect the interests of his stepdaughter. Time had not dimmed his taste for unsuccessful litigation. In 1831 he was instrumental in causing the local clergyman to be dismissed by intervening in a quarrel about money between the vicar and the magistrate. The vicar found him an unwelcome ally, because by taking his side Josephson destroyed his credibility. In 1838 he appeared in court on behalf of Mrs Levey, the manageress of the Theatre Royal, in a foredoomed attempt to prevent her actors accepting roles at a new, rival theatre, and he also failed in a libel suit against Abraham Cohen the printer of the *Australian*. As a result of all this the *Sydney Gazette* wrote that he was 'wealthy son of Abraham' who seemed 'libel mad'.[15]

Upon his release from prison Josephson retired to Penrith, where he opened an inn at Emu Ford and prospered. There is no doubt that he took his religious faith seriously. Two itinerant English Quakers who encountered him at Penrith recalled:

> a Jew, professing Christianity, the father-in-law of the landlord of the inn, told us, that, as we had come among them to preach the gospel, we would be free of all charges. We acknowledged his kindness and explained how our expenses were paid, to which he replied he hoped we would not debar him from this privilege.[16]

Jacob Josephson died at the age of seventy-two on 6 December 1845, the year in which Sydney's York Street Synagogue was opened. Though he was to be buried in the churchyard of St Peter's he is listed as having given the generous sum of £10 5s to the synagogue's building fund.

Donors to the synagogue included Uriah Moses of Windsor, who gave £10. Moses was one of Windsor's oldest inhabitants, having arrived in New South Wales in 1798 and settled in the town as a small landowner and farmer and later as a general dealer and baker. He had grown up in Petticoat Lane, where he worked in his mother's glass shop, but he was caught putting his trade to poor use by cutting out the glass in the window of a nearby draper's shop and stealing its stock. Still a teenager, he was sent to Australia for life, but never forgot his Jewishness. During his years in Windsor he was associated with both Abraham Elias and John Moses and in 1830, at the age of fifty, he married Ann Daly, the 21-year-old assigned servant-girl of his friend Abraham Elias, at St Matthew's, Windsor.[17] They had twelve children, nine of whom survived and, presumably because Ann was a Christian, they were all baptised and brought up in that faith. Some of them, particularly Henry Moses, were to become leading figures in the commercial life of New South Wales. Henry, who was born on 6 November 1832, became a director of the Commercial Bank, the Commercial Union Assurance Company and the Perpetual Trustee Company, and the owner of numerous rural and city properties before his death in 1926.

Joshua Frey Josephson, charcoal drawing by Charles Rodius. The son of Jacob Josephson and Emma (née Wilson) began public life as a child musical prodigy in entertainments produced by Barnett Levey. Josephson grew up to become Mayor of Sydney, a member of the Legislative Assembly, a judge, a company director and a pastoralist!

When at the age of sixty-nine Uriah Moses took to his bed for the last time, his Christian family felt that their Jewish husband and father should be baptised. They asked their Anglican minister to perform the rites but the minister was uneasy. After all, the old man had lived his whole life as a Jew, had kept in touch with his Jewish friends, and did not know a word of the catechism. The family's reassurances that Uriah wished to be baptised sounded hollow, though it must be presumed that they were given in good faith because one may hardly baptise an adult against his will unless he is in *extremis*, and Uriah was not to die for another two or three weeks. The vicar wrote to his superior, Bishop W. G. Broughton, who gave the eager advice: 'Should our fallible judgement, after our best efforts to discern the truth, be misled, we may humbly hope that He will not lay it to our charge'.[18] So Uriah was baptised on 24 November 1847, and departed this life on 5 December. His wife remarried on 4 March 1869 to 'M. James Powell, a Gentleman at Randwick'.

Christianity's most respectable convert in colonial Australia was undoubtedly the Rev. Mr Frederick Mayers, who arrived in Van Diemen's Land in 1837 and went to Hamilton to become a chaplain. The *Hobart Town Courier* of 20 January 1837 recorded:

> We had the pleasure of hearing the Rev. Mr Mayers on Tuesday last and were highly gratified with the ease of his delivery and perspicacity of his discourse . . . gratification is experienced, in listening to arguments in favour of Christianity from the mouth of a converted member of the Jewish faith, combating against his own national prejudices and convinced of the truth of the evidences in favour of the Gospel.

Three years later Mr Mayers had left for home, afflicted by ill health and oppressed by his small stipend.[19]

Less edifying, but far more colourful, are the stories of the convicts Samuel Hyams and Mark Salom of Launceston, both of whom became Christians. Sam Hyams started off badly and became worse before he got better, so that eventually he was described as 'one of the lowest and most depraved old hands' by the Rev. A. Stackhouse in a pamphlet published in Tasmania in 1859 and entitled *Darkness Made Light: The Story of Old Sam the Christian Jew* by the Secretary of the *Tasmanian Auxiliary to the London Society for Promoting Christianity amongst the Jews*.

Sam Hyams picked a pocket in the crowded gallery of the Drury Lane Theatre on 17 October 1807, by deftly unbuttoning a man's waistcoat as he pushed against him and extracting over seven pounds in cash. The victim later explained during Sam's trial at the Old Bailey that he dared not complain because 'there was a parcel of Jews there', but he went outside and called a constable. Sam defended himself by pleading to be 'totally innocent and ignorant' of the charge, and with great sangfroid declared, 'I feel inward satisfaction that my fate is to be decided by a British jury; I shall now throw myself on the mercy of the court'. Profoundly unimpressed, the jury found him guilty and the 17-year-old pickpocket was sentenced to fourteen years transportation to Van Diemen's Land,[20] where he arrived on the *Indian* in 1809.

Illiterate, and incapable of keeping out of trouble, Sam soon ran up a long police record both in Launceston and in Melbourne, where he was one of the earliest settlers and worked as John Batman's servant. Later he claimed to have sheared and shaved William Buckley, the 'wild white man', for which he was rewarded with a bottle of brandy. 'It is my duty to state his character is of the worst description', states one of the police reports concerning his many arrests for such transgressions as selling liquor without a licence, harbouring runaway convicts and dealing in stolen goods. His most complicated case concerned a stolen pig, but he was discharged because apparently it had attached itself to his own herd.[21] In his old age he married a woman who introduced him to the New Testament and this, combined with what the Rev. A. Stackhouse described as 'strange notions about certain dreams and visions', brought him to the baptismal font. Until his death in December 1858 he was supported by a small stipend from the church and by a hawker's licence, and with their aid he roamed Launceston collecting money for a Mission to the Jews.

His fellow-apostate, Mark Salom, was very different. He had been a sailor and had lived in Australia until he returned to England, ran foul of the law, and on 1 February 1841 was sentenced to seven years transportation. He arrived at Hobart Town aboard the *Elphinstone* in 1842, and on 4 February 1842 was granted a Certificate of Freedom with remarkable rapidity. Perhaps it had been achieved by the same self-confidence with which, in 1834, during his first stay in Launceston, he had hired a theatre and sold tickets at seven and sixpence each for 'An Entertainment'. When every seat was occupied he walked on to the stage and began to sing 'Bath bricks a penny a lump', which effectively emptied the place and left him to pocket the proceeds.[22]

Once free, Salom turned to the Hobart Synagogue for financial help, and when this was refused he joined the Christian church. He became a hawker in Launceston, where in the words of a local magistrate 'he had rendered himself obnoxious to the lower members of the Jewish persuasion . . . no time is lost in reviling and taunting [him] as he passes along the streets'. In 1847 he successfully prosecuted a Jew for saying to him, 'You B———y, I suppose you're looking after more "shofel pitchers" [passers of bad money]'.[23]

Baptisms performed on children by force or by stealth were a grave threat to Jewish life in the centuries before our own. In 1817 an armed detachment sent by the Archbishop of Ferrara wrested a 5-year-old Jewish girl from the arms of her family because she had been secretly baptised by her nurse as an infant. In 1838 in the same city the young brother of a new priest was forcibly dragged from his home to be baptised. In 1858 the 6-year-old son of a well-to-do physician in Bologna was abducted by the church because of an infant baptism. World-wide protests failed to bring the boy back to his parents, and the kidnapped child grew up to become a priest.

So it is easy to imagine the consternation of the Jewish community in Hobart Town in 1846 at the news that Mary Ann Lazarus had been baptised by a government chaplain against the consent of her parents. Fortunately for the community, and for the girl's parents, Lieutenant Governor Sir Eardley Wilmot was as annoyed as they were, and an Australian battle for a girl's soul was averted.

Mary Ann Lazarus was one of six children. Her father, Henry Lazarus, was a watchmaker who in May 1833 had been sentenced in Hobart Town to life imprisonment for attempting to defraud Judah Solomon of £145 by the use of a forged bill of exchange.[24] Faced with the problem of supporting the family, his wife Hannah placed two of her daughters in the Queen's Orphan School where the oldest, Mary Ann, began to shine as the star of the chaplain's lessons in religious instruction. In July 1846 the 14-year-old girl, who had been assigned outside the institution to work as a servant, approached the chaplain, the Rev. Mr Forster, and begged to be baptised. The ceremony was performed on the following Sunday.

Her mother was horrified. To excel at religious instruction was praiseworthy and quite acceptable, but to be baptised was to defy her family and her past. She asked the chaplain who had authorised him to convert her child, and whether he had received her sanction. He replied, 'Oh, certainly not. I know you would not have given it'. In the mother's own words:

> I then asked him again, who had authorised him to do so. When he said 'I had the authority of my Bishop' I replied that he was not my Bishop nor had he anything to do with me or my children. He seemed to treat the matter very coolly. I then said, do not think for a moment, Mr Foster, that I will allow this to pass unnoticed. He replied 'Very well. I hold myself responsible. There is no one to blame but me'. I told him I would see my daughter die or kill her rather than she should change her religion. Mr Foster then said I should commit a great sin so doing but I replied I should not commit so great a sin as he had by causing her to rebel against her parents.

It was a debatable point of view, but the tone of the confrontation is significant. The fact that the whole matter was immediately laid before the Lieutenant Governor of the colony by Louis Nathan, the very respectable president of the Hobart Town Synagogue, is strong evidence of a feeling of security on the part of the colonial Jewish community, even in the face of the church. Indeed Nathan wrote of a 'flagrant breach of the principles of toleration . . . a violation of the rights of conscience'.

The Lieutenant Governor angrily protested to the Bishop of Tasmania, and asked him to investigate the complaint and to take any action considered necessary. This in turn produced a sharp retort from the Bishop, stating that the letter trespassed upon the bounds of ecclesiastical authority, although he admitted that the baptism had been performed. The Lieutenant Governor complained to London about the 'unfortunate meddling' of the chaplain, and to the synagogue's president he communicated his 'deep regret' about an event which he felt was 'most improper'.

The Hobart Town Hebrew Congregation provided an epilogue to the story by sending copies of all the relevant correspondence to Sir Moses Montefiore in London to press their case at Whitehall. The answer Sir Moses received from Downing Street was not nearly as satisfactory as the Australian response to the event. Officialdom at home took the side of the Bishop and sarcastically wrote to Sir Moses, 'Lord Grey anticipates your concurrence in his own opinion that [the report of the Bishop] absolves the officiating minister, and the Bishop from all just reproach for their conduct'.

Christian evangelical attempts to capture the Jews was a persistent feature of Australian colonial life. On 16 December 1841 the long sermon given by the Moderator of the Church of Scotland addressed to 'the Children of Israel in all the lands of their

Dispersion!' was reprinted in the *Port Phillip Patriot*. The Moderator asked, 'What avails you *Tallith* or *Tsistsith*—to what purpose your *Tephillin* or *Mezuzoth*? We wish we could persuade you to read and examine the New Testament for yourselves'.

Five years later the same newspaper defended the proposal to admit Jews to the British parliament and attacked opposition by the Anglican bishops in the House of Lords: 'Bigotry must have its nest egg ... Deprived of the power of burning and hanging heretics the Bishops are the last lurch of intolerance. Alas for the Bishop of London's nest egg. It is already addled; it will soon be crushed'.[25]

The other side of the conversion story came from the Jewish community itself. With few women and scores of single men, most of whom had grown up in the isolated world of the ghetto, there were deep and powerful emotional bonds of loyalty that could not be easily broken. From the second Jewish wedding in Australia in 1833[26] to the consolidation of the Jewish communities in the late 1840s, the marriage canopy brought many non-Jewish women into the Jewish faith. Though nearly all the early Jewish convicts married in church and saw their children baptised, some brought their families with them to the synagogue when the first Jewish congregations were formed. These moves by no means increased or even maintained the size of the infant Jewish communities, but they were a partial recognition that intermarriage in Australia had been almost inevitable. Once the Jewish population had grown and there were eligible women within the community, the synagogues, almost automatically, began actively to discourage the acceptance of proselytes to Judaism in order to protect their own families from assimilation.

Van Diemen's Land

THE QUAINT EGYPTIAN FAÇADE of the Hobart Synagogue masks one of Australian Jewry's oldest buildings. Like some transposed and unfinished pyramid its stone walls and its windows slope inwards in faithful imitation of the pattern first set by the Sydney Synagogue and reproduced by Jewish congregations throughout the Australian colonies. Within its walls, darkened cedar timber, curved steps and wrought iron railings contrast curiously with Egyptian columns and carved lotus petals and palm leaves. An elegant and un-Egyptian chandelier hangs perilously low over the reading desk. Old wooden honour boards and marble plaques record the names of those who have contributed to the synagogue from its earliest years. The back of each seat still clearly shows the number inscribed upon it when the synagogue was dedicated in 1845. Beside the doors at the rear of the building, hidden beneath the women's gallery, are three rows of simple wooden benches set aside for the convicts and for the poor. It is one of the few Jewish places of worship in the world with seats set aside for convicts—if indeed there is any other.

Tasmania's story began in 1642 when Captain Abel Janszoon Tasman first charted part of the island's mountainous southern coast and named it Van Diemen's Land in honour of Anthony Van Diemen, Governor-General of the Dutch East Indies. Van Diemen's Land became a separate colony for administrative purposes in 1825. The transportation of convicts to the island ended in 1853, and when responsible government was granted the citizens seized the opportunity on 26 November 1855 to change the name to Tasmania. They had no desire to continue their association, by name and reputation at least, with one of the most dreaded names of the convict era.

The first European settlement was early in the nineteenth century, after the naval and military men of Sydney realised that the southern flank of Australia needed protection from French ambition and territorial expansion. This concern heightened when ships of a French geographic expedition lingered in waters that could become a strategic barrier in the event of an unwelcome confrontation.

Sydney's alarm was echoed in London, and the British government reacted with uncharacteristic speed by dispatching two ships under the command of Captain David Collins to establish an outpost in the region. After an unsuccessful attempt to settle near present-day Sorrento, sixty miles from the future site of Melbourne, the expedition sailed on to Van Diemen's Land to join a small detachment of exiles and soldiers who had been sent from Sydney to secure the island from foreign intrusion.

On the Derwent River, beside a magnificent deep-water harbour and in the shadow of the densely timbered Mount Wellington, the permanent settlement of Hobart Town began. The name continued in use until 1881, when it was officially shortened to Hobart. In 1807 the authorities in Sydney began to reinforce the island population by transferring emancipists and their families from the isolated, and uneconomic, Pacific outpost of Norfolk Island to the broader and more promising pastures of Van Diemen's Land.

Among these reluctant pioneers was Bernard Walford, who had arrived on the third fleet of transports to New South Wales. He joined the Jewish prisoners Samuel Jacobs, Henry Lazarus, Michael Michaels and Joseph Raphael, and 'the convict overseer' Joseph Meyers, who had reached Van Diemen's Land in 1804 after the abortive settlement near Melbourne. Bernard Walford was born in Vienna and went to London as an adult, so his foreign accent would have singled him out and kept the colony conscious of his origins. In Petticoat Lane, in 1788, he stole a basket of laundry and for his crime was sent out to Australia for life. He served part of his sentence on Norfolk Island, where he married Jane Molloy and fathered a fine brood of children and became a farmer. By 1807 he was the owner of a forty acre property on the island, and when he was transferred to Van Diemen's Land he was compensated by a grant of ninety acres with which to make a fresh start.[1]

His new farm sustained his family for ten years, after which he settled in Hobart Town to work briefly as a baker and then for eight years as a tavern keeper.[2] He was the only one of the early Jewish arrivals to care deeply enough about his faith to arrange a Jewish funeral for himself, and in June 1828, three months before his death, the *Hobart Town Courier* wrote that he had 'distinguished himself in obtaining a place of rest for all those who depart this life in the faith of the synagogue'. While his life ebbed he wrote to Lieutenant Governor Sir George Arthur piously offering him his 'heartfelt thanks' and promising to send word of his kindness 'to our revered and highly respected Priest in England. Myself, my brethren, and I flatter myself, my children, after me, will continue to hold the same respect for your Excellency, as you so justly deserve'.[3] With piety, tact and obsequious tolerance he mentioned that he was even 'more thankful' that the grant had been sanctioned by 'the highest authority of the Church of England resident in the colonies'. His very simple, barely legible tombstone lies in the Hobart cemetery, beside the Derwent River. It is the earliest relic of Jewish life in Van Diemen's Land.

When Walford died there were barely one hundred Jews in the whole island colony. All had come in chains and most were still serving their sentences. None was married to a Jew. There were no Jewish children other than those sent out as prisoners. Walford clearly believed that his own children would regard themselves as Jews despite his wife's Irish name and presumably Christian faith. Indeed when Walford's oldest son lay dying in 1846, he vainly begged the newly organised synagogue for permission to be buried as a Jew, and to be granted a grave in the cemetery that had been secured by his father.[4] Another son, Benjamin Walford, married the daughter of the wealthy merchant Joseph Solomon of Launceston. The marriage was viewed with horror by Joseph, who had high social pretensions and who almost disinherited his daughter as a result.[5]

During the first unhappy quarter-century of the history of Van Diemen's Land, the records show that 125 Jewish convicts, of whom 7 were women, were sent to the island. Only 4 men arrived as free settlers. As in New South Wales, free immigration did not expand until the 1830s but, even then, fewer than 130 free Jewish settlers arrived between 1830 and 1850. Unlike New South Wales, the number of convicts landed in Van Diemen's Land during this period equalled that of free migrants; 160 Jewish convicts were sent to the island in those twenty years.

A census of the island in 1842 listed 259 Jews out of a total population of 42 000. Most of the Jews were male shopkeepers and petty tradesmen, which must have made a strong impression in a community in which, the same census notes, there were only 802 shopkeepers. This means that one shop in four was owned by a Jew, and this proportion would have been very much higher in the main shopping streets of Hobart and Launceston, the towns in which most of the Jews lived.

As in New South Wales, the basic ingredients for a community were missing. There were no Jewish families on the island before 1830, and police dossiers recording the careers of 75 000 convicts sent to Van Diemen's Land during its years as a penal colony tell many sad, brutal, though occasionally heroic, stories. There were very few happy endings. Towards the end of the convict period the London papers could still write rhapsodically of the island's 'rippling streams and murmuring rills, verdant meads and flowering dales' but acknowledge that it was also 'the compulsory retreat of vanished exiles, a nursery of villainy, a hot bed of iniquity, a stronghold of the devil, a breathing hole of hell, the continued scene of black, foul and brutal murder'.[6]

Among the first one hundred Jews, less than one in six met with some measure of commercial success or rehabilitation following his period of servitude. Five men escaped from custody and were never recaptured, seven died in gaol, and at least fifteen spent more than twenty years in gaol. Of the four women, three had been prostitutes and none appears to have been rehabilitated. On the credit side there were four successful merchants, six tavern-keepers, and eight who scraped together enough money to buy a licence and become hawkers and pedlars. It is difficult to imagine a less viable community. They came to the colony with no money and few gained their freedom.

Few trades or skills were represented. The grim, handwritten Black Books which carefully set out the punishments and pardons of the Van Diemen's Land convicts also take care to describe the background and career of each prisoner. As numbers rose, the need to maintain accurate and detailed records increased. The dossiers record that among the first 112 Jewish prisoners there were nine pedlars and old-clothes men, six street-sellers, three shoemakers, three tailors, two hatters, two butchers and three watchmakers and jewellers. There was one musician, a pen-cutter, a porter, a glass-cutter, a cigar-maker, and a fishmonger. Some came as children, and to trace their lives is to see vividly the system of conviction, transportation, imprisonment, rehabilitation, and sometimes further imprisonment. These children bring the pages of the convict records to life, because their destinies were the most deeply affected by the penal system.

Convict punishment, from the Cornwell Chronicle (Launceston), 9 September 1837. This is a rare printed critical comment on the convict system. The hangman standing on the hill exclaims, 'Its complete butchery but I must need to do it I suppose'. An official in a top hat observes, 'I will give the dammed wretched 100 lashes and I will send him to be hanged'.

Philip Levi was only sixteen in 1822, when he was sent from the Old Bailey to Australia for life for having stolen a watch from the wife of a Jewish merchant in the Minories.[7] At the time of the trial he was a spectacle-maker. He was 5 feet 3 inches tall and had brown hair, dark-grey eyes and a scar on his left cheek-bone. In his first four years in Van Diemen's Land he received a total of 225 lashes for neglect of duty and for theft. In 1830, brutalised and bestial, he was appointed flagellator at the prisoners barracks in Hobart Town, but was removed from his terrible calling because of 'improper and violent conduct at the Police Office'. In 1834 he was found guilty of trying to obtain eight shillings and six pence by false pretences, and was sent to the chain gang. In his despair he induced 'others to become unruly', and two more years on the chain gang were decreed after which he was to be sent to the dread prison at Port Arthur, 'there to undergo severe discipline'. He collected an additional three-and-a-half years in gaol sentences, 150 lashes, and numerous minor punishments for 'absconding', 'pilfering meat', 'stirring up trouble', 'pilfering copper', and 'conniving at a fellow prisoner having his irons broken'.

At last he was freed, but within a year he was back in chains for twelve months, convicted for 'indecent exposure'. Four years later he was fettered again, this time for

The penitentiary at Port Arthur in a north-east view of the settlement, unsigned and undated pencil sketch,
c. 1854. Port Arthur became the third largest town in the colony. Penal servitude there was greatly feared and
the convicts were subject to a cruel regime and relentless isolation. It remained a prison until 1878.

stealing a cheese. It is understandable that after a life of such brutality and despair he should have ended in the New Norfolk Lunatic Asylum, where he died on 30 September 1849 at the age of forty-three.

Lyon Levy was thirteen when he was caught at a dispensary in Bishopsgate in the act of stealing a hat and some gloves. His pathetic appeal to the judge was recorded by the court stenographer: 'I beg for mercy'. It was to no avail, because in 1822 he arrived in Van Diemen's Land. It was noted in the little convict's dossier that he was 'put to learn many trades but does not appear to have the capacity'. He spent three years at the dreaded prison settlement at Macquarie Harbour, nearly 200 miles from Hobart Town in the wild south-west of the island, and then was returned to Hobart Town, where he 'most daringly' tried to steal 338 yards of printed cotton from the window of a shop in the main street of the town on 15 February 1826. During 1826 and 1827 he received no less than 300 lashes for a whole miscellany of minor crimes. His next period of freedom was tragically cut short by a ten year prison sentence for sodomy. Eight years later he returned to Hobart Town only to gather more convictions for drunkenness, larceny and neglect of duty. The last entry on his pitiful record was made in 1862 from prison, where he was listed as an 'Invalid, Port Arthur, Chronic Ophthalmia'. At fifty-seven, he had been a convict for most of his life.[8]

Not all the children's stories ended so unhappily. Emanuel Levy was a 16-year-old member of a street gang that robbed a little boy of his timepiece as he came home from school along Hackney Road.[9] When the 9-year-old victim stood in the witness box at the Old Bailey, he vividly presented enough evidence to send his assailant to Van Diemen's Land for life: 'They crowded me up, they pushed me, they got me between one another, and I was standing between them, they pushed against me and squeezed me, they crowded me up and said stop young fellow, then they snatched at the watch and broke the chain'.

Levy reached Van Diemen's Land in 1812. After several years in the chain gangs and at least 150 lashes later, he escaped from custody and was rumoured to have become a bushranger. The *Hobart Town Gazette* published his description as 'A Jew about 5 feet 4 inches high, large full eyes and bow legged', and only later was it announced that he was merely 'absent without leave' and had returned to captivity. By 1820 Levy had settled on a thirty acre farm in the Tasmanian county of Ormaigh, where he ended his days in peace. The last entries in his dossier record an isolated reprimand received in 1821 for appearing dirty at church, and a conviction in 1833 for being drunk.[10]

Fate dealt even more gently with Abraham Rheuben, another 16-year-old. A tailor's apprentice and a pickpocket from Whitechapel, he was sent to Van Diemen's Land in 1827 for having stolen one sovereign and half a crown.[11] Rheuben served his sentence with only one punishment, of twenty-five lashes, for neglect of duty and insolence as an assigned servant. He married Rosetta Marks in Hobart Town and had ten children, joined the Hobart Town Synagogue as a member in the year that it was dedicated, and rebuilt his life so successfully that in his sixties, as a respectable and wealthy merchant, he became the first Jewish alderman of the Hobart City Council. He died on 25 September 1876, aged sixty-six. In a second marriage, which was childless, he had married Sarah Abrahams in 1866. He is one of the few Jewish convicts whose descendants in Australia still belong to the Jewish faith.

Among those first arrivals in Van Diemen's Land was Michael Michaels of Sheerness whose transportation had far-reaching consequences. He claimed to have been born in Liverpool and was the son of Jonas and Esther Michaels (née Russell but born Levy). Michaels was sentenced at the Old Bailey in 1802 to transportation for life on two related counts. At the Tower Hill market in London, Michaels had offered Captain Lucas, the master of a coastal vessel, a watch for a bargain price. Having sold the watch and pocketed the money, Michaels then pretended to change his mind, took the watch back and substituted his own counterfeit shillings in return. He confessed that he had already served a year in prison for a similar offence. While in Newgate prison awaiting transportation Michaels was visited by his brother David, who had apparently been commissioned by his family to give him one guinea to help on his way into exile. Enraged by this callousness, Michaels produced a knife and ripped open his brother's stomach.

Michael Michaels sailed on the *Calcutta* and became one the first Jews to set foot in Victoria. The first free Jewish settlers in Van Diemen's Land and subsequently in Victoria owed their arrival to the story of the former convict, Michael Michaels.[12] After the abortive settlement on Port Phillip Bay had been shifted to Van Diemen's Land and further south to the Derwent River, Michaels was appointed an overseer of his fellow convicts. He became one of the earliest traders in the colony and set up in business as Hobart Town's first pawn-broker and money-lender, in Elizabeth Street. In a colony starved for cash, Michaels prospered. The 1810 muster listed him as the owner of an eighty acre farm at Cornelian Bay. In 1812, only eight years after his arrival as a convict, Michaels sold his farm and sailed for England, having appointed the very respectable Dr Bowden as his agent to collect notes of hand amounting to the very large sum of £1333. This small fortune was no mean achievement in the light of the little settlement's statistical return of 1804, which recorded that his fortune consisted of thirteen hens. Michaels would never recover the money that had been left behind. The emancipated convict was able to return to England and live at 2 Swan Street, East Smithfield, where he died in 1824. But, as we shall see, the memory of the lost treasure of Van Diemen's Land lived on.

Sheerness provides the unlikely link in a chain of improbable events that would shape the creation of the Jewish communities of both Van Diemen's Land and Victoria. The story began with Michael Michaels but leads to the mishaps and adventures of two brothers, Judah and Joseph Solomon, who dominate the early Jewish history of the colony in totally different ways.[13]

The Solomon brothers arrived in Hobart Town in 1819, with life sentences for the strange offence of 'hiring burglars to repossess stolen goods'. They were convicted of hiring thieves to steal 78 watches and other silver articles belonging to Abraham Abrahams, who was the former father-in-law of Judah's wife Esther. The brothers claimed they were merely 'reclaiming' unpaid goods. In reality the conclusion of the Napoleonic Wars had brought widespread unemployment, and a crime wave engulfed England. The Solomons had large families and they had hired men to steal from warehouses and bulk stores in the town and on the waterfront. Sheerness lay along the southern bank of the River Medway on the Isle of Sheppey, alongside the coastal towns of Gravesend, Rochester and Chatham. Charles Dickens, who grew up in the market town of Rochester with its ancient cathedral and ruined castle, recalled it in the opening of *Great Expectations*:

> Ours was the marsh country, down by the river, within, as the river wound, twenty miles of the sea . . . the dark flat wilderness beyond the churchyard, intersected with dykes and mounds and gates, with scattered cattle feeding on it was the marshes; and that the low leaden line beyond was the river; and that the distant savage lair from which the wind was rushing, was the sea . . .

The convicts were ever-present. They came ashore from the hulks in work parties, manacled and guarded. Dickens' young Pip confronts an escaped convict who will be sent to Australia: 'A fearful man, all in coarse grey, with a great iron on his leg. A man with no hat, and with broken shoes, and with an old rag tied round his head. A man who had been soaked in water, and smothered in mud, and lamed by stones, and cut by flints, and stung by nettles, and torn by briars; who limped, and shivered, and glared and growled'.

A Jewish community was established in Sheerness by 1790. Behind the wharves and sheds of the port stretched a jumble of wretched houses and shops made of mud and pebbles brought from the beach, and fir beams and weather-board salvaged from the sea, and canvas sails daubed with tar to keep the chill winds out, and all prone to devastating fires. The Jewish community, including the Solomon brothers, traded as slop-sellers and jewellers who specialised in supplying goods to the sailors of the Royal Navy. The Jews would row out to the hulks and sell fresh vegetables and old blankets and coats to the convicts, who would pay for their purchases with trinkets hidden in their deep pockets and in the lining of their clothes. The Parliamentary Select Committee on Secondary Punishments knew Sheerness as a place where thieves disposed of coins stolen on the hulks which lay offshore. The honourable members were told, 'There are a great many Jews that infest the place'.[14]

Sheerness would play a vital and disproportionate role in the history of colonial Jewish Australia. For many convict transport ships it was the last stop before the long voyage to Australia, and the Antipodes were an ever-present reality. The Solomon brothers were mature men. Judah, at thirty-eight, left behind eight children. Esther his wife was pregnant and was a niece of the wife of London's Chief Rabbi Solomon Herschell, and it may have been doubly difficult for him to obtain a divorce. Joseph, aged thirty-nine and with four children, thoughtfully divorced his wife in a Jewish religious ceremony before leaving England. Joseph was illiterate. Judah could read and write. The two men brought with them the capital sum of approximately sixty pounds with which to begin life anew.

The early advertising columns of the Hobart Town newspapers show that the two brothers prospered from the beginning. Within a year of their arrival they were granted permission to open a general store at the corner of Argyle and Liverpool streets, Hobart Town. Their fate touched the hearts of the Jewish congregation at Sheerness. Probably the elders of the community felt a twinge of remorse, because the men had been convicted upon the complaint of Abraham Abrahams, the former father-in-law of Judah Solomon's wife and an honoured member of the Jewish community, who was presumably the legitimate owner of the stolen goods. And so in 1822 the brothers received a gift of money from the Sheerness Jewish community, brought out for them by Henry Davis (Esther Solomon's brother who would marry the sister of Judah's mistress). As a result of this windfall the firm of J. & J. Solomon added jewellery and liquor to its merchandise and opened a branch store in Launceston. The historian Hamish Maxwell-Stewart has explained their *modus operandi*:

> The general store was not an end in itself but merely a means of getting access to the type of business that the Solomons operated in Sheerness (and I don't mean hiring burglars). Let me explain—the principal market for the goods sold in the Solomons' shop were settlers. The main problem that bedevilled the early colonial economy was lack of cash. The Solomons could have, like everybody else, accepted promissory notes—a form of I.O.U. which could itself be traded on. They appear, however, to prefer to be paid with a promise of wheat to be supplied at harvest time. What was the advantage to be had in amassing huge amounts of wheat? The answer is that it gave the Solomons access to the commissariat: the branch of the Government which supplied the public works convicts with their free lunch. Some idea of the scale of

this trade can be obtained when it is considered that each convict in Government employment had to be provided with a pound of flour every day of the year.[15]

Fortune smiled on the Solomon brothers in 1822. The administration changed its rules and announced that it would accept only bulk transactions of wheat, and, at almost the same time each brother was given an early ticket of leave. Joseph leaped at the opportunity to travel north and invest part of their shared capital by opening a store strategically located in Launceston. This enabled J. & J. Solomon to supply basic commodities to both the Southern and Northern Commissariat and to receive in return cash, that rarest of all colonial commodities. It is not surprising to find that the brothers were present in December 1823 when two hundred citizens gathered to subscribe two hundred Spanish dollars each to found the Bank of Van Diemen's Land which could, in turn, look after their money with reasonable security.[16] The brothers began to deal extensively in land. Five of the first 144 transactions recorded in the colony's first Registry of Deeds, for the year 1827, were made in their name. The records show that between 1821 and 1839 the Solomon brothers issued 136 writs for the recovery of more than £18 000.[17]

After eight years of close and prosperous partnership, marked only by an occasional conviction for selling liquor after licensed hours, the two men went opposite ways. Joseph gradually assumed responsibility for the northern branch of the firm and in following years opened stores in Evandale and Campbell Town.[18] Factors other than geography appear to have brought about an estrangement which ended with a formal dissolution of partnership in 1841.

As early as 1828 Joseph had begun to describe himself in legal documents as a 'Gentleman', though Judah, in the same documents, was content to be called a 'Merchant'. Ironically, Joseph's English divorce opened unexpected doors to respectability while Judah's marriage bonds brought him bitterness.

Judah built a mansion in Argyle Street in the heart of Hobart Town and, upon land which was once its garden, the Hobart Synagogue still stands. He prospered, though the Chief Police Magistrate of Hobart complained that his store and home were 'the resort of most of the pickpockets in town'. For illegally supplying liquor 'he was frequently fined—the conviction was invariably squashed by the ability of Mr S's counsel'.[19]

Apparently Judah had no desire to see his wife again, and he took his housekeeper, Elizabeth Howell, to be his mistress. In 1822 she bore him a son who in honour of Judah's partner and brother was named Joseph.[20] His Antipodean domestic arrangement was however shattered by the arrival of Esther, his true and legal wife, together with three of his legitimate children, a son-in-law and four grandchildren on the Juliet in December 1832. Esther pretended to have had no idea that Judah lived with Elizabeth Howell. The rest of the family seemed to be able to cope with this fact but Esther never would. She claimed half of his fortune and moved into his mansion, Temple House. It should be noted that there are now two Joseph Solomons in Van Diemen's land. Judah's brother in the north of the island who had married 'up' and 'out', and Judah's illegitimate son who will eventually be converted to Judaism and marry beneath the *chuppah*.

Judah Solomon's Temple House still stands in the centre of Hobart on the corner of Liverpool and Argyle Streets. The garden beside the mansion became the site for the Hobart Town synagogue.

After vainly trying to cope with two families in one house, Judah moved out of his home in Argyle Street leaving it in possession of his wife, who had written to the Lieutenant Governor and complained that Judah 'threatens to dash my brains out'. It was the first shot in what became her ten-year battle to block Judah's pardon, which would have allowed him to return to England and obtain a Jewish divorce from the appropriate rabbinical authorities. At the same time, Esther, as his legitimate wife, laid claim to half of Judah's property. Esther told the Lieutenant Governor in 1845, 'Although my husband was one of the highest in the colony as regards mere wealth he was and is one of the very lowest in morals'.[21]

It was a bitter personal battle which no doubt was made more painful when Joseph received his conditional pardon.[22] Judah ignored an order from the Lieutenant Governor to return to his wife, then suffered the humiliation of having enlisted the support of all major merchants and magistrates in Hobart Town only to see most of them withdraw when asked by the colonial authorities whether they were aware that they acted on behalf of a man who was living in sin. His support fell away. As one man asked rhetorically, 'I should be one of the last men in the Colony to lend my sanction to any such act of immorality. How could any respectable colonist admit to the Lieutenant Governor that they had known and even condoned such immoral behaviour?'[23] In despair Judah blamed his wife for his conviction, accused her of setting up business in London as a prostitute, and said that she owned a gaming-house. It was an odd allegation to make about the mother of ten children stranded by the deportation of her husband.[24]

Judah's wealth and his power as a trader enabled him, despite his wife, to play a significant role in the life of Hobart Town. He gave generously to its charities and lavishly to the synagogue. The little Jewish congregation accepted his help and he served as its treasurer in its earliest years. Both brothers and their extended family were deeply involved in the settlement of Melbourne and the founding of the Port Phillip Association that founded the township of Melbourne. When Judah died in 1856, still without his marital freedom or an official pardon, his estate was estimated to be worth almost £30 000.[25]

Joseph severed his links with his past when in 1833 he married Mrs Eliza Backhouse[26] at St John's Church, Launceston and the following year was granted a free pardon. His four children came out from England to join their prosperous father and Lion Henry Solomon, his eldest son, married in the same church in the same year. At Evandale, as a sign of his new status, he proudly built a country mansion which he named Riverview. His son-in-law Joseph Cottrell, formerly Chief Constable of Launceston, together with Judah's son-in-law Joseph, represented the family at the creation of the new settlement at Port Phillip.

Joseph died in 1851 at the age of sixty-seven, a wealthy but still illiterate citizen for whom deportation had brought great blessing.[27] Three generations later, in 1909, his brilliant young great-grandson, Albert Edgar Solomon, became Premier of the state of Tasmania. His death in office at thirty-eight cut short what promised to be one of the most brilliant Australian political careers.

In England there is no doubt that stories of their life in the colonies made a vivid impression upon the Sheerness community and upon the extended family of the Solomon brothers who were the children of a foreign-born clothes dealer named Levy. Unwilling to be branded as Jews, the Levys changed their surnames: three— Henry, John and Elizabeth—replaced Levy with the surname Davis; while Esther, George, Phillip and Michael borrowed the name of the major street in their home town of Sheerness and called themselves Russell. And so Judah's wife Esther was born Levy, became a Russell, married an Abrahams and then a Solomon! The convict dossier of the Jewish bushranger Edward Davis reveals that he was also born in Sheerness. In this tight little community, Aaron Abrahams, the brother-in-law of Judah and the son of the prosecutor of the Solomon brothers, married Michaels' niece, and by way of a dowry was told that he could collect the debts owed to Michael Michaels in Hobart Town.[28]

Thus three young men, Davis, Russell and Abraham, were the first free Jewish migrants to Van Diemen's Land. Henry Davis was the pioneer, arriving in 1822. His brother John Davis would marry Louisa, the 14-year-old daughter of Judah and Esther Solomon and his own first cousin at the Great Synagogue in London on 26 March 1826.[29] Henry Davis is a complicated character and not particularly admirable. Even though Judah Solomon's wife was his sister, he does not seem to have had the courage to warn her about Judah's extra-marital living arrangements. Davis brought with him five hundred pounds and asked the authorities for a grant of land, an application made in the usual manner to Earl Bathurst before leaving England.[30] He didn't get the land grant, because there were no secrets in Hobart Town and it must have been known that most of the money belonged to the Solomon brothers. The money was duly delivered to Judah and Joseph. On the basis of the importation of goods worth more than three hundred pounds, Davis became a landholder. He began business in Hobart Town as an auctioneer and draper, and afterwards moved to Launceston where in 1826 he opened a hotel, and immediately fell deeply into debt.[31]

Aaron Abraham arrived in Van Diemen's Land from Sheerness in 1825, and began proceedings to recover the money owed to his uncle-in-law, Michael Michaels.[32] To his dismay, he found that the debtor had died and the estate was now in the hands of the colony's autocratic chaplain and senior magistrate, Rev. Robert Knopwood, who had inherited it in good faith from Michaels' agent. Knopwood emphatically believed that the money belonged to him, and Abraham was wise enough not to argue. He turned to Davis for help in raising enough money to return to England, just as George Russell arrived in the colony without a penny to his name and the money for his passage to Australia still to be repaid.[33] Davis was now so deeply in debt that he was forced to escape to New South Wales in order to avoid his creditors. It proved to be a futile gesture. He was flung into the debtors' prison in Sydney and, in order to save his Tasmanian property, concocted the fiction that his sheep and his hotel actually belonged to Russell and Abraham.

Aaron Abraham left Van Diemen's Land for home and family in 1829.[34] George Russell became an early settler in New Zealand and one of the pioneers of the city of Auckland.[35] Henry Davis remained in Australia, and in 1823 married Hannah Howell, whose sister Elizabeth was the de facto wife of Judah Solomon. Twenty-five years later their daughter Sarah married Judah's illegitimate son Joseph at the Hobart Synagogue.[36] The disastrous business career of Henry Davis included at least two bankruptcy cases in Launceston and one in Melbourne. Sadly, the deaths of two of his daughters provided both Launceston and Melbourne with their first Jewish funerals. Davis died in Hobart Town in 1841, a broken and penniless man whose place as the first free Jewish migrant to Van Diemen's Land had long been forgotten.

The birth of a small, organised Jewish community in Van Diemen's Land brought about a series of political and personal setbacks that fortunately has no Australian parallel. Jewish participation in the public life of Van Diemen's Land was not taken for granted. The colonial administration saw no need to contribute to the spiritual well-being of a non-Christian community. Symbolically, the only boon it granted its Jewish citizens was the cemetery in Hobart in 1828.

Four years after Bernard Walford's death a request by Henry Davis for a similar grant in Launceston was rebuffed.[37] He had 'met with the misfortune of losing an infant and have been compelled from necessity to enter the Remains in a private ground belonging to myself their [sic] being no consecrated Burial place for the

Hebrew persuasion on this side of the island'. The Launceston Jewish community could not then have mustered more than six or seven adults, so the Crown's refusal to help was understandable if only for reasons of precedent.[38] However, there was a difference in need between that of the small independent Christian churches whose members could share facilities with others of the same faith, and that of a non-Christian religion that asked for equality and could not, in conscience, share any existing burial ground. But the government refused to concede this point.

The Jewish community's first sign of life occurred in the following year, 1833, when the first Jewish wedding was celebrated. An emancipist, Mark Solomon, married Miss Hannah Marks in Hobart Town 'attended by most of the children of Israel on this side of the island'. The officiating layman was the tailor, Manley Emanuel, who had been sent to Van Diemen's Land with a seven year sentence for receiving stolen goods. The bridegroom was a publican whose first wife, the mother of three young children, had died two months before. The new marriage began in this shadow and ended abruptly. Mark Solomon died within four years and Hannah married again in June 1840, and so provided Hobart with its third Jewish wedding as well as its first.[39]

The community grew very slowly. The *Hobart Town Courier* observed 'with great pleasure' that on the Jewish Day of Atonement in 1836 'all the shops of that denomination were shut'. The paper drew a general measure of consolation from this display, 'not only as a proof that religious observances were more sacredly attended to in this colony than heretofore but that the population of the town is increasing in the acquirement of morally and virtuously disposed inhabitants'.[40] The island's first organised Jewish congregation was born six years later, as Edward Isaacs, a young member of the synagogue's choir, subsequently recalled:

> In the year 1842 I arrived in Hobart Town in company with a number of young Jewish men (the majority under twenty years of age) and all having been brought up rather orthodox. We were very much surprised on discovering there was no place of worship in connection with our faith. (Service was held on New Year at the Rose and Crown Hotel for want of better accommodation.) Shortly after my arrival I was requested to call a meeting of all the Jewish young residents which I did and the meeting was held at the house of Mr I. Friedman . . . Subsequently Mr Nathan convened a meeting which was attended by, I believe, every Jew in town. He told them what the boys had done and what they should do . . .[41]

It is not surprising that the first meeting of young men who wished to build a synagogue had been held at the home of Isaac Friedman, who was one of the few men in the community with a wide background of Jewish religious knowledge.[42] He was one of the first Hungarian migrants to Australia, and his varied ventures as tailor, pawnbroker (in Hobart Town he issued his own tokens), general dealer, and innkeeper in Sydney, Appin and Maitland were a prelude to his ten-year appointment, in 1858, as minister of the Sandhurst Synagogue on the Victorian goldfields.

Louis Nathan was another who helped to give his community a measure of badly needed respectability. He had come to Hobart Town in 1834 with his wife and four children after having been deeply impressed with the success of his brother-in-law and emancipist, Moses Joseph, the future President of the Sydney Synagogue.[43] Even though Nathan and his family arrived over thirty years after the birth of the colony, they must still be numbered among the very small group of early free Jewish migrants. Nathan opened a general warehouse in Hobart Town, and by 1841 his business had grown large enough to warrant his sending home for his wife's brother Samuel Moses, who arrived in 1842 with his wife, their three children, and two servants.[44] The firm of Nathan Moses & Co. rapidly became one of the largest importing and exporting houses in Van Diemen's Land. A branch was opened in Launceston and by the end of the decade it was the only large Jewish-owned business left on the northern side of the island. Their close link with the family firm of H. E. Moses of Cannon Street in London, and their trade with China and the South Seas, laid the foundations of a fortune.

When Louis Nathan decided in 1847 to leave Van Diemen's Land for home, the newspapers paid tribute to 'the peculiar part he had played among us'. The *Hobart*

Nathan Moses & Co. Wholesale and Retail shop on Liverpool Street, Hobart Town, water-colour by T. E. Chapman, c. 1844. Louis Nathan and Samuel Moses formed a most successful partnership, with capital of one hundred pounds provided by their respective uncle and father-in-law Henry Moses of Cannon Street in the City of London. The firm became one of the largest importing and exporting houses in Van Diemen's Land, enabling both partners to retire to England in their early fifties.

Town Advertiser credited him with 'unostentatiously . . . breaking down prejudice and folly' through his 'extensive and honourable transactions', 'unblemished credit', and 'munificent benevolence'; 'He it was who struck the last blow at prejudices which to our shame be it spoken, environed them in the colonies'.[45]

Nathan's brother-in-law Samuel Moses remained in the colony and continued to conduct a flourishing and thoroughly respectable business.[46] He became not only the first Jewish Justice of the Peace in Van Diemen's Land in 1852, but also the first Jew to be judged worthy of playing host to the Governor when, in 1857, a 'sumptuous ball' at his impressive Hobart mansion was graced by the vice-regent.[47] Moses returned to live in London in 1859. He bought a home in Lancaster Gate and the family mysteriously assumed the more respectable though much less biblical surname of Beddington while the Nathans became Walford.

The impetus to create a congregation had come from Edward Isaacs, its status from Louis Nathan, and its money and land from Judah Solomon. Two men, Jacob Frankel and Phineas Moss, shared with Isaac Friedman the little congregation's religious expertise. The Polish-born Jacob Frankel arrived in Hobart in the year the synagogue was born, and gave his drapery business the unpretentious name of The Cheap Slop. Frankel, like Friedman, had received a traditional Jewish education in Europe. He had already served as minister to a congregation in England and would later work with congregations in Melbourne, Wellington and San Francisco.[48]

Boa Vista, the mansion of Samuel Moses, from H. M. Hull, The Experience of Forty Years in Tasmania, Hobart Town, 1859. This was the family home of Samuel Moses, 'an upright and enterprising citizen'. The Jews of Hobart Town were thrilled when the Governor attended a ball held there in 1857. Situated in New Town, the mansion has been demolished.

Phineas Moss, the synagogue's first secretary, was an English Jew and one of Australian Jewry's most interesting characters. He was born in Portsea, Hampshire, in 1795 and evidently received an excellent Jewish and general education. He came to Hobart Town in 1835 as a free settler, and began work as a clerk at the police station at Bothwell. And he was the guiding spirit of the rural Bothwell Literary Society. In 1841 he returned to Hobart to work as Chief Clerk in the Department of Convict Discipline. It was his task to enter into the infamous Black Books information regarding the punishments of convicts sent in from all over the island. He also had the more cheerful task of supplying books from libraries established by the government at the main prisons. Moss was therefore the first Jew to work in the civil service of any Australian colony. In 1846, in response to an inquiry from England concerning the fate of a Polish Jew, the Colonial Secretary turned to Moss for advice. In Hobart Town he busied himself with higher education. He organised a library for the adults at the Hobart Town Synagogue, gave a lecture to the Mechanics Institute on 'Pneumatics' and to the Royal Society of Van Diemen's Land on the 'Science of Astronomy among the Ancient Jews', and ran courses in 'Pyrnomics' and Natural Philosophy at Bothwell.[49]

Moss published in London in 1853 the first Jewish Calendar for Australia, dedicated 'To the honourable and pious matrons and mothers of the House of Israel, in this island and in other lands of the Southern Hemisphere'. The Calendar's erudite introduction sets out a detailed explanation of the Jewish year and its Holy Days with 'remarks and explanations' showing the Hebrew names of the months and the 'approximate English date' to enable the reader to fix the date of the Jewish festivals. Solemnly Phineas Moss warned: 'ye, virtuous parents, who seek the welfare of your children, place this manual in their hands and may they become impressed with the fear of the Almighty and not deviate from it then when they arrive at old age!' It is appropriate therefore that the main English prayer at the laying of the foundation-stone of the Hobart Town Synagogue should have been written and read by the Calendar's author.[50]

The building of the synagogue in Argyle Street 'for the worship of Jehovah by the descendants of the people of Israel' was officially begun on Wednesday 9 August 1843. With careful dignity Louis Nathan paid tribute to Judah Solomon for generously donating to the congregation the garden of his mansion and former home for the building of the first synagogue in Van Diemen's Land. Conscious that this was a historic moment, he laid within the walls a bottle containing relics of the time, and mortared the foundation-stone with a silver trowel.

The land on which the synagogue was to be built was, on 29 February 1844, conveyed to Judah by his brother Joseph; on 9 October 1844 conveyed by Judah to Samuel Moses, David Moses and Isaac Solomon in trust for the Hebrew Congregation. In view of the convict status of Judah, in October 1844 these gentlemen made a formal application for a grant to the property, and the grant was duly issued on 27 February 1845.[51] The Hobart Synagogue was dedicated on 4 July 1845, two years after the laying of its foundation-stone. Only 'bad health' prevented Lieutenant Governor, Sir John Eardley Wilmot from attending the service. Like his predecessor Sir John Franklin, he did not approve of government aid to the synagogue, but he was tactful enough to accept the congregation's invitation and send his wife in his place.

A poster of the early 1830s encouraging families to migrate to Australia.

ABOVE LEFT: *Phineas Moss, Secretary of the Hobart Synagogue, watercolour by an unknown colonial artist. His beautiful handwriting can be seen in the grim convict record books of Van Diemen's Land. Moss, who was also a fine Hebrew calligrapher and secretary of the Hobart Synagogue, wrote frequently to the London Jewish Chronicle extolling the beauty of his new home and encouraging Jewish migration.*

ABOVE RIGHT: *A colonial portrait of the family of Samuel and Rosetta Moses, c. 1853. The children are thought to be Clara, who died in 1853, and Ernest Leopold Moses.*

'Solomon in all his Glory!!', undated hand-coloured engraving by George Cruikshank. Ikey Solomon, well known as a 'ladies' man' and a dandy, owned a jewellery shop in Bell's Lane near Petticoat Lane, London.

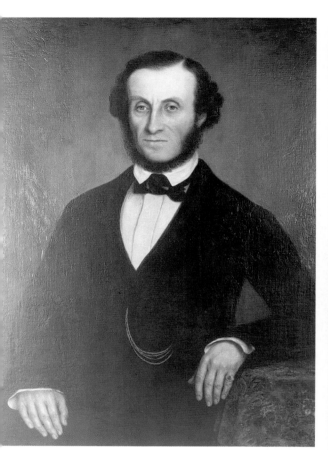 

ABOVE LEFT: John Solomon, by Richard Noble, 1862. The prosperous merchant is John Solomon, oldest child of Ann and Ikey Solomon. Both John and Moses, his younger brother, came out to Australia in 1828 in the vain hope that the authorities would assign their mother and her much younger children to their care. As family life became increasingly complicated in Hobart Town the two young men settled in Sydney, where they prospered. John Solomon, eventually a successful bullion dealer, commissioned these two impressive portraits.

ABOVE RIGHT: Elizabeth Solomon, by Richard Noble, 1862. Elizabeth Solomon is depicted as an elegant and serene wife at home in wealthy circumstances.

Interior of the Hobart Synagogue. The reading desk stands in the middle of the syagogue. On the walls are memorials to its founders. At the back are the cedar benches once set aside for convicts.

The dedication had been delayed by difficulties in obtaining the splendid interior fittings of marble, timber and bronze. The special choir which sang at the dedication service was organised by the young men whose initiative had brought about the congregation's first meeting. The music was written by the Jewish immigrant John Henry Anderson, and orchestrated and conducted by Joseph Reichenberg, a Roman Catholic who had formerly been the bandmaster of the 40th Regiment. With elaborate ceremony the doors of the little synagogue were flung open, and to the sounds of the psalms the scrolls were brought into the building. One hundred guineas were collected at the service and the non-Jewish visitors were duly impressed by the beautiful music and the fervent prayers for the welfare of Queen Victoria and all the royal family.

Encouraged by these first moves to build a synagogue in Hobart Town the Jews of Launceston had formed a congregation of their own and had asked Lieutenant Governor Sir John Franklin for a grant of land for both a cemetery and a synagogue. The Jews of Hobart Town quickly submitted their own claim for 'aid from government funds'.[52] It was a time of economic depression, and though five hundred pounds had been collected from both Jews and Christians in the southern part of the island, the Hobart Town Jews felt that they might as well apply for some of the money which the government was giving to all other established churches.

Yet taken together both petitions were ill-timed and both congregations should have sensed that the Lieutenant Governor was no advocate of aid to the Jewish religion. The Jews of Van Diemen's Land must have been aware that an Act of the Legislative Council authorised by Franklin in 1837 referred specifically to the granting of public money to Christian religious institutions, and restricted the power of the State to make grants of land even to the churches recognised in the Act.[53]

In addition, members of the Hobart Town community, in their first flush of enthusiasm as a newly organised congregation, had already clashed with the authorities when they asked that Jewish convicts be allowed to attend the Jewish High Holyday services. It was true that at the time they had no building of their own and services were being held in a tavern owned by the emancipist Israel Hyam, but still there was room for tolerance: the request was denied, and the official refusal contrasted strangely with the compulsory Sunday morning church parades to which Jewish convicts still had to muster week after week. Permission for Jewish convicts to attend synagogue was finally granted in 1847.[54]

Relationships deteriorated even further when Ellis Casper, a recently arrived convict, was refused permission to attend his son's funeral. Casper and his son had been involved in 'an extraordinary robbery' of gold-dust worth £4600 in 1839 and Franklin may have felt that insufficient time had passed since their sensational exploit in London.[55] Phineas Moss took up the cudgels when the then Lieutenant Governor withdrew permission for Jewish convicts to attend the synagogue. Moss told the Jews of England:

> it will scarcely be credited in civilised and liberal England, that the Lieutenant Governor, Sir William Denison, who is unfortunately known to be a High Church-man, refused absolutely either to allow them to refrain from labour, or to attend their religious rites on those days; and in consequence our unfortunate brethren will now be totally deprived of the means of obtaining those consolations which our holy religion especially affords. Surely if anything were wanted to complete the intellectual wretchedness of the convict, this is one of the best means of its successful infliction; but I am certain it is not the intention of the home authorities to allow such BARBARITY. I cannot soften the harsh term . . .[56]

The Jews were not alone in believing that vice-regal bigotry bore the responsibility for both decisions and the *Hobart Town Advertiser* declared, 'Oh! What an outcry there would have been, had the slaves in the West Indies been prevented from attending to their prayers on a Sabbath!'[57]

It was rumoured that the Launceston congregation's petition had been tersely set aside by the Lieutenant Governor with the words, 'A private room will do well enough for them!'[58] Sir John Franklin was not popular and the Launceston newspapers seized upon this issue to assail his policies and his sense of justice:

> Sir John Franklin was too much of a Christian—alas! that we write it—to do them justice . . . Aversion to any form of religion, like that imputed to Sir John Franklin, if expressed in the execution of his office, is lamentable indeed . . . the government should adopt as a maxim 'to give to all or to give to none'.[59]

Grievously offended by Franklin's rebuff the Jews of Launceston wrote directly to Lord Stanley of the Colonial Office in London, appealing for justice, and to Moses Montefiore, asking him to intervene on their behalf. Franklin forestalled the Jewish petition by explaining to London, 'I have not felt myself justified in Countenancing at the Public Expense a religion essentially hostile to that of Christ, until I shall be honoured by your Lordship's instructions upon the subject'. The Lieutenant Governor knew that Whitehall was not likely to reproach him, because Lord Stanley's firm opposition to any kind of Jewish emancipation was well known.[60]

In London the matter was handled delicately, for Montefiore was a man to be reckoned with. As Lord Stanley tactfully explained to Montefiore, it was impossible to sanction a grant of land or government aid to a religious organisation that numbered less than the statutory minimum of 200 members.[61] The Van Diemen's Land census of 1842 had shown that Launceston had a total Jewish population of only 58. The Jewish petition that had been sent to England bore the names of only 29 men, of whom half were of convict origin.[62]

With government aid denied, a public appeal was announced in Launceston for money to build a synagogue. The *Launceston Examiner* of 6 July 1843 called upon its readers to help: 'Every pious mind, next to desiring an accordance in view and sentiment with himself, must wish to see the Jew provided with a tabernacle to worship the one Jehovah'. The editor discreetly reminded his readers that 'strangers', i.e. Hiram and his subjects, were allowed by God to help Solomon build the first Temple in Jerusalem. State aid would not be offered until 1855 when the Secretary of State informed Moses Montefiore that the sum of one hundred pounds had been placed in the Estimates for the support of Jewish worship. Phineas Moss wrote, 'This event however inconsiderable in a pecuniary view at first sight will be of importance ultimately in proving the equal status of Jews with the other subjects of Her Majesty in the Colonies generally'.[63]

The foundation-stone of the Launceston Synagogue was finally laid on 26 September 1844. The street was filled with onlookers as the members of the congregation marched in pairs to the building site. Their meagre numbers were eked out by the town's Masonic fraternity complete with robes, regalia and swords, and by the full band of the 90th Regiment. It was clearly a demonstration of tolerance and a public expression of disapproval for all that had happened.

As Benjamin Francis, the emancipist President of the congregation and prosperous auctioneer of the city, hopefully declared in the pouring rain that almost marred the ceremony, 'The bright sun of modern intelligence however is fast dissipating the noisome vapours of intolerance and bigotry'.[64] Public opinion supported the community. When in 1846 Sir Moses Montefiore became a baronet, the *Hobart Town Advertiser* declared it:

> a tribute not to his wealth, but to his merit—to his open charity—his persevering efforts for the freedom, the rejuvenation of his race. This is as it ought to be. The Hebrew is now what he should be. He is one of the people. His character, not his

creed, is the distinction in society. Pity it should be so long coming; that the industry, the energy, the intellect of the Hebrews should so long have been forced by national injustice into channels unworthy of them, calculated to injure the country in which they were placed, to deteriorate their own character.' [65]

The little Launceston synagogue took two and a half years to build. Once again the townspeople turned out in force for the occasion and the synagogue was filled with visitors 'of every denomination'. The *Examiner* of 28 March 1846 thought the synagogue was an 'unqualified success', that it was 'unequalled as a specimen of colonial architecture', and proudly wrote of the interior's 'taste and elegance'. The consecration service may well have been the only time the little synagogue was filled with people. Across Bass Strait the settlement at Port

The Synagogue on St John's Street, Launceston. The same Egyptian-style exterior seen in Hobart, Sydney and Adelaide was adopted by the Jews of the northern district of Tasmania. The synagogue fell into disuse shortly after its consecration in 1846 when virtually the entire Jewish population moved across Bass Strait in search of gold.

Phillip flourished while the economy of northern Tasmania began to stagnate. David Benjamin, President of the congregation at the time of its dedication, was already busy with a branch of his firm in Melbourne and had virtually ceased to live in Launceston. Indeed none of the congregation's committee members in 1846 were living in Tasmania ten years later.[66]

An English migrant to Hobart Town wrote home:

I arrived here safely on 9 August 1846 and found to my astonishment a Synagogue, which for its completeness is unequalled in any provincial town at home. It is solidly and elegantly built of the beautiful firestone with which the colony abounds, the interior fittings of polished cedar (rivalling mahogany), with the chandeliers and other accessories, are of the most elegant description. There is a small but talented choir, and it is remarkable, that it is attended by the ladies on sabbaths and festivals to an extent exceeding anything I have witnessed in England . . . there is a splendid race of young folks arising who will at a further period, I doubt not, be a credit to our nation. Education of a high order is easily attained and it is not neglected; the precocity of intellect is remarkable in children here, apparently keeping pace with the rapid productions in nature in this favoured clime.

In the same issue of the London *Jewish Chronicle*, the paper's 'own correspondent' declared the Tasmanian climate 'delightful'. Oblivious to the suffering of the convicts, he wrote that Hobart Town was 'large and well laid out' and travel in the countryside possessed 'a feeling of security that quite astonishes a stranger who has been infected at home with false accounts of the dangers he will have to encounter here'.[67]

Once the synagogues were built, instructions were given by the government that 'all prisoners of the Jewish persuasion not actually under a sentence would have leave to refrain from work and attend Synagogues in Hobart Town and Launceston'. The Hobart Town congregation made provision for prisoners to receive two meals on the Sabbath, and a query was sent to the Chief Rabbi in London asking whether a convict could be counted as a member of a minyan (quorum) and be called to the Torah. The answer was affirmative for the first question and in the negative for the second.[68] Phineas Moss wondered why the free settlers in Van Diemen's Land should be saddled with the obligation to care for the Jewish convicts once they emerged from gaol. He very cautiously wrote to the *Jewish Chronicle* of London asking for help:

> The Israelites of Van Diemen's Land are, in respects to indigent of their brethren, under very peculiar circumstances: and the maintenance of them entails, to use the word literally, a heavy burthen where it ought least to be felt ... A very great expense, therefore, has to be borne for strangers. Numbers of our erring and un-fortunate brethren, chiefly from Britain, who are constantly emerging from a state of bondage and regaining their freedom, require in almost every instance pecuniary assistance to enable them to recommence life and regain a place in society, and it is this which presses unfortunately most heavily on us. I think it is but fair, therefore, that some part of this expense ought to be borne by the Congregations at home ... [It is] a great injustice to our community to continue with our limited number to maintain the British poor.[69]

Only a month before the dedication of the Hobart Synagogue, it had been announced that emancipist holders of conditional pardons would be allowed to settle on the mainland without having to make special application to the authorities. This liberalisation of the penal laws resulted in a substantial movement of men from the poorer southern island with its limited land to the growing communities of New South Wales (which then included Victoria) and South Australia.[70] Even before the lure of the gold rush, a labour shortage resulted from the migration of thousands from Van Diemen's Land to the mainland, and the editor of Melbourne's *Port Phillip Patriot* wrote that the change of regulations had been 'cunningly devised to relieve the sister colony of bad characters at the expense of Australia Felix'. Though this process of emigration affected the northern areas of Van Diemen's Land most deeply it was not long before it was felt in the south. The Jewish community shrank. The Launceston Synagogue closed down[71] but the Hobart Synagogue struggled on. It was an older group. Many of its families had already spent twenty years in Van Diemen's Land and had established deep roots within the community.

The locked doors of the old synagogue still face St John's Street in Launceston. It has now been classified by the National Trust of Australia and waits for the day when a new congregation is established in Launceston. In Hobart the congregation remains alive and the synagogue still functions as a place of worship beside Judah Solomon's mansion in Argyle Street. The congregation's presence is felt not only by its history but also by the names borne by dozens of Tasmanians who, though not Jewish themselves, are descended from an extraordinary group of convicts and pioneers.

The Jews of Van Diemen's Land, and of Australia in general, had found a safe haven. In January 1850 a Christian citizen of Hobart Town wrote to *The Colonial Times & Tasmanian* after attending the presentation of a Torah scroll sent from London by Louis Nathan Esquire:

> I was exceedingly struck with the touchingly affecting character of the imposing and solemn rites observed on the occasion—and rendered still more affecting by the deep devotion which so evidently pervaded the large congregation . . . Why, thought I, should Christians persecute Jews? Or why should Jews hate Christians? Do not Christians hail their Almighty Deliverer as strictly descended from the same root as Abraham? . . . As for Jews—do they not see in their own cherished Scriptures that Gentilism itself equally with Judaism will merge in the forthcoming spiritual glories and triumphs of their redeemed and ransomed beloved Sion?[72]

The Jewish community's scholarly Phineas Moss was equally rhapsodic even though this highly intelligent man perceived the indigenous Tasmanians as barbarians and remained oblivious to the fact that they had been hunted to extinction by 'civilised' European invaders who, in turn, had built a colony upon the lash, the tread-wheel and the gallows.

> A few, very few years have elapsed since [the colony] was but one vast wilderness, where solitary wilds only beheld the dark barbarian seeking a precarious existence, himself scarcely raised in intellect above his unresisting prey, whilst the darkened glades in silence and stealth o'er the crag beneath. But civilisation has succeeded barbarism, and the wilderness and the solitary place has indeed been made glad, whilst the desert has blossomed as the rose.[73]

Fagin in Australia

IKEY SOLOMON, one of the best-known convicts in colonial Australia, was to be immortalised as the villainous Fagin in Charles Dickens' *Oliver Twist*. The former members of London's underworld who had preceded him to Van Diemen's Land were clearly delighted to welcome him. The *Hobart Town Chronicle* on 28 November 1829 described the sensation his disembarkation had caused by quoting a report in the London *Morning Paper*, written by an anonymous Antipodean correspondent, telling of his arrival in Australia:

> He arrived on Sunday the 15th of February, 1829, and the following day was seen parading the straggling streets of Hobart Town, with an air of confidence and self-possession, but scarcely did he pass through one of them, or near any of the government or penitentiary establishments, than he was recognised by his former pals and saluted with Oh! Ikey my boy, how are you? Blow me, but I am glad to see you, what a **** lucky fellow you have been! While others pointing him out to their friends remembered: I say, there goes Ikey Solomon; he used to fence my swag. The **** rogue; if it was not for him I should not be here now. The running comments nothing daunted Ikey—he turned a deaf ear to them: he still continued his business and during the week-days drove about in a fashionable English-built gig. His superciliousness and contempt for his former friends roused their vengeance, and they gave information to Colonel Arthur and the Local Government of the sort of personage who had arrived on the island, the circumstances under which he had escaped, and the heavy charges that were against him in England.

Solomon was a fugitive from justice who, with a fine mixture of *chutzpah*, sentimentality and optimism, had chosen to visit a colony of convicts. He was to be returned to England in chains, escape the gallows, and be sent back to Australia where he would die a lonely man deserted by his wife and repudiated by most of his children. He was certainly well remembered by the denizens of Newgate Gaol. On 23 February 1832 a discharged convict identified as 'AB' gave evidence before the Parliamentary Select Committee on Secondary Punishments. A committee member asked, 'Did you ever hear anything said with regard to the receivers of stolen goods in Newgate?' To which 'AB' eagerly replied:

> Yes I did; one man of the name of Ikey Solomon, that lived in Rosemary-lane; they said he was a man that was possessed of a great deal of money and they could bring anything to him, if they had a house full of plate or property of any sort, Ikey would

have it. I heard them boast what a 'dammed good fellow' he was and the likes of that. He is transported, I believe.

The true story of his life is far stranger and more dramatic than Dickens, or any other novelist, would have dreamed of presenting to the public as fiction. Yet he was notorious in his own lifetime, and his exploits were freely discussed in the newspapers and particularly in three pamphlets published at the height of his criminal career. One of them has the resounding title of *The Life and Exploits of Ikey Solomon, Swindler, Forger, Fence and Brothel Keeper with account of Flesh and Dress Houses, Flash Girls and Coves of the Hutch, now on Town. With Instructions on how to guard against Hypocritical Villains and the Lures of Abandoned Females, also particulars of Mrs Ikey Solomon and the gang which infested London for Nineteen Years etc. etc., by Moses Hebron, formerly a Jewish Rabbi, but now a Christian.* This pamphlet does not mention Solomon in Van Diemen's Land and so must have been published before 1828. The second pamphlet, published in 1829, is *Adventures, Memoirs, Former Trial, Transportation and Escape of that Notorious Fence and Receiver of Stolen Goods, Isaac Solomons etc. etc. by a former Police Officer,* and the third bears the comparatively modest title of *The Life and Adventures of Isaac Solomons, The notorious receiver of stolen goods, better known as* IKEY SOLOMONS *from his birth to the present time with a particular account of his Extraordinary Escape from the City Officers; His recapture in New South Wales and Trials at the Old Bailey on eight different indictments; to which are subjoined The Life and Trial of Mrs. Solomons, the wife of the above.* The date of this one must be 1830 or 1831. The second and third pamphlets use the name 'Solomons', as does a book published in 1837, but the more common spelling of the period omits the final 's'.

These pamphlets, and the records of the Old Bailey, supply the background of his early life. Isaac Solomon was born in 1789, one of the nine children of Henry Solomon of Gravel Lane, Houndsditch.[1] He therefore grew up in that 'haunt of pickpockets and prostitutes, rogues and vagabonds'. At the age of eight, it was said, he began to work as an itinerant street vendor, at ten he had already passed bad money, and at fourteen he was a pickpocket and a 'duffer'. This last occupation required imagination and skill, because a 'duffer' played on the cupidity of honest citizens by convincing them that fake jewellery and similar trashy articles were valuable goods that had been stolen or smuggled, and thus had to be disposed of at giveaway prices.

This career was cut short on 17 April 1810, when Isaac was twenty-one. With Joel Joseph, aged twenty-six, he played the usual trick of one man jostling or otherwise distracting the attention of a 'mark' while the accomplice picked his pocket. The victim was Mr Thomas Dodd, who was relieved of a purse containing bank-notes to the value of £40 and a warrant for the payment of £56. The theft, at a large political meeting in the New Palace Yard in front of Westminster Hall, was seen by an alert constable. As the *Times* told it:

> Having made a plentiful harvest, they endeavoured to make their retreat through Westminster Hall; but, unfortunately for them, the doors at the upper end, one leading to the passage of the House of Commons, and the other into Old Palace Yard, were locked, and there was no possibility of escape, a detachment of the Bow-Street Corps being close at their heels.

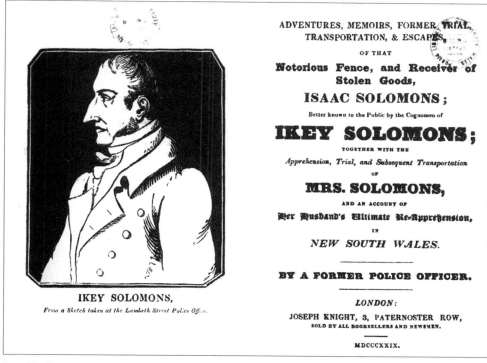

IKEY SOLOMONS,
From a Sketch taken at the Lambeth Street Police Office.

ADVENTURES, MEMOIRS, FORMER TRIAL, TRANSPORTATION, & ESCAPES,

OF THAT

Notorious Fence, and Receiver of Stolen Goods,

ISAAC SOLOMONS;

Better known to the Public by the Cognomen of

IKEY SOLOMONS;

TOGETHER WITH THE

Apprehension, Trial, and Subsequent Transportation

OF

MRS. SOLOMONS,

AND AN ACCOUNT OF

Her Husband's Ultimate Re-Apprehension,

IN

NEW SOUTH WALES.

BY A FORMER POLICE OFFICER.

LONDON:

JOSEPH KNIGHT, 3, PATERNOSTER ROW,

SOLD BY ALL BOOKSELLERS AND NEWSMEN.

MDCCCXXIX.

Pamphlet frontispiece and title-pages (see over).

Joseph desperately attempted to stuff the stolen bank-notes inside the handkerchief around his neck. Solomon deliberately dropped a pocket book as he was being led away. A search revealed four £1 Bank of England notes in his fob-pocket, seven dollars in his breeches pocket and a single bank-note hidden in his right-hand coat pocket. Obviously Joseph and Isaac were not strangers to the law, because they were called 'noted characters' by the police witnesses at the Old Bailey trial, which ended with sentences of transportation for the term of their natural life.[2]

For some reason, Joel Joseph was the only one of the pair to be transported, but both were sent to the convict hulk *Zealand* anchored off Sheerness. There they were issued with clothes, blankets and leg irons.[3] Joseph was transferred from the hulk and sent to New South Wales on aboard the *Admiral Gambier*, which arrived in Sydney on 29 September 1811. A man 5 feet $7\frac{1}{2}$ inches tall with a dark ruddy complexion, black hair and hazel eyes, he absconded with three others on 2 January 1813 and after two days met a party of Aborigines. One of the convicts was killed and the others were left without food or clothing to find their way along the rugged coastline as far as the little settlement on Broken Bay, where they gave themselves up. Joseph was tried at Windsor, and had to serve until 1819 before he received his ticket of leave. He enjoyed only a year of freedom, though it was as the owner of St Paul's Hotel in Pitt Street, before he died on 28 August 1820 and became one of the first Jews to be

The Universal Pamphleteer.

THE LIFE AND ADVENTURES

OF

ISAAC SOLOMONS,

THE NOTORIOUS RECEIVER OF STOLEN GOODS,

BETTER KNOWN AS

IKEY SOLOMONS,

FROM HIS BIRTH TO THE PRESENT TIME;

WITH A PARTICULAR ACCOUNT OF HIS

Extraordinary Escape from the City Officers;

HIS RE-CAPTURE IN NEW SOUTH WALES;

AND

TRIALS AT THE OLD BAILEY,

ON EIGHT DIFFERENT INDICTMENTS;

To which are subjoined,

THE LIFE AND TRIAL OF MRS. SOLOMONS,

THE WIFE OF THE ABOVE.

THE UNIVERSAL PAMPHLETEER,

Consisting of Scarce, Instructive, and Entertaining Tracts on all Subjects, comprises—
Lives of Remarkable Persons—Facts and Romances from History—Tales and Legends
—Extraordinary Trials, Adventures, Phenomena, and Crimes—Abstracts of Acts of
Parliament—Arts and Treatises, &c. &c.
Each Pamphlet contains eight closely-printed octavo pages; and the Work is embellished
with superior illustrative Embellishments on Wood.

buried in the 'right hand corner of the Christian burial ground . . . allocated to the Hebrews'. He had lived with Ann Cooper, by whom he had a daughter Sophia Hannah Joseph on 13 July 1817.[4]

Meanwhile his accomplice Isaac Solomon had, in some inexplicable manner, contrived to avoid transportation for life and to achieve a remarkable level of comfort on board the *Zealand*. The Jews along the Medway were keeping an eye on him. He may well have been a relative of the Solomons who lived in Sheerness and who plied the Thames buying and selling food, clothing and trinkets to the convicts on the hulks.[5] He certainly had an uncle who sold 'slops', or ready-made clothes, in nearby Chatham, which explains how in his six years as a prisoner he was issued with eight jackets, six waistcoats, five pairs of trousers, seven pair of stockings, fourteen pairs of shoes, eleven shirts, six hats and four blankets. The ways of the law were even more capricious in those days than they are now, and public officials were considerably more open to corruption, so it is possible that the wily Isaac found some loophole through which he might slip. Solomon was released by a bureaucratic mistake on 27 June 1816. He had perhaps been confused with a Jonas Solomon who was a fellow prisoner on the hulks.[6] After four weeks of freedom he had the good sense to voluntarily return to custody, for which he was granted a free pardon on 26 October 1816. A few days later he began work for his uncle in Chatham.

The scene is captured by Charles Dickens, who was born in 1812 and grew up in the Medway port towns of Sheerness, Chatham and Rochester. His family rented a small house next door to the Sheerness Theatre and in 1817 moved to the port city of Chatham, known by some as 'the wickedest place in the world'.[7] In *The Pickwick Papers* Dickens described his earliest and deepest childhood memories:

> 'The principal productions of these towns', says Mr Pickwick, 'appear to be soldiers, sailors, Jews, chalk, shrimps, officers and dockyard men. The commodities chiefly exposed for sale in the public streets are marine stores, hard-bake, apples, flat fish, and oysters. The streets present a lively and animated appearance, occasioned chiefly by the conviviality of the military. It is truly delightful to a philanthropic mind, to see these gallant men staggering along under the influence of an overflow, both of animal and ardent spirits.'

And never far away, or out of mind, lay the prison hulks. In *Great Expectations*, Pip recalled 'we saw the black Hulk lying out a little way from the mud of the shore, like a wicked Noah's ark. Cribbed and barred and moored by massive rusty chains, the prison-ship seemed in my young eyes to be ironed like the prisoners.'

The story of Solomon's life in London is told in elaborate, lurid and conflicting detail in the three pamphlets referred to, but it seems likely that after his first imprisonment the capital he earned in Chatham provided the wherewithal to commence a temporarily honest career. He opened a shop in London—the London Dickens describes in his preface to the third edition of *Oliver Twist* as 'cold, wet, shelterless midnight streets of London; the foul and frowsy dens, where vice is closely packed and lacks the room to turn; the haunts of hunger and disease, the shabby rags that scarcely hold together; where are the attractions of these things?'

According to one of the pamphlets describing the life and exploits of Ikey Solomons, 'Swindler, forger, fencer and brothel keeper', the shop was an adjunct to a brothel where prostitutes were supplied with their clothes and where they were offered board and lodging. The author of this story seems to have possessed a measure of expert knowledge, as he lists the ladies: 'Misses Sparkes, Cruttwell, Jemima Mordaunt, Singing Sal, Cherry Bounce and others all eminent in their vocation'. Ikey would lend money to young gentlemen whose fathers would pay their debts rather than risk public shame and embarrassment. In addition Ikey would boast that half the police officers of London were in his pay and the other half wanted to be. One of the more imaginative pamphlets tells how after some successful years in London he moved to Brighton and became a dealer in china and furniture. By that time he had a mistress, Mrs Gordon, who was one of the 'ladies' of the Prince Regent, later King George IV. She helped him to become one of the suppliers of the famous and fantastic Brighton Pavilion, which Prince George had built in the Chinese style fashionable in Regency England. After this he returned to the metropolis, where he established himself as a jeweller but soon became known as a shrewd dealer in stolen goods and stolen bank-notes.

Unlike the fictitious Fagin, described by Dickens as a 'very old shrivelled Jew whose villainous-looking and repulsive face was obscured by a quantity of matted red hair', Ikey Solomon was tall, slim and rather elegant in appearance, with a long face, dark eyes and hair, and an aquiline nose. He was a successful lady-killer, although at an early age he had married the 14-year-old Ann Julian—a barmaid of the Blue Anchor in Petticoat Lane and daughter of Moses Julian, a coach master of Aldgate— and had several children by her. Ann developed into a worthy business associate.

Ikey and Ann Solomon soon established a network of organised crime based on the classic foundations of prostitution, the 'fencing' of stolen goods, and corruption of officials. In Angel Court, off the Strand, they opened a 'dress house' where prostitutes were fed, housed and clothed in return for a share of their earnings. It was alleged that Ikey bribed the police to protect his establishment, and even 'persuaded' them to give him the contract for their uniforms. Metropolitan London soon proved too small, and Ikey began to distribute stolen goods through agencies in the provinces, thus lessening the chances of identifying the merchandise. Presumably with the help of friends in high places, he became a Navy Agent and thus was able to ship stolen goods overseas. He began to specialise in jewellery, which was broken down and sold through agents. By 1825 it was said he had established a chain of brothels in London, and set up a second metropolitan depot in Lower Queen's Street, Islington. This included a second household and a mistress, and it was said that when Ann discovered his infidelity she threw her rival out. Enraged, Solomon's mistress told the police what she knew, but they refused to act.

The underworld was kept busy in securing enough jewellery and other merchandise to maintain a constant flow of business through Solomon's agencies, and in May 1826 a series of London robberies caused such an outcry that a victim had to be produced. The victim of a daring robbery of watch movements valued at two hundred pounds from a warehouse in the City of London belonging to watchmakers Messrs McCabe and Strachan obtained a warrant to search the Solomons' premises in Bell Lane, near Petticoat Lane in Spitalfields. It was Sunday morning and, mysteriously, the investigating police officers took some time to arrive, while Ikey left home in a hurry. Ann told the officers that her husband was out but that she was expecting him home for breakfast at any minute and asked them to wait. When Ikey failed to appear a search of the house was begun, and at the top of the house a room with a padlocked door was revealed. As the door and its padlock were probed and tested Ikey suddenly appeared, looked surprised and fumbled in his pockets for the key. Assuring his visitors that he would just go downstairs and find the key, he disappeared. While the police politely waited, strange noises were heard from inside the locked room. When the door was finally broken down by force there were clear signs that someone had just finished cutting a hole in the ceiling and retrieving most of the hidden property. Only five of the expensive stolen watch movements and a cloud of lime dust were to be seen, and a warrant was promptly issued for Solomon's arrest.

Months of inactivity passed and Ikey was said to have travelled north, boldly escaping arrest despite being recognised frequently, for 'his good nature and liberality produced so favourable an impression on those who had known him that he was not delivered to justice'. Finally, presuming that the coast was clear and incautiously using the unpersuasive alias 'Jones', he returned to London to stay at the house of Mrs Jane Oades at Lower Queen Street, Islington, which was then on the outskirts of London. On 23 April 1827 he was recognised in nearby New North Road, and arrested. In his pockets were watches, jewellery and cash amounting to £45 and 180 sovereigns. A search of his room revealed vast quantities of stolen handkerchiefs, trinkets and bundles of linen, lace and cloth—quite enough to fill a coach and 'more than a man could carry'. The police had discovered 'a most valuable, extensive and general assortment of almost every article of British Commerce', and it was rumoured that he had been betrayed by a neglected mistress. Mrs Oades later testified in court, with a straight face, that 'During the time the prisoner continued at my lodgings he always behaved like a gentleman'.

Despite the cache of stolen goods, when Isaac Solomon was brought before the sitting magistrates at Lambeth Police Court he was charged only with having in his possession the movements of five stolen watches, and was remanded for a week. His arrest revealed unexpected evidence that he belonged to a Masonic Lodge, because the personal possessions taken from him at the police station included 'an old-fashioned seal, the mounting of which resembled a Masonic arch, and a plain seal with the initials I.S. surmounted by Masonic emblems with an anchor underneath'.

He was brought before the magistrates again on 3 May, this time to face charges of possessing stolen goods worth more than £1400, which was an immense sum in those days. His underworld connections tried to help him by making two attempts to break into the police warehouse and spirit away the evidence, but could not save him from being committed for trial at the Old Bailey. A warrant was issued for his removal to Newgate Gaol, with the strict injunction that every care should be taken to prevent his escape. Justice had caught up with Solomon, and it seemed that only the hulks, the gallows or Australia lay before him. A daringly executed plan rescued him from all three.

Obviously he had plenty of powerful friends on both sides of the law, because the first step in the plan involved the issue of a writ of habeas corpus. This meant that he had to be taken from Newgate to the Court of the King's Bench at Westminster, so that a Justice could hear arguments as to whether his defenders should 'have his body' until he had to appear at the Old Bailey. In some mysterious manner Ann's father, Moses Julian, who was a coach driver, managed to inveigle his way up onto the front of the coach. As the plotters anticipated, bail was refused and he was ordered back to Newgate, and the London *Times* of 28 May 1827 was to describe what happened next:

> Two turnkeys—Smart, who had been in that situation 17 years, and a young man— were sent with him. Solomons' wife accompanied him in the coach, and her father sat on the box with the coachman. They left Westminster for Newgate about half- past 12 o'clock. Solomons sat between the turnkeys on one side of the coach, his wife sat on the other. Solomons requested the turnkeys to allow the coach to go a little out of the direct way, that he might set his wife down at a friend's. To this, they consented, having no suspicion that an escape was meditated. The coach having been driven for a longer time out of the route to Newgate than the turnkeys had in- tended, Smart began to expostulate with Solomons, and told him it was impossible to continue any longer in that direction. Solomons assured him they were then just at the place, and the coach, which by this time had reached Bishopsgate, suddenly turned into Petticoat Lane and stopped. The door was quickly opened, and out jumped Solomon. A party of Jews, who were waiting, instantly shut the coach door and kept it closed. As soon as the turnkeys could get out, they saw Solomons at a dis- tance, running as if for his life, they raised a cry of stop thief, and pursued with all their might, but Solomons was seen to turn down one of the alleys off Petticoat Lane, and has not since been heard of . . . the city officers appear confident that he cannot long escape their vigilance. [Note the plural form of Solomon's name.]

But the city officers were not to see him again for a very long time. This escape, which must have involved the whole underworld network and bribery of many people including the coachman and possibly even Smart the turnkey—because he was summarily dismissed—enabled Ikey Solomon to vanish. During the subsequent uproar, Ikey's counsel, Mr James Isaacs, presented himself to the magistrates con- cerned with the case to assure them that he had nothing to do with the escape. Obviously they thought differently, because he was told indignantly that they 'wanted nothing to do with him'. The keeper of Newgate was admonished, and the Secretary of State demanded a detailed report.[8]

The *Times* followed up their story with a description of how the frustrated police turned upon Ikey's family. The home of his father-in-law in Petticoat Lane was searched, and though the police found no trace of the fugitive they discovered 'an immense quantity of property'. It included '50 gold and silver watches and more than 200 gold rings and seals; and several dozens of valuable shawls the whole of which were taken away by the officers'.

A reward was offered for Ikey's capture, and the search continued. In June his wife Ann was arrested and charged at Lambeth Street Police Station for being in possession of stolen property. Bail was allowed, and she was released under 'the presumption that the property was in the possession of her husband'. Within days, Ikey's son John was arrested on similar charges, but these too were dropped. Though Ikey was only thirty-eight, John was over twenty and was described by the *Times* of 22 July as 'a young man of good appearance, as yet in his minority', who 'seemed perfectly undismayed at his situation'. The *Times* reporter, who wrote 'The hand of fate seems to press heavily on the family of the Solomons', described the way in which the magistrate spoke to John 'most feelingly and emphatically, on the course he should hereafter pursue in life'. Apparently John took the admonitions to heart, because he never stood in a dock again and managed to avoid all the disasters that awaited the rest of his family.

However, it seems that Ann was too set in her ways to take notice of the storm signals. The police were poised to pounce on the Solomons. When they heard that Ann had bought a watch that could be identified as stolen, they had the excuse to swoop on her home. On 31 August the *Times* reported that an immense quantity of

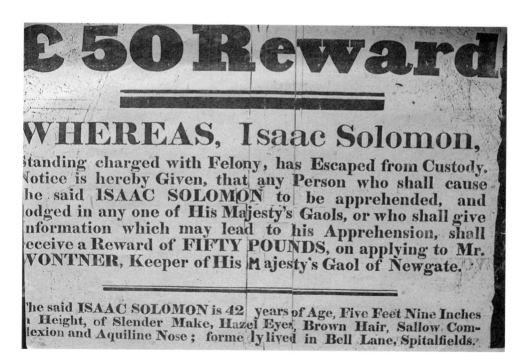

Reward poster for the capture of Ikey, printed in London, 1829. Before Ikey could be arrested and sent home for trial the colonial government had to await the necessary documents from London. This poster was among the papers sent to the Colonial Secretary in Hobart Town which enabled his arrest and deportation.

gold and silver watches, counterfeit money, trinkets and clothes had been seized—
in fact such a profusion of goods that very little, apart from the said watch, could
actually be identified. And worse, the watch was still ticking! In other words, it was
proof that Ann knew where it was hidden and had wound it up.

The watch gave the law the opportunity to remove Ann Solomon from England
for fourteen years. Justice moved swiftly. She was brought to trial at the Old Bailey on
18 September 1827 on the charge of having received, at Christchurch, a watch stolen
from the shipmaster Joseph Ridley. The next day the *Morning Post* reported that 'every
avenue leading to the court was thronged with persons of the Jewish persuasion'.
On 23 September Ann returned to court. The *Morning Chronicle* said Ann was 'much
agitated'. The evidence against her was overwhelming, though she protested 'I am
innocent. I do not know anything at all about it'. The *Morning Chronicle* was impressed:
'The appearance of Mrs Solomons seemed to excite the most intense interest. She was
most elegantly dressed. On hearing the sentence she fainted, but recovered before she
left the dock, and exclaimed as she was leaving the Court, "Oh, my poor children—
my poor children"'. It was no surprise to the public when she received a sentence of
fourteen years transportation.[9]

From the Old Bailey, Ann was sent to prison where, according to the second
pamphlet written about Ikey Solomon, she 'made some disclosures which obtained
her permission to take three of her children to New South Wales to be under her fostering care'. She petitioned the King, claiming that she was now 'deeply impressed
with shame and sorrow' and that she was 'a poor weak Woman, led astray from the
paths of rectitude by others'. It was all in vain. Ann's fate was sealed and she sailed for
Australia on 10 February 1828 aboard the *Mermaid*, which sailed from Woolwich with
ninety female convicts many of whom were accompanied by their children.[10]

Ann, whose conduct on board was deemed by the surgeon, James Gilchrist, to
be 'becoming and Exemplary', apparently contrived to take all four of her younger
children, aged between two and eight, with her in the *Mermaid*, but the government
refused permission for John and his younger brother Moses, aged seventeen, to go
with her. The public purse was not prepared to finance the emigration of young
adults whose parents had been sentenced to deportation, and so the two young men
took passage for Sydney on the *Australia*.[11] In the following year Ann's two brothers
were sent to Australia. Jacob Julian, aged eighteen, who had arrived in Sydney as a
convict on the *Hooghley* (2) in 1828, and his older brother Moses, who was sent to Van
Diemen's Land on the *Roslin Castle*. There remains a tantalising question. The surname
of Ann's family is the same as that often used by Esther Abrahams of the First Fleet.
Julian is not a usual Jewish family name and the Jewish community of London was
not large. Can this be a mere coincidence?

Meanwhile, in London, the police continued to hunt for Ikey and anyone who
might be associated with him. The *Times* of 25 October 1827 reported their raid on
the house of his brother Benjamin, whom they took before the Lord Mayor to be
charged with felony. They had insufficient evidence that articles found in his home
were stolen goods and he was discharged, vowing to be revenged.

Anyone with the name of Solomon trod warily. In June 1827 a 19-year-old labourer named Isaac Solomons, born in London and resident near Petticoat Lane and described as being '5 feet 7 inches, ruddy complexion, brown hair, hazel eyes', was tried at the Old Bailey on a charge of stealing a watch. In his defence he was careful to state, 'I am no relation to Ikey Solomon, and trust my name will not prejudice me', but it may have been a vain hope. He was sentenced to fourteen years and joined the growing number of Jews being transported, to receive a colonial conviction at Windsor in 1839, a ticket of leave for Maitland in 1840, and a conditional pardon in 1841.[12] John Solomon 'a young man of perfectly good appearance, as yet in his minority' was charged at Lambeth Street on Saturday 30 June with receiving stolen property, having negotiated the rental of the house in which a substantial portion of stolen property was found. John was discharged for lack of sufficient evidence.

A week later Ikey's father, Henry Solomons, stood in the dock for having stolen property in his possession. A search of his home at 24 Gravel Lane, Houndsditch had revealed 27 watches, 7 brooches, 14 watch-keys and 28 rings, all of which had been stolen the day before. Henry Solomons simply denied everything:

> I am upwards of seventy years old, and have worked hard to support my family. I never got a penny dishonestly in all my days—I have worked for every factory in London. I hate the very thoughts of a thief and a receiver . . . I have been ill upwards of three years and cannot get out of bed without my wife or daughter putting my stockings on . . .

Ikey's sister Sarah Nathan blamed her brother. She remembered that 'a lad brought this locked box to the house. We were not friends with my brother'. However, Henry Solomon's denial and his story of decrepitude were difficult to believe because the police had arrested him at some considerable distance from his house. The court leniently sentenced him to six months servitude in the House of Correction 'in consequence of his great age' and he was promptly transferred from Newgate. The family saga was not over. On 24 October 1827 Benjamin Solomon, Ikey's brother, stood before the Lord Mayor at the Mansion House having been found with property that appeared to have been stolen from a church. The charge was vague and the church unknown. Even though his wife had not been able to account for a watch which mysteriously 'fell from her person', Benjamin was discharged from custody.

Ann Solomon arrived in Hobart Town on the *Mermaid* on 27 June 1828. She was neither the first nor the only member of her family to be deported to Australia. The story of the Solomon family was so well known that the news was picked up by the *Sydney Gazette* of 4 July. She was assigned to the family of Richard Newman, a Hobart police officer, but it seems that she was a servant in name only. Later, in a court case involving the Solomons and the Newmans, a fellow prisoner assigned to a neighbouring household testified that 'She had never seen Ann doing any work since she was with the Newmans . . . had always seen Mrs Newman doing the drudgery of the house'.[13]

Clearly there was no shortage of money in the Solomon family, so perhaps the servant was paying the mistress to do the work. When Moses and John Solomon arrived in Sydney they began business as general dealers with a large stock of goods for sale, and on 26 September 1828 John petitioned the Governor to be allowed to proceed to Van Diemen's Land to take his mother 'off the Government stores' and 'bring her with her young family to Sydney'. The somewhat impertinent request was refused.[14] John wrote to the Colonial Secretary on 23 February 1829, 'I have purchased the premises of Mr Underwood of New Norfolk, for the sum of £500. I have deposited the sum of £200 into the hands of Mr Gellibrand—Mrs Solomon having the remainder in her possession. May I beg that you will have the kindness to allow him to see her for a few minutes'. It was signed 'Your Humble Servant, John Solomon'. Evidently Ikey had given the bank-notes to his wife, judging them safer in her possession.

Within the Colonial Secretary's file is an account of the official interview with Ann, who could only sign her transcript of the conversation with a cross. She had lived in Commercial Road in the East End:

> 'I have one girl 7, one girl 5, one boy 9, one boy 3 years old. My husband, I believe, has gone to America. I have two children gone to Sydney. John 21 and Moses 18 as gentlemen free settlers. My father is a coach proprietor and lives in Aldgate named Moses (Julian). I believe my husband was a jeweller.' Mr Boyd, the Chief Clerk in the Police Court said to her 'Who is your husband?' She made no reply. He then said 'Your husband is Ikey Solomon of whom so much is heard'. She burst into tears, put her hand to her face and made no answer. The question was not pursued further.

It was just as well, because her family lived in defiance of the law. No one could have doubted that her father had bribed the regular driver of the coach taking prisoners through the streets of London and allowed his son-in-law to escape. The facts spoke for themselves but, without a confession, it was hard to prove.

When Ann's adult sons John and Moses learned that by chance Ann was shipped on a vessel bound for Van Diemen's Land, they were forced to sell their Sydney business and move to Hobart Town, where they began business afresh in Macquarie Street. Their mother was not permitted to stay with them, so they lived with the Newmans as lodgers. According to the Sydney *Monitor* of 17 March 1830 the two young men 'conducted themselves with propriety', and their business prospered. By 1830 John was trading from premises 'opposite the White Horse Inn, Liverpool Street'. In 1831 his store was called The Tasmanian Auction and Commission Mart, which is interesting because Van Diemen's Land was not officially named Tasmania until 1855. In July 1832 he was licensed as an auctioneer, by September he held the licence of the William IV Hotel, and in April 1833 he received a grant of valuable land at the corner of Goderich and Bathurst streets, Hobart Town. For John Solomon at least, self-imposed exile became a blessing and his future career in New South Wales brought him impressive success.

No doubt the Solomon family knew how the 'daring escape' of Ikey was planned, but they may not have been kept informed about all his subsequent adventures. These were told to the world by the London *Times* of 19 July 1830, which said that the escape had cost Ikey 'enormous expense'. Evidently he had spent the first night

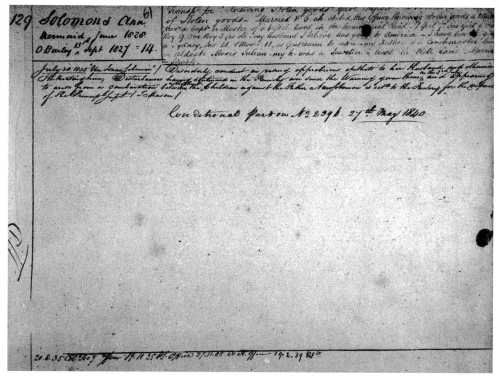

Ann Solomon's convict record. Each convict had an entry in The Black Books which noted date and place of trial, personal status and appearance, religion, behaviour on board ship, and imprisonments, punishments and time off for good behaviour. Only the Van Diemen's Land books survive.

hidden in a house in the City of London, and the next few weeks in Tottenham. When the first hot pursuit had subsided, Ikey had himself smuggled aboard a ship loading ballast in the Thames—no doubt with further addition to his expenses. The ship sailed for Denmark and he landed there safely. Even though he carried eight hundred pounds with him he could not begin trading in a country where he did not speak the language. So he took ship for New York, where he started dealing in watches and trinkets.

Even in those days of slow communications, so interesting a criminal as Ikey Solomon could not escape newspapermen for long. Word of his place of refuge soon reached Van Diemen's Land, where the *Hobart Town Chronicle* of 30 August 1828 reported:

> The Notorious Ikey Solomons, the receiver of stolen goods, who escaped to the United States and whose wife is now in Hobart Town, cuts a conspicuous figure in New York as a gentleman of large fortune under the name of Mr William Jones. But Jonathan smokes him. ['Jonathan' was slang for America or Americans, as we now use 'Uncle Sam'; 'smokes him' was slang for 'knows what he's up to'.]

This report indicates that Ikey had not only returned to his old alias of Jones, but that he was trading successfully whether legally or otherwise. The pamphlets describing his life indicate that he had plunged at once into the underworld. One of them reports:

> Ikey embarked with three others in a system of forgery of notes of the National Bank of New York . . . whilst he entered ostensibly into the jewellery business, in reality [he] negotiated fraudulent debentures on the local Government and discounted stock of the English, which was then at a premium. The frauds were at length discovered, and warned by a friendly municipal [official] he started off to his wife and children.

It seems that news had at last reached him of Ann's arrest and deportation, and that he started off at once for Van Diemen's Land. After a stormy and 'near fatal' voyage to Rio de Janeiro, then a regular port of refreshment for Australia-bound ships, he found one sailing for Hobart. This voyage was a strange decision, commented upon by newspapers as far away as Cape Town, where the *South African Advertiser* of 25 September 1830 opined that he must have made his way to Hobart 'as if by instinct'. The Sydney *Monitor* of 17 March expostulated that it was 'extraordinary, if not fatuitous'. For one person, at least, it was extremely disconcerting. The Rev. Dr William Henry Browne, LL D, who was appointed Colonial Chaplain in 1828 and was to remain in the colony for forty years, had no sooner landed than he hastened to Colonel George Arthur, Lieutenant Governor of Van Diemen's Land, with a burden of bitter complaint. Arthur translated it into a letter to the Bishop of London:

> Dr Browne who was recently appointed to this Colony arrived last week in the *Coronet* . . . his outward voyage has been exceedingly unpleasant from that disrespect and insult to which clergymen are sometimes exposed from men of low and irreligious minds. The vessel unfortunately put into Rio, where an additional passenger unfortunately applied for accommodation to provide which the Chaplain's cabin was, most insultingly, forcibly entered, and the stranger being a Jew, made his associate in a berth scarcely six feet square. On their arrival here the stranger proved to be the runagate Ikey Solomon. Your Lordship may be assured I am fully disposed to afford Dr Browne every protection in my power, indeed I wish it were possible to punish the master of the vessel by sending him back to England with his passenger who has escaped from the hands of Justice.[15]

But however much Arthur might fume, he was powerless, for Ikey had committed no crime in Van Diemen's Land. On 17 October 1828 the Solicitor General advised Arthur that 'he was not aware of any ground on which [Solomon's] arrest in law be justified, and that only if he had committed any particular felony, he would be prepared to advise that a warrant be issued, and upon such warrant he might be arrested and legally conveyed to England'.[16] The Lieutenant Governor immediately wrote a private letter to Robert William Hay, Under-Secretary of the Colonial Office:

> I think it proper to inform you that 'Ikey Solomon' has arrived here, his sons having shortly before preceded him, on ascertaining that their mother was detained as a convict in the colony—'Ikey' was taken on board the *Coronet* at Rio under the name of Sloman . . . in the absence of all evidence of his crimes it has been considered advisable not to take him into custody.[17]

While Arthur awaited an answer from London, Ikey remained free. For a few weeks he maintained the alias of Sloman, though many people had recognised him as soon as he walked the streets of Hobart Town, and he had moved in with the Newmans as another lodger. He used the capital he brought with him to buy a shop in the same street as his sons', and for a little while all went merrily. But very soon, as seems inevitable when two families share the same house, quarrels of increasing magnitude developed between the Solomons and the Newmans. They attracted the attention of officials, who must have been waiting for any opportunity to move against the Solomons, and prompted a legal battle in which Ann was the first victim.

The official investigation showed that Ann had never been treated as an assigned servant, and Newman, who was a constable, had not bothered to report that the notorious Ikey Solomon was living in his house. It seems certain that the Solomons were paying for more than board and lodging with the Newmans but, to avoid censure, Newman claimed that Ann's behaviour had changed since the arrival of her family. And, presumably to ingratiate himself, he reported that Ikey planned to take her out of the colony at the first opportunity. Ikey, he wrote, had stated that even if Ann should be sent to the Female Factory (a combined workhouse and prison) he would use sufficient influence to free her again.

As soon as the Colonial Secretary heard this, his immediate and inevitable response was to order that Ann should be sent to the Factory and never assigned as a family servant again. Arthur must have had some doubts about the wisdom of this move, because he feared that it might prejudice the far more important case he was attempting to build up against Ikey Solomon, but eventually he agreed. Ann was committed to the dreaded Factory, whose inmates were employed upon such tasks as carding wool but which was a repository for incorrigible harridans and an unofficial brothel patronised by the soldiers of the colony.[18]

The Solomon family fought back. John wrote to the Colonial Secretary, and laid the blame on the Newmans. He said that his mother had 'lived happily in Mrs Newman's service, being treated more as the Mistress' sister than as a servant', and that he and his brother had been on the best of terms with Mr Newman until the latter found it necessary to apply to them for 'pecuniary aid'. Possibly this was some polite blackmail by Newman. The Solomons lent him £25, but when he asked for more they refused. Mr Newman then presented an 'exorbitant' bill for their accommodation, and in the subsequent quarrel Mrs Newman struck Ann Solomon and drove her from the house.

As he had done when in New South Wales, John applied for his mother to be assigned to him and wrote that the children's situation was 'desperate', since he could care only for his sister, also named Ann. The three younger children were being maintained in the official orphanage. The long weeks passed, but nothing happened except for John and his sister Ann being summoned to an official interview. Finally Ikey Solomon abandoned his caution and wrote directly to the Lieutenant Governor. He dropped the name Sloman and stated that he had read of his wife's 'unfortunate situation' while he was in America and had travelled immediately to Hobart Town 'solely from those natural causes, feelings, and affections unnecessary, he trusts, to explain to your Excellency'.

Solomon blamed the quarrels with the Newmans upon their constant demands for money, as a result of which his wife had been committed to the Factory, 'In which place of oblivion she is now confined to the utter discomforture and bereavement of your memorialist'. He said that he was now aged fifty, and had travelled 30 000 miles to this place expressly to settle and pass the remainder of his life 'on the bosom of his wife and family'. He asked that his 'beloved wife' should be assigned to him, and stated that he was willing to enter into a bond of indemnity to prove his good faith. He had already secured a leasehold for four hundred pounds and wanted to settle in Hobart Town.

Arthur's reply was curt: 'the ends of justice would be entirely defeated, if his wife, so soon after her transportation to this colony, should be assigned to her husband'. But the ends of justice were soon overlooked when, on 16 March 1829, Mrs Ann Solomon was released on sureties worth almost £3000 and assigned to her husband. Ikey had bonded himself for £1000, his son John for £500, and seven friends for £200 each. The money would be forfeit if she 'at any time be clandestinely removed from the said island of Van Diemen's Land'. Five of the bondsmen were publicans, and almost certainly were friends of young John Solomon. They included the very successful entrepreneur and former convict from Sheerness Judah Solomon; the publican Benjamin Walford, son of one of the first Jewish convict-settlers in Van Diemen's Land; and John Pascoe Fawkner, the son of a convict and future pioneer of the settlement at Port Phillip. Fawkner would fight for the cause of Jewish emancipation in the first Legislative Council of Victoria.

After Ann was released, Ikey may have been under the delusion that even the arm of the law was not long enough to stretch the thousands of miles between London and Hobart. But even while the Sydney *Monitor* of 6 February 1829 was reporting that Ikey and his wife were living 'in comfortable circumstances in Hobart Town', the documents concerning Ikey's arrest, trial and escape were on their way from Whitehall to Hobart. They were accompanied by a letter from Under-Secretary Twiss to Colonel Arthur, in which he wrote, 'I am directed by the Secretary of State Sir George Murray, that you will take immediate steps to apprehend him'.[19]

Nemesis was swift and dramatic. The *Monitor* of 17 March 1830 described the fatal day to its Sydney readers in full and lurid detail:

> At about 2 pm two constables, in the disguise of out-settlers, came into his shop, one of whom said, he wanted some tobacco and the other a pipe. On coming in, they asked for the old gentleman, as they preferred dealing with him to the young ones. Ikey who was behind the counter, started up and said: 'I am the person' and instantly one of the men seized him and said: 'You are the person we want.' On his apprehension, Ikey turned as pale as death, and after recovering from the stupor of a few moments exclaimed: 'So help me Heaven! I am a done man now; its all over for me; I am done for!' He made a rush towards a desk at the upper end of the counter, on which there was lying a penknife, which he endeavoured to seize hold of, no doubt for the purpose of committing suicide, but was prevented in the attempt by

the constables, to whose assistance four of the military who were stationed outside, came with drawn bayonets and fire arms. Having rendered him powerless, they handcuffed him, and brought him before the Police Magistrate of the Colony. After identification as Isaac Solomon, he was committed to gaol, to guard against the possibility of escape, he was heavily ironed.

The Hobart Town *Colonial Times* of 6 November 1829 saw his seizure in more judicious terms, and published in its editorial:

> The domestic arrangements of this family have been viewed with jealousy by many industrious well behaved persons in unfortunate circumstances who were at a loss to reconcile the apparent injustice of a certain marked indulgence they received that had been refused to others and much more deserving objects. Ikey Solomon has been caught in his own trap.

The *Launceston Advertiser* of 16 November commented: 'So Mr Ikey Solomon is put in limbo. He goes home to old England. He is dreadfully cut up and says he will starve himself to death. His wife, poor woman, is returned to the factory'. On 23 November the same newspaper remarked, 'the idea of Ikey Solomon starving himself was a very good one and he certainly appeared very faint (during his appearance in the Hobart Court when he was formally remanded) . . . But people seldom die of starvation, except by compulsion, and Solomon lives still'.

Solomon's detention was followed by the official confiscation of the property in his house and shop. His wife was returned to prison though this time she was sent to the Cotton Factory, which was slightly less oppressive than the Female Factory. Her children were returned to the orphanage, and she was allowed to see them once a week. Her two older boys were forbidden to communicate with her. With their father in prison their mother's hope for a measure of freedom seemed doomed.[20]

John and Moses turned to the courts. They engaged Joseph Tice Gellibrand, the best legal adviser in the colony, as their barrister and introduced a writ of habeas corpus before the Chief Justice, Sir John Lewes Pedder, who was known for giving prisoners the benefit of every possible doubt. The legal position was far from clear because, instead of sending a properly worded warrant for Solomon's arrest, the English authorities had sent an order through Colonel Arthur's dispatch box. The *Colonial Times* of 20 November hoped that a 'legal hitch' would not prevent his deportation to England, and wrote in an editorial

> a criminal is a criminal, whoever he might be, Christian or Jew, a Crowned Head or a peasant, an emigrant or a convict [but] it must be admitted either that the Home Government has a very exalted opinion of their own power in controlling, in a summary manner, the proceedings of their Colonies, or they consider the institutions of Van Diemen's Land as perfectly insignificant.

So badly did the case appear to be proceeding that Arthur called a meeting of the colony's Executive Council and a warrant for Solomon's arrest was drawn up in case the court discharged him.[21] When the warrant was shown to Mr Justice Pedder, he described it as 'the most unmeaning and unintelligible instrument he had ever seen'.[22] The legal arguments dragged on for a month.

Ikey Solomon made a wild and foolish attempt on 29 December 1829 to influence Arthur in his favour by offering to become a police spy 'for detecting all such offences or anything else that the Government may appoint me to do to the uttermost of my ability'. Ingeniously he dredged up an incident in his recent past when a forger of notes of the Bank of the Derwent had been arrested following information he had supplied. The Lieutenant Governor noted on the letter that 'no notice should be taken of this application'.[23]

On Saturday 2 January 1830 Mr Justice Pedder finally decided in favour of theoretical liberty.[24] Bail was set at £2000 for himself and four sureties of £500 upon condition that Ikey proceed to England at the first opportunity to surrender himself for trial. The Judge knew that Solomon would find it nearly impossible to raise such huge sums, and he remained in gaol while preparations were made for his deportation. The *Colonial Times* of 8 January fumed: 'So much for all the able and unanswerable arguments of his Counsel and the effect they have produced!—it amounts to nothing else but incarceration under another shape'. The *Tasmanian and Austral-Asiatic Review* declared on 5 February, 'it was perfectly clear from the very first that Solomon would be sent to England' while that 'glorious privilege, the Right of Habeas Corpus, turned out to be just unsophisticated humbug'. The *Australian* in Sydney reprinted the Tasmanian newspapers' analysis of the case and on 26 February commented bitterly that 'the existence or non-existence of the Habeas Corpus Act can be of little consequence in a country where the Governor has practically absolute power'.

As January ended Solomon was taken, in deep secrecy, on board the *Prince Regent* and, with the colony's Chief Constable as his guard, set sail for England. Overnight Ikey became 'the unfortunate man Solomon' and on 29 January the *Colonial Times* expressed sympathy for his family: 'Our hostility towards him has ceased now that the nondescript character he assumed whilst he sojourned upon our shores has terminated by his having left them'.

Ikey Solomon arrived at Portsmouth on 27 June, and eleven days later stood in the dock at the Old Bailey. He was charged with eight crimes, of which five were capital offences. His trial created a sensation, and was very fully covered in the London *Times* and the *Morning Post*.[25] The second of the pamphlets previously mentioned gives a vivid picture of the scene at the Old Bailey:

> shortly after the opening of the Courts, every avenue leading to the New Court, in which the case was appointed for trial, was thronged almost to suffocation. The decided majority of the crowd seeking admittance was evidently the descendants of the patriarchs. As was but naturally expected the utmost anxiety was evidenced on the part of all those of the Jewish persuasion to catch a glimpse of the person and the features of the prisoner. At 8 am the Common Sergeant took his seat on the bench and shortly afterwards Ikey was placed at the bar. In the Newgate Calendar he was described as a dealer and the age given 45. He did not however, appear nearly so old. During the time the indictments were read, he frequently and piercingly surveyed

the persons in the body of the Court as if he were prepared to find an accuser in everyone his eyes rested upon.

Following the reading of the indictments Solomon expressed the modest hope that 'under all circumstances, His Majesty's Government will be induced to spare his life and that they will permit him to join his wife and family who are still residing in Van Diemen's Land'. Despite a late start to the proceedings, the first two charges were dealt with quickly. Ikey Solomon, who naturally denied everything, was found not guilty by the jury. The trial had started well for him, and Mr Phillips, his barrister, had proved himself an able defender of his celebrated client.

Three of the capital charges were heard and disposed of with equal speed. According to the *Times*, the trying of these charges found the prisoner far more at ease. He 'did not evince that agitation on hearing the verdicts which he manifested on being first placed on the bar', but the charges were 'weak in point of proof as compared with the other indictments on one of which, it is said, a conviction must inevitably take place, owing to the recent possession of the property'. The prosecution experienced great difficulty in their attempts to prove the offences, even though they were able to call as witnesses more than sixty people 'who had been kept in London at great inconvenience and expense'. Many years had passed since some of the offences had been committed. Some of the important witnesses were absent or had died, and some of the charges were invalidated by the ruling that a person could not be called upon to account for the possession of goods found in his custody three months after they had been stolen.

So far all was well, but on 12 July 1830 Ikey Solomon was brought back before the bar of the court for trial on the last three capital charges. In the course of the morning he was found guilty of two of the three charges, involving the purchase of goods knowing that they were stolen, and sentenced to fourteen years transportation. Legal quibbles concerning the disposition of the stolen property, and the question of which Act of Parliament was involved in his conviction, postponed his transportation for nearly a year. He was kept imprisoned at Newgate Gaol, but on 31 May 1831 he sailed for Van Diemen's Land on the *William Glen Anderson* and arrived at Hobart Town on 1 November 1831.

On this second voyage to Van Diemen's Land he sailed in chains, with no opportunity to bribe the shipmaster to let him bully his way into a chaplain's cabin.[26] Nevertheless, the long journey was not devoid of drama. An uprising among the prisoners was thwarted by information given to the ship's authorities by Solomon, and the story of this assistance was later told by Lieutenant Colonel H. Breton to the Select Committee on Transportation of the House of Commons in 1837: 'There was a plan formed by two desperate characters, and the man who came forward was Ikey Solomons; and the argument he made use of was this, that he had a great deal to lose, and nothing to gain, if they took the ship, and therefore he came forward to tell us'.

At the Hobart Town waterfront, the colonial authorities interviewed each convict upon his arrival and copied into the police dossiers the prisoner's own account of his crime and conviction and the details of his home and family in England. This was done because the official legal reports on individual prisoners sometimes took months to arrive, and the officials wanted to hasten the dispatch of prisoners to prison, chain gang or assigned masters. The convicts, unaware that their statements could not be checked against their records, usually kept them fairly accurate. The voyage itself had been intimidating enough, but it was daunting to be hauled out of the ship's hold in chains and made to stand in the bright sunlight before an officer in full dress uniform who sat behind a table laden with official papers and whose sword was carefully placed across the table. A military secretary sat beside the officer, waiting to write down whatever was said. The tableau would generally be enough to elicit the truth.

Ikey Solomon was not to be intimidated. He was very familiar with the system through his previous time in Hobart Town and he knew perfectly well that the documents were not on board. And so he told the authorities a strange story which was duly noted at the top of his dossier. Admitting that he had been sentenced in England for fourteen years for receiving stolen goods, he went on to state that in 1810, under the alias of Moses Joseph, he had been sent out to Australia as a convict for having stolen a pocket book. He claimed that three or four years later he had been pardoned and had returned to England. It was an interesting lie. It evoked memories of his first English trial, and of the fate of his long-dead companion in crime, Joel Joseph, who had been sent to Australia and pardoned shortly before he died.

Solomon obviously hoped that this misleading story of past good behaviour would help to change the course of his future and cause a repetition of official forgiveness. It was not a tactical success, but his intervention on board ship must have been the reason why this notorious fellow was given only five years in gaol and assigned to menial administrative work. He was to spend six months at Richmond Gaol and a year at the infamous prison at Port Arthur, and received several minor convictions for 'abusive language' and 'disorderly conduct' and for making 'malicious charges' against a government architect. For some time he worked as a 'javelin man', or assistant prison guard and warder.

He was rescued from servitude by Hobart Town's prominent Jewish merchant and emancipist Judah Solomon (see Chapter 15). Solomon, who may have been a relative and who came from Sheerness, offered surety for Ikey, the government accepted the bond, and Ikey left Port Arthur with a ticket of leave and the ruling that he should live at New Norfolk, twenty-five miles from Hobart Town.[27]

With high hopes, Ikey Solomon rented a house in the little country town, and there waited to be joined by the wife and family from whom he had been parted six years before. But it was a bitter reunion when he managed to draw the remnants of his family together. His two older sons had left Van Diemen's Land and settled in Sydney. His wife was living with George Madden, a convict on ticket of leave, who had been transported for robbing a betting shop in England. Madden, who was younger than Ann, was working out the rest of his time by serving as a constable. He was said to be wealthy, and it was well known that he possessed the means to return to England once he had been fully pardoned. Ikey's daughter Ann had fallen in love

Ikey Solomon's convict record. In this record we can see Ikey's fictitious story: 'Transp[orted] for Rec[eiving] Stolen Goods. Gaol Report Before Transp[ortation]. Hulk [Report] Good. Married 5 children. Stated This Offence Receiving Stolen Goods. Transp[orted] before 20 years ago for [stealing] a Pocket Book. Pardoned 3 or 4 years afterwards. Moses Joseph was sent to Sydney for the Same Offence'. The dossier also shows that he was immediately employed as a 'javelin man' (guard) at the gaol in Richmond.

with a boarder in her mother's Hobart Town home, and wanted to have nothing to do with her father. His 17-year-old son David claimed the ownership of the house which Ikey had bought in Hobart Town seven years before. As David had collected the rent throughout Ikey's imprisonment, this was a severe blow to Ikey's finances. Only his youngest daughter Sarah, who was thirteen when he was released from prison, seems to have kept some kind of affection for him. She remained within his care, and twelve years later was married in a ceremony held at her father's home.

Either by threats or persuasion, Ikey established his wife, his daughters Ann and Sarah, and his son David in his New Norfolk home. Bringing them together under his roof caused instant pandemonium. A voluminous file in the Archives of Tasmania tells the story of the miserable, apparently interminable quarrels that wracked the family, and bears witness to an extraordinary degree of official concern about the family of a former convict. In view of all that was to happen, the Lieutenant Governor must often have regretted that he sent Ikey to England for trial. Had he been allowed to remain peacefully in Hobart Town the family would have undoubtedly remained united.

The domestic battle erupted into the open when Ann and her children charged Ikey officially with 'drunkenness and violent conduct at sundry times, ever since he returned'. They were determined to see the last of him. The charge was dismissed by the Deputy Police Magistrate on 3 July 1835, but 'equal blame' was attached to both parties on the charge of 'violent and abusive conduct'. Both husband and wife were threatened with prison should 'disorderly proceedings' be repeated. The Chief District Constable was told to keep a watchful eye on them. But the disturbances continued. Ikey's wife called him 'a beast' and 'a wretched dog'. David called his father 'an old vagabond, old beggar and a nasty stinking wretch', and at last Ikey was provoked into prosecuting his wife. The gates of the Female Factory closed behind her once more, for having used 'opprobrious epithets to her husband and ill treating him'.[28]

With their mother in prison again, the children sprang to her defence. Young Ann Solomon's paramour, a Mr J. G. W. Wilson, wrote a letter to Colonel Arthur in which he accused Ikey Solomon of maltreating both wife and daughter. This letter was characterised by the magistrate involved in the case as an 'effusion of a love-sick swain'. Ann returned to Hobart Town and continued to fight for her mother's release. After waiting with 'no avail' four or five days to see the Chief Magistrate, she went with her young sister to the Lieutenant Governor, who 'received them kindly' and promised to 'look into' the matter. Nothing happened. Ann claimed that she was destitute, and that her father had bribed a Constable Brooks to testify against her mother. The magisterial reaction to this allegation was that 'a little retirement would be very beneficial to Mrs Solomon's character'. The Chief Magistrate added:

> Isaac is now so unhappy at their absence that he has repeatedly applied to me to assist him in recovering them. He is quite willing to support them, if they will reside with him, but it is hardly to be expected that, having rented a house at £40 a year at New Norfolk, whence he is not allowed to remove, he should be required to keep up another establishment at Hobart from their wilful opposition to his wishes.

After some interdepartmental discussion the authorities decided to withdraw from the whole dispute, as the property and personal quarrels were of 'a private nature'. Despite certificates by three neighbours testifying to Mrs Solomon's adultery, she received her ticket of leave and, 'in order to protect her children', permission was given to her to live in Hobart. The thick official file concludes with a terse letter which David Solomon wrote from Hobart Town to his father at New Norfolk:

> Mr Solomon,
>
> Unless you send me my things down by the fust convayance I shall emediatley go to Capt Forster about them.
>   You have got a bed and beding, a box of Tules a gun and rod, fiddle dressing table and two Boxes of Closes and a box of Sunderies and dining table of Mying.
>
> D. Solomon.

The letter was delivered at the office of the Colonial Secretary by one of Ikey's neighbours who attached a sympathetic note: 'The letter sent from the son to his father is a precious morceau, and I hope that Mr Solomon's case is well looked into. He has been used ill'.

Considering his long history on the wrong side of the law, the sympathy that Ikey Solomon now enjoyed from neighbours, police and administrators is impressive, and indicates that by this time in his life he was both plausible and pathetic. He certainly became quite well behaved. His police record shows only one regrettable lapse, when he was 'severely reprimanded for making use of obscene language to Rheuben Joseph in the presence of many respectable females, having confessed contrition and apologised to Rheuben Joseph'. Three years later, in 1838, Ikey received permission to leave New Norfolk and effected some kind of reconciliation with his wife, because he returned to his property in Hobart Town and made a fresh start in business as a tobacconist. Judah Solomon withdrew his surety for Ikey in July 1838 and the bond was taken over by Henry Solomon, a jeweller and a cousin. On 27 May 1840 both Ann and Ikey received a conditional pardon. Ikey Solomon received a Certificate of Freedom in 1844.[29]

Ikey Solomon had not been forgotten in London. In 1839 a sensational robbery of Brazilian gold-dust sent to Falmouth resulted in the arrest of four accomplices. As *The Chronicles of Newgate* put it, 'the whole affair had been planned and executed by members of the Hebrew persuasion'. The receiver of the stolen gold was Emanuel

Solomon and his tobacconist's shop in Hobart Town, c. 1846. Ikey was a tall man and is probably the figure standing in the doorway of his dilapidated shop. The Jewish daguerrotype pioneer George Barron Goodman visited Hobart Town twice (in 1842 and 1844) and this photograph may have been taken during one of these visits.

Moses alias Money Moses, a publican who kept the Black Lion Inn of Drury Lane and who was described as 'one of the most daring and successful fences ever known in the metropolis'. The *Chronicles* reported: 'Moses, it may be added, was a direct descendant of Ikey Solomon'. It may have been a metaphorical remark but Money Moses was sent to Van Diemen's Land in 1841 where he promptly died of a broken heart.[30]

In Hobart Town Ikey Solomon became a member of the recently formed Hebrew Congregation. He paid his membership fees and gave some small donations, though by this time he certainly was not a rich man. In April 1844 he was in arrears with his membership fees, and owed the congregation the sum of four pounds and eleven shillings.[31] Evidently the passage of time failed to solve his matrimonial problems, because on 25 May 1840 George Madden charged him with assault. According to the newspaper reports, Solomon caught Madden on his premises and assumed he was there 'for improper purposes'. Madden denied this, but 'Solomon's rage had risen too high to be appeased, and he was proceeding to chastise him but for the interposition of friends'. Ikey was bound over to keep the peace. Exactly four months later Ann charged Ikey with brutal treatment and, after a 'considerable time in court', the case came to an inconclusive end.[32]

In early 1843, Ikey Solomon applied to the government for a family servant to be assigned to him, but this was refused on the grounds that he had been living apart from his wife for some months.[33] He rejected the charge, firmly declaring:

> . . . it would not occasion much trouble on the part of the authorities to ascertain beyond doubt the truth of my denial . . . I can only say I am the father of a large family, and if family differences have taken place between them and me I cannot suppose that such differences would be sufficient to warrant the Police Magistrate's refusal of the assignment to my wife of a servant . . . I have been many years in the colony, and never charged with one single act of dishonesty but on the contrary it is well known that I have used every exertion in my power for the support of my family . . . there seems unfortunately to be a prejudice against me which I am undeserving of, as I can conscientiously say that whatever I may have been thought of previous to my arrival here, my conduct since has been marked for honesty and perseverance.

As the Colonial Secretary commented, 'the denial of the servant was derived from the scenes I have witnessed in this office between Solomon and his wife. I know that they have been living apart from one another and though Solomon may be living quietly now from what I have seen and heard I think it little likely that any control would be exercised over a female assigned servant'.

The records of the Hobart Hebrew Congregation show that on 27 January 1847 Sarah Solomon, aged twenty-five and living with her father at New Town Road, Hobart, married Godfrey Barnett Levy, a draper. On 3 September 1850, Ikey Solomon died in Hobart Town at the age of sixty-six. Yitzhak ben Zvi was his Hebrew name. His was the eighth Jewish funeral at the old Hobart Jewish cemetery. Letters of administration, not exceeding the value of seventy pounds, were granted to Ann Solomon, the widow of the owner of the little tobacconist's shop in Elizabeth Street,

Hobart Town. John Solomon flourished in Australia. He ran the Tasmanian Auction and Commission Mart in Liverpool Street in Hobart Town. He was licensed as an auctioneer in 1832 and ran the public house the William IV. In 1834 he returned to Sydney and became a successful 'merchant and gold bullion dealer'. When John Solomon died in 1889 he left an estate valued at £181 000.

THERE IS A GREAT DEAL of evidence to support the theory that Charles Dickens' character Fagin in *Oliver Twist* was based on Ikey Solomon.[34] Ikey's sensational trial was in 1835: the first chapters of *Oliver Twist* appeared in *Bentley's Miscellany* in 1837. In November 1838 a stage version was performed at the Royal Surrey Theatre, and Dickens referred to Ikey by name in the program notes.[35] This was not the first play to feature Ikey. R. W. Elliston, the father of two sons who had emigrated to Australia, wrote a play called *Van Diemen's Land* in 1830 and as one of his characters used a Jew named 'Barney Fence'. After Ikey's trial, the play was revived and 'Barney' became Ikey Solomon, and in 1835 a second edition of the play had been printed and was in circulation.[36]

William Makepeace Thackeray was also impressed by the drama of Ikey Solomon. In the late 1830s Thackeray used the pseudonym Ikey Solomons Junior to enhance his contributions to London's magazines. Although there is no direct link between the character of Fagin and the life of Ikey, memories of Ikey were fresh when *Oliver Twist* was written. Certainly a lively young London court reporter like Dickens who had worked at the Old Bailey would have known all about Ikey—for, as his biography in the *New Newgate Calendar* remarked, 'There are few offenders whose name and whose character are more universally known than Ikey Solomon'. And a regular observer of the procession of wretched criminals through the Old Bailey and on to the gibbet, the prison hulks or to Australia would have picked up the language of London's underworld. Dickens therefore took the letters of the familiar Yiddish word *ganif* (thief) and by changing the letters around named his villain Fagin.

Perhaps the key to Ikey's character is given in a letter written by William Allenby, a former convict constable, to the Governor of Van Diemen's Land in 1844. He claimed the reward of five hundred sovereigns which he said the British government had offered after Ikey escaped from custody (actually it was only fifty sovereigns) and mentioned that a convict named Rust would testify that in prison, on the morning of the escape, the irrepressible Ikey Solomon had tried to sell him a diamond pin. Under any circumstances, such cool roguery has a glamour of its own.

The 'Jewboy Bushranger' and Family

FOR TWENTY-FIVE YEARS after the First Fleet anchored, the tiny colony centred on Sydney was barred from the interior of Australia by the ramparts of the Blue Mountains. The community was oriented towards the sea, even though there were convicts who believed that China or the utopian country of the King of the Mountains promised freedom for those who could find a way through the towering masses of rock. At last, in 1813, the young explorers William Lawson, William Charles Wentworth and Gregory Blaxland found a way through the mountains and into the vast empty spaces of arable land that lay behind them. Early settlement in such areas meant the establishment of homesteads or little townships at great distances from each other, linked by lonely tracks straggling through the bush and a long way from the law. As settlers both bond and free began to familiarise themselves with the bush, and as young males grew up and discovered that the country offered little future to a man without either land or capital, an increasing number became outlaws. They were given the romantic-sounding name of 'bushrangers', but those who suffered from them did not find them romantic. In Van Diemen's Land in the 1820s, escaped convicts who had taken to the bush were the terror of free settlers until a massive government operation succeeded in catching and hanging more than one hundred in one year. In New South Wales by the 1860s the outlaws were almost uncontrollable, until their reign ended with the capture and execution of the Clark brothers.[1]

Few bushrangers had a more dramatic reputation than Edward Davis, the 'Jewboy bushranger' whose father was a respectable emancipist and whose brother founded one of Australia's great newspapers. Their separate destinies tell a unique story about transportation to Australia. Sixty years after Edward Davis died on the gallows, men still gossiped and wrote about the strange fates of all three members of his family.[2]

The story of Edward Davis began on 29 March 1832, when a 16-year-old lad named George Wilkinson, late of Ealing and a labourer, was indicted for stealing 'one wooden till, value 2 shillings and 5 shillings in copper money, the property of Phillis Hughes'.[3] The daughter of Phillis Hughes, of Brentford, told the court how she had heard the rattle of money as she sat in the parlour behind her mother's shop:

> I looked through the window and saw the prisoner in the shop with the till in his hand—he saw me, then put it down, and ran off, and I after him—I never lost sight of him till Hughes stopped him; he moved the till about two yards—there was about five shillings and five pence in copper in it.

A Mr William Hughes deposed: 'I live near the prosecutrix. I was at my door. I saw the prisoner run out of the prosecutrix's shop and stopped him. I am quite certain of his person'. Young George Wilkinson claimed that he was innocent: 'A lady in Gravel Lane missed her son for a fortnight and sent me to look for him at Brentford. I heard an alarm, and saw the lad run out of the shop—I immediately pursued, and was taken'. The judge did not believe him. He was convicted and sentenced to transportation for seven years. In the printed calendar of prisoners dealt with by Newgate Gaol authorities in 1832, George Wilkinson is listed in May as being aboard the hulks under sentence of transportation. In July his name no longer appears, presumably because he had been transported.

All this would seem to have very little to do with a Jewish bushranger called Edward Davis, but he and George Wilkinson were the same person. After the *Camden* anchored in Sydney Harbour on 17 February 1833, the *Australian* reported that she carried a number of free settlers as well as 198 convicts. Among the convicts two were listed as Jews: George Wilkinson and Raphael Gabey. The latter, who was born in Amsterdam and described himself as a tobacconist, was under life sentence for picking pockets at Chester. Described as 5 feet 4 inches in height, with a muddy complexion, light brown hair, and grey eyes, he received his ticket of leave for the Paterson district in 1844. This was altered to the Maitland district in 1847, and he received his certificate of freedom in 1849.[4]

Detailed descriptions of the convicts were first recorded in the manuscript indent of convict ships of the year in which the ships arrived. George Wilkinson's particulars are in the indent of 1832–33, pages 171–2, no. 33–492. Further details, such as evasions and condemnations, were later added to these records, and the corrected and extended information was reprinted yearly in books entitled *Names and Description of all Male and Female Convicts Arrived in the Colony of New South Wales*. In both the printed and written convict books for 1833 we find a recognisable portrait of George Wilkinson:

> Age 18; able to read and write; religion Jew; single; native place, Gravesend; trade, stable boy; tried at Middlesex 5 April 1832; sentenced to 7 years; former convictions 7 days; height 4 feet 11½ inches; complexion dark ruddy and much freckled; hair dark brown to black; eyes, hazel; particular marks or scars, remarks, nose large, scar over left eyebrow, MJDBN inside lower left arm, EDHDM love and anchor lower left arm, 5 blue dots between thumb and forefinger of left hand; father Michael John Davies, 3 years; mother Anna [Hannah] Davis, 1832.

Both indents give as the reason for his condemnation that he 'robbed a till'. The description shows that, like many of the convicts, he was of small stature. As his trade is noted as 'stable boy'—a rather unusual occupation for a Jew—it is possible that he intended to become a jockey. He certainly was to become known as an excellent horseman.

The printed and manuscript books differ on a major point. In the manuscript his name is listed as George Wilkinson, but underneath, initialled by the registrar, is the name Edward Davis. In the printed register he appears as 'Edward Davis, alias George Wilkinson'. The unusual notation 'father Michael John Davies, 3 years' refers to the fact that Michael Davies had arrived in New South Wales three years before, in the convict transport *Florentia*. He had been sentenced in July 1830 at the Kent Quarter Sessions to seven years transportation for obtaining goods under false pretences. The week after he arrived in Sydney, his oldest son John received a similar sentence at Old Bailey, and was sent to Van Diemen's Land aboard the *Argyle*.

Various official records of the father and his sons paint a fairly detailed picture of the family. There were four boys, John, Edward, Charles and David, and four girls, Ann, Jane, Frances and Sophia. Ann lived with her uncle, Thomas Jones, a fruiterer at Covent Garden, and the other three girls and David and Charles came to Australia with their mother Hannah in 1832. Father had been a managing clerk in an attorney's office in Fenchurch Street. He was forty years old, and had been born in London. His 18-year-old son John also worked in an attorney's office.

The records of the county of Middlesex relate how John was convicted of buying candles and pickles from two different shops under false pretences and with a false name. These crimes, at the time of his father's arrival in Australia, must have been committed out of desperation. Young John had precipitately become the head of a large family. His brother David was only seven years old, Edward was fourteen, Frances was twelve and the three other children probably were younger. The family's financial plight must have been appalling.[5]

It is also easy to understand why Edward gave a false surname to the court when he stood trial three years after the transportation of both his father and his brother. After all, to have had both father and brother sent to Australia as convicts was no recommendation for mercy. Once the trial was over and he was bound for Botany Bay, he dropped the alias. The details of the family names and relationships also illuminate the mysterious letters tattooed on Edward's arm. Information that his mother's name was Hannah and not Anna enables us to read the letters EDHDM as Edward Davis Hannah Davis Mother and their place beside the word 'love' and the anchor becomes meaningful. MJDBN probably relate to Edward's father Michael John Davies and the BN may well be linked with the Hebrew word *ben*, meaning son. It is also possible to decode the initials as *ben Meir*, meaning son of Meir, the words which appear on the tombstone of Edward's younger brother David, who was buried at Port Macquarie in 1836 at the age of twelve. It would have been easy for the prison clerk to misread the tattooed M for N. The five blue dots were typical of the secret signs used by the gangs of London's underworld, and merely serve to remind us that Edward had grown up in the East End with his family far away.

The young convict proved incorrigible. Eleven months after his arrival, Edward used the Christmas period of 1833 to elude the rum-sodden guards of Sydney's Hyde Park Barracks. He was caught and condemned to twelve further months of imprisonment. Two years later he absconded again and received an additional year's sentence. This time he was removed from the convict gangs at Penrith, and sent out as an assigned servant to Edward Sparke, a pioneer farmer at Maitland.

Servitude at the mercy of a settler far from any witnesses often was far worse than being subject to the regulations of a chain gang working on the public roads.

'The Chain Gang', drawing by Frederic Mackie, c. 1853.

On 10 January 1837 Davis ran away for the third time, was captured again, and had two more years added to his sentence. He was sent back to Sydney, and on 21 July 1838 he escaped for the fourth and last time, returning to the Maitland district and to that part of the bush he had come to know well. Six months later he suddenly emerged as Teddy the Jewboy, the leader of a gang of convicts who also had absconded from the farms of their masters.

Apparently Davis formed his band of bushrangers in the summer of 1839 in the Hunter Valley district, in the land he knew from his time on the farm. For two long years he imposed a reign of terror from Maitland along the Great Northern Road to New England and down to Brisbane Waters near Gosford. During this time, most of the outrages committed in this vast territory were indiscriminately ascribed to the 'Jewboy gang'. On 12 January 1839 they robbed Mr Biddington's servant near Wightnab's station on the Namoi River. The *Sydney Gazette* reported on 3 April 1839:

> The country between Patrick's Plains and Maitland has lately been the scene of numerous outrages by bushrangers. A party of run-away convicts, armed and mounted, have been scouring the roads in all directions. In one week they robbed not less than seven teams on the Wollombi Road, taking away everything portable.

Davis was so firmly established in the district of Maitland by 1840, and so well known throughout the country, that G. E. Boxall's *History of the Australian Bushranger*, which when published in London in 1899 was one of the first histories of bushranging, states: 'next to Jackey Jackey and perhaps Matthew Brady, more yarns have been told about the Jewboy, this hero of the roads, than any other bushranger in the pre-gold digging era'. There were even tales of Davis robbing the rich and protecting the poor. W. H. Fitchett's *The Story of the Bushrangers*, published in 1909, records: 'The flogging by the Jewboy of a squatter of Wollombi at the public triangle and with the public flagellator's cat enshrined him as a hero in the heart of a certain class of the community'. The Sydney *Herald*, on 8 December 1840, complained that 'the Davis gang was doubtless helped by convict servants, as they showed great knowledge of the robbed establishments and families'. Yet another tale, repeated by Boxall, told of Davis 'rounding up' the Chief Constable of the district, together with a party of policemen and volunteers who had gone out to search for him and, having 'yarded them like a mob of cattle', taking their horses and money and riding away laughing.

There was a hint of romance in stories told about the gang. It was rumoured that Isabella Kelly, the 'red headed termagant of the Manning River area' chased the gang after having been robbed, and upon catching them recovered her money. She was said to have fallen passionately in love with Davis, so that she became a regular visitor to his hideout and brought him food and ammunition. But she became so 'amorously exacting' that the 'jewboy fled to another district'.[6]

Edward Davis had no scruples about robbing other Jews. In November 1840 he and his gang raided the well-known inn belonging to Henry Cohen at Black Creek near Maitland and, even though the hostelry stood on 'one of the most frequented roads of the Colony', they completely ransacked it. However, it was done very stylishly. The Sydney *Herald* of 23 November reported that there were twenty-six men in the inn when it was raided. Most of them, bullock-drivers and others, were former convicts, and the members of the gang greeted them heartily:

> On their arrival they shook hands with them, treated them to brandy and enquired after acquaintances, both male and female, and in fact showed such an understanding between the parties that Mr Day (the Police Magistrate of the near-by town) cancelled two of their tickets [of leave].

A few weeks later the gang repeated its success, and a report of their adventures was published in the *Herald* of 10 December 1840:

> The bushrangers who were at Newcastle lately, and more recently at Pitchers' farm, on the Hunter, have paid us a visit en passant, and now that they have found themselves in every necessary, have left the district for a bold dash somewhere else. On 29 November, Dr McKinlay, a medical man who was proceeding with a guide towards Mr Chapman of the Grange, from Mr Coar at Wallingra, to visit a lady reported to be ill, was 'bailed up' with his guide, and commanded to 'bundle back' to Mr Coar's Wallingra again, otherwise his brains would be blown out. Being unarmed, he made no resistance. They all proceeded to Mr Coar's where, to the astonishment of the captured party, the house was in possession of bushrangers, handsomely

dressed and 'armed to the teeth'. They demanded the Doctor's watch and money, but by intercession of Mr Coar's man (who was lately a patient) who 'begged him off' everything was returned to him again. The Doctor says he was treated in the most gentlemanly fashion, and that he never spent a happier night in his life. They insisted on his making himself quite at home, and not to be alarmed, as they did not intend injuring him, and pressed him to eat some eggs, beer, damper, and butter. They then cleared a sofa for him to lie on, and covered him with their greatcoats, the pockets of which were stuffed with ball cartridge and buck shot. The Doctor's guide had his arms tied behind him, and was thrust under the pianoforte, *sans ceremonie*, the chief telling him that if he either broke the peddle or fell asleep, he would blow his brains out. They were detained prisoners until the morning, and then marched off towards Mr Chapman's.

Their (i.e. the bushrangers') attire was rather gaudy, as they wore broad rimmed Manilla hats, turned up in front with abundance of braid pink ribbons, satin neck cloth, splendid brooches, all of them had rings and watches. One of them (a Jew I believe) wore five rings. The bridles of the horses were also decorated with a profusion of pink ribbons. The leader was formerly an assigned servant to Edward Sparke Esq. of the Upper Hunter and another (named Shea) was lately an assigned servant of Mr Coar; the third, I believe, a Jew named Davis, a very wary determined fellow.

The correspondent of the *Herald* had mixed up two members of the gang. Davis himself had been Sparke's servant. The newspaper story added that by the next morning the bushrangers had stolen over £75 in cash in five separate attacks, taken three horses and a gold watch, and flogged an unfriendly farmer. The gang now consisted of seven men: Davis, Marshall, Shea, Chitty, Everett, Glanville, and one whose name is not known.

Less than two weeks later, they made their last attack upon society. On Monday 21 December 1840, at four in the morning, they raided William Dangar's property, Juranville, and two hours later they entered the village of Scone. The events of that day can be reconstructed from the depositions of eyewitnesses and evidence given at the subsequent trial in Sydney.[7]

When they arrived at Scone, the seven bushrangers divided into two parties. Marshall, Shea, Chitty and the unidentified bushranger rode into the yard of Dangar's store, whilst Davis, Everett and Glanville entered Mr Chivers' public house, the St Aubin Arms. The inn faced the store across the road, so the two parties could join together again without delay. When they entered the store the clerk, John Graham, recognised them by their gaudy clothes. He snatched up a pistol, fired a shot at one of the intruders, and then ran out of the store towards the near-by village gaol to tell the police and raise the alarm. But Shea felled him with two bullets. Meanwhile, the other party had seized the St Aubin Arms. They entered the various rooms, robbed them, and confiscated whatever weapons they found. Glanville broke into the bedroom of the landlady, Mrs Chivers, and ordered her to hand over her money box. It contained seventy pounds.

Davis himself did not take part in the robbery. In his role as leader he let his men do the dirty work. While they turned the house upside down, he chatted amiably to his involuntary hostess. His behaviour was recalled by Mrs Chivers at the time of the trial:

> Davis was at the bar when I came out of my bedroom, and told me not to be afraid, as no one would hurt me. While standing at my bar, he did not offer any violence; they were all very civil, and said they would not hurt anyone. Davis must have been in my bar all the time and when the shots were fired.

This amiable atmosphere was dissipated by Shea's two shots and the news that a man had been murdered. Davis was reported as saying, 'I would give £1,000 that this had not happened, but as well a hundred now as one', and some of the others are supposed to have said, 'now as we have commenced murdering, it matters little what may follow, as our lives are at last forfeited'. Within twenty minutes they had bundled up their loot and galloped away.

It was then about nine in the morning. From Scone they went to plunder the farm of Messrs Paterson and Goldfinch, and then to the home of James Norrie, where they took all the money they could find, demanded breakfast, and quixotically paid their host one pound for their food. At the trial, Paterson declared that the bush-rangers were 'very agitated'. Norrie recalled that Davis had hustled him into the house, threatening 'to shoot a man in a moment' and stating that they had shot one already. Under cross-examination, however, Norrie wavered and confessed that he was not really certain who had made this admission of guilt.

As the bushrangers rode away towards the ranges, wearing their 'gaudy dress', it was no longer a reckless ride into adventure. 'Ruggy' Everett 'wore the death flag, showing no quarters, being a black handkerchief attached to his hat'. About noon they arrived at Atkinson's Page River Inn, which they had robbed three weeks before. Despite the blood they had shed and their alleged agitation they were cool enough to take refreshments at the inn, rob the thirty people who were on the premises, have their horses well groomed, and vanish into the bush once more.

By the end of the day they had ridden thirty miles from the scene of the murder, but just as they were settling down for the night they were sighted by an avenging posse which several days earlier had been assembled to pursue them. Led by a former army officer, Captain Edward Denny Day of the 46th and 62nd Regiments who had just been appointed Police Magistrate at Muswellbrook, it included the Chief Constable of the district, several local settlers, an Aboriginal tracker and some five ticket-of-leave men. Five miles out of town Captain Day was told that the bushrangers had crossed the Hunter River the previous night. Day proceeded to Scone and to the Court House where Mr Robertson, the Police Magistrate, and two other magistrates were sitting. Afraid that the desperadoes would return, the worthy magistrates even refused to supply Captain Day with a fresh horse; however Day was now joined by four more men. A twenty mile ride down to the Page River in pouring rain soaked their guns, which had to be dried and reloaded. Six miles from the river at Doughboy Hollow, at six o'clock in the afternoon, Captain Day saw through the cover of some trees carts, a fire, some tethered horses and a number of men in shirtsleeves quietly going about their business. The hunt that had lasted two years was over. Only one man, Edward Davis, could be seen hard at work preparing ammunition and casting cartridges.

The end was dramatic. In true Wild West fashion, Captain Day and his men dashed into the camp at full gallop, cheering as they attacked. Though resistance was obviously hopeless, the bushrangers fought back in a last desperate stand. Shea and Everett ran up a hill overlooking the camp, and fired down on the posse. Davis rushed to the opposite side of the gully in order to cover himself from the cross-fire, and the battle became a duel between the two leaders.

'I fired', said Captain Day at the trial, 'and he returned it at me. After he got at the cover of the tree, he fired again at me, resting the gun on the fork of the tree'. One of Davis' shots grazed Day's ear, and Davis was in turn wounded in the shoulder. It was soon over. The bushrangers had to surrender when they ran out of ammunition, and five of the gang, including Davis, were captured within five minutes. Glanville got away and was captured next morning a few miles from the scene of battle, having been tracked down by the Aboriginal. The unknown seventh bushranger escaped, although some newspapers asserted that he had been mortally wounded.

Reports of the victory varied. The *Australian* claimed that Captain Day had recaptured five hundred pounds in cash, and over fifty guns. The Sydney *Monitor* warned the public that the 'property said to be taken from various stations by Davis' gang is much exaggerated'. In reality not much more than seventy pounds was found, as well as some trinkets, eleven guns and about twenty pistols, for which there was no ammunition. The money was promptly claimed by Mr Chivers of the St Aubin Arms and the bushrangers' treasure vanished.

The captives appeared anxious to confess, and Captain Day stayed up all night to hear their stories. Davis and Marshall voluntarily gave him the history of their activities. Shea confessed that he had shot the storekeeper's clerk at Scone. More than one of them said that up until that morning they had done nothing to place their own lives in jeopardy with the law. Davis repeated again and again that he had always been opposed to the shedding of blood for, he said, if they had done so, they would not have reigned a week. As he said this, he turned to his comrades and exclaimed bitterly, 'You see, we have not reigned a day'. All of them, according to Captain Day, said they would rather be hanged than go as prisoners for life to dreaded Norfolk Island.

The next morning the six bushrangers were taken back to Scone and on 23 December 1840, in the presence of J. A. Robertson JP, an inquest was held on the death of the unfortunate Mr Graham and the gang was charged with murder and robbery. Captain Day refused to appear before the formerly unhelpful Police Magistrate, and the matter was taken out of local hands and transferred to Sydney. On 24 February 1841 the gang was committed to trial at the Supreme Court before the Chief Justice, Mr Justice Dowling, and a jury of twelve. The trial attracted great attention. An unusual number of assigned servants and ticket-of-leave holders were observed filling the public galleries.

The newspapers were quick to notice that Davis wore a sober dark suit while his comrades wore prison garb. He was also the only prisoner with a counsel for the defence: the Sydney solicitor William Alexander Purefoy, who tried in vain to save Davis' life. Purefoy was engaged, and paid, by the Jewish community of Sydney. According to A. Marjoribanks, an English visitor to New South Wales who witnessed the last moments of Edward Davis, the Sydney Jews did not turn their backs on the 'Jewboy bushranger' when the shame of a public execution of a Jew seemed possible. In *Travels in New South Wales* he wrote:

> Every possible means were used by the Jews in Sydney, who are a numerous and opulent body, to save the ring leader from being hanged, that being a punishment to which few of that race have been subjected in any age or country, and the counsel whom they employed on his behalf . . . might have succeeded in saving his life had it not been for the circumstances that the magistrate swore . . . that it was the Jew who twice took deliberate aim and fired at him.

The Attorney General pointed out that all the prisoners had been assigned convicts. They had set no value on the system that had assured them a leniency and a kindness unknown to the law except in modern times. Instead they had combined to keep the whole country from the sea coast to the Liverpool Ranges in a state of terror and confusion. Whoever had fired the first shot, all were guilty as aiders and abetttors of the crime. Captain Day was called upon to give evidence. He readily admitted that Davis had told him he had opposed the shedding of blood and would rather be hanged than go for life to Norfolk Island. Mrs Chivers testified that Davis had been in the store when the murder was committed. Mr Purefoy launched 'an able address on behalf of Davis' but did no more than delay the inevitable verdict. The jury retired at 6.15 p.m. and took an hour and a quarter to decide that all the prisoners were equally guilty.

The bushrangers were astounded. During the trial, Everett and Shea had behaved with provocative and insolent good humour. While the jury was considering its verdict, all six of the gang had waved and chatted and joked to friends and acquaintances among the courtroom crowd. So casual was their behaviour that they were ordered into the cage, where they began to quarrel among themselves. They blamed Davis for their ruin, and accused him of brutally alienating friends who had once hidden and helped them and who could have been expected to come to their aid.

The Chief Justice donned the black cap, called each man by name, and told them all that the last scene but one had now arrived. Slowly and in great detail he described the crimes they had committed. He recalled that some of them had said they would prefer to meet their doom than to be transported to Norfolk Island. Their awful wish, he could assure them, would be gratified in order to make an example of them, and to deter others from pursuing a similar course of guilt and crime. He trusted that they would employ the few moments still granted to them to make peace with their Creator, then passed the sentence of death upon them 'in the usual form'.

From the terrible change that had come over the face of Davis, it was obvious that he had anticipated judicial mercy. The Sydney *Herald* of 25 March 1841 reported:

> When Davis heard the sentence he was seen to shed tears, whilst some of the others, observing Mr Lane, the Superintendent of Hyde Park Barracks, in court, vented their anger in wishing he might break his neck. The prisoners were removed to

gaol about 14 minutes after sentence had been passed, each pair being handcuffed between 3 constables and some hundred persons marching along with them.

An unsuccessful appeal was made to the Executive Council, which replied, 'The Council, after an attentive and mature consideration of the case of the several prisoners, has decided that the sentence of the law be allowed to take its course'.[8] Five days before the execution, on 13 March 1841, the *Australian* reported:

> The Hunter River bush rangers who are under sentence of execution were warned by the Sheriff not to entertain the smallest hope that the order for their execution would either be deferred or rescinded. The Executive Council which sat relative to this case, on reviewing the Judge's report, were unanimously of the opinion that the extreme effect of the law ought to be carried into effect upon each individual culprit. Towards Davis public sympathy seems to be a good deal excited. The culprits have been attended for several days past by the ministers of their respective persuasions. We learn that a very urgent appeal has been made to the Council particularly on behalf of Davis. The friends of this unhappy criminal relied mainly on the point adduced in evidence that he was averse to the shedding of blood but the Council in having their attention addressed to the point, immediately referred to the evidence of Mr Day, who swore that Davis placed a musket in the fork of a tree, and deliberately took aim at him twice to take his life.

One thousand people gathered in the gallows yard behind the Old Sydney Gaol in Lower George Street to see the final drama. Jacob Isaacs, the reader at the synagogue, accompanied the Church of England chaplain and the Catholic priest as they led the doomed men through the door of the gaol. The *Australian* of 18 March 1841 reported:

> Davis, in truth, it must be said, appeared with a mind unsettled; the enquiring eye turning in glances round the yard, and then upon the group of some hundreds of spectators assembled on the hill above, seemingly in search of some friend or acquaintances. In health and strength and energies, to all which the buoyancy of almost youth, scarcely arrived at the prime of manhood, these six unhappy men saw placed before them their coffins, and suspended from the beam of the scaffold the ropes. The Deputy Sheriff read the warrant, that further time could not be stayed, the culprits rose and one by one mounted the platform. Davis remained last.
> All the culprits, except Everett, deeply lamented their having committed the crimes, and acknowledged the justice of their sentence. Everett ascended the scaffold hurriedly and in an evident state of excitement. He was followed by Chitty, Marshall and Glanville, all three of whom sung spontaneously the Morning Hymn, found in many editions of the Protestant Book of Common Prayer. 'Awake my soul and with the sun'. In the short interval which elapsed before the withdrawal of the fatal bolt, Marshall and Glanville were engaged in loud and apparently fervent prayer, and we observed Davis thank the Jewish minister for the attention paid to him in his last minutes.

All the witnesses were deeply impressed. Despite the malicious rumour mentioned by A. Marjoribanks that 'not a single Jew attended the execution', at least one Jewish youngster watched the last moments of the Jewish bushranger. 'It was a horrible sight', wrote Morris Asher in his 'Reminiscences of an Octogenarian' published in the *Sydney Mail* in 1907:

> All the men were good looking young fellows. They were all repentant, and said that it was through bad treatment that they took to the bush. This doubtless was so, for the treatment of prisoners generally in those days was, to say the least, very cruel. The clergymen having remained with the wretched men, as long as the terms of the warrant would allow, the executioner proceeded to his office of placing the caps over their faces, and thereby closing upon them forever the light of this world. At this dreadful juncture, the clergymen attendant, two of whom were observed with tears trickling down their aged cheeks, took an affectionate farewell. The signal being given by the Deputy Sheriff, the bolt was of a sudden withdrawn and the six misguided young men were launched into eternity.

A bizarre note had been struck by Everett's behaviour. William George Mathews, a free settler of 1834 who served as Overseer of Convicts and later as a prison clerk, later recalled that Everett had 'behaved with great levity. He flung his shoes among the persons assembled, saying that he would make a liar of his mother, who always said that he would die in his shoes, meaning that he would be hanged'. Mathews claimed Davis was 'the only repentant man of them'.[9]

Edward Davis was buried by himself in a corner of the Devonshire Street Jewish Cemetery. Someone must have saved his body from a common criminal's grave. Perhaps his parents, who knew of his trial and execution, came forward to claim it. Perhaps it was for them that he searched the faces of the crowd on the hill.

There was only one other Australian bushranger who was a Jew. In 1853 Joshua Lazarus and an unnamed companion held up a farm-hand in the outback of South Australia, declaring, 'It is no use talking. We are bushrangers. We take what we want'. Indeed, immediately afterwards Lazarus took £160 from an Indian doctor, Angelo B. Rodriguez, who worked as a shepherd at Mosquito Creek. As the bushrangers left they paused to shake hands with their elderly victim, and express a hope that they would all meet in heaven. Stirred by their apparent piety the old man protested that they had left him penniless, and in response they threw him a derisory two shillings and sixpence. The callous attack threw the colony into an uproar, and within days Lazarus 'the notorious bushranger' was captured and promptly sentenced to imprisonment for life.[10]

WHETHER OR NOT the parents of Edward Davis were present at his execution, there is no doubt that his arrest caused consternation to at least one member of his family. As Edward faced justice in Sydney, his brother John Davies precipitately resigned from his position of Chief Constable of Penrith and left for the newly established township of Melbourne, taking with him his newly acquired non-Jewish wife. He had been Chief Constable only since 1 November 1840, when he was appointed on an annual salary of eighty pounds.[11]

John had made good use of his ten years in Australia. Even though it had begun badly with a written report from the surgeon of his convict ship that he was 'audacious, incorrigible and impudent', it ended well. He had spent his time on board ship as a barber, and when he landed in Hobart Town it seems that he was assigned to a solicitor as a servant and only blotted his record by a brief romance with the wife of a ticket-of-leave man. The official record has vanished, because his page in the Tasmanian convict dossiers is one of the few torn out by a later but influential hand.[12] It should be noted that the family surname seems to have waxed and waned, as 'Davis' and 'Davies' were used, at the beginning at least, with the greatest of ease. The family's association with their place of birth and punishment at Gravesend, Sheerness and Kent is also meaningful, and there seems to have been some significant closeness between the Davis, Russell and Solomon families in Melbourne and Van Diemen's Land.

Be this as it may, John Davies/Davis served his sentence with good enough grace to be allowed to leave Van Diemen's Land before his seven year sentence was fulfilled. He received permission to travel to New South Wales as an assigned servant. The records show that he spent a month on the prison hulk in Sydney, gave evidence in a trial, and was then sent to Port Macquarie.[13]

While Edward was forming his band of outlaws his brother joined the police. For four brief months John Davies reigned as Chief Constable at Penrith until his link with the 'Jewboy bushranger' on trial in Sydney proved to be intolerable, and his resignation from the police force was announced in the *Government Gazette* on 16 March 1841. His personal dilemma won him official sympathy. He went to Melbourne with a high recommendation from Sir John Jamison, the Chairman of the Penrith Bench of Magistrates, and used this to support his apparently unsuccessful applications for the post of Chief Constable of Portland and later for a job in the Water Police Department.[14] There were no vacancies in the police forces of what was then western New South Wales, so John Davies became a reporter on the *Port Phillip Patriot* and later the *Port Phillip Gazette*, where he left this impression:

> [He was] a chubby, red cheeked, dark haired, unmistakably Jewish visaged personage. He had a whole foundry of brass in his face, and was not only self assertive but cheeky. Though comparatively illiterate, he owned other gifts to make up the deficiency, could scrape together readable paragraphs, and as a collector of news was invaluable. It would be hard to find a better general intelligence forager, and at a time when the few officials in Melbourne were insolent and overbearing, no man knew better how to overcome them with his bluster.[15]

Davies also became a frequent performer on the Melbourne stage. Even his own editor was impressed, and on 28 October 1842 wrote:

> Mr. Davies, at present reporter to this office, having engaged the Theatre for Thursday night next, will take a benefit on bidding farewell to the Melbourne stage. Mr. Davies has been deservedly a favourite from his talents as an actor; and if his faults behind the curtain have involved him in censure, submission has expiated fully, the feelings which are common to human temper and human judgement . . . Tickets may be had of Mr. Davies himself and as he is pretty well known, we need not describe his personal appearance at his residence in Bourke Street or at the Gazette Office.

It was far from the final appearance of Davies on the stage in Melbourne or in the public eye. He continued to work both as a journalist and as a comedian. In fact Davies never left the stage. He remained fascinated by the theatre and in his later years became a partner in Hobart's Theatre Royal. The *Port Phillip Gazette* on 18 May 1845 wrote, 'In fact there are frolic and merriment associated with the very idea of Mr. Davies' name appearing on the playbill—Why is it not there more frequently?' His career in Melbourne came to an abrupt conclusion in 1846 when he was charged with, and convicted of, criminal libel for an article that denigrated the wife of the editor of a rival newspaper. The *Gazette* of 22 April reported:

> The editor of the *Port Phillip Patriot*, the irascible John Fawkner, apologised to William Kerr and his wife. Kerr was the editor of the *Port Phillip Courier* and there was little love lost between the two newspapers. Davies was found guilty of criminal libel but his apology in court mitigated his offence and he was fined £15.

After five stormy years it was time to leave Melbourne, and Davies achieved this by finding a vacancy in the police force again. This took him north to Wellington, in New South Wales, and its neighbouring town of Montefiores, where he served in a series of official positions. He was Chief Constable of Wellington, Inspector of the Slaughter Houses, Inspector of Weights and Measures, Inspector of the Distillery, Bailiff of the Court of Petty Sessions, and in 1848 finally became Chief Constable of Bathurst.[16]

Newspaper reports show that as a constable Davies was certainly efficient, but despite these resounding titles there is more than a hint that he carried out his duties in a less than upright manner. His departure for Bathurst whipped up a storm of criticism. A letter to the *Bathurst Advocate* of 26 May 1849 asked sardonically:

> Mr. Davies, what induced you to leave Wellington, where you had less to do? Having the same amount of salary—were the pickings not so plentiful as here? Here the duties are more arduous, and yet you give up quietness for activity and trouble. Did you give £30 to change with your predecessor—was this a quid pro quo?

Davies appeared in court charged with accepting a bribe, and Benjamin Isaacs, the Jewish owner of the *Advocate*, wrote on 9 June 1849:

> [Davies] was severely reprimanded on one of the charges and acquitted of two others . . . We have been informed that Mr. Davies would certainly have been dis-missed had it not been for the strong recommendation of the Police Magistrate.

Bathurst was not satisfied, and a series of poems appeared in the paper about 'Jack'. Their flavour may be tasted by the one entitled 'Jack Crib and his Family Crew', published on 26 May 1849:

> *His father, what was he? a thief,*
> *His sister? a brazen faced w——*
> *His mother? a b——h for mischief,*
> *His brother? the Cain of our shore,*
> *And Jack, 'tis the common belief*
> *Was as bad, if not worse, than the four!*

Davies sued Isaacs for libel and had little difficulty in winning his case. Isaacs was fined forty pounds and sent to prison for two months. In Melbourne the news that someone had actually been convicted for libelling John Davies was greeted with derision. The *Melbourne Morning Herald* drily commented, 'To parties here who knew Davies' real character this sentence will excite more than mere surprise'.[17] In court Davies had flatly denied that Edward was his brother. He fell back upon Edward's alias of George Wilkinson, and said that Edward had been adopted by his father and 'passed' as his brother. Even if this had been true, Davies would still have had to explain Edward's Jewish appearance, his burial as a Jew by the Sydney congregation who would have been delighted to disclaim him, his indent entry, his tattoos, and even his nickname 'Jewboy'. There was, however, no need to go into these details, because the *Advocate's* attacks had been so savage that there was no doubt of their libellous intent.

The trial marked the end of the Bathurst careers of both John Davies and Benjamin Isaacs. After his release from prison, Isaacs went to Windsor to become the owner of the Windsor *Telegraph*. Davies returned to Van Diemen's Land. Newspaper editors allowed themselves a great deal of latitude in those days. Undeterred by Davies' libel victory over its colleague, the *Bathurst Free Press and Mining Journal* of 1 October 1851 wrote:

> It may be satisfactory to a few of our Bathurst readers to learn that Mr. John Davies the pompous, impudent, bloated and unprincipled bully who formerly did the dirty work of the Bathurst police force, is now luxuriating as emigration clerk at Launceston on 30 shillings a week, the inhabitants of which place are wonderfully surprised with the versatility of his genius. Upon receipt of this intelligence we can easily fancy many of them glancing towards their ledgers with a deep sigh.

There is no record of this appointment. In fact Davies had moved to Hobart, where his father had worked for several years as an innkeeper, and in 1852 he became the licensee of the Waterloo Hotel.[18] In the same year he became co-publisher of the *Hobarton Guardian*, which he soon incorporated into the *Hobarton Mercury* and published by himself. Then in 1853, true to his old love for the theatre, he became one of the two lessees of the Hobart Town Theatre Royal, which he completely remodelled and reopened in 1857.

One of the most interesting insights into the life of Tasmania's Jewish community was unwittingly provided by two attempts by Davies to become a member of the Hobart Town Synagogue.[19] John's father had been a member, and had left in debt and disgrace after maliciously accusing Edward Magnus, a fellow Jew, of an assault on a servant girl employed by Henry Jones of Elizabeth Street. The accusation, made by anonymous letter, resulted in Magnus being given three months hard labour.[20] When John Davies applied for membership in 1851 the sins of his father were remembered by the teacher and minister at the synagogue, who had been the employer of the girl. It was suggested to Davies that marriage to a non-Jewish wife disqualified him from membership, but he indignantly and truthfully observed, 'I have been informed from most respectable sources that parties circumstanced as I am by marriage are now members of the congregation'.

The congregation found a solution which was both a compromise and a snub. The Hobart Synagogue Minute Book records that the Board Meeting of 2 March 1851 unanimously resolved 'That seat No. 156 be appointed for the use of Mr. John Davies whenever he be present in the Synagogue but that the Committee decline any payment or pecuniary remuneration for the same and that this resolution be communicated to him by the hon. secretary'. Seat 156 can still be seen at the rear of the Hobart Synagogue. It is the last seat on the benches formerly reserved for convicts from nearby Hobart Gaol, who had been allowed to join the congregation in worship when the synagogue was built. Four years later Davies made a final attempt to join the synagogue

John Davies, photograph by J. W. Beattie, c. 1860.

'for which I am desirous of paying the highest amount usually subscribed'. Once again he was snubbed, probably because by 1855 he had become well known for public litigation and violence.

Four serious court cases concerning assault and libel marked his first ten years in Hobart as a newspaper proprietor. His victims were all fellow journalists. One brawl, with a former editor of the *Mercury*, was so severe that Davies was sent to gaol for a month. When the victim died shortly afterwards, it was said that Davies had killed him.[21] A vitriolic broadsheet greeted his election to the colony's House of Assembly in 1861, and a technicality involving a government printing contract prevented him from taking his seat until 1862, when he became a member of the House for the northern electorate of Devon. In 1871 he became the Member for Franklin, which he remained until his death.

John Davies died on 11 June 1872 and was buried as an Anglican. By that time the *Mercury* was Hobart's only daily newspaper and his two sons had taken over the management. The *Mercury*'s obituary notice, on 12 June, was tactfully silent about the years that preceded John Davies' association with the newspaper, but dwelt lingeringly on 'the gloom' which shrouded the city upon news of his death. It spoke of his 'indomitable energy and earnestness', though it admitted that he was 'much misunderstood' and that 'whatever he thought he said'. We do not know whether anyone in Hobart remembered the truth about 'Jack Cribb'. The account of the funeral reported that it was attended by 'a large concourse of people, representing all classes of the community'. There were judges, members of parliament, and the members of the Ancient and Independent Order of Odd Fellows, of which Davies had

'Delicately Patronizing', cartoon from Fun, or the Tasmanian Charivari, 20 April 1867. John Davies, a powerful figure in Tasmanian colonial politics, prepares for a parliamentary tour of his constituency in the north of the island. Pages of his own newspaper, the Hobart Mercury, lie open on his desk.

been a Grand Master. But it appears that apart from a Mr Levy, no member of the Jewish community was there.

Looking back, John Davies seems the classic newspaper proprietor of the type described so often in fact and fiction: ruthless, domineering, selfish, courageous, colourful. In all these aspects he bore a close resemblance to his father, Michael John Davies, whose career was at least as dramatic, if not as successful.

257

Michael John Davies began his colonial life in Sydney, as an assigned servant to a Mr Richard Smith, until he 'misbehaved' and was sent to Port Macquarie in March 1831. After obtaining his ticket of leave he unsuccessfully sought a publican's licence for the Royal Admiral Inn in George Street, Sydney, in 1838. For a little while he kept an unlicensed hotel in George Street, where he was allowed a billiards table, and he tried again for licences at Port Macquarie in 1839 and Newcastle in 1842. He owned land in Newcastle, and hoped to emulate Henry Cohen at Port Macquarie by building a wharf and stores to handle the developing coastal trade. When this project failed he moved to Melbourne—where in 1847, after some effort, he obtained a licence for the Shakespeare Hotel—and then to Hobart Town. He was dogged by constant financial problems, and on each move he left a trail of debts including his subscription to the Melbourne Hebrew Congregation. One of his longest stays in any one place was after he again returned to Sydney, where he kept the 'well known china shop' at 161 Pitt Street.[22]

There were those who remembered his origins. The *Australasian Chronicle* of 8 December 1840 records that he was fined four pounds at the Sydney court one month before the capture of Edward, for assaulting a steward on a boat for calling him 'a convict scoundrel'. *Bell's Life in Sydney* described him on 8 August 1859 as 'the celebrated patriot and orator and crockery dealer . . . a remarkably irascible old gentleman' and gleefully reproduced a courtroom exchange between Davies and Mr Cory, a Sydney barrister:

> *Cory*: I believe you were sent out here for practising a curious kind of law.
> *Davies*: I am a better gentleman than ever stood in your shoes and was a lawyer before you were hatched.
> *Cory*: Now Sir, were you not sent to this colony for illegally practising law?
> *Davies*: I can teach you law at any rate. I could borrow £10,000 if I wanted to, so it's no matter how I came out.
> *Cory*: I ask you, Sir, were you not sent out for practising law?
> *Davies*: I did not get out like you. I paid for my passage like a gentleman, that's more than you can say.

Michael Davies laid himself open to public attack. *Bell's Life* and the *Herald*, reporting a rally held in Sydney in January 1859 to protest against State aid to religion, sarcastically wrote about 'the Rev. Michael John Davies . . . of the open air cathedral on the Race Course'. Davies declared to the crowd that he was 'a poor humble Jew and a "china man" (cries of "You are a delft man"—Laughter—"Where is your pig tail?")'. The laughter turned to cheers when Davies declared that the Jews of Sydney ought to be ashamed of themselves for requesting State Aid while Joseph Simmons, the President of the Sydney Synagogue, pointedly told the meeting that Davies was 'not the authorised agent of any body of men'.

In one way and another Michael made enough money to retire on in 1863, and five years later he was able to establish his youngest son George Lewis Asher Davies, born in Australia, as the proprietor of the *Australian* at Windsor. George provided him with five grandchildren and, at the age of eighty, the old man published in Sydney a little pamphlet called *Devotions for Children and Private Jewish Families in English*. It was the first Jewish prayer book published in Australia.[23]

The *Mercury* on 25 May 1866 reported the death of John Davies' mother Hannah 'At Sydney, after a long and painful illness, on Sunday 15 April'. Aged seventy-seven, she was buried in the Devonshire Street Jewish Cemetery. Her husband Michael out-lived her by eight years. When the time came for the *Mercury* to record his death, the notice did not appear until 6 January 1874, although he died on 27 December 1873, at Windsor, at the age of eighty-five.

Early in the twentieth century Sydney remembered Michael John Davies as 'a highly respectable citizen' whose 'wayward lad' was 'the only one of a large family that lapsed'.[24] By that time Sir John George Davies, Knight Commander of the Order of St Michael and St George, was the Speaker of the Tasmanian House of Assembly, an office which he held from 1903 to 1913. A son of John Davies, a nephew of Edward Davis the bushranger, and grandson of a convicted attorney's clerk, he was living testimony to the strange consequences which transportation of convicts had upon the destiny of Australia. A second son, Charles Ellis Davies, served as Mayor of Hobart for six terms, Chief Magistrate of Hobart in the 1890s and a member of the House of Assembly for twenty-three years. Like his brother he also was knighted, indeed he held so many worthwhile communal offices that he was often called the uncrowned King of Tasmania. At the end of the nineteenth century Charles visited London and the world of his grandfather. Without a hint of irony or embarrassment he wrote:

> It is the Sunday morning market of squalid London. We found it teeming with people of the poorer classes, who emerged out of the many narrow streets and alleys thereabout . . . Petticoat Lane . . . has been aptly termed 'a vista of dinginess.' On the stalls in the street, amid the shoutings and babbling of the vendors, and the noisy bargainings, may be seen old servitors' liveries, dirty and rejected soldiers' uni-forms, once esteemed beautiful ladies' dresses of every colour, old silks and satins, gentlemen's cast off clothing, and so in endless profusion, the dealers being mostly of the Jewish persuasion.[25]

In the course of one generation the Hon. Charles Ellis Davies MLC had successfully forgotten his own origins.

The Samsons of Swan River

SOLOMON LEVEY was buried in England, but there is little doubt that his heart was broken by the Swan River. Thomas Peel's inability to make the colonisation scheme work was compounded by his allowing Levey, through lack of information to the contrary, to imagine that all was going according to plan. Their ill-fated scheme provides the first mention of a Jew in Western Australian history, yet Levey did not send any Jews to the new settlement. Once his partnership with Peel was sealed, he ceased to stir London audiences with glowing stories of Australian opportunities. Perhaps he sensed a belief among his friends and clients that he was no longer a disinterested adviser.[1]

It is claimed that the first Jew to have been in Australia was Jan Simonsz, alias Jan Israel, or Serdam, who was a member of the Dutch Willem de Vlamingh expedition of 1696–97 which mapped the coast and named the Swan River.[2] The first Jews to participate in the Swan River settlement were the brothers Lionel and William Samson, who went there despite Solomon Levey and not because of him. Their official application to join in the creation of the western settlement helped to set the

'View of the Early Settlement of Perth and the Swan River'.

seal of doom on the Peel–Levey partnership. Family tradition recalls that the Samsons' Australian adventure began on a crowded London street when the two men met Captain James Stirling, the arch-rival of Peel and Levey.

Lionel Samson found himself listening to a description of the magnificent potential of a yet-unformed colony. Stirling was lobbying for the right to develop the land he had just explored, either with a proprietary charter or as a colony with himself as Governor. As Lionel listened, he considered his own way of life. He had recently inherited his father's seat on the London Stock Exchange, yet London and the monotonous respectability of Threadneedle Street seemed to offer a dreary future. The Jewish community still buzzed with the gossip that followed the departure for New South Wales of J. B. Montefiore, who had spurned his father's place on the Stock Exchange and chosen the drama of adventure in the colonies. The Samson brothers had thought of travelling to Canada, but Stirling's enthusiastic description of the land he had just explored at the south-western corner of Australia changed their minds. If Montefiore could go to the east coast, they would go to the west.

It was a fateful decision. Lionel Samson wrote to Under-Secretary Twiss in the same week that Thomas Peel arranged his new alliance with Solomon Levey.[3] Samson explained that it was 'The intention of my brother and myself to emigrate to the new settlement at Swan River and to embark a thousand pounds in this venture'. His letter reached Whitehall on 27 January 1829, and Peel's new plan was unfolded in the same office on the next day. For Under-Secretary Twiss, Lionel Samson's letter was the first and, for a time, the only indication that even without the aid of Peel there were men of substance who would settle at the Swan River and provide the lonely western coast of Australia with a British colony. His simple application, unlike Peel's, made no elaborate demand for special treatment involving millions of acres and first choice of land. It was a routine request that assumed the western colony would function in the same way as the colonies on Australia's east coast, and must have made Twiss look differently at Peel's plan.

Lionel Samson was the only Jewish migrant to Australia to receive a regal farewell from England. The Samsons moved in exalted circles and a few days before his departure Lionel was a guest of King George IV at a grouse shoot. When the noble hunter accidentally knocked and cracked his signet ring, he gave it to Lionel as a good-luck token for his journey to the new world. The ring still belongs to the Samson family.

The brothers arrived in Western Australia on 5 August 1829 on board the *Calista*, the second immigrant ship to reach the settlement, and immediately began business as general dealers and grocers at the coastal port of Fremantle.[4] They brought with them 'a shipload of merchandise, wines and spirits and a hold packed with groceries'. The firm they established is now the oldest Australian business still owned and managed by its founding family. The brothers were the earliest official auctioneers[5] at the Swan River settlement, and Lionel was the first merchant in the colony to be granted a licence to deal in liquor. His name appears on the colony's first grant of country land, made on 29 September 1829, when 4696 acres on the banks of the Swan River were allotted to him.[6]

Their primitive shop became Australia's most westerly post office and Lionel Samson was the colony's first postmaster: an unpaid and expensive position of which the only privilege was being able to open and read his own mail first. Lionel, though normally a charitable and friendly man, would later recall how he dreaded the arrival of ships that brought mail to the colony. Often the settlers would be forced to borrow money from their postmaster to pay the postage due on letters waiting for them, and at the same time they would demand and receive gallons of the Samsons' brandy 'on tick'.[7]

The condition of the settlement and the state of commercial affairs is evoked by a wistful note in the second issue of the *West Australian* on 29 October 1831, two years after the establishment of Lionel Samson's business: 'We hope soon to see something like regular shops established at Perth and Fremantle'. Despite Stirling's official position, he did not fare much better than Peel. Drought and famine, poor soil and penury were the lot of the settlers. At the colony's first horse races, held at South Beach on 2 October 1833, Lionel Samson unsuccessfully fielded a horse perceptively named More in Sorrow than in Anger.

The battle to exist continued for decades. Ten grim years after the establishment of the colony there were barely two thousand settlers in and around Perth. It took twenty years before the colony could claim a total population of five thousand.[8] There were no convicts to provide cheap labour and no regiments of soldiers as profitable customers for stores. Government of the little colony was a simple matter and there was no chance for great fortunes to be made through trade. And even if there had been great business opportunities, it was generally acknowledged that Lionel Samson's public spirit and generosity easily eclipsed his business acumen. Eighteen years after Lionel had settled in Fremantle his home and store still left a great deal to be desired. The *Swan River News and Western Australian Monthly*, published in London on 1 March 1847, wrote:

> And now let us get on toward Mr Samsons' which is that large building apparently without chimneys and seemingly but half finished. Messrs Samsons are the largest merchants in the colony, and are deservedly liked and esteemed for their constant exertions to merit the confidence of their connections.

A view of Fremantle, aquatint by J. Cross, London, 1832. Fremantle became the first port of call for ships sailing on the Great Circle Route with the prevailing south-easterlies. The Samsons' post office and general store is among the small cluster of buildings. The scene was painted shortly after settlement began in 1829.

Lionel obviously tried hard. The records of the struggling colony list the many ships from England that brought the Samsons a variety of merchandise. They also show how his business involved him in several trips to England and kept him in touch with his family and with the Jewish community there. And so, at Brighton in 1842, at the age of forty-four, he married his young second cousin, Fanny Levi, grand-daughter of the Anglo-Jewish banker and grandee Abraham Goldsmid.[9]

Family tradition tells a romantic story. As a young man, Lionel had fallen deeply in love with Fanny Levi's mother. She had gently rebuffed him, saying that she was too old for him and that one day he would marry her daughter. Lionel made her keep her promise. His chance came when he travelled home to England, met his 17-year-old cousin Fanny and secretly fell in love. His account of his very proper and yet strange romance is told in a letter in the South Australian Archives. Dated at Perth on 27 March 1841, it was written to his second cousin and future brother-in-law Philip Levi of Adelaide:

Lionel Samson. Samson arrived on the second immigrant ship to Western Australia. A man of great energy and vision, he became one of the most successful businessmen in the colony. He served as Postmaster-General, was involved in whaling and real estate, and was an original director of the Bank of Western Australia.

> By this time I flatter myself I am as well known to you as if we had met, first from what your good father has written and from other branches of your family . . . I have now to give you some tidings which no doubt will much surprise you. It interests you much as a fond brother and concerns myself most vitally. When at London I was constantly at the habit of being at Balham. I had not repeated my visits before I felt a strong affection for dear Fanny. I did not make this known to herself or any soul . . . but while at Plymouth I wrote your cousin (my dear brother Louis) of the state of my feelings and solicited his interference in this serious affair. He wrote a reply to me at Plymouth but unfortunately I had left before it arrived . . . he made known my wishes to your dear parents who at once conveyed them to dear Fanny and I am proud to say she expressed her pleasure and entire consent, of course, quite uninflu-enced by anyone . . . I propose, please God, to be in England in two years (at the latest). You will no doubt consider I have acted foolishly not making known my wishes while at home, patience, all for the best . . .

Fanny Levi belonged to the cultured and affluent strata of the Anglo-Jewish com-munity, and to a family which had close connections with the Goldsmids, the Rothschilds and the Montefiores. Nothing could have been more different from the circles in which she moved than the sunbaked little settlement on the banks of the Swan River. She could scarcely have imagined how primitive her life would be, yet the idea of marrying Lionel Samson and travelling with him to the other side of the world was not as bizarre as it might seem. Her brother Philip Levi already lived in South Australia, so she would have had some inkling of conditions in the colonies, though it must have been hard for her to understand the immense distance that separated Fremantle from the comparatively civilised little city of Adelaide. Nor could she guess that tragedy awaited her family in Australia.

Fanny Samson, née Levi. After her second cousin, Lionel Samson, travelled home to England to marry her, she became the first Jewish women in Western Australia. Fanny's Australian relatives were members of the Levi family of South Australia.

The *Inquirer* of 16 August 1843 reported that Lionel Samson and his new wife, together with his mother-in-law and her two younger daughters, had arrived in Fremantle, but Mrs Sarah Levi and her daughters continued to Adelaide. Her husband Nathaniel had preceded her, lured by reports which their son Philip sent home about the potential of South Australia. When she arrived she found that her husband had died, and been buried on 21 July. Sarah, the daughter of Abraham Goldsmid, was then forty-six. She lived until 1889.

In Fremantle, Fanny Samson was totally isolated. When an order of French nuns arrived in 1855 to live and work in the colony, she was the only woman in Western Australia with sufficient education to speak to them, interpret for them, and teach them the rudiments of English.[10] When she arrived, Lionel's brother William was thinking of leaving the colony for South Australia, and on 2 December 1846 the *Inquirer* reported that he had sailed for Adelaide. Probably he was no longer content to remain the junior partner in the family firm, and expected that any children of Lionel and Fanny Samson would further deplete his chances of advancement.

Though it must have made sense to move to the thriving colony of South Australia from the languishing settlement on the Swan, strangely enough it was to be a step into obscurity for William Samson. In Western Australia he had been a leading member of society. He married a Christian girl, Elizabeth Mary Pace, on 18 June 1840. Her father was a shipmaster and her mother managed a general store and hotel in Fremantle. The *Inquirer* of 12 April 1841 recorded his appointment as a Justice of the Peace, and the first annual return of the Bank of Western Australia, in 1837, listed him and his brother as partners. In April 1841 this bank merged with the Bank of Australasia, of which William Samson is shown as one of the local directors. On 1 February 1844 the *Swan River News* reported that he had become a member of the Governor's Executive Council.

This latter appointment preceded Jewish political emancipation in Britain by fourteen years: Lionel Rothschild was permitted to take his seat in the House of Commons only in 1858, having been first elected in 1847. William Samson was the first Jew in Australia to become a Justice of the Peace, and when Lionel Samson joined the Western Australian Legislative Council in December 1849 he became the first Jew to sit in an Australian legislative chamber. He served until October 1856, followed by a second term from October 1859 to July 1868. However, this did not create a formidable legal precedent. A Jew was Sheriff of London in 1837, and Jewish aldermen began to sit on many city councils in the same period. And, of course, the Samsons were old friends of Captain Stirling, the colony's first and most famous Lieutenant Governor, who might have found it difficult to exclude them from colonial government.

For a number of years the Samsons were a Jewish minority of two in the colony they helped to establish. Inevitably their status evoked some chagrin. When a zealous Italian missionary was refused naturalisation, his protest to the Colonial Secretary attacked the eminence of the Samsons and misguidedly resurrected the question, settled almost a century before, about the Jewish ownership of land in a Christian country. The *Swan River Guardian* of 19 October 1837 reported him as asking, 'How is it, that Jews in our Colony have received large Grants, and are in possession of Landed Property? Was there enacted a law in their favour ... if it is true that Jews have obtained Grants, the Crown was grossly defrauded and the real bona fide Settlers have been deprived of that land'. Naturally the missionary added, 'This is not personal against Messrs Samson, nor any of the professors of the Jewish creed'. In 1846 two Spanish monks established a Mission Station at New Norcia. When Padre Salvado, an accomplished pianist, decided to give a concert in Perth to raise funds for the mission, 'a Mr Samson, a Jewish merchant, contributed greatly by personally soliciting attendance among the English gentry who were his customers'[11]

Those who professed the Jewish faith in the first fifty years of settlement in Western Australia were very few. David Benjamin was a 24-year-old cabinet-maker and carpenter who came out as a bonded craftsman to work with the Australind Company in an ill-fated attempt to build a model settlement near Bunbury. He married Mary Anne Jane Whitely, and following the birth of their first children set out for Ballarat and the gold fields. The Western Australian Local Ordinances of 1848–1852 and the Statutes of Western Australia 1854–1859 show that Abraham Myers was naturalised in 1849 and Hyman Lipschitz in 1859, and there were at least fifteen Jews among the 9636 convicts transported to Western Australia between 1850 and 1868.[12] Very few stayed in the colony after serving out their time.

Lionel Samson brought to the colony in 1854 his nephew Horace Samson, an inept draughtsman and lithographer who designed and printed Western Australia's first and famous Black Swan postage stamps. Elias Solomon became the manager of Lionel Samson & Son and sat as a member of the first Commonwealth Parliament. Lionel and Fanny Samson had five children, Michael, Louis, Caroline Adelaide, Elizabeth Mary, and William Frederick, but none of them married a Jew. The first Jewish congregation in Western Australia was not established until 1887, in Fremantle, though a synagogue was not built until 1902 when the congregation was already in decline. The Perth congregation built their synagogue in 1897. So when Lionel Samson died in 1878 he had to be buried by a Congregational minister, who did his best to give him a Jewish funeral. His grave was the first in the little Jewish section at the back of the Fremantle cemetery. His brother in Adelaide was buried as a Christian. The Samson brothers and Solomon Levey are Jewish history's only link with the earliest settlement of Western Australia.

South Australia

ENGLISH CITIES TEEMED with the dispossessed while villages withered and died. Precious yeoman stock was robbed of its heritage by enclosures and the Industrial Revolution. England's future in a new era seemed burdened by unimaginable population pressures. The years ahead demanded spectacular solutions. The well-publicised problems of the Swan River settlement coincided with news of the discovery of fertile land near the mouth of the Murray River and to the east of the Great Australian Bight.

Powerful voices were heard favouring the creation of a new Australian colony. Whitehall resisted. The harassed Colonial Office saw no need to begin to build yet another Australian settlement and to be burdened with all its expensive paraphernalia of administration and protection. Yet the lure of empty land was more powerful than rational argument and the government succumbed.

New theories of colonisation were in the air. The South Australian settlement would be fashioned in the image of Edward Gibbon Wakefield's utopian vision of systematic colonisation. There would be a fixed and uniform price for land, and profits from its sale would be used to import selected migrants. The cost of settlement was to be borne by the sale of shares in a company empowered to develop the new province, and South Australia would be a colony open to 'emigrants of every sect' but closed to the transportation of convicts.[1]

An Act of Parliament at Westminster in 1834 appointed eleven Royal Commissioners to organise its settlement. Their principal tasks were to raise the capital and supervise the sale of land needed to finance the colony's first steps. Through the discreet intervention of Sir Moses Montefiore it was proposed, and accepted by the King, that one of the Commissioners should be Jacob Montefiore.[2] Jacob could claim a certain expertise in Australian affairs. In Sydney his young brother Joseph Barrow Montefiore was at the peak of his Australian career, and in the *Sydney Gazette* of 22 July 1834 had hopefully announced that his family's firm in London was ready to invest a quarter of a million pounds in New South Wales. Jacob was to become, in 1836, a member of the Standing Committee formed by some merchants of the City of London to watch over the mercantile and commercial interests of New South Wales, through official and regular communications between the colonial community and the home government.[3]

Jacob Montefiore immersed himself in the affairs of South Australia, becoming one of the most active of the Commissioners. When Colonel William Light laid out the city of Adelaide, the capital of the new colony, one of the highest points of North Adelaide was named Montefiore Hill. Colonel Light's statue stands there today, on what is known as Light's Vision.

Though there were no Jews on the first migrant ships to South Australia, a trickle of Jewish settlers began to arrive during the first months of settlement. An early visitor was Solomon Levey's son John, who arrived in September 1836 on his way to Sydney in search of his patrimony. He was so impressed with South Australia's future that, before leaving Australia again, he applied for a grant of land in the new colony.[4] Phillip Lee and his wife arrived from London on 26 November 1836 in the *Tam o' Shanter*, the eighth ship to call at the colony, and in the *Register* of 12 August 1837 announced 'to the inhabitants of Adelaide that his wine and coffee rooms were open for the reception of gentlemen'. Lee was not only a licensed victualler, he was also a musician. The *Register* of 19 May 1838 reported that he led 'the orchestra' at Adelaide's first entertainments at the

Jacob Montefiore. A cousin of the illustrious Sir Moses Montefiore and one of the eleven commissioners apppointed by William IV to oversee the establishment of South Australia, Montefiore represented the House of Rothschild in Victoria during the gold rush.

Theatre Royal in a room above the Adelaide Tavern in Franklin Street. As the colony developed he moved out of town to try his luck as a farmer and cattle breeder, but returned in time for the foundation of the Adelaide Hebrew Congregation.

The early records of the colony mention a family named Marks and another named Jacobs who both began farming in the new district but who do not seem to have stayed in the colony. The merchant Joseph Lazarus arrived in Adelaide in the first years of its settlement and on 10 March 1838 took space in the *Register* to announce the opening of his Adelaide Store for the sale of goods sent from his agent in London and including 'pork, cheese, sugar, flour, clothing and ironmongery'.[5]

By the time South Australia was ten years old the Jewish population numbered fifty souls, among whom were many members of Anglo-Jewry's inner circle. Their presence was remarkably clear proof of Jacob Montefiore's confidence in the new colony's future, for nearly all were related to him either through marriage or by blood. The first to arrive was Jonas Moses Phillipson and his 16-year-old brother-in-law Philip Levi, who was to become the brother-in-law of Lionel Samson of Western Australia when the latter married Levi's sister Fanny. The two young men spied out the land and both induced their families to join them in Adelaide. Philip's father Nathaniel Philip Levi was the son-in-law of Abraham Goldsmid and the future father-in-law of Lionel Samson. He arrived in Adelaide in 1842 and in that same year his name appears on the list of first holders of occupation and pastoral licences.[6] In accordance with his high social status Levi began to build what the *Register* of 10 March 1847 called an 'extensive' house on Adelaide's South Terrace in preparation for the arrival of his wife. Fate unkindly intervened and Philip was left to thank the Governor 'for the facilities so readily offered by you towards obtaining a burial place for my Father and those Members of the Jewish persuasion that may hereafter die in the Province'. The alacrity with which Major Frederick Holt, Governor of South Australia, acceded to this request may be seen as characteristic of the religious tolerance which the founders of the colony wished to prevail within it.[7]

Philip Levi. This 'merchant prince of South Australia' pushed back the boundaries of pastroal settlement. He survived two protracted droughts that were 'enough to break a Rothschild'.

Philip Levi had an extraordinary career. He began at a clerk's desk in the Customs office, became the proprietor of a store in Adelaide, and through the development of a small farm near the town began to interest himself in the development of the pastoral industry. His story includes a cross-country ride to overland sheep from New South Wales to South Australia, and a period in the 1860s when he could 'count his stock on a thousand hills [and] owned quite 172,000 sheep and cattle'. The fluctuation of prices caused by the American Civil War, and a series of disastrously dry years brought Philip Levi's vast empire to an end in the late 1860s.[8] He had pushed back the frontiers of settlement for hundreds of miles in both central and southern Australia. His business in Adelaide had flourished with the help of his brothers Edmund and Frederick, and his sister's son N. E. Phillipson became a pioneer of development in the northern regions of central Australia. Ironically, Levi and J. M. Phillipson were both founders of the socially exclusive Adelaide Club, whose century-old tradition of anti-Jewish discrimination ended in the 1970s.

The Commissioners of South Australia concluded their work in 1839, but on 24 May 1842 the *Register* reported that Jacob Montefiore was touring South Australia to 'inform himself from personal observation of the progress actually made in the development of our great capabilities'. Seventy of Adelaide's social élite gathered at Isaac Solomon's Shakespeare Tavern to honour 'one of the most zealous friends of the

Colony' who had worked 'indefatigably both as a member of the South Australian Commission and as a private citizen'. The colony was still affected by the general Australian economic depression, though the recently opened copper mines, which were the first mineral workings in Australia, softened some of its impact. So Montefiore was able to tell his enthusiastic and grateful hosts, 'If you have not the reality of wealth, you have now the prospect of it'.

Jacob Montefiore's faith in the colony was also represented by his nephew Eliezer Montefiore Levi, who later reversed his second and third names to give pride of place to the more illustrious surname; the shipbroker Solomon Mocatta; and the auctioneer William Samson from Western Australia. The younger Levi boys Frederick and Edmund settled in South Australia, married their first cousins Cecilia and Gertrude Goldsmid, and brought them to live in Adelaide.[9] Joseph Henriques of Jamaica arrived in 1842 and later married one of the daughters of J. B. Montefiore. His 24-year-old brother Nathaniel died in Adelaide on 2 January 1851.

Joseph Barrow Montefiore came to South Australia in 1846 to commence his second Australian business career and to act once again as agent for his brother Jacob. The *Register* of 29 July 1846 reported:

> By brig *Medway* Mr J. B. Montefiore and Mrs Montefiore and Misses Esther, Evelina, Justina, Augusta, Josephine, Marion and Edith, Master Horace Montefiore—another Miss Montefiore and two female servants, a harp, a piano and 300 packages.

Not only was it J. B. Montefiore's second migration to Australia; it was also his second association with the colony. In more prosperous times he had acted as the first Agent-General for South Australia in Sydney.[10] No doubt his appointment was not unconnected with his surname. It terminated abruptly, however, because no amount of social status could shield his firm from the approaching economic depression, and South Australia was soon left with an insolvent representative in New South Wales. After his insolvency, J. B. Montefiore lost all interest in New South Wales.

It must have seemed appropriate that in Adelaide, J. B. Montefiore found the success for which he had searched so long. He never returned to Sydney. He became one of the original trustees of the State Savings Bank and a member

Joseph Barrow Montefiore. 'A most valuable acquisition to the colony' was the advice from London to the Colonial Secretary in Sydney. Montefiore was a pioneer pastoralist and trader in New South Wales, New Zealand, South Australia and Victoria.

of the governing body of the Chamber of Commerce. He was actively associated with some of the leading mining companies in the colony and became a member of the Adelaide Stock Exchange. He joined with his nephew and son-in-law Eliezer Levi Montefiore in founding a firm of importers and ship agents, and together they prospered. While still in his fifties and with his fortune restored, J. B. Montefiore retired in 1860 and returned home to England to become an honoured member of the Jewish community and a leader of the aristocratic Reform Synagogue in London.[11]

At Port Adelaide, some six miles from the centre of the settlement, Solomon Mocatta established a shipping agency. He had come to Sydney in 1838 and two years later had settled in South Australia. In Adelaide lived the middle-aged Sephardic Jew, Benjamin Mendes Da Costa, and his sister Louisa. Da Costa was a merchant in Adelaide from 1840 to 1848, when he returned to England. In the years immediately before his departure, Bishop Short was organising the foundation of a Church of England college for boys. By way of a parting gift Da Costa donated six town acres in the centre of Adelaide to the college, which was built in 1849 in the suburb later to be called St Peters. Da Costa Building stood on immensely valuable land on the corner of Gawler Place and Grenfell Street, and the private Anglican school may attribute at least part of its present solidity to the donation of a London Jew descended from the Sephardim of Portugal who had fled to England to excape the fires of the Inquisition.

In Adelaide's snug nest of Anglo-Jewish respectability might be found the Solomons, one of the most remarkable emancipist families in Australian history. Elias Solomon of Western Australia and Vaiben Louis Solomon sat in the first Commonwealth Parliament, the latter being a son of J. M. Solomon, known as Sudden Solomon because his ministry was defeated on his first parliamentary day as Premier of South Australia. No hint of their origins has ever been recalled yet, in South Australia, Emanuel Solomon and his family dominated the formation and continued existence of the Jewish community.

However, the first Australian portraits of the Solomon family are to be found in the convict indents of New South Wales. Emanuel Solomon and his brother Vaiben were found guilty of breaking into a house in Durham and stealing coats and other clothes, and were sentenced to seven years transportation. Vaiben was sixteen, and 5 feet 2 inches tall. Emanuel was one year younger and two inches taller than his brother. Both were dark-complexioned with black hair and dark eyes. Their father was a lead-pencil maker and the boys had been trained in their father's trade.[12]

Upon their arrival in Sydney the boys were sent south to serve their initial sentence in Van Diemen's Land, where the Black Books continue their story.[13] Vaiben had five 'crimes' marked upon his record. Three are connected with the weekly Sunday church parades. For being disorderly at church and for being absent from the muster, he earned five weeks hard labour. For his third offence he received twenty-five lashes. He must have hated the forced attendance at Christian services. Emanuel's dossier describes a more violent youngster. In January 1820 he received fifty lashes for escaping into the forests behind George Town in the north of the island. Later that year he received twenty-five lashes for neglect of duty and fifty for having an iron pick in his possession. On 31 March 1821 both young men were caught stealing some clothes, sentenced to three years transportation, and sent to the dreaded penal settlement at Newcastle in New South Wales. Clearly, in the light of their original sentence, the magistrate considered that the brothers were incorrigible. In the fragmentary records of the Newcastle prison colony there is an entry for Emanuel Solomon in January 1823, showing that he received twenty-five lashes for 'repeated irregularities'.[14] It was his final punishment as a convict.

Following their release from prison both Vaiben and Emanuel settled in Sydney. In 1826 Vaiben asked that the government assign David Myers, a Jewish watchmaker and convict, to his service, claiming that he was a relation and that Myers could be 'of great service to the Petitioner'. The Colonial Secretary snarled:

> I do not conceive it would come within either the spirit or the letter [of the Governor's instructions] to assign convicts to every uncle, aunt or cousin ... Solomons is not a watchmaker, he is a pencil maker and keeps a little shop in Sydney and stands in the market like most Jews and is but a short time from Port Macquarie where it is supposed he got acquainted with his relative![15]

Emanuel first visited South Australia in 1838 and quickly decided to make his home in the 2-year-old colony. When the Sydney Synagogue held its first building appeal in 1839, Mr Emanuel Solomon 'of Adelaide' gave a donation of twenty pounds. In Sydney the brothers established the South Australian Packet Office at the Liverpool Wharf and their ship, the 125-ton brig *Nereus*, began to build up a mutually profitable trade between South Australia and the mother colony in New South Wales. Its successor, the *Dorset*, was described as 'a beautiful seaboat' and for almost eight years was the only regular trader between Port Adelaide and Sydney: local gossip decried the *Dorset*, but one satisfied customer wrote, 'the provisions and the wine was excellent; in fact I never had so pleasant a passage in my life (so contrary to what I had anticipated from all I heard in Adelaide)'.[16]

The firm of V. & E. Solomon conducted their Adelaide business from Sydney House, in Gilles Arcade off Currie Street. Emanuel's business ventures in Adelaide grew and diversified. In January 1841, at the cost of three thousand pounds, he opened Adelaide's first real theatre, 'a spacious and handsome edifice', and imported the Jewish actor John Lazar from Sydney to manage it. By that time he had become known as 'one of our most successful and enterprising colonists' and could be seen at the Queen's Birthday levée given by the Governor. In 1845 he described himself as 'the oldest and most experienced auctioneer in the colony' and four years later one journalist wrote:

> There are two things to which Mr Emanuel Solomon seems naturally prone. One is the faculty of knocking up tenements in brick and mortar and the other, the art and mystery of knocking down commodities by means of the magic hammer. From each of these pursuits he has more than once retired ...

And in truth Solomon had retired on a number of occasions and announced his intention to return to England. On 6 February 1846 he sold his auction rooms and business to William Samson, but on 2 June changed his mind and set himself up in business again, in partnership with his nephew and in opposition to Samson.[17]

Emanuel Solomon had left his convict past so far behind him that when Abraham Polack's son-in-law G. B. Goodman was said to have 'bolted' from Adelaide to Melbourne without paying his debts the *Register* of 18 March 1846 scoffed, 'We can inform our Port Phillip contemporary that Mr Goodman's residence with Mr Solomon, whilst sojourning in Adelaide, is sufficient voucher for his respectability'. His links with Sydney were gradually broken. In 1844 his partnership with his brother officially ended and in 1860 Vaiben died. Their younger half-brother Isaac had come to live in Adelaide, and it was at Isaac Solomon's Temple Tavern that a meeting was held in 1848 to form the Adelaide Hebrew Congregation.[18] Judah Moss Solomon, a nephew of Emanuel and Vaiben, had also settled in Adelaide, and he became the first President of the Congregation. During J. M. Solomon's public career he was Mayor of Adelaide and a member of both the House of Assembly and the Legislative Council.

In his old age Emanuel Solomon also served in both the colony's legislative institutions. In 1863 he briefly represented West Adelaide and in 1867 he was elected to the South Australian Legislative Council. In 1871, two years before his death, he celebrated the twenty-fifth anniversary of the foundation of South Australia by person-ally inviting five hundred of the 'old pioneers' to a banquet at the Town Hall.[19] The distinguished old man recalled his landing in a bankrupt colony devoid of 'a silver shilling', whose government immediately leaned upon him for four thousand pounds credit. It must have been an uncomfortable and even eerie moment for his family when Emanuel began to tell the eminently respectable audience how he had been commissioned to transport ten convicts from Adelaide to Van Diemen's Land and how he had chained them up in the ship's hold. Perhaps he was subtly challenging them all to recall the origins of their host and their nation.

The beginnings of a formally organised Jewish congregation in Adelaide came slowly. By 1846 religious services were being held from time to time at the Currie Street home of the recently arrived merchant Burnett Nathan, whose

Emanuel Solomon, sketch by S. T. Gill, c. 1840.
Emanuel Solomon and his younger brother Vaiben were sent to Australia as convicts in 1818. Their success as extraordinary. He opened South Australia's first theatre and was a member of both the colony's legislatures.

'wholesale and agency business was closed on Saturdays and on all Jewish holidays'.[20] He was discreetly described by the *Register* of 27 June 1846 as a 'fortunate newcomer', being both wealthy and enthusiastic enough to furnish his home 'after the English fashion . . . with articles manufactured in the colony. This performance has not only tested the colonial workmanship but provided a beneficent spirit among his friends'.

Within his home Nathan placed 'a most splendid repository for the voluntary offerings of his fellow worshippers whose contributions will, it is hoped, now enable the children of Israel to erect a Temple to their God, in Adelaide'. This box, the newspaper remarked, was 'somewhat of a sarcophagus form', but made of the finest variegated Australian cedar and 'a superb specimen' of colonial workmanship. Upon its lid was inscribed in Hebrew 'All the scattered ones of Israel'. The box made its first appearance in May 1846 at the wedding of Charles Jacobs of Sydney to Miss Elizabeth Joshua of Adelaide. The ceremony was performed by Burnett Nathan 'under authority from Sydney'.[21] *The Royal South Australian Almanack and General Directory* wrote in 1847 that 'the number of Jews in the province is about 80. They have no synagogue . . . nor do they meet regularly in any place on their Sabbath. The feasts of New Year, Tabernacles, Passover, Pentecost are generally attended to'.[22]

Land for the first Adelaide synagogue was purchased following the formal creation of the congregation in 1848, and building began in the following year. Henry S. Coronel wrote home to his parents in London:

> I am happy to inform you that a congregation is about to be formed here and a syna-
> gogue to be consecrated to the God of our fathers which I expect will take place near
> Passover . . . I am in high hopes that the erection of a synagogue will make the Jewish
> community here more united than they are now. There are 150 Jews in all, making
> about 50 families . . . Business is dull, money scarce, shop keepers complaining, markets
> somewhat glutted with goods and the country altogether not as represented at home.[23]

The poor economic conditions meant that another five months would pass before the small stone building was ready. The consecration ceremony of a synagogue tall enough to contain a gallery for women and large enough to accommodate 150 worshippers took place prior to the High Holydays of 1850.[24] It was able to serve the needs of the Adelaide community for the next twenty years. Two narrow windows shaped in 'the Egyptian style' flanked a small rounded porch. Polished cedar pews and bronze chandeliers adorned the simple interior and the curtain in front of the sacred ark was brightly embroidered with the Hebrew characters for the word 'Adelaide'. The dedication service closed with the Hallelujah Chorus, which 'was harmoniously and delightfully performed after which some thirty members of the congregation assembled around a festive board in the large room at the Temple Tavern, where a sumptuous dinner, a recherche dessert and excellent wines were unsparingly provided in Mr Lazar's best style'.[25] From London, where Jews were still politically unemancipated, J. B. Montefiore pointedly reminded the South Australian Society:

> the principles of civil and religious liberties are intertwined with the foundations of
> South Australia and the members of the different denominations enjoy in Adelaide
> the opportunity of worshipping God according to the dictates of their consciences.[26]

Melbourne Hebrew Congregation, watercolour (from an illuminated address presented to the Lord Mayor of Melbourne, 1889).

A Jewish pedlar on the road to Sydney, watercolour in the style of S. T. Gill, c. 1852. 'Sydney 15 miles' says the signpost. The Jewish pedlar with his pack has the same hat, beard and nose (!) as those sported by the gold buyer in S. T. Gill's engraving from Eagle Hawk.

The Adelaide Synagogue. The original synagogue built in the Egyptian style (1850) *stands beside the new building* 'in the Italianate style' (1872) *in the centre of town in Rundle Street, on land granted by the government.*

The Jewish community of South Australia was unique. Social and political discrimination was rare. The Jews of Adelaide were almost entirely English-born and had come to the new colony as free migrants. They participated in the life of the community far more freely than in Hobart Town, Melbourne or even Sydney. Yet the trades they represented were the traditional occupations of colonial Jewry. They were among the leading drapers, publicans, tobacconists, auctioneers, actors and dealers of Adelaide. In 1850 most of the Jewish community lived in Hindley Street: then as now one of the busiest shopping and entertainment centres of Adelaide. The only Jews who lived outside Hindley Street were J. B. Montefiore, E. L. Montefiore, David Benjamin, Philip Levi, the recently arrived Daniel Baruch (Australia's first Jewish doctor), Solomon Mocatta and John Lazar. It is not surprising that following the celebration of the High Holydays in the newly consecrated synagogue the *Register* of 9 September 1850 noted that 'The number of our principal shops of business closed on the occasion gave quite a holiday appearance to Hindley St. and attested to the respectability of our Hebrew townsmen'.

The gold rush proved a heavy blow to the young and fragile South Australian colony whose mineral wealth was severely limited. Adelaide was often an uncomfortable place:

> There are hot winds and now and then we are smothered by clouds of dust, which blow almost up to the sky, though they are not of long duration. A few miles from the town it is very different more like the scenes of Old England, beautiful and salubrious. As to provisions, we give away to the dogs that which many of my former colleagues at home would consider a luxury.[27]

Hindley Street in 1852, from the Illustrated London News. *Virtually the entire Jewish community of early South Australia had shops in Hindley Street.*

Discovery of gold in the neighbouring eastern colonies almost crushed the brave South Australian social experiment, as the population packed up and made their way to find their fortunes. On 22 March 1852 a young Jewish migrant to Adelaide wrote home in dismay:

> Things are very bad and in an unsettled state, almost every man having left Adelaide for the diggings. Many a man here who was worth thousands a few months ago is almost penniless now. We must all partake more or less of this bitter draught of adversity. It will tend, in a great measure, to put an end to that rotten system of credit which has been too extended for so small a community as ours. The house of Montefiore & Co. is going through the court; many others of less note have gone.[28]

The colony which Jacob Montefiore helped to create scrupulously respected the Jewish community's right to share in whatever aid the State gave to religious organisations. The first debates in the Legislative Council about State aid for religion coincided with the first Jewish services in Currie Street, and a token grant was assigned to the Jewish community. The *Launceston Examiner* of 23 September 1846 reported:

> The Council of Adelaide voted the sum of 58 shillings to the Jewish persuasion as a precedent of recognizing their equal claim with Christian churches. The amount, though small, was calculated in the same proportion as the allowances to other sects, which are regulated according to the numerical return of the population.

Once the principle of equal civic rights and entitlements had been theoretically settled the community was content to leave their grant alone. By the time the Jewish community had grown large enough to begin to build a synagogue the era of State aid to religion in South Australia had virtually ended. The congregation itself was wisely and firmly committed to the principle of the separation of Church and State.[29]

A dazzled young Jewish migrant to Adelaide told the Jews of England that he had found the Promised Land:

I am happy to say that we enjoy every privilege without any barrier or distinction in this country; in a word we enjoy civil and religious liberty without there being the slightest fear of the admission of a Jew into the Legislator upsetting the government. We expect at the next election to have a member of the Jewish faith, one of high distinction, and who will we believe, be allowed to take the oath most binding on his conscience and not have to wait upon the pleasure of lords or bishops or a Newdegate. They are by no means afraid of unchristianising the constitution of South Australia. The Almighty will forever guard His chosen people . . . I am proud as an Israelite, to say they (the Jews) form the most liberal and wealthy, taking them as a body and considering their number.[30]

A curious footnote to Australian Jewish history was written by the second Governor of South Australia, Colonel George Gawler, who combined extensive experience as a colonial administrator with an unbounded admiration for the Jewish people in general and for the Montefiore family in particular. Following his term as Governor, Gawler published a pamphlet that anticipated the role of the Zionist movement in the Middle East: *The Tranquillization of Syria by the Establishment of Jewish Colonies in Palestine*. His vigorous and imaginative financial policies in South Australia were bitterly criticised by his successor, and in the *Register* of 7 October 1846 Gawler chose to defend himself by quaintly citing 'some members of the Hebrew nation . . . intimately acquainted with my proceedings in South Australia, and upon this acquaintance they would, I hope, do me justice to acknowledge that bad faith never formed a portion of my public policy'. In no other Australian colony did a governor defend himself by mentioning that he had the sympathy and support of the local Jewish community, a fact which reflected a Jewish community that had no parallel in early colonial Australia.

The Jews of Melbourne

HE RENTED HOME and store of Michael Cashmore had the distinction of being Melbourne's first brick building. Proudly its two storeys rose above the surrounding shingle roofs. Below, at the north-eastern corner of Collins and Elizabeth streets, lay an apparently permanent quagmire known to everyone as Lake Cashmore, 'not sufficiently deep to drown a man, but quite sufficient to half do it'.[1] From 1840 to 1855 the brash Jewish merchant from Houndsditch cajoled and badgered his fellow citizens into paying attention to his hosiery, drapery and ready-made clothes. He filled the columns of the local papers with bombastic doggerel and endless lists of wares.

Cashmore missed the first Jewish religious services in Melbourne, which were held in 1839, the fourth year of the town's existence. A small group of men gathered for prayers at Portland House, the Collins Street clothing store of the draper Moses Lazarus, and formed The Society for the Relief of Poor and Infirm Jews. Two years later, on 12 September 1841, at the home of Asher Hymen Hart, the Jewish Congregational Society came into formal existence and Michael Cashmore was elected the first President 'by a majority of voices'.

No major Australian city took longer to establish than Melbourne and no Australian city grew as rapidly once it began. The ships that were eventually to sail southward to establish the settlement at Hobart Town anchored in Port Phillip Bay in 1803. They landed a disheartened collection of guards, migrants and prisoners at the present site of Sorrento and for fifteen weeks struggled to survive, while their commander Captain David Collins, waited impatiently for permission to move away from a harbour believed to be without fresh water and productive land.

The explorers Hamilton Hume and William Hovell reached Port Phillip in 1824 by an overland route from the settled areas of New South Wales, and a second and less ambitious effort to secure a strategic outpost in the region was attempted at Western Port Bay in 1826. Among the squad of prisoners sent from Sydney to do the heavy work was Walter Levy, a young London hawker who earned his passage to Australia by stealing a watch and chain and then running straight into the arms of a passing guardian of the law. Levy worked in Sydney as a carpenter but could not keep his fingers off other people's property, and his journey to Western Port Bay was the outcome of an appearance at the Magistrates Court. It was a sentence of death, because conditions at the temporary settlement were so grim that within a few months the 32-year-old convict was brought back to die at the Sydney Hospital.[2]

Word of the frail outpost in a promising and empty new region was noted with shrewd interest by Solomon Levey before he left Sydney, and he spoke of it to his eager audience in London. Unaware that it would be abandoned, Michael Phillips wrote to the Colonial Office declaring that he had 'fixed upon that part of the Colony called Western Port as the most desirable; the soil is congenial for the production of grain'.[3] With a flourish he asked for a land grant of 4000 acres and a contingent of thirty convicts to help him build his part of the Empire. It was futile to ask for aid on such a scale, so Phillips settled for 2560 acres within more reasonable distance of Sydney. Had he persisted in his plan for a farm at Western Port he might have been the founder of one of the six states of the Australian Commonwealth.

In Van Diemen's Land more practical plans were being laid. New grazing lands to help to feed the growing herds of sheep and supply the convict establishment were urgently needed and John Batman, an adventurous and energetic settler, applied for permission to move across Bass Strait to the mainland. The eloquent Scot and Australian nationalist the Rev. Dr James Dunmore Lang recalled:

Michael Cashmore. Cashmore and his very large family rented Melbourne's first multi-storeyed brick building on the corner of Elizabeth and Collins Streets, which came to be known as 'No 1, Melbourne'. Cashmore was a founder of the National Australia Bank and the first Jew elected to the Melbourne City Council.

> I happened to be in Van Diemen's Land towards the close of 1835. It [the settlement of the Port Phillip District] was almost the only topic of conversation at the time in any quarter on either side of the island. Every respectable person you met with was actually in the speculation himself or had some son or brother in it, or had sheep and cattle in it or had shares.

Government procrastination had driven Batman to enlist an association of supporters to charter a schooner, and he triumphantly set sail as the leader of his own expedition. He returned with an agreement from the Aboriginal tribes, who had been duped into unwittingly surrendering 600 000 acres of land to his Port Phillip Association. Lang was horrified by these 'adventurers' who had blandly ignored the proclamation of British sovereignty over eastern Australia in 1788 and 'had sought to establish a principle in regard to the purchase of land from the aborigines which could not be tolerated with the limits of the empire'.[4]

At almost the same time John Pascoe Fawkner, the Launceston newspaper proprietor, set sail for Port Phillip with his own ambitious plans. Fawkner had been to Port Phillip as a child, because his father was one of the convicts in the abortive 1803 settlement at Sorrento. Fawkner wasted no time making agreements with Aborigines but settled his expedition at the site of the future city of Melbourne. The two groups came together and the new town was begun.

The complex story of Batman's Port Phillip Association deeply involves Judah and Joseph Solomon of Van Diemen's Land, though their names are missing from the first published petitions of the Association because they were still officially prisoners of the Crown. Once Joseph received his pardon, his name appears upon the list of seventeen partners who undertook to open up the new territory.[5] Among the seventeen, only Joseph Solomon, and through him his brother and partner Judah, represented purely commercial interests. All the others were connected in some way with the land or the professions, so it is obvious that Joseph's role in the Association was that of a significant provider of capital. His name appears tenth upon the list of partners. His son-in-law, Anthony Cottrell, the husband of Frances Solomon, is eleventh.[6] When Batman first surveyed the vista around the Port Phillip District he took care to name one of its features Mount Cottrell and another Mount Solomon in honour of 'his friend' in Van Diemen's Land, even though Joseph Solomon was still a silent partner in the whole venture.[7]

As a practical sign of serious intent, the Port Phillip Association hastily, and hopefully, divided up their territory into seventeen defined land sections.[8] Because they had 'bought' the land from the Aborigines and not from the Crown, their claim was highly speculative. Far more official notice was likely to be taken of their physical presence as squatters on land claimed by the British monarch than as purchasers of tribal property. At least, the Association clearly recognised that the real owners of that vast territory marked Australia Felix on the maps were the indigenous inhabitants.

Joseph Solomon's section was portion six, and his farm was one of the first three to be established within the Port Phillip District.[9] Judah Solomon's part in the founding of Melbourne was represented by his son Michael, who had arrived in Van Diemen's Land with his mother Esther when he was fifteen years old. Michael Solomon crossed Bass Strait with the earliest settlers to Port Phillip and from 1835 to 1841 held the licence for a sheep run at Keilor and from 1837 to 1842 at Carrum. He married Sarah, the daughter of Henry Solomon (brother of Judah and Joseph Solomon), in a Jewish ceremony in Hobart Town in 1840. Michael's occupation on his marriage document is 'farmer'. The marriage was ill-fated and so was his pastoral career, and his life would end in tragedy.

The arrival at Melbourne of a flock of 2400 sheep owned by Michael's cousin Joseph Solomon and Anthony Cottrell was noted both by the Hobart Town newspapers and by the first officials to arrive in the new region.[10] Solomon's sheep were in the care of Michael, who had set up a farm of his own adjoining Cottrell's claim, close to the banks of the Salt Water River now known as the Maribyrnong River.[11] The river crossing near the two farms became known as Solomon's Ford and the stones that constituted the ford marked the only way westward from Melbourne to Geelong.

Young Joseph (who was known as Johnny) Solomon of Melbourne married Judah Solomon's illegitimate daughter Sarah (daughter of Elizabeth Howell) at St John's Church at Evandale, Tasmania on 2 August 1838, and returned with her to Melbourne in the *Henry* on 24 September. The two young people were first cousins.[12] Over the years great confusion has been caused by the fact that there were three Joseph Solomons in Van Diemen's Land, all members of the same family. The senior was Judah's brother. The second was Judah's illegitimate son. The third, who was born in England in the year the two brothers were deported to Australia, was the son of Samuel Solomon, another brother of Judah and Joseph. Joseph Solomon sold his interest in the Port Phillip Association in 1839 for £411, but Judah retained his share. When Judah died in 1856 he left Solomon's Station to his son Joseph (Sarah's brother). Unlike Judah's illegitimate and favourite son, whose name is inscribed upon a marble plaque on the wall of the Hobart Synagogue, the Joseph Solomon of Melbourne took no interest in Jewish affairs. He and his wife Sarah were married and buried as Christians in the Church of England section of the Melbourne General Cemetery. Sarah died on 20 March 1881 at sixty-one; Joseph on 25 April 1890 at seventy-one.

The Port Phillip colony was established without official supervision. John Pascoe Fawkner firmly believed that his fellow settlers were building a paradise on earth. He proudly wrote on 20 March 1840 in his newspaper, the *Port Phillip Patriot*, that Australia Felix had a 'park like appearance'. While an early visitor to Melbourne observed wrily that the settlement 'presented the appearance of a village in the interior of India' Fawkner saw a 'substantial, well built and populous town in a spot where, 18 months ago, were to be seen only the few rude huts of the first settlers'. From the verandah of his hotel 'you could see the peaks of the Villaminerta range of hills [You Yangs]— the settlement—a range of forest beyond which are William's Town and the shipping at the Anchorage and across the Bay to Indented Head'.[13] Alfred Solomon, one of the thirteen children of Joseph and Sarah, affectionately recalled in 1906 his earliest years at his parents' farm by the Salt Water River:

> The river teemed with fish in the season, and like the swamp which then existed near the site of Maidstone, was covered with wildfowl. Though not in very large numbers, plover, quail, snipe, native companions, turkeys and occasionally a flock of emus were found on the plains. Cockatoos, parrots and pigeons with many kinds of smaller birds, lived in the trees and scrub. At night the weird cry of the curlew could be heard. The river valley was the haunt of the kingfisher and the laughing jackasses announced the approach of morn and evening. Hawks, owls and other birds of prey, played their part in the order of nature, and the eagle from the mountain ranges visited the settlers' flocks and carried off their lambs.[14]

The Governor of New South Wales completed an official tour of inspection of the new colony in March 1837, after which arrangements were made to survey the district and hold the first two land sales—which allowed purchasers to secure a legal title to the land on which they lived. The next three sales were held in Sydney, where prices were naturally higher and more speculative. Very few Jews bought land in early

Melbourne and their absence from the list of landowners is evidence of their own economic struggle to exist.[15]

Joseph Barrow Montefiore briefly visited Melbourne in 1840. Montefiore paid £440 for an allotment at the corner of Spring Street and Flinders Lane, £245 for land in Lonsdale Street, £260 for a small plot at William's Town, and £325 for twenty-five acres at Portland. Perhaps these expensive and speculative purchases in a very young colony played a part in Montefiore's subsequent financial collapse.

The local Joseph Solomon paid £39, at the second land sale, for an allotment close to the site of the Melbourne Post Office, and later he was able to purchase 600 acres in the area he had originally leased as a pastoral property. There were some bargains to be picked up. On 12 September 1839 the *Port Phillip Patriot* advertised Block no. 2 on Flinders Street:

> [It possessed] the double advantage of a warehouse, coupled with the quiet retirement of a Country life . . . In the distance the darkly timber clothed tops of the Black Mountains and as the eye draws nearer its home, the beautiful waters of the 'Yarro Yarro' meandering in its sinuous course, and at last, the wonderful township of Melbourne.

At the Sydney sales Samuel Benjamin and Elias Moses began to invest in land purchase in Melbourne. The two men were merchant pioneers and partners in the country town of Goulburn, and had reason to be conscious of the developments in Melbourne. They advertised that their own store was the last place to purchase supplies on the track between Sydney and Melbourne, and Benjamin's two brothers were among the earliest settlers at Melbourne. Over the next ten years Benjamin and Moses continued to purchase land in settlements along Australia's eastern coast. Samuel Benjamin's brothers David and Solomon were the only local Jewish businessmen who could afford to make substantial land purchases during the town's first fifteen years.[16]

Melbourne's first period of growth coincided with a general decline of colonial business and agricultural development throughout Australia. By the end of the 1840s, before the gold rush and its spectacular burst of activity, the size of the Jewish population in the whole Port Phillip District slowly increased from 57 in 1841 to 200 in 1850, while the total population of the colony grew from 11 738 in early 1841 to 45 495 in 1850.[17] Melbourne's fresh water came from the Yarra River, which was soon polluted with offal from tanneries and butcher shops. Each rainy day turned the streets into muddy and impassable quagmires. Hundreds of overflowing backyard cesspools menaced the health of the general population. There was no public provision for the sick, the very poor or the infirm, and the mentally ill were thrown into prison. Every institution had to be created out of nothing, while the government resided in Sydney and was derided in Port Phillip as greedy and unresponsive to the needs of the new settlement.

The middle class in Port Phillip was very small and, just as in Van Diemen's Land, the Jewish contribution to the commercial life of the new community was out of all proportion to its numbers. Before the gold rush, virtually the entire Jewish community was involved in the clothing trade. In Melbourne in 1845 there were 25 clothing shops owned by Jews and 22 owned by non-Jews.[18] In 1850 there were 30 drapers and haberdashers in Melbourne, of whom 16 were Jewish.[19] There were several Jewish publicans, but all went bankrupt.[20] John Davies, reporter with the *Port Phillip Gazette*, was probably related to the Solomons. There was a lodging-house owner, a punt operator, a butcher, a ships' chandler, a clerk and an auctioneer. Most of the principal drapery shops in Collins Street were owned by Jews but only David Ribiero Furtado, a Sephardi dealer in currency exchange, can be numbered among the early merchants of Melbourne. There were two Jewish farmers, Joseph 'Johnny' Solomon and Michael Solomon.

The names of the drapery stores reflected the origins and sympathies of the early Jewish community in Melbourne. Moses Lazarus owned Portland House, Edward and Isaac Hart managed Waterloo House, Michael Cashmore's shop was called Victoria House, the partners Harris and Marks owned the London Mart and the Liverpool Mart, and Moses Benjamin's store and shop was called Albert House.

Competition was intense, and the storekeepers filled the newspapers with spectacular advertisements. Cashmore 'summonsed' all of Melbourne to his store in an advertisement in the form of a writ, signed by Henry Makewell, Charles Wearwell and George Verycheap. David Benjamin of Cheapside House boasted, and endlessly repeated, that his 'adage' was 'Small profits—quick returns'. David and his brother Solomon Benjamin later announced, not quite truthfully, that their presence was required in England and that 'they were determined to sell the whole of their valuable and extensive stock of drapery at unprecedented prices, for cash only'.[21] Harris and Marks then imaginatively announced the dissolution of their partnership and offered their stock at 'an immense sacrifice'. As the Melbourne press recounted it:

> Immediately on this notice appearing, all the respectable haberdashers of the town held a meeting, at which it was determined that all like Harris & Marks [should] 'dissolve partnership' sell 'for cash only' at an 'immense sacrifice'. Handbills to this effect were forthwith posted all over the town being, with the exception of the names of the firm, exact copies of Harris & Marks' bills, and altogether the affair caused a good deal of excitement among the haberdashers, and laughter among the disinterested.[22]

Solomon Benjamin. Benjamin arrived in Van Diemen's Land in 1838 and opened a branch of the family's Launceston business in Melbourne in 1840. Cheapside House became the oldest drapery store in the District of Port Phillip, and Melbourne's first High Holyday services were held there in 1841.

Harris & Marks, London Mart. This drapery store, built in 1840, stood on the corner of Elizabeth and Collins Streets, opposite Michael Cashmore's shop. Economic depression brought the partnership of Jacob Marks and Samuel Henry Harris to an abrupt end very soon after it was built. Marks was a nephew of Solomon and Barnett Levey. Harris began his Australian career as a convict and rose to wealth and respectability.

The Jewish shopkeepers were in a perpetual state of confrontation with the police because of their habit, brought from London's East End, of displaying their wares in the street. The *Port Phillip Herald* of 4 April 1845 reported that the Chief Constable had begun 'a regular fire of information, pains and penalties upon a large portion of the Hebrew traders of Melbourne for the unlawful exposition of saleable goods'.

Unlike almost every other early settlement on the eastern coast of Australia, few convicts were stationed at Port Phillip though, in time, many emancipists and ticket-of-leave men from the Sydney district and Van Diemen's Land made their way to the new town. They gathered in groups at the corner of Collins and Elizabeth Streets, next door to Cashmore's store, waiting for offers of casual work. Michael John Davies and his son John, who both spent some time in Melbourne, were typical of this class of men. Samuel Hyams, the baptised Jew, came from Launceston to be John Batman's personal servant. Samuel Harris and Nathaniel Nathan, former convicts from the Sydney district, opened clothing stores in Melbourne and became respectable members of the community.

Samuel Harris had two drapery stores, in partnership with Jacob Marks, and bought five city allotments in Sydney for £4102. He was one of the four readers at the High Holyday services in Melbourne in 1840. Nathaniel Nathan, whose convict indent showed him as 'cook, butcher, drover' came to Melbourne after being involved in a scandal at Maitland, when he became too friendly with a servant girl in the household of Abraham Elias. At least he married the girl, and would spend many years and many fruitless congregational meetings demanding that the Melbourne Synagogue accept proselytes.

One of the most unusual emancipists at Port Phillip was John James Levien, who came to Australia in 1832.[23] His mother was the sister of the Anglo-Jewish leader and statesman Sir David Salomons, who became the first Jew to be elected alderman, sheriff and Lord Mayor of London and the first Jew to speak in the House of Commons, after leading the fight for full political emancipation. At the age of eighteen John attempted to present a forged bank order for two hundred pounds to a banking house in the Strand, and foolishly pretended to be the stockbroker for whom he worked.

He must have had some doubts about his ability to carry out his plan because in his pocket he carried a phial of poison and poignant farewell letters to his mother and sister. He swallowed the poison when he was questioned by a suspicious clerk, but lived to be sentenced to death at the Old Bailey. The jury made a strong recommendation for mercy on account of his previous good character and his youth, and so he was sent to Australia instead of to the gallows.

Transportation to the colonies brought about the migration of many members of Levien's family to Australia and New Zealand. John was initially sent to Van Diemen's Land as a convict, and his parents and most of his siblings arrived in New South Wales at almost the same time. Undoubtedly the shame of their son's arrest and concern for his future brought his parents to Sydney. His older brother Benjamin Goldsmid Levien established a plant nursery at Geelong in 1840. John's son, Jonas Felix Levien, was the first Jewish child born in Victoria, and became one of the earliest Australian-born ministers of the Crown in the Victorian Parliament. Jonas married his first cousin Clara, the daughter of his uncle John James Levien, so the family must have forgiven their wayward son and brother.[24]

Benjamin Goldsmid Levien. This grandson of the Anglo-Jewish banker Abraham Goldsmid Levien was one of the first settlers in Geelong, where he established a plant nursery. He was the father of the first Jewish child born in Victoria.

Once John Levien had served the first three years of his life sentence in Van Diemen's Land he received a conditional pardon and was permitted to join his father, Solomon Levien, in New South Wales. John migrated to Melbourne in 1841 and worked alongside Anthony Cottrell, the husband of Joseph Solomon's daughter, in a butcher's shop in William's Town.

As boatloads of hopeful immigrants arrived in Melbourne the government faced problems caused by their promise of aid to formally constituted charitable organisations. In those days, social welfare was not considered the direct business of representatives of the Crown. The Jews of Port Phillip, led by Solomon and David Benjamin, hastily created a means for claiming assistance, and a Jewish benevolent society was born. It was Melbourne Jewry's first organisation.[25] The community was so small that were it not for the timely arrival of the brothers Isaac

Asher Hymen Hart. Hart was the first lay reader of the synagogue service in Melbourne and the first President of the Melbourne Hebrew Congregation.

and Edward Hart in 1840, High Holyday services would have been held without the statutory presence of ten men required for Jewish public worship. Edward Hart was a particularly welcome arrival as he was able to act as cantor and chanted the prayers with grace and accuracy. In the following year a third member of the Hart family arrived, Asher Hymen Hart, and an organised Jewish congregation came into existence.[26]

Like so many others, Asher Hymen Hart first tried his luck in Sydney before coming to Melbourne. He brought with him a combination, rare in the colonies, of Jewish learning, a Jewish library and strong religious beliefs. At the High Holyday services of 1841 the congregation had doubled in size and prayers were led by Asher Hymen Hart and sung by Edward. Among those present was Louis Nathan from Hobart Town. The example set by the tiny Melbourne group helped inspire Nathan to agree to become the first President of the Hobart Town Hebrew Congregation in the following year.

There was clearly a need for a Jewish religious organisation. Not only had there been three previous years of High Holyday services but there had already been one Jewish burial in Melbourne, that of the daughter of Henry Davis in 1840. Strictly speaking the girl was not Jewish as her mother was Hannah Howell and her aunt was the mistress of Judah Solomon, but Michael Cashmore volunteered to read the funeral service and the burial place was donated by Abraham Abrahams, a general dealer of Lonsdale Street. The land was at Merri Creek, between Northcote and Merri Creek bridges, and the funeral was an unforgettable experience because the ground turned out to be a field of stone and the grave was painstakingly quarried out of the rock while the mourners waited by the coffin. Urgent steps had to be taken to procure a new Jewish cemetery, but a second attempt also failed when a half acre at Pentridge bought from Abraham Abrahams proved equally unsuitable.

Hart could see little purpose in maintaining a Jewish charitable organisation in a community so small that everyone knew everybody's problems. As he observed:

> The natural tie of Jew and Jew was strong enough without requiring any formal pledge to assist one another. And if any poor brother found his way to Melbourne from the neighbouring colonies, he would find friends to assist him. The want of bodily food to the Australian Jew was not to be compared to the want of spiritual food . . . a permanent place of worship was the great want to be supplied.[27]

And so before the High Holydays in 1844, Hart reconstructed the Jewish benevolent society and turned it into a congregation. Its first High Holyday services were conducted in the unoccupied Port Phillip Hotel in Flinders Street, and thereafter at the home of Solomon Benjamin. Asher Hymen Hart was formally appointed President in 1844, and on 21 January its name was changed from The Jewish Congregational Society to Khal Kodesh Shearith Yisrael, The Holy Congregation of a Remnant of Israel. Solomon Benjamin was its treasurer and Michael Cashmore became secretary. The committee consisted of John Hart and his brother Edward Hart, Isaac Lazarus Lincoln and John Levy. Every member of the committee was a draper apart from Asher Hymen Hart, the President, who had been a linen merchant but was forced to become an auctioneer following a disastrous fire in which he lost his stock and his Jewish library, 'a very choice little lot . . . for this part of the world'. He was left with 'only the trousers and shirt in which he stood'.[28]

Appropriately, the honorary treasurer was the only local Jewish settler wealthy enough to make any substantial purchases of land in early Melbourne. Edward and John Hart worked as partners. Isaac Lazarus Lincoln was a draper in Collins Street, and like A. H. Hart he became an auctioneer and commission agent. He had the distinction of being, in Hart's words to the Chief Rabbi in London, 'a self taught though skilful operator', who performed Melbourne's first circumcision ceremonies.[29] John Levy was the first cousin, and soon to be father-in-law, of a later arrival, Nathaniel Levi—the first Jewish member of the Victorian Parliament and a leader of the Melbourne Jewish community in the latter half of the nineteenth century.

The new congregation promptly applied to the authorities in Sydney for a grant of land for a Jewish cemetery, and in April 1843 the news was received that Sir George Gipps had agreed to the request. The *Port Phillip Herald* of 27 April 1843 was quick to compare this courtesy with the attitude of Sir John Franklin in Van Diemen's Land:

> The Promptitude with which his Excellency complied with this application stands out in bright relief, as contrasted with the illiberal treatment which the Jews of Launceston experienced at the hands of their late Lieutenant Governor, Sir John Franklin.

The Rev. Dr James Allen, son-in-law of George Augustus Robinson, an evangelical missionary working with the Aborigines and whalers at Clarke Island in Bass Strait, happened to be in Melbourne on 16 August 1843. Lewis Hart had died the day before, and word spread through town that a Jewish funeral was to take place in the newly allocated burial ground near Flagstaff Hill, on the site of the present Queen Victoria Market. Driven by curiosity Allen went 'to see a Jew interred' and described the event in his daily journal:

> Four gentiles bore the bier, the coffin was plain and no ornament, it was covered with a black paul [sic], the Jews followed, the relatives (men only) in black cloaks they had several books and they walked by pairs, arm in arm, the bier in front, into the middle of the burial ground then they referred to the books, it seemed for instructions relating to the ceremony. The gentiles were all shut out with the exception of those necessary for the interment. Of course, I was without and many more that the novelty of the ceremony had drawn me to the place . . . They placed a bucket containing water and a cloth. After they had satisfied themselves with the books they proceeded to the grave and the coffin was lowered down. One of them had a broad white scarf and several of them carried books but it seemed only for instruction relating to the ceremony. There was no prayer when the coffin was lowered, his friends came forward and took the spade and threw with it a little earth into the grave and this all the Jews present (about 20) did. They then proceeded into the middle of the ground and washed their hands and wiped them on the cloth. They then turned their faces to the east and several of them seemed to read in the books and bowed their heads three times with their hats on but there was no seeming order for they were in little groups and some of them conversing. The scene deeply impressed me with the truth of the word of God so much so that tears flowed from my eyes as I left the grounds and I thanked the Lord for giving me such a testimony to the truth of the Bible. 1st the separation from the gentiles. 2nd the ceremonial washing. 3rd their books which I have no doubt were Moses and the prophets for their foundation. 4th the gentiles bearing the corpse so that the Jews might escape the defilement of the dead . . . 5th Their facing the east and bowing as it was near sundown . . . I was fully satisfied.[30]

Asher Hymen Hart wrote a letter on 25 April 1844, published in the London *Voice of Jacob* on 29 November, describing the same sad event and how after a respectful interval the community had subsequently applied for an additional grant of land on which to build a synagogue:

> We have now a regular Jewish congregation, under the denomination of the Holy Congregation of the Remnant of Israel and having applied to the Governor for a piece of land for a Burial Ground, which application being granted and the ways and means having been raised to rail round the ground, it was no sooner finished than my brother died suddenly; and thus by the will of the Supreme, he became its first tenant.
>
> We have also written to London for a *Sepher Torah* [a scroll of the Law]. We have regular service every Friday evening and Sabbath morning, as also on Holidays; and are regulated by a code of Laws, which are printed;—and to crown all, I yesterday

received a communication acquainting me that his Excellency the Governor had granted the prayer of a memorial addressed to him, and that half an acre of ground, in a most splendid situation, and of great value, was at the service of the Jews, for the purpose of a Synagogue, although I must not forget to assure you that there is very little probability of its being built, for some years to come; since we have at present no funds for that purpose. The Jewish community here, consists of, say 11 families (married) and the entire number in and about Melbourne, is between 80 and 90— men women and children.

Proudly the editor of the local *Port Phillip Patriot* told his fellow citizens that the Jews of Melbourne had been granted land:

His Excellency the Governor . . . has been pleased to grant a site for the erection of a Synagogue on which our fellow townsmen may worship God according to the practice of their fathers. The promptitude [is] contrasted with the illiberal treatment which the Jews of Launceston experienced'.[31]

Three years later the congregation knew that it was time to begin to make use of the Bourke Street land grant. Even though immigration to Melbourne was virtually at a standstill the congregation understood that to delay any longer might have given the government cause to revoke the gift. The community was so small that the first set of plans had to be rejected when it was discovered that the estimated cost of construction would be £435. The final compromise plan envisaged a tiny building of twenty by thirty feet which would cost no more than £270 and which could, with great difficulty, seat 150 people.[32]

And so at the unlikely, but discreet, hour of eight o'clock in the morning of Wednesday 25 August 1847, the community gathered on the site in Bourke Street to hear Asher Hymen Hart solemnly address the 'Almighty Architect of the Universe', asking for blessing upon this 'minor sanctuary' and upon 'our Sovereign Lady Queen Victoria', and the foundation-stone was laid.[33] In the evening forty or so gentlemen held a celebratory dinner in Collins Street at the Shakespeare Hotel owned by Michael John Davies. Despite a donation of £80 from the Benjamin brothers and 'a most unusual appropriation' of £2 10s from the watching crowd of workmen, the little community could raise only £160 and the new building, consecrated in March 1848, bore a considerable debt. The burden became even heavier with the employment of a minister, and precipitated a Jewish application for government money to aid the congregational budget. It was an unwise step for it caused a long, acrimonious and undesirable public debate about the status of the Jewish community in the colony.

Belligerently Hart bullied the Jews of Melbourne into observing their faith. After the High Holydays of 1846 he resigned as Honorary Reader of the prayers: 'I will not any longer (to be plain) submit to the insult of attending the Synagogue on Sabbaths and Holydays without the means of celebrating public worship'. In response seven members of the congregation faithfully promised to attend service every Sabbath or subject themselves to a fine of five shillings for being absent, so that the quorum necessary for public worship was financially guaranteed.[34] The system seems to have worked for a while.

Hart was a proud member of the Jewish community. All the executive members of the synagogue were office-bearers in the two early Masonic Lodges of Melbourne, and his prayer to the Great Architect of the Universe was not accidental. Hart, as Senior Worshipful Master of the Masonic Lodge, joined in the solemn ceremonies of 1846 which marked the laying of the foundation-stones of Melbourne's first bridge and first hospital. That evening the Mayor of Melbourne spoke of the need to build hospitals and declared that while religion preached about charity in the past, it never built hospitals. At the end of the speech Hart rose from his place and pugnaciously told the Mayor that the Jews 'in the earliest days' had built hospitals of their own.[35]

The early records of Melbourne Jewry clearly show the problems of a struggling and isolated community. While the Sydney Jewish community found £4000 for its synagogue, the Melbourne Hebrew Congregation had great difficulty in raising £300 towards its building and lived in hope of government aid.

Asher Hymen Hart's name was put forward in July 1842 as a candidate for the Melbourne Municipal Council. To his chagrin his name was seconded by James Simeon, an early Jewish settler at Port Phillip whom Hart knew to be a liar and a cheat. Hart protested to the *Port Phillip Herald* on 12 July 1842 for publishing a report of the meeting in which his name was coupled twice with that of 'a person, who however respectable he may be in your estimation, I assure you I have not the slightest ambition to become familiarised with'. Hart offered himself as a last minute candidate for the Lonsdale Ward in the Melbourne Municipal elections of November 1845, and was narrowly defeated. According to the newspaper, 'Irish interest was again triumphant'.[36] Michael Cashmore became Port Phillip's first elected Jewish representative when he was elected unopposed to represent La Trobe on the Melbourne Town Council.

The congregation divided itself into two sections, the privileged and non-privileged members.[37] An applicant for promotion to privileged membership had to have been an ordinary member for at least six months, and be considered beyond the reproach of the congregation. Typical of the ill will this regulation created is a letter from Benjamin Francis to the Melbourne Hebrew Congregation in 1850.[38] Francis had come to Melbourne from Van Diemen's Land, where he had been President of the Launceston Congregation. His dismay at not being accorded immediate privileged membership must have been intensified by the usual sensitivity of an emancipist.

Francis had a chequered career. It began in Sydney in 1819 with a sentence of transportation for life, and included a period as convict overseer at the Parramatta Hospital, a dramatic and illicit love affair, a season of voluntary exile at the prison colony at Port Macquarie, some years as a publican in Sydney and Penrith, a successful business career as an auctioneer in Sydney and Launceston, and partnership as a Melbourne auctioneer with Edward Cohen, the future Mayor of Melbourne.[39] Blandly ignoring the reasons for his sensitivity the congregation replied, 'the regulation may be unpleasing to a respectable man like yourself so well known among us

I admit . . . the law was made to guard respectable men against the encroachment of blackguards'.

The Jews of Melbourne imposed a snobbish division upon their small community, rudely scrutinised the credentials of all newcomers, and quarrelled intolerantly with the Jews of near-by Geelong when the latter established a congregation and applied for permission to receive land from the government for a burial ground.[40] Melbourne felt it had the sole right, bestowed by Sydney, to sustain the Jewish faith in southern New South Wales. It was a claim of Hebraic 'apostolic succession' handed from the Chief Rabbi in London through the congregation in Sydney, and the conservative members of the Melbourne congregation used this link with England to block any significant religious concession to their new colonial environment.

From the outset, the Melbourne congregation, led by Hart, felt deeply about intermarriage. Hart made sure that no one who had married out of the Jewish faith could become a privileged member of the congregation, nor could even be called up to the reading of the Torah. The status of the children of mixed marriages caused a series of congregational crises precipitated by requests from Jewish husbands of Christian wives to have their sons circumcised. At one stage a number of special congregational meetings were called by petition to discuss the whole matter. In July 1845 Hart proposed to the congregation:

> All persons of the Jewish Faith wishing to have their Wives and females that they may be cohabiting with up to this day July 27 1845 be made 'Geurists', shall make application to the Honorary Secretary in writing within one month from this date and that the President shall write in the name of the Congregation to the 'High Priest' [sic] of London.

Michael Cashmore was not in favor of ignoring the sacred bonds of matrimony and proposed that the words 'Females they are cohabiting with' be left out of the motion. Once again Hart won the day, though he clearly felt that the opinions of his opponents carried some weight. In one of the first letters sent by the congregation to the Chief Rabbi in London, Hart asked what could be done about accepting proselytes in a community that had no Rabbi and no rabbinical council. When the Hobart Town Congregation received its first minister in 1846, the Melbourne congregation wrote to him and asked whether he was empowered to receive converts.[41]

When the first 'neat and compact' Melbourne Synagogue was built the congregation hired Walter Lindenthal, a young language teacher, as the Reader whose task was to conduct the service of the synagogue and create a school for their children. Asher Hymen Hart wrote:

> In order that there may be no mistake I wish you to understand that a commercial not a classical education is required among our members who being engaged in business wish their children to be educated accordingly.[42]

Lindenthal was the son of the minister of a small provincial synagogue in England, but he could not read the unvocalised Hebrew of the Torah scrolls nor could he satisfactorily conduct the long service on the Day of Atonement. He then failed to pay his man-servant his wages on time and was summoned by his servant before the Court of Requests. The congregation felt that their teacher had placed himself in a 'disgraceful position' and Lindenthal was summarily dismissed and removed from the synagogue's premises.

Melbourne's second choice fell upon the schoolmaster at the Sydney Synagogue and in 1849 the Edinburgh-born Moses Rintel was appointed Reader of the congregation. He remained in Melbourne as a Jewish minister for thirty-one years.[43] Significantly both men had been chosen because of their qualifications as teachers. The congregation could call upon its members to conduct a service of worship but the instruction of children demanded not only the financial commitment of the entire group but the time and special skills of an expert.

FOR MELBOURNE'S FIRST twenty years, Collins Street was lined with the shops of Jewish traders whose wares spilled over the footpath. An English woman wrote: 'Melbourne is very full of Jews; on a Saturday some of the streets are half closed'.[44] An American, William Kelly, was less than impressed by his visit to Melbourne in 1853:

> The auction mart . . . might have been mistaken for a Jewish synagogue; for, during the loud excitement in the street, the Hebrew family, congregated in a dense mass about the pulpit, perching themselves on every elevated point or prominent position, so that the Christian community only occupied a very narrow rim of background in the throng. I never saw such an overwhelming multitude of sharp nasal promontories and tawny visages, every dark eye glistening with anxiety and every pointed beak seemingly whetted for business; for wherever clothes of any kind are in question, be they new or old, there do the descendants of Moses love to assemble . . . they fairly outstrip and distance all competitors. Most, if not all, of the Melbourne Jewish clothiers have direct connexion with the great Houndsditch and other East London outfitters and if any foreign importation comes upon the market, they buy it over the heads of all Christian competitors, at prices far beyond the limits of remuneration, so as to retain exclusive possession of the trade.[45]

After years of agitation the colony of Victoria formally 'separated' from the mother colony on 1 June 1851. September 13, 1850 was selected for the community's formal celebration, until it was discovered that the chosen day was Yom Kippur. The *Melbourne Morning Herald* quickly reassured the Jewish community that neither the Mayor nor the agitators for independence 'had the most remote intention of hurting the religious feelings of any section of the community' and the colony's celebration was promptly postponed.

Six weeks after the formal transfer of power from Sydney to the newly named colony, Victoria and its hinterland faced ruin. The spectacular discovery of gold fields near Bathurst was enticing every hopeful man to find their fortune in New South Wales. In an attempt to forestall the depopulation of the brand new, self-reliant colony Asher Hymen Hart took the initiative of calling a public meeting to raise a reward for the discoverer of a gold field within two hundred miles of Melbourne. The

Australian press had been filled with lurid tales of murder and mayhem at the gold fields of California and Hart was of two minds when he declared, 'Gold was one of the greatest curses with which they could be afflicted [but] he felt assured that there was plenty of gold within reach'. A Gold Committee was formed and a reward fund of two hundred guineas was pledged. Hart was a committee member, and its elected treasurer was his cousin Henri John Hart. Joy, and great relief, reigned when on 26 July 1851 the *Melbourne Morning Herald* proudly announced 'Our Gold Field—Eureka! We have gold—gold in abundance'. Within hours the great Victorian gold rush began: 'Despondency has fled and from the gloom of discontent comes an outburst of bright hope'. Eager for revenue the new colonial government decreed that no one could be permitted to dig for gold without first buying a valid, and expensive, monthly licence. It was a punitive system designed to keep the poor in their place, and pressure caused by finding the money for the licence before finding any gold would eventually lead to bloodshed and rebellion.

The gold fields lay sixty miles north of Melbourne, and Port Phillip Bay was suddenly crowded with ships. The public was assured, 'The earth of Ballarat is a teeming store of riches'.[46] The tracks through the bush swarmed with motley crowds of fortune-seekers from all over the world carrying gold-cradles, picks and shovels, and the Jewish community of Melbourne changed beyond recognition. In December 1851 three-quarters of the Melbourne Police Force resigned and made for the bush. The Melbourne press reported that prospectors were 'digging up small nuggets with a pocket knife', however the newspapers also reported that shopkeepers were making money by simply staying at home: 'The shops are crammed. The most expensive articles of dress are in the greatest possible demand'.[47] Within days many of the well-established drapers and auctioneers of Collins Street announced that they had become gold buyers, and managed to make considerable fortunes until the banks took over the task of managing this limitless source of new-found wealth. Benjamin Francis and Edward Cohen were among the first to announce that they would hold a weekly auction of gold.[48] David and Solomon Benjamin exported gold bullion worth £42 000 in January 1852. Edward and Isaac Hart sent £900 and Montefiore & Co. £850. Asher Hymen Hart promised miners that he would buy their hard-won gold dust at the highest prices, and was so successful that by November 1854 he was able to retire and return to live in London. In 1852, in gratitude to the Great Architect of the Universe who had providentially brought these Jews to a world flowing with wealth, it was decided to send a collection of gold dust to London to be shaped into a Kiddush cup and presented to 'the Rev. Dr Nathan Marcus Adler, Chief Rabbi of the British Jews, as a token of high esteem' Forty-one ounces of gold were collected and a four-inch tall wine cup decorated with laurel wreaths, kangaroos and emus was solemnly presented to the much revered gentleman.

The number of Jews in the District of Port Phillip grew from 200 in 1850 to 2900 in 1860. It was now possible to build in Bourke Street a Jewish house of worship of great dignity whose noble façade obscured the little synagogue and old class room at the back of their plot of land. The newly formed Legislative Council, which met in St Patrick's Hall next door to the synagogue, confronted the issue of Jewish emancipation on 20 December 1851. The Jews of Melbourne asked for a 'proportionate allowance' from the public purse, which they said was their 'just right' in accordance with the 'liberal views of the age'. William Westgarth, the renowned democrat, undertook to present the Jewish Petition, and the Council debated 'That this house recommends to the executive government, that the members of the Jewish persuasion in this city be allowed to participate in the reservation (in the budget) for religious purposes under the head of Schedule C'. John O'Shanassy, a draper and a leader of the Irish Catholic community, seconded the motion and Dr Francis Murphy was in favour of an Act being passed. Colonial Secretary William Lonsdale agreed that the equal treatment of Jews could be gained only by the passage of a specific Bill to amend the Church Act. The amendment was passed but the technical difficulty of defining religion apart from Christianity meant that the legislators were still debating the issue in February 1854. Once again the non-conformist and old friend, John Pascoe Fawkner, enthusiastically supported the principle of equal treatment:

> [I] knew that the Jews were an orderly and charitable people. The Bible had been received from the Jews and the world was under a 'great obligation' to them which they could never discharge; the great founder of Christianity was a Jew. David was a

The Melbourne Synagogue from the tower of the Victoria Supreme Court in the 1880s. The original schoolroom and minister's residence can be clearly seen at the back of the building. The Synagogue faced Bourke Street.

Jew as were the Apostles. The house should spare no exertions in order that Victoria might be the first of the British Colonies to extend to the Jews the full rights as British subjects.

The Colonial Secretary agreed that they were all deeply indebted to the Jews, at which Fawkner interjected, 'Then pay them!' The vote was taken and, after the laughter had died down, the motion to include the Jews as part of the religious community of Victoria was lost by one vote. The Argus wrote, 'Endow every religion and let TRUTH not change her course by intolerance'.[49]

The Jews of Melbourne lost patience and, by this time, could muster five hundred protesters. On 22 February 1854 'a large and influential body of Jews' assembled in the Bourke Street Synagogue to demand equal treatment in the proposed Constitution Bill. David Benjamin was in the chair and Asher Hymen Hart told the indignant crowd that 'Religion was between man and his Maker. What were the Israelites? They were a good, upright, faithful and moral people ready to shed their blood in defence of the country which protected them'. In stirring phrases Michael Cashmore proposed that they asked 'neither for toleration in a Colony where all Her Majesty's subjects are upon an equality nor favour from those who are bound to mete out justice to all, they claim as a right being good citizens and loyal subjects, that they not be excluded'.

Beyond the Metropolis

LOOKING INTO THE FUTURE on 2 September 1848, Benjamin Isaacs, printer and editor of the *Bathurst Advocate*, wrote in his editorial:

> That our colonial territory is to be for ever considered as it hereto has been, a mere pastoral country, may suit the purposes of some short sighted man, but can never benefit the colony. But this character of the country is not true. It is a land of corn and wine and oil, it is a land of iron, copper, lead and coals, it is a land adapted to the production of silk, cotton, flax and hemp and that which is required is the investment of capital and the introduction of labourers.

These were prophetic words in young colonies which received three distinct Jewish colonial diasporas. The first scattered Jewish rural population emerged in the shadow of the convict system. The second diaspora reflected the enterprise of free settlers as rivers and roads began to ferry the rural wealth of an emerging continent to the bustling towns on the coast. The gold rush of the 1850s created a third Australian Jewish diaspora. Suddenly the interior was peopled by eager immigrants whose search for wealth lured them far beyond the former boundaries of settlement.

From the days of Governor Phillip onwards, it was a fundamental aim of administrative policy to encourage the settlement of convicts on the land. This was partly common sense, and partly an expression of a mystique which declared that there is a spiritually cleansing power in performing basic hard work with the soil. The convict community had to be made self-supporting, because it could not live forever on hard tack and salt meat. So the land had to be cleared and farms established. On the one hand, any convict who proved himself worthy could eventually obtain land. A ticket-of-leave man could rent, but not buy, a property; an emancipist stood a good chance of obtaining a grant. On the other hand, it was essential to decentralise the new communities and prevent Sydney and Hobart Town from being flooded with ex-convicts who were likely to get into mischief. It was therefore common for convicts to be given their tickets on condition that they did not leave their particular country areas. Many such men made friends within the districts where they had first worked as assigned servants or on road-making gangs, and eventually married and settled down there. Sustained contact with the land would, it was believed, cleanse men of criminal proclivities and create a sturdy new yeoman class in the 'Britannia of the Pacific'.

Among the Jews, this development was somewhat different. In central Europe, where so many families had originated, the relentless hostility of the Christian church had for centuries barred them from entry into most trades and all guilds. Eastern Europe had welcomed them as dealers, artisans and traders who could fill the gap left open by aristocrats for whom trade was offensive and peasants too simple or ignorant to engage in it. For the Jews of Europe, urban life had of necessity become second nature, and many emancipated or free-settling Jews in Australia had quickly established themselves as traders.

The Jews of both New South Wales and Van Diemen's Land spread out from the first areas of settlement as hawkers and licensed hotel-keepers. They were particularly suited to the latter occupation by the Jewish aversion to drunkenness, which enabled them to prosper because they were not tempted to drink up their profits. It was a business that had been a traditional Jewish preserve in the Polish and Russian Pale of Settlement. Sometimes a pedlar was able to profit from the popular thirst for strong liquors—like Joseph Raphael, of whom the *Australian* of 2 September 1826 wrote:

> [He] arrived at Newcastle on Sunday last, and on the following day he commenced to sell a variety of goods by public auction. He treated his customers with such potent libations of peppermint and brandy during the sale that more than one half of the fair bidders became subject to its all-powerful influence; and were conveyed at mid-day to their respective habitations unconscious of the precious exhibition they were making to their more sober neighbours.

It is not surprising to read in the *Monitor* of 13 March 1830 that Raphael had become the landlord of the Manchester Arms, George Street—though the *Gazette* of 28 February 1832 reports his insolvency.

Often such wandering pedlars, who were able to spy out the land for themselves, discovered a spot where a tavern could do good business and opened the first general store and pub in the district. The lightly disguised reminiscences of Alexander Harris an Emigrant Mechanic has left us a vivid portrait of just such a nomadic entrepreneur in the 1830s. Harris was droving cattle in the north of New South Wales when he came upon the campfire of a dealer whose three packs were laden with his wares.

> He was a merry, free hearted fellow, and made us have a drop of capital brandy with him; and our tobacco being nearly worn out, we supplied ourselves with a pound of negro-head a-piece; but his profits were exorbitant, viz., from 100 to 200 and even 300 per cent. on what the goods cost him. However, in these shopless wastes there is no help for it; one must either give what they ask or go without the article, for the supply is so much less than the demand, that it is rarely they take anything of consequence back to Sydney. We stopped at the dealer's fire all night; he was a merry fellow, and kept everybody about him in excellent humour. He was a Jew.[1]

For those obliged as a condition of their tickets-of-leave to stay in one spot, life in the sparsely populated interior was lonely and unprofitable by contrast with the teeming ghetto streets of London's East End. For most it became an impatient wait as they worked hard for years to accumulate enough cash to survive the move to town, and wrote anguished petitions to the Colonial Secretary begging permission for the move. Phillip Joseph, who arrived in the *Mangles* in 1824 with a sentence of fourteen years and received his ticket-of-leave for assisting in the capture of a bushranger, became a shopkeeper at Newcastle and asked for his ticket to be extended to Parramatta 'owing to decrease in local population'. The Colonial Secretary replied, 'his object in having his Ticket altered for Parramatta is to live in Sydney I have no doubt. There is plenty of business in Maitland for small shop keepers. Allowed for Maitland'.[2]

Free men and former officers who began their colonial life with the blessing of the authorities and generous grants of land owned the great properties in rural Australia. They lived in a manner resembling that of the country gentlemen of England. But for Jewish ticket-of-leave men it was a very different matter. The Polish-born ex-clerk Joachim Boaz, who arrived and received his ticket in 1815, 'for nine years rented a small farm in the District of Evan until very recently when [he] was forced to relinquish it in consequence of being several times robbed of his all'—and then became a shoemaker. Joseph Marcus rented a farm at Georges River in 1810 and within three years had fallen so deeply in debt that the Provost Marshal of the colony confiscated and sold his eight acres of maize, wheat and potatoes. The *Sydney Gazette* of 14 July 1810 reported that he was given three months hard labour for selling grain, which the government store supplied for use as seed.[3]

Benjamin Cohen was the pound-keeper at Parramatta in 1814, while nearby lived Jacob and Esther Isaacs at Petersham. Jacob, a hatter, arrived in the *Baring* in 1815 with a fourteen-year sentence. At the Isaacs' Tea Garden, which soon became a licensed tavern, Australia's first child to have two Jewish parents was born in 1817. She was Rachel Isaacs, who in 1836 escaped conviction on a charge of having stolen seventeen pounds from Mr Moses of the Australia Inn but two years later was convicted for stealing money.[4]

John Moses, the confectioner and pastry-cook who supplied the Lieutenant Governor of Van Diemen's Land with confectionery while serving his sentence there, moved to New South Wales and held the licence for the King's Head at Penrith. He had to be brought into Sydney at Passover time because he was 'the only person who knows the art' of baking unleavened bread. Later he returned to Hobart, where he purchased the Hobart Town Theatre for £2025 in 1839. By 1844 he had returned to New South Wales to live in Yass with his brother Isaac, and he died in Sydney in 1883.[5]

Joel Joseph supplied the first carriage and horses to take provisions to the village of Bathurst, the first settlement west of the Blue Mountains, and he equipped the expedition that explored the Lachlan River. At Windsor in the 1820s Solomon Josephs was a tavern-keeper and Abraham Elias a shopkeeper and small farmer.[6]

The first Jews content to remain in rural areas were the free settlers of the 1830s, who came prepared to be pioneers. They often brought with them enough capital and cargo to see their families through the first difficult years, and they were prepared to travel to find the most promising speculative opportunities. Even though Sydney remained the heart of the commercial and administrative life of the colony, small

Jewish communities grew up in a number of developing country towns. And the country produced some compensations for lonely storekeepers and dealers. When actor and theatre manager Joseph Simmons left the city to become a country shopkeeper at Bathurst one of Sydney's journals consoled him with the promise of future greatness:

> Unquestionably, the Country Storekeeper is a head of the People, and in some districts he is the most important personage—one without whose assistance the affairs of the interior could scarcely be carried out. His stores form a 'magazin' of multifarious matters, a sort of mercantile Bazaar, at which you can be supplied with almost everything from a needle to a bullock dray . . . He is, and must be, the purveyor of everything, or he is nothing. He is also a general agent and banker . . . Let it not be supposed that in a country store situated some miles from the metropolis, a man becomes altogether isolated, far different, the diversity of characters with which his business brings him in contact must . . . afford him a great deal of amusement.[7]

When the economy began to tumble in 1841, Sydney's Jewish community was so closely interwoven by trade and family connections that the fall of one business affected many more, and the depression destroyed the financial stability of almost every Jewish merchant and dealer. In mid-1841 the *Sydney Gazette* declared that 'men who were, twelve months ago, reported to be worth thousands, are now little better than beggars'. The depression undoubtedly prevented a large number of Jewish families from moving out of the rural areas to the city—so that when gold was discovered in the early 1850s sizeable Jewish communities already were established in the gold-bearing regions.

The Jewish population of Australia's eastern coast continued to increase, from 856 in 1841 to 1086 in 1846 and 1334 in 1851.[8] Though this was an increase of 30 per cent, the proportion of Jews in the general population declined from 0.7 per cent in 1841 to 0.47 per cent in 1851. There were 462 Jews in Sydney in 1841 and 633 in 1848. Only in the metropolis of Sydney did the number of Jews show a very small proportional increase. In 1848 there were 633 Jews in Sydney, 81 in Melbourne, 37 in Port Macquarie, 20 in Illawarra, 14 in Berrima, 60 in Goulburn, 21 in Yass, 10 in Windsor, 11 in Penrith, 24 in Bathurst, 40 in Maitland and 11 in Geelong. Only in Goulburn in 1851 did a rural centre before the gold rush reach a total Jewish population of 75.

In early colonial days one of the easiest and quickest ways for an emancipist to accumulate capital was to possess a liquor licence, though it demanded a special kind of stamina to be a publican in a rough and raucous place like Sydney. Outside the city a publican's life tended to be more easy-going, and no doubt it took longer to accumulate enough money to turn to a more respectable occupation. By the end of the 1840s very few Jews remained among the ranks of the tavern-keepers of Sydney, though many were scattered through the country towns. In Goulburn in 1849, six out of eight of the licensed dealers in spirits were Jewish. In Queanbeyan there were two out of four, in Maitland four out of twenty. Jewish publicans were to be found at Carcoar, Yass, Gundagai, Albury, Scone, Armidale and Muswellbrook. Together with their wives and children they constituted a very large proportion of the Jewish population of rural Australia.[9]

The pioneer Jewish settlers of rural New South Wales were a varied and versatile crew. Their place in the life of the rural community gave them a leading role in the political and commercial life of the colony which easily eclipsed the achievements of their cousins and brothers in the city.

George Cohen was Gunnedah's first storekeeper and postmaster. Benjamin Isaacs was the proprietor of the *Bathurst Advocate* in 1848. At the same time the turbulent John Davies was the sleepy little town's Chief Constable and Joseph Simmons owned the general store and local liquor licence. At nearby Summer Hill the Travellers Inn was owned by Samuel Phillips. By the 1840s he was the leaseholder of 16 000 acres near the Bogan River. Lewis Wolfe Levy established one of the first stores in Tamworth. By 1871 Levy was a member of the colonial Parliament and a director of many prominent Sydney companies. Godfrey Alexander, David Cashmore and C. Simmons were all pioneer merchants at the isolated southern coastal settlement of Portland. Philip Philips was an early storekeeper in Geelong and a pioneer of the Victorian town of Colac. At Yass, Henry Hart, Moses Moses, and his brothers Isaac and John, must have monopolised the early liquor trade in the district. And by 1845 there were enough Jews in the district to warrant the establishment of a Jewish cemetery. Almost forty years had passed since Moses Moses and Samuel Lyons had stowed away on the *Kangaroo* in the Derwent in the hope of escaping from Van Diemen's Land. Moses had been a member of the first Yass Town Council and in 1840 built 'the best hotel out of Sydney'. His tombstone in the dusty rural cemetery reads, in Hebrew and English, that he died 'in good old age . . . one of the oldest inhabitants of the town of Yass . . . much respected . . . many friends deplore his loss'.[10]

Morris Asher of Albury came to Sydney in 1838 and early in his career helped to drive seven bullock teams laden with merchandise to the new settlement at Port Phillip. News that the Aborigines had murdered some shepherds in the Murray River district sent the convoy back to Sydney, and Asher began a period as a pedlar in the Grenfell and Monaro districts. He then travelled to New Zealand, where he fought as a volunteer in the Maori Wars, then became the owner of two whaling stations and a trading post which linked the islands with Australia. In 1847 Asher settled in Albury, where his general store was the town's first brick building and where he eventually

Morris Asher of Albury. Asher opened his first store in Albury in 1840. After some years in New Zealand he returned to Albury to become a leading member of the Murray River District.

became a publican, building three hotels in the town. He had returned to Sydney by 1859, and won the Riverina parliamentary seat of Hume; and he was later official appraiser for lands in the Riverina district. Asher died in Sydney on 29 October 1909, aged ninety-one.[11]

The *Sydney Gazette* reported on 12 March 1833 that Abraham and Saul Lyons owned the Rose Inn at Maitland, and on 30 June 1836 that Israel Joseph had founded a general business there. At Singleton in the same year Nathan Joseph established a business, and Aaron Isaacs owned a store at Paterson in 1842. At Port Macquarie the emancipist Henry Cohen, hotel owner and storekeeper, owned a ship named after his wife which plied between Sydney and Port Macquarie in the first decades of free settlement.

Henry Cohen's involuntary exile brought his large family to Australia. Nancy, one of his daughters, married Joseph Simmons the well-known actor, and set sail with her mother Elizabeth and nine siblings to follow their father to New South Wales. Upon arrival in Sydney, Simmons applied to the Colonial Secretary to have his father-in-law assigned to him. When this option was promptly declined the Cohen family settled in Port Macquarie, and a complicated and remarkable rural Australian dynasty began. We need to meet another settler with the same surname. Abraham Cohen, who arrived as a free settler on the *Warrior* in 1835, began his career in Sydney as printer of the *Australian* and then attempted to make his fortune by opening stores in quick succession at Port Macquarie, Tamworth and Goulburn. He married Sophia, daughter of Henry and Elizabeth Cohen of Port Macquarie, and they proceeded to have ten children. Among this family was Nathan, who was twice Mayor of Tamworth; Fanny, who became Lady Benjamin Benjamin; and Edward, who was Mayor of Melbourne and a Member of the Legislative Assembly of Victoria.[12] One of Abraham Cohen's children was Henry Emanuel Cohen, a Member of the Legislative Assembly of New South Wales, Judge of the Supreme Court, and the first Judge of the Commonwealth Arbitration Court.

Settlement of rural districts proceeded slowly from the comparatively small inner ring of Parramatta, Windsor and Penrith, following the harbours, bush tracks and rivers.

To Berrima, seventy-five miles south of Sydney on the road to the southern highlands, came Joseph Levy, whose store sold the usual sundry goods, slops and rations. He founded the little town's Imperial Brewery in 1837, and was soon producing 'the best colonial beer, equal to any in the colony' and disposing of it at his hotel, the Victoria Inn. Levy had already gained a measure of dubious fame by appearing as a character in the early Australian autobiographical satire *Ralph Rashleigh*, written by the convict James Tucker. Levy is described in the book as a 'bandy-legged, chocolate-cheeked Jew' who was the convict overseer of a gang employed in clearing land and who appeared to 'delight in oppressing his men as much as possible'.

Joseph Levy came to Australia in 1819 as a 19-year-old convicted thief. His victim told the Surrey Quarter Sessions how Levy 'came up to him and thrust his arm across his breast and pushed him on the footpath, at the same time looking steadfastly in the

The town of Berrima in the 1850s. Dense smoke rises from the chimney of what is probably Joseph Levy's house and hotel. Behind the houses can be seen the stone walls of the Berrima Gaol.

face. He then suddenly ran from him in a stooping posture'. As he ran he took with him a watch and chain, but was captured hiding under a nearby cart. Twenty years later Levy was the owner of the Berrima Store, the brewery and an auctioneer's licence, and was able to offer a reward of five pounds for the recovery of his chestnut filly, stolen from him by a convict known as Big Jem.[13]

Berrima was also the home of a young Joseph Levy, the 10-year-old son of the town's butcher who made the tragic mistake of giving evidence to the police about a man who had been seen 'cruelly stabbing a mare'. By the time the case was brought to court the culprit had bribed the boy to deny the whole story. The prisoner was acquitted for lack of evidence and the young witness sentenced to seven years transportation for perjury. In October 1841 Joseph Levy, 'height 4 feet 7 inches, age 10, fair complexion, brown hair, small nose, born in Sydney', arrived in Van Diemen's Land to be sent to the children's prison on Point Puer at Port Arthur. On 25 January 1842 the boy, who had turned to the police to complain about human cruelty to an animal, received '25 stripes on the breach' for 'gross misconduct'. His dossier shows that during the next three years he received over one hundred lashes for 'misconduct' and spent more than fifty days in solitary confinement. He was returned to New South Wales in November 1848 with his sentence completed and his life shattered.[14]

Bathurst's Jewish community developed in the 1840s. Though one of the earliest country towns, Bathurst's development was slow due to the difficult and perilous road over the Blue Mountains. Joseph Simmons had established stores at Bathurst and nearby Carcoar by 1845, and owned extensive tracts of land in the district. The emancipist and hawker Aaron Gainsborg opened Bathurst's first jewellery and watch-making store and in 1844 became the owner of a liquor licence. In 1848 Benjamin Isaacs was the owner, publisher, editor and (when his compositor was drunk) printer of the *Bathurst Advocate*; despite the religious interests of almost all his readers, Isaacs felt impelled to continually print items of Jewish interest in his newspaper. It was in Bathurst too that John Davies ruled as Chief Constable and it was because of him that, in 1848, Isaacs spent two months in prison for libel before moving on to become the owner of the *Windsor Telegraph*.

The Wellington Valley lay fifty miles north-west of Bathurst along the Macquarie River. Among its first landowners was the Sydney merchant Joseph Barrow Monte-fiore. Although not a farmer, he developed his original grant of 2560 acres in 1828 into 7000 acres by 1838, while leasing a considerably larger area from the Crown. The two Quakers James Backhouse and George Washington Walker visited the pro-perty in 1835 and wrote 'a Sydney merchant' had 'erected some good wooden build-ings; consisting of a dwelling house, prisoners' huts, a large wood shed etc.'[15] Strangely the ultimate purchaser of 16 000 acres of Montefiore's land was Joseph Aarons jnr, a baptised Jew and the son of two Jewish convicts. He grew up in Sydney and in 1839 opened a store in Bathurst, followed by a hotel, and then made a fortune dealing in livestock. He became Wellington's first Mayor.[16]

For many years Montefiore's prop-erty, Nanima, was managed by his brother-in-law George Mocatta. Mocatta acquired Blackdown Station near Bathurst in 1840, and by 1849 he was listed as the leaseholder of 20 000 acres in the Darling Downs, which made him one of the very few large scale Jewish pastoralists before the gold rush.[17] Another was Saul Samuel, also of the Wellington Valley, who eventually made Jewish political history by becoming the British Empire's first Jewish Minister of the Crown. Samuel was related by mar-riage to both the Montefiore and the Mocatta families, and by 1848 his stock grazed on 200 000 acres by the Macquarie River. As land was the key to respectability, it is not surprising to find that in May 1848 'Saul Samuel Esq. of Wellington' was the first Jew to be appointed a magistrate in New South Wales. Samuel's success in spite of his

Sir Saul Samuel. The first Jewish magistrate in New South Wales and a leading businessman in Bathurst, he became a member of the Legislative Council in 1854 and later of the Legislative Assembly. In 1880 he became Agent General of the colony in London, having previously served as colonial Treasurer and Postmaster-General.

lack of previous experience as a grazier was described by the man who seconded his first nomination for parliament in 1854:

> I have known Mr. Samuel for 14 years. At the commencement of our acquaintance Mr. Samuel arrived at Wellington as the proprietor of a newly purchased sheep station and although he knew next to nothing whatever of sheep, in a very short time, it was the best managed and most profitable concern in the district.[18]

Apart from George Mocatta and Saul Samuel, J. B. Montefiore, Michael Phillips and Michael Hyam, the only other Jewish names to appear as owners or leaseholders of extensive tracts of land in early New South Wales were Isaac Levey, brother of Barnett and Solomon Levey, and Abraham Moses. Levey made his fortune by buying land cheaply near Yass and Goulburn during the economic depression of the early 1840s, and Abraham Moses was the first Jew to receive a licence to pasture stock beyond the established boundaries of settlement in the foothills of the Australian Alps, to the south, in 1837.[19]

The pious Abraham Moses, who arrived in Sydney in the *Palambam* on 10 January 1833, brought to New South Wales not only his family but also Norman (Nahum) Simon, his own private *shochet* (ritual slaughterer of kosher meat) and Hebrew teacher for his children. Yet Simon appears to have neglected his duties very soon, because on 17 July 1835 the *Australian* reported that he had acquired an auctioneer's licence and opened a store—Berrima House—at Berrima. Moses began his colonial career in Sydney as the owner of the Joiners' Arms in King Street, and after two years profitable trading he opened 'commodious stores' at Monaro Plains, two hundred miles south-west of Sydney. Moses supplied goods to the scattered settlements of the southern tablelands and the Australian Alps from 1837 to 1841. He carried mail as far as the Snowy River, a distance of one hundred miles, and, conscious of the opportunities presented by the vast fertile territory, built a store at Dr Reid's Flat (near the Tambo River, north of Tambo Crossing), which soon became known as Jews' Flat. The great depression of the early 1840s sent Moses back to Sydney where he began to build up a prosperous business as a trader in the city, as an importer and exporter, and as a major landholder. Moses died in London, in 1873, supposedly leaving an estate of £650 000. In reality, his assets barely exceeded £3000.[20]

To Jews' Flat came the settlers Solomon Solomon and Samuel Shannon and their families. Both men were free migrants of the mid-1830s, and their families became part of the pioneering population of the southern highlands of New South Wales. Solomon took over the store and public house of Abraham Moses at Jews' Flat and carried on his business there until 1854, when he transferred his properties to his brother Maurice and moved to Cooma. The firm Solomon Pty Ltd still exists and is Cooma's 'senior store'. Members of the family are still shareholders of the firm. The Solomons founded stores in Eden on the south coast of New South Wales and in nearby Bombala, where Moses Joseph of Sydney owned a large property. Samuel Shannon opened a general store at Jews' Flat and later became one of the earliest storekeepers at Cooma.

'As solid as a Goulburn Jew' became a colonial byword, and there was good reason for this expression of grudging respect. Until the gold rush, Goulburn possessed the third-largest Jewish settlement on the eastern side of Australia. It was an impressively prosperous community and the town's bustling main street was lined with patriarchal names.[21] Goulburn, 120 miles south of Sydney, began as a garrison town at the gateway to the fertile southern tablelands and became the crossroads for the inland development of southern New South Wales. In 1836 the town consisted of 'a courthouse of slabs, covered with bark, a lock-up house, a few huts, occupied by the mounted police and constables, a cottage of roughly cut timber and a small inn, affording tolerable accommodation for such a place, as well as a better house or two at a short distance'. The small inn was The Travellers' Home Inn, owned by Solomon Moses, who advertised 'the best of Wines, Spirits, and Bottled Porter and well aired beds'.[22]

Solomon Moses was from Sheerness and had undoubtedly been tempted to come to Australia through the success of the brothers Judah and Joseph Solomon in Van Diemen's Land. Following his marriage in Sydney in January 1835 (the third Jewish marriage in Australia) he set out for the new settlement. The little tavern, which he built on land purchased from Abraham Moses of Jews' Flat, brought Solomon Moses good fortune. The district flourished, and in 1841 he opened the Royal Hotel in the new settlement of Goulburn, which had been moved back from the flood-prone banks of the river.[23] The *Australian* of 22 December 1841 described the new building as 'an ornament to the Southern Districts and is not to be equalled in Sydney, the New Royal Hotel excepted'. In July 1838 Moses suffered the terrifying experience of being unjustly arrested and sent to Sydney on suspicion of having received stolen notes after the robbery of the Maneroo Mail coach. Following his interrogation and release he returned to Goulburn, and received vice-regal patronage later in the year when Governor Sir George Gipps and all his entourage chose to stay at the Royal Hotel while on tour of the southern counties. A levée was held in the hotel, while in the drawing-room Lady Gipps graciously received the ladies of the district.[24]

Elias Moses and his brother-in-law Samuel Benjamin owned the Argyle Store in George Street, Sydney, whose wares included:

> Grindery of every description, Pistols and Fowling pieces, Gunpowder and shot, Haberdashery, Drapery, Hosiery and Saddlery, Sole and Kipp Leather, Wines, Spirits, Tea, Sugar, Tobacco, Groceries, General Assortment of Clothing, Crockery, Iron-mongery, Wilkinson's Sheep Shears, Wool Packs, Bags and Bagging, Paints, Oil and Turpentine with an extensive assortment of every description of Goods on the most reasonable terms.[25]

The two men became partners in Sydney in 1833 and soon branched out to Windsor. Elias Moses married Julia, the daughter of Abraham Moses, in April 1840, and her father's tales of the great new fertile regions of the south induced the two men to sell their George Street store and move to Goulburn in 1842.[26] At almost the same time they established an outpost even further to the south, at Queanbeyan. Benjamin and Moses prospered despite the severe economic depression which had seized the whole country and had temporarily ruined the wool industry. Outside Goulburn they built one of the largest 'boiling down' factories in the colony, to reduce to tallow the almost valueless carcasses of the district's vast herds of sheep and cattle.[27]

At the small settlement of Bungonia, some eleven miles south-east of Goulburn, Nathan Mandelson and his wife opened the Hit or Miss Inn in 1837. Mandelson, a pastry cook from Warsaw, was married to Phoebe Cohen of Leicester, a cousin of both Lady Judith Montefiore and Baroness Rothschild. They offered 'travellers up and down the Maneroo . . . good stabling and feed for horses'. As the district developed Bungonia itself declined and Mandelson moved to Goulburn in 1840, where his new hotel became an important landmark. In June 1851 Mandelson offered two hundred guineas reward to 'the first party who discovers a goldfield in the Police District of Goulburn'. The prize was soon claimed and the coach service from Goulburn to the new goldfields at Braidwood was owned and managed by Nathan Mandelson. Samuel Emanuel, brother-in-law of Mandelson, moved to Goulburn in 1845 and opened the Bee Hive Store, which became one of the most important firms in the district. Emanuel later became the member for Argyle in the Parliament of New South Wales.[28]

Goulburn's best-known emancipist was probably Samuel Davis, who established the Australian Store in 1838. He had been sent to Australia in 1831 at the age of seventeen for stealing sacred ornaments from the Ark of the Duke's Place Synagogue. Ironically, by the time of the gold rush Davis the sacrilegious collector of sacred silver had become one of the town's most important purchasers of gold. Davis went to the Goulburn district as an assigned servant and as soon as he was free he opened a store in the town's main street. It developed into the firm of Davies Alexander & Co.[29] The London *Voice of Jacob* of 6 June 1845 reported that Jewish High Holyday services had been held in Goulburn at the home of Elias Moses in 1844 and that seventeen people had attended. An acre of land was set aside for a Jewish cemetery and today the graves are all that remain of the first inland Jewish community in Australia.[30]

In the fertile Hunter River district, in and about Maitland, the 1841 census shows that there were forty-six Jews. One of the earliest Jewish settlers was Philip Joseph Cohen, from Sydney, who opened a soap factory in December 1833. Cohen's father-in-law, Solomon Levien, came to Maitland in the same year, gained his first experience as a publican at the Rose Inn and then moved to Sydney. Samuel Cohen, who was no relation to Phillip Joseph Cohen but was Nathan Mandelson's brother-in-law, settled in Maitland in 1836. Though Cohen had merely intended to visit Australia and then return to London, he found the long sea voyage so unpleasant that he preferred to stay where he was. His brother David came to Maitland and, together with Lewis Wolfe Levy who had originally settled in Tamworth, founded the well-known firm of David Cohen & Co.[31]

Despite financial trouble in 1843 the firm grew into a powerful business and Samuel Cohen became an important landowner and businessman with extensive mercantile interests throughout the Hunter Valley and New England. Cohen was elected a member of the Legislative Assembly for the district of Morpeth in August 1860. It was a brief political foray. Several months later he was defeated at a general election after failing to vote on the vital Robertson Land Bill that tried to entitle

LEFT: Henry Cohen of Port Macquarie, by an unknown colonial artist, c. 1850. Cohen, the patriarch of a large and successful colonial family, was transported to Port Macquarie in 1833 for dealing in stolen promissory notes. His wife followed him with nine of their ten children (two more were to be born in Australia). Having served his time, and after eleven years in business in Port Macquarie, he moved to Sydney and established the firm of Henry Cohen & Co., which opened branches throughout eastern Australia. He was elected president of the York Street Synagogue in 1859.

BELOW: 'The Gold Buyer—The Market Price Discussed—Eagle Hawk', hand-coloured engraving by S. T. Gill. The Jewish owner of a general store on the Victorian gold-fields carefully weighs the nuggets brought in for sale by the Irish digger. A large poster on the wall boasts 'Best Price Given for Gold', and we know that whatever price is paid will be recouped by the purchase of pickaxes, flour, tea, a billy, a spade or even soap

A ritual Kiddush cup, by C. F. Hancock, London, made from Victorian gold and complete with miniature kangaroos and emus. It was presented to Chief Rabbi Adler in 1853.

the small farmer to settle on unsurveyed land. Cohen explained that if the carrying of the Land Bill depended on his vote on the Sabbath, he would not record it. Since he had been in New South Wales he had protected the electors' Sabbath and he would protect his own even if they did not help him!

It had been in Cohen's house in Maitland in 1843 that fifteen Jews gathered to hold High Holyday services, and in 1859 he was the prime mover in the secessionist movement which created Sydney's second synagogue. He died in 1861, having created a business which would flourish in Sydney, Newcastle and Maitland for more than a hundred years. Even today it still exists, on a smaller scale, with the descendants of Samuel Cohen as its directors.[32] There are remnants of Jewish life still left in Maitland. A small overgrown graveyard sits in the middle of a farm. The Jews of Maitland built a handsome house of worship in the centre of the town in 1879, but the synagogue closed its doors in 1901 and the building is now used as a bank. A plaque pays a forlorn tribute to its status as a 'historic building' but, curiously, fails to mention that it was Maitland's synagogue.

At the other end of the Jewish social scale in Maitland were Samuel Levy and his wife Esther. Levy's colonial career is a saga of human suffering. He arrived in Sydney in 1810 and was almost immediately sent to the four-year-old settlement of Hobart Town. There he was sentenced to death in 1811 for being one of three men who stole eight sheep. His sentence was commuted to transportation for life and he was taken to Newcastle, where he spent thirteen terrible years, followed by two years at Port Macquarie. He wrote to the Governor asking for permission to return to Sydney 'having contended with hardships and privations which in former times were scarcely to be endured by Human Beings'. He was now 'of the advanced age of 60 and had long labor'd under severe Bodily infirmities brought on by his former sufferings'.[33]

Levy was assigned to Joseph Raphael, the quarrelsome Sydney dealer and former convict who claimed that he had been eight times to beseech mercy from the Governor on Levy's behalf 'on account of his age and of his being of the Jewish persuasion'. Raphael's good intentions rapidly evaporated and he soon denounced Levy for 'gross insolence and gross disobedience' and the unfortunate convict was sent to a chain gang working on the roads near Windsor. Again Levy wrote to the Governor. This time he could mention his 'advanced age of sixty-five' and that he was now afflicted with 'Rheumatism and pains in his limbs', and he hopefully asked to be assigned to the care of Israel Chapman. Before an answer could be given Levy had been convicted in Windsor of theft and had been sent to spend twelve months at the northern prison settlement of Moreton Bay.

Upon Levy's return he was assigned to a non-Jewish merchant in Sydney, who sent Levy off as a pedlar hawking his master's goods. He became well known in the Hunter River district and, when he was arrested in 1835 at Maitland for 'being improperly at large' and having no pedlar's licence, two petitions were organised in Maitland by Solomon Levien on behalf of his unfortunate fellow-Jew. The petitions were successful and Levy was allowed to remain in the district. Providence even bestowed upon him a belated measure of happiness, for in 1837 Esther Isaacs, the widow of Jacob Isaacs, applied to the Colonial Secretary for permission to marry the

70-year-old convict. Her request caused confusion within officialdom and, forgetting that three years before Moses Joseph had married in Sydney, the Colonial Secretary wrote on the application, 'This appears to be the first application for the marriage of a Jewish prisoner'. The problem posed by the request was whether a prisoner could be married by someone other than an official chaplain. Levy and his new wife were married in the Sydney Synagogue, and were still living in Maitland in 1847 when the colonial government finally granted the old man a conditional pardon for 'anywhere except the United Kingdom'.

THE SCATTERED BUSH STORES of the Jews made their owners frequent and obvious targets for highway robbery. Samuel Benjamin of Goulburn was held up by three bushrangers in January 1845 as he was travelling by coach to his branch store at Queanbeyan. The raid was interrupted by the arrival of the local keeper of the gaol, who chased the outlaws and captured one of them. In the following month eight armed and mounted men attacked the public house of Isaac Davis and the store of Isaac Levy at Burrowa, some forty miles beyond Yass. Davis died from gunshot wounds defending his wife and two little children, and his funeral was the third at the Jewish cemetery of Goulburn.[34]

Abraham Moses was bailed up by a bushranger while out on business in the lonely Australian Alps. On being ordered to dismount Moses asked the outlaw to hold his horse, and as soon as one foot was out of its stirrup he kicked the bushranger under the chin. The bushranger went sprawling and Moses galloped away. His son-in-law Elias Moses of Goulburn was not so lucky. He was robbed of his possessions and left tied to a tree, but at least his life was spared.[35]

In Yass, Moses Moses suspected that one of the customers at his hotel was the bushranger Massie. He burst into the dining room, attacked the outlaw and seized him by the throat. Moses, a 'very powerful man' who had been a professional boxer, soon had the upper hand and sent for the police, but the bushranger escaped as soon as they led him out of the hotel. However, the residents of Yass were so pleased with Moses that they presented him with a suitably engraved medallion.[36]

Barnett Levey's nephew, Jacob Marks, was robbed by three armed bushrangers at his store at Curryong Creek. In a bitter fight for his cash, Marks was shot twice and badly wounded. His wounds refused to heal and he closed down his business, asking the government for 'a small portion of land for the purpose of turning his attention to agricultural pursuits ... affording him the means of subsistence'.[37] When his petition was refused, Marks became a draper in Melbourne, married his first cousin, and found the strength to become a wealthy and respected citizen in the new colony.

More distant than the towns and villages of Sydney's rural hinterland, and beyond that part of the continent called New South Wales, new settlements and colonies were being created. Fear of foreign aggression and hunger for new lands often combined to give birth to struggling stockades and villages, and discoveries and dreams drew many settlers across the world from Britain. In each colony there were Jews, and each state of the Commonwealth of Australia can trace the birth of its Jewish community to its earliest years.

The Feared Outpost Prisons

ONVICTS WHO WERE PUNISHED by transportation from England to Australia sometimes suffered yet another transportation. If they were foolish or rebellious enough to behave badly, they could be sent from Sydney or Van Diemen's Land to Norfolk Island, Newcastle, Port Macquarie, Macquarie Harbour, Maria Island, Port Arthur or Moreton Bay. Each of these was a dreaded place of further punishment for convicts who refused their first opportunity of rehabilitation. Curious personalities sometimes emerged from the tales about these prison hells, such as Lewis Lazarus, the explorer, James Lawrence, actor and diarist, and James Woolfe, the pirate. But in general, it is the outcasts of Australian Jewry of these times whom we encounter in the prisons.

The site for Newcastle was discovered in 1796 by Lieutenant John Shortland. He was pursuing some convicts who had stolen a boat, and when he entered 'a fine river' some one hundred miles north of Sydney he named it the Hunter, after the Governor of that time. Cliffs on the coastline were found to be rich in coal, and enormous deposits of oyster shell promised a useful source of lime for Sydney's new buildings. Convicts were sent to work the coal and burn the lime, and 'Coal River' soon became a handy place in which to dump troublesome prisoners. They were worked so hard and treated so savagely that some chose suicide as the quickest way of escape, but coal-workings and lime-pits had the desired effect on most prisoners sent to New-castle and the majority decided to reform. Few stayed very long, and they usually settled in Sydney when their sentence was completed. Among the Jews sent to New-castle were Ikey Solomon's companion Joel Joseph in 1813, Samuel Lyons in 1819, and Vaiben and Emanuel Solomon in 1821.

As the rural settlement of New South Wales expanded, Newcastle became com-paratively civilised and the authorities had to look further afield for an appropriately isolated penal settlement. They chose Port Macquarie, 250 miles north of Sydney and discovered by Surveyor-General John Oxley in 1818. Port Macquarie was estab-lished by Governor Macquarie as a place of punishment in 1821, but by this time settlement was spreading so rapidly along the coast that in less than ten years it had lost its isolation and had been opened up for free settlement. There were convicts at Port Macquarie until 1847 and at Newcastle until 1855, but they were greatly out-numbered by free settlers. Very few Jews were sent to Port Macquarie, the most notable being Michael John Davies in 1832 and Henry Cohen in 1833. Both were allowed to take their families into exile with them, and both became part of the

Newcastle, with a distant view of Point Stephens, drawn by I. R Brown, published in Sydney, 1812. In March 1804 a group of Irish convicts rebelled against the military regime, only to be defeated by Major George Johnston and a detachment of twenty-five soldiers. Following the execution of their ring-leaders thirty-four convicts were sent northwards to Coal River, now to be called Newcastle, and a convict settlement for secondary punishment was created.

commercial life of the new region.[1] All that remains today of a small but once-flourishing Jewish community are some well-worn tombstones.

By Governor Sir Thomas Brisbane's time it was necessary to look even further for places of banishment. Sir Thomas decided in 1824 to re-open the Norfolk Island penal settlement, which had been abandoned in 1809; in 1823 he sent John Oxley northwards to seek an isolated outpost with the double advantage of suitability both for a penal settlement and to show the flag against French encroachment. Oxley found Moreton Bay, and named the river which ran into it the Brisbane. Sir Thomas sailed north to inspect and approve it, and on 30 August 1824 the first convict ship left Sydney for Moreton Bay. Within a few months the settlement had moved inland to the banks of the river, to make a wretched beginning to the story of Brisbane, capital of the future colony of Queensland.

Despair and misery reigned at Moreton Bay.[2] The commandant, Captain Patrick Logan, was said to have been appointed at the suggestion of his fellow officers in Sydney in order to get rid of him. Only the most incorrigible prisoners from Sydney and Port Macquarie were sent there, and until Port Arthur was established in Van Diemen's Land in 1830 it was the most brutal penal settlement in Australia. Prisoners murdered one another in order to obtain a quick release on the gallows. Punishments were decreed in hundreds of lashes, and sometimes the sound of the whip was heard from sunrise to sunset.

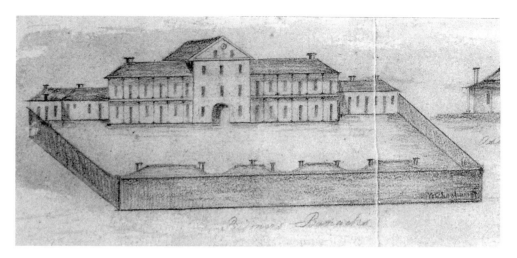

Moreton Bay Prisoners' Barracks. The most degraded and incorrigible convicts were sent northwards to Moreton Bay, and a contemporary ballad recalls their treatment:

For three long years I've been beastly treated; heavy irons each day I wore.
My poor back has been lacerated, and oftimes painted with crimson gore.
Like the Egyptians or ancient Hebrews, we were sorely oppressed by Logan's yoke,
Till kind Providence came to our assistance and gave this tyrant his total stroke.

(Quoted in C. M. H. Clark, A History of Australia, vol. 2, p. 176.)

The *Chronological Register of Convicts at Moreton Bay*, an ornately decorated, leather-bound volume now in the Oxley Memorial Library, Brisbane, records the names of the 2373 convicts sent from Sydney to Moreton Bay between 1824 and 1839, 1 per cent of whom were Jews. Listed as numbers 36 and 725 was Lewis Lazarus, whose seven years at Moreton Bay made him the first Jew to live in the future State of Queensland. His colonial adventures fill a closely written dossier among the papers of the Colonial Secretary in Sydney.[3]

Lewis Lazarus first appeared in the Old Bailey at the age of thirteen, and was found guilty of stealing eight brushes worth two shillings. This earned him a whipping and a month in gaol, but a year later, in 1818, he was charged with stealing a watch and was transported. He was to spend twenty-two years of his life in Australia as a convict, and receive more than three hundred lashes. He escaped twice. On the first occasion he survived in the bush for four months despite being speared by Aborigines, and on his second escape he was able to make his way from Moreton Bay to Port Macquarie through rugged and unexplored territory. His account of the journey raised great official interest because it opened up new overland tracks between the two settlements, but did not save him from being sent back to Moreton Bay. He was put to work in the hospital, where he stayed for six years. Then the penal settlement's hated Commandant, the sadistic Captain Logan, vanished in the bush, and Lazarus as an experienced bushman was promised a conditional pardon for finding him.

Lazarus did find Logan, but ten days too late. The Commandant had been speared by Aborigines, who hid his body in the bush. Lazarus almost died from an infection contracted as he carried the decomposed body back to camp. The authorities kept their word, and Lewis Lazarus, Moreton Bay's first Jewish resident and self-taught explorer, was returned to Sydney in 1832.

Joseph Hyams, is number 1160 in the *Chronological Register*. A native of London, he arrived in the *Somersetshire* in 1814. He had a life sentence to serve, but almost immediately was allowed to start work as Australia's first dentist. He advertised that in his rooms at 31 Pitt Street he could 'respectfully offer his services in the light of his profession— scaling, cleaning and drawing the Tooth, when necessary, without causing pain, and supplying the vacancy with others of pure Ivory— also corns extracted without charge'.

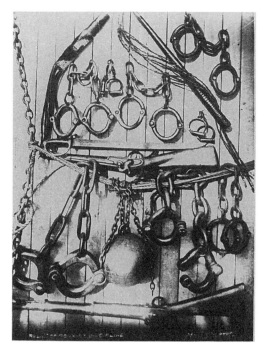

Manacles, handcuffs and whips of the convict system.

The first Medical Board of New South Wales found in 1820 that Hyams and his Jewish convict colleague Simeon Lear were not 'duly qualified to practise as physicians or surgeons', and published a warning about them in the *Sydney Gazette*. This may have caused Hyams to turn to crime, because in 1827 he was transported to Moreton Bay for robbery. Following this experience, which he vehemently denounced as a miscarriage of justice, he was returned to Sydney and ended his days as a guardian of the trees planted in Hyde Park.[4]

A typical story from the first brutal period of Moreton Bay is that of Isaac Wolf, number 2618. Wolf, a London errand-boy, was transported for life in 1821 for the singular crime of picking a policeman's pocket of eight shillings, in the crowd going into the East London Theatre. He was seen by another policeman, and at the age of eighteen arrived in Sydney in the *Mary*. In Sydney he stole half a chest of tea, for which he spent four years at Moreton Bay. Despite a note in his convict indent that he was blind in the right eye, he was placed in charge of a flock of sheep. On New Year's Eve 1838, the flock of this one-eyed shepherd was attacked by native dogs, and he was given twenty-five lashes for 'allowing several of the sheep to be lost'. Three months later he was given a further fifty strokes for losing three more sheep.[5]

Some prisoners, like Samuel Alexander, numbers 970 and 2042, were truly incorrigible. He served two sentences at Moreton Bay: the first for stealing port at

Windsor in 1826, and the second because after his return to Sydney he was found to be 'incorrigible and running away'. Three years later he was sentenced to death in Sydney for being a smuggler, but was reprieved and sent to Norfolk Island for ten years. His return to the mainland was noted by the Sydney police, who classified him as 'head of a mob of thieves'.[6]

Hyam Alexander, who became an early Jewish settler in Queensland, arrived in Australia as a convict in 1819. His original crime puts him in a category of his own.[7] As a young furniture upholsterer he was caught at an election meeting near Covent Garden while quietly cutting through the overcoat and suit pockets of the Right Hon. Thomas Lord Foley, with his upholsterer's knife. He almost got away with fifty pounds, a watch and a purse, but instead found himself in the Old Bailey. His colonial record was so bad that he was still a prisoner of the Crown in 1854, when he was allowed to settle in Ipswich. He finally received his ticket-of-leave in 1857.

The last of Moreton Bay's military commandants advised the Governor in Sydney in 1839 that there were hardly enough convicts left to protect property and stock. It was suggested that the country be opened to free settlement. Three years later, on 15 February 1842, the *Government Gazette* announced that 'all settlers and other free persons shall be at liberty to proceed thither in like manner as to any other part of the colony'.

The first free Jewish settlers were half-brothers Judah Moss Solomon and Isaac Solomon, together with hotel-keeper Benjamin Lee, who came from Sydney when Moreton Bay was first opened for free settlement. The Solomons belonged to the family of Emanuel and Vaiben Solomon, and travelled northward to conduct the first land sales in the region. In Brisbane, Judah's first son Moss Judah became the third free child to be born in the settlement. Both Judah and Isaac had already spent some time with Emanuel Solomon in his first months in Adelaide, and both eventually returned to live in South Australia. It was in Isaac's hotel that the Jewish community of Adelaide was first organised.[8]

In the first year of free settlement George Mocatta, who at that time owned a property near Bathurst, joined with Benjamin Lee and a Sydney businessman in sending 1600 head of cattle overland from central New South Wales to Moreton Bay. The journey took three months and was reported eagerly in the Sydney press, for it indicated a new phase in the development of the northern regions.[9] Mocatta, who must be counted among the pastoral pioneers of Queensland, established a sheep station at Grantham on the Darling Downs close to today's Toowoomba, and probably it was to this outpost of civilisation that he took his sheep. In 1848 Mocatta moved on further north to the Burnett River district, which today is noted for its sugar-cane plantations. In its earliest years of settlement George Mocatta leased from the government no less than 92 000 acres on seven leases which were set aside for 30 000 sheep. It was the foundation of a fortune which enabled the pioneer to leave the district in 1855, transferring most of the properties to Montefiore, Graham & Co.[10]

Moses Joseph of Sydney bought land in Brisbane in August 1842 and appointed the Solomons as the Moreton Bay representatives of the Sydney Synagogue, authorising them to gather donations for the York Street Synagogue.[11] It was not surprising that no subscriptions were collected. Apart from their friend Benjamin Lee, there were no other Jews in the settlement. Lee remained in Brisbane longer than did the Solomons. Between 1843 and 1846 he held a victualler's licence for the Shepherd and Flock Inn at North Brisbane, then moved to the Sovereign Hotel in Queen Street while at the same time buying and selling as a general dealer.[12] By 1848 the census recorded a grand total of eight Jews amid the Moreton Bay population of 2257. Lee and his family had been joined by emancipist Marcus Berkman, a Berlin-born pedlar who received his ticket-of-leave in 1844 and became an early settler of Warwick,[13] and by Joel Henry Asher, who owned the California Store near the town ferry and then worked briefly as an auctioneer and agent in Brisbane.

For many years the principal Jewish connections with Brisbane Town were more evident in the advertising columns of the colony's newspaper than in the streets. Sydney's business houses, tailors and importers kept in close touch with the new region by sending their representatives to the north and inviting customers to visit them in return. Henry Hayes & Co. of George Street addressed large advertisements to 'our friends in the interior'. The Spyer Brothers and Samuel Lyons told the northern colony of cash advances on wool and tallow sold in Sydney, while Benjamin & Moses offered property for sale in Brisbane. Robert Graham, the Presbyterian partner of Jacob Levi Montefiore, opened a store in Brisbane, and Montefiore's brother Frederick spent some time working in early Brisbane. Sydney's Jewish community was also in-directly involved in the development of the colony, with early, obviously speculative purchases of land by Samuel Benjamin, Elias Moses and Moses Joseph.[14]

Famine, drought and economic depression dogged Brisbane's first years as a free community. It was not until 1865 that fifteen Jewish families gathered together to form a congregation. It was a further twenty-one years before a synagogue was built. Even today the Jewish community in Queensland is one of the smallest in Australia, reflecting its late start and the general northern preoccupation with agricultural development.

In 1788 Governor Phillip had sailed from England with instructions from George III to secure Norfolk Island as quickly as possible 'to prevent [it] being occupied by subjects of another power'. The small, formerly volcanic island, measuring five miles by three, became the temporary home of many of Australia's earliest settlers, including Esther Abrahams, John Harris and Bernard Walford. The island's first period of settlement ended in 1809 when the transfer of farmers to Van Diemen's Land was completed. It was not until 1824 that it was decided to reopen Norfolk Island as 'a penitentiary' for the worst criminals and 'colonial offenders' of New South Wales and Van Diemen's Land. The new régime was harsh. Convict women were excluded, homosexuality flourished, and prisoners sent to Norfolk Island were not expected to return.

A 'new plan' based on moral considerations was authorised by the British government in 1839, and Captain Alexander Maconochie of Van Diemen's Land was appointed Superintendent. Maconochie had been horrified by the degradation of prisoners at Port Arthur, and on Norfolk Island he began a Mark System of Convict

Discipline that gave credit to prisoners for good conduct and enabled them to redeem themselves and gain their freedom.[15]

In this new and hopeful atmosphere, Australia's strangest Jewish congregation assembled for worship on Norfolk Island in early 1840. Guided and inspired by Captain Maconochie, the nine Jewish prisoners on the island were told in December to write to the Sydney Synagogue and ask for prayer books and Passover food. Their 'reader', Levy Abraham, proudly wrote:

> [We have] experienced every encouragement from Capt. Maconochie R.N., Civil Superintendent of this Island in the pursuit of our religious duties as far as practicable, in having a ward solely appropriated to our use as a place of worship and furnished with what was immediately necessary for that purpose.

This amounted to an unheard-of concession. The Norfolk Island prisoners were all colonial offenders. Several had been in and out of prison for more than twenty years. In Maconochie's words they were 'deplorably sunk and demoralised'. The congregation responded to their plea with a box of prayer books, some works of religious instruction, unleavened bread for Passover, and an almanac with all the Jewish festivals and holidays prudently marked in red to protect the benevolent Captain 'against any misrepresentation that might possibly be made by persons in the condition of the applicants in order to obtain indulgence or exemption from labour'.[16]

One of the convicts in the congregation, James Lawrence,[17] has left us a long, imaginative account of his life and adventures. Boastfully he describes a life of crime which began in the chorus line of the Drury Lane Theatre, then proceeded to New

The convict barracks on Norfolk Island following their final evacuation in 1856.

York where he stole a thousand pounds from an uncle in Greenwich Street and pocketed the entire proceeds of a theatrical benefit in Buffalo. Lawrence claimed that his first six years in Australia as a convict earned him an astounding 1225 lashes for sundry punishments. He appeared on stage in Sydney and Launceston and was a member of Barnett Levey's theatrical company before being sent to Norfolk Island for fraud.

Lawrence made history in the South Pacific. In the interests of morale, Captain Maconochie allowed the prisoners to present a play called *The Castle of Andalusia* on the Queen's birthday holiday in May 1840, and Lawrence took the leading role of Don Caesar. In his letter to the Sydney Synagogue, Abraham complained that Lawrence's behaviour was so objectionable that 'he has been indispensably separated from us'. He apparently did not regain permanent freedom. The Melbourne Hebrew Congregation's Burial Book records his death in prison near Melbourne in 1863.

The congregation at Norfolk Island even included a pirate, albeit a reluctant one. James Woolfe, alias Mordecai, had come to Australia in 1828.[18] He had been sentenced in London at the age of twelve to seven years transportation. Woolfe's first act of piracy occurred in 1839 when he and eight others escaped from Port Arthur in a large six-oared whale-boat, only to be captured four months later at Twofold Bay on the south-eastern coast of New South Wales. Four years later he was still a prisoner of the Crown, working with the crew of the brig *Governor Phillip* which carried convicts and sailors from Sydney to Norfolk Island. At seven in the morning on 21 June 1842, with cries of 'Throw these bastards overboard and they will tell no tales!', Australian maritime history was made as the convict crew tried to take control of the ship and lock the soldiers and officers below decks, but five mutineers were killed and six captured, including James Woolfe. Woolfe emerged as a most unwilling pirate. He rescued one of the soldiers thrown into the sea and saved the life of another held captive on the deck. All prisoners were found guilty of mutiny, four were hanged, and Woolfe and one other sent to Van Diemen's Land for life.

At the prison at Port Arthur, history repeated itself. Once again Woolfe was employed as a convict seaman, this time on the waters of the Tasman Peninsula. A sudden squall upset his boat and Woolfe was able to save the life of an officer. Before he could receive a pardon he was off again on his third fruitless attempt to escape from gaol. In 1845 in Hobart, James Woolfe and five others were sentenced to death for being part of a robbery with violence. The judge declared that Woolfe was 'especially culpable as his life had been spared before on conviction of piracy', but His Honour had 'no doubt under the present lenient administration that their lives might be spared and they would be spared, and they would be sent to Norfolk Island'. And so it was. Woolfe returned to Norfolk Island and continued to work on the boats.

In a petition for mercy written in 1848, Woolfe tells how he rescued the convict stock-keeper and recovered the body of the Chief Constable following the wreck of a whale-boat on the island's reef. Four days later he rescued the crew of a whaler's boat, overturned while trying to cross the bar. By this time James Woolfe the pirate had spent twenty years in Australia as a convict and had been sentenced to death twice.[19]

Convicts at work at Port Arthur, hauling logs as a human 'centipede', 1836.

Captain Maconochie's four years on Norfolk Island marked the heyday of the sad little Jewish community, whose numbers never quite reached the traditional *minyan* (quorum) of ten men needed for a complete service of Jewish worship. Most of those listed in the letter to the Sydney Synagogue were back on the mainland within two years and their names continue to appear in the court records of the colony. When Maconochie was relieved, Norfolk Island reverted to its tradition of brutality and hopelessness until the prisons were closed in June 1856 and the descendants of the *Bounty* mutineers were brought there from Pitcairn Island. The last Jewish convict on Norfolk Island was Isaac Levey, who had been sent to Van Diemen's Land in the *William Jardine*. He was freed on 15 June 1854.[20] After the final removal of the convicts, Norfolk Island played no further part in the history of Australian Jewry.

Ophir

ON 12 AUGUST 1850 a well-behaved but vocal crowd gathered at Circular Wharf on Sydney Cove in the pouring rain to demonstrate their feelings of 'irritation, disgust and contempt' with the 'mother country' for continuing to transport convicts to the bustling colony of New South Wales. Five thousand Australians voted to send a delegation to the Governor and marched up the hill to the gates of Government House where they were met 'by soldiers and loaded muskets'. A defiant Governor Charles FitzRoy was convinced the meeting had been organised by the Sydney 'mob', but the *Illustrated London News* wrote that the rally was 'analogous to that which effected the separation of the American colonists from the British Empire'. At Port Phillip the *Melbourne Morning Herald* thundered, 'The British Government had done away with black slavery but they manufactured white slaves to send them out here'.[1]

The indignant protests of the colonials were not enough to sway the determination of British officialdom, but gold would effectively bring the transportation system to an end. On 5 May 1851 a Sydney newspaper reported that gold had been found the previous January 'West of the Blue Mountains' by Edward Hammond Hargraves, a miner who had just returned from the Californian goldfields. The discovery had been made beyond Bathurst in a rivulet of the Macquarie River, which was soon named Ophir after the goldmines pursued by King Solomon. The discovery certainly ended the deportation of prisoners to eastern Australia as the British government could hardly send convicted felons to the goldfields as a punishment for criminal behaviour.

For several members of the Jewish community the excitement was long overdue. In 1845 the Sydney jeweller E. D. Cohen had notified the press, and the curiously apathetic public, that 'a new age' was about to dawn. *The Cumberland Times and Western Advertiser* of 20 December 1845 reported:

> We yesterday saw a specimen of virgin gold which has been purchased by Mr E. D. Cohen from a person who had come down from the country and who stated that he had discovered it in the mountains . . . Mr Cohen purchased a small specimen from the same individual about 12 months ago, some of which he melted down and it proved to be pure gold.

And Cohen's son Moses later recalled:

> Shepherd Macgregor gave it to me in front of the shop to carry it in and I helped to clean it with him and Father, and when he was paid for the clean gold, he gave me a shilling for helping clean it, and said, you are the first Australian white boy to carry

and help clean and spend the first shilling from the first gold got in Australia, dug out of the ground at Summer Hill Creek near Wellington New South Wales.[2]

The news was noted in Melbourne in the *Port Phillip Patriot*, which carried the story on Christmas Eve 1845. Quoting the *Sydney Morning Herald*, the editor claimed that he had found the cure for unemployment: 'Out of Sydney all you idlers, make engagements with the squatters, and who knows but in addition to your wages you may be rewarded by the discovery of a gold mine'.

It is clear that the authorities had known about the existence of gold for some time. In 1823 a government surveyor named James McBrien noted in his field book that he had discovered gold in the Fish River; curiously, nobody paid him the slightest attention. The Polish explorer and geologist Paul Strzelecki found gold-bearing rock formations in the County of Wellington in 1839. Official caution, prompted by the presence of thousands of convicts, quietly restrained public action and announcements. On 17 May 1849 the *Sydney Morning Herald* mentioned a rumour that a Mr Davidson of Wellington had picked up some specimens of gold mixed with quartz, but called the report 'a mere idle hoax'. The prolific Melbourne press sarcastically diagnosed a case of 'the yellow fever' and described an earlier report of a gold discovery near the Grampians as 'a six day wonder'. Thomas Chapman, the young ticket-of-leave shepherd, felt so intimidated by the threat to his life caused by his 'secret' that he fled to Sydney and found a job in a pub. Apparently Australians needed to hear about the glittering excitement of the Californian gold rush before they could understand the rich possibilities of an economy based on gold.

A year before Hargraves' discovery was proclaimed Solomon Meyer, who owned the Australian Store at Carcoar, published a sensational advertisement in the *Bathurst Free Press* of 5 January 1850. He headed it '£500 reward!' and continued:

It has been currently reported that an extensive gold field has been lately discovered in the vicinity of Carcoar . . . Every sensible man must be surprised at the ridiculous preference which people are inclined to give Californian gold over Carcoarian Gold, for this simple reason, that they have heard of the former, but not seen the latter . . .

The reward, however, was no more than an advertising gimmick. Meyer offered it to any individual who could obtain his supplies more cheaply than he could buy them at the Australian Store. But those advertisements were prophetic and it is no wonder that Solomon Meyer was among the colonies' first gold buyers. Together with another Jew, Raphael Tolano of Carcoar,[3] he offered in the *Bathurst Free Press* of 17 May 1851 the 'highest prices for gold', while J. Solomon & Co. of Bathurst advertised that at their Bee Hive Store 'The utmost value in cash or kind will be given for wool and Bathurst Gold in large and small quantities'.

In London the editor of the *Jewish Chronicle* became obsessed with the Australian gold rush, hoping its lure would painlessly cure the embarrassment of the ever-growing and conspicuously poverty-stricken Jewish community in the East End. The *Chronicle* reprinted letter after letter about conditions in Australia sent to the newspaper by proud but anxious parents. From Melbourne came this anonymous contribution written on the day after Christmas in 1851. It contained not only the promise of instant wealth but also the magic name of Montefiore, indicating that emigration to Australia was now a respectable option for rich and poor:

Everything you may read concerning the diggings in Victoria however amazing it may appear, you may place every reliance in the truth of the same. For some little time Sydney had the laugh at us, and their papers exulting in their success; little expecting that when once gold should be discovered here we should, as we have done, beat them altogether. Their gold fields have, in many cases, been overpraised; ours spoken of as much under the truth as theirs over.

Indeed, it is astonishing to see the gold flying about in Melbourne. I was present but the other day at the stores of Messrs Benjamin [Solomon, David and Moses] when I myself witnessed four men, who had been at work for about three weeks, receive a cheque for 1400 and some odd pounds. Yes, my dear Sir, hundreds are though almost nothing of—thousands! . . . I often witness at the store of A[sher] H[ymen] Hart esq five, ten and fifteen pounds weight brought in . . . as our coreligionists are among the large purchasers here, you can satisfy yourself or any other person who feels an interest, by making enquiries among the London merchants trading in this part of the hemisphere that California, the once famed California, is now completely eclipsed. The Britishers (so termed here) need no longer go among the American ruffians to be scoffed and ill treated among them: No! our Queen (God Bless Her!) owns one of the richest continents in the whole world.

It is but seven months since that gold was discovered near Bathurst, about fifty miles from Sydney. It was reported that all who went there made their fortune in a few weeks; but in truth, such was not the general case; for out of every hundred there were but ten who did well.

Many flocked to Balarat [sic] and the same exaggerated reports which characterise these theories were rife here. Thousands were disappointed and returned worse off than when they went, until the second diggings (so commonly termed here) were discovered and great and marvellous in the extreme are the doings there . . . We had an arrival amongst us recently, namely Jacob Montefiore esq together with his lady and family. He attended divine service on the first Sabbath of his arrival and after being called to the Torah said *Birkat Hagomel* [the Blessing for having been delivered from danger] very feelingly for their safe arrival from a distance of 10,000 miles and explained his delight at beholding so regularly organised a congregation at such distance from our native land. Persuade no one to leave who can get a living at home, as I can assure you that the work has proved too hard for many who have been accustomed to labour all their lives.[4]

Every corner of Australia felt the impact of the gold discoveries as the male population packed their bags and left for the diggings. In the newly proclaimed separate colony of Victoria it was reported that Geelong was in ferment and that people were leaving Melbourne in thousands. The country town of Kilmore predicted that by the end of the week that gold was found in Buninyong, only the sick, the halt and women would be left in town. The *Melbourne Morning Herald* composed a hymn in praise of the gold mania.

> *Almighty Gold! Whose magic charms dispense*
> *Worth to the worthless, to the graceless grace*
> *To cowards valour and to blockheads sense!*[5]

View of the Bathurst Diggings, 1851. This scene was repeated in and around Ballarat where, in September 1851, some one thousand men scratched for alluvial gold. Within a month there were three thousand 'diggers' in Ballarat. Hunger, typhoid, dysentery and flies beset the fortune-seekers, whose numbers daily increased.

The newspaper believed that Victoria's new-found wealth would 'keep [her] pure from the convict blood of the neighbouring colonies'. It was a faint hope. From the town of Ross in the interior of Van Diemen's Land, the son of Abraham Vallentine wrote in 1852 to his father, who promptly published the letter for all to see in the communal journal:

> Everybody in this part of the world is gold mad. The gold discoveries in Sydney you have heard of, but the discovery in Port Phillip is beyond description. The gold is found in tons . . . It is nothing new to see one of your servants leave you and go away for a month or two and return with one hundred pounds or a thousand pounds or even three thousand pounds which has been got in a very short time. It has upset everything and when it is to end God only knows.[6]

'In my opinion' huffed a well-bred settler to the *Illustrated London News* of 21 December 1850, 'this place is inevitably and irretrievably ruined; I cannot see it in any other light . . . The gold fields are inexhaustible . . . At the moment I cannot get a pair of boots made or mended in Melbourne . . . I get my bread at Collingwood by sufferance . . . The Judge's servants are gone, his sons clean the knives and shoes and reckless vagabonds arrive from all over the world'.

From Hindmarsh, in the colony of South Australia, the son of a Mr Farrow warned the English Jewish community:

> I am off to the diggings in three or four weeks and I hope to be successful. If I am I shall come to England. Port Phillip is only four hundred miles from here by water and in a direct line. The diggings are only three hundred and sixty miles away; the passage costs three pounds and a license thirty shillings. I want a pick-axe and shovel and a tin dish to wash the gold in . . . Anybody in England who has a wish to come here, advise them not to do so, for they ought to have a summer or two's experience of the climate before they go digging. Then they might be unsuccessful and happen to be short of cash; and having no one to give them a crust, they might lie and die— for this is a rum country for a greenhorn . . . I guess I shall look rather curious with a brace of pistols stuck in my belt. Everybody at the diggings is armed and I go with the full determination to shoot the first person that meddles with me. There are 40,000 people at the diggings and of this number 30,000, at least, are old convicts.[7]

An equally sober warning to would-be migrants to Victorian goldfields was published in the *Jewish Chronicle* of 6 November 1852:

> If you know any who thinks of coming out try by all means in your power to stop at home . . . thousands lose their all, a few are benefited . . . Many are carried off by dysentery, after a few days painful illness; they die among strangers . . . It is not safe to go about Melbourne after dark; the wretched villains who lurk in the sombre corners of the streets, have a knack of rushing out upon persons and seizing them by their throats and choking them.

H. S. Ansell in Geelong told a different story about opportunities waiting for the Jewish poor:

> The great field for emigration is open for our poor brethren to these parts . . . Carpenters, shoe makers, cabinet makers and all such mechanics are getting here from 15 shillings to 25 shillings per day. It is only proper that the poor Jew should endeavour to participate in the good things here . . . Our leading men would be doing a great service to the Jewish young men out here by sending out a few respectable single girls for it would save many a young man from marrying a Christian.[8]

Young Mr Ansell's plea did not fall on deaf ears. The *Jewish Chronicle* gave a great deal of publicity to the formation of a committee to send single Jewish women to Australia:

> We understand that Nathaniel Montefiore Esq has consented to accept the office of president of the Committee for aiding Jewish emigrants to Australia. The committee will consist both of ladies and gentlemen and their assistance will be rendered to such single females only as shall produce testimonials that they will have a home to go to on arrival at the selected colony. By such a judicious arrangement the evils to which single female Jewish emigrants are likely to be subjected will, in the case of Jewesses, be avoided.[9]

The newspaper vigorously supported a distinguished committee of Anglo-Jewish grandees who had joined forces in a scheme to send their Jewish poor to the ends of the earth. The community believed that there were powerful reasons to send the East

End Jews to Australia rather than to the United States of America. After all, wrote the editor of the *Jewish Chronicle*:

> Females can only emigrate to a country where the laws are respected, and when no disorder arising from the sudden advent of Mammon can be lasting. In this respect Australia is far different from California. There gold is not a blessing but a curse. It has not become so in Australia; nor will it be if emigration from the other country is properly supplied . . . California is a republic in its most offensive form. Australia is a British colony and that speaks its praise for the sovereignty of the crown is there acknowledged by a loyal community. In California the country is a desert and peopled with men deserving no higher name than semi barbarians. In Australia the population has attained a high social and commercial position under a constitutional legislature.

Migration of Jews from Poland and Russia, 'fleeing from the land of cruel despotism' to Great Britain, was causing immense social stress, as the *Jewish Chronicle* described:

> Anyone who will take the trouble to visit the populous quarters where the poor reside, as Middlesex Street and the vicinity; anyone who will condescend to go about on a winter's night, and unexpectedly call at some of the miserable hovels (houses we cannot call them) situated in the narrow courts and alleys, often inhabited by two or three families, including a great number of children, often so densely crowded, that one unaccustomed to such a dwelling can hardly draw breath; anyone we say . . . will see children running about half naked, mothers whose haggard looks betray their anguish in not being able to satisfy the hunger of the infants and fathers afflicted with illness.[10]

'Alarming Prospect: Single Ladies off to the Diggings'. The shortage of women on the goldfields became a major concern in England. Charitable emigration societies, both Christian and Jewish, attempted to solve the problem by recruiting young indigent women to travel to Australia.

Knowledge of this social crisis reached Whitehall, and the Colonial Land and Emigration Office agreed to help the Jewish community send the poor to the other side of the world. The Jewish Ladies Benevolent Loan and Visiting Society led by Grace Josephs of 10 Doughty Street, Mecklenburgh Square joined hands with the organisation headed by Caroline Chisholm to sort out and gather the appropriate emigrants. The Commissioners 'would not object to their putting on board at their own expense preserved [kosher] meats' if 'a party of persons of the Jewish faith sufficiently numerous to constitute one or more messes (which generally include 6 to 8 persons each) should at any time be approved'. The highly respected Caroline Chisholm met with Nathaniel Montefiore's Emigration Committee in August 1853 and told the Committee that the would-be emigrants 'were, of course, expected to be of the working class', stating that 'she had ever found the poor grateful, of which she quoted several personal examples'. To demonstrate the prosperity of Melbourne she produced a Melbourne newspaper that advertised an excursion ticket by steamer to nearby Geelong costing 40 shillings.[11]

In the first week of April 1854 the *Ballarat* set sail for Melbourne with Caroline Chisholm and 34 assisted Jewish migrants. They were supplied with a dismal shipboard diet, comprising $17\frac{1}{2}$ hundredweight of 'Jewish meat', 280 pounds of suet and 280 pounds of preserved carrots. Before the ship sailed it was visited by Sir Anthony and Lady Rothschild and Mr Nathaniel Montefiore, who gave the travellers bedding, Bibles and prayer books.[12] By June 1854 the Jewish Emigration Society had sent 85 settlers to Australia and 45 to America. Despite the kindness and concern of the indefatigable Caroline Chisholm, young Henry Harris in Melbourne was not impressed by the prospect of an influx of respectable, indigent Jewish females, and wrote home to his father:

> I saw an account in the *Jewish Chronicle* about sending single girls out here. I should advise them to consider well before they do so. Respectable Jewish single girls, I should think, could get better situations as cooks or servants in England without coming out here and to come on the spec of marrying. It is, I fear, a very bad spec, as one half of the Jewish young men are not getting more than a living for themselves much less for a wife . . . I do candidly tell you Melbourne is the last place I should pick out to send a lot of virtuous Jewish girls to . . . Most of the young men who are in business live at boarding houses and sleep four or five in one room.[13]

As the migrants poured in, there was a long debate in the Legislative Council of New South Wales on a motion to pay a stipend for a Jewish minister. George Moss, who modestly called himself 'An Israelite' (*Ish ha-Israeli*), wrote to London: 'Mr Wentworth, who introduced the motion is well entitled to the thanks of our co-religionists, wherever located, for his exertions in our cause; as is also Mr [Robert] Nichols, another member. This gentleman is of Jewish descent'. (Nichols had employed Moss to collect delinquent fees for the *Australian* newspaper, so the relationship to his grandmother Esther Abrahams was obviously no secret.) George Moss added, 'There is a great field for Jewish emigration. Jewish married families with £500 and friends at home would do well here'.[14]

'New Chums, Refreshing Sleep. 10/- a night!', Melbourne, 1852. Some 100 000 arrived in Melbourne in 1852. It was the greatest gold rush ever seen and the 16-year-old village was unable to cope. Desperate immigrants spent all their savings before they even began the long hike through the harsh and unfamiliar Australian bush to find their fortune.

But in 1853 the Jews of London were warned that the goldfields were in 'a frightful state of disorganisation where pandemonium reigned':

> Australia is yet drunken with success and the civilising influence of women is not yet felt. Woman unprotected is not yet safe in the gold regions of Australia. Aye but the girls will say, they have friends. We reply those friends are too busily occupied just now in procuring gold.[15]

'Advance Australia, thou fair foster child of thy mother England!' declaimed young David Isaacs 'late of Liverpool' to the *Jewish Chronicle* on 26 May 1854:

> To follow gold seeking occupations here I have seen the merchant leave his counting-house, the clerk his office, the shepherd his sheep, the reaper his sickle, the poet his rhymes, the author his works, husbands leave their wives, parents their children and children their parents. Gold has infused discontent into their hearts.[16]

The initial Victorian gold-licence fee of 15 shillings a month, enforced for every prospective miner whether they were successful or not, brought the goldfields to a state of rebellion. Jews were among those who fought against the troopers at the Eureka Stockade on Bakery Hill in Ballarat, beneath the blue and white flag of the Southern Cross. The loquacious and indefatigable future legislator Charles Dyte and the inn-keeper Henry Harris helped frame the resolutions at Eureka. The Polish-born watchmaker and storekeeper Manasha 'Yorkey' Flatow was arrested on suspicion of having been associated with burning down Bentley's Eureka Hotel, which triggered the rebellion.[17] Young Teddy Thonen, whose language was German, was one of those shot down by the troopers on that fateful day, as rebel leader Raffaello Carboni romantically recalled: 'Five feet high, some thirty years old. Shrewd, yet honest, benevolent but scorning the knave; of deep thought though prompt in action. Thonen possessed the head belonging to that cast of men whose word is their bond'.[18] The more prosaic truth is that the gregarious Thonen was known in Ballarat as 'The Lemonade Man' because he sold sly grog.

Another Polish watchmaker, Hyman Levinson, who was born in Posen and grew up in London, found himself in the midst of the battle. He was less than heroic, but his account of the battlefield has the mark of truth:

> When I arrived in Ballarat I brought my tent with me from Melbourne. It took me about a week to find a suitable place for it. There was only one formed road. I selected my spot on the slope of a high hill. A road was being cut then along that hill. On the one side of it the ground was very high, on the other it was low. One had to come down from the road to my tent. I procured a carpenter to put up the frame for my tent, and on Wednesday it was finished. On Thursday evening I pre-pared to start business. I was cleaning the small window, which was a necessary feature for my watchmaking business, about ten o'clock, when Charles Dyte came running along, calling out: 'Hyman, put up your shutters!' 'Why?' 'The riot's begun'. Nothing was to be done. I had my stock of watches in my trousers pocket. I stood and waited for developments. Suddenly a digger with a revolver in his hand burst into my tent.
>
> 'Hullo mate'. I asked 'What are you going to do?'
>
> 'I'm going to shoot that —— fellow' and he pointed to Captain Wise in com-mand of the military.
>
> I objected. 'There'll be a volley and we'll both be shot.' He persisted. 'Well, I said, I don't want to interfere, but I'll have to go for protection.'

This Levinson did, and the rebel was duly arrested and word spread through Ballarat that Levinson the Watchmaker was an informer:

> I tried to explain but it was useless. They were all Germans! They all attacked me. I was struck again and again. My window was smashed and the tent pulled down. I ran and they pursued me. I ran to a store where I had bought my provisions but the situation was too dangerous for its occupants and they turned me out. I ran down the road with my pursuers after me. As I ran I saw my friend Samuels at his door. He happened to know German so he stopped my pursuers and asked them what was the matter, so as to give me time.[19]

AS THE GOLD RUSH BEGAN, the first era of an emerging nation's colonial history ended abruptly. For the Jews of Australia it meant the sudden emergence of a Jewish com-munity of free citizens and settlers. Between 1851 and 1860, 740 000 people poured into Australia, including many Jews who, like all the other fortune hunters, sought wealth on the goldfields or from supplying those who were digging for gold. The Jewish population trebled, and the little congregations established in the 1840s suddenly became self-sufficient. New communities grew up in all the major cities. A glittering future obliterated the grey shadows of the past.

In Melbourne on 20 February 1853 the congregation resolved 'That in consequence of the extraordinary influx of Jewish Emigrants in to the colony of Victoria and Melbourne in particular the Congregation of the first Jewish Synagogue has deemed it necessary to find the means for building a Synagogue on the ground belonging to the present Congregation'. It would be 'an extensive building'. The congregation was 'important' but the congregational leadership felt that the Jewish community lagged 'far behind her many neighbours of other denominations' through the 'apathy displayed by the large numbers of new arrivals'.

The Jewish population of Australia at the end of 1851 was said to number 1887 men, women and children, consisting of 979 in New South Wales, 364 in Victoria, an estimated 100 to 150 in South Australia, 9 in Western Australia and 435 in Van Diemen's Land.[20] These Jews formed the only non-Christian minority in the Australian colonies apart from Aboriginal people and Chinese gold-diggers. The Jews had built synagogues and part-time schools in Sydney, Melbourne, Hobart Town and Adelaide. Few in number, they seemed to dominate the markets, auction rooms and clothing shops, and the jewellery trade, throughout the eastern Australian colonies. They established general stores and hotels at many country crossroads where towns would one day grow. They contributed Yiddish and Hebrew words to Australian slang: cobber (friend), shikker/shikkered (drunk) and shemozzle (confusion). Their sons grew up to become members of colonial and local councils, and the judiciary. There were Jewish cemeteries in Sydney, Launceston, Hobart Town, Port Macquarie, Goulburn, Yass, Adelaide and Melbourne.

In Sydney, a small Jewish library was founded by George Moss, and the committee charged with its administration had remitted seventy pounds to England for the purchase of suitable books. A booklet listing the contents of the library, and its rules, was published in Sydney in 1848.[21] Also in Sydney, the Jewish community founded the Hebrew Benevolent Society in 1833, which later merged into the Sir Moses Montefiore Jewish Home for the Aged. The Ladies Dorcas Society for the relief of distressed Jewish women was opened in 1844, and still functions as The Hebrew Ladies Maternity and Benevolent Society. A short-lived Righteous Path Society and a Hebrew Mutual Benefit Society were established in Sydney in 1848,[22] and Jewish philanthropic societies were founded in Hobart Town in 1836 and Melbourne in 1848.

The congregations in Melbourne, Sydney and Hobart Town employed ministers or readers to conduct their services and to teach their children. The Reverend Herman Hoelzel arrived in Hobart Town in 1853 and claimed, incorrectly, to have been appointed by the Chief Rabbi in London to be the 'presiding Rabbi of the Jews of the Australian Colonies'.[23] Hoelzel told the *Hobart Town Courier* that from his earliest youth he had decided to spend his life among Englishmen. The newspaper considered him to be 'a perfect orator', able to speak extemporaneously with 'grace and fire'.

The gold rush gave Australian Jewry a chance to survive as a viable community. The Victorian census of 1861 recorded 2903 Jews in the colony (1857 males and 1046

Phillip Solomon's and John Levy's store on the goldfields at Maryborough,Victoria, in 1853. Half the Jewish population in the 1850s was to be found on the goldfields and in the villages and fly-by-night bush towns.

females). Synagogues were founded in Ballarat, Sandhurst (Bendigo) and Geelong, and a second congregation in Melbourne. In New South Wales, with 1759 Jews (1072 males and 687 females) the impact of gold fever was less dramatic. Nevertheless, there were significant clusters of Jews in Goulburn, Tamworth, Yass, Maitland and scattered through the goldfields. The Jewish population of Australia in 1861 was 0.48 per cent of the total. The proportion has not changed greatly since that year, and very few of the 700 Jewish children in colonial Australia had Jewish grandchildren. It is estimated that there are now 100 000 Australian Jews, constituting one of the few communities in the Diaspora that is growing in number. Foundations stretching back to the convict era have given Australian Jewry a sense of pride and identity.

When the young amateur poet Elias Davis died on the goldfields in 1854 his 'old schoolmaster' in Liverpool wrote an elegy dedicated to his pupil and to all those who had left Europe for Australia, most of whom would never be seen again:

> The stranger has laid him in a stranger's grave
> Where the south wind whistles and the gold streams lave
> Sad thirst for the gold of a that far-off clime
> Insatiate from drinking, unquenched by time
> Horrid rush to that cheerless howling waste
> To gratify humanity's most sordid taste.
> He worked not like others, alone for the gain
> And his labour, like theirs, was not all in vain;
> A parent's declining years to bless—
> He desired no more, he toil'd for no less.[24]

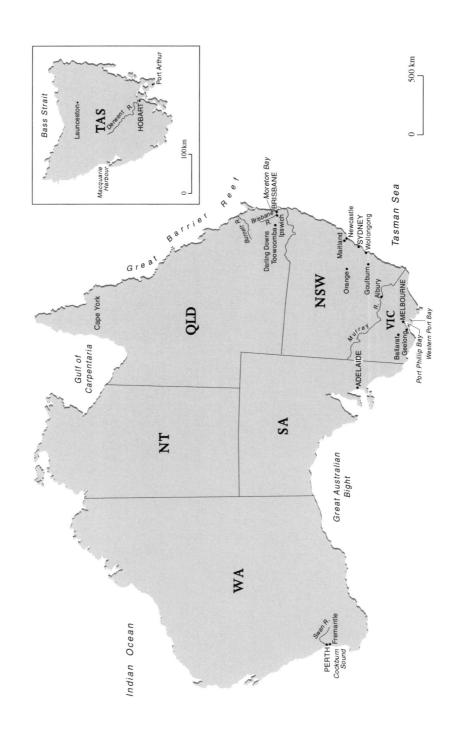

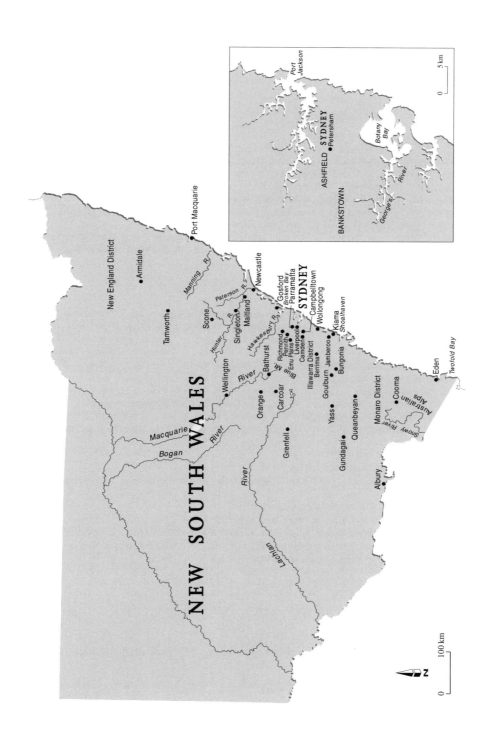

Notes

1 The Outcasts

1 Endelman, *The Jews of Georgian England 1714–1830*, pp. 25, 114ff.
2 J. Rumney, 'Anglo Jewry as Seen through Foreign Eyes 1730–1830', *JHSE*, vol. 13, 1932–35, p. 331; E. N. Adler, *London*, Philadelphia, 1930, pp. 153–7.
3 Francis Place, MS. in British Museum, quoted in J. Rumney, ibid., p. 331.
4 *Public Advertiser*, 15 November 1771. Crook (ed.), *The Complete Newgate Calendar*, vol. 4, pp. 71ff.
5 G. Reitlinger, *English Jewry at the End of the 18th Century*, London, 1961, p. 61.
6 R. D. Barnett, 'Anglo Jewry in the Eighteenth Century', in V. D. Lipman (ed.), *Three Centuries of Anglo-Jewish History*, London, 1961, p. 61. F. Goldsmid, *Remarks on the Civil Disabilities of British Jews*, London, 1830, pp. 69ff.
7 Endelman, *The Jews of Georgian England 1714–1830*, p. 3.
8 Sachar, *The Course of Modern Jewish History*, p. 33.
9 Ibid., p. 27.
10 Pellatt, *Brief Memoir of the Jews in Relation to their Civil and Municipal Disabilities*, p. 28.
11 Quoted in J. Rumney, 'Anglo-Jewry as Seen through Foreign Eyes 1730–1830,' *JHSE*, vol. 13, 1932–35, pp. 323ff.
12 Disraeli, *Tancred*, Book V, ch. 6.
13 *Jewish Chronicle*, 7 May 1852; Dickens 'Old Clothes', *Household Words*.
14 Cecil Roth, *A History of the Jews in England*, Oxford, 1941, pp. 255ff.
15 Endelman, *The Jews of Georgian England 1714–1830*, pp. 172ff. In 1830 Francis Henry Goldsmid calculated, on the basis of Jewish burials in London, that there was a Jewish population of 17 986. Endelman notes that the population of Anglo-Jewry increased by 2500 per cent between 1700 and 1830 due to an almost uninterrupted flow of largely destitute Ashkenazi Jews from Holland, the German states and Poland.
16 MS. Add. 5832, British Museum.
17 Knaff and Bald, *Newgate Calendar*, vol. III, pp. 284ff.
18 *Public Advertiser*, 15 November 1771; 'The Origins of the Jewish Orphanage', E. S. Conway, *JHSE*, vol. 22, 1970, pp. 53ff.
19 Dickens, correspondence, Mocatta Library, London.
20 Shaw, *Convicts and the Colonies*; C. Bateson, *The Convict Ships 1787–1868*.
21 Endelman, *The Jews of Georgian England 1714–1830*, p. 341. A letter from Moses E. Levy in *The World*, 12 December 1827, put the Jewish population of London at 3000 families. Assuming there were five persons per family, that would make about 15 000 Jews living in London.
22 Levi, *The Forefathers*.
23 Price, *Jewish Settlers in Australia*.

2 The First Fleet

1 *Journal of the House of Commons*, 1778–80, vol. 37, p. 311.
2 R. Lubofsky, *Lord George Gordon* in *A Portion of Praise*, Melbourne, 1997, pp. 193ff. Solomons, *Lord George Gordon's Conversion to Judaism*.
3 James Picciotto, *Sketches of Anglo-Jewish History*, pp. 183ff.
4 Memo by Arthur Phillip, 1786, CO 201/2, p. 92.
5 John Nicol, who sailed as a steward on board the *Lady Juliana*, believed there were 'a number of Jewesses' on board his convict transport ship. When the First Fleet arrived in Tenerife, 'One, Sarah Sabolah, had a crucifix, and the others soon got them and passed themselves for Roman Catholics, by which means they got many presents from the people on shore and laid up a large stock for sea'.

There is no documentary evidence for the existence of the mysterious Sarah with her fake crucifix. See T. Flannery (ed.), *The Life and Adventures of John Nicol, Mariner 1776–1891*, Melbourne, 1997, p. 126.

6   CO 201/3.

7   *Historical Records of New South Wales*, vol. 2, 1894, p. 35.

8   OBSP, 1783–84, Case 560, p. 767.

9   Directory of the Justices of the Peace, AO 1/296, p. 3, 11/1.

10   Burial Records, St Philip's, Sydney, 112/180.

11   OBSP, 1784–85, Case 1024, p. 1367; Norfolk Island Victualling Book, 1792–95; Mutch Index, ML A1958; Burial Records, St John's, Parramatta.

12   OBSP, 1783–84, Case 556, pp. 765, 863; Judges Reports, HO 10/6.

13   *Gloucester Journal*, 14 December 1789, quoted by Ruth Campbell in *RAHS*, J&P, vol. 68, no. 3, December 1982, p. 169.

14   OBSP, 1782–83, Case 632, p. 840, see also p. 941; Cobley, *Sydney Cove 1788*, pp. 75, 247, 248; Mutch Index, ML A1958.

15   *Port Phillip Patriot*, 1 June 1840.

16   Gillen, *The Founders of Australia*, pp. 213ff.; Cobley, *The Crimes of the First Fleet Convicts*, p. 202.

17   Gillen, *The Founders of Australia*, pp. 269ff.; Cobley, *The Crimes of the First Fleet Convicts*, pp. 161ff.

3   The First Lady

1   *Sydney Gazette*, 20 June 1827; Ellis, *John Macarthur*, p. 327.

2   G. F. J. Bergman, 'Esther Johnston the Lt. Governor's Wife: The Amazing Story of a Jewish Convict Girl', *AJHS*, vol. 6, no. 2, 1996, pp. 90ff.

3   OBSP, 1786, no. 7, part 1, Case 664, p. 994.

4   List of Female Felons at Newgate Prison, Pri. Com. 2/175; Judges Reports, 1788, HO 47/7; List of convicts sent to NSW in 1787, in *The Voyage of Governor Phillip to Botany Bay*, Adm. 51/4376, parts 8, 9; Bowes, A Journal of a Voyage from Portsmouth to New South Wales and China in the *Lady Penrhyn* (ML).

5   Bateson, *The Convict Ships 1787–1868*, p. 95; HRNSW, vol. 1, part 2, pp. 59, 747.

6   Johnston's life story is told by A. T. Yarwood in *Australian Dictionary of Biography*, vol. 2, p. 20. George Johnston kept a diary, which was unknown to historians. This diary of three volumes disappeared after the death of Mr Percival Johnston, allegedly because his son, Mr Douglas Hope-Johnston, intended to write a biography of George Johnston which would, of course, have revealed the origin of Esther Johnston (copy of affidavit by Mr Hope-Johnston in ML).

7   Cobley, *Sydney Cove 1788*, p. 153.

8   Register, St Philip's, Sydney.

9   Rumsey, *The Pioneers of Sydney Cove*; Norfolk Island Victualling Book, p. 55b, AO.

10   Ibid., pp. 55b, 80a; Robert Johnston's life story is in *Australian Encyclopaedia*, vol. 5, p. 140.

11   *Sydney Morning Herald*, 14 May 1904; Grants of Land Register, Series I, p. 54 and Series II, p. 325, Registrar-General's Department; NSW Muster, 1800, no. 77, AO.

12   R. M. Younger, *Australia and the Australians*, Adelaide, 1970, p. 80.

13   NSW Muster, 1800, no. 77, AO.

14   Wheate and Graham, *Captain William Bligh*; Evatt, *The Rum Rebellion*.

15   'Song on New South Wales Rebellion' in Bligh Papers, ML, quoted in Evatt, *The Rum Rebellion*, p. 144. Jack Bodice is a reference to John Macarthur.

16   See Chapter 17.

17   Registrar-General's Department, Grant Books, Series I, p. 295.

18   *Sydney Gazette*, 7 January 1810.

19   HRNSW, vol. 7, pp. 216ff.

20   *Sydney Gazette*, 7 January 1810.

21   NSW CS, Letters received, Memos 1810, no. 167a.

22   Registrar-General's Department, Grant Books, Series VIII, p. 36.

23   CO 201/15, 20 January 1799; see also Isaac Nichols in *Australian Dictionary of Biography*, vol. 2, p. 283.

24   Registrar of Probates, Supreme Court of NSW, vol. 1, Will 59.

25   *Sydney Gazette*, 26 August 1820 (also written as Stuart).

26 *HRA*, Series I, vol. 1, pp. 227, 677.
27 Ibid., vol. 8, pp. 157, 257; Government and General Orders, No. 72, ML A339.
28 Macquarie's letter of 19 February 1819 in George Johnston Papers; Governor Macquarie, Diary, vol. i, pp. 104ff., ML MS. A774; *HRA*, Series I, vol. 10, p. 280.
29 Registrar of Probates, Supreme Court of NSW, vol. 1, Will 196.
30 *Australian*, 20 March 1829.
31 *Sydney Morning Herald*, 28 August 1846.
32 *Sydney Gazette*, 2 July 1819.
33 *Jewish Chronicle*, 27 January 1854 letter dated 20 September 1853; I. Porush, 'The Story of State Aid to Jewish Establishments in New South Wales', *AJHS*, vol. 1, no. 10, 1943, pp. 350ff. and vol. 2, no. 1, 1944, pp. 29ff.
34 For a biography of G. R. Nichols, see *Australian Encyclopaedia*, vol. 6, p. 340 and *Australian Dictionary of Biography*, vol 5, pp. 335ff.
35 Stenmark, *Sir David Martin*, 1996.

4 A Policeman's Lot

1 Collins, *An Account of the English Colony in New South Wales*, vol. 1, pp. 77ff.
2 OBSP, 1783, no. 109, p. 193; G. F. J. Bergman, 'John Harris, the First Australian Policeman', *AJHS*, vol. 5, no. 2, 1960, pp. 49ff.; OBSP, 1783–84, Case 576, p. 775.
3 Cobley, *The Crimes of the First Fleet Convicts*, pp. 117ff.
4 Bench of Magistrates, Proceedings, 15 August 1789, ML.
5 Collins, *An Account of the English Colony in New South Wales*, p. 85.
6 *HRA*, Series I, vol. 1, pp. 138ff.
7 King, Journal on Norfolk Island, 1791–94, p. 428.
8 Ibid., p. 530; King, Letter Book of Norfolk Island, pp. 243, 271, 292, 302; *HRNSW*, vol. 5, pp. 274ff.
9 Ibid., *HRNSW*, vol. 4, p. 331.
10 CO 201/3.
11 Registrar-General's Department, Register II of Grants, no. 241.
12 *Bell's Messenger Weekly* (London), 6 March 1800.
13 Philip Gidley King, Papers, vol. 9, nos 77, 75, ML.
14 *HRNSW*, vol. 5, pp. 274ff.
15 Ibid., vol. 4, p. 279.
16 Ibid., p. 331.
17 *HRA*, Series I, vol. 3, p. 323.
18 *Monthly Magazine and British Register*, vol. 17, no. 1, 1804, pp. 83ff.
19 *HRNSW*, vol. 5. pp. 274ff.
20 Registrar-General's Department, Register of Land Grants, vol. 3, pp. 126, 243; vol. 4, p. 62.
21 Ibid., vol. 8, p. 43; *Sydney Gazette*, 20 June 1812.
22 See *Australian Dictionary of Biography*, vol. 4, pp. 350–1, for C. L. Lack's biographies of John Harris and George Harris.
23 NSW CS, Letters received, pp. 92–8, AO 4/1741; Marriage Register no. 207, St John's, Launceston; Memorandum by the Surveyor-General of Van Diemen's Land, 9 May 1832; *Launceston Examiner*, 28 August 1882; *Cornwall Chronicle*, 19, 22 February 1851.

5 The Honest Jew of Parramatta

1 OBSP, 1787–88, Case 6, pp. 13ff.; G. F. J. Bergman, 'James Larra, the Commercial Nabob of Parramatta', *AJHS*, vol. 5, no. 3, 1960, pp. 97ff.; 'Some Additional Notes on the Life of James Larra', *AJHS*, vol. 5, no. 4, p. 186.
2 Collins, *An Account of the English Colony in New South Wales*, vol. 1, p. 391.
3 Ibid., p. 327.
4 Registrar-General's Department, Register of Land Grants, series IIIc, folio 12, where a copy of his Final Pardon is hidden away.
5 HO 11/1, pp. 62, 182.

6. Registrar-General's Department, Marriage Register, vol. 4, no. 179.
7. Registrar-General's Department, Register of Land Grants, series II, vol. 2, p. 182.
8. Bench of Magistrates, Minutes Book.
9. Registrar-General's Department, Register of Land Grants, series I, register 3, p. 40.
10. Roth, *A History of the Jews in England*, p. 226; Cramp and Mackaness, *A History of the United Grand Lodge of the Ancient, Free and Accepted Masons of New South Wales*.
11. *Memoirs of Joseph Holt, General of the Irish Rebels in 1798*, London, 1838, vol. 2, pp. 123, 182.
12. See note 4.
13. pp. 196–7.
14. HO 10/31.
15. *HRA*, series I, vol. 3, note 50, p. 768; vol. 4, p. 578; vol. 5, pp. 18, 257. *AJHS*, vol. 5, no. 4, 1961, pp. 186ff.
16. Ibid., vol. 3, p. 501; vol. 4, pp. 117, 437, 474, 521, 529; vol. 5, pp. 137, 704; vol. 7, p. 178. *Sydney Gazette*, 10 April, 2 October 1803; 22 August, 1, 15, 22 September 1805.
17. *HRA*, series I, vol. 6, p. 732. Registrar-General's Department, Register of Land Grants, vol. 3, p. 243; vol. 4, p. 52; vol. 5, p. 150. *Sydney Gazette*, 15 January 1809.
18. NSW CS, Letters received, Memos 1810, CS, Memo 2, no. 186.
19. Wentworth, *A Statistical, Historical and Political Description of New South Wales*, pp. 551; Supreme Court, Papers, ML.
20. 'A.L.F., late of N.S.W.', *The History of Samuel Terry* (pamphlet), London, publ. after Terry's death.
21. Handwritten note by William Palmer on a copy of the *James Tegg Monthly Magazine* (Sydney), 1836, pp. 177ff., ML.
22. CS, Letters and Petitions received, 1818, p. 92, AO 4/1741, statement dated 9 November 1818.
23. See note 21.
24. Bigge, Report of the Commissioner of Enquiry, Appendix, p. 95.
25. *Sydney Gazette*, 25 March 1815.
26. John Earnshaw, 'John Lang—Alexander Harris', *Bulletin* (Sydney), 17 January 1954.

6 The Man They Couldn't Hang

1. G. F. J. Bergman, 'The Story of Two Jewish Convicts: Joseph Samuel, "The Man They Couldn't Hang", and Isaac Simmons, alias "Hickey Bull", Highwayman and Constable', *AJHS*, vol. 5, no. 7, 1963, pp. 320ff.
2. OBSP, 20 December 1795, no. 293, pp. 759–62; PSC, Indent of Convict Ships, 1801–14, p. 21, AO 4/4004.
3. OBSP, 1796–97, case 160, p. 241; PSC, Indent of Convict Ships, 1801–14, p. 122.
4. Bench of Magistrates, Proceedings, 7 May 1803 (12/39), AO 1/299. Simmons signed a deposition dated 23 July 1803 (12/42) with a mark.
5. Lang, *Fisher's Ghost and Other Stories of the Early Days of Australia*, pp. 24ff.
6. The story of Luker's murder and the attempts to execute Samuel may be found in the *Sydney Gazette* of 4 and 18 September and 2, 25 and 28 October 1803, and in the *Sydney Herald* of 23 May 1831.
7. *Sydney Gazette*, 18 August and 22 December 1805, and 18 May 1806.
8. NSW CS, Letters received, Petitions for Mitigation of Sentence, 1817, vol. L–S, p. 299, AO 4/1852.
9. Governor Bourke Dispatches, 1833, p. 690, ML A1211; 1835, p. 745, ML A1214.
10. OBSP, 1796–97, Case 332, p. 318.
11. *The Tasmanian*, 2 August 1828. OBSP, 1822–23, p. 511; CON, 31–1, no. 189; CSO, 1/336/7715.

7 Izzi, the 'Noted Trap Man'

1. G. F. J. Bergman, 'Israel Chapman, Australia's First Police Detective, and Noel Chapman, Chief Constable', *AJHS*, vol. 6, no. 7, 1969, pp. 392ff.; N. Keesing, 'Israel Chapman in Fiction', *AJHS*, vol. 6, no. 7, 1969, pp. 411ff.; Lang, *Botany Bay, Fisher's Ghost and Other Stories and Assigned to his Wife, or the Adventures of George Flower, the Celebrated Detective Officer*.
2. This Abraham Pollack was probably the emancipist Abraham Polack whose London Tavern in George Street is easily recognisable.
3. OBSP, 1817–18, Case 191, p. 75.

[4] PSC, Ship Indent of *Glory*, p. 76, AO 4/4006.

[5] NSW Returns for Overseas of the Crown, ML A2131; Mutch Index, ML; Register, St Philip's Church, 401/27.

[6] See biography of Israel Chapman by Hazel King in *Australian Dictionary of Biography*, vol. 1, p. 217.

[7] NSW CS, Letters received, p. 63, AO 4/1864.

[8] T. O'Callaghan, 'Police Establishment of New South Wales', *RAHS, J&P*, vol. 6, p. 308: 'Israel Chapman is the only record of detective service I can find in the various records of police in NSW until the sixties of last century'.

[9] Ibid., 9 June 1825, 18 July 1827; *Australian*, 23 March 1826.

[10] *Sydney Gazette*, 2 May 1827.

[11] NSW CS, Letters received, 26/6025, AO 4/1903, depositions *re* case Sudds–Thompson no. 1975–8864; Clark, *A History of Australia*, vol. 2, pp. 71, 72.

[12] *Australian*, 21 September 1827.

[13] Government Despatches, 1826, pp. 369, 377, ML 1198.

[14] *Sydney Gazette*, 4 March 1826.

[15] *Sydney Gazette*, 25 March 1826.

[16] *Sydney Gazette*, 31 March 1829, 16 February 1830; Great Britain and Ireland CO Miscellaneous Letters re NSW, 1832, p. 134, ML A2146.

[17] *Sydney Gazette*, 11 October 1834; *Monitor*, 2 April 1836, 7 March 1837.

[18] CS, Letters received, 43/9003 and 47/5969, AO 2/7823.

[19] NSW Probate Office, Series I, no. 2178; *Bell's Life in Sydney*, 6 January 1850.

[20] *Empire*, 1, 2, 16 June 1852; Sydney Quarter Sessions, 1852, ML No. 62, 2928; Burial Register, York Street Synagogue.

[21] Ward (ed.), *The Penguin Book of Australian Ballads*, p. 41.

8 The Redemption of Sydney Sam

[1] PSC, Indent of Convict Ships, *Marquis of Wellington*, p. 32, AO 4/4005; for a biography of Samuel Lyons, written by P. E. LeRoy, see *Australian Dictionary of Biography*, vol. 2, pp. 141–3.

[2] OBSP, 1814, Case 251, p. 151.

[3] OBSP, 1814, Case 208, p. 126.

[4] NSW CS, Letters received, 1816, p. 57, CS, 14.

[5] Ibid., pp. 66, 73.

[6] HRA, Series III, vol. 2, pp. 201–8.

[7] Record Book, Court House, Hobart Town, 7 May 1817.

[8] *Hobart Town Gazette*, 31 July 1819.

[9] CS, Petitions for Mitigation of Sentence, 1822, Petitions 58 and 59, AO 4/1866.

[10] In the possession of Mr John Holman, Erambie North, Molong, NSW.

[11] NSW CS, Letters received and Petitions, 1823, K–Y letter 14, 16 April 1823, AO 4/1870.

[12] *Australian*, 9 February, 5 April, 1826.

[13] Mundy, *Our Antipodes*, pp. 19ff.

[14] *Sydney Gazette*, 2 January, 5 February, 6 March, 29 June 1827; *Australian*, 14 February, 29 June, 10 and 19 August, 12 and 21 September, 2 and 10 October 1827.

[15] Darling to Lord Goderich, 20 October 1831, Governor Darling Dispatches, 1831, part 4, p. 444, ML A1269.

[16] Register, St Philip's Church.

[17] Martin, *The History of Austral-Asia*; *Monitor*, 1 January 1834; *Sydney Evening News*, 7 March 1914.

[18] *Australian*, 30 December 1834.

[19] *Australian Almanac and Directory*, 1835, p. 339; *Sydney Times*, 1 October 1836; *Australian*, 4 October 1836.

[20] ML 365W.

[21] Autobiography of William Augustine Duncan, 1811–54, MS., ML A2877.

[22] *Sydney Herald*, 5 November 1842.

[23] *Australian*, 29 November 1836.

[24] *Sydney Morning Herald*, 15 August 1844.

[25] HRA, Series I, vol. 14, p. 560; *Sydney Gazette*, 5 May 1829; Governor Gipps Dispatches, 1845, p. 145, ML A1246.

[26] Ibid., p. 37.

[27] 'The Foundation of the York Street (Sydney) Synagogue', *AJHS*, vol. 6, no. 1, 1964, p. 38; York Street Synagogue, *The 1845 Report*.

[28] *Sydney Morning Herald*, 19 and 21 October 1844.

[29] *Sydney Gazette*, 30 December 1832; *Australian*, 26 August 1841; *Sydney Morning Herald*, 22 February 1841; Register of Probates, Supreme Court of NSW; records of Sydney University show that the legacy was not paid.

[30] *Sydney Morning Herald*, 12 March 1844.

[31] *Sydney Morning Herald*, 15 August 1844; *AJHS*, vol. 4, no. 5, p. 315; Parkes Correspondence 23/250, 23/144–45, ML.

9 'Mr Levey is a Jew'

[1] CS, Copy of Returns of Absolute Pardons Granted 1810–19, AO 4/4427; NSW Government Dispatches, 1819, vol. 3, p. 827, AO; Memorials for Land 1825, Petition 467, AO 4/1843; G. F. J. Bergman, 'Solomon Levey—from Convict to Merchant Prince', *RAHS, J&P*, vol. 49, no. 6, 1963–64, pp. 406ff. and vol. 54, no. 1, pp. 22ff. (the basis for this chapter); Hasluck, *Thomas Peel of Swan River*.

[2] *OBSP*, August 1813, Case 982, pp. 511–13.

[3] Indent of the *Marquis of Wellington*, 1815, AO 4/4005.

[4] *OBSP*, 1814, Case 208, p. 126; *Sydney Gazette*, 16 May 1818.

[5] Letter to John Horton, 11 July 1826, CO 201/179, 1826.

[6] *OBSP*, 1813, Case 574, pp. 313ff., HO 10/1; Muster, 1816. *Sydney Morning Herald* 2 November 1848.

[7] See chapter 21.

[8] Broadsheet dated August 1824, Dixson Library Add. 59; *Tasmanian and Austral-Asiatic Review*, 5 March 1830; *Sydney Gazette*, 20 December 1817.

[9] *Sydney Gazette*, 5 April 1807, 21 September 1809; 16 September 1820.

[10] Register of Pardons, 8 January 1819, p. 67, AO 4/4427; Bonwick Transcripts, Box 88, pp. 18ff.; Banks Papers, vol. 22, pp. 33, 179, 183; *Sydney Gazette*, 26 January 1814, 7 August 1813.

[11] Bigge Enquiry Appendix, BT Box 24, p. 5160c, October 1820, ML; Memorials for Land, 1825, Petitions 466 10 January, 2 May 1825, AO 4/1843.

[12] NSW CS, Letters received pp. 330, 217ff., AO 4/1760.

[13] Registrar-General's Department, Marriage Register; Muster, 1822.

[14] Bigge Enquiry Appendix, BT Box 25, pp. 5354ff., ML.

[15] *Sydney Gazette*, 13 January 1821; Bigge Enquiry Appendix, vol. 129, pp. 62712–14.

[16] Memorials for Land, 1825, Petition 467, 19 November 1825, AO 4/1843.

[17] *Australian*, 21 June, 22 September 1825.

[18] D'Arcy Wentworth, Treasury of the Colonial Revenue Accounts, p. 8, ML MS. A766.

[19] *Australian*, 23 December 1824.

[20] *Sydney Gazette* and *Australian*, 16 December 1824.

[21] ML Q/9911b.

[22] Wentworth Papers, Misc. p. 160; the original contract for the partnership is in the Hutchinson Papers (Norton and Smith Papers), ML; *Australian*, 8 October 1825; Fowles, *Sydney in 1848*, p. 57.

[23] *Australian*, 24 June 1826, 11 November 1829; *Sydney Gazette*, 18 January 1826, 10 January 1827, 4 January, 25 June 1827, 17 October 1828, 24 February 1829.

[24] *Australian*, 8 August, 22 December 1825, 21 June 1826; *Sydney Gazette*, 8 March, 5 August 1826, 16 May 1827; King Papers, vol. 1, Corr C 1976, pp. 436–43, ML.

[25] Memorials for Land, 1825 Petition 467, AO 4/1843.

[26] *Australian*, 16 March 1826; *Sydney Gazette*, 12 April 1827; P. A. Morton, 'The Vaucluse Estate', *RAHS, J&P*, vol. 15, 1944 pp. 300ff.; E. C. Rowland, 'Cranbrook', *RAHS, J&P*, vol. 31, pp. 400ff.

[27] *Sydney Gazette*, 14 October 1826, 9 November 1827.

[28] *Australian*, 11 April 1827; *Sydney Gazette*, 4 August 1828.

[29] Ledger Book of the Board of Directors of the Bank of New South Wales, Bank Archives; Bigge Enquiry Appendix, vol. 129, pp. 627–91.

[30] *Sydney Gazette*, 4 March 1826.

[31] CO 18/13, pp. 258ff.; *Swan River Guardian*, 4 April 1837.

[32] CO 18/1, pp. 81–2; HRA, Series III, vol. 6, pp. 610–11. The story from Peel's point of view may be found in Hasluck, *Thomas Peel of Swan River*.

[33] Ibid., p. 89.

[34] CO 397/1, pp. 8ff.; CO 18/1, p. 61; HRA, Series III, vol. 6, p. 593.

[35] CO 18/13, pp. 258ff.

[36] CO 18/14, p. 311; CO 397/1, pp. 80–1; HRA, Series III, vol. 6, pp. 610–11.

[37] Hansard New Series, vol. xxi, pp. 1736ff.; *Sydney Gazette*, 10 December 1829.

[38] CO 18/13, pp. 267ff.

[39] CO 18/14, pp. 321, 331–2.

[40] CO, Swan River Papers, vol. 7.

[41] CO 397/3.

[42] CO 397/1, pp. 387ff.

[43] CO 18/7, pp. 33ff., 54.

[44] CO 18/7, p. 335.

[45] CO 18/13, pp. 258–9.

[46] CO 18/3, p. 260.

[47] CO 397/3, pp. 302ff.

[48] CO 18/13, pp. 261, 285; CO 397/3, pp. 154ff.

[49] CO 18/3, p. 31.

[50] Norton and Smith Papers, Hutchinson Papers, Box 143, letter dated 27 May 1833, ML.

[51] WA CS, Settlers, vol. 27, pp. 103–4, WA Archives.

[52] CO 18/13, p. 287; CO 397/3, p. 333; WA CS, Letters, vol. 6, p. 157.

[53] Norton and Smith Papers, Hutchinson Papers, Box 143, copy of the last Will of Solomon Levey, ML; documents relating to Cockburn Sound, Location 16, Application File 128/19/4, Land Titles Office, Perth.

[54] Lands and Survey Description Book of WA, Land Titles Office, Perth.

[55] CO 397/2, pp. 382ff.

[56] Miscellaneous deeds, Norton and Smith Papers, Box 125, ML.

10 'Enter Barney!'

[1] J. E. Foster, 'Barnett Levey', *RAHS, J&P*, vol. 2, 1925, pp. 306ff.; A. W. Hyman, 'Barnett Levey, The Father of the Theatre in Australia', *AJHS*, vol. 1, no. 7, 1942, pp. 223ff.; Bertie, *The Story of the Royal Hotel and the Theatre Royal*; biography by G. F. J. Bergman, *Australian Dictionary of Biography*, vol. 2, pp. 108–10; Irvin, *Theatre Comes to Australia*; E. Irvin, 'Barnett Levey's Theatre Royal—A Reassessment', *AJHS*, vol. 7, no. 3, 1972, pp. 185ff.; Thorne, *Theatre Buildings in Australia to 1905*; HRA, Series 1, vol. 13, pp. 81–3; G. F. J. Bergman, 'Barnett Levey', Blue Mountains Historical Society paper, October 1964.

[2] CS, Letters received, 1822, pp. 217–20, AO 4/1760. In Barnett Levey's handwritten application to take up residence in New South Wales, his first name appears as 'Bernard'.

There was another Barnett Levey (or Levi) in the colony. A convict who had arrived in 1814 at the age of twenty-one, he was the brother of two other convicts, Abraham Levey and Hannah Fox. In the 1830s he settled in Windsor, but was allowed to attend the market in Sydney. He was often in trouble and known as the 'most notorious thief and pocket picker which the colony has ever produced' (*Bell's Life in Sydney*, 12 January 1861). Nevertheless he received his pardon on 5 September 1862.

[3] *Sydney Gazette*, 22 June 1825.

[4] Material for Land 1825, Petition 466, 2 May 1825, AO 4/1843. Registrar-General's Department, Grant Books, vol. 28, p. 9; Dowd and Foster, *The History of the Waverley Municipal District*.

[5] *Sydney Gazette*, 22 June 1825.

[6] *Sydney Gazette*, 10 November, 1 December 1825.

[7] *Sydney Gazette*, 8 May 1830. E. Irvin, 'Sydney's First Skyscraper and Theatre', *Architecture in Australia*, December 1968, p. 1121, reprinted *AJHS*, vol. 6, no. 6, 1969, pp. 305ff.

[8] *Sydney Gazette*, 15 October 1827.

[9] CS, Letters received, 1827, 27/6873, 23 July 1827, AO 4/1939.

[10] HRA, Series I, vol. 13, p. 81.

[11] Ibid.

[12] Ibid.

[13] CS, Letters received, 1827, 27/5586, 12 June 1827, AO 4/1934.

[14] Ibid.

[15] CS, Letters received, 1828, 28/8420, AO 4/2196a; 1830, 30/7134, 20 September 1830, AO 4/2082; Act 9e, George IV, no. XIV, Governor in Council I, IX, 1828.

[16] MS. Add. 159, Dixson Library.

[17] CS, Letters received, 1830, 30/230, 7 January 1830, AO 4/2063.

[18] Ibid., 30/1734, AO 4/2082.

[19] CS, Letters received, 1834, 34/838, AO 4/2221.2.

[20] Irvin, *Shakespeare in the Early Sydney Theatre*, pp. 125ff.

[21] CS, Correspondence re Land, AO 2/7906.

[22] CO, Miscellaneous Letters re NSW, 1830, pp. 118–20.

[23] CS, Letters received, 1833, Miscellaneous Letters, Petition 32/838, AO 4/2196.1.

[24] CS, Letters received, 1834, Attorney-General, 32/51264, AO 4/2221.2.

[25] *Sydney Herald*, 26 August 1832.

[26] Irvin, *Theatre Comes to Australia*; Irvin 'On Staging a Play at Sydney's First Theatre Royal', *Masque*, April–May 1969 (Sydney).

[27] 'Barnett Levey's Theatre Royal—An Assessment', *AJHS*, vol. 7, no. 3, 1972, p. 186.

[28] Will No. 998, Book of Wills, Registrar of Probates, Supreme Court of NSW, Sydney.

[29] *Sydney Gazette*, 20 June 1828. H. F. Rubinstein of London, a descendant of Barnett Levey's brother Isaac Levey, wrote a set of five one-act plays entitled *Israel Set Free* (London, 1936). The fifth play deals with the life of Barnett Levey and is called *To the Poets of Australia*, referring to an advertisement in the *Sydney Herald* of 25 October 1832 in which Levey offered a silver medal for an 'approved Opening Address to be spoken on the first night of the opening of the Theatre Royal, Sydney, composed and written by a Native of the Colony'.

11 Judah's Voice

[1] A biography of Joseph Simmons, by the late Mrs H. L. Oppenheim, is in *Australian Dictionary of Biography*, vol. 2, pp. 445–7; it omits Simmons' activities in the Jewish community and includes erroneous material about his later life and death. See also J. M. Forde, 'Old Sydney', *Sydney Truth*, 30 July 1911; *Sydney Gazette*, 30 June 1811.

[2] *Sydney Gazette*, 21 January 1834.

[3] Irvin, *Shakespeare in the Early English Theatre*, pp. 125ff.

[4] *Sydney Gazette*, 17 September 1836, 10 October 1837.

[5] CS, Letters received, 1844, AO 4/2655.

[6] *Sands' Sydney Directory*, 1880–90.

[7] A biography of John Lazar, by G. L. Fischer, is in *Australian Dictionary of Biography*, vol. 2, pp. 98, 99.

[8] Governor Bourke Dispatches, 1837, ML A126715, pp. 253–5, and 1838, pp. 255ff., ML A1277.

[9] *Commercial Journal and Advertiser*, 15 August 1840; *South Australian Register*, 2, 9 January 1841.

[10] CS, Letters received, Miscellaneous Persons 26 July 1841, AO 4/4561.1.

[11] CS, Letters received, 1844, AO 4/2653, and 1846, AO 4/2731.5; Miscellaneous Persons, p. 269, AO 4/3548. The title of Lazar's Christmas Pantomime sounds suspiciously like a child's Hebrew reading exercise that declined the pronoun 'this'.

[12] E. Irvin, 'From the London Theatres', *Theatre Notebook* (London), vol. 22, no. 4, pp. 169ff.; *Sydney Gazette*, 15 September 1838; *Sydney Herald*, 19 September 1838; *Commercial Journal and Advertiser*, 16 January 1839.

[13] *Port Phillip Gazette*, 16 April 1845; Goldman, *The Jews in Victoria in the Nineteenth Century*, pp. 22, 23, 50.

[14] Goldman, *The Jews in Victoria in the Nineteenth Century*, pp. 22, 24, 230, 231, 406, 407; *South Australian Register*, 5, 8 January 1848; Finn, *The Chronicles of Early Melbourne*, vol. 2, pp. 457ff.

[15] J. L. Montefiore was a member of the Sydney Synagogue from the time of his arrival, and in 1845 fought for the claim of the Jewish community for a share in State aid and later for aid to denominational schools. In 1868 he secured official recognition of the Sydney Hebrew Certified Denominational School by the NSW Council of Education. In 1875 he was appointed a commissioner for the Philadelphia International Exhibition and returned to London via the United States. (*AJHS*, vol. 4, no. 6, 1957, pp. 244ff., 314ff.; M. Z. Forbes, 'Jewish Personalities in the Movement for Responsible Government in New South Wales', *AJHS*, vol. 4, no. 6, 1957, pp. 307ff.

16 CS, Letters received, 1843 (AO 4/4561.1 with 43/5494); ibid., 1847 (AO 4/2771.1 with 47/3785), CS, Special Bundle 1843–50 (AO 4/474), April 1847.

17 Bertie, *Isaac Nathan*; Mackerras, *The Hebrew Melodist*; G. F. J. Bergman, 'Isaac Nathan, Father of Australian Music', *Bnai Brith Bulletin* (Sydney), vol. 7, no. 3, pp. 3ff. Isaac Nathan's great-great-great-grandson, the conductor Charles Mackerras, re-orchestrated the overture to Isaac Nathan's opera, *Don John of Austria*, and conducted its first performance since 1847 with the Sydney Symphony Orchestra in the Sydney Town Hall on 19 May 1963.

18 *Port Phillip Gazette*, 13, 17 February 1841; *Australian*, 27 February, 7 August 1841.

12 Judah's Face

1 Police returns from Port Macquarie, 35/5239, 22 July 1835, AO 4/7326; PSC, Indent of Convict Ships, Indent of *Arab*, p. 140; Register of Flash Men, p. 72, AO 2/673.

2 Jacky Jacobs: see Register of Flash Men, pp. 96, 114. Emanuel (Money) Moses: CON, 63–1.

3 The Levi brothers: Lazarus, CON, 18–13; Samuel and Philip, Personal Notes, p. 87, Allport Collection, Hobart.

4 *Sydney Gazette*, 13 October 1827; 1828 census, PSC, Indent of Convict Ships, AO 4/4004.

5 Ward, *The Australian Legend*, p. 18.

6 Mansfield, *Analytical View of the Census of New South Wales*, p. 13; *Australian*, 10 August 1841.

7 Eliza Shaw, Letters to friends in England 1829–33, ML 3/164.

8 G. F. J. Bergman, 'The Hundred Jews of S.S. *Palambam* in 1832: Rectification of an Error', *AJHS*, vol. 5, no. 7, 1963, pp. 339ff. The Jewish passengers were Mr and Mrs Samuel Benjamin and two children, Mrs Esther Solomon and two daughters, Mr and Mrs Elisha Hayes and children, Mr and Mrs Abraham Moses and four children, Mr John Moses, Mr and Mrs Israel Myers, Miss Catherine Phillips, Mr Joseph Moses, and Norman (Nahum) Simon (CSO, 1/632/14277, AOT).

9 List of Convict Ships sent to VDL, 1825–54, p. 114, ML A1059; CON, 40–7, 32–4, 72–7, vol. 2, p. 434.

10 *Sydney Gazette*, 29 April 1824.

11 *Sydney Herald*, 2 December 1833.

12 *Colonial Times*, 15 July 1834.

13 *Sydney Gazette*, 28 November 1818; Clark, *A History of Australia*, vol. 1, p. 356; *Sydney Gazette*, 15, 22 April 1824.

14 *Hobart Town Advertiser*, 6 November 1846.

13 The Birth of the Synagogue

1 CO, 201/14, p. 308, 1 November 1799.

2 *Sydney Gazette*, 4 March 1804; HRA, Series I, vol. 9, p. 517.

3 Marsden to Wilberforce, 27 July 1810, original in Guildhall Library. S. P. G. Bonwick Transcripts, Missionary 1, Box 49, pp. 87ff., ML.

4 Levy: Records, St Philip's Church, Sydney, 112/180. Uziel Baruch: Cobley, *Sydney Cove*, p. 257. Solomon Bockerah: Petition for Land to Governor Macquarie, 2 January 1810, AO, 4/1821.

5 The 1845 York Street Synagogue Report, p. 7; *Sydney Gazette*, 2 September 1820.

6 *Settlers and Convicts*, p. 55.

7 *Report of the London Society for Promoting Christianity Amongst the Jews*, no. 13, 1821, p. 18ff. Joseph Marcus was born in Mannheim in 1758 and studied at yeshivot (rabbinical seminaries) in Poland and in Jerusalem. He was sentenced at the Staffordshire Assizes for breaking and entering, and was sentenced to death. He arrived on the *William Pitt* in 1792. He was listed in the 1828 census as a householder in George Street, Sydney, and he died on 26 November 1828. His tombstone stands in the Pioneers' Cemetery at Botany Bay and is inscribed with the final stanza of the Hebrew hymn 'Adon Olam'.

8 Petition in CS, Letters received, 1828, 28/6877, AO 4/1990.

9 St James' Register, 20/61, Mutch Index.

10 Abraham Elias married Harriet Robinson, twenty-four, at St Matthew's, Windsor, in 1822. Daughter of Edward Robinson, she was colonial born, and died at Freeman's Reach, Windsor, on 3 March 1877. Simmons died on 2 May 1849. Will, dated 16 March 1849, Sydney Probate Offfice.

11 *The 1845 York Street Synagogue Report*, p. 7; C. Roth, 'Rabbi Aaron Levy's Mission to Australia', *AJHS*, vol. 3, no. 1, 1949, pp. 1ff.

12 The ill-fated wedding in 1788 of John Hart and Florah Lara was the first of a Jewish couple in Australia (see Chapter 2).

13 OBSP, 1816–17, Case 1283, p. 433; Parramatta Gaol Admittance Book, 1835–36, no. 664, p. 114, AO 4/4008.

14 Joseph–Nathan marriage: no. 143, AO 4/4511, and AO 4/4512, p. 37; Moses Joseph: PSC, Ship Indent, p. 39, AO 4/4012.

15 CS, Letters received, 1832, 32/707, AO 4/2132.

16 Howard T. Nathan, 'The Benefits of a Conviction', *AJHS*, vol. 13, no. 1, 1995, pp. 5f.

17 PSC, Butts of tickets of exemption from government labour 1831–32, 32/142, AO 4/4285; Goldman, *The History of the Jews in New Zealand*; NSW Govt Dispatches A1242, 1847, pp. 511ff., ML A1242; *Sydney Chronicle*, 22 January 1848; *Sydney Morning Herald*, 7 February 1849; Licences 94–97, Licences for Dispatching Stock, Liverpool Plains Pastoral District, Supplementary Lists in New England District; Sydney Probate Office, 1889.

18 *Voice of Jacob*, vol. 1, p. 34; *Monitor*, 8 August 1828, 26 September 1832, *Hill's Life in New South Wales*, 23 September, 14 December 1832; Marks, *The First Synagogue in Australia*; Maclehose, *The Picture of Sydney and Strangers' Guide in New South Wales for 1838*.

19 V. Cohen, 'The Reverend Solomon Phillips and his Descendants', *AJHS*, vol. 1, no. 3, 1940, pp. 73ff.

20 Series I 97, p. 409, 8 April 1850, Registrar-General's Department.

21 I. Porush, 'From Bridge Street to York Street', *AJHS*, vol. 2, no. 2, 1944, pp. 61ff., and vol. 3, no. 3, 1950, p. 152.

22 *The Voice of Jacob*, 16 August 1844.

23 Fowles, *Sydney in 1848*, pp. 64, 66; Balfour, *A Sketch of New South Wales*, p. 54; Morais, *The Jews of Philadelphia*, p. 14.

24 Getzler, *Neither Toleration Nor Favour*, chs 2, 3.

25 HRA, Series I, vol. 25, pp. 83, 202; Grey to FitzRoy, 13 April 1847.

26 I. Porush, 'The Story of State Aid to Jewish Establishments in N.S.W.', *AJHS*, vol. 1, no. 10, 1943, and vol. 2, no. 1, 1944, p. 32.

27 *Sydney Gazette*, 15 October 1833, 12 August 1841, *Australian*, 31 March 1839, 12 July 1843, 27 October 1845, 12 March 1846.

28 The three editions were dated 27 May, 24 June and 5 September 1842; D. J. Benjamin, 'The Sydney *Voice of Jacob*', *AJHS*, vol. 3, no. 10, 1900, pp. 443ff.

29 *Australian*, 6 March 1838.

30 Sydney Synagogue Minute Book, 1837–47, 6 May 1840, p. 41. G. F. J. Bergman, 'A Note on The Reverend Michael E. Rose, Australia's First Jewish Minister', *AJHS* vol. 6, no. 5, 1968, pp. 287ff., and no. 6, 1968, p. 360.

31 PSC, 36/7615, petition dated 21 September 1836; Sydney Synagogue Minute Book, 1837–47, 20 May 1840, p. 44; *Voice of Jacob*, vol. 4.

32 *The 1845 York Street Synagogue Report*, p. 9; *Sydney Morning Herald*, 12 September 1844; *Voice of Jacob*, 25 April 1845.

33 Land for Churches, Schools, Parsonages, and Cemeteries, 1825–54, Section VI 48/9413 and M7807, 13 September 1848, AO 2/1852; Sydney Synagogue Letter Book, no. 2, 10 June 1849.

14 Emigration

1 David Monroe, letter dated 17 August 1842 (ML).

2 *The Gentleman's Magazine*, vol. 74, August 1804, p. 755.

3 Madgwick, *Immigration into Eastern Australia 1788–1851*, pp. 49, 54.

4 Bateson, *The Convict Ships 1787–1868*, p. 135. HRA, vol. 1, p. 316; King's Letter Book, L 187, p. 85. OBSP, 1789–90, Case 538, p. 664.

5 CO, 207/2.

6 2 March 1823.

7 HRA, Series I, vol. 12, pp. 736ff.

8 ML 4/5198; *Australian*, 26 September 1827; *Sydney Gazette*, 29 September and 5 October 1827.

9 CS, Letters received re Land, AO 2/7906.

[10] *Sydney Gazette*, 7 July 1828.

[11] CS, Letters received 21 January 1828, 28/632, AO 4/1963, and 28/4943, AO 4/1983.

[12] *Sydney Gazette*, 16 June 1828; *Australian*, 9 July 1828; G. F. J. Bergman, 'Walter Jacob Levi and Governor Ralph Darling, The Sad Story of a Gentleman Planter', *AJHS*, vol. 6, no. 8, 1970, pp. 461ff.

[13] *HRA*, Series I, vol. 13, p. 132.

[14] Ibid., vol. 14, p. 243.

[15] A biography of Montefiore, by I. Getzler, is in *Australian Dictionary of Biography*, vol. 2, pp. 250ff.

[16] Picciotto, *Sketches of Anglo-Jewish History*, vol. 1, p. 206.

[17] CS, Letters received re Land, 4 September 1830, AO 2/7390.

[18] CS, Letters received re Land, 34/7994, November 1834, AO 4/2240-S; *HRA*, Series I, vol. 18, pp. 8ff.

[19] *South Australian Register*, 21 December 1844.

[20] *Currency Lad*, 1 September 1832; *HRA*, Series I, vol. 14, p. 672; *Sydney Gazette*, 6 April 1833, 22 May 1834; Shipping List, 11 August 1835, AO 4/5209.

[21] CSO, 5/77/1724, AOT.

[22] *Sydney Gazette*, 16 June 1837.

[23] *Australian*, 28 May 1828 (original statement in *Sydney Gazette*, 19 May 1828; CS, Letters received re Land, 7 February 1833, AO 2/7827.

[24] *Sydney Gazette*, 19 May 1828; *Australian*, 28 May, 30 July 1828; *Monitor*, 26 January 1829.

[25] *Australian*, 27 January and 7 February 1834.

[26] *Australian*, 29 November 1833, 13 January 1835, 2 May 1840.

[27] *Hunter River Gazette*, 11 December 1841, 30 April 1832; *Maitland Mercury and Hunter River General Advertiser*, 14 January and 29 July 1843, 13 July 1844.

[28] Quoted in Tucker, *Jemmy Green in Australia*.

[29] *Sydney Morning Herald*, 21 September 1844; P. J. Marks, 'Early Jewish Education in Sydney', *AJHS*, vol. 1, no. 2, 1939, pp. 25ff.; G. F. J. Bergman, 'Phillip Joseph Cohen', *AJHS*, vol. 8, no. 2, 1975, pp. 48–81.

[30] *HRA*, Series I, vol. 14, pp. 243ff.

[31] CS, Letters received re Land (H), AO 2/7887.

[32] CS, Letters received, 1829, 29/509, AO 4/2014.

[33] CS, Letters received re Land (H), AO 2/7887; *HRA*, Series I, vol. 14, p. 618.

[34] Register for the County of Northumberland, 1823–37, AO 7/459; CS, Letters received re Land (H), AO 2/7887; Governor Darling Dispatches, p. 453, ML A1204.

[35] Governor Darling Dispatches, p. 610, ML A1211.

[36] CS, Letters received, 1832, 32/6184, AO 4/2153; 1833, 33/1039, AO 4/2180.2.

[37] McCaffrey, *History of Illawarra and its Pioneers*, pp. 112ff., 132ff.

[38] Bridge Street Synagogue Marriage Register, 8 February 1835.

[39] Spark Diaries, 1836–56, ML A4869–4870.

[40] CS, Letters received, 41/7285, AO 4/2535.4; McCaffrey, *History of Illawarra and its Pioneers*, pp. 132ff.

[41] Jameson, *New Zealand, South Australia and New South Wales*, p. 121.

[42] Goldman, *The History of the Jews in New Zealand*, pp. 35–50; G. F. J. Bergman, 'Abraham Polack (1797–1873), Rise and Fall of a Jewish Emancipist', *AJHS*, vol. 7, no. 5, 1972, pp. 348ff.

[43] Printed Indent of Convicts, 1831, p. 71; TL 37/1691, CP 47/595.

[44] G. F. J. Bergman, 'David Poole, The First Jewish Lawyer in Australia', *AJHS*, vol. 7, no. 3, 1972, pp. 239ff.; Supreme Court Papers of VDL, File S.C. 207/85, AOT; *Sydney Gazette*, 1 August 1828; Sydney Probate Office, Register of Wills, no. 365(1); *Australian*, 20 March 1829; *Voice of Jacob* (London), 29 October 1841; *Australian*, 11 January 1833, 3 May 1835, 19 April 1836; *Sydney Gazette*, 5 June 1834, 16 September 1841; *Australasian Chronicle*, 7 January 1840.

[45] *Australian*, 5 June 1841; *Sydney Gazette*, 5 July 1842; Eric Ramsden, 'Alexandre Salmon, an English Jew who made History in Tahiti, and his Family', *AJHS*, vol. 1, no. 3, 1940, pp. 57ff.; A. M. Gurau, 'Jews in the Pacific Islands of the South Seas', *AJHS*, vol. 1, no. 8, 1942, pp. 257ff.

[46] PSC, Ship Indent 1814–18, AO 4/4005.

[47] *Jewish Chronicle*, 'Sydney, 25 January 1853'.

15 The Lost Sheep

[1] *The Obligations of Christians to Attend the Conversion of the Jews* (pamphlet) by a Presbyter of the Church of England, London Society for Promoting Christianity Among the Jews, 1808.

[2] R. Bentley, Our Antipodes, London, 1852, vol. 1, p. 96.

[3] H.W. Meirovich, 'Ashkenazi Reactions to the Conversionists 1800–1850', JHSE, vol. 26, 1979.

[4] The Mystery Unfolded, or, an exposition of the extraordinary means employed to gain converts by the agents of the London Society for promoting Christianity among the Jews; with the whole proceedings of Mr Frey, from his arrival in London, to his dismissal from the London Society, with some particulars of his reception in America. The interesting case of Jacob Josephson, a convert accused of purloining the communion plate at Stanstead, etc. etc., London, printed by and for the author, 1817, British Museum.

[5] PSC, Indent, p. 60, AO 4/4006.

[6] CO, 201/118.

[7] NSW Govt Dispatches, 1819–20, ML A1192; List of applicants to bring wives and children from England, 20 February 1819; a biography of Joshua Frey Josephson, by H. T. E. Holt, can be found in Australian Dictionary of Biography, vol. 4, pp. 492–3.

[8] W. C. Wentworth, Correspondence 1825–42, p. 195, 22 October 1825, ML A1440; Sydney Gazette, 15, 24 April 1824.

[9] Australian, 17, 24 March 1825.

[10] Sydney Gazette, 9 December 1824.

[11] Sydney Gazette, 17 February 1825; G. F. J. Bergman, 'Abraham Polack, Rise and Fall of a Jewish Emancipist', AJHS, vol. 7, no. 5, pp. 348ff.

[12] CS, Petitions for Mitigation of Sentence, 1825, Petition 119, to Sir Thomas Brisbane, AO 4/1874.

[13] Sydney Gazette, 10 November 1825.

[14] Australian, 18 November 1824, 6 October 1825; Sydney Gazette, 13 May 1820, 20 January 1821, 5 February 1824; Bigge Enquiry, Appendix B.T., Box 52, pp. 1135–6, ML.

[15] NSW Govt Dispatches, 1830, pp. 871–905, ML A1267–12; Sydney Gazette, 13 March, 12, 17 May 1838.

[16] Backhouse, A Narrative of a Visit to the Australian Colonies, p. 337.

[17] OBSP, 1797–98, Case 73, p. 87; Letter Books 1836–37, 1837–41, Magistrates, Patrick Plains, AO 4/5658, 4/5659.

[18] Stiles, Rev. H. T., Correspondence, 1832–56, letter dated 6 December 1847, p. 79, ML.

[19] GO, Inward Dispatch, vol. 42, pp. 95–102, 17 February 1840, and vol. 34, p. 56, 1840, AOT.

[20] OBSP, 1807–08, Case 688, pp. 459ff.; CON, 13/1, p. 21.

[21] CSO, 5/69/1503, 1/195/4613, AOT; Goldman, The Jews in Victoria in the Nineteenth Century, p. 14.

[22] Whitefield, The Cyclopaedia of Tasmania, vol. 2, p. 61.

[23] Hobart Synagogue Minutes, 7 May 1845; Hobart Town Courier, 4 October 1839; CSO, 24/28/750, 14 September 1847, AOT.

[24] CSO 11/28/546, CON 16/1, p. 52.

[25] Port Phillip Patriot, 3 March 1846.

[26] Sydney Synagogue Marriage Register, 21 January 1833, John Barnett married Sarah Francis, converted to Judaism on 18 January 1833 by Michael Phillips and J. B. Montefiore; Moses Brown officiated. In the first eight years of Jewish marriages in Sydney (1832–40) four of the first forty weddings included a convert to Judaism.

16 Van Diemen's Land

[1] OBSP, 1789, Case 819, p. 964; Piper Papers, vol. 1, pp. 84ff., ML A254; List of Settlers on Lady Nelson for the Derwent, 9 November 1807.

[2] Hobart Town Gazette, 2 April 1820.

[3] Hobart Town Courier, 14 June 1828; CSO, 1/269/6497, 25 May 1828.

[4] Hobart Synagogue Minute Book, 16 July 1846. Bernard Walford (jnr) applies on his death bed to be buried as a Jew. Refused.

[5] Hobart Probate Offfice, Register of Wills, 18 May 1851.

[6] There appears to be no proof of the frequent statement that Jewish religious services were first held at the home of Judah Solomon in 1830 (AJHS, vol. 2, no. 1, p. 4). Port Phillip Patriot, 6 August 1847, quoting London Weekly Journal, 13 January 1847.

[7] CON, 63/2, no. 236.

[8] OBSP, 1817–18, Case 1080, p. 342; CON, 31/27; Hobart Town Gazette, 18 March 1826.

[9] OBSP, 1810–11, Case 839, p. 448.

[10] CON, 13/1, p. 13; *Hobart Town Gazette*, 11, 13 June, 31 August 1816; HRA, Series III, vol. 3, p. 573; CON, 31/27, L46; CP 1026 granted on 2 September 1826; *Hobart Town Courier*, 10 December 1834.

[11] CON, 31/34, no. 521; *Mercury*, 26 September 1876; *Tribune*, 26 September 1876; Hobart Hebrew Congregation Registers.

[12] 1811 Muster, AO 4/1233; OBSP, 1801–02, Case 262, p. 188; CSO, 1/242/5844.

[13] Solomon, The Queer Colony; a biography of Joseph Solomon, by H. J. Solomon, is in *Australian Dictionary of Biography*, vol. 2, pp. 458–9; CON, 31/38, no. 216 (Judah) and no. 217; HO, 11/3 (Joseph); PSC, Ship Indent *Prince Regent*, 1819; CSO, 16/6/203, letter dated 28 April 1842 from Judah Solomon to Governor; Hobart Probate Office; *Hobart Town Gazette*, 10, 17 February, 17 March 1821; CSO, 16/6/203; see in particular, letter from Esther Solomon 27 January 1845.

[14] Evidence to Select Committee on Secondary Punishments 1832, p. 53. Fire had swept through Sheerness in 1827 and 1830 and the town is described in *The Gentleman's Magazine*, 16 January 1830.

[15] Maxwell-Stewart, 'Land of Sorrow, Land of Honey'.

[16] HRA, Series III, vol. 4.

[17] Registry of Deeds, Hobart, Book 1, 1827. Lieutenant Governor's Court Register of Judgments in Civil Cases, 1821, LC 3/3 and 1822–1824, LC 8/2, Lc 83. Supreme Court Register of Writs, 1824–1830, SC, 177/1–4, AOT.

[18] CSO, 1/336/7708; also Entry 108, folio 72, and Entry 144, folio 90.

[19] CSO, 16/6/203: letter from Chief Police Magistrate, 8 July 1834.

[20] Judah Solomon's Will, Register of Wills, Hobart Probate Offfice.

[21] CSO, 16/6/203, Letters of March 1835 and 16 November 1837; CO, 280/258; 27 January 1845.

[22] CP, 333, 13 March 1833.

[23] CSO, 16/6/203, 21 October 1837. Twenty-eight Hobart businessmen supported Judah's application for a pardon; twelve withdrew, six remained, ten were undecided.

[24] Ibid., letter from Judah Solomon to Lieutenant Governor, 5 December 1835.

[25] Papers of the Port Phillip Association, SLV.: Charles Swanston buys the rights from Joseph Solomon for £411 on 20 May 1839 and he attests the purchase on 18 October 1847 (Hobart Probate Office). Judah died 18 February 1856.

[26] *Independent* (Launceston), 23 November 1833.

[27] *Launceston Examiner*, 21 May 1851.

[28] Register of Pardons, vol. 1, p. 274, AO 4/4427; *Sydney Gazette*, 12 December 1812; Return of the Livestock at V.D.L., 4 August 1804, CO, 201/35; CSO, 1/224/5447; Roth, *The Rise of Provincial Jewry*, p. 98; CSO, 1/242/5844.

[29] John and Louisa Davis and four of their children came out to Australia with Mrs Esther Solomon on the *Juliet* in February 1839.

[30] CO, 201/106, 6 November 1821.

[31] CSO, 1/153/3700; *Hobart Town Courier*, 8 March 1833, 31 March 1837.

[32] CSO, 1/242/5844. Abraham arrived as a steerage passenger in the *Cumberland* (*Hobart Town Gazette*, 24 January 1825).

[33] CSO, 1/224/5447.

[34] CSO (WA), vol. 1, p. 185, Abraham listed as passenger on board the *Ephemina*, 30 October 1829, en route from VDL.

[35] Goldman, *The History of the Jews in New Zealand*, pp. 52ff.

[36] CSO, 1/6 pp. 8–9; *Hobart Town Courier*, 30 August 1823.

[37] CSO, 1/613/13989, Launceston, 17 September 1832.

[38] *Elliston's Hobart Town Almanack*, 1837–38.

[39] *Hobart Town Courier*, 20 December 1833; CSO, 1/611/13954; CON, 13/1.

[40] *Hobart Town Courier*, 23 September 1836.

[41] *Australian Israelite*, 22 November 1872.

[42] E. F. Kunz, 'The Reverend Isaac Friedman', *AJHS*, vol. 6, no. 5, 1968, pp. 279ff.

[43] Herbert I. Wolff, 'A Century of Hobart Jewry', *AJHS*, vol. 2, no. 1, 1944, pp. 5ff.; L. M. Goldman, 'The History of Hobart Jewry', *AJHS*, vol. 3, no. 5, 1951, pp. 209ff.

[44] *Hobart Town Courier*, 12 August 1842.

[45] *Hobart Town Courier*, 26 February 1848; *The Voice of Jacob* (London), 23 June 1848.

[46] *Jewish Chronicle* (London), vol. 1, p. 163, 1845.

[47] *Hobart Town Courier*, 10 July 1857.

[48] *AJHS*, vol. 1, no. 10, 1943, p. 356.

[49] G. F. J. Bergman 'Phineas Moss, Public Servant and Author', *AJHS*, vol. 6, no. 5, 1968, pp. 267ff., and no. 6, 1968, pp. 361–2; CSO, 50/16; CSO, 22/52/304 and 22/41/1310; CSO 20/29/681; HRA, Series I, vol. 25, p. 177; Moss writes to Governor about inquiry forwarded from England regarding whereabouts of Anzel Davidowicz Davis: 'very few foreign Jews retain their common Judaic or surnames on their arrival in England (*AJHS*, vol. 1, no. 10, 1943, p. 356); *Launceston Examiner*, 19 June 1844; *Hobart Town Courier*, 27 May 1842; *Papers and Proceedings of the Royal Society of Tasmania*, vol. 3, no. 2, 1859, pp. 221–7; *Sydney Times*, 27 May 1837.

[50] *Hobart Town Courier*, 11 August 1843; Supreme Court of VDL, Grant Book 18/59/3828.

[51] *Colonial Times*, 15 August 1843.

[52] A detailed description of the struggle for State aid can be found in Getzler, *Neither Toleration Nor Favour*, chs 5 and 6. The preamble to the code of laws of the Launceston Synagogue of 1846 traces the community's history back to December 1838 when 'seven men formed a Jewish Benevolent Society'. See also Hobart Town Synagogue Minute Book 1, 1 May 1843; CSO, 8/165, letter to Louis Nathan, 30 May 1843.

[53] 1 Vic., No. 16, 1837, 'Support for certain Christian ministers and erection of places of divine worship'.

[54] *Hobart Town Advertiser*, 20 September 1842; *Hobart Town Courier*, 30 September 1842; *Hobart Town Synagogue Minutes*, 25 April 1847.

[55] *New Newgate Calendar*, pp. 480ff.

[56] 'Intolerance at the Antipodes', *Jewish Chronicle*, 19 May 1848.

[57] *Hobart Town Advertiser*, 30 September 1842.

[58] *Morning Chronicle*, 28 February 1844.

[59] *Launceston Examiner*, 8 March 1843.

[60] Ibid., 24 May 1843; *Voice of Jacob* (London), 24 November 1843.

[61] *Launceston Examiner*, 6 July 1844.

[62] CO, 280/157 (reel no. 520), Launceston 20 May 1843.

[63] *Jewish Chronicle*, 1 February 1856.

[64] *Launceston Examiner*, 2 October 1844; *Voice of Jacob* (London), 28 February 1845.

[65] *Hobart Town Advertiser*, 6 November 1846.

[66] *Launceston Examiner*, 30 September 1842, 8 May 1844. Committee consisted of: President, D. Benjamin; Treasurer, Moses Moss; Secretary, John H. Anderson; and B. Francis, A. H. Nathan, J. Lyons, Joseph Nathan.

[67] *Jewish Chronicle*, 20 August 1847.

[68] Hobart Synagogue Minutes, 25 April 1847; Getzler, *Neither Toleration Nor Favour*, pp. 66ff.

[69] *Jewish Chronicle*, 16 June 1848.

[70] *Sydney Morning Herald*, 17 July 1845.

[71] By 1871 only three Jews lived in Launceston. The synagogue closed, and was re-opened in 1939, but closed again at the end of the 1960s. At present, only a handful of Jews live in the north of the island.

[72] 'M. B. of Sandy Bay', 8 January 1850.

[73] *Jewish Chronicle*, 6 July 1849.

17 Fagin in Australia

[1] Arthur Griffith, *The Chronicles of Newgate*, London, 1884. The author belonged to the late 63rd Regiment, and was one of H.M. Inspectors of Prisons.

[2] OBSP, 1810, Case 491, pp. 267ff.

[3] Hulk Records of the *Zealand*, PRO, London.

[4] AO 4/4430; *Sydney Gazette*, 16 January, 13 February 1813, 2 October 1820; AO 4/1855, no. 151; York Street Synagogue committee report, 1845, p. 3.

[5] The story of Judah and Joseph Solomon and their extended family is told in Chapters 19 and 20.

[6] Tobias, *Prince of Fences*, pp. 18ff.

[7] Ackroyd, *Dickens*, pp. 20ff.

[8] CO, 2/S: correspondence, Twiss to Arthur, 7 May 1829.

[9] OBSP, 1826–27, Case 1922, pp. 731ff.

[10] CSO, 1/354/8078; Indent CON 40–9, No. 129, AOT.

[11] *Monitor*, 17 March 1830.

[12] OBSP, 1826–27, Case 1464, p. 562; TL 40/873.

[13] CSO, 1/354/8078, AOT.

[14] CS, Letters received, 1828, 28/7646, petition dated 26 September 1828, AO 4/1993.

[15] Letter from Arthur to the Bishop of London, Aa75/3, 17 October 1828, ML.

[16] CO, 33–4, pp. 665–7.

[17] CO, 33–4, p. 661.

[18] CSO, 1/354/8078, AOT.

[19] CO, 2/S, vol. 15, pp. 105, 109.

[20] *Hobart Town Courier*, 28 November 1829.

[21] EC, 2/1 Minutes of the Executive Council of VDL, pp. 478ff.

[22] *Tasmanian and Austral-Asiatic Review*, 5 February 1830.

[23] CSO, 1/430, File 9642.

[24] *Hobart Town Courier*, 9 January 1830.

[25] *Times*, 2, 9, 10, 13, 14 July 1830; *Morning Post*, 9, 10, 13, 14 July 1830. See Middlesex County Records, HO 11/8, p. 48; OBSP, 1829–30, Cases 1273/4, 1319/20, 1399/1400, 1435.

[26] CON, 31–9, no. 1407, p. 156.

[27] CSO, 1/849/17494.

[28] CON, 40–9, no. 129.

[29] CP 2397; CF 705.

[30] Griffith, *The Chronicles of Newgate*, op. cit., p. 473.

[31] Ledger Book, Hobart Town Hebrew Congregation.

[32] *Hobart Town Courier*, 25 May, 25 October 1840, 19, 26 March 1841.

[33] CSO, 22/68/1507.

[34] The first to draw attention to the possibility that Dickens might have chosen Ikey Solomon as a model for Fagin was Edwin Pugh, in *The Charles Dickens Originals*. He was followed by Landa, *The Jew in Drama*, pp. 159ff.

[35] Playbills 313, 19 November 1838, British Museum.

[36] Moncrieff, *Van Diemen's Land*.

18 The 'Jewboy Bushranger' and Family

[1] F. Sullivan, *The Bloodiest Bushrangers*, Adelaide, 1973.

[2] Only once in colonial records was Edward's surname written correctly: in the account of his trial in *The Australasian Chronicle*, 25 February 1841. He was the subject of J. M. H. Abbott's novel *Castle Vane* (Sydney, 1920). See also G. F. J. Bergman, 'Edward Davis, Life and Death of an Australian Bushranger', *AJHS*, vol. 4, no. 5, 1956, pp. 205ff.

[3] OBSP, 1831–32, p. 381.

[4] PSC, Indent of Convict Ships 1832–33, p. 23; TL 44/2310, AO 4/4193.

[5] Indent of the *Argyle*, CON 14/2; AOT 68/95 states that Ann Davies was the wife, not the niece, of Thomas Jones; Middlesex Records, MJ/SR 4240, Indents 4, 5.

[6] Joy and Prior, *The Bushrangers*.

[7] *Scone Advocate*, 20 August 1920; evidence given by Joseph Chivers at inquest in Scone, 23 December 1840; *Sydney Morning Herald*, 26, 29, 31 December 1840, 25 February, 25 March 1841; *Australian*, 23, 29 December 1840, 25 February 1841; *Monitor*, 29 December 1840.

[8] Minute no. 6, Executive Council of VDL, vol. 5, 1837–41.

[9] ML Newspaper Cuttings, vol. 116, p. 110, F991,1,N.

[10] *South Australian Register*, 24 January, 18 February 1854.

[11] NSW *Government Gazette*, no. 79, 2 December 1840, p. 1309; NSW Returns of the Colony, 1840, p. 200.

[12] Personal notes about John Davies by Alfred Nicholas, Allport Collection, Hobart. A biography of John Davies, by F. C. Green, can be found in *Australian Dictionary of Biography*, vol. 4, pp. 27–8.

[13] PSC, Hulk *Phoenix* Entrance Book, no. 538, AO 4/6282.

[14] Letter, 42/2302, SLV; NSW Returns of the Colony, 1842, p. 328.

[15] Finn, *The Chronicles of Early Melbourne*, pp. 467, 846.

[16] *Bell's Life in Sydney*, 19 February 1848; NSW *Government Gazette*, no. 8, 26 January 1847; CS, Police Letter Book, 30 March, 8 April 1847, AO 4/3851. *Citizen*, 20 March 1847; NSW Returns of the Colony, 1848, p. 294.

[17] *Melbourne Morning Herald*, 10 October 1849.

[18] List of licensees, AOT.

[19] Records, Hobart Town Hebrew Congregation, letters, 24 February 1851 and 25 May 1855.

[20] CSO, 20 March 1888, 27 October 1845.

[21] *Tasmanian Daily News*, 16, 28 June, 5 July 1855; *Hobart Town Advertiser*, 23 July 1860; S. Prout Hill, note in Allport Collection.

[22] CS, Police Letter Book, AO 4/3851; *Sydney Gazette*, 17 January, 7 May 1839; Surveyor's correspondence, 30 October 1837, 30 July 1838, 19 March, 13 April 1839, 7 April 1842, AO 2/7839; *Bell's Life in Sydney*, 28 March 1856.

[23] *Bell's Life in Sydney*, 8 January 1859; *Sydney Morning Herald*, 4 January 1859; *Sands' Sydney and Suburban Directory*, 1859, 1864–73; Register of Wills, Series II, no. 1217, Supreme Court of NSW, Probate Office; Michael John Davies, *Devotions for Children and Private Jewish Families in English*, Sydney, 1867 (in Ferguson, *Bibliography of Australia*). The only existing copy, known to have been in the Mitchell Library, is lost.

[24] J. M. Forde, 'Old Sydney', *Sydney Truth*, 20 September 1908.

[25] *Australian Dictionary of Biography*, vol. 8, p. 233; Davies, *A Trip to Europe*, pp. 82ff.

19 The Samsons of Swan River

[1] This chapter is based on G. F. J. Bergman, 'Solomon Levey—from Convict to Merchant Prince', *RAHS, J&P*, vol. 49, no. 6, pp. 406ff. and vol. 54, no. 1, pp. 54ff.

[2] Mossenson, *Hebrew, Israelite, Jew*, p. 3.

[3] CO, 18/6, letter dated 27 January 1829.

[4] Lionel Samson bought land at the first sale of Fremantle Town allotments, 5 September 1829 (*WAHS, J&P*, vol. 1, no. 1, p. 13).

[5] Wilson, *Western Australia's Centenary*, pp. 365ff.; CSO (WA), vol. 52, pp. 219–21.

[6] CSO (WA), vol. 1, papers 13, 14, 28, 29, 28 August to 22 September 1829.

[7] O. Silbert, 'Lionel Samson, The Pioneer Merchant of West Australia', *Westralian Judean*, 1 September 1932, p. 448; *Inquirer and Commercial News*, 20 March 1878; NSW A1294, pp. 369–75; CSO (WA), Dispatches of Governor Stirling, vol. 15, letter from Lionel Samson dated 7 May 1831 from 'G.P.O. Fremantle'.

[8] A. C. Staples, 'Early Days in W.A.', *WAHS, J&P*, vol. 5, no. 7, pp. 83ff.

[9] Index of Marriages, December quarter 1842, General Register Office, London; the marriage was performed by Moses Rintel.

[10] D. J. Benjamin, 'Western Australia Jewry 1829–1897', *AJHS*, vol. 2, no. 5, 1946, pp. 231ff.

[11] P. M. Culp jnr, 'Spanish Impressions of Colonial Australia', *RAHS, J&P*, vol. 60, no. 4, 1974, p. 249.

[12] See Mossendon, *Hebrew, Israelite, Jew*, pp. 251ff.

20 South Australia

[1] Pike, *Paradise of Dissent*.

[2] Munz, *Jews in South Australia*, p. 11, quoting the diaries of Sir Moses and Lady Montefiore.

[3] *Sydney Gazette*, 8, 11 October 1836.

[4] Opie, *South Australian Records*, p. 16. John Levey Roberts arrived in the *Cygnet* on 11 September 1836, the fifth ship to bring settlers to South Australia. See CS, Letters received, 40/1826, 18 December 1840, AO 4/2385.

[5] An Isaac Jacobs arrived in the colony 10 February 1837 (Opie, *South Australian Records*, p. 24). Marks and Jacobs are mentioned in the 1841 census of the Province of South Australia. There is no record of the arrival of Joseph Lazarus.

[6] There is some doubt about the date of N. P. Levi's arrival. He may have first come to Adelaide with his son Philip in 1838 (Opie, *South Australian Records*, p. 49) and then returned to England, being at home at Balham when Lionel Samson paid his respects to his daughter Fanny. A Mr Levi appears to have arrived in the *Orisa*, 10 March 1840 (Opie, p. 93).

[7] Letter dated 10 October 1843, GRG 24–1–1843/247, SA Archives.

[8] *Pastoral Pioneers of South Australia*, vol. 1, pp. 28ff.

[9] A. M. Hyamson, 'An Anglo-Jewish Family', JHSE, vol. 17, 1953, p. 4.

[10] Letter from J. B. Montefiore, 15 July 1837, SA Archives, 'We feel much indebted to His Excellency for the selection of our Firm'; CS, Letters received, 39/9105, AO 4/2363.2.

[11] Munz, *Jews in South Australia*, pp. 14ff.

[12] PRO Durham, letter 17/57, and PRO letter 16/3, 10 May 1868; PSC, Ship Indent re *Lady Castlereagh*, p. 34, AO 4/4006.

[13] CON, 31/38, AOT.

[14] CS, Newcastle, Monthly Return of Punishments 1810–25, January 1823, AO 4/1718.

[15] CS, Miscellaneous Persons, Out-letters, p. 3, AO 4/3520.

[16] Opie, *South Australian Records*, p. 50; *Sydney Gazette*, 22, 27 November 1838, 6 August, 15 October 1839; *South Australian Register*, 22 June 1839.

[17] *South Australian Register*, 30 May 1840, 2 January 1841, 7 January 1843, 10 January 1845, 6 February, 18 March, 2 June 1847, 18 July 1849.

[18] *Sydney Morning Herald*, 3 April 1844.

[19] *South Australian Advertiser*, 29 December 1871.

[20] *Royal South Australian Almanack*, Adelaide, 1848, p. 109; *South Australian Register*, 27 June 1846.

[21] *South Australian Register*, 30 May 1846.

[22] p. 109.

[23] 'A letter dated 2 February 1850 from Mr H. Coronel our agent who went out to the colony last year', *Jewish Chronicle*, 2 April 1850.

[24] *South Australian Register*, 5 September 1850.

[25] *Ibid.*

[26] *South Australian Register*, 30 October 1844.

[27] *Jewish Chronicle*, 2 August 1850.

[28] *Jewish Chronicle*, 23 July 1852.

[29] Getzler, *Neither Toleration Nor Favour*, pp. 74ff.

[30] *Jewish Chronicle*, 30 May 1851. Newdigate was the anti-Jewish MP for North Warwickshire.

21 The Jews of Melbourne

[1] See L. M. Goldman 'The Early Jewish Settlers in Victoria and Their Problems', *AJHS*, vol. 4, nos 1, 2, 7, 8; Finn, *Chronicles of Early Melbourne*, p. 457; Brodzky, *Historical Sketch of the Two Melbourne Synagogues*.

[2] HRA, Series III, vol. 1, p. 555; OBSP, 1816–17, Case 1525, p. 502. PSC, Indent of Convict Ships, 1818, re *Neptune*.

[3] Michael Phillips to Earl Bathurst, 4 January 1827, HRA, Series I, vol. 13, p. 132.

[4] New South Wales Legislative Council, 20 August 1844.

[5] *Victorian Historical Magazine*, vol. 18, p. 104; Port Phillip Association Papers, pp. 47–53, SLV.

[6] On 20 November 1866 John Pascoe Fawkner wrote to the government setting forth his claim to be the true founder of Melbourne:

> these 17 workers deserve some notice by the way—they were a strange medley. Captain Swanston, a M.C. of V.D. Land, John Bateman, an Illiterate man, said to be one of Col. Arthur's spies in V.D.L. Col. Arthur himself in the name of his nephew and J. Solomon, a Jew and at the time a Prisoner of the Crown—The Company consists—or did consist originally—of Col. Geo. Arthur, Lt. Governor of Van Diemen's Land, Judah Solomon at the time a convict, therefore his name was withheld, J. T. Gellibrand, Captn. Swanston, M.D. of V.D.L., Mr. Cotterill, J. H. Wedge, Mr. Simpson, J. Paul, Chairman of the Convict Board and Mr. M. Connelly.

(The letter is included in the Port Phillip Association Papers, p. 66, SLV.)

[7] John Batman's Diary, SLV.

[8] Turner, *A History of the Colony of Victoria*, p. 133.

[9] Bonwick, *Discovery and Settlement of Port Phillip Bay*, map after p. 140, and p. 274.

[10] *Bents News*, 19 February 1836; Billis and Kenyon, *Pastures New*, pp. 38ff.; Governor Bourke Dispatches, A1267–14, 1836, p. 1738, ML.

[11] Kenyon Index, Licence 4/11, Deep Creek 40, SLV.

[12] Melbourne Hebrew Congregation, Letter Book 1, SLV 45/86 M 55773, refers to Joseph's relationship to Henry Davis (letter to J. Solomon, 13 November 1844); also the will of Joseph Solomon (Melbourne Probate Offfice). Bonwick (Discovery and Settlement of Port Phillip Bay, p. 85), a contemporary of Solomon, describes Joseph as Judah Solomon's 'nephew'. Brodzky (Historical Sketch of the Two Melbourne Synagogues, p. 22) writes of 'The case of a Jewish girl named Davies'.

[13] Port Phillip Patriot & Melbourne Advertiser—Australia Felix, 3 February 1842, 20 February 1839.

[14] Jones, Solomon's Ford, p. 56, quoting Thomas Flynn, The History of Braybrook (MS).

[15] A. L. Benjamin, 'Jewish Colonists in Melbourne's Early Land Sales', AJHS, vol. 2, no. 5, 1946 pp. 217ff.

[16] CS, Letters received re Land, 28 October 1840, 23 December 1841, AO 2/7799.

[17] Voice of Jacob (Sydney), 27 May 1842; Melbourne Hebrew Congregation, Letter Book 1, 3 September 1850.

[18] The Port Phillip Separation Merchants and Settlers' Almanac, Diary, published in 1845 for 1846; Melbourne Directory for 1845, Melbourne, 1844, pp. 63ff.

[19] A list of drapers, haberdashers and slop-sellers who attempted to set the hour of 7 p.m. as closing time (except on Saturday nights) during the winter months included Isaac Hart, A. E. Cohen, Colin Isaacs, Michael Cashmore, Elias Ellis, S. H. Harris, Edward Hart, A. E. Alexander, James Simeon, John Levy, Nathaniel Nathan, Moses Lazarus, Cashman Lazarus. David and Solomon Benjamin did not join this attempt to regularise shop hours, perhaps because they already closed for the Sabbath (Melbourne Morning Herald, 29 May 1850).

[20] The Jewish publicans were: Henry Davis, who came from Launceston and opened the Royal Exchange Hotel which, within months, had failed (Port Phillip Gazette, 15 December 1841). Michael John Davies, of the Shakespeare Hotel; insolvent by 1847 (Port Phillip Herald, 7 January 1847). Isaac Lazarus Lincoln; failed as a hotel-keeper in early Seymour (in 1846). Benjamin Goldsmid Levien; owned the Victoria Hotel near the Maribyrnong River between 1840 and 1843. John Davies tried to start a hotel in Melbourne in 1841; within weeks his Imperial Hotel was insolvent. He later went to Van Diemen's Land, again as a publican. He has been confused by Goldman with John Davies the actor and newspaper proprietor, the son of Michael John Davies and brother of the bushranger Edward.

[21] T. Cohen, 'Michael Cashmore', AJHS, vol. 6, no. 3, pp. 144ff.; L. M. Goldman, 'The Early Jewish Settlers in Victoria and Their Problems', AJHS, vol. 4, no. 7, 1958, p. 354. T. Cohen, 'Solomon and Cashmore: Chain Migration and Early Jewish Settlement in Australia, AJHS, vol. 15, no. 3, 2000, pp. 315ff.

[22] Port Phillip Patriot, 28 August 1843, Goldman, The Jews of Victoria in the Nineteenth Century, p. 45.

[23] OBSP, 1832, Case 1885, pp. 780ff. John Levien was described as a 'clerk'.

[24] A. M. Hyamson, 'Benjamin Goldsmid Levien', AJHS, vol. 2, no. 6, 1945, pp. 349ff.; CON, 31/28, no. 712; G. F. J. Bergman, 'A Jewish Farmer's Religious Scruples and Letter from Geelong 1856', AJHS, vol. 6, no. 3, 1967, pp. 157ff.

[25] Brodzky, Historical Sketch of the Two Melbourne Synagogues, pp. 20ff.

[26] CS, Shipping Records, 1838, 8 June 1838, AO 4/5213.

[27] Brodzky, Historical Sketch of the Two Melbourne Synagogues, p. 22.

[28] Voice of Jacob (London), 6 December 1844, p. 57.

[29] Goldman, The Jews in Victoria in the Nineteenth Century p. 58; Voice of Jacob (London), 28 August 1846, p. 194.

[30] Papers of Dr James Allen (son-in-law of George Augustus Robinson) of Clarke Island in Bass Strait. Transcribed manuscript supplied by the late Stephen Murray-Smith, 4 June 1981.

[31] Port Phillip Patriot, 19 February 1844.

[32] The Story of the Melbourne Hebrew Congregation, issued by the congregation in commemoration of its century, pp. 9ff.

[33] Port Phillip Gazette, 28 April 1847.

[34] The Story of the Melbourne Hebrew Congregation, p. 9.

[35] Port Phillip Gazette, 21 March 1846; Finn The Chronicles of Early Melbourne, p. 235.

[36] Port Phillip Patriot, 3 November 1845.

[37] Laws and Regulations of the Holy Congregation of a Remnant of Israel, 1844.

[38] Melbourne Hebrew Congregation, Letter Book 1, 16 April 1850.

[39] Petition to Governor Brisbane, CS, Letters received, 449; AO 4/1872. CS, Letters received, 1822, AO 4/1752; Police Correspondence from CS, 1829, p. 308, AO 4/3828. Australian Israelite, 20 May 1873.

[40] The Melbourne Synagogue wrote to Geelong that 'they had come to the unanimous determination that they cannot sanction anything in connection with a separate congregation in Geelong' (Melbourne Hebrew Congregation, Letter Book 1, 16 September 1849).

[41] Minutes of the Melbourne Hebrew Congregation (MHC), 23 January 1848. The Laws of the congregation (1844) stated that 'No application for conversion to the Jewish faith be received by this Congregation or entertained in any shape' (MHC Minute Book, 11 August 1844; MHC Letter Book 1, 19 July 1844). This was Abraham Levy's second application for the conversion of his wife (18 July 1845). Five members call a meeting 'to consider on the propriety of making guerists (converts)', and Nathaniel Nathan's son is allowed to be circumcised as 'a special case' (MHC Minute Book, 3 August 1845; see also letter dated 27 June 1848 in MHC Letter Book 1).

[42] Melbourne Hebrew Congregation, Letter Book, 21 December 1847.

[43] M. H. Kellerman, 'Walter L. Lindenthal, a Critical Study', *AJHS*, vol. 3, no. 3, 1950, pp. 109ff.

[44] Clacy, *A Lady's Visit to the Gold Diggings of Australia 1851–52*, p. 30.

[45] Kelly, *Life in Victoria*, pp. 118ff.

[46] *Melbourne Morning Herald*, 6 September, 1, 4 October 1851.

[47] *Melbourne Morning Herald*, 1, 2 December 1851.

[48] *Melbourne*, 22 October, 1 November 1851.

[49] *Argus*, 2 January 1852, 16, 23 February 1854.

22 Beyond the Metropolis

[1] An Emigrant Mechanic, *Settlers and Convicts*, p. 136.

[2] CS, Letters received, 1831, 31/6897, 2 August 1831, AO 4/2116.

[3] Re Boaz: ML 2/8243, p. 174; CS, Petitions for Mitigation of Sentence, p. 19, 20 October 1825, AO 4/1873; re Marcus: CS, Letters received, Memo 1810, L–Y, no. 204; *Sydney Gazette*, 14 July 1810.

[4] Re Cohen: *Sydney Gazette*, 9 April 1818; re Jacob Isaacs: PSC Ship Indent, AO 4/4005; re Rachel Isaacs: Gaol Recognition Book, 1837–38, AO 4/6300.

[5] Re John Moses: *Colonial Times*, 15 March 1836; *Sydney Gazette*, 28 October 1830; *Hobart Town Courier*, 13 July 1838; *Commercial Journal and Advertiser* (Sydney), 6 February 1839.

[6] Re Joel Joseph: Bigge Enquiry, Appendix, B.T. Box 25, p. 5487; re Solomon Josephs and Abraham Elias: *Sydney Gazette*, 31 July, 4 December 1823, 20 April 1824, 1 August 1831.

[7] *Heads of the People* (Sydney), 6 November 1847.

[8] Official return of census for 1841 (NSW); NSW Returns of the Colony, 1850, pp. 560, 566.

[9] NSW *Government Gazette*, no. 171, 28 December 1849; John Moses, *Bell's Life*, 28 July 1849; *Australian*, 1 May 1841; *Sydney Morning Herald*, 9 April 1849.

[10] Re Samuel Phillips *Sydney Morning Herald*, 6 January 1845; AO 2/7950 Land Correspondence; *Sydney Morning Herald*, 21 April 1845. Re Lewis Wolfe Levy: *AJHS*, vol. 6, no. 8, 1970, pp. 474ff. Re David Cashmore, Goldman, *The Jews in Victoria in the Nineteenth Century*, p. 27. Re Godfrey Alexander *Sydney Morning Herald*, 4 January 1862; R. H. Montague, 'G. Alexander: Sydney's First Chiropodist', *AJHS*, vol. 6, no. 8, 1970, pp. 531ff. Re Isaac Moses, *Sydney Gazette*, 5 January 1837; *Sydney Morning Herald*, 16 January 1838, 7 January 1840. Re John Moses, AO 4/2650.4.

[11] Morris Asher, 'Reminiscences of a Nonagenarian,' *Sydney Mail*, 31 July and 14, 21, 28 August 1907; M. Z. Forbes, 'Jewish Personalities in the Movement for Responsible Government in New South Wales', *AJHS*, vol. 4, no. 6, 1957, pp. 307ff.; *Sydney Morning Herald*, 30 October 1909.

[12] CS, Letters received, 1843, 43/7474, AO 4/4560.2; S. Schultz, 'Early Jewish Settlers in Port Macquarie', *AJHS*, vol. 3, no. 8, 1953.

[13] J. Tucker (attrib.), *The Adventures of Ralph Rashleigh: A Penal Exile in Australia, 1825–1844*, London, 1929, ch. 11; *Australian*, 2 October 1838, 5 January, 12 October 1839, 2 June 1840.

[14] CSO, 16/2/58 and CON, 35/1, no. 1400, AOT; CS, Assignment List of Convicts Sentenced to Transportation for Colonial Offences and sent to V.D.L. 1832–53, AO 4/4523; NSW Prison Department, Sydney Gaol 1819–23, Gaol no. 1527, AO 4/6297.

[15] CS, Letters received re Land, AO 2/7930; *Extracts from the Letters of James Backhouse*, part 3, p. 21.

[16] A biography of Joseph Aarons, by D. I. McDonald, is in *Australian Dictionary of Biography*, vol. 3, p. 1.

[17] CS, In-letters, AO 4/2326.2, 36/4930; *Sydney Gazette*, 1 July 1837; Supplementary List of Runs, Darling Downs District, Gazetted 1849, no. 58.

[18] List of Licences for Depasturing Stock beyond Boundaries of Settlement, Bligh Pastoral District, no. 4, 1848, 115, 116, and Wellington Pastoral District, no. 5, 1848, 91, 92, 93; *Sydney Chronicle*, 6 May 1848; *Bathurst Free Press and Mining Journal*, 16 October 1854.

[19] CS, Letters received re Land, AO 2/7906; Scarlett, *Queanbeyan District and People*; AO 2/7933.

[20] Abraham Moses arrived in the *Palambam* in January 1833. The first part of the story of his colonial career is told in a petition for land at Monaro, CS, Letters received, 25 February 1839, AO 2/7933.

[21] S. B. Glass, 'Jews of Goulburn', *AJHS*, vol. 1, no. 6 to vol. 2, no. 3; Backhouse, *A Narrative of a Visit to the Australian Colonies*, pp. 439ff.

[22] *Sydney Gazette*, 19 July 1836; *Australian*, 20 December 1836.

[23] C. Roth, 'Rise of Provincial Jewry', *The Jewish Monthly* (London), 1950, p. 96.

[24] *Sydney Gazette*, 10, 24 July 1838.

[25] *Sydney Morning Herald*, 29 October 1838.

[26] S. B. Glass, 'Jews of Goulburn', *AJHS*, vol. 1, no. 8, p. 283.

[27] *Sydney Morning Herald*, 24 February 1845.

[28] Re Nathan Mandelson: application for naturalisation, NSW Government Dispatches, 1843, A1232, pp. 215ff; *AJHS*, vol. 1, no. 8, 1942, pp. 282ff.; *Bathurst Free Press and Mining Journal*, 7 June 1851. Re Samuel Isaac Emanuel: *Sydney Morning Herald*, 13 July 1868.

[29] OBSP, 1830–31, Case 414, pp. 202ff.; PSC Ticket-of-Leave Butts, AO 4/4103, TL 36/784, CF 38/460.

[30] S. B. Glass, 'Jews of Goulburn', *AJHS*, vol. 1, no. 10, 1943, p. 373.

[31] Re P. J. Cohen: CS, Letters, received re Land, 7 February 1833, AO 2/7827. Re Solomon Levien: CS, Letters received, Postmaster-General 1834, 7 January 1834, AO 4/2257; CS, Letters received, 1835, AO 4/2283.7, 35/2069.

[32] G. F. J. Bergman, 'Samuel Cohen, an Early Settler and a Parliamentarian with a Conscience', *AJHS*, vol. 6, no. 6, 1969, pp. 334ff.

[33] Re Samuel Levy, alias Samuel Lazarus, alias Lawrence Jones: CS, Petitions for Mitigation of Sentence, 1823, letter 10, AO 4/1870 and Petition 73, 1824, AO 4/1882; CS, Letters received, 1827, 27/10405, 5 November 1827, AO 4/1953; CS, In-letters re Prisoners, 1835, 35/5545, AO 4/2296; *Sydney Gazette*, 16 November 1811, 13 December 1826; Chronological Register of Convicts at Moreton Bay, no. 1448; CS, Letters received re Prisoners, 1835, 35/5545, AO 4/2296; CS, In-letters re Convicts, 1837, 37/4256, 37/3404, 37/4256, AO 4/2352; CS, Letters to PSC, 1847, p. 425, 14 October 1847, AO 4/3692.

[34] *Sydney Morning Herald*, 7 January 1845; *Sentinel*, 19 February 1843.

[35] *AJHS*, vol. 3, no. 1, pp. 53–4.

[36] *Sydney Mail*, 14 August 1907.

[37] CS, Letters received re Land, 39/6555, AO 2/7914.

23 The Feared Outpost Prisons

[1] Prisoners to Port Macquarie, AO 4/3897, p. 418; Surveyor's Correspondence, AO 2/7839; *Sydney Morning Herald*, 24 February 1845; TL 40/356, Printed Indent 1833, p. 20; S. Schultz, 'Early Jewish Settlers in Port Macquarie', *AJHS*, vol. 3, no. 8, 1953, pp. 341ff.

[2] William R–S, *The Fell Tyrant*, pp. 20ff.

[3] CS, Letters received re Prisoners, 1840, 40/8189, AO 4/2513; Petition for TL; OBSP, 1816–17, Case 868, p. 302, and 1817–18, Case 97, p. 40; *Isabella* Ship List, 1818, p. 89, AO 4/4006.

[4] CS, Letters received, AO 4/1917.1; CS, Copies of Letters to Moreton Bay, 1824–31, p. 295, AO 4/3794; *Somersetshire* Indent, AO 4/4005; *Sydney Gazette*, 24 December 1814, 29 July 1820; CS, Letters received, 1836, 37/6607, 19 July 1837, AO 4/2362.4; CS, TL Applications, 1833, 33/3138, AO 4/2180.2.

[5] OBSP, 1820–21, Case 639, p. 238; AO 4/4009, p. 47; AO 4/2460.3.

[6] Entries for 31 December 1838, 19 March 1839, Book of Trials, Oxley Memorial Library; Criminal Court, Sydney, 20 November 1833, 25 January 1834; Register of Flash Men, AO 2/673.

[7] OBSP, 1818–19, Case 396, pp. 172ff. PSC, TL Butts, 1843, 43/2412, AO 4/4181; 57/20, AO 4/4231.

[8] CS, Letters received re Land, AO 2/7974; *Sydney Morning Herald*, 2 April 1844; *South Australian Register*, 8 April 1841, 13 February 1847, GRG, 24 1 1840/554, SA Archives; *Sydney Morning Herald*, 2 July 1845; *South Australian Register*, 10 September 1848.

[9] *Sydney Gazette*, 24 September 1842.

[10] J. Campbell, 'The Early Settlement of Queensland', *Ipswich Observer*, 1875, p. 6; Murphy and Easton, *From Wilderness to Wealth*; Register of Applications, Commissioner for Crown Lands (NSW), 1848–68.

[11] Sydney Synagogue Minute Book, 13 November 1832.

[12] *Moreton Bay Courier*, 4 July 1846; *Sydney Morning Herald*, 7 May 1845; Court of Requests (Petty Sessions), May 1844–51 includes twenty instances of cases tried for recovery of small debts by Lee (CPS 1/1, Queensland State Archives).

[13] Printed Register, 1834, p. 117, Roslin Castle, OBSP, 1833–34, Case 140, p. 107; TL, PSC TL Butts, 33/2282, AO 4/4193; CS, Letters received *re* Land, AO 2/7796; *Moreton Bay Courier*, 1 September 1849, 18 December 1847, 6 April 1850.

[14] *Moreton Bay Courier*, 7 November 1846, 15 March, 10 June, 8 July, 30 December 1848. CS, Letters received *re* Land, 2/7792, 2/7799, AO 2/7894; HRNSW, vol. 1, no. 2, p. 89.

[15] A biography of James Maconochie, by J. V. Barry, is in *Australian Dictionary of Biography*, vol. 2, pp. 184–6.

[16] Sydney Synagogue Minute Book (also Bridge Street Synagogue Letter Book 26, December 1840 and Minute 17 February 1841); the Jewish prisoners were Levy Abraham, Aaron Wolff, Seronie Solomon, James Lawrence, John Davis, Lewis Solomon, John Roberts, Ralph Simmons, Samuel Alexander.

[17] James Lawrence, Diary; Ship Indent, for *Indefatigable*, May 1815, p. 47, AO 4/4005; Lancashire Quarter Sessions, 27 April 1814; Aaron Price, Norfolk Island History.

[18] List of Convict Ships to VDL, A1059–4, ML; NSW Prison Department, Description Book, 1831, AO 4/6297; *Hobart Town Courier*, 23 February 1838, 28 June 1839, 30 January 1845; *Sydney Morning Herald* and *Australian*, 15, 21 October 1842. Woolfe's life is imaginatively told in *A Tale of Norfolk Island by a Chaplain*, ML.

[19] CON, 44/3, Convict's Petition, 1848, AOT.

[20] Returns of Prisoners at Norfolk Island 1844–1856, D113, ML.

24 Ophir

[1] *Sydney Morning Herald*, 12 June 1849; *Melbourne Morning Herald*, 22 August 1849.

[2] Note written by Moses Cohen, P1/C, ML.

[3] Raphael Tolano was an emancipist who arrived as a convict in 1837 (Indent, for the *Charles Kerr*, 1837, p. 161).

[4] 'From our Correspondent' Melbourne, 26 December 1851, *Jewish Chronicle*, 28 May 1852.

[5] *Melbourne Morning Herald*, 27 September, 4, 9 October 1851.

[6] *Jewish Chronicle*, 2 July 1852.

[7] Ibid., 4 February 1853.

[8] Ibid., 26 November 1852.

[9] Ibid., 4 February 1853.

[10] Ibid., 30 October 1846.

[11] Ibid., 5 August 1853.

[12] Ibid., 12 April 1854.

[13] Ibid., 11 November 1853.

[14] Ibid., 27 January 1854.

[15] Ibid., 25 March 1853.

[16] *Melbourne Morning Herald*, 15 August 1854, from a letter written 20 September 1853.

[17] Bruce T. Colcott, 'A Jewish Connection to the Eureka Incident', *Jewish Genealogy Downunder*, vol. 1, no. 4, November 1999, p. 3.

[18] Rutland, *Edge of the Diaspora*, pp. 52, 412.

[19] Levinson, A Record of Some Memories.

[20] C. A. Price, 'Jewish Settlers in Australia', *AJHS*, vol. 5, no. 8, 1964, appendix 1. Dr Price estimated 100 Jews in South Australia, but research for this book indicates 150.

[21] L. A. Falk, 'The Sydney Jewish Library, 1846', *AJHS*, vol. 3, no. 3, 1950, pp. 133ff.

[22] G. F. J. Bergman, 'Righteous Path Society and Hebrew Mutual Benefit Society, Two Early Benevolent Societies in Sydney', *AJHS*, vol. 6, no. 4, 1968, pp. 215ff.

[23] I. Porush, 'Rev. Herman Hoelzel—The First Qualified Jewish Minister in Australia', *AJHS*, vol. 2, no. 4, 1945, p. 172ff.

[24] 'Lines on the Death in Australia, of Elias Davis', *Jewish Chronicle*, 19 May 1854.

Abbreviations

Adm.	Admiralty
AJHS	*Journal of Australian Jewish Historical Society*
AO	Archives Office of New South Wales
AOT	Archives Office of Tasmania
AP	Absolute Pardon
BM	British Museum
CF	Certificate of Freedom
CO	Colonial Office
CON	Convict Record Book, Archives Office of Tasmania
CP	Conditional Pardon
CS	Colonial Secretary
CSO	Colonial Secretary's Office
EC	Executive Council
GRG	Government Record Group
HO	Home Office
HRA	*Historical Records of Australia*
HRNSW	*Historical Records of New South Wales*
HTHC	Hobart Town Hebrew Congregation
JHSE	*Journal of Jewish Historical Society of England*
ML	Mitchell Library, State Library of New South Wales
OBSP	*Old Bailey Sessions Papers*
PRO	Public Record Office (London)
PSC	Principal Superintendent of Convicts (New South Wales)
RAHS, J&P	*Royal Australian Historical Society, Journal and Proceedings*
SLV	State Library of Victoria
TL	Ticket-of-Leave
WAHS, J&P	*Western Australian Historical Society, Journal and Proceedings*

Conversions

1 inch	2.54 centimetres
1 foot (12 inches)	30.5 centimetres
1 yard (3 feet)	0.91 metre
1 mile	1.61 kilometres
1 acre	0.4 hectare
1 ounce (oz)	28.3 grams
1 pound (lb)	0.45 kilogram
1 hundredweight	50.8 kilograms
1 bushel	36.4 litres
1 gallon (8 pints)	4.55 litres

Currency

On 14 February 1966, Australian currency changed from pounds, shillings and pence (£, s, d) to dollars and cents at the rate of £1 = $2. Twelve pence made up one shilling and twenty shillings made up one pound. A guinea was a pound plus a shilling.

Select Bibliography

Archival sources

United Kingdom

Board of Deputies of British Jews, Minute Book 1, November 1760–April 1828 (Board of Deputies, London).

Corporation of London, Records (Guildhall, London).

Dickens Correspondence (Mocatta Library).

Hulk Records (PRO).

Judges Reports, 1788, HO (PRO).

List of Female Felons at Newgate Prison (PRO).

Middlesex Session Book (Middlesex Records Office).

New South Wales

Great Synagogue, Sydney

Sydney Synagogue (Bridge and York streets), Minute Books 1 and 2, 1837–1860; Birth, Marriage and Burial Registers, and plan of the Devonshire Street Cemetery Jewish Section.

Sydney Synagogue (Bridge Street), letters, 1840–1842 (copies).

Sydney Synagogue (York Street), letters, 1844–1845 (copies); Letter Book 1, 1846–1859.

Mitchell Library, and Archives Office of New South Wales

Alphabetical Return of Convicts, 1810–1820.

Anon., A Tale of Norfolk Island by a Chaplain, 1845.

Banks, Joseph, Papers.

Bench of Magistrates, Proceedings, 1788–1812.

Bigge Enquiry, Appendix.

Bonwick Transcripts.

Bourke, Governor, Papers.

Bowes, Arthur, A Journal of a Voyage from Portsmouth to New South Wales and China in the Lady Penrhyn, 1787.

Certificates of Freedom, 1827–1867, Butts.

Clerk of the Peace, Quarter Sessions (Bathurst, Maitland, Newcastle, Parramatta, Windsor), 1827–1837, Depositions of papers.

Conditional Pardons (copies).

Convict Pardons, 1826–1870 (copies).

Convict Ships arriving at Port Jackson 1788–1849.

Cumberland, County of, Bench Book, 1788–1821.

Free Pardons.

Harbour Master, Daily Reports from Vessels Arriving at Port Jackson, 1820–1850.

Hawkesbury Benevolent Society, Registers.

Hulk *Phoenix*, Entrance Book.

Hutchinson Papers.

Indents of Convict Ships, 1788–1841.

Index of Vessels Arriving at Port Jackson, 1837–1850.

Johnston, George, Papers (Dixson Library).

King, Governor, Letterbook of Norfolk Island; Papers.

Lawrence, James, Diary (Dixson Library).

Macarthur Papers.

Montefiore, J. L., Don John of Austria; Marguerite; The Duel (MSS.).

Mutch, T. D., Birth, Marriage, Death Registers.

New South Wales, Census, 1828, 1833, 1836, 1841.

———— CS, Letters Received; In-letters.

———— Criminal Court Procedures.

———— Government Dispatches.

———— Governors' Dispatches.

———— Musters, 1800, 1811, 1814, 1818.

New South Wales Pioneers Index 1788–1918, CD-Rom, Pioneers Series, Royal Melbourne Institute of Technology, 1994.

Norfolk Island Victualling Book 1792–1795.

Northumberland, County of, Register, 1823–1837.

Norton and Smith, Papers.

Parkes Papers.

Permission to Marry Book.

Piper Papers.

Price, Aaron, Norfolk Island History (Dixson Library).

Register of Flash Men (AO 2/673).

Returns of the Colony, 1822, 1823, 1825–1850.

Shaw, Eliza, Letters to friends in England, 1829–1833.

Shipping Lists of Convicts: to and from Moreton Bay 1827–1839; to and from Norfolk Island 1828–44, 1850; to and from Port Macquarie 1821–1842; to and from Van Diemen's Land 1812–1840; to Newcastle 1811–1822.

Spark, A. B., Diaries, 1836–1856.

Styles, Rev. H. T., Correspondence.

Supreme Court on Circuit, Quarter Sessions (Sydney and Country), 1824–1860.

Tasmanian Convicts: The Complete List from the Original Records, CD-Rom, Royal Melbourne Institute of Technology, 2000.

Tasmanian Pioneers Index 1803–1899, CD-Rom, Pioneers Series, Royal Melbourne Institute of Technology, 1993.

Tickets of Leave, 1827–1875, Butts.

Victorian Pioneers Index 1837–1888, CD-Rom, Pioneers Series, Royal Melbourne Institute of Technology, 1994.

Wentworth, D'Arcy, Papers.

———— Treasury of the Colonial Revenue Accounts.

Wentworth, W C., Correspondence and Papers.

Various locations

Bank of New South Wales, Board of Directors, Ledger Book (Bank of New South Wales).
Grants of Land Registers (Registrar-General's Department, Sydney)
Marriage Register, St John's, Parramatta (St John's).
Marriage Register, St Philip's, Sydney (St Philip's).

Tasmania
Archives Office of Tasmania

Arthur File.
Convict Ships Arriving in Van Diemen's Land, 1812–1853.
Executive Council of VDL, Minutes.
Male and Female Convicts' Registers, VDL.
Musters 1811, 1818–1821, VDL.
Probate Register, Supreme Court of Tasmania.
Record Book, Court House, Hobart Town.
Solomon, H. J., The Queer Colony, MS. on the Solomon family 1820–1920.

Various locations

Elliston's Hobart Town Almanack, 1837–1838.
Hobart Town Hebrew Congregation, Minute Books 1–3, 1842–1875; Birth, Marriage and
    Death Registers; Correspondence and Ledgers (Hobart Synagogue).
Marriage Register, St John's, Launceston (St John's).

South Australia

Adelaide Hebrew Congregation Minute Books, 1848–1851 (Adelaide Synagogue).
Colonial Secretary's correspondence with J. L. and J. B. Montefiore, 1848–1851 (SA Archives).

Victoria
State Library of Victoria

Batman, John. Diary.
Jewish Congregational Society Melbourne, Minutes, 1841–1843.
Melbourne Hebrew Congregation, Letter Book 1; Minute Book 1, 1843–1853.
Port Phillip Association, Papers.

Queensland
Oxley Memorial Library

Book of Trials, Moreton Bay, 1835–1838.
Medical Records, Moreton Bay, 1829–1834.
Register of Convicts, Moreton Bay, 1829–1834.
Spicer Journal.

Queensland State Archives

Court of Requests, Records, 1844–1851.
Register of Applications, Commissioners of Crown Lands, 1848–1868.
Stock Run Registers, 1848–1868.

Western Australia

J. S. Battye Library

Colonial Secretary's Office Records, In-letters; Out-letters (copies).

Contemporary books and pamphlets

A. L. F., *The History of Samuel Terry, in Botany Bay, who died lately, leaving a princely fortune of nearly one million sterling*, London, 1838.

Backhouse, James, *A Narrative of a Visit to the Australian Colonies*, London, 1843.

—— *Extracts from the Letters of James Backhouse*, London, 1838.

Balfour, J. O., *A Sketch of New South Wales*, London, 1845.

Barrington, G., *The History of New South Wales*, London, 1802.

Bigge, J. T., *Report of the Commissioner of Enquiry into the State of the Colony of New South Wales*, 3 vols, London, 1822 (Adelaide, 1966).

Bonwick, J., *Discovery and Settlement of Port Phillip: being a history of the country now called Victoria*, Melbourne, 1856.

Clacy, Mrs Charles, *A Lady's Visit to the Gold Diggings of Australia 1851–52*, London, 1853 (Melbourne, 1963).

Collins, D. A., *An Account of the English Colony in New South Wales*, 2 vols, London, 1798, 1802.

Colquhoun, P., *A Treatise on the Police of the Metropolis by a Magistrate containing a detail of the various crimes and misdemeanours by which public and private property and security are, at present, injured and endangered*, London, 1795.

Crook, G. T. (ed.), *The Complete Newgate Calendar*, 5 vols, London, 1926.

Disraeli, Benjamin, *Tancred*, London, 1847.

Elliston's Hobart Town Almanack 1837–1838.

Emigrant Mechanic, An [Alexander Harris], *Settlers and Convicts, or Recollections of Sixteen Years Labour in the Australian Backwoods*, Melbourne, 1883 (Melbourne 1969).

Flanagan, Roderick, *History of New South Wales*, London, 1862.

Fowles, Joseph, *Sydney in 1848*, Sydney, 1848 (Sydney 1962).

Great Britain, House of Commons, *Report of the Select Committee on Transportation*, 1812.

—— *Report of the Commissioner of Enquiry into the State of the Colony of New South Wales*, see Bigge, J. T.

—— *Papers Relating to the Conduct of Magistrates in New South Wales, in Directing the Infliction of Punishments Upon Prisoners in that Colony*, 1826.

—— *Report from the Select Committee on Transportation*, 1840.

Holt, J., *Memoirs of Joseph Holt: General of the Irish Rebels in 1798*, edited by J. Crofton Croaker, London, 1838 (Sydney, 1988).

Holy Congregation of the Remnant of Israel, *Laws and Regulations of the Holy Congregation of the Remnant of Israel*, Melbourne, 1844.

Hunter, J., *An Historical Journal of the Events at Sydney and at Sea 1787–1792*, London, 1793 (Sydney, 1968).

Jameson, R. G., *New Zealand, South Australia and New South Wales: A Record of Recent Travels in These Colonies*, London, 1842.

Kelly, W., *Life in Victoria*, 2 vols, London, 1859.

Knaff, A. and W. Bald, *Newgate Calendar*, London, 1824–28.

Lang, J. G., *The Forger's Wife or the Adventures Of George Flower, the Celebrated Detective*, Sydney, 1855.

—— *Botany Bay, or True Tales of Early Australia*, Hobart, 1859 (London, 1861).

———— *Fisher's Ghost and Other Stories of the Early Days of Australia*, Melbourne, n.d.

London Society for Promoting Christianity Among the Jews, *Report*, London, 1821.

Maclehose, James, *The Picture of Sydney and Strangers' Guide in New South Wales for 1838*, Sydney, 1838.

Mansfield, Ralph, *Analytical View of the Census of New South Wales*, Sydney, 1847.

Marjoribanks, A., *Travels in New South Wales*, London, 1847.

Martin, M. R., *The History of Austral-Asia*, London, 1836.

Moncrieff, W. T. [nom de plume], *Van Diemen's Land, Richardson's Minor Drama*, London, 1831.

Montefiore, J. L., *A Few Words upon the Finance of New South Wales*, Sydney, 1856.

———— *A Catechism on the Rudiments of Political Economy*, Sydney, 1861.

Morais, H. S., *The Jews of Philadelphia*, Philadelphia, 1894.

Mundy, G. C., *Our Antipodes, or, Residence and Rambles in the Australasian Colonies*, London, 1852.

The Mystery Unfolded, or, an exposition of the extraordinary means employed to gain converts by the agents of the London Society for promoting Christianity among the Jews: with the whole proceedings of Mr Frey, from his arrival in London, London, 1817.

Nathan, I., *The Southern Euphrosyne and Australian Miscellany, etc.*, Sydney, 1849.

Nicol, J., *Life and Adventures of John Nicol, Mariner 1776–1801*, edited by Tim Flannery, Melbourne, 1997.

Old Bailey Proceedings (*The Whole Proceedings of the King's Commission of the Peace, Oyer and Terminer, and Gaol Delivery for the City of London and also the Gaol Delivery for the County of Middlesex, held at Justice Hall in the Old Bailey*), 1776–1833 (microfilm), Harvard University Library, Cambridge MA.

Pelham, C., *The Chronicles of Crime or the Newgate Calendar*, 2 vols, London, 1841.

Pellat, A., *Brief Memoir of the Jews in Relation to their Civil and Municipal Disabilities*, London, 1829.

Péron, F., *A Voyage of Discovery to the Southern Hemisphere, performed by order of the Emperor Napoleon during the years 1801, 1802, 1803 & 1804 etc.*, London, 1809.

Phillip, Arthur, *The Voyage of Governor Phillip to Botany Bay*, London, 1789.

Polack, J. S., *New Zealand: Being a Narrative of Travels and Adventures*, 2 vols, London, 1838.

Return of Corporal Punishments inflicted by Sentence of the Sydney Police Bench from the 4th to the 30th September 1833 in the presence of E. A. Slade J. P. Superintendent Hyde Park Barracks, facsimile in *Convict Discipline 1833*, Melbourne, 1977.

Sailman, M., *The Mystery Unfolded*, London, 1817.

Sainty, M. R. and K. A. Johnson, *Census of New South Wales, November 1828*, Library of Australian History, Sydney, 1985.

Solomon, I. (Ikey), *The Life and Exploits of Ikey Solomon, etc.* (pamphlet), London, c. 1828.

———— *Adventures, Memoirs, From Trial, Transportation and Escape of . . . Isaac Solomon, etc.* (pamphlet), London, c. 1829.

———— *The Life and Adventures of Isaac Solomon, etc.* (pamphlet), London, 1830 or 1831.

Stackhouse, A., *Darkness Made Light: The Story of Old Sam*, Tasmania, 1859.

Statistical Account of Van Diemen's Land, vol. 1, 1804–48, Hobart Town, 1856.

Sydney Synagogue, *Laws and Rules for the Management of the Sydney Synagogue*, Sydney, 1833.

Tench, Watkin, *A Complete Account of the Settlement at Port Jackson, in New South Wales*, London, 1793 (Sydney, 1961; Melbourne, 1996).

Wentworth, W. C., *A Statistical, Historical and Political Description of the Colony of New South Wales, and its Dependent Settlements in Van Diemen's Land*, London, 1819.

William R–S [nom de plume], *The Fell Tyrant, or the Suffering Convict*, London, 1835.

Williams, W., *Party Politics Exposed by an Immigrant*, Sydney, 1834.

York Street Synagogue, *The 1845 York Street Synagogue Report*, Sydney, 1845.

Later works

Abbott, J. H. M., *Castle Vane: A Romance of Bushranging on the Upper Hunter in the Olden Days*, Sydney, 1923.

Abbott, G. J. and Nairn, N. B., *Economic Growth in Australia 1788–1821*, Melbourne, 1969.

Ackroyd, P. A., *Dickens*, London, 1991.

Aron J. and Arndt J., *The Enduring Remnant: The First 150 Years of the Melbourne Hebrew Congregation*, Melbourne, 1992.

Back to Shoalhaven, Nowra, 1926.

Bateson, C., *The Convict Ships 1787–1868*, Glasgow, 1969.

Bermant, C. *The Cousinhood: The Anglo-Jewish Gentry*, London, 1971.

Bertie, C. H., *The Story of the Royal Hotel and the Theatre Royal*, Sydney, 1927.

—— *Isaac Nathan: Australia's First Composer*, Sydney, 1922.

Billis, R. V. and Kenyon A. S., *Pastures New: An Account of the Pastoral Occupation of Port Phillip*, Melbourne, 1930.

Blainey, Geoffrey, *The Tyranny of Distance*, Melbourne, 1966.

—— *A Land Half Won*, Melbourne, 1980.

Boxall, G. E., *The Story of the Australian Bushrangers*, London, 1899.

—— *History of the Australian Bushrangers*, London, 1908 (Sydney, 1924).

Brodzky, Isadore, *Sydney Takes the Stage*, Sydney, 1963.

Brodzky, Maurice, *Historical Sketch of the Two Melbourne Synagogues*, Melbourne, 1877.

Chesney, K., *The Victorian Underworld*, London, 1991.

Clark, C. M. H., *A History of Australia*, vols 1, 2, Melbourne, 1962, 1968.

Cobley, J., *Sydney Cove 1788*, London, 1962.

—— *Sydney Cove 1791–1792*, Sydney, 1965.

—— *The Crimes of the First Fleet Convicts*, Sydney, 1970.

—— *The Crimes of the Lady Juliana Convicts 1790*, Sydney, 1989.

Cramp, K. R. and Mackaness, G., *A History of the United Grand Lodge of the Ancient, Free and Accepted Masons of New South Wales*, Sydney, 1938.

Davies, C. E., *A Trip to Europe*, Hobart, 1900.

Digby, E. (ed.), *Australian Men of Mark*, vol. 1, Sydney, 1889.

Dowd, B. T. and Foster, W., *The History of the Waverley Municipal District*, Sydney, 1959.

Ellis, A. S., *Elias and Rebecca Ellis: The Phillips Connections and Some of their Descendants*, privately published, Perth, 1975.

Ellis, M. H., *John Macarthur*, Sydney, 1973 (1st edn, 1955).

—— *Lachlan Macquarie: His Life, Adventures and Times*, Sydney, 1955 (1st edn, 1947).

Emsley, C. (ed.), *The Newgate Calendar*, London, 1997.

Endelman, T. M., *The Jews of Georgian England 1714–1830: Tradition and Change in a Liberal Society*, Philadelphia, 1979.

Evatt, H. V., *The Rum Rebellion*, Sydney, 1965 (1st edn, 1938).

Finn, E., *The 'Garryowen' Sketches: Historical, Local and Personal; by An Old Colonist*, Melbourne, 1880.

—— *The Chronicles of Early Melbourne 1835 to 1852: Historical, Anecdotal and Personal, by 'Garryowen'*, 2 vols, Melbourne, 1888.

Fixel, H., *Hobart Hebrew Congregation: 150 Years of Survival Against All Odds*, privately published, Hobart, 1995.

Frost, A., *Botany Bay Mirages: Illusions of Australia's Convict Beginnings*, Melbourne, 1995.

Getzler, I., *Neither Toleration nor Favour: The Australian Chapter of Jewish Emancipation*, Melbourne, 1970.

Gillen, Mollie, *The Founders of Australia: A Biographical Dictionary of the First Fleet*, Sydney, 1989.

Goldman, L. M., *The Jews in Victoria in the Nineteenth Century*, privately published, Melbourne, 1954.

—— *The History of the Jews in New Zealand*, Wellington, 1958.

Green, G. L., *The Royal Navy & Anglo Jewry 1740–1820*, London, 1989.

Hasluck, A., *Thomas Peel of Swan River*, Melbourne, 1965

Holden, R., *Orphans of History: The Forgotten Children of the First Fleet*, Melbourne, 1999.

Hughes, R., *The Fatal Shore*, London, 1987.

Hyamson, A. M., *A History of the Jews in England*, London, 1907.

Irvin, E., *Shakespeare in the Early Sydney Theatre*, Sydney, 1969.

—— *Theatre Comes to Australia*, Brisbane, 1971.

Jervis, J., *The Story of Parramatta and District*, Sydney, 1933.

Jones, Valantyne, J., *Solomon's Ford: Which Ford? Which Solomon?*, Melbourne, 1983.

Joy, W. and Prior, T., *The Bushrangers*, Sydney, 1963.

Keesing, N., *Gold Fever: Voices from Australian Goldfields*, Sydney, 1971.

Kunz, E. F., *Blood and Gold: Hungarians in Australia*, Melbourne, 1969.

Landa, M. J., *The Jew in Drama*, London, 1926.

Levi, J. S., *The Forefathers: A Dictionary of Biography of the Jews of Australia 1788–1830*, Melbourne, 1976.

Levinson, H., *A Record of Some Memories of Hyman Levinson*, edited by Augusta Levinson Knapp, London, 1920.

Linebaugh, P., *The London Hanged: Crime and Civil Society in the Eighteenth Century*, London, 1991.

Lipman, V. D. (ed.), *Three Centuries of Anglo-Jewish History: A Volume of Essays*, London, 1961.

McCaffrey, J., *The History of Illawarra and its Pioneers*, Sydney, 1922.

McGuire, P., *Inns of Australia*, Melbourne, 1952.

Mackerras, Catherine, *The Hebrew Melodist: A Life of Isaac Nathan*, Sydney, 1963.

Madgwick, R. B., *Immigration into Eastern Australia 1788–1851*, Sydney, 1969.

Maitland and Krone. *The Cyclopedia of Tasmania*, Hobart, 1900.

Mansfield, Ralph, *Analytical View of the Census of New South Wales 1846*, Sydney, 1847.

Marks, P. J., *The First Synagogue in Australia* (pamphlet), privately printed, Sydney, 1925.

Maxwell-Stuart, H., 'Land of Sorrow, Land of Honey: A Short Life of Judah Solomon', lecture at the Hobart Hebrew Congregation, 19 January 1997.

Mitchell, F. F., *Back to Cooma Celebrations*, Sydney, 1926.

Mossenson, D., *Hebrew, Israelite, Jew: The History of the Jews of Western Australia*, Perth, 1990.

Munz, H., *Jews in South Australia 1836–1936*, Adelaide, 1936.

Murphy, J. F., and Easton, E. W., *From Wilderness to Wealth*, Brisbane, 1950.

Neal, D., *The Rule of Law in a Penal Colony: Law and Power in Early New South Wales*, Cambridge, 1991.

Opie, E. A. D., *South Australian Records, Prior to 1841*, Adelaide, 1981.

O'Sullivan, J., *The Bloodiest Bushrangers*, Adelaide, 1973.

Parkes, Henry, *Fifty Years in the Making of Australian History*, 2 vols, London, 1892.

Pastoral Pioneers of South Australia. Publishers Limited, 1925–27, Adelaide, reprinted from *Adelaide Stock and Station Journal*.

Picciotto, J., *Sketches of Anglo-Jewish History*, 2 vols, London, 1875.

Pike, D., *Paradise of Dissent: South Australia 1829–1857*, Melbourne, 1957.

A Portion of Praise: A Festschrift to Honour John S. Levi, Melbourne, 1977.

Porush, I., *The House of Israel*, Melbourne, 1977.

Price, C. A., *Jewish Settlers in Australia*, Social Science Monograph of the Australian National University, Canberra, 1964 (also in *AJHS*, vol. 5, no. 8, 1964).

Pugh, E., *The Charles Dickens Originals*, London, 1912.

Reed, H., *The Marks Family*, privately published, Sydney, 1972.

Roberts, S. H., *The Squatting Age in Australia 1835–1847*, Melbourne, 1935.

Robinson, P., *The Women of Botany Bay*, Sydney, 1988.

Robson, L. L., *The Convict Settlers of Australia: An Enquiry into the Origin and Character of the Convicts Transported to New South Wales and Van Diemen's Land 1787–1852*, Melbourne, 1965.

Roth, C., *A History of the Jews in England*, Oxford, 1949.

—— *Anglo-Jewish Letters (1158–1917)*, London, 1938.

—— *The Rise of Provincial Jewry*, London, 1950.

Rubinstein, H. F., *Israel Set Free*, London, 1936.

Rubinstein, H. L., *The Jews in Victoria 1835–1985*, Sydney, 1986.

—— *Chosen: The Jews in Australia*, Sydney, 1987.

Rumsey, H. J., *The Pioneers of Sydney Cove*, Sydney, 1937.

Rutland S. D., *Edge of the Diaspora: Two Centuries of Jewish Settlement in Australia*, Sydney, 1988.

Sachar, H. M., *The Course of Modern Jewish History*, New York, 1963.

Salmon, E., *Alexandre Salmon, 1820–1866, et sa femme Arii-tamai, 1821–1897*, Paris, 1964.

Scarlett, E. L., *Queanbeyan District and People*, Queanbeyan, 1968.

Shaw, A. G. L., *Convicts and the Colonies: A Study of Penal Transportation from Great Britain and Ireland to Australia and Other Parts of the British Empire*, London, 1966.

Solomons, I., *Lord George Gordon's Conversion to Judaism*, London, 1915.

Stenmark, M., *Sir David Martin*, Sydney, 1996.

The Story of the Melbourne Hebrew Congregation, Melbourne, 1941.

Tardif, P., *Notorious Strumpets and Dangerous Girls: Convict Women in Van Diemen's Land 1803–1829*, Sydney, 1958.

Thorne, Ross, *Theatre Buildings in Australia to 1905*, Sydney, 1971.

Tipping, Marjorie, *Convicts Unbound: The Story of the Calcutta Convicts and their Settlement in Australia*, Melbourne, 1988.

Tobias, J. J., *Prince of Fences: The Life and Crimes of Ikey Solomons*, 1974.

Tucker, J., *Jemmy Green in Australia*, edited by Colin Roderick, Sydney, 1955.

Turner, H. G., *A History of the Colony of Victoria from its Discovery to its Absorption into the Commonwealth of Australia*, 2 vols, London, 1904.

Ward, Russel, *The Australian Legend*, Melbourne, 1958.

Ward, Russel (ed.), *The Penguin Book of Australian Ballads*, Melbourne, 1964.

Wheate, P. and Graham, C., *Captain William Bligh*, Sydney, 1972.

Whitefield, E., *The Cyclopaedia of Tasmania*, Hobart, 1900.

Wilson, J. G. (ed.), *Western Australia's Centenary 1829–1929*, Perth, 1929.

Younger, R. M., *Australia and the Australians: A New Concise History*, Adelaide, 1970.

Index